Beijing
The Complete **Residents'** Guide

Passionately Publishing...

EXPLORER

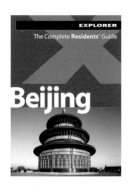

Beijing Explorer 1st Edition ISBN 13 - 978-9948-03-327-1 ISBN 10 - 9948-03-327-2

Printed and bound by Emirates Printing Press, Dubai, United Arab Emirates.

Explorer Publishing & Distribution
PO Box 34275, Dubai
United Arab Emirates
Phone   +971 (0)4 340 8805
Fax   +971 (0)4 340 8806
Email   info@explorerpublishing.com
Web   www.explorerpublishing.com

Welcome

Your life in Beijing has just become a lot simpler. This book is going to help you get to know the city, its people, their customs and more. Becoming a fully fledged resident of China has never been more enjoyable.

Over the following pages you'll find everything you need to know to make the most of your life in Beijing, and settle in to one of the world's most dynamic cities. From *hutong* adventures to finding your dream home, we'll tell you how and where to do it.

Firstly, the **General Information** (p.1) chapter will bring you up to speed with Beijing's history, geography and customs, and offer suggestions for places to stay and how to get around.

The **Residents** (p.57) chapter is the one for life admin. It will help you decide where to live, with an area by area run down on where is best for families, bohemians or young professionals.

There is also essential information on visas, schools, health care, and all the formalities involved in the big move.

Next comes **Exploring** (p.151), which takes you through Beijing's varied neighbourhoods, highlighting the beautiful architecture, places of interest, parks, tours, galleries and museums.

Turn to the **Activities** (p.205) section when you are feeling frivolous or you have more time on your hands. These pages tell you the best spas and beauty salons for a good pampering, and where to indulge in hobbies as diverse as climbing, kite flying and dragon boat racing.

For most, the **Shopping** (p.245) chapter will prove invaluable when kitting out your new life. This section will tell you where to go for all you shopping needs, no matter how large or small.

Then, to celebrate all your achievements, turn to the **Going Out** (p.299) chapter for a run down of Beijing's premier places for eating, drinking and dancing until early morning.

To help you navigate your new home town, we've included a chunky **Maps** (p.351) chapter at the back. You'll notice coloured icons dotted throughout the book; these refer to this chapter, and should help you find the bar, park, shop or association you're looking for. Turn to the inside back cover for our map of the metro system.

And if you think we have missed something, whether it's somewhere to drink, or a spectacularly talented basket weaving tutor, please let us know. Go to www.explorerpublishing.com, fill in the Reader Response form, and share the knowledge with your fellow explorers.

The Explorer Team

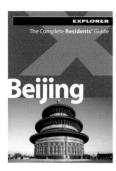

There are so many things the Beijing Explorers love about this buzzing city: watching old-timers waltzing in the park (p.190); hearing new music from young bands at D-22 (p.343); sharing steaming hotpot with friends on a cold day (p.301); walking the Great Wall from Simaitai (p.198); soaking up the calm of the Forbidden City (p.180) in the snow; joining the crowds at Temple Fairs (p.55) during the Spring Festival; riding through the hutongs; buying tacky Mao memorabilia (p.284) and just enjoying the thrill of the future capital of the world.

Andrew Peaple After years toiling as a financial journalist in London, a love of Chinese food, history and culture brought Andrew to Beijing. It's his second stint out east, after living in Japan for three years. His love of cricket didn't rub off on the Japanese, but maybe the Chinese will prove more willing. **Best city memory?** Playing drinking games with some of the Red Army one bank holiday.

Flora Bagenal Flora is a property editor and freelance news journalist for *The Sunday Times*. She first came to China aged 17 and, despite seeing toads skinned, decided to return on a one-way ticket in 2006. When she is not writing and ordering pickled cucumber, she volunteers, teaching old Beijingers Olympic English. **One reason you'd never leave Beijing?** Friends.

Greg May Greg is an Iowa-born writer, editor and critic, living in Beijing who works for TripAdvisor, IDC, and *That's China*. When not trying new restaurants, he's adding to a vast DVD collection that may make some custom agent's family quite happy when he heads back to America. **Best view?** After the Great Wall (p.197), try the CCTV tower (old or new). Both offer great vantage points.

Jonathan Haagen Jonny is a feature writer for the *Economist Intelligence Unit*, *Newsweek Select*, *China Daily* and local magazines. His first book, *Climbing Strange Mountain*, was published in China last year. He remains because he's just too busy to leave. **Best city memory?** The week the municipal government took half the cars off the road.

Juliet Holdsworth Juliet's visits to China began in 1999. Over the next six years she found any excuse to return: as a language student, an intern in the Redgate Gallery (p.177), a wine consultant, and even, for want of a thrill, a lackey for a Russian property company. She made a more permanent move in 2005 where she began her career as a freelance writer. **Worst thing about Beijing?** The smog.

*Having trouble navigating your way around sprawling Beijing? Look no further than the **Beijing Mini Map**, an indispensable pocket-sized aid to getting to grips with the roads, areas and attractions of this mega-metropolis.*

Kit Gillet Kit has lived in Beijing since 2005, spending his days exploring the alleys and restaurants that make the city so amazing. He writes for local magazines and guidebooks and enjoys nothing more than exploring the country and interviewing its illuminating characters. **Ultimate Beijing must-do?** Watching the early morning exercisers outside the Temple of Heaven (p.188).

Lauren Mack An insatiable appetite for exploring and a love of travel led Lauren east. Three days after graduating from Columbia University's Graduate School of Journalism, she landed in Beijing, where she works out of the coffeeshops in Wudaokou as a freelance writer. **Best place to drink with the locals?** At a street side game of mahjong.

Natasha Dragun Natasha began her adventures in China more than 10 years ago, and despite an inauspicious slip into a public toilet on her first visit, she has never looked back. Natasha has written for many travel and lifestyle publications and is also the editor of a local magazine. **Best city memory?** First snow – it's like a blanket of shhhh over a city that never sleeps.

Peter Ellegard A travel writer and photographer, Peter has spent 25 years globetrotting. He presented a travel series for CCTV9, has written extensively about China and an image taken there won him the British Guild of Travel Writers' Photograph of the Year award in 2005 and 2006. He also contributed images to this book. **Best city memory?** Visiting traditional *hutong* homes.

Sally Xu Sally studied English literature in college, but unfortunately never finished the whole works of Shakespeare. She has translated dictionaries, film scripts and once dreamed of being an astronaut. With her feet on the ground, she likes nothing more than travelling to new parts of the world. **Ultimate Beijing must-do?** Buy a good map.

*Now that you've moved to Beijing, it won't be long before you're playing host to wave upon wave of visiting family and friends – and we've got the perfect guide to help them get the most out of their sightseeing. Packed with info on Beijing's shops, restaurants and tourist spots, you can't go wrong with the **Beijing Mini Explorer**.*

Samantha Wilson In 2004 Samantha left on a trip through South and Central America, Israel and the Middle East, finally landing in Beijing. She writes regularly for several international magazines and has put her name to guide books on Sichuan Province and Israel. **Favourite daytrip?** Hiking the Great Wall from Jinshaling to Simatai (p.198).

Sherisse Pham Sherisse has lived in Asia for the past five years. She is a freelance writer who enjoys digging out the city's best gems and trumpeting them to the world. She has written for a number of magazines and publications including *Frommer's*, and Zagat Survey and is currently based in Beijing. **Best view?** The balcony of No Name (p.309) restaurant.

Tom Husband Tom spent his first year in Beijing drinking. He is delighted to be able to pass on his expertise, as he has become a sofa jockey since. This descent into slipper-wearing was latent in his character, and is in no way related to the quality of Beijing's fantastic nightlife. **City must-do?** Race ice bikes on Beihai lake (p.191) in the winter.

Will Davies Will fled London and his life as an investment banker four years ago, ending up in Beijing, where he works as a journalist. He has travelled throughout Europe, Africa, America, and Australasia, but Asia appealed the most. Will had not visited China before moving there, and now appears to be stuck. **One reason you'd never leave Beijing?** The authorities have my passport.

Thanks...

As well as our team of authors, whose expert advice and dedicated research skills have been invaluable, several others have contributed towards making this book a success. Our thanks go to: Peter Ellegard for last minute images (opera, foot massage, hot pot, acrobatics, cha, tombs, kite and hot springs) in the checklist (p.153), Marko Ferenc for additional pictures, Julien Wagner, Sacha Dunas and everyone at World Events for their local nous, Sally for the swift replies, Jo Holden MacDonald, Kaye Holland and Audrey Lee for the proofing, and Kimia dates from Iran, for being there when we needed them most.

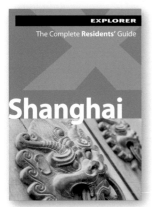

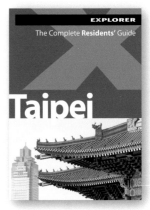

Where are we exploring next?

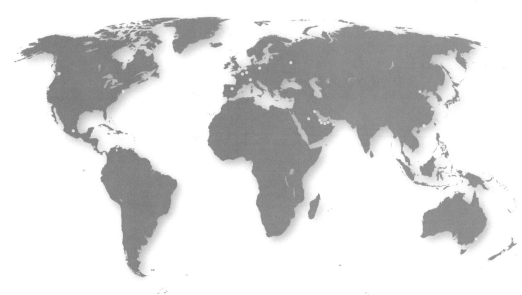

- Abu Dhabi
- Amsterdam
- Bahrain
- Barcelona
- Beijing
- Berlin
- Brussels
- Dubai

- Dublin
- Geneva
- Hong Kong
- Kuala Lumpur
- Kuwait
- London
- Los Angeles
- Mexico City

- Moscow
- New York
- New Zealand
- Oman
- Paris
- Qatar
- San Francisco
- Saudi Arabia

- Shanghai
- Singapore
- Sydney
- Taipei
- Tokyo
- Vancouver

Check out our website for more details

Where do you live?
Is your home city missing from our list? If you'd love to see a residents' guide for a location not currently on Explorer's horizon please email editorial@explorerpublishing.com.

Advertise with Explorer...
If you're interested in advertising with us, please contact sales@explorerpublishing.com.

Make Explorer your very own...
We offer a number of customization options for bulk sales. For more information and discount rates please contact corporatesales@explorerpublishing.com.

Contract Publishing
Have an idea for a publication or need to revamp your company's marketing material? Contact designlab@explorerpublishing to see how our expert contract publishing team can help.

www.explorerpublishing.com

Life can move pretty fast, so to make sure you can stay up to date with all the latest goings on in your city, we've revamped our website to further enhance your time in the city, whether long or short.

Keep in the know...

Our Complete Residents' Guides and Mini Visitors' series continue to expand, covering destinations from Amsterdam to New Zealand and beyond. Keep up to date with our latest travels and hot tips by signing up to our monthly newsletter, or browse our products section for info on our current and forthcoming titles.

Make friends and influence people...

...by joining our Communities section. Meet fellow residents in your city, make your own recommendations for your favourite restaurants, bars, childcare agencies or dentists, plus find answers to your questions on daily life from long-term residents.

Discover new experiences...

Ever thought about living in a different city, or wondered where the locals really go to eat, drink and be merry? Check out our regular features section, or submit your own feature for publication!

Want to find a badminton club, the number for your bank, or maybe just a restaurant for a hot first date?

Check out city info on various destinations around the world in our residents' section – from finding a pilates class to contact details for international schools in your area, or the best place to buy everything from a spanner set to a Spandau Ballet album, we've got it all covered.

Let us know what you think!

All our information comes from residents which means you! If we missed out your favourite bar or market stall, or you know of any changes in the law, infrastructure, cost of living or entertainment scene, let us know by using our Feedback form.

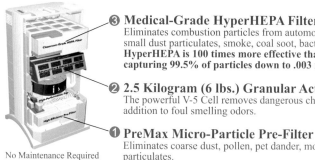

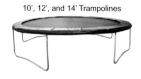

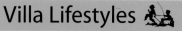

Contents

Contents

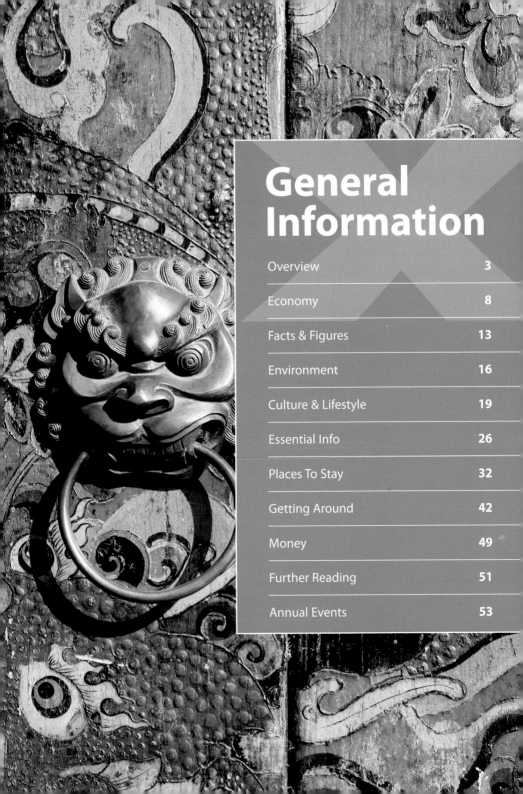

General Information

Geography

The People's Republic of China is in eastern Asia. It ranks behind Russia and Canada in area and is almost identical in size to the United States. China considers Taiwan as its 23rd province (*sheng*), making it the world's third-largest nation. Mainland China covers about 9.6 million sqkm. It measures 5,250km from east to west, and 5,500km from north to south. It shares borders with 14 countries; the longest is with Mongolia, at nearly 4,700km, and the shortest is with Afghanistan, at less than 80km. It has a coastline measuring 14,500km, lapped by the Yellow Sea, East China Sea, South China Sea and part of the Pacific Ocean. There are five autonomous regions, four municipalities (including Shanghai and Beijing) and two special administrative regions; Hong Kong and Macau (see Government & Politics, p.12).

Size Matters

As well as being the third-largest country on earth, China is home to the world's third and sixth-largest rivers (Yangtze and Yellow), the highest point (Everest), the second lowest point (Turpan Depression), and the most people (1.3 billion).

Physical Geography

China's vast size comes with dramatically varying landscapes. Its west is mostly mountainous, with high plateaus that drop down in steps to the bountiful plains of the east coast.

The mighty Himalayas form a border with four of China's neighbours – Nepal, Bhutan, India and Pakistan – and encompass the world's highest peaks. At 8,850m, Everest (Qomolangma) towers above all others, while other notable peaks in Chinese territory include K2 (8,611m) and Shishapangma (8,013m).

To the north-east of the Himalayas, the Tibetan plateau extends over a huge area, with an average elevation in excess of 4,500m. Some of Asia's longest rivers begin there, including the east-flowing Yellow (Huanghe) and Yangtze (Changjiang), plus the Mekong, which flows south. Great swathes of China's north-west are desert, the most notable being the Taklamakan and Gobi. Also in the north-west is the Turpan Depression, which lies at 154m below sea level and is the lowest place in China, and the second lowest inland area on the planet.

Beijing

Beijing lies in the northern part of the Huabei plain, in north-eastern China. It is bordered by Hebei province and Tianjin municipality. It is cradled by the Xishan and Jundu mountains to the west, north and north-east, on a plain that gently slopes east and south-east to the Bohai Sea, an inlet of the Yellow Sea.

Beyond the mountains lie the advancing sands of the Gobi Desert, just 200km from Beijing. The city covers a total area of 16,410 sqkm (about the size of Kuwait) and had a population of 15.38 million at the end of 2005, according to figures from the Beijing Municipal Bureau of Statistics (www.ebeijing.gov.cn).

The Yongding, Chaobai and Juma rivers flow through the city from the mountains to the north-west, continuing on to the Bohai Sea. Beijing is also the northern terminus of the ancient Grand Canal, which runs for nearly 1,800km from Hangzhou. The urban centre of Beijing is in the south-eastern part of the municipality and is in a grid pattern, with Tiananmen Square (p.183) and the Forbidden City (p.180) at the heart. Several sections of the Great Wall of China (p.3) lie within the municipality.

Chinese Literature

China has a longer literary history than any other country. The invention of paper 2,000 years ago, woodblock printing during the Tang Dynasty (618 - 907) and movable type printing during the Song Dynasty (960 - 1279) helped popularise the written word. China's classical literature dates back to the Eastern Zhou Dynasty and includes the Five Classics, *said to have been compiled by Confucius. Among them are* I Ching *(the Book of Changes),* Chun Qiu *(Spring and Autumn Annals) and* Lunyu *(Analects of Confucius).*

History

Beijing has been influential throughout China's history. The first recorded human habitation in China was at Zhoukoudian, in the south-western suburbs of today's city, where Peking Man roamed forests and lakes more than half a million years ago. The farming settlements that grew around the area 4,000 years ago were the beginnings of civilisation in the region.

Ancient Beijing & The Great Wall

In the turmoil of the Warring States Period (475 - 221 BC), the city of Ji was built where Beijing stands today, becoming the capital of Yan state. When China was unified under the first Qin emperor, Qin Shihuang, Ji became a key trading and military post for the next 1,000 years. It was under Qin that the Great Wall was begun, forming a supposedly impenetrable barrier to the north. Over following centuries it was renamed Yanjing (Southern Capital) by the Khitans, then Zhongdu (Central Capital) by the Jurchen. The Jurchen were ancestors of the Manchus and established the Jin Dynasty (1115 - 1234). The city flourished and its population reached one million. Then Genghis Khan and his Mongol hordes swept through the Great Wall, capturing the city and vanquishing the Jin.

Kublai Khan

By 1279, the reunification of China was complete with the defeat of the Southern Song by Genghis Kan's grandson, Kublai Khan. He established the Yuan Dynasty and made Zhongdu the capital, under the new name Khanbalig. For the first time, the city was the political and cultural centre of China. Splendid, ornate new palaces replaced the fire-ravaged Jin buildings. These impressed Venetian traveller Marco Polo when he visited the Yuan court. It was under Kublai Khan that the city's rectangular, grid-style layout was adopted. The Grand Canal, originally started in the 5th century BC, which linked Hangzhou and the Yangtze River (Chang Jiang) with the Yellow river (Huang He), was also extended north to Khanbalig.

Ming & Qing Dynasties

The Mongol empire lasted until 1368, when a revolt led by former monk Zhu Yuanzhang restored Chinese rule under the Ming Dynasty. The first Ming capital was established in Nanjing. However, in 1406 Emperor Yongle began a huge reconstruction programme at Khanbalig to turn it into the Ming capital. Initially called Beiping (Northern Peace), its name became Beijing (Northern Capital). High walls were built, along with the grand palace buildings of the Forbidden City. Eunuch General Zheng He led naval expeditions as far as Africa and the Middle East, but after Yongle's death, Ming China became more inward-looking and the Great Wall was extended. The Portuguese were allowed to set up a trading base in Macau in 1557. The Manchus took advantage of the growing unrest in China, slipping through the Great Wall with the help of a Ming general and taking control. The ensuing Qing Dynasty lasted from 1644 to 1911, expanding China to include Manchuria, Mongolia and Tibet.

Foreigners & Opium

Openness to the west evaporated in the 18th century. International trade was limited to the port of Canton (present-day Guangzhou) and exports heavily outweighed imports. But then the west introduced China to opium. As people became addicted, Qing indignation grew, until the seizure of opium from the British at Canton led to the Opium Wars. China finally capitulated, signing the Treaty of Nanking, which ceded Hong Kong to the British and allowed trade to reopen. The Treaty of Tianjin opened up more ports and brought diplomatic missions to Beijing. Increasing foreign influence fuelled protests, culminating in the Boxer Rebellion in 1900, during which thousands of Chinese Christians were killed by peasant mobs. Attacks on foreign interests grew, and at one point embassies had to be rescued by a multinational force after being under siege for 45 days.

Chinese Labour Corp

China supplied 140,000 labourers to the British army during the first world war. The Chinese Labour Corps fought in France on the understanding the German run parts of China would be returned to the Chinese after the war. But, the Treaty of Versailles awarded Shandong to Japan, fuelling resentment among those who would later start the May Fourth Movement.

The End Of Empire

The end of imperial China was close, and reforms were imposed on the Qing Dynasty under the Boxer Protocols. The whiff of revolution grew, led by the Hawaiian-educated doctor Sun Yatsen. When the Empress Dowager Cixi died in 1908 and was succeeded by 2 year old Emperor Puyi, it signalled the Qing's demise.

Foreign-financed railways became the target for national anger and violence, and Sun Yatsen's Alliance Society took advantage, with nationwide uprisings. The Provisional Republican Government of China was set up in 1911. However, Sun Yatsen lost out to imperial army chief Yuan Shikai for the post of president after Yuan gained the emperor's abdication. After declaring himself emperor, Yuan died as China descended into warlord-dominated violence.

A nationalist group called the May Fourth Movement grew out of anger over Japan being given Shandong province after World War I. It was embraced by students and intellectuals and quickly grew. The group laid the foundations for the Chinese Communist Party in 1921, at which Mao Zedong was present.

An alliance followed with the Nationalist Party, the Kuomintang. But after Sun Yatsen's death, a power struggle ensued. In 1927, some 5,000 Communists and trade union representatives were massacred. The following year a national government was set up by the Kuomintang under Chiang Kaishek. After repeated clashes, the Communists embarked on the Long March in 1934, with Mao leading the way. Less than a quarter of the original 90,000 survived the year-long, 8,000km march from Jiangxi province to Shaanxi, but it cemented Mao's position as Communist leader.

Japanese Colonialism

Japan began flexing its colonial muscles after the Meiji Restoration in the late 1860s, which restored imperial rule and began a period of military growth. In 1872, the Japanese briefly occupied Taiwan. In the following negotiations China was forced to hand over sovereignty of the Liuqiu islands, which are still part of Okinawa province today.

The First Sino-Japanese War, in 1894, was over control of Korea. The weakening Qing Dynasty was

Cheeky Cixi

Empress Dowager Cixi was the daughter of a low ranking civil servant who became de facto ruler of an empire. In 1851, aged around 16, she was selected as a concubine to the Emperor Xianfeng. She quickly moved through the ranks, beginning as a 'noble person', the fifth level in the concubine hierarchy. Within six years, she had given birth to the emperor's only male heir, Zaichun (later Emperor Tongzhi). He was just 5 years old when he ascended, and while officially a consort to her son, Cixi effectively ruled China from 1860 to 1908. Cixi is commonly (though not universally) viewed by historians as an avaricious schemer, who built a vast personal fortune and extravagant palaces while China's economy floundered.

Expat Women
Helping Women Living Overseas

Our mission is to help you succeed overseas by providing you with a first-stop website to share stories, network globally, develop personally and find the best resources!

Visit Now: www.ExpatWomen.com

no match for Meiji Japan, which invaded Taiwan and Manchuria, overwhelming Chinese forces. The Treaty of Shimonoseki ceded Taiwan to Japan. China also had to pay reparations and allow Japan to open factories in its ports and operate ships on the Yangtze River. With civil unrest growing, Japan again invaded Manchuria in 1931, setting up a puppet state under Puyi, the last Qing emperor. It then invaded the rest of China in 1937. Atrocities included biological warfare and the Rape of Nanking, in which 300,000 people, including women and children, were massacred. Relations between China and Japan remain fragile to this day, exacerbated by claims by some Japanese that the massacre never happened.

Much Read Book

Mao Zedong's Little Red Book *was largely the brainchild of People's Liberation Army chief Lin Biao, who compiled a collection of Mao's thoughts in a single volume. Officially known as* Quotations from Chairman Mao Zedong, *the pocket-sized book was first published in April 1964. It contains 427 Maoist quotations in 33 chapters. During the Cultural Revolution, it was required reading in schools and workplaces. It became an icon of the era, waved enthusiastically at public events and brandished by rampaging Red Guards. More than 900 million copies have been printed.*

'The things I've seen...'

The People's Republic

Full-scale civil war broke out between the Communist Party (CCP) and Kuomintang (KMT) in 1946. In major battles in 1948 and 1949, the KMT were soundly beaten. Communist forces entered Beijing peacefully in January 1949, while Chiang Kaishek fled with his remaining forces (and China's gold reserves) to Taiwan, then known as Formosa. Mao Zedong proclaimed the People's Republic of China (PRC) on October 1, 1949, in Tiananmen Square. The early years of the PRC saw a rebirth of the economy, with land redistributed to peasants and a five-year plan that boosted industrial production. The Hundred Flowers experiment of 1957 allowed some freedom of expression, encouraging 'a hundred flowers to bloom' in the arts and 'a hundred schools of thought to contend' in sciences. This was quickly dropped in the face of public criticism. Then came the Great Leap Forward. It was an economic and social plan intended to boost steel production by encouraging backyard blast furnaces, but resulted in the collapse of agricultural production. An estimated 30 million Chinese died of starvation. The Cultural Revolution, from 1966 to 1970, followed the acrimonious break-up of relations between China and Russia, and was aimed at bolstering Maoist ideals. A collection of Mao's sayings were put together into what became popularly known as the *Little Red Book*. This was used as a key education text and a rallying symbol for the Red Guards – fanatical followers of Mao, who were mostly students. Charged with sweeping away old ideas, manners and customs, the Red Guards led a purge of the arts. Priceless treasures from China's past, including temples, monasteries, cultural relics and works of art were destroyed, and many schools and universities were closed. The 60s and 70s also saw Beijing's extensive Ming Dynasty city walls and most of its Ming-era gates torn down. Mao died in 1976.

New Constitution

Following the Cultural Revolution, stability was restored, with Premier Zhou Enlai leading efforts to improve relations with the rest of the world. Under Deng Xiaoping, from the late 70s China adopted several market economy policies and established Special Economic Zones. It also introduced the one-child policy, to stem population growth. The 1982 Constitution embraced many changes aimed at modernising China's economy, the social rights of its citizens, and encouraging foreign investment. This set the foundations for much of China's economic success.

New Millennium

With the economy rapidly expanding there are worries about a potential meltdown. Although inflation has crept up, indications suggest continued growth. From being a bankrupt, peasant economy half a century ago, China is now one of the world's leading economic dynamos. The 2008 Olympics will enable it to show the world how much the country has achieved, and leave onlookers with one overriding message: there's more to come.

Beijing Timeline

500,000 yrs ago	Peking Man lives near Beijing, in the area where the village of Zhououdian is now.
475 BC	Warring States Period. The city of Ji becomes the capital of Yan state.
221 BC	Qin Dynasty. The Great Wall is begun and an underground mausoleum built at Xi'an, guarded by thousands of terracotta warriors.
206 BC	Han Dynasty. Chinese culture and goods are exported to central Asia, the Middle East and Europe along the Silk Road. Other cultures reach China in return.
618-907	Tang Dynasty. The Khitans move south from the Liaohe River and occupy Ji, making it their second capital. They rename it Yanjing (Southern Capital).
1115-1234	Jin Dynasty. The Jurchen take over Yanjing and rename it Zhongdu (Central Capital), building beautiful palaces.
1215	Genghis Khan leads his Mongol army into Zhongdu, giving the city provincial status.
1271	Kublai Khan, grandson of Genghis, establishes the Yuan Dynasty and renames the city Khanbalig, which means Dadu (Great Capital) in Chinese.
1293	The Tonghui Canal opens, connecting Khanbalig with the Grand Canal and the Yellow River, Yangtze River and Hangzhou.
1368	Ming soldiers seize the city, renaming it Beiping (Northern Peace). The capital is moved south to Nanjing.
1406	Ming emperor Yongle starts a 15 year project to build 12m walls around Beiping.
1417-1420	The palace buildings and gardens that now form the Forbidden City are built. Yongle transfers the capital from Nanjing and names his new capital Beijing (Northern Capital).
1644	The Manchus found the Qing Dynasty and begin to build a series of gardens including Yuanmingyuan (Old Summer Palace).
1839-1862	Opium Wars. China loses and is forced to cede Hong Kong to Britain and open up treaty ports to foreign powers.
1851-1864	Nanjing falls to an army of religious zealots led by Hong Xiuquan. All 100,000 take their own lives rather than surrender to the Qing soldiers that retake the city.
1899-1901	The Boxer Rebellion. In one conflict, a 45 day siege of foreign legations in Beijing is ended by a multinational rescue force.
1911	Collapse of the Qing Dynasty and end of imperial China. The Provisional Republican Government of China is set up. Yuan Shikai becomes the first president.
1915	Yuan Shikai declares himself emperor but dies within a year. China falls under the control of feuding regional warlords.
1928	With Beijing still under warlord rule, the Kuomintang nationalists change its name back to Beiping and make Nanjing capital of the Republic of China.
1937	Beiping falls to Japanese forces during the Second Sino-Japanese War. It reverts to Beijing. Some 300,000 Chinese are massacred in The Rape of Nanjing.
1945	Beijing becomes Beiping once more, with Japan's surrender in World War II.
1949	Communist forces enter the city on January 31 without a fight. Mao Zedong announces the creation of the People's Republic of China on October 1 in Tiananmen Square. The city becomes Beijing again.
1965	Beijing's Ming city wall is torn down to make way for the Second Ring Road. Ming gates are also demolished.
1997	Hong Kong becomes a Special Administrative Region of China after the handover from the United Kingdom.
1999	Macau joins Hong Kong as a Special Administrative Region, when it is handed over by Portugal.
2001	Beijing is named as host for the 2008 Olympics.
2005	Government plan limits expansion of Beijing to two semi-circular bands east and west of the city centre.
2008	The airport opens its futuristic Terminal 3. The city hosts the 2008 Olympic Games.

China Overview

China has been one of the world's fastest-growing economies for more than 25 years and it continues to power forward, defying fears of a meltdown. In the first half of 2007, the Chinese economy grew at 11.5%, its fastest since 1994, according to the Asian Development Bank (ADB). The surge has been buoyed by exports, investment and increased domestic consumption.

China's foreign exchange reserves are also rising as its juggernaut economy, now the world's fourth largest, motors on. International Monetary Fund figures for June 2007 show that reserves rose by $266 million over the previous 12 months, giving a current account surplus of over $1.3 trillion. This represents 50% of the entire foreign exchange reserves for developing Asia.

Average Salary

Finance directors

Country	Annual base salary (€)	Annual total cash (€)
USA	195,727	248,535
UK	158,582	205,528
China	59,213	67,658

Marketing directors

Country	Annual base salary (€)	Annual total cash (€)
USA	161,335	209,342
UK	149,294	182,885
China	62,078	75,691

Human resources directors

Country	Annual base salary (€)	Annual total cash (€)
USA	149,530	190,218
UK	135,673	165,687
China	53,657	64,499

Source: Mercer Human Resource Consulting

The World Bank says China's trade surplus reached $137 billion in 2007. It is one of the biggest lenders to the US, and in 2005 loaned America $242 billion.

At the same time, private consumption is growing briskly, as incomes grow. The World Bank forecasts China's growth in 2007 will be 11.3%, well above the Chinese government's target of 8% and a level likely to be maintained for the next three years, according to the Economic Research Institute of the Renmin University of China.

Official government figures put China's GDP at ¥20.94 trillion ($2.68 trillion) in 2006. Standard & Poor's has steadily raised China's credit rating. It now stands at A, reflecting its stability. But, inflationary pressures are increasing. The National Bureau of Statistics predicts China's consumer price index (CPI) for 2007 will have reached 4.7%, a figure the bureau's head calls 'moderate and tolerable.' But, the CPI hit 6.5% in both August and October, partly as a result of increases in food costs caused by global fuel price rises. In 2006 the CPI rose by 1.5%.

Industry

Over the last 30 years, China has gone from collective farming to a market-based economy. It has closed large, inefficient factories and encouraged high-tech industries and heavy manufacturing. Car making, trains, aircraft, ships and military equipment have long been the driving force for the economy. Electronics and telecommunications joined them in recent years. Toys and clothing are other key industries.

Other than Hong Kong and Macau, China's main trading partners are the US, Japan, Korea, Germany, the Netherlands, the UK, Singapore and Italy. Key exports are electrical machinery, power generation equipment, clothing, iron and steel, optics and medical equipment, furniture, chemicals, toys, vehicles and plastics and electronics. Much of its exports come from the Pearl River delta (the special economic zone of Shenzhen, as well as Hong Kong and Macau) and Shanghai and the Yangtze delta.

Despite the fast-growing economy, the country's GDP per capita still lags behind international standards, at just one fifth of the world average.

The average income of Chinese rural residents stood at ¥3,587 ($460) in 2006, equivalent to ¥10 ($1.20) per day. Much of China remains a rural subsistence economy, resulting in a growing disparity between city and countryside. The average annual disposable income per capita in urban areas was ¥11,759 (about $1,500) in 2006. In essence, the spare money that city folk have is worth three times the total income of their rural compatriots. According to the World Bank, about 150 million people in China live on less than $1 a day. The Chinese government has vowed to tackle urban unemployment and reduce it to below 4.6%, by creating at least nine million new jobs.

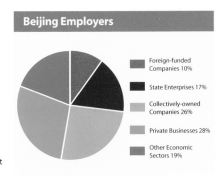

Beijing Employers

- Foreign-funded Companies 10%
- State Enterprises 17%
- Collectively-owned Companies 26%
- Private Businesses 28%
- Other Economic Sectors 19%

Beijing Overview

While Beijing does not have a manufacturing base comparable to Shanghai or Shenzhen, as China's capital, it plays a pivotal role in the county's economy. Many banks (including the Bank of China), insurance companies and other financial institutions are headquartered here. Service industries around finance, IT, and scientific research and development accounted for 47% of the city's GDP from 2002 to 2006.

The 2008 Olympics has also provided a massive boost to the city's economy and infrastructure. Billions of dollars are being spent on facilities, transport, telecommunications and environmental improvements. The total invested in infrastructure between 2002 and 2006 reached almost ¥284 billion (more than $38 billion), with an annual increase averaging 16%. During this period, 60km of rail tracks were laid as part of an expansion of the subway and rail networks. Real estate development during the same period totalled ¥691 billion (about $93 billion). In the first three quarters of 2007, a further ¥74.7 billion (about $10 billion) was invested in infrastructure.

The city's citizens have also grown more affluent. The internet is now a part of everyday life for Beijingers, with 95.7 computers for every 100 households. City dwellers like to keep in touch with each other by telephone, too. In 2006, there were 57.3 landlines for every 100 homes, and 99.4 mobile phones for every 100 people. By the end of 2006, Beijing also had more than two million private cars, adding to the city's pollution problem.

The Financial District (p.90)

Growth

Beijing's gross domestic product grew at an annual rate of 12.1% between 2002 and 2006, a rise of 1.3% on 1997 to 2001. Its per capita income reached $6,210 over the same period, almost double the 2001 level and two years ahead of the municipal government's goal. And, the government says this was achieved with lower resource consumption and waste emissions. In 2005, Beijing's GDP totalled ¥69 billion, while the city's revenue reached ¥92 billion, an increase of 23.5% over the previous year.

Trade

Beijing's international trade has soared in the run-up to the Olympics, more than tripling between 2002 and 2006, to $158 billion. The capital also saw foreign investment reach $15 billion, an increase of almost 50% over the same period.

Employment

China's urban unemployment level is officially around 4.5%. Like other major cities, Beijing suffers from an influx of migrant workers from poor rural areas who arrive hoping to find employment to send money back to their families.

Leading Industries

Other than tourism and the finance sector, Beijing's major industries include electronics, chemicals, car making, machinery, metallurgy, textiles, garments, and household appliances. In 2005, the total deposits in *yuan* and foreign currency of Beijing's financial institutions reached ¥2,897 billion.

Income for insurance businesses, both domestically and from overseas, totalled ¥4,982 billion, and the trading volume in Beijing's various financial markets reached ¥932 billion.

Beijing is developing a 'Silicon Valley' over the next few years, with plans for 10 semiconductor chip assembly lines by 2010.

It is also China's centre for higher education and scientific research, with more than 70 universities and 560 research institutes.

Mini Explorer

Don't let the size of this little star fool you – it's full of insider info, maps, contacts, tips and facts for visitors. From shops to spas, bars to bargains and everything in between, the Mini Explorer range helps you get the most out of your stay in the city, however long you're there for.

Tourism

As China's cultural heart and capital, Beijing is a must-see for visitors to the country. The most celebrated sights are the Forbidden City, the Great Wall, the Temple of Heaven and the Summer Palace; all of which have UNESCO World Heritage status. The number of foreign tourists entering Beijing has soared recently, helped by hype about the 2008 Olympics. There were 3.63 million in 2005, generating foreign exchange income of $3.62 billion.

By the end of 2005, the city had 594 star-graded hotels, with an average daily room rate of ¥425 (about $55). The Olympics were forecast to bring 500,000 people into Beijing for the three weeks from August 8. Hotel prices have reportedly quadrupled during this period, with many major hotels only taking bookings covering the whole three-weeks.

Some overseas tour operators believe expectations are too high, and that hotels will be forced to slash prices close to the event, just as happened in Sydney 2000. Ticket holders for Olympic events will be able to use public transport for free.

Getting Gobby

Beijing is using the Olympics to try and eradicate the image of the Chinese as a nation of spitters. Spitting in public is one of the main complaints from tourists in China, and is against the law. Yet it persists. A noisy growl and hock is the soundtrack to any day on Beijing's streets. So, authorities have been waging a campaign. During the week-long Labour Day holiday in May 2007, more than 100,000 paper bags were handed out for people to spit into, while on the spot fines of up to ¥50 ($6.70) were dished out to 89 people for spitting in public. Volunteers have also been patrolling the streets with tissues and asking offenders to clean up their spit. The habit is regarded as one of the 'four new pests' of modern Beijing, the others being queue-jumping, swearing and smoking. The original 'four pests' of Chairman Mao's day were rats, flies, mosquitoes and sparrows. Uniformed queuing inspectors have been targeting bus stops and subway stations to ensure people don't push in. Nearly three million etiquette pamphlets have been handed out to civil servants and other workers, including taxi drivers, bus conductors, waiters and waitresses, encouraging them to be polite to visitors. There is even a civic index covering health and public order rules, attitudes towards strangers and etiquette while watching sports events. In 2006 it reached 69.06 points, 3.85 points above 2005. The target for the Olympics is between 72 and 78.

2008 Olympics

Beijing's key sights have undergone major renovations for the Olympics. The Hall of Supreme Harmony in the Forbidden City, for example, was closed throughout 2007. The games are also proving a big spur for investors; capital investment in 2007 was estimated at ¥381 billion (about $50 billion). This includes the Olympic venues and infrastructure, transport, energy and water supplies, and environmental improvements. The major Olympic venues have been purpose-built, with an eye on environmentally-friendly methods. They include:

- National Stadium – nicknamed the Bird's Nest, it will host the opening and closing ceremonies, athletics and football. It will seat 91,000, dropping to 80,000. See p.228.
- National Aquatics Centre – The Water Cube will host swimming, diving and water polo events. It will seat up to 11,000 during the games, and 6,000 afterwards. See p.228.

Other venues in the Olympic Green (map 4 F2) include the National Indoor Stadium (gymnastics, trampoline, handball), National Fencing Hall (temporary – fencing, modern pentathlon), Olympic Green Tennis Centre and the Olympic Green Archery Field and Hockey Field, both of which are temporary.

New venues in other parts of the city include the Wukesong Indoor Stadium (basketball), Laoshan Velodrome (cycling), Shunyi Olympic Rowing-Canoeing Park and the Peking University Gymnasium (table tennis). Not all these have been built for the Olympics, however. Among existing venues being used are the Olympic Sports Centre Stadium and Gymnasium (handball, water polo, modern pentathlon), the Workers' Indoor Arena (boxing) and the Workers' Stadium (football). See the Activities chapter, p.205, for a full listing of events and venues.

Key Projects

The Olympics is driving much of the construction in Beijing. Of the 37 venues being used, 31 are in the capital and 19 are new. Most interest centres on the Olympic Green, which has 13 venues, including the iconic National Stadium (see above).

Beijing's Capital International Airport is also undergoing massive expansion, with the opening of ¥27 billion ($3.6 billion) Norman Foster-designed Terminal 3 in February 2008, the world's largest terminal building.

Beijing's new subway Line 5, which runs north-south through the heart of the city, has opened ahead of the Olympics. Three more subway lines are due to be added in 2008, taking the total track length to 200km (125 miles).

The Bird's Nest (p.216)

International Relations

China's economic clout gives it plenty of political power internationally. It maintains good relations with the rest of the world, despite some sensitive issues, because of its value as a trade partner. Other countries are also keen to win the 'approved destination' status that will allow Chinese tourists to visit.

China and Japan have made recent efforts to improve their relations, which remain delicate because of the latter's pre-second world war invasion (see p.4) and denial of the Rape of Nanking.

China is a member of international organisations including the UN, the International Monetary Fund and Unesco, and is one of the five permanent members of the UN Security Council. It is also a member of the G-77 coalition of developing nations and, although not a member, Chinese president Hu Jintao has addressed outreach sessions of G8 several times. China is also a member of the Asia-Pacific Economic Cooperation forum (a body of Pacific Rim countries) and an observer of the Non-Aligned Movement.

It has tended to take a back seat in international affairs, but is beginning to play a more active role, particularly as peace-broker in international wrangles involving North Korea and Iran.

Party Time

The Communist Party of China (CPC) has more than 70 million members and is the largest political party in the world. It was founded in 1921 in Shanghai and Mao Zedong was present at its first congress. Strictly speaking, China is not a one-party state. There are eight minor parties, but they are all under the auspices of the CPC.

Government & Politics

China has been run by the Communist Party of China since the party's foundation in 1949. The head of state is President Hu Jintao, who is also general secretary of the Communist Party and chairman of the Central Military Commission. Hu was elected president in 2003 by the 10th National People's Congress (NPC), which also elected Zeng Qinghong as vice president.

The NPC is the highest political body in China and is a single legislative chamber. It comprises nearly 3,000 deputies who are elected for five-year terms by local people's congresses. Each deputy has a vote for general secretary and vice president, the result decided by simple majority. The NPC meets for two weeks each year to decide policy issues, laws and the budget.

When the NPC is not in session, the Standing Committee, with up to nine members, is effectively China's cabinet.

The State Council is the main administrative body of the government, and is responsible for the day-to-day running of the country. It is chaired by the prime minister, currently Wen Jiabao, who can have up to four deputies.

Below state level, there are 22 provinces (Anhui, Fujian, Gansu, Guangdong, Guizhou, Hainan, Hebei, Heilongjiang, Henan, Hubei, Hunan, Jiangsu, Jiangxi, Jilin, Liaoning, Qinghai, Shaanxi, Shandong, Shanxi, Sichuan, Yunnan and Zhejiang), plus Taiwan, which China sees as its 23rd province.

There are also five autonomous regions (Guangxi, Inner Mongolia, Ningxia, Xinjiang and Tibet) and four municipalities (Beijing, Shanghai, Tianjin and Chongqing), all of which come under the jurisdiction of the State Council.

All ministries and institutions, including news agencies, come under the State Council. The Ministry of National Defence comes under the State Council but the council does not control the military. Provinces have governors elected by local congresses. Municipalities are large cities with the same status as provinces. Autonomous regions are ethnic, province-level areas, which have an elected chairman instead of a governor. The special administrative regions of Hong Kong and Macau have a high level of autonomy under China's 'one country, two systems' policy, brought in when they were transferred back to China (from Britain and Portugal respectively) in the 1990s.

Population

According to the most recent survey by China's National Bureau of Statistics, Beijing's population reached 15.4 million in 2005. However, latest estimates by the city's Commission of Population and Family Planning put the total at 17.4 million. This figure comprises 12 million permanent residents and 5.4 million transients. A report by Peking University's Institute of Population Research predicts that the influx of economic migrants from other parts of China will boost Beijing's population to 20 million by 2020. Beijing Municipal Bureau of Statistics data shows that the city's population has doubled since 1978, when it stood at 8.7 million, although the rate of increase has slowed recently. The capital's birth rate has stayed close to the six per 1,000 mark for the last 10 years, dropping to just over five per 1,000 in 2003. The current level is significantly down on pre 1990 figures and represents just one third of the 17.29 per 1,000 recorded in 1987. This indicates that China's family planning initiatives and one-child policy have had a major impact on family sizes. The average household size is 2.7, below the national average of just over three people. Beijing's resident population is 50.6% male and 49.4% female. The average life expectancy for men in the city is 74 and 78 for women, according to the most recent national census, in 2000.

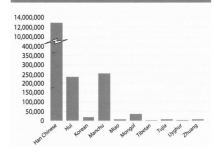

Population by Nationality

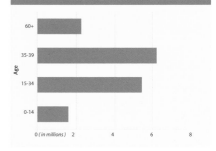

Population by Age Breakdown

The five-starred Red Flag

National Flag

China's national flag, the five-starred Red Flag, was the winning design in a country-wide competition held in 1949. It was first erected by Mao Zedong in Tiananmen Square on October 1, 1949, the day the People's Republic was founded. It is flown on buildings and parks across China on the same date each year, China's National Day. The flag features a red background symbolising revolution, with one large five-pointed yellow star and a semi-circle of four smaller ones in the top left corner signifying the unity of the Chinese people under the leadership of the Communist Party of China. The flag is raised at sunrise and lowered at sunset every day in a ceremony in Tiananmen Square performed by People's Liberation Army soldiers. It is flown throughout the year on key public buildings, airports, ports, railway stations and border posts and by schools during term times.

Time Zones

Athens	-6
Bangkok	-1
Berlin	-7
Canberra	2
Dallas	-14
Denver	-15
Dubai	-4
Dublin	-8
Hong Kong	0
Johannesburg	-6
London	-8
Los Angeles	-16
Manila	0
Mexico City	-14
Moscow	-5
Mumbai	-3
Munich	-7
New York	-13
Paris	-7
Perth	0
Prague	-7
Rio de Janeiro	-11
Santiago	-12
Sydney	2
Tokyo	1
Toronto	-13
Wellington	4

Local Time

Despite its size, the whole of China observes the same time as Beijing, which is eight hours ahead of UCT (Universal Coordinated Time, formerly known as Greenwich Mean Time, or GMT). Daylight saving is not observed, so clocks stay the same all year. The table lists time differences between Beijing and various cities around the world, not incorporating daylight saving time in any country.

Public Holidays

China has four main public holidays, three of which are 'golden weeks'. Although golden weeks are officially three days long, most offices close for the whole week, and New Year's Day follows the same pattern.

The first golden week marks the Spring Festival (Chinese New Year) and starts on the first lunar day of the first lunar month of the Chinese calendar (usually falling in late January or early February). The second starts on Labour Day and the third on China's National Day. Foreign consulates also close on Christmas Day,

Public Holidays 2008

New Year's Day	Jan 1
Spring Festival	Feb 7-9
International Women's Day	Mar 8
Qingming Festival	Apr 5
Labour Day	May 1
National Youth Day	May 4
CPC Founding Day	Jul 1
International Children's Day	Jun 1
Dragon Boat Festival	Jun 8
Army Day	Aug 1
Mid-Autumn Festival	Sep 14
National Day	Oct 1

Boxing Day and at Easter, and a few western companies prefer to stay open during some golden weeks.

Secondary schools get 10 or 11 weeks of holiday and primary schools 13 weeks. Both are spread over summer, Chinese New Year, March and April. Other traditional Chinese holidays include the Qingming Festival, when family tombs are traditionally visited and swept, the Dragon Boat Festival (Duan Wu Jie), and the Mid-Autumn Festival (see p.55).

Temple of Heaven (p.188)

Summer Palace (p.182)

Qianmen Gate (p.182)

SOLUTIONS **AND** ANSWERS
FOR THE EXPATRIATE COMMUNITY

Expat Show gathers Beijing's expatriate community for a unique annual event.
To learn more about the exhibitors, activities, and other useful information please visit :

Climate

Beijing's climate is influenced by the Mongolian plateau to the north-west. It has distinct seasons marked by frequent extremes. Summers are long, hot and humid (due to its proximity to the Yellow Sea), with an average temperature in July of 30ºC (87ºF), but summer highs frequently top 40 ºC (104ºF) and (though rare) can reach 50ºC (122ºF) in August. Storms are most likely in summer, bringing torrential rain which can lead to temporary flooding of roads. More than half the city's annual 27.6 inches (700mm) of rain falls in July and August, so an umbrella is handy. The Beijing Olympic Games were put back by two weeks from the original start date of July 25 (to August 8) because of fears over the heat, humidity and rain. The Beijing Meteorological Bureau incorporates the Beijing Weather Modification Office, and is tasked with controlling the weather for Beijing and surrounding areas. The method of seeding clouds with silver iodide from aircraft and rockets is being used to ensure downpours ahead of the Olympics, in an effort to reduce pollution levels and ensure rain-free event days.

Winters are long and cold but largely dry, with cold fronts from Siberia bringing bitter weather, bone-chilling winds and clear skies. Temperatures in January average -10 ºC (14ºF). Beijing is prone to sandstorms in spring. They sweep in from the expanding Gobi Desert, generally from March to May, and smother the city in a choking, yellow fog which

Seedy Business
China indulges in more cloud seeding than any other country. It is generally used to increase rainfall in dry areas, and is used by more than 20 countries around the world, but its effectiveness remains a cause for debate among scientists.

can linger for days and leaves everything coated in a film of sand. The number of sandstorms is increasing; between February and April 2006 alone the city was hit by 10 storms, one of which lasted 10 days and dumped 300,000 tons of sand on the capital. The rise in frequency is blamed on the desertification of China's arid north-west, made worse by soil erosion as a result of deforestation, farming and overgrazing by livestock.

Beijing's best weather is in September and October, a period called 'golden autumn' for its clear blue skies.

Temperature & Humidity

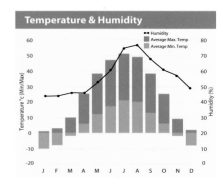

Average Rainfall

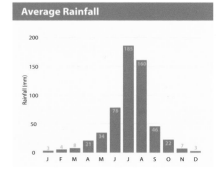

Average Monthly Snowfall

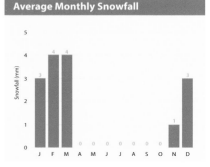

Environment

Flora & Fauna

According to the regularly told joke, the only wildlife you will see in Beijing is likely to be on a plate. The Chinese, another joke runs, have a tendency to eat anything that flies except aircraft and anything with legs except tables. Their reputation for eating birds and animals that would be off-limits in other countries is well-deserved. However, it is also possible to see a surprising amount of wildlife away from the dining table. Unfortunately, the birdsong you might hear in inner-city areas such as the traditional *hutong* neighbourhoods is more likely to emanate from caged birds left outside homes or being taken for a walk by their owners. Beijing's markets are a major source for the trade in caged birds, despite Chinese government legislation protecting many of the country's species. Even with an ever-expanding population, the capital and its environs provide a diverse habitat for both flora and fauna. You will see wildlife everywhere, from city centre parks and suburban wetlands to mountains, forests, and the Yellow Sea coast.

Flora

Beijing's parks are home to many old and stately trees. Among the most impressive species is the Platydadus Orientalis, otherwise known as Oriental Arborvites, which can reach 65 feet (20 metres). Some in Zhongshan Park (p.171) date back 1,000 years. Beihai Park (p.191) contains an example of Sophora Japonica, the native Chinese scholar tree, planted during the Tang Dynasty (AD 618 - 907), while another, almost 900 years old, has pride of place in the Forbidden City (p.180). Beyond the city are forested areas which act as a barrier to the encroaching sands of the Gobi Desert and help to lessen the impact of spring sandstorms.

Fauna

You won't find many beasts in Beijing itself but, according to a late 90s survey, the mountain areas close to the capital are rich in wild animals. The researchers found evidence of populations of wild boars, jackals, wolves and panthers in the forested suburbs. The Sungshan National Nature Reserve to the south-east and Wuling Mountain Municipal Nature Reserve, a two-and-a-half-hour drive north-east of Beijing, are both said to be home to the rare Chinese leopard. The endangered Pere David's deer, once hunted exclusively by emperors, has been re-established in the Milu Wildlife Park after breeding pairs were imported from Britain's Woburn Abbey, where they were saved from extinction.

Feathery Friends

With strict rules regarding pets in many apartment buildings, birds are popular companions. Guanyuan Market (p.281) is a good bet for adding some creature comfort to your new life. See p.280 and p.105 for more information on buying a pet or bringing your own to Beijing.

Birds

Beijing's suburban wetlands and reservoirs are particularly rich in birdlife and attract many different species. The wetland areas include Ye Ya Hu (Wild Duck Lake) and Guanting Reservoir in the north-west, Sahe Reservoirs and Bahe Wetland Park, in Choayang District. City parks such as the Summer Palace (p.182) and Kunming Lake, Beihai Park (p.191) and the Beijing Botanical Gardens (p.190) are also rich in birds, with species such as mallard and teal ducks, goosanders, kingfishers and blue magpies. Mountains and forest areas

Yinding Bridge, Houhai

including the Great Wall at Badaling and Wuling Mountain are good for bird spotting. Here you can find raptors including falcons and sparrowhawks, plus woodpeckers and parrotbills. Beijing lies on a major migration route for raptors (all of which are endangered in China) but increasing human disturbance, illegal hunting and pressure on their habitats has left them vulnerable. As a result, the Beijing Raptor Rescue Centre was set up in 2001 to care for injured birds and those seized from traders by authorities.

Beidahe, on the coast east of Beijing, is on the migration route from Siberia and a good place for bird-watching, as it attracts more than 250 species.

Numbers of swifts have plummeted in the last 25 years. As a result, nestboxes have been put up around Beijing by wildlife preservation authorities to encourage breeding. Birds have also been bought in local markets and taken to wildlife parks for release.

Marine Life

Several rare species have been discovered in the Beijing area after a two-year study of an aquatic nature reserve at Huairou Reservoir, where the Huaisha and Huajiu rivers cross. The 23 species of fish found included the Chinese nine-spine stickleback. Water shrews, white-tailed sea eagles and mandarin ducks also live in the reserve. Other rivers and lakes around the city provide habitats for a cross section of aquatic life.

Environmental Issues

Despite (or perhaps becuase of) China's international reputation as a heavy polluter, Beijing has been talking up it's environmetal credentials. It has set out to stage a 'green Olympics' and aims to make the event as environmentally-friendly as possible. The city has invested ¥120 billion ($14 billion) on environmental protection measures in the last 10 years. Its annual spend has steadily increased since 1999, when the total stood at ¥5.4 billion ($0.7 billion).

But, pollution remains a major worry, especially with the number of private cars hitting three million for the first time, in May 2007. Measures to restrict car usage during the Olympics are being considered. One plan already tried is to ban cars on certain days. The city succeeded in taking 900,000 municipal vehicles off the roads during the three day forum on China-Africa Co-operation in late 2006. A million cars later stayed off the road each day for four days in a test in August 2007. Levels for acceptable vehicle emissions have also been tightened and the city's government said those not meeting the new standards will be scrapped. More than 2,500 polluting buses and 5,000 taxis were withdrawn during 2007.

Beijing's Environmental Protection Bureau set a target of 245 'blue sky days' (when air quality levels are grade II or better) for 2007 after meeting their targets of 241 in 2006 and 234 in 2005. The capital launched its air quality initiative after achieving just 100 blue sky days in 1998.

Water Usage

The city set a target in 2007 to treat 90% of waste water and 97% of waste solids in its eight central districts. Beijing also uses waste methane gas to produce electricity. In addition to these initiatives, the city pumps ten million cubic metres of rainwater a year back into rivers and lakes to improve water quality. It has set a target to recycle 500,000 tonnes of waste water by the end of the tenth Five Year Plan period. Another measure was pumping oxygen into the Tongzihe River to raise oxygen levels. Dirty industries in the Beijing area have also been closed down or relocated to further reduce pollution, and illegal buildings torn down.

Culture

As China's political and cultural heart, Beijing has a strong sense of tradition. Head to a park early in the morning or at a weekend, and you will see locals engaged in activities at the very core of the country's cultural psyche. Groups of people will often be practicing tai chi (p.241), the slow-motion ritual. Originally developed as a martial art, it is now used to maintain fitness and inner peace. Another ritual commonly seen in public places is calligraphy. Practitioners use giant brushes dipped in water-filled buckets to trace the outlines of complex Chinese characters on paving stones, only for them to evaporate in minutes.

Music is another key cultural tradition. Beyond traditional Peking Opera (p.347) performances, locals enjoy gathering at places like the Open Corridor near the Temple of Heaven (p.188) to play traditional instruments or sing. Others engage in lively games of cards or mahjong (p.153). You can find teahouses (p.324) throughout Beijing, and locals love gathering to chat over a pot or their individual flasks or jars. They may discuss politics, but it isn't controversy that draws them there; it is the sense of community spirit and comradeship which endures. Venture onto the vast expanse of Tiananmen Square and you will find families and groups of friends picnicking or enjoying the age-old custom of kite-flying.

Sadly, how much longer such traditions will continue is another matter. Look closer and you will see that most of the people in the parks are elderly. Like every other country, the young are being seduced by the digital age and the traditions of their ancestors do not seem to have the same appeal.

Street Wise

There are a variety of ways of writing addresses in Beijing, but Pinyin words are used throughout this guide. Common examples that you'll notice are lu *(road),* jie *(street) and* dadao *(avenue), and compass points –* bei *(north),* nan *(south),* dong *(east) and* xi *(west). Think of this as the first of many impromptu Mandarin lessons you'll receive during your time in Beijing.*

Language

Other options **Learning Mandarin** p.142

Beijing's official language is Mandarin Chinese (*Putonghua*). A notoriously difficult language to learn, it has no set alphabet and instead uses characters, a type of pictogram, of which there are approximately 50,000. Luckily for Mandarin learners, not all are in everyday use and knowledge of about 3,000 should be enough to read a newspaper. Learning spoken Mandarin is made easier through the use of Pinyin, a system that uses the Roman alphabet to represent pronunciation sounds.

Refrain, however, from breathing a sigh of relief, since spoken Chinese is a tonal language and, in itself, tricky to master. Each character is assigned one of five tones in the spoken form: first tone (high and level), second tone (rising from medium to high), third tone (starting low, dipping lower and then rising again), fourth tone (sharply falling from high to low) and the fifth neutral tone. Characters with the same Pinyin 'spelling' have numerous meanings, each dependent on the particular tone used during pronunciation. A well-known but clear example of this potentially confusing aspect of spoken Chinese uses the word 'ma': pronounced with the first tone (*mā*) it means 'mother'; with the second tone (*má*) it means 'hemp'; with the third tone (*mǎ*) it means 'horse'; with the fourth tone (*mà*) it means 'to swear or reprimand'; and with the fifth tone (*ma*)

Pinyin

Pinyin was first approved in China in 1958, and had replaced several other Romanised forms of Mandarin, (including Wade-Giles and Gwoyeu Romatzyh), as the standard method by 1979. Some Pinyin consonants are particularly confusing when compared with their English equivalents: c, for example, should be pronounced like the 'ts' in 'hits'; q should be pronounced like the 'ch' in 'cheeky'; sh as in 'shout' but with the tongue curled back; x as the 'sh' in 'ship'; z as the 'dz' sound in 'buds'; and zh as the 'j' in 'judge' but with the tongue curled back.

it takes on the grammatical use of a question particle. A slip of the tonal tongue can, therefore, prove embarrassing.

For a foreign student of Mandarin this can pose serious comprehension problems. Regardless of whether you can understand or not, Chinese people greatly appreciate foreigners trying to learn the language and take such efforts as a sign of respect. Learning at least a few phrases is therefore a good way of ingratiating yourself with locals, particularly as many do not speak English.

In business or administrative situations, it is, however, advisable to stick to your native tongue. Starting off with the few Mandarin phrases that you have practised may give the impression you understand more than you do. Fortunately, as well as

Basic Mandarin

General Words

Yes	shìde	是的
No	búshì	不是
Please	qǐng	请
Thank you	xièxiè	谢谢

Greetings

Good morning	zǎo an	早安
Hello	nǐ hǎo	你好
Goodbye	zàijiàn	再见
How are you?	nǐ hǎo ma?	你好吗？
Fine, thank you	hén hǎo, xièxiè nǐ	很好，谢谢 你
Welcome	huānyíng	欢迎

Introduction

My name is (first name)	wǒ jiào...	我叫...
My name is (last name)	wǒ xìng...	我姓...
Where are you from?	nǐ shì nǎlǐ rén?	是哪里人？
I am from (country/city)	wǒ shì (country/city) rén	我是 (country/city) 人

Questions

How much?	duōshǎo?	多少？
Where?	nǎr?	哪儿？
When?	shénme shíhou?	什么时候？
How?	zěnme?	怎么？
What?	shénme	什么？
Why?	wèishénme?	为什么？
Who?	shéi?	谁？

Taxi Or Car Related

Is this the road to (place)?	zhège lù dào bú dào...?	这个路到 不到...？
I'd like to go to (place)	wǒ yào qù...	我要去...
Stop	tíng chē	停车
Turn right	wǎng yòu guǎi	往右拐
Turn left	wǎng zuǒ guǎi	往左拐
Straight	yìzhí zǒu	一直走
Ahead	zài qiánmiàn	在前面
North	běi	北
South	nán	南
East	dōng	东
West	xī	西

Turning (street corner)	lùkǒu	路口
First	dì yīge	第一个
Second	dì èrge	第二个
Road	lù	路
Street	jiē	街
Avenue	dàdào	大街
Roundabout	huándào	环岛
Traffic light	hónglǜdēng	红绿灯
Near	jìn	近
Petrol station	jiāyóuzhàn	加油站
Airport	fēijīchǎng	飞机场
Hotel	jiǔdiàn or bīnguǎn	酒店 or 宾馆
Restaurant	fàndiàn or cānguǎn	饭店 or 餐馆
Please slow down	qíng nǐ kāi màn yìdiǎnr	请你开慢 一点儿

Accidents & Emergencies

Police	jǐngchá	警察
Licence	zhízhào	执照
Accident	shìgù	事故
Papers	wénjiàn	文件
Insurance	bǎoxiǎn	保险
Sorry	duìbuqǐ	对不起
Hospital	yīyuàn	医院
Doctor	yīshēng	医生
Ambulance	jiùhùchē	救护车

Numbers

One	yī	一
Two	ér	二
Three	sān	三
Four	sì	四
Five	wǔ	五
Six	liù	六
Seven	qī	七
Eight	bā	八
Nine	jiǔ	九
Ten	shí	十
One hundred	yì bǎi	一百
One thousand	yì qiān	一千

Local Dialect

Beijing locals generally add 'er' to the end of words, often as a diminutive to emphasize smallness or used as a term of affection. So where other Standard Mandarin speakers would say *men* for door, in Beijing dialect, or Beijing *hua*, it would be menr – similar to a Scotsman saying 'wee door'. But Beijing *hua* also has a rich lexicon of idioms and slang, some of which have passed into national usage. Among them are *si zhou zi*, which means stubbornness, and *huai le cu le*, to make a mess.

standard Mandarin, English is broadly accepted as the language of business in Beijing. Many firms hire English teachers to train their Chinese employees. Many restaurants and bars also cater to the expat population and now have bilingual menus. Venture outside these 'safe-havens', however, and you'll be faced with page upon page of Chinese characters. Smile and point for a new culinary experience. It is also a good idea to take a card with your destination and return address written in Chinese characters to show to taxi drivers.

Mastering Chinese script is even more of a challenge than speaking the language. But you quickly learn to recognise important signs – such as those for men's and ladies' toilets. A lack of native English proofreaders means that numerous examples of 'Chinglish' can be found anywhere from shop signs to instruction manuals, many needing code-breakers to decipher. Luckily, most street signs avoid this trend and stick to Pinyin, making navigation relatively easy.

Other than Mandarin, which is spoken by more than 835 million people worldwide, the main Chinese dialects are Wu and Cantonese. Wu covers south-eastern Jiangsu province and neighbouring Zhejiang plus Shanghai and is spoken by 77 million people. Cantonese covers Hong Kong and Guangdong province, uses traditional Chinese characters as its written form and is spoken by 71 million people worldwide.

Race Relations

Beijing is a melting pot of cultures and nationalities. They co-exist happily most of the time, but there are occasions when tensions do run high. The most recent example was in spring 2005, when thousands of Chinese protestors took to the streets of Beijing and threw stones, bottles and eggs at the Japanese Embassy. Japanese cars and shops were wrecked by rioters in other cities, including Shanghai, and there were calls for boycotts of Japanese goods. It was sparked by a new history textbook in Japan which, China claimed, ignored Japanese wartime atrocities during its occupation of China from 1937 to 1945. Relations have since improved, but a new Japanese film claiming the Nanjing Massacre never happened – 300,000 Chinese lives were lost – could stoke up tensions again.

Religion

The relaxation of controls over religion at the end of the 70s resulted in a surge of spiritual activity. But, there are still far fewer places of worship than before the Cultural Revolution.

There still isn't total freedom of worship. For a congregation to be held, places of worship must register with the government's department for religious affairs and not be seen as a threat to society.

Roman Catholic churches come under the jurisdiction of the state-controlled Chinese Patriotic Catholic Association (CPCA), rather than the Vatican, as the Communist Party does not accept any organisation owing allegiance to a foreign influence. Bishops are chosen by the CPCA and not Rome. This caused a divide and forced some bishops to go 'underground'. However, the government is becoming more conciliatory, and the Vatican has endorsed some CPCA-appointed bishops. There are active Catholic and Protestant churches. Special services are held to mark Christmas and Easter, in addition to weekly services.

Temples representing all three traditional beliefs in China – Taoism, Buddhism and Confucianism – are dotted around, while Muslim and Jewish congregations also have places to worship. Kehillat Beijing was the first congregation to be established following Deng Xiaoping's open door policy almost 30 years ago. There are now about 800 Jews in the city, and weekly services are held at the Capital Club Athletic Centre in Chaoyang (www.sinogogue.org, 010 6467 2225) as well as at a Jewish centre in the same district.

Three mosques cater to the Muslim population. Islam came to China via the Silk Road 1,500 years ago and today there are an estimated 20 million Chinese Muslims. They are primarily the Uyghurs and Hui in the north-west of the country, notably in the autonomous region of Xinjiang and neighbouring areas.

Places Of Worship

Bai Ta Si (White Dagoba Temple)	Xicheng	010 6616 0211
Baiyun Guan (Taoist Temple)	Haidian	010 6346 3531
Beijing Gangwashi Church	Xicheng	010 6617 6181
Cathedral Of The Immaculate Conception (Nan Tang)	Xuanwu	010 6603 7139
Chabad Lubavitch Of Beijing (Jewish)	Chaoyang	010 6486 1321
Chongwenmen Protestant Church	Chongwen	010 6513 3549
Congregation Of The Good Shepherd	Chaoyang	010 8486 2225
Dong Yue Miao (Taoist Temple)	Chaoyang	010 6551 0151
Dongsi Mosque	Dongcheng	010 6525 2770
Fahai Temple	Cuiwei Mountain	010 8871 5776
Haidian Protestant Church	Haidian	010 6257 2902
Jietai Temple	Western Hills	010 6980 6611
Kong Miao Confucian Temple	Dongcheng	010 8401 1977
Kuanjie Protestant Church	Dongcheng	010 6522 9984
Lidai Diwang Miao (Temple Of Past Emperors)	Xicheng	010 6653 0060
Niu Jie Mosque	Xuanwu	010 6353 2564
The River Of Grace Church	Chaoyang	131 2690 5684
Source Of Law Temple (Fayuan Si)	Xuanwu	010 6353 4171
St Michael's (Dongjiaominxiang Cathedral)	Dongcheng	010 6513 5170
Temple Of Azure Clouds	Haidian	010 6259 1155
Wangfujing Catholic Church (East Church)	Dongcheng	010 6524 0634
Wanshou Temple	Haidian	010 6841 3380
West Church	Xizhimen	010 6615 6619
Xiapo Mosque	Chaoyang	010 8562 6316
Xishiku Catholic Church	Xicheng	010 6617 5198
Yonghe Temple (Lama Temple)	Dongcheng	010 6404 3769
Zhushikou Protestant Church	Chongwen	010 6301 6678

National Dress

While China has no official national dress, the *cheongsam* (for men) and *qipao* (for women) are often associated with the country. Introduced by the Manchu Qing Dynasty, which ordered all Han Chinese to adopt the styles, they replaced the traditional *hanfu* gown that had been popular from the days of Confucius. *Cheongsams* were the formal dress for men in pre-Communist China and consisted of a formal jacket (traditionally black for funerals) over a long tunic. Although the female version is often called the *cheongsam*, the correct name is the *qipao*. Tight-fitting, and usually with a slit up one thigh, the elegant dress became synonymous with decadent, early 20th century Shanghai.

The familiar blue Mao suit was brought in by Communist Party leader Mao Zedong in the early days of the People's Republic of China. It was based on the suit said to have been introduced by the father of modern China, Dr Sun Yatsen, after the imperial age ended in 1911.

Culture & Lifestyle

Watchtower on the Great Wall (p.197)

Tai-chi in action

The Gate of Heavenly Peace (p.183)

The Temple of Heaven (p.188)

The Mao suit was ubiquitous for three decades until China's more open policies heralded more liberal attitudes towards dress. While you occasionally see rural workers and old people still sporting the Mao suit, it is the *qipao* which has made a comeback. It is popular as evening wear for parties or formal events and is used as the basis for uniforms by many businesses, including airlines.

China's 55 ethnic minority groups all have their own dress. They often have everyday wear, which sometimes includes hats with wide brims, and formal wear for special occasions, festivals and tourist shows. They frequently include intricate headdresses with fine, hand-worked silver designs. Among the most lavish costumes are those worn by women of the Miao, Yao, Zhuang and Yi minorities of south-west China.

With Beijing's extreme seasons you will need a large wardrobe. Dress for humid summers and chilling winters – and always carry an umbrella. Smart attire, especially for business, is expected, as the Chinese can't see the logic in scruffy clothes unless you are poor. Women can be fashionable, though perhaps not too skimpily dressed. You might want to carry a handkerchief, scarf or cotton face mask to keep the pollution out too.

Face Facts
When invited to a meal, never insist on paying your share of the bill. This would imply the host cannot afford it and result in a loss of 'face'. The face games don't end there. China has an intricate system of subtle-but-important social codes that can potentially cause irreparable damage. For example, you should never yell at someone in public or imply that a colleague can't perform their job.

Food & Drink

Other options **Eating Out** p.300

Order a Chinese take-away elsewhere in the world and it is likely to be oily, bland, swimming in MSG and smothered in salt. This is not representative of the food served up in China. It could be argued there is no such thing as Chinese food in China, as Chinese cuisine actually breaks down into eight major schools – Anhui, Fujian, Guangdong, Hunan, Jiangsu, Shandong, Sichuan and Zhejiang. All are named after the places they originate from and each varies greatly in food preparation methods, serving style, taste and ingredients. They can be grouped into four key regional cuisine styles: northern, southern, eastern and western. Unsurprisingly, Beijing comes under the northern category.

Northern cuisine has developed from the Shandong style and features such specialities as Peking duck (also called Beijing duck) and Mongolian hotpot. A type of Chinese fondue, hotpot consists of a circular pot full of oil placed on a heater in the centre of the table with raw strips of meat and vegetables dropped in by diners to cook. One ingredient the more squeamish might want to avoid putting in the pot is solidified duck blood.

Pick A Pecker

Be prepared for anything when you eat in Beijing. Chicken and duck are often served complete with the head, beak and neck still in situ. Chicken feet are also loved by locals but likely to turn the stomach of non-Chinese. For even more exotic meals, try the night food markets just off Beijing's main shopping street, Wanfujing (p.290). Fried, skewered seahorses, scorpions and silk worms are just some of the tasty snacks available, along with goat genitalia. There is even a penis restaurant (Guolizhuang; 3Dongshishitiao, 010 6405 5698) that serves up horse penis and testicles, dog penis, donkey penis and snake penis. For those unconcerned about preservation, tiger penis is rare, but quietly available in some restaurants.

The Chinese tend to eat much earlier than people in west, particularly Europeans, and finding somewhere to eat after 21:30 can be difficult. Rice may be served with the meal but is often served at the end. Sliced fruit and melons indicate the meal is over. Desserts are usually only offered if you are dining from a western menu. Mooncakes, made with salted egg yolks, are a popular tradition during the Mid-Autumn Festival, which usually falls in September.

Doing Lunch
Long business dinners are the norm for corporate entertainment, with many deals negotiated through a fog of cigarette smoke and baijiu *fumes. To* ganbei, *literally meaning to 'dry your cup', is a form of toast-making instigated by the host or other important guests, in which you are expected to gulp down the contents of your glass in one go.*

Food has traditionally been cheap. The vending stands and little street cafes where many Chinese stop to have breakfast on the way to work cost a pittance for a bowl of noodles, rice congee or other staples. However, the rising cost of fuel has pushed up food production costs, and the resulting increases in food prices have been largely responsible for a sudden surge in inflation. Beijing's food differs markedly from the cuisines of other parts of China. The eastern cuisine styles of Shanghai and Zhejiang are richly-flavoured and sweet. By contrast, in the Sichuan and Hunan cuisine styles, the food is hot and spicy and a speciality is beancurd (*doufu*). Cantonese cuisine comes under the southern style and is what most visitors would be familiar with from the Chinese restaurants of their home countries. The food can be exotic, as the Cantonese have a reputation for eating almost anything.

Chopsticks

Chopsticks remain the eating tool of choice in Beijing's Chinese restaurants, although most mid to high-end eateries will provide a knife and fork on request. Table manners are generally not strict and, particularly in the cheaper establishments, slurping, burping and spitting out bones on the table are common. There are, however, some important rules of social etiquette, especially regarding seating arrangements (VIP guests always sit to the right of the host) and payment (see Face Facts on p.24).

Drink

Alcohol is liberally consumed in Beijing. Chinese red wines such as Great Wall and Grace Vineyard which, until recently were unpalatable, have improved radically, and at prices as low as ¥30 per bottle are good value alternatives to imported wines. Chinese beers such as Tsingtao and Harbin are sold for as little as ¥4 per 700ml bottle, and the Xinjiang (north-west China) brewed black beer sold in the expat-popular Uighur restaurants is worthy competition for overpriced, imported Irish stout. For something a little stronger, try *baijiu*. Literally 'white liquor', this grain-based spirit, brewed to slightly different recipes throughout China, often reaches 50% alcohol and is potent enough to alter both your taste buds and your perception of the world. A gentler liquid refreshment is 'pearl milk tea' (*zhenzhu naicha*), a sweet, milky, black tea filled with chewy sago balls and sold either warm or cold in plastic cups from small kiosks everywhere.
For something a little purer, try some of China's health-promoting green tea (*lucha*). Consumed faithfully by the Chinese, who believe that it staves off cancers and prevents premature ageing, green tea comes in different forms from different regions and can be bought from local stores or large tea markets, such as those in Caobao Lu and Datong Lu. And if your clothes are feeling a little tight, drink some oolong tea, which is believed to have metabolism-boosting and fat-burning properties. Sweet-smelling teas such as jasmine (*molihuacha*) and cholesterol-lowering *pu'er* tea are also popular.

Raw and ready

Beef noodles ¥7

In An Emergency

When trouble strikes there are two important phone numbers that you should remember; that of your local consulate or embassy (see table) and 110, the number for emergency police assistance. You should be connected to an English-speaking officer, but if this is not the case, you can call the foreigners' hotline of the Public Security Bureau (010 8402 0101) which will help you locate your nearest police station. If you find yourself a victim of petty crime, such as pickpocketing, you can either go to your nearest police station or report it via a special hotline (010 6401 1327).

Emergency Numbers	
Emergency Numbers	
Ambulance	120
Fire	119
Local Directory	114
Police	110
Police Traffic	122
Public Security Bureau Division For Foreigners	010 8402 0101
Utilities	
City Emergency Power Supply Bureau	95598
Medical Services	
Beijing Union Hospital	010 6529 5284
Beijing United Family Hospital ▶p.117	010 6433 2345
Hong Kong International Medical Clinic	010 6553 2288
International Medical Centre (24 hr)	010 6465 1561/3
International SOS (24 hr alarm centre)	010 6462 9100

Medical Emergencies

Beijing's medical facilities for foreigners are superior to those in many of China's other major cities. There are several hospitals with English-speaking or foreign staff, including the Beijing United Family Hospital (p.118) and the International SOS Clinic (p.118), which both have 24 hour emergency hotlines. Services don't come cheap however, with an initial consultation costing around ¥800, as opposed to about ¥50 in a local hospital. The emergency number for ambulances is 120, but because of Beijing's traffic jams and the inconsistent standard of facilities within ambulances, it's probably wiser to take a taxi to the hospital.

Embassies & Consulates

There are two main diplomatic areas in Beijing where the majority of embassies and consulates are located: Sanlitun and Jianguomenwai.

Women

Beijing is a relatively safe city for women. Although foreign women may receive lingering glances from local men, it rarely goes any further and women should feel free to dress as they wish. Beijing's buses and the subway are safe for women travelling alone, and taxis are also generally safe; just refrain from taking unlicensed cabs or from travelling alone at night if you are drunk (or intend to have a quick nap en route). In 2006, there were some incidences of attacks on women that gave rise to speculation that crimes against foreigners in Beijing are increasing. Although these were rare cases, it always pays to be vigilant. If you feel at all threatened, immediately call the police on 110. See Crime & Safety p.28.

Children

Beijing is a fantastic place to bring up kids. Not only is it safe, there are world-class international schools, dozens of child-friendly attractions and hundreds of activity groups to keep tots entertained and parents sane.

Embassies & Consulates	
Australia	010 6532 2331
Belgium	010 6532 1736
Brazil	010 6532 2881
Canada	010 6532 3536
France	010 8532 8080
Gabon	010 6532 2810
Germany	010 8532 9000
India	010 6532 1908
Ireland	010 6532 2691
Italy	010 6532 2131
Japan	010 6532 2361
Liberia	010 6532 5617
Myanmar	010 6532 0359
The Netherlands	010 6532 0200
New Zealand	010 6532 2731
Nigeria	010 6532 3631
North Korea	010 6532 1186
Pakistan	010 6532 2504
Russia	010 6532 1381
Singapore	010 6532 3926
South Korea	010 6505 2608
Spain	010 6532 3629
Sweden	010 6532 9790
Thailand	010 6532 1749
UK	010 5192 4000
USA	010 6532 3831

The best place to find a full directory of what's on offer is www.tbjkids.com, an online version of the *That's Beijing Kids* (p.204) magazine. During the hot summer months, follow local residents to Tuanjiehu Park where you'll find a clean, but crowded, beach and wave pool bang in the middle of the city (see p.189). During winter there's ice skating at Le Cool Ice Rink (see p.217), or, for the more adventurous, there's the Qiaobo Ice & Snow World near Shunyi, which has a 150m bunny slope for kids over 3 years old (see p.224). For less active entertainment, the Beijing Aquarium (p.174) is large and modern and has an impressive selection of aquatic life.

When it comes to mealtimes, there are loads of family-friendly restaurants, including the award-winning Grandma's Kitchen (p.304) and Annie's (p.315), the latter being well equipped with several highchairs. Babysitting is not common in Beijing, since most expat families have their own *ayi* (nanny), who often tackles cooking and household chores too, see Domestic Help on p.102 for a list of agencies.

Access Granted
The Summer Palace (p.182) has been fitted with wheelchair ramps, while the Grand Hyatt (p.34) and the Jianguo (p.35) hotels have specially equipped rooms for guests with mobility issues.

People With Disabilities

Arriving at Beijing Capital International Airport you could be fooled into believing that the city is very accommodating to residents with disabilities; facilities are good and staff are friendly. But once you enter the city itself, the helpful smiles soon disappear, along with the lifts and ramps. Although the government, in the run up to the 2008 Olympics and Paralympics, has added dropped kerbs and ramps around Beijing, they are often too steep for wheelchair access. What's more, the tactile pavements that can now be found in most districts are littered with concrete posts, bits of wire and parked motorbikes, making them minefields for the visually impaired. In a similar vein, many tourist attractions have been made to look accessible. The Forbidden City, for example, is one of the few places to show the International Disability Access sign. Go inside, however, and you'll discover steps and a lack of ramps. Newer subway stations (particularly on Line 5) have lifts, but many older stops don't even have escalators. And although government regulations now insist on making buildings wheelchair accessible, they are not always enforced.

What To Wear

Walk Beijing's streets and you'll see labels (and flesh) galore. Although Chinese girls traditionally keep their top halves covered, hemlines are soaring. Hip-hop wannabes and local art school students add further colour, with psychedelic clothes and dyed manes. So, although there are no rules of dress in Beijing, one factor that may affect your choice is the weather. In summer, the air is dry and the sun is scorching, so wear lightweight clothes (with sleeves in the evening to protect against mosquitoes). In winter, temperatures can fall to -10 degrees, so thermal underwear, scarves, hats and gloves are a must. Beijing is reportedly the centre of China's fur trade, and you can see members of the Russian community wearing mink coats throughout the winter months. Spring and autumn are mild, usually only requiring a sweater or light jacket, but beware of sandstorms in March and April, when a large cotton scarf wrapped tightly around your head can provide some protection.

Dos & Don'ts

For westerners, who may be used to seeing smokers shunned at every turn, the prevalence of cigarettes may come as a surprise. Bars and restaurants are full of patrons who have mastered the art of simultaneous eating and smoking. This isn't surprising in a country that is thought to smoke 30% of the world's cigarettes. Drinking laws are similarly relaxed, although recent crackdowns on drug dealers prove that the government draws the line on certain types of revelry.

It is, however, the unwritten rules of culture that are harder for foreigners to follow. Remember, for example, not to ask for extra rice at the end of a meal, or you risk implying that your host has been stingy. And do not insist on paying your share of the bill if you have been asked out for a meal; this is considered most insulting. This important idea of 'face' is an attempt to avoid conflict and preserve dignity. Talking about politically sensitive issues will not ingratiate you with the locals either. Neither will dropping or crumpling business cards, which in China are seen as an extension of the owner and should be given and received with two hands. The same rule applies when exchanging money. There is never any need to tip, and waiters have been known to chase down departing patrons to return extra money.

Soldiers in Tiananmen

Photography

Although most Chinese people don't mind having their photo taken, it's always best to ask before snapping. Quickly showing the image in the digital viewer usually makes things easier. Airports are off limits for photography, although snaps from inside the terminal are unlikely to be reprimanded. Photographing military installations is forbidden and can result in a lot of hassle, and cameras are not welcomed at public disturbances. Temples often charge for taking pictures inside and it is customary to refrain while services are in progress.

Nimble Fingers
Traffic police published a report in 2007 stating which bus routes are the most prone to pickpockets. You are most likely to encounter light fingers on inner-city routes 9, 57 and 44.

Crime & Safety

Other options **In An Emergency** p.26

In comparison to most of the world's capital cities, Beijing is a safe place with a low (but growing) crime rate. In particular, juvenile crime is on the rise, with government statistics suggesting a jump of 33% between 2003 and 2006. These crimes are usually petty ones, like pickpocketing, which is common in Beijing's tourist areas.
Isolated attacks on foreign females, including two murders in 2006, have prompted advice for women not to walk alone in empty streets after dark and to always use reputable taxi companies. The year 2006 also saw some fights between groups of local and foreign men in popular nightlife areas, all involving too much alcohol and testosterone. Drugs are prevalent, though harsh sentences for those caught dealing and using are strictly enforced.
Fraud is something that a foreigner is far more likely to encounter. Counterfeit money is common, and sometimes used by taxi drivers as change. Avoid exchanging money on the black market; not only are you likely to be given fake notes, but you also run the risk of being charged with breaking exchange laws.

Victims Of Crime

If you find yourself a victim of serious crime, you should immediately call the police on 110. Then, contact your local embassy or consulate for advice on whether you need a lawyer. You may find that reporting a petty crime is more trouble than it's worth. Bikes, for example, are stolen so often and re-sold so quickly, that by the time the report is made, the bike is often long gone.

Small but indispensable…

Perfectly proportioned to fit in your pocket, this marvellous mini guidebook makes sure you don't just get the holiday you paid for but rather the one that you dreamed of.

Dubai Mini Visitors' Guide
Maximising your holiday, minimising your hand luggage

EXPLORER

Traffic Accidents & Violations

Government figures released in autumn 2007 claimed there were 57,168 road fatalities in Beijing over the previous twelve months. That's 157 per day. Contrary to what these horrifying statistics may imply, a Road Traffic Safety Law does exist, which, among other things, dictates what you must do if involved in an accident.

Firstly, in a major accident, call the Traffic Police on 122. Do not move your vehicle until they arrive. Secondly, if anyone is injured, all those involved should visit the hospital together. And finally, do not sign any police reports unless you are given a full translation or can read Chinese. Since July 1 2007, you don't have to wait for the police in the case of a minor accident. Instead, just fill out a Car Accident Rapid Handling Agreement (机动车交通事故快速处理协议书) from the police and give it to your insurers.

Speeding on Beijing's roads incurs fines of between ¥200 and ¥2,000 plus three black points on your licence. If you're caught on camera, penalty notices are sent in the post and contain details on where you must pay and how much. Drink driving is illegal in Beijing and those caught with more than 20mg of alcohol per 100ml of blood face fines of up to ¥500 and up to 12 points (the maximum) on their licence. For anything over 80mg per 100ml blood, drivers face fines of up to ¥2,000, the loss of their licence for six months and a possible 15 days in prison. All drunk drivers are put on a blacklist and repeat offenders will lose their licence for at least five years. Serious accidents caused by breaking traffic rules can lead to criminal investigations and detention.

Lost & Stolen Cards

MasterCard	800 110 7309
Amex	800 744 0106
Visa	800 110 2911

Getting Arrested In Beijing

Foreigners in Beijing should not feel beyond the arm of the law. In fact, recent arrests suggest that foreigners may be targets for the city's police. Foreigners arrested in Beijing will be taken to a Public Security Bureau, where they will be questioned, probably fined, possibly detained or even deported. Authorities are entitled to detain a person for up to 15 days without charge, and foreigners for up to four days without informing their embassy or consulate. Foreigners are not allocated state lawyers and are rarely granted bail. Any foreigner who is arrested should contact their embassy or consulate as soon as possible to get information on their rights.

Prison Time

While UN officials and foreign journalists often report that conditions in Chinese jails are poor, state newspapers and government reports claim that the system favours modern methods of rehabilitation.

In general, visitation rights are limited, but Beijing Prison has opened its doors to members of the public. Facilities are certainly spotless, and each cell even has its own fish tank. Access beyond these model prisons is more restricted.

Few prisoners get parole, unless they are terminally or critically ill, very old and weak, or pregnant and lactating. Some 70 crimes carry a possible death sentence, including drug dealing, political activism and murder. Official execution statistics are unavailable, but Amnesty International claims more than 1,010 people were executed in China in 2006, two thirds of the global total for that year. China's Deputy Health Minister, Huang Jiefu, acknowledged China's controversial trade in the organs of executed prisoners in 2005, and vowed to try and put an end to the problem.

Police

Within Beijing's Public Security Bureau there are seven branches of police. The regular police wear dark blue uniforms and hats, and carry batons instead of pistols. Traffic Police have similar uniforms but wear white helmets and usually drive motorbikes. The household registration police are the ones you'll find knocking at your door to check if you have an up-to-date residency permit.

Hopefully, you will never come face-to-face with the Criminal Investigative Police, who are either uniformed or in civilian dress and deal with serious crimes involving, for example, narcotics, organised crime or fraud.

Beijing's Fire Brigade is also part of the police force, and is stationed around the city. The Special Duties or Riot Police are only seen at times of civil unrest. The People's Armed Police Force wears olive green uniforms and stands guard at party and government institutions.

Don't confuse the police with the PLA (People's Liberation Army), which you'll see marching around the city. They're easy to spot, with olive green uniforms, and many appear to be quite young. In the run up to the Olympics, many everyday police officers have been sent to English language classes, and although most speak no more than a few words, they are generally approachable and helpful. To avoid trouble, foreigners shouldn't involve themselves in police matters involving Chinese citizens, and should not take photographs of arrests.

The Whole World's Your Home

Explorer Residents' Guides are going global with new titles for locations as far flung as Dublin and New Zealand. So if you fancy living abroad check out the complete list of current and upcoming Explorer guides on our website www.explorer publishing.com. Remember, life's a trip... all you need to do is pick a destination.

Lost & Stolen Property

If you have something stolen, report the crime at the nearest police station within 24 hours and, for insurance purposes, do not leave without getting a police report. Although translators should be at hand, be prepared for a long process. If you leave something in a taxi, check the receipt for the taxi number and contact phone number. For anything lost within Beijing Capital International Airport, go to Room 12026, near door 15 on the first floor, where you will find the lost property department or call 010 6454 0110.

Lost Passports

If you lose your passport, immediately inform your embassy and then visit counter number 37 in the reception hall of the Exit & Entry Administration Department of the main Public Security Bureau (公安局, 2 Andingmen Dongdajie, Dongcheng). For details of what documents to bring, visit www.bjgaj.gov.cn.

City Information

The Beijing Tourism Administration is a government department dedicated to helping visitors and residents get the most out of the city. It runs tourist information centres in many districts, where the staff all speak some English. You can pick up maps and shopping guides and find out what's on in the city's theatres.

The website is a good place to find practical tips for travel, visa and customs information (www.english.visitbeijing. com.cn). You can also call an English-speaking member of staff on the 24 hour Tourist Hotline (010 6513 0828). The China National Tourism Office has several branches

Beijing Tourism Offices Overseas		
Australia	Sydney	(+61) 2 9299 4057
France	Paris	(+33) 1 5659 1010
Germany	Frankfurt	(+49) 69 520 135
Singapore	Singapore	(+65) 337 2220
United Kingdom	London	(+44) 20 7935 9787
USA	New York	(+1) 888 760 8218

around the world (see table). Two other helpful websites that offer information on tourist attractions and practical travel tips are www.thebeijingguide.com and www.beijingpage.com. The official website of the Beijing Olympic Games provides Olympics related news (www.en.beijing2008.cn).

Places To Stay

Whether you're travelling on a shoestring or are aided by a hefty expense account, you'll almost certainly be able to find somewhere suitable to stay. From simple hostels (p.40) and budget motels to charming courtyard guesthouses and gleaming five-star hotels, the options vary widely in price and service. And if you're planning on staying for longer than a few weeks, there are dozens of serviced apartments available for rent (see p.38). Beijing's tourist industry is flourishing. According to www.chinahospitalitynews.com and the Beijing Municipal Bureau of Tourism, the city's high-end hotels are enjoying average occupancy rates of 75.3%, with peaks of over 95% during holidays or trade fairs, so make sure to book ahead.

Hotels
Other options **Landmark Hotels** p.34

Beijing's hotel industry is booming. According to real estate advisors DTZ, there will be 800 hotels in the city by the end of 2008, up from 700 at the end of 2007. This will provide up to 130,000 rooms. Hotels are clustered in several different areas. Upscale business establishments can be found in the CBD around Guomao subway station, along Xicheng's new 'Financial Street' and in the Lufthansa business district beside the Airport Expressway. Many tourist favourites are in Wangfujing, near to the Forbidden City and Tiananmen Square, as well as in Dongcheng district's remaining *hutongs*, where a rising number of courtyard hotels can be found.

All of the big brands have staked their claim, so names such as Park Hyatt, Ritz-Carlton and Shangri-La are among the 18 new upscale hotels being built. You'll pay anything from ¥2,000 to more than ¥60,000 for the honour of staying in one of these opulent establishments, but can of course expect spacious, gadget-filled rooms, lavish spas, world-class restaurants and sometimes, a personal butler. With these luxury hotels you can usually trust the five star ratings, but the local government's own star rating of

Red Capital Hotel (p.36)

The Peninsula (p.35)

cheaper hotels tends to fall short of western expectations. Many midrange places, for example, claim to be three or four star but often lack character, facilities and English speaking staff. At prices of between ¥500 and ¥2,000 per night, you may do better at a traditional courtyard hotel, which makes up for a lack of amenities and mediocre restaurants with bags of historical charm.

For something completely out of the ordinary, try Commune by the Great Wall (see Four Star list, below), an ambitious hotel in which local and international architects designed 11 contemporary villas on a mountain beside the Great Wall. Whole houses are rented out from ¥12,500 per night.

Budget Hotel Accommodation

The budget accommodation sector, which until recently was dominated by some pretty shabby digs, has improved dramatically with the arrival of chains such as Super 8 Motels, Home Inns and Motel 268 (see table). These all offer simple, clean accommodation for prices averaging ¥250 per night. By the end of 2007, the number of budget hotels in Beijing was predicted to reach over 200, providing more than 13,000 rooms.

Hotels

Five Star			
China World	中国大饭店	010 6505 2266	www.shangri-la.com
Grand Hyatt	东方君悦大酒店	010 8518 1234	www.beijing.grand.hyatt.com
Hilton	希尔顿酒店	010 5865 5000	www.beijing.hilton.com
Kempinski	凯宾斯基饭店	010 6465 3388	www.kempinski-beijing.com
Kerry Centre	嘉里中心饭店	010 6561 8833	www.shangri-la.com
Peninsula	北京王府半岛酒店	010 8516 2888	www.beijing.peninsula.com
Raffles	北京饭店莱佛士	010 6526 3388	www.beijing.raffles.com
Regent	丽晶酒店	010 8522 1888	www.regenthotels.com
Ritz-Carlton	丽思卡尔顿饭店	010 6601 6666	www.ritzcarlton.com
Shangri-La	香格里拉酒店	010 6841 2211	www.shangri-la.com
Sofitel Wanda	万达索菲特大酒店	010 8599 6666	www.sofitel.com
St Regis	北京国际俱乐部饭店	010 6460 6688	www.stregis.com/beijing
Four Star			
Commune By The Great Wall	长城脚下的公社	010 8118 1888	www.communebythegreatwall.com
Jianguo	建国饭店	010 6500 2233	www.hoteljianguo.com
Novotel Xinqiao	新侨诺富特饭店	010 6513 3366	www.accorhotels.com/asia
Park Plaza Wangfujing	王府井丽亭酒店	010 8522 1999	www.parkplaza.com/beijingcn
Three Star			
Bamboo Garden	竹园宾馆	010 5852 0088	www.bbgh.com.cn
Beijing Shatan	北京沙滩宾馆	010 8402 6688	www.shatanhotel.com
Holiday Inn Central Plaza	中环假日酒店	010 8397 0088	www.ichotelsgroup.com
Motel 268 Wangfujing	王府井莫泰268	010 5167 1666	www.motel168.com
Two Star			
Comfort Inn	凯富酒店	010 8523 5522	www.choicehotels.com
Fangyuan	芳园宾馆	010 6525 6331	www.cbw.com/hotel/fangyuan
Home Inn	如家快捷酒店	010 6317 3366	www.homeinns.com
Luxury Boutique			
Hotel Côte Cour	No Chinese Name	010 6512 8020	www.hotelcotecoursl.com
Red Capital Residence	新红资客栈	010 8403 5308	www.redcapitalclub.com.cn
Budget			
Jinjiang Inns	锦江之星旅馆	010 400820 9999	www.jinjianginns.com
Super 8 Motels	速8酒店	010 400810 7822	www.super8.com.cn

Landmark Hotels

24 Xiaoshiqiao Hutong
Jiugulou Jie
Xicheng
旧鼓楼大街小石桥胡
同24号
西城区
🚇 *Gulou*
Map 8 C1 **1**

Bamboo Garden Hotel 竹园宾馆

010 5852 0088 | *www.bbgh.com.cn*
This popular courtyard hotel is on a traditional *hutong* near Beijing's Drum Tower. All rooms are nostalgically decorated with faux Ming and Qing dynasty furniture, heralding the days when it was the private residence of an imperial minister. Bathrooms are modern and there is broadband access throughout. The two main restaurants serve authentic imperial cuisine.

1 Jianguomenwai Dajie
Chaoyang
建国门外大街1号
朝阳区
🚇 *Guomao*
Map 11 F3 **2**

China World 中国大饭店

010 6505 2266 | *www.shangri-la.com*
The luxury China World is a landmark hotel on top of one of Beijing's best, and most exclusive, shopping malls. The sumptuous lobby is a popular meeting place for businessmen and residents who often retire to Aria, the hotel's renowned restaurant and wine bar. There is Wi-Fi access throughout.

1 Dongchangan Jie
Chongwen
东长安街1号
崇文区
🚇 *Wangfujing*
Map 10 F3 **3**

Grand Hyatt 东方君悦大酒店

010 8518 1234 | *www.beijing.grand.hyatt.com*
This is next to the mammoth Oriental Plaza mall and just 15 minutes from Tiananmen Square. Its 825 rooms are neither huge nor inspirationally decorated, but they fulfil the needs of the executive traveller. Made in China (p.309) offers Dongbei cuisine with a modern twist and the intimate Redmoon Bar is good for a *Lost in Translation* encounter.

1 Dongfang Lu, Dong
Sanhuan Beilu
Chaoyang
东三环北路东方路1号
朝阳区
🚇 *Dongzhimen*
Map 5 C4 **4**

Hilton 希尔顿酒店

010 5865 5000 | *www.beijing.hilton.com*
The Hilton is at the heart of Beijing's Lufthansa business district, only 25 minutes from the airport. Its once seedy reputation has improved following a major facelift, and it now houses the popular Zeta Bar (p.340), as well as arguably the city's best toilets. Wine connoisseurs will appreciate the hotel's very own wine humidor and sommelier.

70 Yan Yue Hutong
Dongcheng
演乐胡同70号
东城区
🚇 *Dongdan*
Map 11 A3 **5**

Hotel Côté Cour

010 6512 8020 | *www.hotelcotecoursl.com*
More hip than many of Beijing's courtyard hotels, Hotel Côté Cour has taken on the 'boutique hotel' mantra with style and gusto. The 14 rooms and suites are lovingly decked out with goose down duvets, Chinese silk, polished brick floors, flat screen TVs and free Wi-Fi. Remember though, small doesn't necessarily mean cheap.

Jianguo 建国饭店

5 Jianguomenwai Dajie
Chaoyang
建国门外大街5号
朝阳区
🚇 *Yonganli*
Map 11 E3 6

010 6500 2233 | www.hoteljianguo.com
A long-standing favourite, the hotel underwent a makeover in 2006 and, as a result, room standards (in building A) and prices have risen. It offers a slice of greenery in the heart of the business district, in addition to a large indoor pool and health club. Extensive business facilities are available, as are suites with kitchenettes for extended stays.

Kempinski 凯宾斯基饭店

50 Liangmaqiao Lu
Chaoyang
亮马桥路50号
朝阳区
🚇 *Dongsishitiao*
Map 5 c4 7

010 6465 3388 | www.kempinski-beijing.com
Although older than many of Beijing's top-end hotels, the Kempinski remains popular, especially with German businessmen who value the professional service and the spectacle of Chinese waitresses serving good beer in Bavarian dress at the nearby Paulaner Brauhaus. Inside the hotel complex there is the fantastic Kempi Deli (p.264). Refurbishments began in 2007.

Kerry Centre 嘉里中心饭店

1 Guanghua Lu
Chaoyang
光华路1号
朝阳区
🚇 *Guomao*
Map 11 F2 8

010 6561 8833 | www.shangri-la.com
Despite being a little worn around the edges, the Kerry Centre Hotel's 487 rooms are spacious and clean. Its most famous draw is its bar, Centro (p.329), which consistently wins awards for the city's best cocktails. Always packed, it is a regular haunt for expats and lone business travellers, who appreciate the sultry waitresses.

Peninsula 北京王府半岛酒店

8 Jinyu Hutong
Wangfujing
Dongcheng
王府井金鱼胡同8号
东城区
🚇 *Dengshikou*
Map 10 F2 9

010 8516 2888 | www.beijing.peninsula.com
A member of the prestigious Peninsula Group, this hotel oozes exclusivity, from the attached shopping arcade filled with Cartier and Gucci boutiques, down to the slightly pompous behaviour of staff members. Club Deluxe rooms allow you access to the Club Lounge, offering unlimited free drinks and snacks. Suites are spacious, with TVs in the bathroom.

Raffles 北京饭店莱佛士

33 Dongchangan Jie
Wangfujing
Dongcheng
东长安街33号
东城区
🚇 *Wangfujing*
Map 10 F3 10

010 6526 3388 | www.beijing.raffles.com
This historic hotel dates from the 1900s, when it was a focal point of Beijing socialite life. In 2006 it was completely refurbished and now houses 171 immaculate rooms decorated in an elegant mix of Chinese and French design. Lunch at Jaan, the hotel's fine dining restaurant, is an absolute treat. *Conde Nast Traveller* placed the hotel on its hot list in 2007.

Red Capital Residence 新红资客栈

9 Dongsiliutiao
Dongcheng
东四六条9号
东城区
🚇 *Dongsishitiao*
Map 9 A3 **11**

010 8403 5308 | *www.redcapitalclub.com.cn*

This eccentric courtyard guesthouse, set down a *hutong*, is a refreshing contrast to Beijing's other corporate offerings. Filled to the (slightly dusty) rafters with communist kitsch knick-knacks, its Bomb Shelter Bar and five suites evoke a bygone era. Rather than luxury, you pay for a memorable experience in a place filled with historical charm.

Regent 丽晶酒店

99 Jinbao Lu
Wangfujing
Dongcheng
王府井金宝街99号
东城区
🚇 *Dengshikou*
Map 7 A2 **12**

010 8522 1888 | *www.regenthotels.com*

Opened in 2007, the Regent is the pinnacle of luxury. All 500 guestrooms are spacious, sumptuously decorated and have flatscreen TVs. The buffet breakfast is considered by many to be the best in town. Tiananmen Square and the Forbidden City are nearby, making the hotel a good choice for tourists.

Ritz-Carlton 丽思卡尔顿酒店

1 Jinchengfang
Dongjie
Xicheng
金城坊东街1号
西城区
🚇 *Fuxingmen*
Map 6 E2 **13**

010 6601 6666 | *www.ritzcarlton.com*

This addition to Beijing's five-star hotel scene has received rave reviews since it opened in 2006. Located on the city's new Financial Street, it is convenient for business travellers who will also appreciate its chic decor, gadget-filled rooms, comfortable beds and 1,500sqm spa.

Sofitel Wanda 万达索菲特大酒店

93 Jianguo Lu, Tower C
Wanda Plaza
Chaoyang
建国路93号万达广
场C座
朝阳区
🚇 *Da Wang Lu*
Map 7 C2 **14**

010 8599 6666 | *www.sofitel.com*

Opened in October 2007, the Sofitel Wanda is a stunning mixture of opulent Tang dynasty and modern French design. All 417 rooms have all-feather beds, LCD TVs in the bedroom and bathroom and free wireless internet. The hotel's signature Le Pré Lenôtre (p.314) restaurant is inspired by the three michelin star rated, Le Pré Catelan in Paris.

St Regis 北京国际俱乐部饭店 （圣瑞吉斯饭店）

21 Jianguomenwai
Dajie
Chaoyang
建国门外大街21号
朝阳区
🚇 *Jianguomen*
Map 7 A2 **15**

010 6460 6688 | *www.stregis.com*

Not the newest, but certainly one of the best hotels in Beijing, and the choice of President Bush and his entourage when they visit. From the grand marble lobby, to the personal butler service and the excellent Danieli's restaurant, this hotel exudes class. Other highlights include a natural hot spring spa, a bowling alley and a rooftop putting green.

Life in the fast lane?

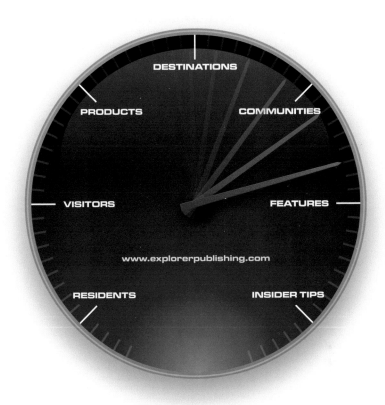

Life can move pretty quickly so make sure you keep in the know with regular updates from **www.explorerpublishing.com**

Or better still, share your knowledge and advice with others, find answers to your questions, or just make new friends in our community area

www.explorerpublishing.com – for life in real time

Hotel Apartments

If you're staying in Beijing for more than a few weeks, you may want to consider renting an apartment. They are less claustrophobic than a hotel room, with a kitchenette for those nights when you can't bear the thought of another takeaway. At the top end of the scale are the fully serviced hotel-style apartments, which can be rented out daily, monthly, weekly and even yearly, with longer terms securing discounted prices. Most come with the added benefits of a hotel like a gym, pool, security staff and daily maid service. One-bedroom apartments start from about ¥17,000 per month.

Self-catering apartments are often in residential complexes and can be rented directly from the owner or through an agency. Ranging wildly in price but certainly cheaper than fully serviced apartments, they start from around ¥5,500 per month for a one-bedroom place. Check out www.moveandstay.com/beijing for an overview of what's on offer or see local magazines (p.51).

Hotel Apartments

Ascott Beijing ▶ p.39	北京雅诗阁服务公寓	010 6567 8100	www.the-ascott.com
Beijing Landmark Apartments	北京亮马河大厦	010 6590 6588	www.beijinglandmark.com
Beijing New World Apartments	北京新世界公寓	010 6702 9902	www.nwcl.com.hk
Boutique Beijing Fortune Land	北京富邦国际酒店	010 8771 8866	www.boutiquehotelsandresorts.com
China World Apartments	国贸公寓	010 6505 2288	www.cwtc.com
Fraser Residence	辉盛庭国际公寓	010 5870 9188	www.frasershospitality.com
Kerry Residences	嘉里公寓	010 8529 8383	www.beijingkerrycentre.com
Lost Inn	螺丝钉时尚驿居	010 8706 1690	www.lost-inn.com
Luxury Serviced Residence ▶ p.39	北京丽舍服务公寓	010 6566 2200	www.the-ascott.com
Millenium Heights	尊萃豪庭公寓	010 8518 1188	www.orientalplaza.com
Oakwood	奥克伍德公寓	010 8446 5824	www.oakwood.com
Palm Springs	棕榈泉国际公寓	010 8595 7777	www.marriott.com
Rosedale Hotel & Suites	珀丽酒店	010 5960 2288	www.rosedalebj.com
Somerset Grand Fortune Garden ▶ p.39	盛捷福景苑高级服务公寓	010 8451 8888	www.somerset.com
Somerset ZhongGuanCun ▶ p.39	北京盛捷中关村服务公寓	010 5873 0088	www.somerset.com
Westin Executive Residences	威斯汀大酒店	010 6606 8866	www.starwoodhotels.com
ZhongGuanCun Residence ▶ p.39	北京中关村租赁公寓	010 5873 0088	www.the-ascott.com

Guest Houses

The term 'guesthouse' is hard to define in Beijing. Some, like the well-known Haoyuan Guesthouse, are more like hotels, offering beautifully decorated rooms filled with mod cons for around ¥800 per night. Others resemble a traditional B&B, offering simple accommodation in a private house. Staying in one of these offers visitors a chance to see how the locals live, and many hosts are more than happy to act as both guide and chef. Prices in these traditional guesthouses are low, even lower than in Beijing's budget hotels, and can start at around ¥65 per person per night. Make sure to check out www.bb-china.com for comprehensive listings of Beijing's most attractive B&Bs and guesthouses.

Guest Houses

4 Banqiao Courtyard	板桥四号客栈	010 8403 0968	www.4banqiaocourtyard.com
Beijing Courtyard Guesthouse	帽儿28B&B	136 6121 9901	www.bb-china.com
Gu Xiang 20	古巷20号商务会所	010 6400 5566	www.guxiang20.com
Haoyuan Guesthouse	好园宾馆	010 6512 5557	www.haoyuanhotel.com
Liyi's Inn	丽宜客栈	136 2113 7003	http://liyis-inn.tripod.com
LuSongYuan Hotel	侣松园宾馆	010 6404 0436	www.sinohotelguide.com
Sihe Hotel	四合宾馆	010 5169 3555	www.sihehotel.com

Hostels

Hostels provide by far the best value accommodation. Long gone are the days when the best you could expect was a bland YMCA offering. In the past few years scores of hip private establishments have opened their doors, many of them offering dorm beds in renovated courtyard houses for as little as ¥55 per night. Some, like the Red Lantern House, also offer comfortable doubles with en suites for ¥220 per room per night, which would be just as suited to couples as backpackers. A common lack of en suite bathrooms and temperamental heating or air-con may, however, make some hostels unsuitable for families with young children or elderly travellers. Business travellers might find the lack of phones in rooms problematic, although many hostels now provide free internet. Online bookings at a large selection of hostels can be found at www.hostelbeijing.com.

Hostels			
4 Banqiao Courtyard	板桥四号客栈	010 8403 0968	www.4banqiaocourtyard.com
9 Dragon House	鑫茂青年酒店	010 8403 6146	www.hostels.com
Beijing Downtown Backpackers	北京东堂客栈	010 8400 2429	www.backpackingchina.com
Beijing Far East Youth Hostel	北京远东饭店国际青年宾馆	010 5195 8811	www.fareastyh.com
Beijing Jade Youth Hostel	北京智德青年旅馆	010 6525 9966	www.xihuahotel.com
Beijing Lotus Hostel	北京莲舍	010 6612 8341	www.lotushostel.cn
Hutong Inn	枣园居宾馆	136 6118 1267	www.beijinghutonginn.com
Lama Temple Int'l Youth Hostel	雍和国际青年旅舍	010 6402 8663	na
Leo Hostel	广聚元饭店	010 8660 8923	www.leohostel.com
Peking Int'l Youth Hostel	北平国际青年旅舍	010 6526 8855	www.hostelbeijing.com
Qianmen Hostel	前门客栈	010 6313 2369	www.qianmenhostel.com
Red Lantern House	红灯笼客栈（古园宾馆）	010 6611 5771	www.redlanternhouse.com
Sleepy Inn Downtown Lakeside	北京丽舍什刹海国际青年旅舍	010 6406 9954	www.sleepyinn.com
Templeside House Hostel	广济.邻 国际青年旅舍	010 6617 2571	www.templeside.com
Youyi Youth Hostel	友谊青年酒店	010 6417 2632	www.poachers.com.cn
Zhaolong Int'l Youth Hostel	兆龙国际青年旅馆	010 6597 2299	www.zhaolonghotel.com.cn

Campsites

Other options **Camping** p.209

Camping is becoming popular among Beijing expats who crave respite from the city's smog. There are some fantastic spots only about an hour north of town, all surrounded by green mountains, gorges and waterfalls. Although adventurous types feel happy marching off on their own with nothing but a map and tent, others may prefer something more established, such as Camping Beijing, a campsite of 100 lots and 10 bungalows about 50km north of the city centre. A spot for a three-person tent costs ¥195 per night, and includes 24 hour security and the use of a hot water and shower block (www.campingbeijing.com). Yunmengshan is a forest park straddling Miyun County and Huairou district about 85km north of the city centre. Ask at the park's main gates for directions to the very basic campsite in a clearing in the forest (www.yunmengshan.net). Green Dragon Gorge in Huairou district is another popular spot to set up tent (www.bjhr.gov.cn/eng/qinglongxia.htm). U-Do Adventure (www.udoadventure.com) organises alpine trekking and camping around Beijing while Mountainyoga also runs camping retreats by the Great Wall at which you sleep in native Indian tipis (www.mountainyoga.cn). The best time for camping is late spring and early autumn when the weather is mild. For more information on camping, check out the Activities section on p.205.

The definitive media group

Connected to a huge network of consumers,
Media Manbu is one of the only media companies
reaching Chinese, English and Japanese communities.

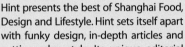

Getting Around
Other options **Exploring** p.151

Considering that the municipality of Beijing is the same size as Belgium, it is hardly surprising that a simple trip from one end of the city to the other can often take more than 90 minutes But it's not just the immense proportions of the capital that make travelling across it so time-consuming, traffic jams also play a major role. The city of 'nine million bicycles' has modernised, and cars have become the favoured form of transport among a rapidly growing middle class. Every day, 1,000 new cars are registered, and the roads are paying the price.

Changan Jie, a long boulevard that bisects the city from east to west, is Beijing's very own Champs-Élysées, lined with major hotels and shopping malls. Tiananmen Square and the Forbidden City lie at its centre, with Xi Changan Jie to the west and Dong Changan Jie to the east. Changing its name twice more, it becomes Jianguomennei Dajie until it crosses the Second Ring Road where it turns into Jianguomenwai Dajie. Note here the use of compass points: *xi* (west), *dong* (east), as well as *nei* (inside), and *wai* (outside), which are seen in many of Beijing's street names. Cutting through this main east-west thoroughfare are Beijing's six ring roads. The two innermost are the Second and Third Ring Roads, inside which you'll find downtown Beijing and most of the city's major attractions and entertainment areas. During the daily rush hours of 07:30 to 10:00 and 16:00 to19:30, traffic on these roads is at a standstill. The Fourth Ring Road can also be crippled by congestion, making a detour to the outlying Fifth Ring Road a lengthy but sometimes worthwhile trek if you need to get across the city quickly. Lying 10km from the city centre and close to many Olympic venues, it has earned the nickname Olympic Avenue. Finally the Sixth Ring Road, which lies almost 20km from downtown, is useful for those who live in the villa communities of Shunyi to the north-east of the city.

Taxis and buses, though cheap and numerous, are subject to the same traffic jams as private cars. The subway is a much faster option but current lines are few, and do not reach many parts of the city. Things are changing, however, as the government realises the necessity of a strong public transportation network. 2007 saw the opening of subway Line 5, with 90% of Line 4 scheduled for completion by 2008. Line 10 should also be finished in time for the Olympics. By 2015 the government hopes to have opened another 561km of lines, aimed at carrying eight million passengers a day. Until then, you can always explore Beijing by bicycle, a method made easier by the wide cycle paths throughout many parts of the city.

Chinese Script
Most of mainland China has adopted the use of simplified Chinese characters. They were largely introduced by the government via two documents in 1956 and 1964, although were already in common usage. The aim was to cut the number of strokes used per character to make writing Chinese easier. Further simplifications were proposed soon after Mao's death in 1977, but were then withdrawn because the timing meant they were unpopular. The Kangxi Dictionary – the standard Chinese dictionary of the 18th and 19th centuries – contained a mind-boggling 49,000 characters. Thankfully, studies have shown that full literacy only requires knowledge of between 3,000 and 4,000 characters.

Air Travel

Beijing Capital International Airport
Beijing Capital International Airport is made up of two terminals: the older Terminal 1 covers around 60,000sqm while Terminal 2, opened in 1999, covers an area of 336,000sqm. Terminal 2 is supposedly able to handle 26 million passengers a year, but since the airport's traffic is increasing annually by 20%, its facilities are being pushed to the limit. Queues at check-in and through customs and immigration can be painfully long. International transfers are particularly time-consuming, as you are forced to fill out several forms and to queue up twice at immigration (to get out and then in again). This situation is not helped by a lack of well-informed or English-speaking airport staff. Information on

You're this close to Brits worldwide

 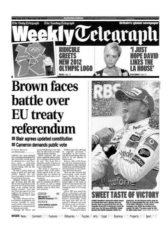

Go online at **telegraph.co.uk/expat** for the most comprehensive range of information services available to Brits outside of the UK - and tap into a world network of well-travelled, knowledgeable and friendly expats, many of whom actively contribute to the site and support each other both locally and from afar.

Produced by the publisher's of the Weekly Telegraph, from the home of The Daily Telegraph and Sunday Telegraph, **telegraph.co.uk/expat** is of real value to Brits worldwide. Go online and see for yourself.

Also online, you can subscribe to the **WeeklyTelegraph** and have the UK's global newspaper delivered direct to your home or office on a weekly basis. Alternatively, subscribe via our credit card orderline +44 1622 33 50 80 quoting ref. EXP08, lines open 0900 - 1700 BST.

Telegraph.co.uk/expat

the expat community online

Airlines

Air Canada	010 6468 2001	www.air-a.com
Air China	010 6656 9226	www.airchina.com.cn
Air France	400 880 8808	www.airfrance.com.cn
Austrian Air	010 6464 5999	www.aua.com
British Airways	400 650 0073	www.british-airways.com
China Eastern Airlines	95808	www.ce-air.com
China Southern Airlines	95539	www.cs-air.com
Continental Airlines	010 8527 6696	www.continental.com
Dragon Air	400 881 0288	www.dragonair.com
Japan Airlines	400 888 0808	www.cn.jal.com
KLM	400 880 8222	www.klm.com.cn
Korean Air	400 658 8888	www.koreanair.com
Lufthansa	400 886 8868	www.lufthansa.com.cn
Malaysia Airlines	010 6505 2081	www.malaysiaairlines.com
Qantas	800 819 0089	www.qantas.com
Scandinavian Airlines	010 8527 6100	www.flysas.com
Shanghai Airlines	010 6459 0901	www.shanghai-air.com
Singapore Airlines	010 6505 2233	www.singaporeair.com
Thai Airways	010 8515 0088	www.thaiairways.com
United Airlines	800 810 8282	www.united.com

flight delays or cancellations is also in short supply. Arrivals are on the first floor, where you'll find several banks for exchanging money and a branch of the Beijing Tourist Information Centre. In the departures hall on the second floor you'll find more banks, a first-aid clinic (in the domestic section) and a limited range of overpriced, tacky souvenir shops, duty free and some pretty uninspiring restaurants. Luggage can be left for up to seven days in the lockers that are found in both arrivals and departures. For property lost in the airport terminals, call 010 6459 8333. For general inquiries regarding flight schedules or the airport itself, call 010 6454 1100. Complaints can be made at 010 6456 1200.

To cope with the 550,000 expected visitors to the upcoming Olympics, Capital Airport has enlisted famous British architect, Lord Norman Foster, to design its new Terminal 3. Due to open in February 2008, the $4.6 billion terminal will cover more land than London Heathrow's four terminals combined and will resemble an airborne dragon. Rumour has it that plans are already being made to build another international airport in the south-east of Beijing.

Airport Services
The airport does not have e-gates although there are electronic check-in counters for Air China at counters 46 and 47 in the departures hall.

Airport Transport
Lying 26km north-east of the city centre, Beijing's Capital International Airport is currently only accessible by taxi or bus, although a planned rail link to and from Dongzhimen is due for completion for the 2008 Olympics. Taxis should take between 45 and 90 minutes depending on traffic, and shouldn't cost more than ¥100, including the ¥15 Airport Expressway toll. You should join the taxi queue outside the arrivals hall and never accept a ride from an illegal cabbie, who will almost certainly rip you off. Six buses run from outside the arrivals hall into the city. The most useful are: bus 1 that runs to Fangzhuang via Dabeiyao, where you can access subway Line 1 at Guomao; bus 2 that runs to Xidan via Dongzhimen; and bus 3 that runs to Beijing Railway Station via Chaoyangmen. For details of operating hours and stops call the 24 hour hotline on 010 6459 4375 or visit http://en.bcia.com.cn.

Bicycle
Other options **Cycling** p.211

Bicycles remain the primary form of transport for many of the city's inhabitants. With its flat, wide roads and generous bicycle lanes, central Beijing is a safe place to cycle, as long as you keep to the tracks and wear a helmet. Most locals don't, but then they seem to have been blessed with an innate warning signal for oncoming traffic. Bear in mind that cars will not give way to either cyclists or pedestrians. Remember too, that Beijing is a huge city, and a major commute by bike may not be realistic. It is advisable to save cycling for short journeys, (especially during rush hours when you can smugly ride pass the queues of frustrated motorists), and for exploring *hutongs*. There is no defining law covering cyclists in the case of an accident. Beware, however, of locals stepping out in front of foreign cyclists. Though rare, this does happen, as a way of squeezing a quick buck from the 'careless' foreigner – generally a few hundred yuan are handed over in compensation to avoid a trip to the police station.

Bus

Travelling by bus is by far the cheapest way of getting around Beijing. Standard fares are ¥1, although air-conditioned buses sometimes cost ¥2. In 2006, the authorities introduced a transport IC card or *yika tong*, a prepaid swipe card that can be bought from most subway and bus stations, post offices and branches of China's CITIC bank. You can add money in multiples of ¥10, with an initial ¥20 deposit. Using an IC card saves bus travellers 60% on fares.

The flipside to this affordable transport is overcrowding; buses are horrendously cramped during rush hours and journeys can be slow due to the lack of bus lanes. But, if you're willing to be patient and get to grips with the Chinese-only bus signs and route maps, you can reach most parts of Beijing on one of the 800 routes.

Although it will seem complicated at first, there are some basic rules: buses with single and double digit numbers are for the inner city; the 100 series are trolley-buses; the 200 series are night buses; the 300 series cover suburban routes and 900 series buses go long distance. The most useful buses for tourists are the double-deckers, numbered 1 to 4, that run throughout the city centre.

To save the hassle of searching for the correct change, you can now buy three, seven and 14 day passes at the same outlets that sell IC cards. If you don't read Chinese, try and find a conductor as soon as you get on and point to your desired destination on a map. Further information (including route maps) can be found at www.bjbus.com.

Car

Other options **Transportation** p.143

Other options **Transportation** p.143

Mao Mobile

For a special car on an extra-special occasion, contact the Red Capital Club (010 6402 7150, www.redcapitalclub. com.cn) about hiring their vintage Red Flag stretch limo, which once belonged to Madame Mao.

Driving in Beijing is not for the fainthearted. Although you are supposed to drive on the right hand side of the road, most local drivers adopt a fluid approach, weaving in and out of lanes to get the best advantage. Many rules are the same as in other countries, but one that does tend to baffle foreigners is the lack of a left-turn signal at intersections. This becomes a survival of the fittest – or fastest – where you must simply push on through and hope to beat oncoming traffic. Beijingers also like to use their horns more than their mirrors, so being alert with your ears is vital.

Speed limits are as follows: 120kph on expressways, 80kph on ring roads, and 60kph on most other inner city roads. Speeding will incur fines and points on your licence, but chances to do this are slim, since traffic on the inner city roads rarely gets above 12kph during rush hours. Even during non-peak times, traffic can be gridlocked within the Third Ring Road. Areas around Xidan, Wangfujing and Changan Jie are best avoided completely, due to congestion.

Beijing is encircled by six ring roads. Only the outermost has a toll (¥15), which makes it the quietest. Its north-eastern section runs through Shunyi, where many expats live in villa communities. The Jingshun expressway also links Beijing to Shunyi and is entered from the Third or Fourth Ring Roads. The Airport Expressway links Beijing Capital Airport with the Third Ring Road at Sanyuanqiao, and is the busiest of Beijing's expressways.

The recently opened Tonghuihe Beilu has helped those driving into Beijing's CBD by easing traffic around Guomao subway station. It starts at Dongbianmen on the Second Ring Road and heads east to the Third and then Fourth Ring Road at Sihui Bridge. In 2006, the Foreign Affairs Office of Beijing Municipality promised that it would improve signs written in English on all roads within the Sixth Ring Road. In 2007, it was announced that vehicle tax would rise from ¥200 to between ¥360 and ¥660 (depending on the vehicle), by the end of 2007 no change had come into effect.

Hiring A Car

To drive in Beijing, you need a Chinese licence (p.66). You can then shop around at different hire companies. Cheap models, including the ubiquitous VW Santana, can be hired for under ¥300 per day. Audis cost around ¥800 per day, and a luxury model, such as a Mercedes-Benz S350, will cost upwards of ¥3,000 per day. These prices usually include a daily limit of 100km, with extra charges if you drive further. Look out for hidden extras such as insurance or higher charges for dropping the car off in different places. For more information, see Vehicle Leasing, p.145.

Car Rental Agencies		
5i5cars Car Rental Co Ltd	010 6856 6866	http://zwey.com
Avis	010 6229 1119	www.avischina.com
Aviss Car Lease Inc	010 8952 1610	www.aviss.com
Beijing Grand View Car Rental Company	010 5128 7373	www.taxi-beijing.com
Beijing Top-A Car Service	010 6438 1634	www.expatslife.com
Chongqing Union Travel Coach Co	010 6161 9853	www.cqcarrental.com
Hertz	010 6595 8109	www.hertz.com.cn

All Hail

There are taxi ranks outside most hotels and shopping malls, or you can simply hail one at the side of the road. Taxis are not allowed to stop on expressways or ring roads, so find a backstreet or sliproad if necessary. An empty taxi will have a lit sign on its roof, simply wave your arm and it should stop.

Taxi

Beijing is swarming with around 70,000 taxis, run by 200 different companies. The newest, and most comfortable, are the Sonata models made by Hyundai, which are yellow and blue or yellow and green and have air-conditioning. Older Citroen and Volkswagen taxis are still around, as are a few red Xialis that you should take only in desperate circumstances, or if you have a sense of adventure and don't mind feeling as though the floor could collapse at any minute.

Taxi travel is very cheap, at ¥2 per kilometre, and the pick up rate is ¥10 (add 20% between 23:00 and 06:00). Licensed taxis all use meters and drivers are generally honest. If you encounter a problem, you can call the taxi complaint hotline on 010 6835 1150.

In 2007, the government imposed etiquette rules for drivers that included not eating garlic before picking up passengers, not having long hair (for men) and not wearing chunky earrings (for women). The effects of these new regulations are yet to be seen. Taxi drivers have also recently been pushed to learn English, and Shouqi Taxi Company has even introduced a translation service that its drivers can call in times of confusion. Even with these valiant efforts, it is still best to have your destination written down in Mandarin characters. Hotel concierges are used to scribbling in the back of guidebooks for confused foreigners and although most Beijing taxi drivers know the city well, having your own map (with place names in Mandarin) is another good idea; the *Mini Map* from Explorer is a handy size. Beijing cabbies have a relaxed view of traffic rules, and although most will insist that you don't need to wear your seatbelt (some may even be offended if you do) it's still best to buckle up.

Taxi Companies	
Jingyuan Taxi	010 6468 8091
Jinjian Taxi Company	010 6374 1666
Shouqi Group	010 6406 5088
Wanquansi Taxi Co	010 6345 3690
Yinjian Auto Services	010 8761 1452
Yuyang Group	010 8760 6626

出 EXIT 电梯 Elevator 西北口 A 东北口 B 出 EXIT

A cosy bus stop

Beijing Train Station

东四 DONGSI

TP4093

Beijing subway

A rare, quiet subway station

Taxi

Train

China's train service is comprehensive safe and punctual, reaching as far as Hong Kong, and it was recently extended to Lhasa in Tibet. Those on popular routes, such as Beijing to Xi'an, were recently updated and are exceptionally comfortable, with air-conditioning and dining facilities. There are four classes of tickets: hard seat (*ying zuo*), soft seat (*ruan zuo*), hard sleeper (*ying wo*) and soft sleeper (*ruan wo*). Short distance trains usually only have hard seats. Long distance routes have a choice of sleeper carriages: the open six-berth hard sleepers and the more expensive, enclosed, four-berth soft sleepers. The Beijing-Shanghai 'Z' category trains also have deluxe soft sleepers: two-berth private carriages with a private washroom. Tickets for all trains can be bought at Beijing Train Station (010 5101 9999) or Beijing West Train Station (010 5182 6273). Queues can be long so many prefer to pay a small surcharge and buy online at www.china-train-ticket.com, www.chinatripadvisor.com or www.train-ticket.net.

Sample one-way ticket prices for hard sleepers include: Beijing to Shanghai, ¥350 (11 ½ hours); Beijing to Xi'an, ¥275 (11 ¾ hours) and Beijing to Lhasa, ¥813 (47 ½ hours). These prices can increase greatly during busy periods, such as national holidays, when attempting to travel is generally inadvisable. Always make sure to buy your ticket several days in advance to ensure a seat or bed. Online timetables can be found at www.chinahighlights.com/china-trains, or visit www.chinatt.org to buy printed versions.

Subway

The subway is often the fastest way of getting around Beijing but its problem lies in a lack of lines, and many areas of the city are unreachable. Currently there are five lines: Line 1 runs underneath Changan Jie, Beijing's major east-west artery. Line 2 is Beijing's loop line, running around the city centre and through Beijing Railway Station. Line 13, which is mostly above ground, links Dongzhimen and Xizhimen to the northern suburbs. The Batong line is fully above ground and links Sihui near the Fourth Ring Road to suburban areas in Tongzhou. The new Line 5, which opened in October 2007, features wheelchair access, air-conditioning, flatscreen TVs and trains that move at 80kph. Paper tickets can be bought with cash, but the re-chargable *yika tong* swipe card is more convenient and can be bought at ticket booths for an initial ¥20 deposit. In 2007, a flat fare of ¥2 with unlimited transfers was introduced. This prompted increased passenger volumes, making trains on Lines 1 and 2 unbearably crowded. To ease the situation, Beijing Subway introduced 72 air-conditioned trains. A series of new lines are planned, with several set to open in 2008. The Airport Line will connect Capital Airport with Dongzhimen. The Olympic Line will stop at the cluster of venues in north Beijing, connecting to the new Line 10, which will run from Wanliu in the west, to Songjiazhuang in the south. Line 4 will go as far as The Summer Palace and down past Beijing South Railway Station to Majiapu. By 2015 the government plans to have 19 lines, covering the entire city and its suburbs. For timetables visit www.bjsubway.com.

Walking

Other options **Hiking** p.216

Many of Beijing's inner-city roads are very big and pedestrian unfriendly. Distances within the city are enormous, so walking as a means of transport is fairly unrealistic. If you decide to take on the challenge, use pedestrian bridges and underpasses taking extreme care at intersections: drivers never give way to foot traffic. Walking around Sanlitun is a little easier, with many streets blocked to cars, but be wary of stray bicycles and scooters. The best places for walking are the old *hutongs*, particularly in Dongcheng where you can explore where many cars cannot reach. Around the Drum Tower (p.179) and Houhai Lake areas (p.165) there are many alleyways filled with small shops, bars and restaurants.

Need Some Direction?

The Explorer Mini Maps pack a whole city into your pocket and once unfolded are excellent navigational tools for exploring. Not only are they handy in size, with detailed information on the sights and sounds of the city, but also their fabulously affordable price mean they won't make a dent in your holiday fund. Wherever your travels take you, from the Middle East to Europe and beyond, grab a mini map and you'll never have to ask for directions.

mini **Beijing** **map**

Money

The use of plastic may be becoming more popular among Beijing's 18 to 24 year olds, but the primary method of payment among most residents is still cash. In banks, shops and restaurants you'll often see locals paying from large, brown envelopes stuffed with wads of notes. However, international credit cards can now be used in many large retailers, all high-end hotels and even some restaurants. Many ATMs throughout the city now also accept foreign debit and credit cards. Only the local Chinese currency of Renminbi (¥) is accepted in Beijing.

Local Currency

Cash Custom
When handing over money, use both hands. This is not grovelling obsequiousness, but a sign of politeness. Chucking someone a crumpled note with one hand may make you seem like a boorish foreigner, who doesn't appreciate the value of money. The same applies to business cards.

Taking its name from the People's Bank of China (Zhongguo Renmin Yinhang), Chinese currency is known as Renminbi or 'people's money'. The basic unit of Renminbi is the yuan (or *kuai* in the spoken form). One yuan is made up of ten *jiao* (*mao* in the spoken form), and one *jiao* is subsequently broken down into ten *fen*. Only yuan come in paper notes, and are available in the following denominations: 100, 50, 20, 10, 5 and 1. Available coins are: 1 yuan, 5 *jiao*, 1 *jiao* and the now rarely used 5 *fen*, 2 *fen* and 1 *fen*.

Until 2005, the Renminbi was pegged at a fixed exchange rate to the US dollar. Pressure from US and G7 finance ministers then pushed the Chinese government to change their policy and to instead peg the Renminbi to a basket of world currencies. Renminbi is a relatively stable currency and is now fully accepted in Hong Kong as well as in parts of some other Asian countries such as Vietnam.

Money Exchange

Currency (C)	1C = ¥	1¥ = C
Australia	6.6	0.15
Canada	7.57	0.13
Denmark	1.46	0.69
Euro	10.85	0.09
Hong Kong	0.95	1.05
India	0.19	5.3
Israel	1.89	0.53
Japan	0.07	14.85
New Zealand	5.63	0.18
Norway	1.35	0.74
Philippines	0.17	5.86
Russia	0.3	3.3
Singapore	5.11	0.2
South Africa	1.11	0.9
South Korea	0.01	123.55
Sweden	1.17	0.86
Switzerland	6.61	0.15
Taiwan	0.23	4.36
Thailand	0.24	4.24
United Arab Emirates	2.02	0.49
United Kingdom	15.17	0.07
United States	7.42	0.13

Banks

Beijing is stuffed full of banks, all battling for the custom of a growing middle class with rising incomes. Major domestic banks such as Bank of China (www.boc.cn), China Merchants Bank (www.cmbchina.com) and Industrial & Commercial Bank of China (ICBC) (www.icbc.com.cn) are easily accessible, with multiple branches located in all of the city's districts. Foreigners can open up yuan or US dollar accounts at most branches (see p.74). All offer local debit cards, internet banking services and currency exchange services, although the latter is not always available at minor branches. It is practically impossible for foreigners to get credit services from domestic banks, but there are several branches of international banks such as HSBC or Citibank; see www.hsbc.com.cn or www.citibank. com for locations. Opening times vary but in general they are open from 09:30 to 16:30 Monday to Friday, sometimes with an hour's break from 12:30 to 13:30, and from 09:30 to 12:30 on Saturdays.

ATMs

There are more than 3,000 ATMs in banks throughout Beijing, as well as in many supermarkets, hotels and shopping malls. Here you can use your domestic debit card to withdraw a maximum of ¥20,000 per day, with a limit of ¥2,000 to ¥3,000 per transaction. If you have a foreign debit or credit card, you can withdraw funds from back home at many branches of Bank of China, ICBC and China Merchants Bank. The latter two are connected to the Visa/Plus card system, while ICBC accepts MasterCards with the Cirrus logo. To locate Beijing ATMs that accept Visa and MasterCard visit http//visa.via.infonow.net/locator/global or www.mastercard.com/atmlocator. There are four Citibank ATMs and 16 HSBC ATMs that accept most foreign credit and debit cards; for listings visit www.citibank.com or call the HSBC hotline on 800 820 8878. Particularly useful HSBC ATMs can be found in the China World Hotel (see p.34) and in Beijing Capital International Airport. To improve security at ATMs, the Central Bank announced in 2007 that all of Beijing's ATMs would be fitted with face-recognition technology to identify criminals and protect against fraud.

Money Exchanges

As long as you have your passport, you can exchange money in most hotels and in major branches of large domestic banks, several of which have exchange counters at the airport. The government standardises rates of exchange, so there is little point in shopping around. Hotels often charge higher commissions than banks, which generally charge either 0.75% to 1% or a fixed fee of up to ¥50 per transaction. Keep your receipts in case you want to reconvert surplus yuan later. Avoid the private money exchanges; these are illegal in China and frequently deal in fake notes. The easiest way to get local currency is to withdraw money using your international debit or credit card at a compatible ATM where you'll pay 2 % to 3% commission.

Spend Trend ◀ ## Credit Cards

Credit cards, though a relatively new concept in China, are becoming increasingly popular among the younger generation, who don't see saving as a number one priority. Olympics fever is further increasing this trend, with Bank of China issuing special Olympic credit cards. Foreigners are, however, rarely offered Chinese credit cards, since the banks are wary of them running up huge credit bills and then leaving the country.

Almost all of Beijing's three, four and five-star hotels accept MasterCard, Visa, American Express, JCB and Diner's Club. Visa and MasterCard are now accepted at some high-end restaurants and in a selection of larger retailers. In smaller shops and markets, you'll have to pay in cash. You can get cash advances with your credit card at large Bank of China branches, but a commission of at least 4% will be added in addition to those charged by your card provider.

For security purposes, it is worth subscribing to a credit card protection policy that will replace your card anywhere in the world in the event of loss or theft. You'll be able to arrange for cash advances to be sent to you if you are stranded without money or cards, get temporary travel documents if you lose your passport and be covered in the event of credit card fraud. You can apply for these protection plans through your home bank or directly with companies such as CCP Direct (www.ccp.co.uk) or Sentinel Card Protection (www.sentinelcardprotection.com).

However, if you lose your card and are not subscribed to such a plan, call Visa 800 440 0027, American Express 800 610 0277, or MasterCard 800 110 7309.

Tipping

Tipping is rare in Beijing. Until recently it was discouraged by the government and banned by restaurant owners. However, waitresses and taxi drivers are becoming more accustomed to getting a few extra yuan. Although not expected, telling your cabbie to keep the change or giving your hairdresser a 5% to 10% tip is acceptable. Expensive bars or restaurants often add a 15% service charge so further tips are not necessary. Feel free to offer a good waiter or waitress a ¥10 or ¥20 note, but try not to let the boss see or it may be nabbed.

Chinese magazines

Newstalk
CCTV (China Central Television) is China's state television broadcaster. Its 24 hour English-language news channel, CCTV9, is perennially dull but it is at least one of the very few free English language channels in Beijing. CRI (www.crienglish.com, p.298), on 91.5FM provides English language radio news. See Television (p.112) and Radio (p.112) for more.

Newspapers & Magazines

China Daily, sold at newsstands all over the city for ¥1, is Beijing's major English-language daily. State-controlled, its mission is to support the policies of the Communist Party. Foreign editors are restricted in what they can write and undergo strict censorship. Consequently, all news and reviews are very China-friendly, with negative comments saved for articles about foreign countries. For less biased international news, you can buy day-old copies of The Times, the Financial Times, the Asian Wall Street Journal, USA Today and the International Herald Tribune at many five-star hotels for under ¥40 each. Also check out the hotel gift shops for imported copies of international magazines including Newsweek and The Economist.

People's Daily (Renmin Ribao) is a leading Chinese-language daily, similar in style and loyal content to the China Daily. The English-language version can be found online at http://english.peopledaily.com.cn. A local publication that frequently pushes the boundaries of state censorship is Caijing, a bi-monthly business magazine whose relative freedom is due in part to its reliance on private investment rather than government funding. It ostensibly uses the cloak of financial reporting to delve into inter-related topics concerning politically sensitive issues such as corruption and pollution. Its English-language newsletter is found at www.caijing.com.cn/English.

For a more light-hearted view of Beijing, there are several English-language entertainment magazines that can be picked up for free in most high-end hotels and in expat-frequented bars and restaurants. The best are That's Beijing, City Weekend, Time Out Beijing and Beijing Talk. All employ foreign writers and editors who produce Beijing-related lifestyle articles, nightlife listings and useful restaurant reviews. Some bars and cafes, such as Aperitivo (p.327) and the Beijing Bookworm (p.324) also stock copies of foreign fashion and lifestyle magazines including Elle and Hello.

Xinhua News Agency, China's government-run press agency, has more than 100 worldwide and 30 domestic bureaus that provide most of the information for much of China's media. Frequently criticised for its stance on censorship, China ranked 163 out of 169 in the 2007 Worldwide Press Freedom Index. Further criticism followed announcements in 2006 that Xinhua would claim full commercial and editorial control over all foreign news agencies, such as Reuters, operating in China.

Books
Other options **Websites** p.52

For an amusing look at a foreign girl's misadventures in the newly-developing Beijing of the mid 90s, pick up a copy of Foreign Babes in Beijing by Rachel DeWoskin, while Ben Whately's Black Dragon River is a brutally honest and painfully hilarious account of his struggles to learn Chinese in the remote Heilongjiang province in China's icy north-east. If you're after some heavier reading China Shakes the World: A Titan's Rise and Troubled Future – and the Challenge for America by former Financial Times reporter James Kynge, is an authoritative account of China's economic situation and its impact on world trade and politics. The Beijing Bookworm (p.254) has a wide range of English-language literature and factual guides on Beijing.

Websites

While most expats rely on free magazines for information about what's on and for useful listings, websites still attract many visitors. *The Beijinger* has a popular classifieds section that includes employment, personals, real estate and 'for sale sections', while *City Weekend* has an expat forum and up-to-date bar and restaurant reviews. Websites such as www.asiaxpat.com and www.thebeijingpage.com are practical information portals for Beijing's expat community.

Blogs

Starting a blog about Beijing seems to have become a new expat trend. Among the dross, and there is plenty, several trusted ones include www.beijingboyce.com, www.danwei.org and the www.thatsbj.com/blog. These aim to provide unbiased news, opinionated reviews and snippets from the foreign press, all sadly lacking in China's state newspapers. Make sure to check out www.sexybeijing.tv, an internet TV blog with some side-splitting postings.

Websites

Business & Industry

www.caijing.com.cn/English	English-language version of leading financial magazine
www.chinahospitalitynews.com	Up to date info on China's hospitality sector
www.chinaretailnews.com	Up to date info on China's retail industry

City Information

http://english.visitbeijing.com.cn	Online city guide from the Beijing Tourism Administration
www.ebeijing.gov.cn	Official website for the municipality of Beijing
www.thebeijingguide.com	Virtual travel guide on Beijing

Culture

www.798art.org/English	Guide to Beijing's premier art district
www.chinesecultureclub.org	Culture institute and event organiser

Directories

www.cityweekend.com.cn/beijing/listings	Community and entertainment listings
www.thebeijinger.com/directory	Community and entertainment listings
www.beijingpage.com	Links to numerous Beijing-related sites

Living & Working

http://beijing.asiaxpat.com	Expat portal with information, classifieds and forums
www.moveandstay.com/beijing	Practical guide for those relocating to Beijing
www.thebeijinger.com	Jobs, real estate, for sale/wanted
www.thebeijingpage.com	Useful info for expats

News & Media

www.chinaview.cn	English-language news service of Xinhua News Agency
www.cityweekend.com.cn/beijing	Lifestyle articles, listings and blog for expats
www.danwei.org	Media, advertising and urban life in China
www.sexybeijing.tv	Internet TV station with podcasts and videos about Beijing
www.thebeijinger.com	Blog, forums, listings and classifieds

Nightlife

http://eng.clubzone.cn	Party and nightclub information
www.beijingboyce.com	In-depth guide to Beijing's drinking scene
www.cityweekend.com.cn/beijing	Restaurant and bar reviews; expat forum
www.zagat.com	Restaurant, nightspots and shop reviews

Online Shopping

www.asc-wines.com	Wide range of wines to buy online
www.amazon.com	Books, CDs, DVDs
www.l-martgroup.com	Internet grocery store with imported goods

Beijing Annual Events

National Agricultural Exhibition Centre
Chaoyang
September

Art Beijing
010 6554 7002 | www.artbeijing.net
Art Beijing moved to the new hall at the National Agricultural Exhibition Centre in 2007, with more than 20,000sqm of exhibits from 165 galleries in China, Asia, the USA, Europe and Latin America. Some 60% were Chinese, in line with Art Beijing's goal to highlight the best in national contemporary art. Now in its fourth year, it is a place to buy art works, and acts as a platform for younger artists to show off their skills.

Raffles Beijing Hotel
Dongcheng
March & November

Beijing International Fashion Week
010 6526 3388 | www.beijing.raffles.com
Held twice a year, Beijing International Fashion Week aims to highlight the growing influence of Chinese designers. There are more than 30 catwalk shows from local and foreign talents, plus competitions for the best model and best young designer.

Haidian Park
Haidian
September

Beijing Jazz Festival
010 6282 2006 | www.beijingjazz.cn
For one weekend in September, respected local and foreign acts perform at China's first and largest jazz event. There are usually two outdoor stages, one for traditional jazz and swing, the other dedicated to modern jazz, funk and world music. Grammy award winner Donny McCaslin performed in 2007. Sessions in bars around the city complement the main events.

Begins at the National Olympic Sports Centre
Chaoyang
October

Beijing Marathon
010 8525 1200 | www.beijing-marathon.com
The Beijing marathon, which was first run in 1981, now attracts 30,000 runners a year. Past races began at Tiananmen Square, but the 2007 event started and finished at the National Olympic Sports Centre, passing several venues for the 2008 Olympic Games en route, including the 'Bird's Nest' stadium (p.228) and the 'Water Cube' swimming centre (p.228).

Haidian Park
Haidian
May

Beijing Midi Music Festival
010 6259 0101 | www.midifestival.com
China's largest outdoor rock festival fills Haidian Park for four days during early May. With more than 90 bands from China and abroad playing on five stages, it attracts 15,000 revellers each day, with indie, rock, electronica, hip-hop and sound art. Tickets cost ¥50 per day.

Various Locations
October

Beijing Music Festival
010 6593 0250 | www.bmf.org.cn/en
This month-long festival, endorsed by the Ministry of Culture, celebrates a wide variety of music, including traditional and Chinese opera and chamber music. The 2007 programme included performances from Die Staatskapelle Berlin and the Orchestre de Paris with soloists including Nigel Kennedy and Lang Lang, one of China's premier young pianists.

Chaoyang Park
Chaoyang
September

Beijing Pop Festival
010 6593 0367 | www.beijingpopfestival.com
This event grows every year, with several thousands now willing to pay ¥200 to ¥380 for a ticket. It attracts some big names too; the 2007 line-up included Nine Inch Nails and Public Enemy. The fact that bands like these were permitted, with their anti-establishment slants, has been seen as a sign of China opening up. Public Enemy could, however, only be referred to as P.E. in all promotional material.

Fayuan Temple
Xuanwu
April

Birthday Of Sakyamuni Buddha

Although it's uncommon to see public displays of faith in atheist China, many people still visit the Fayuan temple in early April to celebrate the birthday of the founder of Buddhism, Sakyamuni. If you're lucky you'll see monks chanting prayers and washing the dust off Buddha's statue.

Various Locations
January or February

Chinese New Year

Also known as Spring Festival, Chinese New Year falls on the first day of the first month of China's lunar calendar, which can be anywhere between late January and early February. Families get together to eat lavish dinners, exchange money in small red envelopes and let off firecrackers, which mercilessly resound around the city for over a week. Many people visit temple fairs during this period (see p.55).

Beijing Tennis Centre
Fengtai
September

Chinese Open

www.chinaopen.com.cn

This 16 day tournament, held at the 10,000 seat Beijing Tennis Centre, attracts big name players from China and the rest of the world. There are women's and men's singles and doubles competitions. In 2007, the men's event was upgraded to the ATP 500 series, and Fernando Gonzalez took the men's singles title.

Various Locations
September - October

The Dangdai International Art Festival (DIAF)

010 6438 2797 | www.diaf.org

For three weeks in September and October, DIAF takes over 798, the old industrial complex in north-eastern Beijing that has become the hub of China's contemporary art world. With dozens of leading galleries participating and works from over 50 nationalities, DIAF adopts an international and multi-discipline approach. In 2007 it cooperated with Art Beijing (p.53) and spread to other locations around the city, including the Caochangdi and Liquor Factory art districts.

Various Locations
May - June

Dragon Boat Festival

The Dragonboat Festival commemorates the poet Qu Yuan (340 - 278BC), who drowned himself in a river during the Warring States Period. People race in boats with dragonheads and eat rice dumplings known as *zongzi*, which legend claims were fed to Qu's ghost by his distressed friends. You can catch these races on the fifth day of the fifth lunar month in several locations in and around Beijing, including the Tonghui River in Chaoyang district and the Ming Tombs Reservoir in Changping district.

Various Locations
May

International Labour Day

International Labour Day, which traditionally celebrated the efforts of farmers, workers and the socialist movement of the 1930s, is of particular significance in communist countries. Farmers and workers flock to the city to mark the beginning of a 'golden week' holiday created by the government to promote domestic tourism. Hundreds of thousands of residents and visitors crowd into Tiananmen Square at dawn to watch the flag raising ceremony or visit other cultural attractions. With more than 100 million people travelling throughout China from 1-7 May, transport can become hectic.

Chinese New Year celebrations

54

Lantern Festival

Various Locations
February

010 6591 5258

The Lantern Festival (*Yuanxiao Jie*) is one of three major festivals in Chinese folklore. Falling on the 15th day of the first lunar month, it marks the end of winter, and people traditionally hung red paper lanterns to encourage the Taoist Lord of Heaven to bring good fortune to their household. Today people still hang colourful lanterns and Chaoyang Park is a good place to see them. Here you'll also find stalls selling traditional sweet dumplings filled with red bean or black sesame paste.

Mid-Autumn Festival

Various Locations
September or
October

Mid-Autumn Festival (*Zhongqiu Jie*) falls on the 15th day of the eighth lunar month, which can be anytime from mid-September to early October. It was traditionally a time when people honoured the moon and round pastries, known as 'mooncakes', were given as offerings and families still come together to make them. With fillings ranging from sweet red bean to salty egg yolk, they are often given as personal and corporate gifts and can be bought, complete with fancy packaging, from most supermarkets and upscale hotels.

National Day

Various Locations
October

China's National Day, on 1 October, celebrates the moment in 1949 when Chairman Mao Zedong stood in front of 300,000 people in Tiananmen Square and declared the founding of the People's Republic. Today, hundreds of thousands crowd into the square to watch the dawn flag-raising ceremony. Firework displays and parades are also held around the city. As the start of one of China's 'golden week' holidays, it marks a time of mass travel across the county, with many workers going back home to their families.

Pine Valley Beijing Open

Pine Valley Golf Club
Changping
April

www.asiantour.com

This is Beijing's only men's professional tournament on the Asian Tour, and was first played in 2007. With a prize of $500,000 it attracts top international and domestic names, including Chinese golf stars Zhang Lianwei and Liang Wenchang. It is played at Pine Valley Golf Club (01 8979 6868, www.pinevalley.com.cn) which is set in over 1,000 acres of land near the Badaling section of the Great Wall.

Temple Fairs

Various Locations
January or February

Temple fairs originated when traders put up stalls around temples to get the custom of the visiting pilgrims. The tradition has flourished and now a number of temples in Beijing hold fairs during the Spring Festival that attract citizens keen to watch folk performances, buy traditional snacks and take part in religious ceremonies. Ditan Park was the site of an altar on which sacrifices were formerly offered to the earth god, and today visitors can watch recreations of the ceremony, while Dongyuemiao temple fair is devoted to re-creating the customs and life of old Beijing.

Tomb Sweeping Day

Babaoshan Cemetery
Shijingshan
April

010 6214 1444 | *www.babaoshan.com.cn*

Tomb Sweeping Day (*Qingming Jie*) was traditionally a time to remember deceased relatives. Families still travel to cemeteries to clean graves, make offerings of food and drink and burn imitation bank notes or paper houses to provide greater comfort to their ancestors in the afterlife. More than 100,000 people flock daily to Babaoshan Cemetery, often taking picnics and flying kites as a way of simultaneously welcoming in the spring.

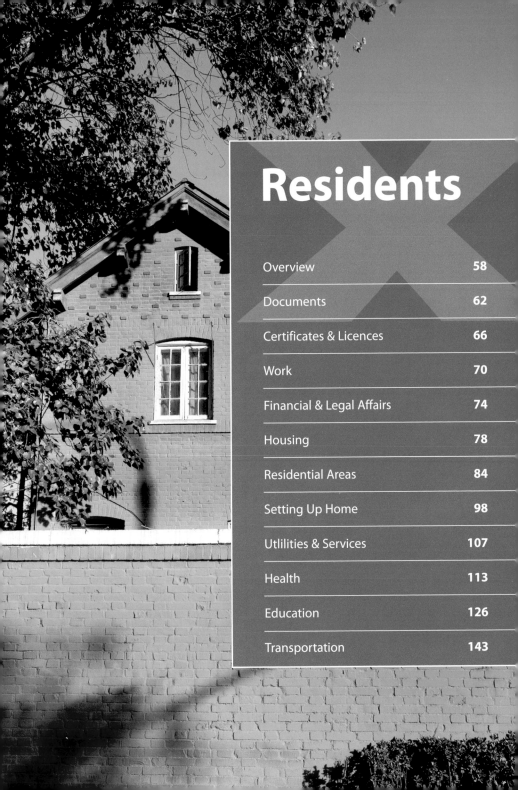

Residents

Residents

Overview

Beijing's international profile soared ahead of the 2008 Olympics. This, combined with China's increasing wealth, has seen more international firms arrive. They have brought an expat influx and subsequent change in atmosphere. Only a few years ago, westerners were a rare sight. Now, there are more than 100,000 living in Beijing. You'll still stand out among the city's 15 million inhabitants (and get some curious stares), but it is becoming easier for westerners to live here.

Although visa regulations have been tightened considerably, teaching English remains one of the easiest jobs to get. The city realises that being bilingual is crucial for future business opportunities, and the government encouraged locals to learn English before the Olympics.

Other opportunities do exist for foreigners, but applicants who speak Mandarin are often considered above those who cannot. This only begins to change at more senior levels. Chinese bureaucracy can appear complicated and unintelligible at first, but remember that rules are set in stone, and if you follow them everything should run smoothly. Employers should help to process the copious form filling. The language barrier is by far the most significant obstacle for anyone moving to Beijing.

Pick Me!

As this book went to print, the recruitment period for Olympic volunteers was ending. However, if BOCOG doesn't get all those that it needs (and foreigners can join) it will re-open the process. Check http://en.beijing2008.cn, or call 12308 (24 hours, with English speakers) for updates.

Considering The City

For foreigners, working in Beijing is an eye opening experience. Business is conducted in a format that will be alien to most, with meetings, bureaucracy and managerial hierarchies following strict cultural traditions. But, foreign workers are treated with a respect and tolerance that few other countries can offer.

Salaries vary greatly and depend principally on whether you work for a Chinese or foreign owned company. Wages offered to foreigners by Chinese companies are often higher than they would give native workers, but still far less than could be expected in most western countries. Foreign owned firms tend to pay rates similar to those in the west, and many offer housing allowances and medical insurance.

China is a cheap country to live in, and many expats find it easy to save money, which is often a big incentive to relocate. Although the city is more modern than other parts of the country, it has managed to retain that incomparable Chinese flavour that attracts both tourists and expats.

Facilities for foreigners are improving daily, and there is a strong community atmosphere. On the downside, the language barrier is a constant thorn in the side of those trying to tackle even the simplest tasks.

Dongbianmen Watchtower

Up until the middle of 2006, getting a business or F Visa (p.62) was relatively simple and finding work with it even easier. Today however, authorities are clamping down on foreigners working illegally, most notably in language schools. It is important to note that you cannot upgrade from a tourist or L Visa (p.62) to a working or Z Visa (p.63) in the country, but this is possible from an F Visa. But, life will be simpler if you secure work before you arrive.

Before You Arrive

Once the decision to move to Beijing has been made, the long list of 'to dos' begins. Arrangements need to be made both in your country and in China, ahead of your arrival.

- To get a work visa (Z Visa) and resident's permit (p.63), you will need confirmation of employment before departure. So task one is to find a job. Employment agencies (p.72) at home and in Beijing are a good place to start, as are expat magazines (p.51) and websites (p.71).
- Ensure all paperwork is sent well in advance from employers in China.
- Apply for your visa one to two months in advance. Additional or unexpected paperwork may take time to gather.
- Put your home property on the market or consider renting it out. If you are renting, be sure to notify your landlord well in advance.
- Ship (p.248) your belongings to China (this can take up to six weeks).
- Book flights in advance (prices increase closer to the date of departure). If taking pets, be sure to notify the airline.
- Get pets (p.104) vaccinated against rabies at least three months before departure.
- Cancel direct debits or standing orders or ensure there are sufficient funds in your bank account to accommodate them (transferring money from China is time-consuming and costly).
- Notifying tax and pension authorities, banks and student loans companies.
- Notify utility companies and cancel mobile phone contracts.
- Research schools (p.127) and housing (p.78). The city is vast, so consider looking for housing and schools close to your work. Your embassy or employer can help provide a list of international schools, fees and acceptance criteria.

Hounded Hounds
Beijing has strict laws restricting large dogs in public areas, and within the Third Ring Road, so this may affect where you choose to live. See pets (p.104) for more.

When You Arrive

Arriving in Beijing can be a somewhat daunting experience. Achieving even basic tasks can be arduous and time consuming. Enlisting the help of your employer or making contact with other new residents before arriving can prove invaluable. Alternatively, hiring a local interpreter may be a good option to consider. On arrival, you will need to:

- Upgrade your entry visa to a full working visa (Z Visa, p.63) and obtain your resident's permit (p.63).
- Find an apartment or house. It is a good idea to stay in a hotel near where you want to live, rather than commute for viewings.
- Visit schools (p.130) or kindergartens (p.127) in your chosen area.
- Set up utilities (p.107). Landlords will normally have done this, or will help set it up.
- Sign up to telephone (p.108), television (p.112) and internet providers (p.110).
- Buy yourself a mobile phone (see Shopping, p.245),
- Buy household items. Most apartments are furnished but this can be removed if you have brought your own. Stores such as IKEA (p.268) and Dazhong (p.262) are good for the basics.
- Apply for a driving licence and take the theory test (only those with a resident's permit may have a Chinese driving licence).
- Register with one of the western hospitals in the city (see p.118).
- Register with the local police station. Your landlord will need to accompany you, so do this when you sign contracts.
- Join local sports clubs or gyms (many larger apartments have facilities and fees can often be negotiated into your rent).
- Register with your embassy (p.26).
- Register any pets (p.104) with the local police station and get a licence. Expats cannot register dogs themselves – this can only be done with a Chinese citizen ID card.

- Find pharmacies stocking western medicines, supermarkets (including those selling imported goods), vets and pet supply shops. See Shopping (p.245).
- Learn some Mandarin (p.20).

When You Leave

Leaving is easier than getting set up, mainly because by now you'll be fully aware of the pitfalls and difficulties involved in Chinese bureaucracy. Be sure to consider the following when planning to leave Beijing:

- Try to leave at the end of a lease, as getting out of rental contracts early is difficult and costly.
- Cancel utilities and subscriptions. Your landlord won't return your deposit until this happens. As utilities and telephone and internet subscriptions are paid in person on a monthly basis (there are no direct debits) this is relatively easy. Gym and cable TV subscriptions are usually paid annually and are non-refundable.
- Ship belongings well in advance (this can take up to six weeks).
- Sell anything you don't want to take with you (some countries – including the US – don't support the same electrical output as China).
- Many countries do not allow pets to enter from China. Consider this before leaving or look into finding a new home for Rover in Beijing.

The Finance District (p.90)

From country to city

The watchful gaze of Mao

Beihai Park (p.191)

Fashion Boutiques p.123
Financial Advisors p.95

Written by residents, the Dubai Explorer is packed with insider info, from arriving in the city to making it your home and everything in between.

Dubai Explorer Residents' Guide
We Know Where You Live

Documents

Arranging paperwork and administrative tasks isn't easy, particularly if you don't speak Mandarin. But bureaucracy is unwavering, so if you follow the rules and accept there are no exceptions then things will be less frustrating. Employers often help, and this should be checked in advance. A company unwilling to help should be treated with scepticism. The following items should be kept easily to hand:

- Passport and copies (by law, you must always carry a copy of your passport and visa).
- Passport photographs.
- Work Permit for Aliens (p.64).
- Resident's card (p.63).
- Police registration certificate (p.64).
- Copies of dependents' passports and visas.
- Marriage certificate (p.68).
- Birth or adoption certificates (p.67).
- Pet vaccination cards (including rabies certificate and blood test result – RNATT) and electronic chip number (p.104).
- Health certificate (p.64).
- Driving licence (p.66).

What The L?

Any friends or relatives coming to visit you in China must apply for a tourist visa (L) at the Chinese consulate before leaving home. They cannot be issued in China.

Entry Visa

Anyone entering China must have a visa issued by a Chinese consulate before they arrive in the country. Entry visas cannot be issued at the airport. Passport holders from Japan, Brunei and Singapore are the exception, and may enter for business, travel or transit for up to 15 days without an entry visa.

To enter China, your passport must be valid for at least six months from the date when you made the visa application.

There are several types of visa and each comes with its own set of stringent rules. A Q1 form, two passport photos and a fee (see below) will need to be submitted, along with any visa-specific paperwork.

L – Tourist Visa

This is the most commonly issued visa, and meant for leisure visitors. Single or double entry versions are available and valid for up to 30 days, after which they can be extended in China. Nationals of some countries (for example, New Zealand) must provide three month's bank statements and original flight tickets, so check with the consulate beforehand. Converting from a tourist visa (L) to a working visa (Z) visa in country is not possible.

F – Business Visa

This is issued to people invited to China for business, research, lectures, cultural exchanges or study programmes of less than six months. It is not a working visa. To apply for this visa you will need the original letter of invitation from the company or establishment in China. Single, double or multiple entries can be obtained. Chinese authorities are clamping

Over-Staying Your Visa

Over-staying your visa is taken seriously, with a fine of ¥500 imposed for each extra day (up to ¥5,000) and possible deportation. Police are getting stricter on this issue, and spot checks are regularly carried out in areas where there are many expats. It is important not to allow your visa to expire and to always carry a copy of your passport, visa and original ID card (if applicable) on you. There are reports of police targeting building complexes where expats live or raiding offices and English language schools looking for foreign residents working on tourist or out of date visas.

down on the illegal use of F visas which, until recently, were widely used to work with. The F visas have for many years been used in Beijing as a long term way into the country for those who don't qualify for a working visa (Z). Companies in the city are often willing however, to hire people holding an F visa and arrange for them to be upgraded to a Z visa. To convert from an F to a Z visa applicants usually have to leave the country.

Z – Work Visa
Issued to people who are to take up prearranged employment in China, and their dependents. See p.64.

Visa Pleaser
See the margin on p.66 for details on where to get official translations of your documents.

X – Student Visa
Issued to those studying in China for up to six months. Applicants need to submit an Entrance Notice of Schools in China and a Foreign Student Visa Application Form (JW201 or JW202). A medical examination certificate is also required for those undertaking studies of more than one year (see p.64). Student visas can be extended in the country and your university or school should help.

D – Permanent Resident Visa
These are issued for up to five years and generally only to foreign children of a Chinese parent, or Chinese people who have relinquished their passport (through marriage to a foreigner). Those investing large sums of money into the country can also apply. There is often some confusion between the D Visa and the Z Visa, as those given the Z will get a resident's permit of up to five years. But, this is considered temporary residence (see p.64). To apply for a D Visa, you need a health certificate and certificate of residence approval (issued in China). A six month visa will be issued, which is upgraded on arrival.

G – Transit Visa
This is needed by anyone who will be passing through China, whose transit time exceeds 24 hours. To apply, you will need to submit all flight tickets for your onward journey.

J – Journalist Visa
A J-1 visa is issued to journalists who are posted to China for at least one year, while those on short term visits will be issued J-2 visas.

Multiple Entry & Fees
If you have applied for multiple entry (eligible on Z, D, X, F and J visas) you will generally be issued a single entry visa, which then needs to be upgraded within 30 days of arriving. This must be done at the Exit & Entry Administration of Beijing (Municipal Public Security Bureau, 2 Andingmen Dongdajie, Dongcheng, 010 8402 0101). There are fees for all visas, which vary according to number of entries requested and in which country you apply (with the exception of the US, where all visas cost ¥750). Fees generally range from ¥195 to ¥460 for one entry and ¥585 to ¥1,380 for year-long visas with multiple entries. Some consulates only accept cash, so it's best to check in advance.

Residence Visa
There is often some confusion over the issuing of D and Z visas. China only allows residents to be in possession of one nationality. The D visa is generally issued to Chinese people (or their children) who have relinquished their Chinese passports and are otherwise difficult to obtain. Those holding Z, X or J-1 visas, and who will be in the country for more than one year, can apply for a resident's permit. These are valid for between one and five years and cover the holder and their dependents (see below).

Working Visa & Temporary Resident's Visa

For those working in China, the Z visa is the closest thing to a permanent resident's visa available.

To apply, you will need to submit a Work Permit for Aliens or, for teachers, a Foreign Expert's Licence. These are issued by authorities in China, and should be supplied by your employer.

Once in China, you must visit the Exit & Entry Administration of Beijing office (Municipal Public Security Bureau, 2 Andingmen Dongdajie, Dongcheng, 010 8402 0101). Here, you can upgrade to a full Z visa and apply for your resident's permit. A health certificate must also be supplied (see below).

Resident's permits are valid for the length of your contract, and should be carried with you. They can be renewed at the Public Security Bureau, as can the working or student visa.

Family members are also eligible for Z visas, provided marriage, birth or adoption certificates are submitted. Dependent parents are also illegible for Z visas. China does not recognise common law couples or homosexual marriages.

Police Registration

Expats in China must register at their local police station as soon as they get their resident's permit. Take your passport and permit and go with your landlord, who will confirm that you live in their property. The landlord should also help you to find the nearest police station and translate forms.

People on L or F visas must stay in approved hotels (there is usually a plaque on show) and complete a form when they check in. The hotel completes the process for you.

If you stay with friends or relatives who are on resident's visas, you must go to the local police station and register. Until recently this was rarely done, but in the build up to the Olympics police are getting stricter. If you do choose to go, you will need to take your passport and visa and those of your hosts, including their ID cards.

Health Requirements

Those requesting working (Z), student (X), residence (D) or journalist (J-1) visas will need to have a health exam on arrival. This can only be done at the Beijing International Healthcare Centre (20 Heping Li Beijie, Dongcheng, 010 6427 4239). It includes blood tests, a general check up, an ECG and blood pressure check. The clinic is open Monday to Friday, from 08:00 to 10:30 and you must not have eaten that day. You will need your passport and three passport photos. Exams and certificates cost ¥700, but many companies will cover this.

Citizenship

Applying to become a Chinese citizen is extremely difficult. Citizenship is rarely granted and not often attempted. The Nationality Law of China states that Chinese citizens may only have one passport and the country does not recognise dual citizenship.

Those applying to become a Chinese citizen would need to relinquish their passport and may have difficulty getting visas to their own country afterwards. Children born to one Chinese and one foreign parent must choose an official nationality for the child.

ID Card

ID cards are only issued to Chinese citizens that have a household registration (*hukou*). This is issued at birth by the local government and records name, date of birth, names of parents and adds spouses, births, deaths, marriages and divorces within the family. It acts as the formal ID in China and must be renewed if the person changes address. Resident's permits (p.63) are issued to temporary or permanent residents.

Documents

Great Hall of the People (p.180)

Pedicab

Beihai Park (p.191)

Colonial style building

Buses at Qianmen Gate

Driving Licence
Other options **Transportation** p.143

There are an estimated 1.7 million cars and 10 million bicycles on Beijing's manic streets, so many foreigners opt for the plentiful, cheap taxis rather than adding to the congestion. Some do brave the streets though, and foreign owned cars are becoming more common. Cars owned by non-Chinese citizens carry black number plates, while Chinese owned vehicles have blue ones. Black and red denotes a diplomat, while white indicates an army or government official. Cars drive on the left in China, the legal driving age is 18 and it is mandatory to have your licence whenever you are behind the wheel. There are occasional spot checks, but foreigners are less likely to be stopped than Chinese citizens.

China does not recognise the International Driving Licence. So, you'll need the local version unless, oddly, you hold a Belgian licence. A reciprocal agreement exists that allows Belgian licence holders to driver in China.

Otherwise, foreigners on A, D, Z, X or J-1 visa for one year or more can apply for a permanent local driving licence. A temporary licence can be issued for those on the visa types above for between three months and one year. Those travelling on a tourist visa (L) need to either use public transport or hire a car with a driver.

To obtain a Chinese licence, foreigners must be between 18 and 70 years old, have a valid foreign driving licence, a valid visa, residence permit, and residence registration certificate. The applicant must also pass an eye test, translate their licence into Chinese, pass a computerised road test (with a score of more than 90 out of 100), and pay a fee of ¥10. FESCO (Beijing Foreign Enterprise Human Resources Service, www.fescochina.com) can help. Foreigners can get their eyes tested at any of the hospitals in the table. Chinese licences are valid for six years, and work on a 12-point system, with points deducted for traffic violations. If you lose all 12 points in a single year, you must pass your traffic test again to regain your licence.

Eye Testing Hospitals

Friendship Hospital	010 6301 4411
Sino-Japanese Hospital	010 6422 1122
Tonghe Hospital	010 6512 9911
Xiehe Hospital	010 6529 6114

Translators
Official translations can be done by China Translation and Publication, sixth floor, Wuhua Complex, A4 Chegongzhuang Dajie (010 6800 2558) or Beijing Notary Public Office, 206 Jixiangli Chaowaidajie, Chaoyang District, (010 6553 8988/9).

The Process

The process involved in getting a permanent (or temporary) Chinese driving licence (C1) is fairly straightforward, if a little long-winded. Applications can be made at the Foreign Affairs Office, Traffic Administration, 90 Laiguangying Xilu, Chaoyang (010 6490 4379). Just complete a driving licence application form and show your passport and translated licence from home. See left for details.

You will need to take a computerised theory test, but a road test is unnecessary for those who have been driving for more than one year. To pass the theory test, which is available in several languages, you need to score at least 90%. When you first apply for your licence and make your test appointment, you will get a road safety booklet with all the potential multiple choice questions. An eye test is also required, which can be done at any of the hospitals above, but they must provide you with a certificate.

Licences generally take about one week to process and there is a fee of ¥20. If you rack up 12 penalty points in a single year, you will have your licence removed until you re-sit and pass the theory test. Speeding offences receive a fine of between ¥200 and ¥2,000.

Driving Test

There are several schools offering driving courses. While the driving techniques witnessed on Beijing's streets might imply little or no testing occurs, students actually must complete a 58 hour course that incorporates a theory test, a training site test (not on public roads) and a final road test. A rather entertaining driving simulator is also

Driving Schools

Fengshun Driving Training Centre	Fengtai	010 6381 9435
Laoshan Driving School	Shijingshan	010 6886 2551
Oriental Fashion Driving School	Daxing	010 5806 1999
Shenghua Driving Training School	Chaoyang	010 6737 2117
Shouqi Fengtian Driving School	Chaoyang	010 8481 2221

often used before students are put behind the wheel of a real car. A three month course costs between ¥3,000 and ¥8,000 and all lessons are held in Mandarin, so you will need to take along a translator if your language skills are not up to the challenge. There are 102 registered driving schools in Beijing so there is plenty of choice, although those listed in the table are particularly recommended.

Motorcycle Licence

If you hold a motorcycle licence, you can apply for a Chinese version by following the same application rules as for a car. Three wheel motorcycles receive a D licence while two wheel vehicles get an E licence.

Birth Certificate & Registration

Because the Nationality Law of China does not recognise dual citizenship, children born in China to one Chinese and one foreign parent must choose a nationality for their child at birth. Those born to two foreign parents should be registered at their embassy and issued with a passport as soon after the birth as possible.

Christenings

Christenings and other ceremonies can be arranged by contacting the relevant clergy. See Religion, p.21, for relevant details. The city's resident Rabbi (www.chabadbeijing. com) can perform Brit Milah or Brit Habat ceremonies, but not circumcision. If you wish to have your baby boy circumcised (al-Khitaan in the Muslim faith) this can be done at any of the western hospitals.

Children Of One Chinese Parent & One Foreign Parent

For children born to one Chinese and one foreign parent a nationality must be chosen at birth. If you want your child to become a Chinese citizen, you will need to take its birth certificate to your local Public Security Bureau and get the child registered on the household registration list (hukou).

If you choose for your child not to become a Chinese citizen, then you will need to go to the relevant embassy and get a consular report of birth certificate. With this you can then get an entry and exit visa for your child at the Public Security Bureau. The next time the child leaves the country, you must apply for a residence visa at a Chinese consulate. If both parents are foreign, the child can have a temporary resident's visa.

Children Of Two Foreign Parents

Parents must take the child's Chinese birth certificate to their embassy, along with their own passports and (if applicable) marriage certificate. Birth certificates are issued at the hospital where the baby is born. Embassies all have slightly different requirements, so it is a good idea to call them before the birth. Upon receipt of the child's passport, parents must apply for a temporary resident's visa at the Entry & Exit Administration of Beijing (Municipal Public Security Bureau, 2 Andingmen Dongadjie, Dongcheng, 010 8402 0101) within one month of the birth. This is extremely important, as it will be necessary to show this when you leave China.

There are no special laws regarding children born to foreign parents and the one child policy does not apply. Either the mother or father can apply for the child's visa.

Adoption

China is a common source country for international adoption, so the process is well-established.

The one child policy and favouritism towards boys mean the majority of children up for adoption are girls under 6 years old. The Chinese Center for Adoption Affairs (CCAA) (7

Baiguang Lu, Xuanwu, 010 6554 8804/5, www.china-ccaa.org) deals with all adoptions and only children registered with them may be adopted.

The first step is to request an application kit, which outlines the long and rather expensive process. Using an adoption agency in your own country is a good idea as the mountains of paperwork can be daunting. You will also need to get in touch with your embassy to ensure that you are meeting the requirements of your home country. Fees differ with agencies and the legal and embassy charges, but you should expect to pay around $10,000. There is a $4,000 compulsory 'donation'. The entire process can take up to one year, but is shorter if you live in China.

People over 35 years of age can only adopt abandoned children and are only permitted to adopt one child. People under 35 can only adopt orphaned or disabled children and may adopt more than one. Couples or single people can legally adopt, but homosexual couples may not.

Forged On Camera
Photographs of the big day are a must for Chinese couples, but are usually taken before the actual wedding. Those with the resources often go to scenic spots in their wedding finery with a photographer in tow, sometimes weeks before the actual event. If this option isn't within their budget, the couple poses in front of landscape scenes in a studio. The frosted, hazy look is one of the most favoured.

Marriage Certificate & Registration

Weddings are big business. While there are enough long-standing customs to merit a chapter unto themselves, western traditions such as ring-giving and altar ceremonies are becoming more popular. Weddings in China (and in particular Beijing and Shanghai) are extremely expensive, and there are many services geared towards helping couples prepare. China only recognises civil marriages, which are usually completed the day before the showpiece event. As a result, wedding parties can take place pretty much anywhere, with plush hotels and restaurants being the first choice for most Chinese couples.

The Paperwork

Marriages are registered according to Chinese laws, regardless of the nationality of the couple. They are administered by the Marriage Registration Office, Bureau of Civil Affairs of Beijing Municipality (First Floor, 8 Huayanli, Chaoyang, 010 6203 5724), which is open from Monday to Friday, 09:00 to 11:30 and 13:30 to 17:00.

While regulations differ according to whether both partners are foreign or one is Chinese, there are two documents that everyone needs: a Certificate of Marriageability (*danshenzhengming*) and a Certificate of Marriage. The minimum age for marrying is 20 for women and 22 for men. This law applies to both Chinese citizens and foreign nationals. Same sex couples cannot marry.

Foreign Couples

Foreign couples can marry in Beijing provided at least one of them has a resident's permit. A couple travelling to China on tourist visas are unlikely to be able to marry. However, most expats tend to go home for their big day and few tie the knot in Beijing. To begin the process, all documents must be translated into Chinese by the Beijing Notary Public Office (206 Jixiangli Chaowaidajie, Chaoyang, 010 6553 8988/9).

Both partners will need a Certificate of Marriageability (*danshenzhengming*, also referred to as a Certificate of No Impediment), which can be obtained from your home country or embassy. It involves swearing an affidavit that you are legally allowed to marry and, if done in your home country, needs to be certified both by your embassy and the public notary office. It should also be translated if your embassy doesn't offer dual language certificates.

Some countries (for example the UK) require you post a Notice of Intent either in your home country or embassy for 21 days before they issue a Certificate of Marriageability. After this has been issued, the couple are considered legally married. Many expats then opt to have a religious ceremony, although this is not recognised in China. For religious ceremonies contact the relevant clergy (see Religion, p.21). Most religions are represented in Beijing and your embassy can provide a list of contacts.

Sino-Foreign Couples

If one partner is Chinese, the marriage must take place in the civil affairs office in the area where the Chinese citizen is registered. The foreign partner must submit the following: passport, Chinese resident's permit, a health certificate from Beijing International Healthcare Centre (p.64), a Certificate of Marriageability (See Paperwork, left) and three photos of the couple together. The Chinese partner must submit a Certificate of Marriageability, birth certificate, *hukou*, health certificate and a letter of permission from their parents. Both partners must submit divorce or death certificates (if widowed) where applicable.

Death Certificate & Registration

In The Event Of A Death

To call an ambulance, dial 120 and specify which hospital you want to go to. Once there, you will be issued with a medical death certificate and the body will be stored until a decision has been made regarding a funeral or repatriation. Specify that you want the body to be kept cold, as this is not always standard procedure. The embassy (see p.26) of the deceased will help with language issues and most have emergency numbers.

Registering A Death

Within two weeks of the loss, and with the medical death certificate in hand, you will need to register the death at the Entry & Exit Administration of the Municipal Public Security Bureau (2 Andingmen Dongdajie, Dongcheng, 010 8402 0101). If you are the next of kin, you can show the person's passport, resident's permit (if applicable), any paperwork from the hospital or police and your own documents plus a Declaration of Death for Foreign Nationals form. If you are not the next of kin, you must get power of attorney to complete this process. This must be obtained from the next of kin and can be arranged through your embassy. Some embassies will send an official to the Public Security Bureau on your behalf. Once you have registered the death, take the certificate and deceased's passport to their embassy and register the death there. It is a good idea to make several copies of the deceased's passport, resident's permit and visa and have these certified at the Beijing Notary Public Office (206 Jixiangli Chaowaidajie, Chaoyang, 010 6553 8988/9). A national death certificate will be issued once the passport is cancelled and the original Chinese death certificate is presented.

Funeral Homes	
Ba Bao Shan Funeral Home	010 6824 3385
Global Doctor	010 8456 9191
SOS International	010 6462 9112

Investigation & Autopsy

The Beijing police will investige if someone dies under suspicious circumstances. The family of the deceased can request an autopsy if they feel it is necessary. The Municipal Public Security Bureau will do this, but the request must be made within 48 hours of the person's death. Private investigators are illegal in China and embassies cannot conduct their own investigations. An autopsy or police report is needed to get a death certificate from local authorities and from the deceased's embassy.

Returning The Deceased To The Country Of Origin

With the paperwork done, you will need to arrange a burial or repatriation of the body. Funeral homes (see table) can help, as can the deceased's embassy. If repatriating, you will need to have the body embalmed and obtain a coffin exit certificate from the Inspection and Quarantine Bureau. You should also arrange for a funeral director in the destination country to collect the body from the airport. And contact the deceased's insurer, or you will bear costs that can run to tens of thousands of *yuan*.

Working In Beijing

The attraction of working in such an exciting economy is proving irresistible for many. As more foreign companies pile into China, opportunities to work in Beijing are opening up, while the Chinese people's insatiable desire to learn English means the most traditional expat market – language teaching – is thriving. While Beijing may not be as glitzy as Shanghai, it has the attraction of being the country's capital and an essential stop for those who want to get ahead.

Working in China can be a huge positive on a CV. It demonstrates a willingness to work in a new culture and experience a different market. As China's importance in the world economy increases, time spent there is a sound investment for the future. But, as with all expat terms abroad, it's wise to keep an eye on opportunities elsewhere or back home. You might find employers in your own country aren't always as excited by your time away as you are.

New business opportunities are opening up all the time. Despite its reputation as a government town, the entrepreneurial spirit sweeping China is alive in Beijing. Local people are hard-working and keen to get ahead, which makes for a good work atmosphere. However, decision making is a slow process and patience is a necessary virtue, but it's also important to be quick-thinking and flexible to keep up with the changing market. Meanwhile, Beijing's more general problems, like the pollution, cold winters and stifling summers, are off-putting to some.

Connections in China are all-important, so take lots of business cards wherever you go. The word *guanxi* describes how Chinese people build networks through friends, classmates, colleagues and family, to be used in their business life. It can be difficult for a foreigner to match the web of contacts Chinese people are able to build, but you should try to nurture the relationships you do form with locals.

Many foreigners get by without speaking Chinese, but the more you can communicate, the better. Speaking Chinese certainly gives you more options when looking for work, though in industries such as finance and professional services, it's not always so important.

Most people coming to live in China find the cost of living much lower than at home, particularly if they're from western Europe or the US. Decent accommodation, meals out, taxis, and even having a cleaner for your apartment, are all reasonably priced. However, the cost of living is rising and Mercer Consulting rated Beijing the world's 20th most expensive city in its 2007 survey. Buying clothes and electronics in shopping malls is not necessarily cheaper than in the west, though there are still plenty of markets (p.292) where you can try your bargaining skills.

Salaries vary greatly between industries and companies. There's also a big difference in packages if you are moved here by an employer, rather than just pitching up to look for work. Fewer companies now see Beijing as a hardship posting, and more are looking to hire locally, as the availability of well-qualified, English-speaking Chinese people increases. This means the days of extravagant expat packages are dwindling. Still, at the top end, employees can push for perks such as help with housing and education costs. If you're moving abroad with a company, it's worth pushing for flights home once a year and help with moving expenses to be included in your contract. Be aware that employment benefits are generally different from norms in the west. While around 80% of domestic and international companies in China will offer healthcare and related insurance, only around a fifth will provide supplementary pension plans. Moreover, only around a quarter offer flexible working hours.

Explorer Online

No doubt now that you own an Explorer book you will want to check out the rest of our product range. From maps and vistor guides to restaurant guides and photography books, Explorer has a spectacular collection of products just waitiing for you to buy them. Check out our website for more info. www.explorer publishing.com

Working Hours

As in most countries, working hours vary depending on industry and company. The basic working day is comparable to the west, beginning at around 08:30 or 09:00 and ending early evening. Chinese workers, however, often work much longer hours, and

Business Councils & Groups

American Chamber Of Commerce	www.amcham-china.org.cn
Australia China Business Council	www.acbc.com.au
British Chamber Of Commerce In China	www.pek.bricham.org
Canada China Business Council	www.ccbc.com
China & New Zealand Business Council	www.canzbc.co.nz
China-Africa Business Council	www.cabc.org.cn
China-Britain Business Council	www.cbbc.org
Confederation Of British Industry, China	www.cbichina.org.cn
Ireland China Business Association	www.irelandchina.org

at weekends. Expats in China can find themselves working later than they're used to back home, particularly when making the adjustment to a new office and way of working. If you're working for an international company, time differences mean it's sometimes necessary to work into the evening to accommodate colleagues overseas. There are three main times of the year when most Chinese people go on holiday for a week; during Chinese New Year, the first week of May and the first week of October.

Finding Work

It is necessary to get a working visa (p.63) before you arrive to work in China, for which you'll need a sponsoring company. Most companies will have HR departments to guide you through the visa process; if not, make sure you check requirements with the Chinese embassy. If you have dreams of setting up your own company in China, it's probably best to take a 'starter' job in order to get your feet on the ground. However, it has been known for people to move to China on a student visa and set up a business straight away.

Useful Websites

www.chinahr.com
www.zhaopin.com
www.dragonsurf.com
www.jobchina.net
www.monster.com
www.innbeijing.org
www.thebeijinger.com

Finding Work Before You Arrive

While lots of overseas companies in Beijing are keen to hire more local staff, many find it hard to find the right calibre of employee. This is particularly a problem in professional areas such as finance and accounting, HR, sales and marketing, and R&D. Engineering companies are also big expat employers in China, though many work outside Beijing. Whatever you do, a big part of your job may involve training and coaching local staff; China in general is in a race to 'upskill', meaning companies are keen to find people with qualifications and experience they can pass on to local workers. Accordingly, most companies are looking for people with relevant work experience already, ideally with a professional qualification or a particular skill. If you are keen to work in China, it's worth stressing any experience to potential employers or recruiting agents. For those looking to teach in Beijing, think seriously about getting a qualification such as a TEFL, as this will help with prospective employers.

In terms of practicalities, if you're not moving with your existing employer, the usual job-seeking channels apply. As elsewhere in the world, the job market has become ever more reliant on the internet. Contact recruitment consultancies at home for opportunities and don't be afraid to write to HR departments at companies that interest you.

Finding Work While You're In Beijing

Most people come to China with a job already arranged, but there are opportunities once you arrive. Get hold of the directories published by different chambers of commerce in Beijing which provide addresses and contact details of people to write to. Networking is important; local listing magazines (p.51) contain details of events hosted by the chambers and business networks, so it's a good idea to attend.

Think also of what makes you stand out – generally it will be your ability to speak English. That can lead to jobs as varied as freelance journalism, editing copy for professional firms, helping out at TV stations or magazines, or working at educational services companies. Another key source is the various free expat magazines (p.51) that are available in bars and restaurants around the city. One thing is for sure, no one ever got anywhere in Beijing by being shy, so get out there.

Recruitment Agencies

There are around 85 recruitment agencies operating in China, according to the China-Britain Business Council's website (www.cbbc.org), with some of the more famous western names among them. Agencies tend to interview job candidates first, at least by telephone.

Recruitment Agencies		
Antal	010 6410 8866	www.antal.com
Career	010 8525 2022	www.chinacareer.com
MRI Worldwide	010 6505 9182	www.brilliantpeople.com

Voluntary & Charity Work

Opportunities for voluntary work are increasing, but you will generally be subject to similar visa requirements to those needed for paid work. Organisations operating in Beijing range from international groups like Greenpeace to INBAR (www.inbar.int), which helps support communities that rely on bamboo for housing. Local listings magazines (p.51) contain details of groups seeking volunteers if you wish to do something worthwhile in your spare time.

Major organisations such as Oxfam, Actionaid Plan International and the Clinton Foundation will advertise for their own salaried staff, while www.chinadevelopmentbrief.com is a good website for seeking out more opportunities. Many of the more recognised names look for staff with good qualifications and significant experience. Less formal positions, such as visiting prisons, are possible but aren't often advertised so keep your ear to the ground. If you're coming from abroad check out organisations such as Voluntary Service Overseas in the UK or the Peace Corps in the US who will be able to help with visa requirements. Make sure you do a good background check on any group you sign up with to make sure they are reputable.

Working As A Freelancer Or Contractor

The main difficulty in setting up as a freelancer is obtaining a working visa. The best method is to find a company or school to serve as a basic employer who can help you fulfill the official requirements. The government introduced a new Labour Law at the start of 2008 which may make working as a freelancer more difficult. The law requires freelancers to sign a contract with the commissioning company, but precise details of how this will work in practice haven't yet emerged.

Once you are in Beijing there are plenty of freelance opportunities, in areas such as journalism, teaching or IT. If you want to develop your own business, some of the best opportunities are in providing services to the ever-expanding expat population. Other openings can be found providing English language services such as translating or editing.

Employment Contracts

It is a good idea to have a written contract with any prospective employer before starting work in Beijing. However, having a contract in place in China is not essential – from a cultural perspective, contracts are not seen as binding as in other countries. It is rare for an employee to take an employer to court over breach of contract. Teachers in particular can find that unexpected alterations to their terms of employment are made when they arrive in China.

Do your best to make sure that precise details about your length of employment are included in the contract, including any probation periods. If your contract is for a year or less, the probation period should only be one month long. You should check salary details, including how regularly you will be paid and in what currency, details of taxes that will be deducted from your pay, the terms of any overtime work that you do, and holiday policies. It's also vital to clarify any 'extras' that come as part of the job so that they are written into your contract, including such things as housing, plane tickets and mobile phone costs. Check in advance on what terms you can leave your job, and the company's procedure if it decides to terminate your employment. As for maternity leave, the law in China is that women over the age of 25 are entitled to four months off work after giving birth; if you're under 25, you are allowed three months.

Labour Law

Business Cards

When giving business cards, always present them with two hands, and ensure they are in good condition. They are considered an extension of the owner, so a crumpled bit of tat casually cast across a table will reflect badly.

The Labour Contract Law, which covers all workers in China, changed on January 1 2008, in an effort to address the rising number of labour disputes. It covers areas such as severance pay, probationary periods, mass layoffs, non-compete clauses and collective bargaining. It requires that contracts be put in writing within one month of employment, and gives clear recourse to employees whose rights have been violated. Much will depend on how the law is implemented, with some experts suggesting it will be more rigorously enforced against foreign companies than domestic ones. An English translation can be found on the American Chamber of Commerce Shanghai's website (www.amcham-shanghai.org).

HR professionals suggest that if you are badly treated at work, you should first complain to your personnel department, preferably in writing, with evidence to back your case. If there's no change after that it could be time to speak to a lawyer. Try to find a reliable Chinese lawyer as they will be more familiar with the local regulations. If your company is seeking to fire you for any reason, they should give you one month's notice, first providing verbal and written warnings in cases of alleged misconduct. Another resource can be your own embassy, which should be able to put you in touch with a lawyer.

Changing Jobs

Given the number of opportunities opening up in China, finding a new job shouldn't be too hard. You have to be careful about visa requirements as it is necessary to change the name of your sponsoring company on your visa and work permit. Teachers in particular need to obtain a 'letter of release' from their previous employer which allows them to change their residence permit. This can be a tiresomely bureaucratic procedure.

Be warned that moving to a new industry altogether can be quite tough; recruitment agencies say that while there are plenty of jobs available in China, they prefer to put forward candidates with relevant experience.

Companies in some sectors will include non-compete clauses. These will prevent you from working for a competitor for a certain period after leaving their employment, which could mean you spend time on so-called 'gardening leave'. Again, it is best to keep a sharp eye on such things when you're settling your initial contract.

Company Closure

As in any rapidly expanding economy, there are soaring successes and some stories of failure. While many international firms are doing well in Beijing, not all are getting their business models right. It's not unknown for even the largest language schools to fold suddenly. So, it's best to have an exit plan (and back-up funds) in case the Beijing adventure goes belly-up. Check the details of any contract closely, and ensure you have the contact details of a lawyer you can trust. If things go really awry, you could also try filing a complaint to China's Foreign Affairs Bureau (外事局).

Bank Accounts

Local banks dominate in China, though a few western institutions, such as HSBC and Citibank, have set up branches recently. Opening a bank account in the local currency is pretty simple. You'll need to show a passport with a valid visa and some proof of address (a lease or utility bills normally work). Banks provide debit cards and ATMs are plentiful. Not all ATMs take foreign debit cards, though Bank of China machines are usually reliable. Should you need to visit the bank, allow plenty of time as the queues can be long and slow moving. If you're going at lunch time, it's often best to grab a queue ticket then have your meal. By the time you've finished, it should be your turn. Banks are generally open from 09:00 to 17:00, though some close early on weekends. Local banks can also provide MasterCard or Visa credit cards.

Banking		
ABC	95599	www.abchina.com
ANZ ▶ p.77	010 6510 2929	www.anz.com
Bank Of China	010 6519 9988	www.bj.bank-of-china.com
CCB	95533	www.ccb.com
China Merchants Bank	010 6642 6969	www.cmbchina.com
Citibank	010 6510 2458	www.citibank.com.cn
HSBC	010 5999 8888	www.hsbc.com.cn
ICBC	010 6610 8048	www.icbc.com.cn
Société Générale	010 8519 2810	www.sgcib.com

Financial Planning

Given the relatively low cost of living in Beijing, many people find they can save some money during their stay. How you make the best of extra cash will depend on how long you expect to be in China and the tax regime in your own country.

There are a handful of firms to help with financial planning. They can recommend plans with respected companies like Zurich, Friends Provident or Generali that are tailored to your needs, including offshore funds. One such firm, Austen Morris Associates, says the offshore route can work particularly well if you intend to live in China for more than three to five years. You are likely to do better by saving overseas. Deposit interest rates at Chinese banks are still relatively low, meaning you won't get much of a return.

Financial Advisors		
Asia Connect	021 6415 1181	www.theasia-connect.com
Austen Morris Associates	021 6390 1233	www.austenmorris.com
Beijing Jingdu Certified Public Accountants	010 6526 4838	www.bjjdcpa.com.cn
China International Tax Consultancy	010 6354 0593	www.citcc.com
Credit Suisse	010 6410 6611	www.credit-suisse.com
Deloitte	010 8520 7788	www.deloitte.com
Devere & Partners	+41 443 898 282	www.devereandpartners.com
Ernst & Young	010 5815 3000	www.ey.com/china
Essential Finance	0852 2893 3200	www.essential-finance.com
Financial Page International	email inquiries	www.fpi.cn
Financial Partners	email inquiries	www.financial-partners.biz
Gilt Edge International	010 8453 4438	www.giltedgeintl.com
HW Intertrust China	010 6514 8686	www.horwathintertrust.com.cn
KPMG	010 8508 5000	www.kpmg.com.cn
Montpelier Nordic	010 5879 4899	www.montpeliergroup.com
PricewaterhouseCoopers	010 6533 8888	www.pwccn.com
Société Générale	010 8519 2810	www.sgcib.com
TA & Associates Asia	010 8520 0256	www.ta-asia.com
Temple Bar	email inquiries	www.templebarint.com
Vocation International Certified Public Accountants	010 8801 8766	www.tzcpa.com

Cost Of Living

Aspirin	¥20
Bananas	¥4
Beer (pint)	¥20
Beer (six pack)	¥30 - 50
Big Mac	¥17.5
Bread (loaf)	¥10
Capuccino	¥25
Car rental (per day)	¥150 - 600
Chocolate bar	¥3
Cigarettes (pack of 20)	¥5 - 50
Cinema ticket	¥50 - 60
Coke (can)	¥12
DVD	¥30
Eggs (per dozen)	¥15
Fresh chicken (per kg)	¥25
Golf (18 holes)	¥500 - 1000
Milk (litre)	¥8.5
Newspaper (international – IHT)	¥24
Newspaper (local)	¥1.5
Orange juice (litre)	¥15 - 25
Petrol (litre)	¥5
Picture printing (roll of 36)	¥30
Pizza (large, takeaway)	¥100
Postcard	¥5
Potatoes (packet of two)	¥5
Rice (1kg)	¥31
Salon haircut (female)	¥300 (top end)
Salon haircut (male)	¥200 (top end)
Stamp	¥5
Strawberries (punnet)	¥32 (in winter)
Sugar (2kg)	¥20
Taxi (10km journey)	¥25
Underground	¥2
Water (1.5 litre) – restaurant	¥25
Water (1.5 litre) – supermarket	¥16
Wine (house bottle)	¥300
Wine (house glass)	¥50 upwards
Wine (off-licence)	¥150 upwards

Such firms can also be useful for advice on pensions if you don't have one provided by your company. Most expats moving with an existing job suspend their pensions back home and take up whatever is on offer through their company in China.

If you want to invest in China's stock market, which has seen a remarkable rise in value in the last couple of years, it can be tricky. Expats can't directly invest, and it's difficult to buy into funds unless you have a bank account in Shanghai, where the country's main stock market is based. Financial advisers also warn that there remain issues over the transparency of some companies listed in China. Perhaps the best way to expose your money to the China growth story is to buy into a mutual fund that invests mainly on the Hong Kong stock exchange, where many Chinese companies are listed.

Taxation

If you live and work in Beijing for less than five years, you'll be liable for individual income tax (IIT) on your China earnings. Stay for more than five consecutive years and you'll become domiciled in China, meaning your worldwide earnings will be taxed in China.

China's income tax is progressive, with rates ranging from 5% to 45% in nine bands, depending on how much you earn. It's also worth keeping receipts (*fapiao*) for things like meals and laundry services, as you can offset these against your taxable income, as well as 'reasonable' relocation costs, business trip expenses and language training. Your employer should be able to handle the administrative side of paying your taxes, by withholding them from your monthly salary. Be sure also to check your tax position in your home country so that you fulfil all the requirements there. VAT in China is 17% for most products.

Fapiao

You may occasionally hear people ask for a *fapiao* after meals. This is not some exotic aperitif, but an invoice, which can be offset against taxable income. Most shops won't provide one unless asked, and the process can be a hassle in some smaller places, but they are worth demanding.

Legal Issues

With the economic reform that began in the late 1970s, China started to reform its legal system. It is still in a period of transition, with laws (such as the Labour Law, p.73) still being refreshed and revised. The evolving system has drawn on a mish-mash of influences, including western and Asian law, Chinese tradition and the government's desire for a 'socialist market economy'.

The National People's Congress, dominated by the Communist Party, is the highest lawmaking body in the land, though cities and administrative regions set local laws. The influence the Communist Party has on how laws are implemented varies from region to region. While its influence is usually significant, there are also signs of emerging judicial independence. Some lawyers at western companies say the process is becoming more fair.

As a rule of thumb, if you're unsure of the legality of something then steer clear. As in most countries, ignorance of the law is no defence. For most expats, the main contact with the authorities will be getting a resident's permit (p.63), or if you are trying to set up your own company. Beijing is a relatively crime-free city for westerners, particularly as the majority stick to well-trodden expat areas. Should you run into legal difficulties, the first steps should be to contact your embassy or consulate (p.26), and then a lawyer.

Marriage

To marry a Chinese person in Beijing, your spouse must be a Beijing resident. Otherwise, you'll have to go to their home town. You'll need a Certificate of Marriageability from your own embassy; this states you are single and able to marry. Take this, your passport and residence permit (don't forget your spouse-to-be) to the Beijing Municipal Civil Affairs Bureau (北京市民政局) to register the marriage where you'll also have to pay a fee. If you are both foreign, one of you must be living in China and you'll need to get married in the town where you are registered. See Marriage Licence (p.68) for more.

Adopting A Child

Adopting a child in China is possible, though it is essential to follow the correct procedures. Refer to your own embassy for advice. The process can take over a year and is subject to laws in both China and your home country. There are also fees involved in processing the required documentation. Chinese law allows adoption only of children aged 13 or under by married couples or single, heterosexual people. See Adoption (p.67) for more.

Yuan

Saint Joseph's Catholic Church

Shiny new banks

Beijing Exhibition Hall

ANZ. The Expat Banking Specialists

Confused about banking in China?

Then let ANZ take the pressure off. Contact our friendly team of English speaking Expat specialists today.

Some useful tips:
- Chinese currency can be called Renminbi (RMB), Yuan and Kuai.

- You can change RMB into foreign currency by providing your employment contract, payment slips and tax receipts to ANZ.

- You can finance your property in Australia or New Zealand using an ANZ offshore mortgage facility.

- It only takes 1-2 working days to receive your money into an ANZ China branch from Australia or New Zealand.

- Avoid lengthy queues by setting up regular ANZ automatic payments back home and for your rent.

It's important to bank with someone who understands your needs and speaks your language, so call us today.

chinaexpats@anz.com

Beijing
Sally Zhao
t: (86 10) 6510 2929 ext 239
e: Sally.Zhao@anz.com

Shanghai
Will Abbott
t: (86 21) 6136 6000 ext 156
e: Will.Abbott@anz.com

Guangzhou
Chris Lefebvre
t: (86 20) 3877 0501
e: Chris.Lefebvre@anz.com

www.anz.com

ANZ
澳新银行

Housing

Nothing demonstrates Beijing's development more than its booming construction industry. No building appears safe from the hungry bulldozers but, while the capital has seen its fair share of destruction, it has also enjoyed unprecedented levels of domestic and overseas investment. As one tatty, characterful old building is pulled down, a shiny new one gets put up in its place. As a result, the range of living options is expanding rapidly.

Most expats choose to rent, as laws regulating foreign ownership are complex and make it hard to guarantee a secure investment. The options for leasing range from very cheap flats in concrete tower blocks to lavish penthouse apartments. Residential areas tend to suit quite specific needs, so it's a good idea to familiarise yourself with the different districts before you decide where to put down your roots.

Renting In Beijing

Rents have been increasing since Beijing was announced as the host for the 2008 Olympics. Rumours that landlords stand to make a huge profit for the duration of the games has fuelled speculation throughout the city.

There are fears that tenants whose contracts finish before the Olympics begin will be unable to renew their lease, or will be asked to pay a dramatic increase. Those signing a lease in the run up to the games should ask for a clause written into the contract stating that this will not happen.

However, it is still possible to lease decent accommodation at reasonable rates. Low to mid-range apartments are generally found in government-built, four to six-storey concrete blocks. A two-bedroom flat in one of these properties ranges from ¥2,000 to ¥8,000 per month.

More expensive apartments are in international serviced and non-serviced towers in purpose-built compounds, and cost upwards of ¥10,000 per month. Families tend to congregate in the north-east of the city, near the international schools, where housing ranges from small two-storey houses to luxury villas with gardens and swimming pools.

Classifieds ◀
Local listings magazines (p.51) are a good bet for finding estate agents (also listed on p.80) and landlords who are renting properties.

Finding An Apartment

A large proportion of expats who move to Beijing arrive on corporate packages that include housing. Some companies used to restrict their staff to living in company-owned buildings, but today it is more common for a package to provide a set budget for employees to find their own home. Those brought over by a company usually deal directly with the firm's HR department, which will liaise with an estate agent to complete the necessary paperwork.

People who don't have the help of a company to find accommodation can deal independently with an estate agent, or even directly with a landlord. International real estate firms tend to deal with higher-end clients, so if your budget is ¥10,000 or less a month, it is best to go through a local estate agent. There are agencies all over Beijing, and you may need to try a few before you find a company you feel comfortable with.

Most agencies cover the area they are situated in, so it is often helpful to first choose the district you would like to live in. The internet is also a good place to look for housing; many of the English language forums include property advertisements and notices posted by people looking for a place to live. They are particularly useful for students or those looking for house shares. Check www.thebeijinger.com, www.beijing.asiaxpat.com, www.expatsinchina.com or www.cityweekend.com.cn/beijing.

Housing

Beijing housing

Negotiating The Lease

Bargaining is common in China and the practice doesn't stop when it comes to accommodation. Most landlords are willing to negotiate on the terms of the lease, whether it is lowering the rent rate, shortening the contract period or throwing in a few extra pieces of furniture. It is usual for a landlord and prospective tenant to spend at least an hour discussing the contract terms before a deal is signed. Standard lease agreements last for a year, although extending the contract period to two years or even 18 months can significantly lower your rent. Payment is typically made in cash, directly to the landlord two or three months in advance. Gas, electricity, water and phone bills can be paid at any bank branch and are usually the responsibility of the tenant. Most mid to high-end apartments are serviced by *wuye* (maintenance men), who can be called out to do general repairs. Make sure you check with your landlord if this service is included in your contract before signing.

Real Estate Agents

Agents are required to be licensed by the local authorities. Make sure you ask to see their stamped business certificate before you enter into negotiations. Real estate agents will charge a commission based on the rent which is usually the equivalent of one month. The landlord almost always pays this but, since commission is based on rent, it is within the agent's interest to persuade you to go as pricey as possible. If an agent appears pushy don't hesitate to ditch them and find someone else, if there is an abundance of anything in Beijing, it is property salesmen.

Real Estate Agents		
Century 21	010 6561 7788	www.century21cn.com/english
Colliers	010 8518 1633	www.colliers.com
Cushman & Wakefield	010 5921 0808	www.cushwakeasia.com
Golden Keys	010 8589 1006	www.zdhouse.com
HRS	010 8559 1011	www.srealty.com.cn
Joanna Real Estate	010 5108 8028	www.joannarealestate.com.cn
Jones Lang LaSalle	010 5922 1300	www.joneslanglasalle.com.cn/en-gb
Knight Frank	010 8518 5758	www.knightfrank.com.cn
Lihong	010 8580 2389	www.lihong.biz
Solution Realty	010 8559 1011	www.srealty.com.cn
Waveland Reality	010 8580 5609	www.wavelandrealty.com

The Lease

Because lease terms are heavily set by negotiation, it is crucial to check the wording of your contract. Make sure you ask for a copy of the contract in both Chinese and English and get an impartial third party to read through it. A common oversight is failing to check who is liable for repairs and get stung when the boiler breaks down or the air-con fails. Usually the tenant is responsible for damage to the property but the landlord must deal with general wear and tear. Landlords are responsible for maintenance of existing fittings and furniture, but remember all contracts vary.

Security deposits are standard practice and are typically the equivalent of one or two month's rent, to be paid on signing the lease. After a contract has been signed both you and the landlord are required by law to register the agreement at the local police station. Some landlords will try to avoid this because registering means they become liable for the compulsory stamp duty, (0.1% of the rent). Expats risk a fine if they do not register within 24 hours of moving into a property.

A full inventory of existing furniture should be included in the contract to avoid disputes when you move out. It is rare for disputes to reach tribunal level; the system is overly complicated and it is often more trouble than it's worth. If no compromise can be reached however, foreigners can sue in the People's Court of the district where the property is located. The statute limitation for rental disputes in two years.

Main Accommodation Options

No Fourth Floor

Step into any elevator in Beijing and you will be presented with row upon row of numbered buttons. Look closely however, and you will notice the absence of any floor containing the number four. This originates from a deep superstition held by most Chinese people, who claim the Mandarin word for the number four sounds like the word for death. As such, most would be unwilling to rent or buy an apartment on the 'death' floor.

Low-End Apartments

At the lower end of the scale, apartments tend to be in four or six-storey concrete buildings, built by the government to replace the sprawling *hutongs*, or communal courtyards of old. These can be basic, but are fully integrated into the community, and a great place to live if you want to practice your Chinese. Rents start at ¥2,500 per month.

Mid To High-End Apartments

New-build, high-rise homes are common for expats and wealthy Chinese. They tend to be clustered in gated complexes, and come serviced and include convenience stores, play areas and gyms. Prices vary dramatically, and while rents start from about ¥10,000 per month in the centre, they can be as low as ¥5,000 on the outskirts.

Houses & Villas

Expats wishing to recreate western suburbia head to the north-west of the city near the capital's airport. There you'll find the space to accommodate townhouses and villas with gardens and garages. Most are located in gated developments or estates and have their own security and other facilities.

Courtyard Houses & Hutongs

While a great deal of Beijing's traditional *hutong* or courtyard houses have been destroyed, it is still possible to find one to rent. Courtyards that have not been renovated tend to be very basic, with just one or two rooms on a single floor. Some do not even have their own bathroom, which means sharing communal toilets and washing out of a bucket. These start at about ¥5,000 a month. Those that have been renovated tend to be of a very high standard. Restored furniture and antique fittings give them a delightful traditional feel but mean rents tend to be over ¥20,000 a month.

Homestay

The best option for an eager Chinese language student is to live with a host Chinese family and become immersed in local life. Bed and board is often offered free or at a very low price in exchange for English lessons. If you're looking for a homestay it is a good idea to post a message on an expat websites (p.52) or contact your university or study programme for details.

Other Rental Costs

Be prepared to pay a security deposit equal to one or two month's rent. You may also need to pay up to three month's rent in advance when you sign a contract. The maintenance fee for your apartment may be included in the rent rate but utility bills should be paid separately at a local bank. Make sure your landlord provides receipts to show that they are up to date with payments before you move in. If you found the property through an agent then their commission fee will need to be paid. If the monthly rent is above ¥3,500 then the landlord should be responsible for this but make sure you check in advance.

Buying Property

It is rare for expats to buy property in China and five or six years ago it was unheard of. In 2002 the government tentatively opened up Beijing's property market to foreign direct investment. There was an initial rush by wealthy individuals and international corporations. Terrified the market would be swept from beneath them by big multinationals, the government introduced restrictions for foreign investment. Expats do continue to buy in Beijing but in smaller numbers and on the understanding that the investment is unlikely to yield rewards in the short term. Individual buyers are now limited to one property and that must be their main residence. Foreigners keen to buy must have lived in China for at least one year and provide a resident's permit to prove it. One way expats get around restrictions is to take out a long-term fixed rate lease of up to 50 years which, if paid in one or two lump sums, is usually significantly cheaper than paying monthly. Often the contract for these deals includes a clause that allows the leaseholder to do what they like to the property if in keeping with municipal planning laws. This allows foreigners the freedom to make a property their own without the hassle or risk of buying it outright. The drawback is that they will not benefit from any appreciation in value from renovations made and will have to hand the place back at the end of the lease period, unless land laws change before the contract is up.

The Process

Before buying a home, expats will need to provide visas, work permits and proof of residency. Buying a property is a serious, long-term commitment and it is essential that you find a trustworthy agent. It is highly advised that you demand to see the following documents before committing to a purchase: Land Use Right Certificate, Project Planning Permit, Land Use Planning Permit and Building Work Certificate. Make sure you also have clear contact details and identification from the landlord. Once an agreement has been made, a sales contract must be signed by both parties and presented to the District Property Exchange Centre to transfer the title and deeds. A stamped and signed sales contract is needed to apply for a mortgage. Money transfers can be made from an overseas bank account directly into the seller's account or you can wire money into your own local bank and exchange it into local currency before handing it over.

Buy To Let

It is illegal for an expat to buy to let in China, since any property owned has to be their main home. However, expats have been known to flout the rules by brokering deals with local agents or registering a second property in the name of a Chinese spouse.

Selling Property

Most sellers get agents to advertise their property and handle paperwork. Agents will ask 1% of the sales price in return. Make sure you have the title to the home, up to date tax documents, and the original purchase receipt to hand. A seller must have paid off the mortgage in full unless the seller's bank can directly transfer the mortgage to the buyer's bank. Factor in spending on renovations and your desired selling price. Sellers must pay a 20% capital gains tax if they sell less than five years after buying.

Mortgages

Prospective buyers can apply for mortgages with international or local banks. A developer selling a new block will often have a pre-existing arrangement with one bank and, as part of the process buyers will have to use it. Expats going to a local bank can borrow up to 70% of the value of a new or recently built property, and up to 50% for an older place. Most banks will want to see proof of income, a valid visa and passport. Repayment methods vary, and it is worth shopping around.

Mortgage Providers

The Bank Of China (BOC)	010 6659 6688	www.boc.cn
The Bank Of Communications (ICBC)	95559	www.beijing.bankcomm.com
HSBC	800 830 2880	www.hsbc.com.cn
Industrial & Commercial Bank Of China (ICBC)	95588	www.icbc.com.cn
Standard Chartered (Shanghai)	021 5887 1230	www.standardchartered.com

Housing

Xicheng District

Xicheng housing

Communist era housing

Your door may not look so grand

Chongwen housing

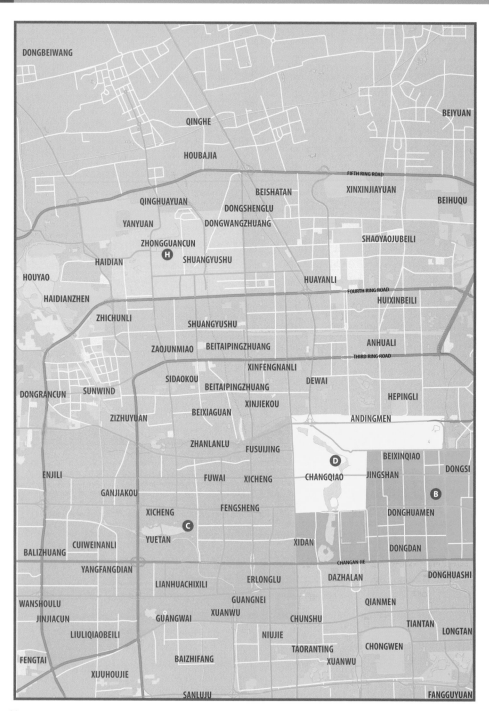

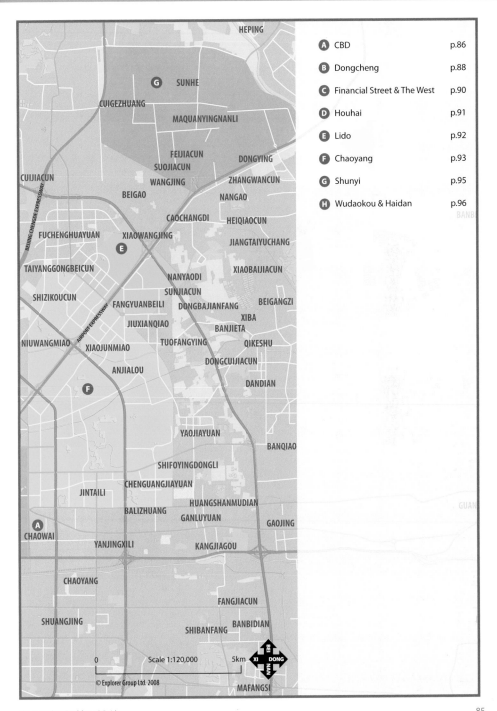

© Explorer Group Ltd. 2008

Area **A** *p.84*
See also Map 11

CBD

Beijing's Central Business District (CBD) lies in the south-east of the city, and runs between Chaoyang Beilu in the north and Tonghui River in the south. It borders Xidawang Lu to the east, and reaches Dongdaqiao Lu to the west. The vast north to south axis of the Third Ring Road cuts the area in two.

Investment has been pouring into the CBD since it was demarcated in 2000, and vast development has followed. The area is characterised by hotels, high-end shopping malls, designer department stores and swish bars and restaurants. Landmarks include the New CCTV Tower, China World Trade Towers, The Place (p.296), The Kerry Centre, Jianwai SOHO and New SOHO. Accommodation tends to be apartments in high-rise, modern developments. Notable residential areas are the complexes near Ritan Park and Jianguomen in the west and the clusters of high-rise buildings around New SOHO.

Best Points
Handy for city workers, high standard of accommodation and good shopping.

Worst Points
Noisy and crowded, bad traffic and expensive rents.

Accommodation

The price of a penthouse apartment in Beijing Yintai Centre is reportedly ¥70,000 a square metre, making them China's second most expensive flats, after Shanghai's Riviera. While not all property in the CBD is that expensive, rents tend to reflect the luxury of the accommodation.

A 135sqm two-bedroom apartment in the Fortune Plaza development next to the Kerry Centre, with air conditioning, sports facilities and 24 hour security, will set you back between ¥10,000 and ¥12,000 a month. A similar apartment in the Central Park or Oriental Rose developments will cost between ¥8,000 and ¥12,000.

To the east, Blue Castle is a well known area among expats. A cosy two-bedroom flat could cost as little as ¥6,000 per month, including management fees and heating, but prices are higher for bigger suites.

Apartments in new developments on the city's outskirts, near the Fourth Ring Road to the east of the CBD, can be considerably cheaper.

Shopping & Amenities

This is Beijing's designer label district. The Silk Market (p.294) on Jianguomen is full of fake Burberry and Calvin Klein, while the boutiques on The Place, China World and Shin Kong Place sell the real deal.

The malls offer a selection of mid-range high street stores including Mango, Zara, French Connection and Benetton, as well as high-end Chinese outlets. The area to the west, near Ritan Park, has a Friendship Store, a Jenny Lou's (p.297) grocery and several good bakeries. The Russian Market on the west side of the park offers cheap clothing and souvenirs, but without the crowds of the Silk Market (p.264). There is a Wal-Mart in the Wanda Plaza on Jianguo Lu.

Entertainment & Leisure

Some of the best bars and restaurants are attached to hotels, including Centro (p.329) cocktail bar in the Kerry Centre and Aria Jazz and Wine Bar in China World Hotel. Philippe Starck's LAN bar is a central feature of this district, with its lavish contemporary design, impressive cocktail list and nightly live music and DJs.

The area around Ritan Park offers a good selection of Asian and western cuisine, with Grandma's Kitchen (p.304) and Steak & Eggs (Xiushui Nan Jie, Jianguomenwai Dajie, Chaoyang, 010 6592 8088, www.steakeggs.com.cn) favourites among expats for family dining and American-style portions. There are several restaurants inside the park itself, including Xiao Wang Fu (p.311), which serves some of the best Peking duck in the city. The Stone Boat Cafe (p.338) in the centre of the park is hugely popular in the summer and offers live music at weekends.

Sports facilities in the area tend to be attached to housing developments, but several offer fitness, dance and yoga classes and membership to non-residents. The Oriental Taipan (p.238) near Sunshine 100 offers treatments and is a popular after-work treat among city types.

Education

Eton International School (p.136) and Eton Bilingual School (p.129) have campuses at Global Trade Mansion off Guanghua Lu. Kids at other international schools commute to campuses in Sanlitun and the north of the city.

Transport

The central axis of the CBD is the golden cross at Jianguomen where subway Lines 1 and 2 meet. The Third Ring Road runs through the middle of the CBD and connects to the airport expressway in the north. Traffic can get really bad at peak times and it is often a lot easier to travel by subway, which stops at all three of the major junctions in the CBD. Beijing Railway Station is one stop further south from Jianguomen.

Healthcare

The Beijing Vista Clinic (p.118) in the Kerry Centre on Guanghua Lu is a private hospital that offers 24 hour emergency treatment (010 6501 4260), general medical services and has a pharmacy with western medicine. The Arrail Dental Clinic (p.121) on Jianguomen Da Jie offers comprehensive non-surgical treatment and English speaking staff. You'll find full dentistry services at SDM Dental (p.121) in China World Trade shopping mall.

The Silk Market (p.294)

The CBD at night

Beijing Railway Station

Area **B** *p.84*
See also Map 10

Dongcheng

The area to the east of the Forbidden City (p.180), inside the Second Ring Road, is one of Beijing's most populated areas. It covers Dongzhimen and the Workers' Stadium, the Lama Temple (p.189), Gui Jie and Jiadakou.

Best Points

Has a real Chinese community feel, excellent transport links and great restaurants.

More and more expats are choosing to live in Dongcheng, but it retains a traditional feel. Most of the area's old *hutongs* have been replaced by high-rise flats, but the community spirit lives on; there are always Chinese pensioners sitting out in the street playing cards or ballroom dancing in the parks.

Accommodation

Mid-level apartment blocks, populated by a mix of Chinese families and expats, are the most common accommodation. The area is particularly popular with students

Worst Points

Can be noisy and very busy and is far from many of the international schools.

and young professionals because the apartments can cost as little as ¥2,000 a month (although rents are rising).

Next to the dilapidated, soviet-style community housing, the Naga development sticks out like a well-designed sore thumb, and the top floor is rumoured to be owned by Jackie Chan. Apartments start from ¥10,000 a month.

Directly north of Dongzhimen is the Lama Temple. The area around it is a maze of old *hutongs* that have managed to escape demolition. Genuine courtyard homes can be found for as little as ¥3,000 (though in a fairly shabby state). Plusher, refurbished courtyards can cost as much as ¥25,000 per month, but both types are rare and in high demand.

Shopping & Amenities

The Sky Mall, on the corner of Dongzhimen Wai and the Second Ring Road, offers a selection of clothing outlets, including Mango, Watson's pharmacy and a large, rather pricey supermarket that sells some international products.

The Russian Embassy is on Dongzhimen Bei Zhong Jie and there are several small Russian stores nearby that sell bread, chocolate, wine and cheese alongside bottles of strong vodka and tins of Spam. The 7-Eleven on Gui Jie is open 24 hours and is popular with Chinese school children looking for instant noodles and sugary snacks. It's really worth a visit just to see the army of shop assistants who greet every customer by saying 'welcome' in unison. If there is a surge of people entering, it can create quite a chorus.

Nearby, Chinese grocery stores and fruit stands sell good, reasonably priced produce throughout the year. Street vendors offer everything from popcorn to hot sweet potatoes and chestnuts.

Entertainment & Leisure

Lanterns line the sides of the road along Gui Jie (known as 'food street'), which has every conceivable type of Chinese cuisine. Stroll from one end to the other and try to resist the overtures of competing doormen.

Towards Jiadakou, Waiting for Godot (p.339) is a popular cafe among freelance journalists, who go there to hide in its dark corners and take advantage of free wireless internet. Café de la Poste (p.313) on the road leading up to Lama Temple serves choice steak and fine French wine. The *hutong* opposite the entrance to the temple is home to the Vineyard (p.325), popular among expats for reasonably priced western food, including full English breakfasts and Sunday brunch.

Education

The international campuses and nurseries in Sanlitun are a short commute. However, the schools in Shunyi are 45 minutes away by road and no school buses currently pick up from within the Second Ring Road. There are a few good Chinese language schools, including Frontiers School (010 6413 1547), which runs daytime and evening Mandarin classes and one-to-one tuition for adults.

Transport
Transport links are excellent. Dongzhimen subway connects commuters to Line 2 and Line 13 and Beijing Railway Station is only four stops to the south. A direct line from the airport to Dongzhimen is due to open in mid 2008 and will whisk passengers to and from the airport in less than 15 minutes. The central bus depot on Dongzhimen Wai is a five-minute walk from the subway, and the area is swarming with taxis day and night.

Healthcare
There are no international hospitals or surgeries in the immediate area, but Beijing International SOS Clinic (p.118) in Sanlitun is 10 minutes away by taxi.

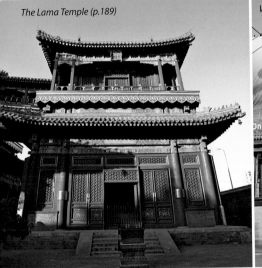

The Lama Temple (p.189)

Wanfujing shops (p.290)

Beihai Lake (p.191)

The Lama Temple (p.189)

Area ❸ *p.84*
See also Map 6

Worst Points
*Remote, with
few residential
communities.*

Best Points
An area on the up.

Financial Street & The West

The west of Beijing is the least populated area of the city and attracts very few international residents. The rapid development around Fuxingmen has brought with it a number of residential blocks, but many currently lie empty or unfinished. As more hotels and high-end shops move to the area, expect this situation to change.

Accommodation

Options are limited to a cluster of high-rise blocks around the financial hub. Guanyuan Apartment block and Grace Court offer flats from ¥15,000 a month.

Shopping & Amenities

Department stores and malls are your main options. Lane Crawford (p.258) in the upmarket Seasons Place Mall opened in late 2007, offering shelf upon shelf of premium brand, designer goods. The area to the east around Xidan subway station has a department store, several bookshops and a science and technology shopping mall.

Entertainment & Leisure

The main attractions are the hotel bars and restaurants that cater for the tourist and corporate trade. The Ritz-Carlton (p.36) and The Westin (p.38) offer a selection of restaurants staffed by top quality chefs. Champagne brunch is a speciality among these establishments and provides an opportunity to gorge on lobster and on chocolate fountains. The Central Conservatory of Music (p.347), The National Theatre (p.347), Beijing Concert Hall (p.347) and the Forbidden City Concert Hall are all in the vicinity, hosting Chinese and international performances.

Education

Anyone with children that plans to move to the area should remember that it is at least an hour's commute each way to the international schools in the north east of Beijing.

Transport

Financial Street is connected to both Line 1 and Line 2 of the subway. However, it is a long way from Capital Airport and traffic towards Tiananmen Square and the city centre can be heavy. Cabs are harder to flag down and taxi ranks are few and far between.

Healthcare

Beijing Emergency Medical Centre (010 6609 8114) on Qianmen Xi Da Jie offers emergency medical care and some first aid training with English speaking staff. Beijing Children's Hospital on Nanlihi Lu (010 6802 8401) is a public paediatrics centre, but not all staff speak English. Xuanwu Hospital on Changchun Jie (010 8319 8899) is a public medical centre staffed by English speaking doctors, offering expertise in neurology, general surgery and medical imaging.

New offices

Area **D** *p.84*
See also Map 8

Houhai

A few years ago Houhai was hugely popular among expats looking for authentic courtyard houses and a bustling local community. However, an abundance of western residents and tourists has brought the inevitable street hawkers, tacky souvenir shops and beggars. The area is now better known for its bars and restaurants.

The Drum and Bell Towers (p.179) are one of the city's most popular attractions, and the *hutongs* around them are a great place for a weekend stroll. The bars, restaurants and boutiques along Nanluoguiang Hutong make it a prime spot for browsing the ethnic clothes shops or sipping cocktails on a restaurant roof terrace.

Best Points
Full of bars and places to eat out. Pretty hutongs *and courtyard houses. Always bustling with activity.*

Worst Points
Increasingly noisy and touristy. Rent is expensive.

Accommodation

There are plenty of online ads touting courtyards for rent. Many of these will be rundown, and despite being small and badly renovated, their novelty factor makes them expensive. Prices start at about ¥5,000 per month.

There are some in great condition, often with western fittings, traditional exteriors and a price to match; duplexes with 24 hour security start at around ¥20,000. There are plenty of agents and private landlords who specialise in high-end courtyard homes. Contact a selection to get an idea of prices.

Shopping & Amenities

Shopping is restricted to boutiques, local fruit and vegetable stands and souvenir shops. You'll have to travel south to the CBD and SOHO or east towards Chaoyang Park (p.191) if you want to find international food and shopping malls. The boutiques along Nanluoguxiang sell kitsch posters, designer clothes, hand-made pottery, jewellery and trinkets, but these tend to be pricey.

Entertainment & Leisure

The bars and restaurants around Houhai Lake are popular evening destinations; in summer the roof terraces and street tables are packed. Favourites include No Name (p.309), which serves hearty Yunan food, the large Hancang Hakka, offering cuisine from China's minority population in the south-west and Hutong Pizza (9 Yindingqiao Hutong, Dongcheng, 010 6617 5916, www.hutongpizza.com) in nearby Yindingqiao Hutong. The bars along Gulou Dong Da Jie and Nanlouguxiang are always busy. You'll also find two of Beijing's best live music venues here: Yugong Yishan (p.344) on Zhangzizhong Lu and MAO Livehouse (p.335) on Gulou Dong Dajie.

Education

It's a fair trek to the international schools and nurseries in Shunyi, but some have campuses in Sanlitun (p.94). Either way, there are no school buses that serve the area, so be prepared for long car journeys if you want to send your children to international schools.

Transport

The addition of Line 5 at the end of 2007 brought a subway link to central Beijing, and Houhai, Beixinqiao and Zhanzizhong Lu stations are within easy reach of the lake. Buses and taxis pile up along Gulou Dong Da Jie and Gulou Xi Da Jie and traffic can get very congested at peak times. The lake and surrounding *hutongs* are accessed by foot only.

Healthcare

The nearest medical facilities are in Chaoyang, a 25 minute taxi ride away, where you'll find several large hospitals (p.93).

Area **E** *p.84*
See also Map 5

Lido

In the north-east corner of Chaoyang, on the way to Capital Airport, is Lido. It is a small residential area in a cluster of international shops and hotels.

There's a good sense of community among local expats, who regularly organise social events and entertainment. The proximity to the airport and good transport links make it a useful spot for frequent travellers and those with children attending schools in Shunyi.

Best Points
Great sense of community, good local shops and amenities. Close to the airport and international schools. Cheaper accommodation.

Accommodation

Many developments are new but prices tend to be reasonable due to the distance from the centre. A two-bedroom apartment in the Landscape or Cando developments, both with 24 hour security, cost as little as ¥3,000 a month. Richmond Park and Upper East Side complexes offer more expensive and extravagant options, with facilities such as a gym, sauna and swimming pool. Prices for a two-bedroom apartment start at ¥12,000.

Worst Points
Far from central Beijing with no bars or late night entertainment.

Shopping & Amenities

Lido offers a good mix of cafes, restaurants and shops to suit western tastes including international supermarket Jenny Lou's (p.264), Starbucks and the Lido Deli (p.348). There is also a pharmacy, several spas and beauty salons, as well as Tom's DVDs (p.277), which is one of Beijing's largest DVD shops.

Entertainment & Leisure

A small selection of restaurants offer a range of international food, including authentic Italian fare at Annie's (p.315) and Pure Lotus vegetarian restaurant (p.322). Apart from a branch of Frank's Place (p.331), a sports bar serving draft beer and hearty food, the Lido is quiet at night.

The Airport Expressway means central Beijing isn't far away and a taxi to Sanlitun takes 10 to 15 minutes. Beijing's art district, 798 (p.176), is a 15 minute walk; its galleries and cafes offer plenty of opportunity for browsing.

Education

Eton International School (p.136), Eton International Bilingual Academy (p.129), and the International Academy of Beijing (p.137) all have campuses in Lido. School buses ferry kids to and from the international schools in Shunyi, a short commute to the north. There are several playgroups and nurseries including 3e International Kindergarten and Elementary School (p.128), for children aged from 18 months to 8 years.

Transport

The airport is a 20 to 30 minute drive on the expressway, which also connects Lido to the Third and Second Ring Roads and central Beijing. The subway doesn't stretch this far, but an airport shuttle bus leaves regularly from the Lido Hotel. Buses 401, 404, and 934 travel between Lido and the central bus depot in Dongzhimen.

Healthcare

Beijing United Family (p.118) is the city's largest international hospital and a first choice for most expats. All doctors are internationally trained and speak English. Amcare Women's and Children's Hospital (p.116) is a public medical centre with several private rooms and delivery suites. Some doctors speak English and translators are available.

Area **F** p.84
See also Map 5

Chaoyang

Chaoyang, the largest district in Beijing, covers the north-east of the city between the Second and Fifth Ring Roads. It includes the residential areas of Sanlitun, Gongti and around Chaoyang Park, which offer mid to high-end accommodation close to some of the city's best shops, restaurants and bars. This makes the area popular among expats. With many embassies and several of the international schools in Sanlitun, it's a good choice for families. The CBD is a short taxi or subway ride to the south, making it convenient for those working in the city.

Best Points
Central location, excellent transport links and a good range of accommodation.

Worst Points
Noisy and polluted. Hawkers and beggars in touristy areas can be a nusiance.

Accommodation

Property in north-east Chaoyang is dominated by apartment blocks and high-rise flats. Housing around Sanlitun, a popular nightlife enclave, tends to be cheaper and more suited to young people or couples without children. A simple two-bedroom apartment in one of the government-built six-storey buildings can cost as little as ¥2,500 a month. Modern high-rises such as Season's Park, between Gongti Beilu and Dongzhimen Wai, are serviced to a higher standard, and come with 24 hour security, parking, and leisure facilities. Prices start at about ¥10,000 for a two-bedroom, 90sqm flat and rise to ¥20,000 for a top floor suite. The residential area on the far side of the Third Ring Road is clustered around Chaoyang Park and tends to be quieter, catering to a wealthier clientele. Flats in Palm Springs, which overlooks the south of the park itself, start at ¥15,000 a month and come with en suite bathrooms and fully fitted kitchens. Just north of Chaoyang Park is Maizidian, where developments are older and less expensive. Rents start from about ¥3,000 for a 90sqm two-bedroom apartment but facilities are basic and public areas such as lifts and corridors can be a little rundown.

Shopping & Amenities

Be it expensive perfume, cheese, books, DVDs or souvenirs, you'll find it in and around Sanlitun and Gongti. The multi-floor department store Pacific Century Place (p.296) on Gongti Beilu stocks international brands including Miss Sixty, Levi's and Clinique. Indoor markets off Sanlitun Beilu such as 3.3 (p.295), Nali Mall and the tourist trap Yashow (p.294), sell knock-off designer labels, shoes, belts, bags, electrical goods, cheap jewellery and other trinkets. Western food can be purchased at Jenny Lou's (p.264), April Gourmet or The Friendship Store (p.264).

Entertainment & Leisure

By day, Sanlitun is a popular cafe spot with tourists and expats, especially for alfresco dining in summer. At night, it becomes one of the most popular spots among expats for evening entertainment. It is possible to find food for every taste and occasion, from Taiwanese noodles at the 24 hour joint Bellagio (p.306) on Gonti Xi Lu, to mussels at the Belgian restaurant Morel's (p.312), on Gonti Beilu. Restaurants near Chaoyang Park are similarly varied, offering anything from Chinese street food to sushi. The Workers'

Chaoyang waterway

Stadium (p.230) is at the centre of the action and boasts some of Beijing's most popular clubs including Mix (p.343), Cargo (p.342) and Vic's (p.344). Venues clustered on Jiu Bar Street off Sanlitun Beilu offer cheap drinks and loud music into the early hours. Further east near Chaoyang is Lucky Street, row upon row of regional Chinese restaurants and bars. Off Lucky Street is Block 8 (p.342), a carpark full of upmarket bars and restaurants, including several sushi joints and i-Ultra Lounge (p.332).

There are several good spas and beauty salons, including Dragon Fly (p.237), off Sanlitun Nanlu, and a whole floor dedicated to nail painting and massages inside Yashow Market (p.294). The Yoga Yard (p.242) on Gonti Beilu offers daytime and evening classes for adults and kids, and the Beijing Bookworm (p.254) on Sanlitun Nanlu has wireless internet, a great range of new and second-hand western books, and offers regular talks with authors. Chaoyang Park (p.191) has a range of outdoor sports and entertainment facilities, including tennis courts, football pitches, a beach volleyball court and a fairground.

Education

Several large international schools have campuses in the Sanlitun and Chaoyang Park areas, including Beijing World Youth Academy (p.134), The Canadian International School (p.134), The British School of Beijing (p.134), The Ivy Academy (p.129), Eton International School (p.136) and Dulwich College Beijing (p.136). The area is also home to several popular nurseries and playgroups, including the Children's House Montessori Kindergarten (p.128), Mamolina Children's Home (p.129) and Sanlitun Kindergarten (p.130).

Transport

East Chaoyang is served by Line 10 of the subway system, which runs from Songjiazhuang in the south to Wanliu in the north-west. It stops at Guanghua Lu, Gongti Beilu and Maizidian Xi Lu. The Third Ring Road runs through the middle of Chaoyang, providing access to the city centre and connecting with the airport expressway to the north-east. Dongzhimen Bus Station off Dongzhimen Waidajie is Beijing's main hub. Taxis are in abundance and can be hailed on every street corner.

Healthcare

The International Medical Centre (010 6465 1561) in the Lufthansa Centre on Liangmaqiao Lu is a 24 hour private hospital with English-speaking doctors. It offers a wide range of services, including emergency treatment, major and minor surgery, family healthcare, sexual health and contraception, dentistry, dermatology and counselling. Beijing International SOS clinic (p.118) on Sanlitun Xiwujie offers comprehensive services, including a 24 hour emergency ward, optometry, counselling and therapy, orthopaedics, dentistry and travel vaccinations.

Chaoyang nightlife

Area **G** *p.84*
See also Map 3

Shunyi

Shunyi is 30km from downtown Beijing – far enough to make it feel like a town in its own right. It sits to the west of the Airport Expressway, between the Fifth and Sixth Ring Roads. Sometimes referred to as the expat village, it is home to most of Beijing's foreign families. It has the feel of western suburbia, with tree-lined avenues and large villas with swimming pools and garages. Many international schools and nurseries are in the area.

Best Points

Feels like home for many westerners. Away from the noise and pollution of the city. Lots of space.

Worst Points

Doesn't feel like China. Isolated, and has relatively expensive accommodation (rents are quite often quoted in dollars).

Accomodation

Accommodation tends to be in gated communities. The sprawling Beijing Riviera is a good example of those at the top end, with 447 villas, ranging from 226sqm to 451sqm in area. Each has European furniture, fitted kitchens, wooden balconies and a walled garden. The clubhouse has a golf course, tennis courts, football pitch, indoor and outdoor pools, a gym and a spa. Rents start at $4,000 (¥29,000) per month. Over the road is Cathay View, a similarly luxurious development, with purpose built courtyard-style homes. Each villa has been designed to replicate the open layout and low ceiling of a traditional home, but comes with mod cons and a private garden. Rent starts at $7,000 (¥51,000) per month. Apartments and town houses in developments like Beijing Euro village or Capital Paradise start at around $1,000 (¥7,000) a month.

Shopping & Amenities

Shunyi has its own shops, salons and markets, with more opening all the time. Pinnacle Plaza, next to Eton International School (p.136) , has clothes, music, electrical goods and sports gear. As well as international grocery stores such as Jenny Lou's (p.264) and April Gourmet (p.264), there is an ethical goods market and The Orchard (Jingshun Lu, 010 6433 6270), an organic farm, restaurant and shop. Expats from across the city make the pilgrimage to The Exquisite Bakery (p.279), in Riverville Square, which stocks everything from Pokemon cakes to Christmas decorations. There are several furniture, interiors and homeware shops, selling Chinese antiques, fabrics and bespoke furniture.

Entertainment & Leisure

Shunyi boasts lots of western dining options, with bagel shops, cafes and pizza parlours. The Orchard is hard to find but serves excellent European food in beautiful grounds. The area has some of the city's best sports facilities. In addition to those attached to residential developments and international schools, there are golf clubs, riding stables, a skate park and fishing lakes. Dance, yoga, fitness and kung fu classes are offered at many of the schools.

Education

Most of the city's international schools are here, including Dulwich College (p.136), Eton International (p.136), The British School of Beijing (p.136), The Swedish School of Beijing (p.138), Western Academy of Beijing (p.138), The International School of Beijing (p.137) and The Children's House Montessori Kindergarten (p.128).

Transport

It's a 40 minute drive to town along the Airport Expressway. Most residents have their own cars (and often drivers too). School coaches run from Shunyi to other campus sites, such as Sanlitun. There is no subway. The number 915 runs to the city centre, but takes over an hour and stops after 20:00. Taxis are rare.

Healthcare

Beijing United Family Clinic (p.118) in the Pinnacle Plaza is a surgery and clinic linked to the Beijing United Hospital (p.118) in Lido. There are also several vets and kennels.

Area **H** *p.84*
See also Map 4

Wudaokou & Haidian

Wudaokou, Beijing's student enclave, is in the heart of Haidian district and a prime spot for affordable accommodation. It is quite far from the city centre, but the distance lends the area its own character.

Best Points
Cheap, sociable and with lots of study facilities.

Restaurants and bars tend to be cheaper and there are several good markets for clothes and electrical goods. The area is also credited with being the birthplace of Beijing's fledgling music scene and is a great place to catch China's indie kids, metal heads, goths and punks.

Accommodation

Worst Points
Accommodation is based around the needs of students. Far from downtown.

A great deal of accommodation in Wudaokou is university residences, offered to students as part of their education packages. Rent prices are the cheapest in the city and a single dorm or room can go for ¥1,000 a month. There is plenty of opportunity for house shares; adverts for roommates can be found in cafes and online.

A standard, fully furnished two-bedroom flat in a development near Beijing Language & Culture University costs around ¥2,000 and has 24 hour security, but won't be anything fancy. Prices go up to around ¥4,000 or ¥5,000 for large three and four-bedroom apartments and duplexes.

Shopping & Amenities

The Wudaokou clothing market is a great place to kit yourself out cheaply. There is a Wal-Mart (p.297) on Zichun Lu and a Carrefour (p.297) on Zhonggauancun to cover household needs. On the same road is one of Beijing's largest electronics markets, and Zhonghai computer market is nearby. Together they provide everything from hard drives to digital cameras.

The Zhonggauancun shopping mall (p.296) has a range of local and western chains including Nike, Lacoste and Sephora. Some of the best English language books and study aids can be found among Wudaokou's large international bookstores.

Entertainment & Leisure

The noisy, smoky and cheap bars and clubs in Wudaokou are the antithesis of those in the city's east. Leading the crowd is the pokey live music venue D-22 (p.343) on Chengfu Lu, its tireless efforts to showcase local talent makes it one of the leading live music venues in China. Two doors down, 13 Club (p.326) charges itself with promoting the country's nebulous heavy metal and rock scene.

The student district is characterised by cheap eats so there are plenty of local restaurants and fast food joints to satisfy those on a budget.

The Summer Palace (p.182), Beijing Zoo (p.189) and the Botanical Gardens (p.190) are this side of town and are all excellent places to escape the city, especially in summer.

Education

Beijing Xiyi Elementary School (p.134) on Beisanhuan Xilu was one of the first local schools to admit international children. There are several local nurseries that take expat kids, however the primary language is Chinese, so most foreign children commute to schools in Shunyi and Chaoyang.

Further education is Haidian's speciality and all the main campuses for foreign and local students are based there. These include Peking University (p.141), Tsinghua University (p.141), Beijing Language & Culture University (p.140) and Renmin University (p.141). There are also a wide range of private schools and tutors offering group or one-to-one Mandarin classes. The best way to find out about these is to check university noticeboards or one of the online expat forums (p.52).

Transport

Wudaokou is 45 minutes by bus, subway or taxi from the centre of Beijing. A taxi can cost as much as ¥40 or ¥50 for a single journey. The Wudaokou subway stop is on Line 13, which connects to Line 2 at Xizhimen in the east and loops all the way round to Dongzhimen in the west, taking 45 to 60 minutes. Bus number 375 runs between Wudaokou and Xizhimen, where you can take the subway to downtown Beijing. The number 690 bus to Qianmen takes more than an hour. On weekends, some of the university campuses put on coaches to take students into town for a night out.

Healthcare

There is a branch of the Arrail Dental Clinic (010 8286 1956) on Kexueyuan Nanlu, offering 24 hour dentistry, general check ups, and the treatment of gum disease. The nearest international hospital is the Beijing United Family Clinic (p.118) in Shunyi.

Haidian housing

Setting up Home

Setting up home in Beijing can be smooth and simple. Moving costs are low, there are plenty of furniture shops with traditional Chinese pieces, and reliable domestic help is relatively cheap. There will be hiccups and stresses, but these are surmountable. Once you have the house set up, settle in and explore the neighbourhood; most areas are blissfully self-contained. The advantages of living in a modern, densely populated city include abundant services within walking distance – dry cleaners, restaurants, grocery stores and tailors are all nearby.

Moving Services

There are several firms that offer relocation services. International companies charge steep prices, usually between $500 and $1,000 per cubic metre. They also provide well-trained staff and can organise visa arrangements, customs clearance, and all packing and unpacking. Generally, a smaller shipment will incur a costlier rate per cubic metre. Multinational employers usually cover the costs of relocating, but if you are moving alone, get quotes from at least three companies. Packing boxes yourself and leaving some stuff at home will help lower the price.

There are several regulations to keep in mind. The usual items are prohibited: weapons and firearms, counterfeit goods, pornographic materials, endangered species, certain milk and meat products, and plants and seeds. Alcohol carries a very high import tax. Other items are less obvious, and materials that might be deemed politically offensive or anti-communist may be worth checking with your local Chinese embassy.

If you are not deeply attached to your furniture, leave some of it behind. Beijing furniture stores (p.267) are stocked with beautiful pieces that sell for a fraction of the price that they would in Europe or North America. Finely crafted, Chinese wooden pieces abound. European styles are harder to find, but it is inexpensive to have furniture

No Loafing

For those who are on a budget or relish doing things independently, a popular choice is hiring a *mianbao che*, literally, a 'bread car', so named for their resemblance to a loaf of bread. These are pint-sized minivans readily available for hire around Beijing. Once you've boxed everything up at home, head to the Dongzhimen long-distance bus station, where *mianbao che* drivers wait for customers. You can negotiate to hire a van for the day (expect to pay between ¥400 and ¥500), and the driver will help shuttle your goods from your old home to your new one.

Relocation Companies

AGS Four Winds	010 6566 3405	www.agsfourwinds.com
Asian Express International Movers	010 8580 1471	www.aemovers.com.hk
Asian Tigers KC Dat	010 6415 1188	www.asiantigersgroup.com
BAL International Cargo	010 6561 4171	www.bim.com.hk
Beijing Belle Transport	010 8453 1240	www.bellepack.com
Beijing Doda International Moving	010 6748 8828	www.doda.com.cn
CIM Continental International Moving	010 8762 5110	www.cimmover.com
Crown Worldwide	010 5801 8088	www.crownworldwide.com
Hiboo International Group	010 5820 6459	www.hiboo.com.cn
Kerry EAS	010 6461 8899	www.kerryeas.com
Move One Relocation	010 6581 4046	www.moveone.info
OTTO Packing & Transport	010 5260 8300	www.ottochina.com
Rhema	010 6586 9115	www.rhemachina.com
Sante Fe	010 6947 0688	www.santaferelo.com
Schenker DB Logistics	010 8048 0126	www.schenker.com
Sirva Relocation	010 5870 0866	www.sirvarelocation.com

Is getting lost your usual excuse?

Whether you're a map person or not, this pocket-sized marvel will help you get to know the city like the back of your hand – so you won't feel the back of someone else's.

Beijing Mini Map
Fit the city in your pocket

custom-made. If you are moving locally, you can hire a domestic company, which charges around ¥2,000 per cubic metre.

Smooth Moves

If moving internationally, get all your paperwork done in advance. If you are transferring with a company, they should take care of most of this. If not, contact your local Chinese embassy before departure to check any changes in regulations. Once you arrive, register with your local police station within 48 hours. This is a straightforward procedure, see p.64 for details. International movers should provide you with an inventory of what is being sent. Don't be afraid to be pernickety and insist on adding extra detail to this list, including specifics about the condition of delicate items. If you're moving with a smaller, local firm, keep a detailed log of what you're sending and the condition of items. It might even be worth photographing more expensive pieces.

Most important of all; allow yourself much more time than you think is necessary. Moving is a hassle, but moving in a hurry can be coronary inducing.

Removal Companies		
Beiao Likang Moving	010 6422 6688	na
Beijing Belle Transport	010 8453 1240	www.bellepack.com
Chang'an Banjia	010 6292 8498	na
Stone Moving Services	010 8431 2266	www.stbj.com.cn
Yunming Banjia Gongsi	010 6203 3265	www.stwl.com.cn

Furnishing Your Home

Furnished apartments are popular and more common than unfurnished apartments. Generally, standard furnished apartments include a bed, bedside tables and a wardrobe for each bedroom, desk, bookshelf, sofa, TV with stand, dining table and chairs, washing machine, refrigerator, stove top, and sometimes an oven and dishwasher. Within the realm of furnished apartments, a very popular approach is to find a brand new apartment in which no furnishings have been purchased yet. You can then negotiate with the landlord to purchase furnishings that match your style or colour preferences, even picking exact models. The result is usually good, but it requires significantly more time and effort than finding an apartment that is ready to move into.

Serviced apartments are a popular option for those coming to Beijing for a short period of time; most require a minimum one month stay. Serviced apartments are often owned by hotels and offer all utilities, internet connection, everything you would

Interior Designers	
Dara	www.dara.com.cn
Radiance ▶ p.269	www.radiancechina.com
Vita Furniture ▶ p.101	www.vita-furniture.com

need for a short stay including utensils, sheets and towels in addition to regular cleaning services. Semi-furnished apartments do exist in Beijing, but there is no general standard. It will usually depend on what was purchased for the previous tenant. If you are furnishing your own apartment, a cheap and convenient option is IKEA (p.268). The Beijing branch is the second largest IKEA store in the world. Local prices are cheaper than those found overseas, with affordable delivery and assembly charges. If you are searching for antique or refurbished Chinese style furniture, head to Gaobeidian (p.294), the large antique furniture district on the eastern side of town. Dozens of stores on one long street sell everything from hand-made opium canopy beds to coffee table bric-a-brac. Gaobeidian is also an excellent place to find craftsmen who will build items to order. Custom-made pieces are reasonably priced, but it is a good idea to take a translator, or to price things before you go to ensure a good deal. For east-meets-west designs, upscale furniture and home decor, Dara (p.268) is a local favourite, with its in-house Asian and European designers. IQAir (www.theiqairstore.com) has four stores selling air purifiers.

Apartment Tips

On the day you move, make sure your landlord or real estate agent helps you with telephone and internet connection, the first water dispenser delivery and utility payment method. For payments, do a dry run of refilling each card at the bank or management office and recharging the meter. This is a big headache for newcomers so take along a notebook. If your apartment does not have maintenance service, get details or phone numbers for a plumber or electrician in the (likely) event of any problems.

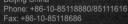

Second-Hand Items

The Beijing expat scene is constantly changing, which means second-hand furniture is usually available somewhere. A good place to start looking is online. Local expat magazine *That's Beijing* maintains a website (www.thebeijinger.com) that has a healthy For Sale/Wanted section. TVs, sofas, and electronic equipment are regularly on offer. If you are involved in the diplomatic communities, some embassies have furniture sales once or twice a year. You need to have diplomatic identification to purchase goods at these garage sales. Embassies import items into China duty free so can only sell items to individuals who have similar diplomatic tax exemptions. Noticeboards at the expat grocery stores such as Jenny Lou's (p.264), April Gourmet (p.264), and the Friendship Store (p.264) are also good sources for used furniture.

Tailors
Other options **Tailoring** p.286

Tailors are plentiful and they can readily whip up soft furnishings to your specifications. Head to the larger markets (p.292) where you can find several tailors in once place and can peruse generous selections of fabrics. It takes approximately one week to complete orders. Expect to pay around ¥400 to ¥600 for curtains, including rod and hooks. The same tailors also make cushions and pillows to order. Re-upholstering will require you to take measurements yourself, or bring in cushions and pillows that the tailors can copy.

Tailors

Tailors		
DaXin Textile Company	Dongcheng	010 8402 3919
Golden Give Star Market	Haidian	010 8837 8056
Silk Market	CBD	010 5169 8800
Yashow Market	Sanlitun	010 6415 1726

Laundry Services

Nearly all apartments come equipped with a washing machine, but dryers are rare so most Beijingers air-dry clothes. If you want the warmth and convenience of a dryer, most appliance stores sell domestic and international models. Check that you can drill a hole in your wall for the ventilation tube required. Alternatively, you can indulge in local dry cleaning and laundry services. Individual apartment buildings do not usually come with launderettes, but laundry services are available at most serviced apartments. If you are not in a serviced apartment, chances are there is a laundry nearby. Look for the sign marked *xi yi*. Small family laundry services vary in quality, so do a trial run with inexpensive clothing first. As with franchises, these smaller operations charge by the item. Services include ironing and next day pick-up is standard. Typical prices are ¥5 for shirts and trousers, suits and jumpers for ¥8, and coats for ¥20 to ¥50.
Fornet (010 6417 7767, www.fornet.com.cn) and Gold Water (010 6463 9411) are reliable franchises with several branches around town. Fornet's pricing scheme does not differentiate between regular laundry and dry cleaning; ¥12 for shirts and trousers, ¥18 for jackets and sweaters, ¥36 to ¥56 for coats and dresses, and ¥56 to ¥80 for quilts and blankets. Gold Water's dry cleaning services cost ¥18 for suits, ¥24 for trousers, ¥28 for jackets, and ¥45 to ¥55 for coats. Its regular laundry charges are slightly cheaper. Prices for both chains include ironing and pressing. In the case of Fornet, prices include delivery services.

Domestic Help
Other options **Babysitting & Childcare** p.103

Domestic help comes in all shapes and sizes in Beijing. Live-out, part-time help is the most common service. Locals and expatriates alike often refer to domestic helpers as *ayi*. The formal translation of *ayi* is 'maternal aunt'. Specifically, you would address your mother's younger sister as *ayi*. Domestic helpers are often women, so using the title *ayi* is both polite and respectful. This is true even if your housekeeper happens to be younger than yourself. Family names are stated before given names in China, and titles are placed after family names. If your housekeeper's name were Liu Shaojun, you would call her 'Liu Ayi'.

Ayis

Many serviced and standard apartments are set up for a live-in *ayi*, usually a separate room with its own entrance where your housekeeper can retire to once she has finished her duties for the day. Most residents employ a live-out *ayi*. Residents with children often have an *ayi* for childcare who works a standard Monday to Friday, 40 hour working week and takes on childcare, light housekeeping and maybe even cooking duties. Those without children typically have a cleaning *ayi* who comes once or twice a week.

The domestic help industry in China is fairly unregulated. Payment is usually in cash and occurs monthly or bi-monthly. An *ayi* enjoys standard state holidays (one or two weeks at Chinese New Year and one week in October to celebrate National Day) in addition to weekends off. Wages for a cleaning *ayi* are roughly ¥50 to ¥80 per three or four hour shift or ¥200 to ¥500 per month for someone who comes once or twice a week. Full-time, live-in or live-out help starts as low as ¥1,400 per month. It is customary to give a *hongbao* – a red envelope filled with around one month's salary to your *ayi* at Chinese New Year.

Some expats are now hiring English-speaking Filipina *ayi*. If you choose to do so, check their visa status. It is illegal to house a foreign *ayi* without a work permit (Z-visa). The best place to find an *ayi* is by word of mouth. Ask friends, colleagues and acquaintances for recommendations. Chances are they will either recommend their own *ayi* or they will know someone who is leaving and would like to help their *ayi* find a new employer.

Domestic Help Agencies		
Beijing Ayi Housekeeping Service	010 6434 5647	www.bjayi.com
Beijing Expat Housemaid Service	010 6438 1634	www.expatslife.com
Beijing Merry Home Consulting	010 8205 0311	www.merryhome.com.cn

Babysitting & Childcare

Most families with children employ nannies or *ayis* (see above). Typical arrangements are to have a full-time nanny from Monday to Friday, with the occasional evening shift. Several family-oriented, high-end hotels offer babysitting services for in-house guests. Generally, gyms and malls do not have babysitters, though IKEA has a very generous supervised play area. Many five-star international hotels such as Shangri-La's China World Hotel (p.34), the Grand Hyatt Beijing (p.34) and the Ritz Carlton (p.34) have babysitting services. The *ayi* agencies listed above also offer babysitting and childcare services.

Babysitting & Childcare		
The Clubhouse At Qijiayuan	010 8532 1782	na
Fundazzle	010 6500 4193	www.fandoule.com
Kindermusik With Sarah	010 8772 3419	www.kmwithsarah.com.cn
KindyROO Early Childhood Development Academy	010 5166 8078	www.kindyroo.com
La Leche League	010 6298 0197	www.llli.org
Make It Easy Beijing	email inquiries	www.makeiteasybeijing.com
Parent Support Group	139 1029 7173	na

There are plenty of kid friendly restaurants around town; American Steak & Eggs (Xiushui Nanjie, Jianguomenwai, 010 6592 8088, www.steakeggs.com.cn) and Grandma's Kitchen (p.304) are perennial favourites. Western eateries such as Annie's (p.315), Brasserie Flo (p.313), and Grandma's Kitchen (p.304) have kiddie corners where the little ones can play while parents and adults dine in relative peace.

Parent groups and organisations such as La Leche League and The Clubhouse at Qijiayuan (see table on p.103) provide expat parents with support, advice, and occasional social activities. Parent Support Group is a group for parents of children with special needs. Beijing also has several activity groups and educational centres aimed at childhood development.

Good Copy
Tom's DVDs (p.277) is an expat favourite that sells good quality copies of current films.

DVD & Video Rental

China's trade in fake goods, from handbags and fashion to electronics and DVDs is well documented. As a result, legitimate DVD rental shops do not exist in Beijing. The city has a prolific counterfeit market where the latest films sell for between ¥20 and ¥30 per DVD, which is cheaper than a Blockbuster rental in most countries. Traders can be found in most shopping areas, and some will do home visits for regular customers.

Pets

There has been an explosion in pet ownership, and owning a cute creature has become quite fashionable. Today, walking a (small) dog in Beijing no longer invites strange stares. Pet stores are found around town, and there are even places to pamper or groom your furry family members. Pets in apartments and compounds are generally accepted, but check with the management office or your landlord beforehand.

Cats & Dogs

Dogs are more common than cats and the most popular mutt about town currently is the Pekinese, while cats tend to be a mixed lot. For now, there are no cat registration requirements. Dogs are another matter and restrictions vary by location. In urban Beijing (roughly inside the Fourth Ring Road) only one dog measuring no taller than 35cm is allowed per household. Guide dogs are an exception.

Diplomats living in embassy compounds have different regulations and generally the size rule does not apply.

To register your dog you need a dog-owner's permit from your neighbourhood committee. They need your passport, proof of residence and, in the case of imported dogs, quarantine certificate. Afterwards, take the same documents plus the new permit and two passport-sized photos (head shot from the front) of the dog to your local police station to register. Some stations may request to see the dog itself. Registration fees are ¥1,000 or ¥500 for spayed or neutered dogs if you can prove the dog was treated by a legally registered and licensed animal hospital. The registration fee entitles you to a free check-up, including a rabies vaccine, at officially licensed animal hospitals. These hospitals will then issue a Beijing Animal Health & Immunity Certificate (also known as the 'Red Vaccination Book'), which you will need to re-register your dog next year, to move to another city in China, and to export it out of China. Annual re-registration costs ¥500.

Households outside the city can have one dog per passport holder. A dog-owner's permit is not required, and registration is merely ¥200, though it does not come with the free check-up. If you live in a villa in the Shunyi district (p.95), you may be able to register your dog at the villa office and bypass the police station. If your dog is caught without registration anywhere in Beijing, the fine is ¥2,000 in addition to the registration fee. Avoiding fines will result in the kennelling of your dog.

Fish & Birds

Most Beijing residents live in apartments, making fish and birds ideal pet choices. Native goldfish are popular in Beijing – the oranda, butterfly, lionhead, and bubble eye are a few notable species. Imported saltwater fish are also available. A variety of birds can be found in pet stores. Many elderly Chinese men keep birds, taking them to local parks in the mornings where they hang up their birdcages and spend time catching up with fellow bird owners over tea or a game of *Weiqi*.

Pet Pampering
For shops selling pet care products (and the animals themselves), turn to p.280.

Bringing Your Pet To Beijing

Pet owners are allowed to import one pet per passport, and you will need an employment visa (Z-visa) to import. Anything other than a companion animal (a dog or cat) is considered exotic and must undergo a special inspection upon entering China. Importing birds to Beijing is not allowed. Companion animals must have official certification of a recent rabies vaccination, an official export certificate from the source country, and a health certificate (between one month and 1 year old) prepared by a qualified veterinarian in your departure country. Pets brought into China must undergo mandatory 30 day quarantine. They are held at a government-run facility and owners will be charged an initial ¥1,000 deposit. Final fees, collected at the end of the quarantine, usually amount to the deposit.

Experienced relocation companies can sometimes reduce quarantines to one week or overnight stays. Some airlines allow small pets on board in soft-sided carriers if they fit underneath the passenger seat. Larger animals are held in pressurised cargo. In the wake of the avian bird flu most airlines do not allow pet birds to travel on their aircraft. The cost of transportation varies with departure points. You should look into having your pet vaccinated against bordatella (kennel cough) at least two weeks prior to departure. Kennel cough is often transmitted among animals in boarding facilities and during transit with other animals.

Taking Your Pet Home

At least three months prior to departure, check the vaccination requirements of your destination country and the latest restrictions of China's Entry-Exit Inspection & Quarantine Bureau (6 Tianshuiyuan Jie, Chaoyang, 010 6421 2748). Pets must undergo a brief health exam at the Beijing Ornamental Animal Hospital (7 Beisanshuan Zhonglu, 010 6204 9631) an official government facility. The exam must take place seven to 10 days before departure and costs at least ¥800. Once completed, you will be issued a Beijing International Companion Animal Health Inspection Form. From here, you need to go to the Entry-Exit Inspection & Quarantine Bureau. Bring the Beijing International Companion Animal Health Inspection Form, your pet's 'Red Vaccination Book', and all other official documents with you. At the end of your visit, the bureau will hopefully issue your pet with an official Animal Health Certificate, valid for 14 days only. Export-A-Pet (+852 2358 1774, www.export-a-pet.com) and World Care Pets (010 6211 6185, www.worldcarepet.com) can help you and your pet prepare for the move home. Most of the international relocation companies (p.98) also offer pet services.

Vets & Kennels

You should only take your pets to legally registered, officially designated veterinary hospitals. These hospitals are required to purchase their vaccines from the Animal Husbandry Bureau which in turn purchases high quality, internationally registered vaccines from Europe and North America. There is some variation in the care provided by official hospitals. Some, for example, offer acupuncture services (generally ¥50 to ¥70 per session) for pets. General check-ups for small pets cost around ¥200. Kennel standards vary widely. Check the facility before boarding your animal to

Veterinary Clinics

Aikang Veterinary Hospital	010 6504 2085
Beijing KPK Veterinarian Hospital World	010 6552 5829
Beijing Ornamental Animal Hospital	010 6204 9631
Dr Tony Beck's Clinic	010 6202 3827
Fanzhuang Banlu Veterinary Hospital	010 6760 5989
International Center For Veterinary Services	010 8456 1939
KK Animal Hospital	010 8046 2358
Wa Wa Pet Hospital	010 8737 1999
Wanghong Veterinary Hospital	010 6344 7717
Wangjing Veterinary Hospital	010 6475 2626

review standards of services such as exercise, grooming, feeding and cage space. High-end kennels provide 24 hour service and maintain boarding logs that owners can request upon retrieving their pets. Prices vary, but expect to pay ¥60 to ¥130 per night depending on the size of the animal.

Grooming & Training

Pet training services are not common in Beijing. Caring for animals as pets is still a new concept, and training schools have not yet found a market. The International Center for Veterinary Services and KK Animal Hospital offer obedience training. Several hospitals in town offer grooming services. A large park on the eastern side of town offers city dogs a day of freedom complete with swimming and jumping facilities.

Pet Shops

It is easy to buy a pet in Beijing and you will encounter hawkers near subway stations or in markets selling puppies out of cardboard boxes. For a less casual transaction, start your search with a qualified veterinarian. Unfortunately, most animals found in pet shops and animal markets are unhealthy. A reputable vet should be able to recommend a licensed breeder or reliable rescue centre. Check postings online at www.thebeijinger.com, as well as noticeboards at expat shops like April Gourmet (p.264), Jenny Lou's (p.264), and The Friendship Store (p.264) to inherit or purchase a pet from a private owner. The Beijing Human & Animal Environmental Education Center (010 6179 1908, www.animalschina.org) is a respected rescue centre where you can adopt older, abandoned pets. At Carepets (010 8677 8529, http://carepets.blog.com.cn) and Beijing Cat (010 6679 6620, www.beijingcat.org) you can adopt stray and abandoned cats. These and other rescue centres vaccinate and spay or neuter their animals. Purebred animals can be found at select pet shops.

Pet Boarding & Sitting

Dogs Day Care In Beijing	010 8377 8817	Cindy, a private caregiver looks after dogs in her home. Service includes walks twice a day.
International Center For Veterinary Services	010 8456 1939	Offers grooming, exercise three times a day, and daily boarding logs, copies of which clients can read.
Qiqi Pets	010 8142 2927	Boarding services include extended outdoor daytime activity, weather permitting.
Sherwood Beijing Equestrian Club	010 5188 4137	Boarding services for dogs only. Fees paid to this club are used to support a veterinary clinic.

Pet Grooming & Training

Coco Pet	010 8401 8650	Offers hair and nail grooming services for rabbits, chinchillas, guinea pigs and hamsters.
Coolbaby	010 6500 6281	Features a dog park spread over 40 acres. Entrance fee of ¥10.
Hip Dog Club	010 6533 6814	Obedience training.
KK Animal Hospital	010 8046 2358	Offers basic grooming services for pets.
Miss Dai's	010 5163 3882	Offers basic grooming services (hair and nails) for cats and dogs.
Pet Care Shop & Grooming Parlour	010 8459 3083	Offers basic grooming services for pets.

Utilities & Services

Utilities & Services

Humidify

Beijing is a very dry place, so consider buying a humidifier. Not only will your skin benefit, but your house will feel warmer, helping the environment and your bank balance. Any electronics store (p.262) will carry a variety. Expect to pay around ¥300 for smaller models.

Power and water are provided by state-owned monopolies. The Beijing Power Company provides the city with electricity, while Beijing Tap Water Company supplies most of your household water, unless you live in a district outside of the city limits. As Beijing is located in a desert, water supplies are a constant concern. The Beijing Gas Company is responsible for your natural gas, which is usually only used for cooking.

Heating is centralised. Most apartment buildings use steam radiators for heat, which is usually turned on in mid-November and turned off in mid-March. Luckily, most rooms also have their own air conditioner and heater units. Air conditioning is typically managed through these units, so electricity costs peak during the summer when they may be left on day and night.

Electricity, gas, water, telephone, and internet costs are not usually included in rent, though the winter heating fee almost always is. These fees are usually paid every other month, in cash, and often your building management company will combine all utilities except telephone and internet into one bill. It is also possible that your apartment will use prepaid cards for some services, in which case your landlord will check the meters when you move in and out and charge accordingly. Be sure to ask your landlord or agent for clear information on when, where, and how to pay these bills.

Hutong Heating

Those in older accommodation will probably need to buy electric blankets and heaters to stay warm. Available in most markets, these items are essential for the bitter Beijing winters.

Electricity

Each district has a branch of the Beijing Power Company, but it's unlikely you'll ever need to go. This is a good thing, since English services are not often available, either in person or over the phone. If your Mandarin is up to the task, dial 95598 for all power-related concerns. Your power should already be connected when you move in. The bill is usually included in the bi-monthly utility bill from your property management company. If not, you will need to pay monthly, in cash, at a bank. Electricity costs average between ¥100 and ¥300 per month for a mid-sized apartment with two people, but can double during the summer if air conditioning is used regularly.

Remember that most North American devices run on 110 volt power, and will not work with 220 volt Chinese current. Even though the outlets may look the same, if you plug an American device in, it may fry. Most laptops, many mobile phones, and some other devices work with both. Be sure to check before plugging in; a compatible power 'brick' will say something like 110-220v or 100-240v.

If your device isn't compatible, you'll need a converter, widely available for smaller devices, but expensive and hard-to-find for larger items. It may be cheaper to leave some things at home and buy local replacements. Outlets in China will not usually have a three-pin plug, but sockets with two flat or two rounded holes are common.

Water

With offices across town, the Beijing Tap Water Company is easy to reach, but English is not usually spoken. A typical bill will be around ¥50 per month for two people sharing an apartment. Beijing tap water (as in the rest of China) is not safe to drink, so is mainly used for showers, bathing and cooking. Some even recommend that you avoid brushing your teeth with the municipal water, due to metals from older pipe systems. Water dispensers are ubiquitous; most homes and businesses will have at least one. These can be bought at any large market or appliance store and range in cost from ¥200 for a basic model, to ¥500 for advanced systems with sanitisers and extra filtration. The water itself comes in large plastic jugs. They can be ordered from a variety of suppliers who offer free delivery, but often only speak Chinese. Several brands are available and the price of a jug ranges from ¥8 to ¥15, with a ¥50 deposit paid the first time you buy. You can find a service simply by looking for the ubiquitous carts stacked high with bottles, or by asking you neighbour or landlord.

Gas

The Beijing Gas Company handles liquid natural gas, but supply issues are dealt with by a landlord or property management company. Some apartments will use propane canisters for the hot water heating and the stove, others will use prepaid cards. Some have centralised meters, which are then tallied into the overall utility bill to be paid to the property manager. Gas is likely to be your least expensive utility, ranging from ¥20 to ¥75 per month for apartment dwellers that don't cook much, up to ¥50 to ¥100 for culinary wizards.

Sewerage

Beijing residents pay sewerage fees through the water bill. The system is reasonably good, though many apartments will have serious problems with odours. More than 60% of Chinese towns and cities lack sewage treatment facilities, but as part of the Olympic bid Beijing set a goal of treating and recycling over 90% of its waste water.

Rubbish Disposal & Recycling

The handling of rubbish and recycling is almost invisible to most expats. A large dustbin on each floor of an apartment, or a central dumpster near a house, will usually be the only spot you need to know. There are no fees, and municipal trucks come nightly to most areas to take rubbish to landfills. Many newcomers are upset at the lack of obvious recycling, but waste is actually sorted at its destination, providing a lot of employment. Workers sort glass, plastic, paper and metal to sell for reprocessing. You may be able to sell some recyclables yourself – stacks of cardboard, for instance, can earn a few *kuai* from the collectors who roam the streets on small carts. Beer bottles are one of the few items where recycling is directly encouraged. A deposit may be charged for each one, and given back on return of the empty bottle.

Telephone

Textual Healing

If you brought a mobile phone from home, ask a shop to help add new software to support Chinese language text messages. This can be very helpful for handling directions and addresses.

There are only two fixed-line providers in town: China Netcom (10060) and China Telecom, through Beijing Telecommunications (10000). If you are renting an apartment, telephone service will usually be active, and you will simply have to take over the payments.

Rates and services are quite similar – ¥21.60 per month as rental for a landline, and broadly equivalent long distance rates. Beijing Telecom offers longer discount hours. A domestic long-distance call costs ¥0.70 per minute (or ¥0.40 during evening off-peak hours). International long-distance is ¥8 per minute (¥4.80 off-peak), though Hong Kong, Macau, and Taiwan are much cheaper (¥2 per minute).

If you do need to have a new line installed, you will probably need to apply in person at the provider's office. There are dozens of branches throughout town, and installation fees are typically ¥200 to ¥250 for a regular landline. Make sure that you apply for both international and long distance services when setting up your new line. Call waiting and caller ID are available for free, but other services (such as call forwarding) cost extra.

Love your Beijing too

To pay your landline bill (which often includes the internet), go to almost any Chinese bank and give the cashier your phone number. Fees are due monthly in cash, and you will need to know the name on the account. Lines at banks can be lengthy, so be patient – grab a number from the dispenser and wait your turn. Alternatively, you can use the new machines available at some banks. A ¥2 fee is added, and at the moment they are only in Chinese, but they can be a great timesaver.

Telephone Companies	
China Netcom	10060
China Telecom/Beijing Telecom	10000

Pay Phones

Pay phones in Beijing have almost disappeared, but you can still find a local alternative – the phone stall. Nothing more than a bank of phones with a roof, you can pay in cash and the folks working there will even give change.

Many foreigners use prepaid IP (Internet Phone) or calling cards to save money on calls home. IP cards are available at most markets, just look for the IP sign. Each card will have a face value, usually ¥100, but are often sold at a discount of 40% to 60%, so make sure to bargain. Long-distance rates through these cards vary by country and provider, but are typically around ¥2 to ¥4 per minute. The cards are simple to use, and often have instructions in English. Dial the phone number on the back, enter your card's pin, and then dial the number you wish to call. These typically expire one year after first use.

Mobile Phones

The mobile phone, or *shouji*, has become an indispensable part of Chinese daily life. Over 500 million people own one in China, making it the world's largest mobile phone market. Signal strength is excellent in most parts of the country. Rural areas, tunnels, trains and even new subway lines are covered. Even if you plan on being in Beijing for only a short while, it's a good idea to have a mobile at hand.

European visitors with GSM phones that use a SIM card are likely to be able to use their existing handset, as long as it is unlocked. North American travellers though, should be careful. Dual-band phones sold in the US and Canada are not compatible with local networks, so you need a tri or quad-band phone. A quick search online for your model or call to your provider should tell you.

If you don't have a phone, don't worry. Beijing's markets (p.292) are sure to provide more options than you need. Phone stores are scattered throughout the city, though larger shops, like those near Wanfujing, are more likely to have staff that speak English. Prices for new phones range from ¥300 to upwards of ¥3,000 for a smartphone or something gold-plated, diamond-encrusted, or otherwise blinged up. Used phones are a bit harder to find, but expat magazines (p.51) and websites (p.52) are a good bet. You can also try the Nurenjie area, which has a massive second-hand market where phones can cost as little as ¥40 or ¥50. When buying a phone, as with anything in China, make sure to keep the receipt. Also, make sure that your phone offers English language instructions.

Unlocking Phones

Foreign phones need to be unlocked to work with a Chinese carrier. Nokia users can get free unlock codes online, but other phones may need to contact their home carriers. Otherwise, the many small phone stores can do the business for a small fee. When making any changes to your phone, ensure that you have backups of your contacts.

SIM Cards

Once you have a phone that will work locally, you will need a SIM card. SIM cards are tied to both a phone number and a provider, so choose carefully. They can be bought at any mobile phone shop, even at the airport, and the numbers will usually be offered on a large sign or list. Prices vary, largely depending on how lucky the number is considered, and range from ¥60 to ¥300. Don't lose the small plastic card attached to the SIM card; it will be needed in case of loss or theft.

Mobile Providers

There are only two providers: China Mobile and China Unicom, each offering pay-as-you-go and subscription services. Don't be fooled by names like GoTone or M-Zone, as they are simply different plans offered by these carriers. China Mobile offers slightly better coverage, while China Unicom is a bit cheaper. The plans change regularly, but some charge a monthly fee on top of usage (in return for lower costs per call), charge for incoming calls, and whether you have a monthly package of text messages or minutes. Rates per minute are in the ¥0.30 to ¥0.60 range, but lower if you sign up for a package. Note that with either provider, you can use an IP phone number which can be dialled before making a call, which cuts costs dramatically. These numbers are usually 12593, 17591, or 17911.

Mobile Service Providers

| China Mobile | 10086 | www.chinamobile.com |
| China Unicom | 10010 | www.chinaunicom.com.cn |

Cheap Overseas Calls

You can use your credit card to pay for international calls from any landline, simply by dialling 108, then the country code. In addition, Voice-over Internet Protocol (VoIP) services have become very popular among expats. These allow cheap, and sometimes free, international calls through your computer. You'll need to have broadband access, though you can always use an internet cafe; most have microphones and headsets that work with VoIP.

VoIP Providers

Gizmo Project	www.gizmoproject.com
Lingo	www.lingo.com
Packet8	www.packet8.com
Skype	www.skype.com
Vonage	www.vonage.com

Skype, Gizmo Project, and others offer reasonable call quality and cheap call rates, usually less than ¥0.30 per minute. You could also consider investing in a stand-alone VoIP device from a service like Vonage, Lingo, or Packet8 if you make a significant quantity of calls. These devices usually offer a flat monthly rate (¥200 and up) and more reliable quality.

Internet

Other options **Websites** p.52

China has joined the global information revolution, but on its own terms. The aptly named 'great firewall' removes access to sites that the government deems inappropriate. These include pornographic sites, some that are critical of the government, and sites such as Wikipedia, Flickr, and parts of the BBC. Still, getting online is pretty simple.

For quick access, internet cafes (*wang ba*) are found throughout the city and fairly cheap; about ¥3 to ¥5 per hour. However, prepare for a haze of cigarette smoke, and perhaps a wait if you visit in the evening. There are wireless hotspots in many coffee shops, restaurants, hostels and hotels. Very few require payment and most don't even need a password.

The last option, outside of your home, is to use cellular data networks. Buy a PCMCIA or USB dongle for your computer at any electronic or mobile phone market, and you can use your SIM card to surf the internet wirelessly. This can be a great option for those on the move, as it is faster than dial-up and reasonably cheap at around ¥0.03 per KB of data. Make sure you test the software when buying it.

At home, choices are limited. The most common is ADSL, now offered almost everywhere. Most agents or landlords will help set it up, as it must be installed in the name of the telephone account holder. It is simple to arrange, though it can take up to a week and costs ¥300 for installation. Pay-as-you-go rates are available at ¥0.05 per minute, but most residents will want to opt for a monthly plan of ¥120 to ¥188 (according to the data rate, of between 512 KB/s to 2 MB/s).

Cheap dial-up access is available anywhere you can find a phone jack. Simply dial 95963 (username and password 263, ¥0.07 per minute), or 16900 (username and password 169, ¥0.05 per minute) to connect. The fees will be added to the next month's phone bill. Remember that you pay a small charge to the phone company as well, of about ¥1.20 per hour.

Two other possibilities are cable internet, offered through Beijing Gehua (www.gehua.com), and broadband, offered through your building or complex. Cable internet varies widely in speed, and is not available in all areas, so ask your landlord or agent, as it can be a bit trickier than ADSL. Rates for both are competitive with ADSL.

Postal Services

China's postal service is cheap and efficient, but reliability varies. The national service is run by China Post. There are dozens of offices, typically open from 09:00 to 17:00 on weekdays and on Saturday mornings. Almost none offer English-speaking service. Some smaller offices may not accept international shipments and some may limit the size of parcels that they will accept. Sending shipments worth more than ¥1,500 is usually prohibited. Make sure your packages are unsealed, as inspection is mandatory. Shipments of DVDs, CDs, and some electronic goods such as hard drives are also either barred or strictly limited. However, sending mail is fairly cheap, costing as little as ¥5 for a letter to other Asian countries, and ¥6 or ¥7 to much of the rest of the world. Typically, letters will take a week to two weeks to arrive. Packages cost more, at around ¥85 for a 1kg package sent economy class.

Shipment by both air and boat are possible, with vastly different prices and travel times; two days at the fastest, two to three months at the slowest.

If you are having trouble sending a package, need English assistance, or your item is large or oddly shaped, your best bet is to try the central post office at Yabao Lu on Jianguomenwai (010 6512 8114).

When having a package sent to you, it's best to list the address in Chinese, though packages in Pinyin stand a decent chance of making their way safely. You may need to go to a local post office to retrieve your post. Make sure you bring your passport and any notification cards.

Express & Courier

You could turn to an international shipping company for more reliable and flexible service. DHL, Fedex/Kinko's, TNT, and UPS all have offices. English service is patchy at best. Deliveries within Beijing or China are best done through EMS (run by China Post, see table), or through a private courier. STO Express, Chenghangdi Express, and

The Great Firewall

Eventually, every expat needs to access a website that is blocked. Wikipedia, parts of the BBC, Amnesty International and certain blogs all have access restricted. If you don't feel like taking a trip to Hong Kong (where internet access is open), then you'll need to find a way through the 'great firewall'. Your best bet is likely to be Tor (www.torproject.org), a free and safe download that allows you to use proxy servers, which should make your surfing untraceable. It's often best to use Mozilla Firefox (www.mozilla.org) as your browser, another free and safe download. Using a proxy slows your connection quite a bit, but Tor allows you to turn the proxies on and off easily.

Not all sites will be available through your average proxy, but the more popular the site, the easier and faster access will be. Paid alternatives are available, but reliability varies.

If it is really desperate, you can always check with your embassy or any friends who work for a news or media organisation. Typically, these have access that is less restricted, and sometimes completely unfettered.

Mini Explorer

Don't let the size of this little star fool you – it's full of insider info, maps, contacts, tips and facts for visitors. From shops to spas, bars to bargains and everything in between, the Mini Explorer range helps you get the most out of your stay in the city, however long you're there for.

Zhaijisong Express all offer similar services, called *kuaidi* in Chinese. Prices depend on distance and size, and a letter or small parcel sent within Beijing may cost as little as ¥10 for same day delivery.

Express & Courier Services

Chenghangdi Express	010 6493 2250	na
China Post	na	www.chinapost.com.cn
DHL	800 810 8000	www.cn.dhl.com
Fedex/Kinko's	800 988 1888	www.fedex.com/cn_english
STO Express	010 8769 7913	na
TNT	800 820 9868	www.tnt.com
UPS	800 820 8388	www.ups.com
Zhaijisong Express	400 678 9000	www.zjs.com.cn/eng

Radio

Radio, like other media, is government-controlled. That hasn't stopped Cantopop and English pop from taking over the airwaves, though taxis will still stay tuned to old-fashioned radio dramas. Try HIT FM at 88.7 to hear some of the same stuff that's on chart stations back home, or 91.5 (Easy FM) which is bilingual – and a good introduction to Chinese pop music. On the AM dial, Radio 774 introduced some English programming in preparation for the Olympics, and has broadcast rights to Olympic events.

Channel Surfing
A whole channel of traditional opera? Try CCTV 11. Or check out the 'Children's, Military, Agricultural' channel, CCTV 7. And learn English the way the Chinese do on CCTV 4, the international channel.

Television

Local television is a favourite target of expat complaints. Government-controlled CCTV runs most channels, broadcasting more than a dozen stations. The only English language channel is CCTV 9. Their programming, like the rest of Chinese television, is heavily censored with little original programming and a heavy focus on documentaries, news and talk shows. Chinese soaps and classic operas are plentiful and make for interesting viewing. CCTV 6 plays movies, but be warned: they will often stop the film halfway through and move onto other programmes. CCTV 5 shows sports, and occasionally airs important basketball or football matches. As your favourite shows will not be airing in China, you'll need to find some of the ubiquitous pirate DVDs to keep up with *Lost* or *Heroes*. Nonetheless, these shows are popular in Beijing; *Prison Break*, was even airing on a regional channel for a while, until the government stepped in.

Satellite Television

If the 50 plus channels on local cable are not enough, you may want to get a satellite dish. The government has outlawed them, but a burgeoning underground market thrives on both expats and locals. Typically, you will have to purchase a dish and set-top box outright, and the price will include installation, setup and a package of channels. There is no annual fee, but you may need to pay for the access card to be replaced, as the codes are changed regularly in an attempt to lock out pirates. Ask who to contact to change the codes, and how much it will cost. Some providers will offer one year of service as part of the package. Look to spend between ¥1,500 and ¥2,500, depending on service and wiring, and bargain hard.

Most channels are available, including the BBC and CNN, sports channels, and even adult programming. Thai, Australian, Japanese, Korean, and Russian programmes are also available from some providers. Many apartment buildings will have advertisements from providers, and expat magazines (p.51) are another good source. BJ STV (www.bjstv.com) has a decent website and is fairly popular.

You can always turn to a local pub for televised sports events. From American football to Irish rugby, it's likely to be on at one of the many bars (p.326) around town.

General Medical Care

Healthcare in Beijing is up to international standards, and the city can boast some of the best hospitals and doctors in China. Expats should have no trouble finding care, as English-speaking staff and high quality facilities are becoming commonplace even in some local hospitals.

Public hospitals often have VIP sections, which cater specifically to foreigners. Perks include English-speaking staff and a route around the long queues. Prices are much higher in these VIP wings, but they can still be half that of a western hospital. One downside to public hospitals is that you normally pay upfront, though credit cards are accepted. Most of them lack direct billing for foreign insurers, but it's relatively simple to get reimbursed, so make sure you keep the paperwork. Another downside is that staff can often seem cold or uncaring. Bedside manner can be very different in China, and some patients may be unhappy with the lack of detailed or open discussion about their care.

You may want to find a general practitioner (GP) if you plan on staying in Beijing. They can handle annual check-ups, physicals, and seasonal health concerns, and direct you to help for larger issues. Inquire at any of the listed clinics (p.120), and ask friends or co-workers for recommendations.

Dental care, cosmetic surgery, psychological care, and other health-related services are now widely available to western standards, though prices can vary widely. The standard of medicines and blood supplies have been the focus of recent government attention, and a variety of support groups have sprung up to help those in need.

One Flu Over The Cuckoos Nest

SARS, avian flu, bird flu... whatever you call it, it's best to be prepared. While the masks may not do much, the recently approved vaccine will. Consider asking a doctor about it before leaving, especially if you plan to travel to rural areas.

Public Healthcare

China lacks a traditional government healthcare system. However, many citizens are covered, at least in part, under their employer's health insurance. Healthcare costs are kept low, and the system is reasonably effective at treating enormous numbers of people. There are public hospitals and clinics throughout the city, which can be intimidating. Two well-regarded options are the China-Japan Friendship Hospital (p.116) and the Peking Union Medical College Hospital (p.116). Prices can start as low as ¥20 for some basic services, though VIP services cost from ¥100 to ¥300 and more.

Private Healthcare

If you (or your insurer) can afford them, private facilities are smaller, more comfortable, and offer faster, friendlier service. Comprehensive providers like Beijing United Family (p.118) and International SOS (p.118) offer 24 hour translation and emergency services. There are also a few smaller options, like the American-Sino OB-GYN (p.118), and the Beijing Vista Clinic (p.118), which offers house calls. A regular check-up will cost about ¥500, a specialist around ¥1,000, and emergency services start at ¥1,500. Expect to spend ¥6,000 or more for each overnight stay.

Streetside safety

Emergency Services

Beijing's traffic and maze-like apartment complexes mean that ambulances can take a while to arrive. Furthermore, drivers don't usually yield to emergency vehicles. It is much faster and cheaper, whenever safe, to take a cab. That said, if you need emergency services, dial 999 or 120 on any phone. English operators are slowly being added, but you should learn your address in Chinese.

It's a good idea to carry an emergency card with information in both Chinese and English. This should list your name, address, passport and citizenship information, current medications, blood type, allergies, insurance information, and 'ICE' or 'in case of emergency' contacts. You should have one of these for each member of your family, and keep them handy. Children should also be informed of what to do in an emergency, and some clinics will provide cards that they can keep. Pre-registering at your hospital of choice can save time and hassle if something goes wrong.

If your family have an *ayi* to take care of children, consider having her trained in first aid and CPR. Several local clinics, including Beijing United (p.118), provide these programmes.

Hospitals ◀

Hopsital listings (both private and public) begin on p.116.

Pharmacies

Your first trip to a Chinese pharmacy can be frustrating. Unless you are at an international clinic, few products will be labelled in English. You are also unlikely to see brands you know or trust. Items as basic as Pepto-Bismol, full-strength aspirin, and cold medications are difficult or impossible to find. It's best to bring these products from home in sufficient quantity for your stay, as well as any medications you might take regularly (with the original prescriptions if possible). Most international hospitals and clinics have well-stocked pharmacies, but prices can be higher than at home.

If you find a medicine's chemical name, or ask your doctor for help, it is possible to find the Chinese equivalent, which can be much cheaper than the foreign versions. Fake medicine can be an issue, so stick to government-run facilities or pharmacies attached to a hospital (though even these have not escaped counterfeit medicines). Some weak or old antibiotics are sold over the counter, which can make treating seasonal flu cheaper and easier.

Check-Ups

Annual health check-ups are offered at all the major hospitals and clinics, as are preventive care ('well-man' and 'well-woman') services. Complete health screening and physicals are available. Beijing United's Family Health & Wellness Centre (p.118) at Jianguomen, offers immigration check-ups, which are required for embassy officials, among others.

Before You Arrive

Get your medical records in order before arriving in China, and request copies. If you already have health insurance, you should contact your provider to ensure that your cards are current and that China is covered. Check that your immunisations are up to date. It's recommended that you be immunised against hepatitis A and B, polio, typhoid, and tetanus. Rabies and Japanese encephalitis shots are a good idea if you plan on heading outside of the cities.

Health Insurance

You are not required to have health insurance in China, but most employers offer a basic plan. You can also buy it individually. Prices can vary widely (from ¥3,000 to as much as ¥30,000 per year), depending on factors such as age and previous medical history. Adding on extras such as dental and optical cover will also raise the rates.

For many expats, health insurance will be offered through your company. Though the plan may be costly, it's unlikely you'll find a better deal, and a safety net is well worth the price.

For those who aren't covered through their workplace, it is not mandatory to have insurance. But, accidents happen, and medical bills can quickly add up. Basic coverage will include in-patient care and emergencies. Assess both the excess (or 'deductible' – the bit you pay before insurance kicks in) and the cost of the insurance plan. A plan with a higher excess will only cover larger emergencies, but it will cost less per year for the plan itself. It's worth considering a plan that offers repatriation of remains, and possibly emergency relocation.

Insurance plans do not usually cover cosmetic surgery or alternative medicines, infertility issues, or pre-existing conditions.

Health Insurance Companies

Bupa	www.bupa.com
Expatriate Insurance	www.expatriate-insurance.com
Global Insurance/Pacific Prime	www.globalsurance.com
GoodHealth	www.goodhealthworldwide.com
Healthline Asia	www.healthlineasia.com
International Medical Group	www.imglobal.com
International SOS	www.internationalsos.com
MedEx	www.medexassist.com
Medibroker	www.medibroker.com
Royal & Sun Alliance	www.royalsunalliance.com.cn

Also, injuries from extreme sports or activities are not normally covered, though you can sometimes get a 'rider' to cover them for an additional fee. If you plan on travelling through China, look into a medical evacuation plan offered by International SOS or MedEx. These offer assistance if you are in a remote area.

There is no complete list of insurance providers, but you can check with the hospital or clinic you plan on using and ask them who they accept or prefer. An insurance broker that offers direct billing with your doctor can save a lot of time and hassle.

When buying a plan, read the fine print, ask questions, and ensure you understand when and how to pay. Costs will vary, but a 30 year old male can expect to spend upwards of ¥4,000 a year with an excess of ¥20,000, and twice that amount for a smaller excess and the addition of dental care.

Donor Cards

A critical shortage of organs has forced the Chinese government to take measures to encourage donation. Some sources claim the shortfall is over a million organs per year. Lack of regulations, and traditional Confucian principles that value keeping a body intact even after death, have hindered most efforts. Unfortunately, as an expat, there is no simple and straightforward way to guarantee that your wishes will be honoured, though informing family members is a good starting place.

Giving Blood

Giving blood is safe and easy in China; there are even buses parked in shopping areas that serve as mobile blood donation centres. Because most Chinese people do not have Rhesus (Rh) negative blood, donating can help fellow expats who may not be compatible with the larger pool of local blood. One in eight Caucasians has Rh-negative blood, compared with only around 1% of the Chinese population, so there can be a severely limited supply.

Giving Up Smoking

There are no area support groups for quitters, and those trying may find it difficult due to the omnipresence of smokers in Beijing. Several clinics offer programmes aimed at the local population, which are not typically in English. Nonetheless, China-Japan Friendship Hospital (p.116) has an outpatient smoking cessation programmes that includes counselling and nicotine replacement therapy.

Alternative therapies are common, and anecdotal evidence is positive; acupuncture, for instance, is available at TCM (traditional Chinese medicine) providers like the Beijing Massage Hospital (www.massage-hospital.com).

Public Hospitals

There are dozens of public hospitals scattered about the city. Technically, expats are supposed to use the VIP wards, but if you decide to brave the waiting times and confusing signage it's unlikely anyone will complain. Unless your Chinese is good, it is best to take a local if you seek help at a public hospital.

9 Fangyuan Xilu
Chaoyang
芳园西路9号
朝阳区
Map 5 D3 **1**

Amcare Women & Children's Hospital 美中宜和妇儿医院

010 6434 2388 | *www.amcare.com.cn*
This excellent, though fairly small, hospital in the Lido area offers paediatrics, gynaecology, obstetrics and family planning. There is a courtyard garden, recreation centre and gym. It is reasonably priced and there's no registration fee. A consultation costs between ¥100 and ¥300. It accepts credit cards and offers direct billing with several international healthcare insurance companies.

95 Yongan Lu
Xuanwu
永安路95号
宣武区
Map 12 C3 **2**

Beijing Friendship Hospital 北京友谊医院

010 6301 4411
Established in 1952, this general hospital is known for organ transplants and the cardiovascular centre. Registration costs between ¥5 and ¥14 or ¥70 to ¥200 for VIP services. Consultations range from ¥70 to ¥300. It has emergency facilities, with a helipad on the roof, and can admit up to 5,000 patients per day. Accepts credit cards.

Yinghua Dongjie
Heping Jie
Chaoyang
和平街樱花东街
朝阳区
Map 5 B3 **3**

China-Japan Friendship Hospital 中日友好医院

010 6422 2952
This is one of the best-regarded public hospitals in Beijing and the primary medical facility for athletes during the 2008 Olympics. There are some English-speaking staff, and 80 beds set aside for expat patients. A wide variety of services are available, combining eastern and western medicine. The choice ranges from TCM to modern orthopaedics. Registration costs ¥100, but inpatient services may require a deposit of as much as ¥10,000.

1 Shuaifuyuan
Wanfujing
Dongcheng
王府井帅府园1号
东城区
Map 5 A3 **4**

Peking Union Medical College Hospital 北京协和医院

010 6529 5284 | *www.pumch.ac.cn*
This is an excellent public hospital well-known for its maternity services. There is an in-house blood bank and most doctors can speak English. Services run from full emergency care to ophthalmology, in addition to TCM treatments including massage and acupuncture. It will cost ¥100 to ¥300 for a consultation, and from ¥800 for a private room per day. Offers direct billing with some insurance companies.

45 Changchunjie
Xuanwu
长椿街45号
宣武区
Map 6 E3 **5**

Xuanwu Pain Treatment Centre 宣武医院疼痛诊疗中心

010 8319 8899
This hospital specialises in imaging, neurology, and electrophysiology in addition to Chinese medicine. There is a small registration fee of ¥5 to ¥10, and widely varying prices for in and outpatient services. A few doctors and specialists speak English.

Other Public Hospitals		
Chaoyang No 2 Hospital	Chaoyang	010 6502 1645
Haidian Hospital	Haidian	010 6258 3042
New Century Children's Hospital	Xicheng	010 6802 5588
Peking University Third Hospital	Haidian	010 6201 7691
Tongren Hospital	Dongcheng	010 5826 9911

Emergency Services Available in Beijing

As an expatriate in China, the emergency response network here may differ from that of your home country. Beijing United Family Hospital and Clinics (BJU), an international standard facility accredited by the Joint Commission International, offers emergency medical services that are available 24 hours a day, 7 days a week.

By calling BJU's emergency hotline, you are put directly in touch with trained emergency medical staff who speak fluent English. They can give you emergency advice and if you need, dispatch an ambulance to you. BJU also has partnerships with the national 120 and local 999 ambulance services, you can call directly, operators at these numbers may speak only Chinese.

When you arrive at the Emergency Room (ER) at BJU, you will be treated by experienced emergency physicians and nurses who speak fluent English and who offer the most up-to-date, international standard level of care available. A 24-hour translation service is available for patients needing assistance beyond English and Chinese.

Since BJU is a full-service hospital, patients coming to the ER can be admitted directly into the hospital for further treatment if necessary. In-house specialists, including a pediatrician, obstetrician, and surgeon are available 24 hours a day. Imaging, laboratory, and pharmacy services as well as hospital operating rooms, an Intensive Care Unit, and a supply of triple-tested blood are also available 24 hours a day.

An Ounce of Prevention
It is said that an ounce of prevention is worth a pound of cure. While living and traveling in China, you may be exposed to preventable diseases or encounter new health challenges. To avoid emergencies, it is recommended to follow a routine of regular health check ups and to keep your vaccinations current. BJU offers routine medical services as well as vaccination and travel medicine counseling.

Being Prepared
Since you never know when an emergency may arise, it's always good to be prepared. The minutes before trained help takes over can be crucial. To teach your family and those close to you how to better react in an emergency, BJU offers First Aid and CPR training courses for you, your driver, and your ayi. These courses, given in Chinese and English, teach how to respond in an emergency and how to start emergency care for infants, children, and adults.

#2 Jiangtai Lu, Chaoyang District, Beijing 100016
北京市朝阳区将台路2号 100016

24 Hour Emergency Hotline
24小时急诊热线: +86 (10) 6433 2345

www.unitedfamilyhospitals.com

Main Private Hospitals

Beijing United Family Hospital opened its doors in 1997, introduing private medicine in China. This move started a trend for private medicine. Typically, such facilities are joint ventures and serve as an alternative to the long lines (and often unfriendly service) at public hospitals. Individual attention and hotel-style rooms can be a sharp contrast to the mass wards at most local hospitals, but the prices are also much higher.

218 Xiaoguan Beili
Andingmenwai
Chaoyang
安定门外小关北里
218号
朝阳区
Map 5 A3 6

American-Sino Obs/Gyn (ASOG) 美华妇产服务

010 6496 8888 | www.asog-beijing.com
The rather clumsy name of this hospital hints at its services. This is a US-based joint venture with comprehensive services for women with full gynaecology and obstetrics care, as well as fertility consultations and treatments. Registration is free, fees start at ¥300, and a natural delivery will cost around ¥25,000. Counselling for teenagers and VIP membership are also available.

5 Sanlitun Xiwujie
BITIC Building C
Chaoyang
三里屯西五街5号北
信京谊大厦C座
朝阳区
Map 9 F1 7

Beijing International SOS Clinic 北京国际救援中心

010 6462 9112 | www.internationalsos.com
At this respected hospital the staff speak European languages including English, French, Italian, German and Spanish. House and hotel calls are on offer, and there is a well-stocked pharmacy, in addition to a 24 hour emergency ward, on-site laboratory, and wide variety of medical services and specialities. Fees start at around ¥800 for members and over ¥1,000 for non-members. First-aid training for *ayis* is also available.

2 Jiangtai Lu
Chaoyang
将台路2号
朝阳区
Map 5 E3 8

Beijing United Family Hospital & Clinics ▶p.117
北京和睦家医院

010 6433 3960 | www.unitedfamilyhospitals.com
The city's first private hospital now offers comprehensive services, including 24 hour emergency care (010 6433 2345), an intensive care unit, independent blood bank and large on-site pharmacy. Staff have been trained internationally and speak many languages. This is also a training hospital, and it runs satellite clinics in Shunyi and Jianguomen. Fees start at ¥900. Also on offer are first-aid training, antenatal courses and classes and La Leche League (p.103).

2 Chaoyangmenwai
Swissotel Office
Tower, 9/F
Dongcheng
朝阳门外大街2号瑞
士酒店办公楼九层
东城区
Map 9 B3 9

Hong Kong International Medical Clinic 香港国际医务诊所

010 6501 4260 | www.hkclinic.com
This clinic focuses on general medicine but also offers paediatrics, ophthalmology, plastic surgery and has a decent pharmacy. It provides HIV tests and physical examinations for Canadian immigration. Also available are house or hotel visits, 24 hour emergency care and a helpline in Japanese, English, and Chinese. Fees start at ¥400 and the clinic offers direct billing with around 15 international insurance companies, including BUPA and William Russell.

50 Liangmaqiao Lu
Lufthansa 1/F (S106)
Chaoyang
亮马桥路50号燕莎中
心写字楼一层
朝阳区
Map 5 D4 10

International Medical Centre 北京国际医疗中心

010 6465 1384 | www.imcclinics.com
Family medicine, counselling, dermatology and paediatrics are available at this facility in Chaoyang. English, Japanese, Chinese and Arabic are all spoken and a drop-in service for travellers is provided. There is also an on-site pharmacy and laboratory. Fees start at ¥450, memberships are on offer and there is no extra registration fee.

Other Private Hospitals

Bayley & Jackson Medical Centre	Chaoyang	010 8562 9998
Beijing United Jianguomen	Chaoyang	010 8532 1221
Beijing United Shunyi	Shunyi	010 8046 5432
Beijing Vista Clinic	Chaoyang	010 8529 6618

Dermatologists

The combination of summer sandstorms and polluted air can leave skin feeling dry and gritty. Even the most ardently anti-grooming males occasionally yield to a little moisturiser, and many seasoned residents find the product becomes as important as soap or toothpaste.

For more serious skin conditions, the hospitals listed on p.118 all have a dermatological facility and Beijing United Family Hospital (p.118) is particularly popular. In addition, there are two specialist clinics in Chaoyang; the Bioscor Beijing Clinic (010 6503 5707) and Confidant Medical Services (010 6559 6769).

Ayi

Most expat parents in Beijing choose to hire an ayi (nanny) to help look after the kids. For information on how and where to find one, turn to p.103.

Maternity

Other options **Baby Items** p.251

Giving birth abroad may seem scary, but Beijing's hospitals offer options that any expat should feel comfortable with. Many doctors at United Family (p.118), American-Sino OB/GYN (p.118), and other hospitals will be excellent, or native, English speakers. You can also expect attentive service, western amenities, and even extras like prenatal yoga. Local hospitals are also an option; Peking Union Medical College Hospital (p.116) comes closest to providing an environment that is up to western standards.

Many Chinese women prefer to give birth using Caesarean sections, allowing them to use epidurals and thus eliminate much of the pain. Choice of midwife is often limited, as are chances for water births, and hospitals often lack neo-natal intensive care units. If you are interested in a homebirth, it can be difficult to find a midwife, and your best bet is to network through groups like La Leche League (p.125), which offers local support in English, French, and Chinese.

Many health insurance policies only cover pregnancy-related costs if the policy was purchased before the pregnancy began. It is often treated as a pre-existing condition, so be sure to check with your insurance provider.

Private Hospitals

Private hospitals offer more personal care, western standards, English-speaking doctors and high prices. A typical pregnancy package can cost upwards of ¥50,000, and more for a Caesarean section. At Beijing United (p.118), for instance, a Caesarean delivery will cost nearly ¥100,000. These packages usually include antenatal and post-natal care, the hospital stay for delivery, medications and the newborn's immunisation. You can expect to spend ¥500 to ¥1,000 for appointments and checkups done individually.

Government Hospitals

Preparation and planning are required if you want to have your child in a local hospital. Regulations may forbid a partner from being present, and if your closest hospital doesn't have a VIP ward it may be unable to accept you. Further, some facilities have a waiting list, and many staff cannot speak English. However, fees can be around a fifth of those in private clinics. Peking Union Medical College Hospital (p.116) has well-trained doctors and staff, and charges between ¥10,000 and ¥20,000 for delivery, depending on the type of birth.

Antenatal Care

It's a good idea to check out the hospital where you would like to give birth. Having your antenatal checkups there can be a great way to assess the staff and facilities. Often, private maternity packages will include antenatal care, though you can also pay per visit, per trimester, or for a complete antenatal package. Prices range from around ¥200 per visit, to ¥5,000 per trimester or ¥15,000 for full antenatal care.

Going Back Home

Many mothers choose to stay in Beijing until shortly before delivery, and go home for the actual birth. Keep in mind that many airlines will not allow you to fly after 36 weeks into your pregnancy, and some have even stricter policies or require a doctor's note. Doctors typically recommend that also you don't fly for four weeks after giving birth.

Take home a copy of your monitoring records; your local doctor should be able to give you a duplicate. Once you've given birth, register for a passport and a visa for your infant, and bring immunisation and medical records when returning to China. You are required to register children with the Public Security Bureau (www.bjgaj.gov.cn).

Post-Natal Care

Post-natal services are usually part of a maternity package, and include midwife support, booster vaccinations and basic checkups. Some clinics offer home visits, and even post-natal massage sessions, for as long as two months after delivery. La Leche League (p.125) offers support for those who intend to breastfeed, and also serves as a network of mothers who can help with any questions you may have.

Maternity Leave

Chinese citizens, and expats working locally, receive 90 days of paid maternity leave, consisting of 15 days prenatal and 75 days after delivery. Employers must ensure that the position stays open during the leave period. Some international firms have a global standard for maternity leave, which may exceed this. If you decide to leave your position after the leave is completed, you are not obligated to compensate your employer, as they receive reimbursement from the government. However, it is a good idea to check in with your workplace periodically while on leave, especially if you would like to extend your time off.

Maternity Hospitals & Clinics

Amcare Women & Children's Hospital	010 6434 2399	Public
American-Sino OB/GYN Service	010 6496 8888	Private
Beijing United Family Hospital & Clinics ▶ p.117	010 6433 3960	Private
Peking Union Medical College Hospital	010 6529 5284	Public

Post-Natal Depression

The best treatment for post-natal depression is rest, and being aware of the symptoms and willing to get help. One in 10 women are said to be affected, and support groups like La Leche League (p.125) offer assistance.

Contraception & Sexual Health

With a population of more than 1.2 billion, and a heavily encouraged one-child policy, birth control in China is easy to find. Condoms are available at supermarkets or convenience stores, and contraception (biyun yao) can be found over the counter at even the smallest pharmacies. It is a good idea to check with a doctor before starting any form of birth control; different pills have different dosages and hormones, and women should get their blood pressure tested as a precaution.

Emergency contraception, in the form of the 'morning after' pill, is also available widely, though typically has side effects. A package of birth control pills for either 21 or 28 days can cost as little as ¥80 from a Chinese pharmacy (Chinese instructions only), or over ¥300 from an international pharmacy, with instructions in English.

Abortions

Family planning is a fact of life under the one-child policy. Abortions are safe, legal and widely available in public hospitals for ¥200 to ¥500. Most western and private medical facilities do not offer this service, though Beijing United Family Hospital (p.118) does.

Gynaecology & Obstetrics

It is important to find a doctor you feel comfortable with, and there is no shortage of options. Decide whether you'd like a smaller clinic or a larger hospital, keeping in mind that costs, availability and the range of services can vary. Many doctors are male, so request a female physician if you have a preference. As always, ask friends and co-workers for any references.

Fertility Treatments

A few clinics offer state of the art medical treatments for infertility, though Beijing is behind Shanghai or Hong Kong. American-Sino OB/Gyn (p.118) is probably your best bet. Some local hospitals now offer treatments, but they usually lack English-language speakers and can

Gynaecology & Obstetrics	
Amcare Women & Children's Hospital	010 6434 2388
American-Sino OB/GYN Service	010 6496 8888
Bayley & Jackson Medical Centre	010 8562 9998
Beijing Obstetrics & Gynaecology Hospital	010 8597 6699
Beijing United Family Hospital & Clinics	010 6433 3960
Beijing Vista Clinic	010 8529 6618
Peking Union Medical College Hospital	010 6529 5284

be unfriendly. Insurance will typically not cover IVF or other fertility treatments, so be prepared to pay yourself. Fees start from ¥20,000, though an ultrasound will usually only cost around ¥150.

Paediatrics

There is no shortage of paediatricians in Beijing. Several hospitals are focused primarily on children's medicine, and many offer some English-speaking doctors and western amenities. To narrow the options, ask for a recommendation from a friend or colleague, or a referral from your insurance provider. Family health plans should cover regular hospital visits and check-ups for your child. The Chinese vaccination schedule includes tuberculosis and hepatitis at birth, a polio shot at two months, DPT at three months, and MMR or measles at eight months. Also consider having your child immunised against meningitis at six months as well as Japanese encephalitis and chicken pox.

Paediatrics	
Amcare Women & Children's Hospital	010 6434 2388
Beijing Children's Hospital	010 6802 8401
Beijing United Family Hospital & Clinics	010 6433 3960
New Century International Children's Hospital	010 6802 5588

Dentists & Orthodontists

Basic dentistry is widely available in Beijing and is clean, safe and inexpensive. General services include x-rays, fillings, cleanings and extractions. Typical costs range from ¥200 to ¥500, and some clinics may charge a registration fee. Almost all hospitals, both private and public, offer dental services. Many newer clinics also offer teeth whitening, orthodontics and oral surgery, though major dental surgery takes place at a hospital.

Dentists & Orthodontists	
Arrail Dental – CITIC	010 6500 6473
Arrail Dental – Exchange	010 6567 5670
Arrail Dental – Haidian	010 8286 1956
Arrail Dental – Somerset	010 8440 1926
Beijing United Family Hospitals & Clinics	010 6433 3960
Careplus	010 6586 2517
Detail Dental ▶ p.123	010 6512 6668
Elite Dental Clinic	010 8256 2566
King's Dental	010 8458 0388
SDM Dental – 21st Century Hotel	010 6466 4814
SDM Dental – Guomao	010 6505 9439
SMD Dental – Golden Resources	010 8859 6912
SMD Dental – Sunshine Plaza	010 6497 2173

Opticians & Ophthalmologists

Eye care is inexpensive and easy to find. Most neighbourhoods will have a small optician that can handle frames, lenses and contacts. Prices start from ¥150. Most opticians can also do prescription sunglasses. Laser eye surgery is a booming industry in China, and larger clinics and hospitals can do these procedures, as well as general optometry. Fees can be as little as ¥5,000 to as much as ¥20,000, depending on the type of surgery. For other, more serious, eye care needs, ophthalmologists are also available at larger medical facilities. As always, check with your insurance provider to see what they cover. Driving licences only require a short eye exam at the testing bureau.

Opticians & Ophthalmologists	
Beijing Intech Eye Hospital	010 6771 5558
Daming Optical – Golden Resources	010 8887 5633
Daming Optical – Wanfujing	010 6513 1327
Perfect Vision Optometry	010 6410 5850

Cosmetic Treatment & Surgery

Cosmetic surgery (*zhengrong*) has become extremely popular in Beijing. Especially common are double-eyelid surgeries, liposuction, wrinkle removal, leg stretching and breast augmentation procedures. More than a million Chinese people a year have some form of cosmetic surgery, making it the world's second-largest market.

Newspapers and television programmes have shown stories of shoddy treatment and botched operations so make sure that you ask questions, investigate your chosen clinic and doctor, and look through their history before jumping on the operating table.

Prices are fairly low (relative to western standards) for most procedures and service is consistently good, with many English-speaking doctors available. For those who want something a little less invasive, Botox and other non-surgical methods are also on offer. Hair implants and hair regrowth treatments are available at many clinics.

Cosmetic Treatment & Surgery	
Beijing Ever Care Xingfu	010 6462 7575
Bioscor Beijing	010 6503 5707
Confidant Medical Services	010 6559 6769
Viv International Medical Beauty Clinic	010 6530 2348

Alternative Therapies

Aromatherapy in Beijing is exclusively linked to spas (p.236). Treatments are not intended to be medical, and are not linked to TCM. Acupuncture and acupressure are used to treat almost anything; helping smokers to quit, curing depression, slowing the process of aging, and treating or preventing many diseases. Typically, thin needles will be inserted into several parts of the body to help channel energies or relieve pressure. Popular among both expats and locals, a session can cost from ¥100 to ¥500, and be tried at most hospitals.

Traditional Chinese Medicine (TCM)

Traditional Chinese medicine, or TCM, has some famous and reputable clinics treating a variety of ailments. English-language practitioners are not common, but plenty of sources are available both for educational and medical purposes.

TCM operates under principles of balance between yin and yang, or cold and hot. Treatments include cupping, scraping, and many medicines. TCM medications are usually made from natural herbs and occasionally minerals or animal parts, and make claims such as 'liver cleansing' or 'iron replenishing'. Various diets

Alternative Therapies	
Beijing Massage Hospital	010 6616 1064
Dongzhimen Hospital	010 8401 3212
Liuzheng Massage Clinic	010 6552 9282
Ping Xin Tang Clinic	010 6523 5566
Tongrentang TCM Clinic – Fengtai	010 6766 8793
Tongrentang TCM Clinic – Jianwai SOHO	010 5869 1171
Tongrentang TCM Clinic – River Garden	010 8046 1907

eatment or enjoyment?

Welcome to the Dental SPA at

ail Dental,where we promise you a perfect Hollywood Smile forever...

- Best equipment
- Cutting-edge technology
- Friendly environment
- Superior clinical skills
- Flexible schedule

e try our best to help you, to serve you, to WOW you.

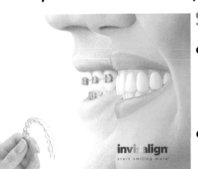

Special services provided

- Invisalign :
  Invisalign gradually moves your teeth through a series of custom-made, removable, nearly invisable Aligners.
- Lumineer :
  American Lumineer no-drill, no-pain, ultra-thin porcelain veneers.

e take assignment from all major dental insurances.

d:Ya'an international village Level1,

  No.2Jin Bao street,Dongcheng district,Beijing

el:010-65126668

www.detaildental.com

make use of traditional Chinese medicinal beliefs, and common therapies include acupuncture, massage, and moxibustion.
TCM is typically intended to be used over a long period of time, as much as six months for some illnesses. Costs can vary widely, from ¥88 per hour of massage to upwards of ¥2,000. However, it can be difficult to know exactly what you are buying, as standards are less than stringent.

Dragon Eyes
The longyan tree, (literally, 'dragon eyes') is unique to China, and is used in TCM to help prevent aging and improve circulation. Eat the fruit, or simply add it to tea.

Healing Meditation

Meditation circles can be found easily, along with many forms of yoga (p.241), including ashtanga, bikram and iyengar. Private and group sessions are usually available, and most are offered in English. Prices range from ¥60 to ¥140 per class to ¥9,800 for a full year. Mats and other supplies are available from any school or studio.

Healing Meditation	
Alona Studio	010 5820 6920
Beijing Yoga	010 8589 3102
Mountain Yoga	010 6259 6702
Nirvana Yoga	010 6593 7509
Yoga Club	010 6200 0127
Yogi Yoga	010 8561 5506

Physiotherapy

There has been great improvement to physical therapy thanks to the 2008 Olympics. Chinese hospitals used to recommend avoiding movement and motion, or use electric currents to stimulate muscles. But with awareness growing around the games, every major hospital can offer basic physical therapy. Even if you're not an athlete, physical therapy can be required for a number of joint and muscle-related problems. As this is still a growing field, prices can vary widely, but expect to pay over ¥600 for a session.

Physiotherapy	
Beijing International SOS Clinic	010 6462 9112
Beijing Massage Hospital	010 6616 1064
Beijing United Family Hospital & Clinics	010 6433 3960
Institute Of Sports Medicine At Beijing Medical University	010 6201 7691

Reflexology & Massage Therapy

Other options **Massage** p.237

Much like acupuncture, massage is often a part of TCM. There are a wide variety of techniques used, from 'fingerpressing' massage used to help boost immunity, to blind masseuses who use *tuina* therapy to treat arthritis and aching muscles.
Chinese massage techniques are often extremely deep, which can be quite uncomfortable to those who are unprepared. Usually, your masseuse will be unable to speak English, which can render attempts to change the depth of the massage useless. Don't be afraid to speak up if you feel that a massage is too harsh or painful.
Massage houses can also serve as covers for illicit adult activities. Knowing which are legitimate, and which are not can take some careful judgement.

Back Treatment

Chiropractic methods are relatively unheard of. Formally-trained chiropractors are rare, though similar treatments (such as those used in physical therapy, acupuncture, or massage) are widely available. Your best bet for back pain or orthopaedic issues is with a major hospital or private clinic. International SOS and United Family Hospital both offer therapies and treatments for everything from spinal injuries to scoliosis. Fees typically cost ¥600 to ¥800 per session. For Chinese treatments, which can include breathing exercises, acupuncture, massage, and cupping, Beijing Qihuang Chinese Medicine Clinic specialises in back pain.

Back Treatment	
Beijing International SOS Clinic	010 6462 9112
Beijing Massage Hospital	010 6616 1064
Beijing Qihuang Chinese Medicine Clinic	010 6503 5867
Beijing United Family Hospital & Clinics	010 6433 3960

Nutritionists

Few clinics have on-staff dieticians, and the field of nutrition isn't common in China. Typically, larger gyms or health spas that cater to western clients will have a nutritionist on staff, and both International SOS Clinic and United Family Hospital can offer diet-related services.

Traditional Chinese medicine is heavily integrated into diet, and any TCM clinic will be able to offer advice on foods to eat or avoid. Fees can be as low as ¥100 at a TCM clinic, much cheaper than a western nutritionist or dietary specialist.

Nutritionists	
Beijing International SOS Clinic	010 6462 9112
Beijing United Family Hospital & Clinics	010 6433 3960
Tongrentang TCM Clinic – Fengtai	010 6766 8793
Tongrentang TCM Clinic – Jianwai SOHO	010 5869 1171
Tongrentang TCM Clinic – River Garden	010 8046 1907

Counselling & Therapy

Psychiatric care is still somewhat new in China, and many avoid treatment for fear of being socially outcast or shamed. Few dedicated facilities exist, few doctors are properly trained, and almost no public counsellors are available who can speak English. Beijing Huilongguan Hospital is the largest public psychiatric facility near Beijing. It can handle adult and child care for behavioural and psychological disorders, and offers psychotherapy. There is a private facility with English-speaking staff, but a general lack of understanding of expat issues in public hospitals. Domestic and personal counselling is available through hotlines and support groups. For more serious care, help is available at larger private clinics and hospitals, though it can be fairly costly (over ¥800 an hour). Make sure that you check with your insurance provider about any coverage that they offer.

Counsellors & Therapists	
Beijing Ankang Hospital	010 6131 6005
Beijing Huilongguan Hospital	010 6271 5511
Beijing International SOS Clinic	010 6462 9112
Beijing United Family Hospital & Clinics	010 6433 3960
Beijing Vista Clinic	010 8529 6618
International Medical Centre	010 6465 1384

Addiction Counselling & Rehabilitation

Addiction is often treated as a mental illness in Beijing. While there are a growing number of options for Chinese citizens, expats with addictions might need to turn to a church or community group, or seek help at a private hospital. Beijing Ankang Hospital does provide drug rehabilitation, but is largely aimed at local residents.

The Beijing International Christian Fellowship (BICF) offers professional and peer counselling, as well as courses and seminars in English. Those battling alcohol addictions can attend their local AA group, which meets weekly and offers a separate group for women.

Addiction Counselling & Rehabilitation	
Beijing Alcoholics Anonymous (General)	139 1138 9075
Beijing Alcoholics Anonymous (Women)	138 0105 2274
Beijing Ankang Hospital	010 6131 6005
BICF Counselling Centre	010 6467 2362

Support Groups

If you are struggling in Beijing it's likely that another expat is too. Lots of support is available, whether you are an expectant (or new) mother, or someone who just wants to learn more about Chinese culture. Most private schools offer meetings for parents to get together, and many communities offer networking nights.

The International Newcomers' Network (www.innbeijing.org), has meetings to explore topics like driving, banking and other basics. Mothers can find help through La Leche, which meets monthly.

Support Groups	
BICF Counselling Centre	010 6467 2362
BJU St Regis Clinic (Men's Support Group)	010 6433 3962
INSPIRED	136 2113 2201
International Newcomers' Network	135 5261 1887
La Leche League	010 6298 0197
Parent Support Group	139 1029 7173

Education

Most places offer after-school programmes, with activities ranging from sport to music and art. Participation is compulsory at some schools, like Harrow International (p.136). Beijing has many sport clubs, including ClubFootball (p.213), which offers football coaching at schools around town, and Sports Beijing (010 6430 1412, www.sportsbj. com) which offers baseball, cheerleading, dance, rugby, tennis and water polo.

The Dulwich College Community Programmes offer a range of activities open to the public, including art, baking, drama, and languages. Boy Scouts of America (www. troop943.com) and Girl Scouts (bjgsinfo@yahoo.com) are active here. Art classes are offered at Kids' Gallery (010 8046 1454, www.kidsgallery.com). For full listings of kids' activities see p.218. English language magazines (p.52) like *City Weekend* (www. cityweekend.com.cn), *That's Beijing* (www.thebeijinger.com) and *Time Out* also offer detailed listings.

Whether your child attends a Chinese or international school, there are education options for most budgets and lifestyles. Education is compulsory (and free, apart from small fees for books and uniforms) for Chinese citizens from age 6 to 15. This ensures each child receives a primary and middle school education. Parents pay modest tuition fees for high school, which ends with the competitive *gaokao* (National University Entrance Examination). This decides which university pupils can attend.

As the cost of education rises and the number of companies paying for tuition decreases, expat parents have increasingly turned to Chinese schools or home schooling. While many international schools only enroll expats, Chinese schools are required by law to accept the children of legal foreign residents. Some are more willing than others. Nationwide, the Ministry of Education has approved 71 academic institutions from primary school to higher education for foreign instruction. Tuition fees at local schools average ¥28,000 to ¥48,000 annually. Tuition fees at international schools range from ¥25,000 for pre-school to over ¥175,000 for high school. In addition, many international schools have a 'capital levy fee' that goes towards school maintenance and improvement. This varies by school and grade, but starts at around ¥16,000. Other expenses like uniforms, lunch, books, and transport are not always included in the tuition. Most after-school activities are though. Some schools, like Beijing City International School (p.132), offer scholarships. Many offer a sibling discount or a discount for a lump sum fee payment at the beginning of the school year. Many offer financial assistance or monthly payment plans.

Beijing's international schools offer many curriculum choices, including International Baccalaureate (IB) programmes, English curriculum (including GCSEs and A-levels) and American curriculum. Other countries' curricula are also represented, including Australian, Canadian, French, German, Indian, Pakistani and Swedish. Class sizes vary by school and grade, but tend to be small, with five to 25 pupils.

Peking University, p.141

It is best to apply to schools as early as possible, as many have waiting lists. Most will accept students mid-way through the year if space is available. Some offer tuition repayment should a student withdraw.

Most schools require an admissions application, pupil's health records, passport and visa information and previous school records. Some, like nurseries and kindergartens, require a birth certificate. Others want recommendation letters, assessments, on-campus interviews, entrance exams and set a minimum level for language skills.

Nurseries & Pre-Schools

Many parents enroll their babies and toddlers in nurseries and pre-schools to give them a head start on education and develop their social skills.

Most schools or kindergarten offer flexible schedules for younger children (typically from around 18 months old) who can attend a few days a week, half day or all day. In pre-kindergarten (ages 2 to 4) and kindergarten (ages 5 to 6), students tend to have a longer school day, typically from 08:00 to 15:00.

With Montessori, Multiple Intelligences Theory and Reggio Emilia, Beijing nurseries and pre-schools offer a wide variety of ways to educate children.

Named after Maria Montessori, Italy's first female doctor, the Montessori approach groups children together across several years, so 2 to 5 year olds will often share the same classroom and teachers. The curriculum focuses on five areas: practical life, sensorial, language, mathematics, and culture. The philosophy behind it is that children can learn at their own pace, with their own choice of activities among a community of students.

Multiple Intelligences Theory is based on a book by Howard Gardner which challenged the traditional psychological view that intelligence is singular. He proposed individuals have seven independent intelligences: linguistic, logical-mathematical, musical, special, bodily-kinesthetic, interpersonal and intrapersonal. Multiple Intelligences Theory approach fosters these intelligences.

Based on teaching methods in early childhood education in Reggio Emilia, Italy, this method puts the child in control of their education by focussing on the child and their strongest competencies. The approach includes building a curriculum based on the child's interests, with small and large group projects.

Many schools offer a bilingual environment, exposing children to both English and Chinese languages (this is a popular choice among expats). Some offer lunch and after-school programmes.

Most teachers are university educated and certified in the various teaching pedagogies, though it's a good idea to make a school visit to determine the level of instruction and allow your child to get a feel for the school.

Tuition fees for international nurseries, pre-schools and kindergartens tend to be steep, ranging from ¥25,000 to ¥103,000. School lunch, uniforms, assistance with English as a second language, transport on a school bus, the capital levy fee and after-school activities may not be included in some fees. Local nurseries like Beijing Huijia Kindergarten (p.128) will accept foreign children and typically have much lower tuition fees.

Playgroups

For parents looking for less structure (or that want to save money), there are plenty of playgroups in Beijing.

Gymboree (010 5869 4087, 010 5166 0516, 010 8248 6191, www.gymboree.com.cn) has three locations while Kindy ROO (010 6553 6362, 010 5166 8078, www.kindyroo.com) has two. Both offer drop-in developmental classes for newborns to 4 year olds. The popular weekly Mommy and Me programme (010 6539 7171 extension 1302, www.etonkids.com) for mums and kids up to 3 years old, is open to anyone. The German Playgroup (010 8046 1840, 135 0120 1368) meets on a regular basis and is open to German-speaking children.

Playground (010 6407 6889, www.myplayground.cn), a children's activity centre located in a renovated courtyard home, has a drop off service for youngsters from toddlers to age 14, who can enjoy free time under adult supervision.

Active Kids
If the thought of keeping your nippers occupied in this strange and forbidding city fills you with worry, turn to p.218 for a few ideas.

3e International Kindergarten 三弈国际幼儿园

18 Jiangtai Xi Lu
Chaoyang
将台西路18号
朝阳区
Map 5 D3 **11**

010 6437 3344 | www.3eik.com

Affiliated with Michigan State University and Beijing Normal University, this bilingual nursery and kindergarten accepts children from 18 months to 6 years old, and follows a mix of Montessori, Multiple Intelligences and Reggio Emilia styles. Classes have 12 to 16 students with a student to teacher ration of 4:1 (nursery) and 8:1 (pre-school/kindergarten). Facilities include a library, kitchen, art room, playground and gym. An elementary programme, starting with first grade, began in 2008.

Beanstalk International Bilingual School 青苗国际双语学校

Building B
40 Liangmaqiao Lu
Chaoyang
亮马桥路40号B座
朝阳区
Map 5 D4 **12**

010 6466 9255 | www.bibs.com.cn

One of several Beanstalk schools in Beijing, this kindergarten accepts children aged 2 to 6. Instruction is in English and Mandarin. Children can attend half or full day. The school has a library, playgrounds inside and out, and music rooms. After-school activities include ballet, kung fu and piano.

Beijing Huijia Kindergarten ▶ p.IFC 北京汇佳幼儿园

Huating Jiayuan
Chaoyang
北四环中路6号华 亭嘉
园B座33C
朝阳区
Map 4 F2 **13**

010 5165 2252 | www.hjkids.com

Sister school to the Beijing Huijia Private School (p.132), there are 16 branches of this Chinese kindergarten around the city. It accepts Chinese and foreign children from 18 months to 5 years old. Classes are in Chinese and the curriculum is based on the Multiple Intelligences method. Huating Jiayuan is at 6 Beisihuan Zhong Lu.

The Children's House

Various Locations

010 6505 3869 | www.montessoribeijing.com/ens

This nursery, pre-school and kindergarten accepts children aged from 1 to 6 and follows the Montessori curriculum. A bilingual programme is available. Children can attend half or full day. All campuses have playgrounds. The China World campus has a kitchen and access to a ballet room, the Lufthansa campus has access to tennis courts, and the Yosemite campus has a library and kitchen. For more details of where the campuses are located, visit the website.

Children's Learning Center Of Beijing 北京爱嘉励儿童双语学校

Gahood Residence
Villa, House 4059
Baixinzhuang
Houshayu
Shunyi
后沙峪白辛庄嘉浩别墅
4059号
顺义区
Map 3 D2 **14**

010 8046 7082 | www.clcbkids.com

This bilingual nursery and kindergarten accepts children from 10 months to 5 years. A trilingual class (Mandarin/English/German) for 3 to 5 year olds is also available. Classes are small (10 to 12 students) and the student to teacher ratio is 2:1 (nursery), 3:1 (pre-school) and 4:1 (kindergarten). Classes are organised in a theme-based curriculum providing flexible enrollment. Half day and full day classes are offered, with extended hours from 07:00 to 17:30 available. Facilities include a playground and garden, and after school activities include Chinese, English, German, arts and crafts, Kindermusik, kung fu, dance and gymnastics.

Der Kindergarten 北京德国幼儿园

Merlin Champagne
Town 40B, 6 Liyuan Lu
Tianzhu
Shunyi
天竺镇丽苑路6号美林
香槟小镇乙40号
顺义区
Map 3 E3 **15**

010 6450 8580 | www.derkindergarten.com

Part of Kinstar International Bilingual School (p.138), this kindergarten accepts German children aged from 2 to 6. It teaches mainly in German, with some Mandarin and English. Classes have eight to 10 students with a student to teacher ratio of 5:1. The school follows the Berlin curriculum, and students can attend for either half or full days. Facilities include a garden, playground and dress up area. Two spaces are available annually for non-German speakers.

Eton International School 艾顿国际学校

Various Locations

010 6533 6520 | www.etonkids.com

Eton International School accepts children from 18 months to 6 years old and follows the Montessori curriculum (see Nurseries & Pre-Schools, p.127 for more on this). Instruction is in English and Mandarin, and the student to teacher ratio is 5:1. Children can attend half or full day sessions, and extended hours are available. Facilities include art and music rooms, libraries, and playgrounds. The Global Trade Mansion Campus also has drama and ballet rooms. For locations of their campuses, check their website.

Ivy Academy 北京市艾毅幼儿园

East Lake Villas, 35 Dongzhimenwai Dajie
Dongcheng
东直门外大街35号东
湖别墅
东城区
Map 4 C2 **16**

010 8451 1380 | www.ivyacademy.cn

This Multiple Intelligences Theory nursery and kindergarten accepts children aged from 2 to 6 years old. Instruction is in English but Chinese is part of the curriculum, which is set by a Multiple Intelligences expert certified by Harvard Graduate School of Education. Student to teacher ratio is 5:1 with a maximum of 60 students. Children can attend two, three or five days a week for half or full days. Facilities include a playroom, library and access to tennis courts. After-school activities include ballet, kickboxing and swimming.

Ivy Bilingual School 艾毅双语幼儿园

Various Locations

010 8446 7287 | www.ivybilingual.cn

This school follows a combination of Chinese national and American curriculae. There are more than 150 students aged 2 to 6 years old, and classes have between 18 and 20 students with a student to teacher ratio of 5:1. The teachers all tend to have college degrees in early childhood education, while English teachers are native speakers of the language. Students can attend half or full day sessions. Facilities include libraries, playgrounds and a pool, and at the new Orchid Garden campus, a football pitch and music and dance rooms. The school has an extensive after-school programme based on Multiple Intelligences Theory (see Nurseries & Pre-Schools, p.127 for more on this). For full details of the schools campuses (including a new site in Shunyi), see the website.

Kids' Gallery 儿童艺廊

Baixin Zhuang Cun Nan, Houshayu
Shunyi
后沙峪白辛庄村南
顺义区
Map 3 D2 **17**

010 8046 1454 | www.kidsgallery.com

The Beijing branch of this international chain offers pre-school and kindergarten classes focusing on the arts, with a wide range of classes to develop creativity and an appreciation of art (think mucking about with paints, plastecine and papier mache). There are some performance elements, like plays, included too. The small school accepts children aged from 2 to 5 years old. Children can attend two, three and five days for half or full days.

Mammolina Children's Home 三为国际幼儿园

A36 Maquanying Siqu (Liyuan Xiaoqu) Xiangjiang Beilu
Chaoyang
香江北路马泉营四区
（丽苑小区）甲36号
朝阳区
Map 3 D3 **18**

010 8470 5128 | www.montessori.ws

This bilingual (English and Mandarin) Montessori school caters for children aged from 2 to 7 years old, with a student to teacher ratio of 7:1. Attendance is on a half or full day basis, and the school offers a limited number of scholarships. Facilities include a 280sqm classroom, a reading area, oriental garden and kitchen. The school also has an upper floor observation balcony for parents to watch over their little ones' classroom activities.

Various Locations ◀ Oxford Baby Bilingual Kindergarten 北京小牛津双语幼儿园
010 6489 5533
This bilingual kindergarten accepts Chinese and foreign children from 18 months to 6 years old at its four campuses around Chaoyang. Day school and boarding are available, The main langauge is Mandarin, but English teachers are native speakers. Branches are located at 308 Huizhongli, Yayuncun (010 6493 6636), 6 Nanxinyuan (010 8731 1098) and 88 Jianguo Lu, SOHO New Town (010 8589 7363).

3 Jiqingli
Chaoyangmenwai
Dajie
Chaoyang
朝阳门外大街吉庆里
3号 朝阳区
Map 7 B1 **19**

Sanlitun Kindergarten 三里屯幼儿园
010 6551 0877
This kindergarten accepts children of any nationality from 18 months to 6 years, but instruction is only in Chinese. Special emphasis is placed on physical exercise. Normal kindergarten classes run every day of the week, while for children under 2 years old there are weekly classes where they must be accompanied by a parent or *ayi*.

Primary & Secondary Schools

Beijing has an array of international schools offering many teaching methods and different curriculae. All the popular national systems are represented including American, Canadian, Chinese, English, French, German, Indian, Pakistani and Swedish. School days are typically 08:15 to 15:30, with after school activities running until 16:00 or 16:30. Schools break for several days or a week for national holiday in the first week of October, Christmas, spring festival (a week between mid-January and mid-February depending on the lunar calendar), spring break and May holiday. Some schools have half days or days off throughout the year for teacher training.

Admissions requirements vary, but most request a completed admissions application, health records, passport and visa information, and previous school records. Some schools ask for recommendation letters, assessments, on-campus interviews, entrance exams and language requirements. It is best to apply to schools as early as possible but most are willing to take students mid-way through the year if space is available.

A popular choice for parents who aren't on a corporate package is to send their children to local Chinese schools. The admissions materials at local schools are typically in Chinese and at most places there's little support for families and students who do not speak the language. Beijing Zhongguancun International School (p.134), Fangcaodi Primary School (p.136), The High School Affiliated to Renmin University of China (p.137) and Beijing Ritan High School (p.132) all have a history of admitting expat children, and have sizeable foreign student populations on campus. Non-Chinese speakers are usually set back several years, normally to first grade. The national curriculum allocates most of the day to Chinese study and maths with a focus on preparing students for entrance exams to middle school, high school and university.

Class sizes vary but average at 35 pupils. Unlike Chinese citizens, local school is not free for expats but tuition is much lower than at international schools. Many parents find the local Chinese education system beneficial for younger children, but turn to international education for high school, unless the child plans to attend university in China.

7 Louzizhuang Lu
Chaoyang
楼梓庄路7号
朝阳区

Australian International School Of Beijing ▶ p.131
北京澳大利亚国际学校
010 8439 4315 | www.aisb.com.cn
This school (kindergarten to grade six) follows the New South Wales curriculum as well as regular Mandarin lessons. Classes have a maximum of 20 students, with some as low as 12 to 16. Facilities include computer and language labs, a library, a football pitch, basketball and tennis courts, a 400 metre track, dance studios, a driving range and a 9 hole golf course. After-school activities include tutoring, football, cricket, piano and dance. Boarding is available.

38 Nanshiliju
Chaoyang
南十里居38号
朝阳区

Beanstalk International Bilingual School 青苗国际双语学校
010 8456 6019 | www.bibs.com.cn
This bilingual school accepts students from pre-kindergarten (age 2) up to grade seven and follows a curriculum featuring elements from the UK, USA and Canada. There are over 300 students at two campuses. The new campus at Nanshiliju includes libraries, computer labs, science and art buildings, a music room, an auditorium, a gym, basketball and volleyball courts and a football pitch. Classes have 20 to 22 students. The other campus is at 6 Dongsihuan Beilu (010 8465 6019).

No 17, Area 4
An Zhen Xi Li
Chaoyang
安贞西里4区17号
朝阳区
Map 4 F3 22

Beijing BISS International School 北京BISS 国际学校
010 6443 3151 | www.biss.com.cn
This pre-kindergarten to Grade 12 school has 400 students and offers a full International Baccalaureate programme. Classes have a maximum of 20 students. Facilities include music and art rooms, a library, computer labs, a design and technology centre, wireless access in many parts of the school, a running track and a multi-purpose sports court. There are also over 50 after-school activities including an a cappella choir, street hockey and a rock band.

77 Baiziwan Nan Er Lu
Chaoyang
百子湾南2路77号
朝阳区
Map 7 D3 23

Beijing City International School 北京乐成国际学校
010 8771 7171 | www.bcis.cn
BCIS is an International Baccalaureate World School with 400 students from nursery (age 3) to Grade 11. Classes have between 16 and 20 students. Facilities include music studios, arts rooms, science and computer labs, design and technology studios, libraries, a theatre, a gym, a 250m track, a football pitch, a climbing wall and a 25m pool. A new 10,000sqm 'eco-garden' 20 minutes from campus offers students a chance to learn about nature. After-school enrichment programmes include Roots & Shoots and Chinese maths. Scholarships (¥80,000 to ¥160,000) for Grade 11 are available.

157 Changhuai Lu
Changping Yuan
Changping District
昌平区昌平园昌怀路
157号

Beijing Huijia Private School 北京私立汇佳学校
010 6078 5722 | www.huijia2000.com
This private Chinese all-boarding school has over 2,000 Chinese and foreign students from Grades one to 12. The school offers the International Baccalaureate programme taught in English and a Chinese national curriculum taught in Chinese. Facilities include a golf course, a library, a pool, piano studios and a basketball court.

12 Xinzhong Jie
Dongcheng
新中街12号
东城区
Map 9 D3 25

Beijing No 55 Middle School & High School
北京市第五十五中学
010 6416 9531 | www.bj55.cn
This local Chinese school has a large number of foreign students in grades three to 12 and a dedicated foreign student department. Students can choose the International Baccalaureate curriculum or Chinese national curriculum. Classes are taught in the high school in Chinese (for non-native speakers) or English. The middle school is in Chinese only. An intensive Chinese programme is available to help non-speakers.

Various Locations

Beijing Ritan High School
010 6503 1815 | http://rtzx.bjchyedu.cn
This Grade one to 12 public school in Chaoyang offers a bilingual programme for elementary students, however instruction for the middle school and high school is in Chinese and follows the Chinese national curriculum. After school activities include band and sport. The elementary school is located at 38 Nanshiliju (010 6438 2945), the middle school at 2 Baijiazhuang Xili (010 6500 4609), the high school at A7 Daojayuan (010 6506 2605), and the high school for the senior year only is at 36 Dongsanhuan Beilu (010 6591 2920).

DULWICH COLLEGE BEIJING

Building Bridges to the World

At Dulwich College Beijing,
we believe in excellence in all that we do:

Academic Achievement
High quality curriculum with standards established in partnership with Dulwich College London, one of Britain's most prestigious independent schools.

Performance
Opportunities for each student to explore their musical and dramatic interests and abilities.

Sport
Each student has an opportunity to access high level training and participate in competitions.

Community
A wide range of community sports and activities for children and adults living in Beijing.

Legend Garden Campus
Shunyi District
Tel: (8610) 6454 9000

Beijing Riviera Campus
Chaoyang District
Tel: (8610) 8450 7676

River Garden Campus
Shunyi District
Tel: (8610) 8046 5132

www.dcbeijing.cn   info@dcbeijing.cn

40 Liangmaqiao Lu
Chaoyang
亮马桥路40号
朝阳区
Map 5 D4 **26**

Beijing World Youth Academy 北京市世青中学
010 6461 7779 | www.ibwya.net
This school caters for both Chinese and foreign students in grades six to 12 and offers the International Baccalaureate curriculum or Chinese national curriculum. The school has 440 students and has a student to teacher ratio of 5:1. The average class size is 25. Facilities include science, computer and multimedia labs, a library, a dance studio, a pool, a recording studio, and basketball and tennis courts. After-school activities include student government, cooking, knitting, musical instruments, chess and Chinese painting. The Northern Campus is on Liangmaqiao Lu, while the Southern Campus is on Maizidian Jie, also in Chaoyang.

49 Beisanhuan Xilu
Haidian
北三环西路49号
海淀区
Map 4 B2 **27**

Beijing Xiyi Elementary School 北京市西颐小学
010 8263 2789 | www.hdxyxx.bjedu.cn
Although classes are taught only in Chinese, this was one of the first schools to accept foreign students in Beijing, and it offers places for students from grades one to six. Alongside the usual subjects, there are also classes in computing, art and Beijing opera. A new building is currently being constructed, and will open soon.

Laiguangying Dong Lu
Chaoyang
来广营东路
朝阳区
Map 3 B4 **28**

Beijing Zhongguancun Int'l School 北京中关村国际学校
010 8440 6540 | www.bzis2002.com
This local school moved from Zhongguancun to a new campus in 2007. It offers an American curriculum approved by the California Department of Education which emphasises maths and science for grades one to eight. Chinese language and culture classes are offered weekly for foreign students. Facilities include science and computer labs, library, gym and auditorium. The school plans to add high school grades in the future.

Sanlitun Campus
5 Sanlitun Xiliujie
Chaoyang
三里屯西六街5号三里
屯校区
朝阳区
Map 9 E1 **29**

British School Beijing 北京英国学校
010 8532 3088 | www.britishschool.org.cn
This pre-kindergarten (age 2) to grade 11 school follows the English National Curriculum (including GCSE) at two campuses. Pre-kindergarten to year six is offered at the Sanlitun campus while the Shunyi campus (Cuizhu Xincun, Linyin Lu, Tianzhu Zhen, 010 6458 0884) offers pre-kindergarten to grade 11. Facilities include interactive white boards in all classrooms, libraries, IT suites, science labs, music rooms, performance hall, football pitch and gym. The Shunyi campus also has a pool and theatre.

38 Liangmaqiao Lu
Chaoyang
亮马桥路38号
朝阳区
Map 5 D4 **30**

Canadian Int'l School Of Beijing ▶p.135 北京加拿大国际学校
010 6465 7788 | www.cisb.com.cn
This Montessori kindergarten to grade 12 school operates under the guidance of the Ministry of Education in Canada, and has a student to teacher ratio of 10:1. Teachers are part of the Canadian Teachers Federation and must meet Ministry standards. Facilities include 90 classrooms with SMART boards, computer labs, visual arts and science labs, libraries, a lecture hall, a theatre, gyms, a pool and a football field.

Naidong Bailou
Sunbai Lu
Chaoyang
顺白路奶东工业区
白楼
朝阳区
Map 3 D3 **31**

Daystar Academy 启明星晨曦教育文化交流中心
010 8430 2654 | www.daystar-qimingxing.org
Daystar is seeking approval as a private Chinese school. It caters for students from kindergarten to grade six, following the Chinese national and English Montessori curricula. Students take Chinese midterm and final exams and Canadian Achievement Tests in English and maths. From 2007 to 2008 there were 33 students but the newly opened 19,000sqm campus accommodates 400 and anticipates a student to teacher ratio of 15:1. Facilities include a gym with dance, art and music studios and outdoor sports facilities. After-school activities include homework support, sport and arts.

The Joy of Learning with SMART Board !!!

CANADIAN INTERNATIONAL SCHOOL OF BEIJING

北京加拿大国际学校

Montessori M1 to Pre-E.   Canadian Grade 1 to 12

The Canadian International School of Beijing is a candidate school for the Diploma Programme. This school is pursuing authorization as an IB World School. These are schools that share a common philosophy – a commitment to high quality, challenging, international education that Canadian International School of Beijing believes is important for our students.

Only schools authorized by the IB organization can offer any of its three academic programmes: the Primary Years Programme (PYP), The Middle Years Programme (MYP), or the Diploma Programme. Candidate status gives no guarantee that authorization will be granted.

For further information about the IB and its programmes, visit http://www.ibo.org

38 Liangmaqiao Lu, Chaoyang District, Beijing, China 100016
Tel: (86-10) 6465.7788 Fax: (86-10) 6465.7789
E-mail: admissions@cis-beijing.com
Website: www.cisb.com.cn

Deutsche Botschaftsschule Peking 北京德国使馆学校

49A Liangmaqiao Lu
Chaoyang
亮马桥路甲49号
朝阳区
Map 5 C4 **32**

010 6532 2535 | www.dspeking.net.cn
This small German embassy school accepts students from kindergarten to year 13. Classes are taught in German and the curriculum meets the German Board of Education standards. Approximately 50 children attend the kindergarten with around 370 enrolled in the elementary and upper school.

Dulwich College Beijing ▶p.133 北京德威英国国际学校

Legend Garden
Campus
89 Capital Airport
Road, Legend Garden
Shunyi
北京市首都机场路
89号 丽京花园
Map 3 C4 **33**

010 6454 9000 | www.dcbeijing.cn
Affiliated with Dulwich College in London, this school has more than 1,000 students from pre-kindergarten to year 11. Pre-school and kindergarten follow a Montessori curriculum at the Riviera, River Garden Villas and Sanlitun campuses. Year three and up follow the English National Curriculum while upper students follow IGCSE and, starting in 2008, International Baccalaureate at Legend Garden campus. Classes have a maximum of 24 students. Facilities include IT suites, media centre, theatre, music rooms, recording studios, pool, gym, dance studio, tennis and squash courts, golf driving range, and cricket, football and rugby pitches. Lunchtime and after-school activities include football, chess, film, dance and music. Year 12 will be added in August 2008 and year 13 will be added in 2009. Other campuses are at Riviera, 1 Xiangjiang Beilu, Jingshun Lu, Chaoyang (010 8450 7676), River Garden Villas, Houshayu, Baixinzhuang, Shunyi (010 8046 5132) and 7 Sanlitun Beixiaojie, Chaoyang, (010 6532 6713).

Eton International School 艾顿国际学校

Palm Spring
International
Apartments, 8
Chaoyang Gongyuan
Nanlu
Chaoyang
朝阳公园南路8号，
棕榈泉国际公寓
朝阳区
Map 7 C2 **34**

010 6539 8967 | www.etonkids.com
Eton International School accepts Chinese and expat pupils from 18 months to 6 years old or 9 years old at the Global Trade Mansion campus (Guanghua Lu, Chaoyang, 010 6506 4805). The schools follow the Montessori curriculum. Instruction is in English and the student to teacher ratio is 5:1. Facilities include art and music rooms, libraries and playgrounds. The Global Trade Mansion campus also has drama and ballet rooms. There are other campuses at Pinnacle Plaza, Tianzhu Real Estate Development Zone, Shunyi (010 8046 5338) and Lido Country Club, Lido Place, Jichang road, Chaoyang (010 6436 7368).

Fangcaodi Primary School 芳草地小学

1 Ritan Beilu
Chaoyang
日坛北路1号
朝阳区
Map 7 B2 **35**

010 8563 5120 | www.fcd.com.cn
This local primary school has been accepting foreign students since 1956. It has grades one to six and follows the Chinese national curriculum. Instruction is in Chinese. Classes include Chinese, English, IT, music and fine arts. Facilities include state-of-the-art classrooms and playing fields, while after school, sports such as badminton, *wushu* (martial arts) and rollerblading are offered.

Harrow International School 北京哈罗英国学校

No 5, Block 4
Anzhen Xili
Chaoyang
安贞西里4区5号
朝阳区
Map 4 C4 **36**

010 6444 8900 | www.harrowbeijing.cn
Affiliated with Harrow School in England, this small school of 200 students offers year seven to year 13 and follows GCSE, AS and A-level curriculum. The school boasts a 100% pass rate on A levels. Professional artists teach at the school and the student to teacher ratio is 6:1. Facilities include music and dance rooms, a recording studio, gym, science and ICT labs, and library. Each student is required to participate in a different after-school activity from Monday to Friday; these include music lessons, drama, chorus, rock bands and sport.

The High School Affiliated To Renmin University Of China (Renda Fuzhong) 人民大学附属中学

37 Zhongguancun Dajie
Haidian
中关村大街37号
海淀区
Map 4 C3 37

010 6251 1966 | www.rdfz.cn/English

This school is run by the state and accepts students in grades seven to 11. It is known for producing high test score and offers A level qualifications. Most of the teachers are Chinese, but more than 20 are expats. Instruction is in Chinese but an intensive Chinese course is available. Of the school's 4,000 students, about 180 are foreign. Facilities include computer and science labs, simulated driving classroom, library and auditorium. After-school activities include chorus, dance, photography, chess team and sport.

Indian Embassy School 印度学校

1 Ritan Donglu
Chaoyang
日坛东路1号印度
使馆
朝阳区
Map 7 B2 38

010 6532 1827

Run by and located in the Indian embassy, this small school accepts students aged from 4 to 11. There are approximately 100 students from 24 different countries. Classes are taught in English and the school follows an Indian-style curriculum, which includes Chinese classes.

International Academy Of Beijing IAB国际学校

Lido Office Tower 3 Lido Place, Jichang Lu, Jiangtai Lu
Chaoyang
将台路机场路丽都
广场丽都办公大楼
3号楼
朝阳区
Map 5 D3 39

010 6430 1600 | www.iabchina.net

Accredited by the Association of Christian Schools International, this kindergarten to grade 10 school has 250 students. Classes have 16 to 20 students and a student to teacher ratio of 8:1. Facilities are extensive with IT and science labs, library, auditorium, playground, basketball court and access to a nearby pool and gym. After-school activities include music, art, quilting, ballet, Chinese, table tennis, yearbook club and sport. The school plans to open grade 11 in autumn 2008 and grade 12 in autumn 2009.

Int'l Montessori School Of Beijing 蒙台梭利国际学校

River Garden Campus Houshayu
Shunyi
后沙峪白辛庄裕京花
园校区
顺义区
Map 3 C2 40

010 8046 3935 | www.msb.edu.cn

This school accepts children aged 1 to grade three. It follows a Montessori curriculum with instruction by native English speakers, with an option to study in Chinese. Facilities at River Garden include a kitchen, art room, library and playground. The new Cherry Tree Lane campus (Xiang Jiang Beilu, Chaoyang, 010 6432 8228) has a football pitch, running track and indoor pool.

The International School Of Beijing 北京顺义国际学校

10 Anhua Jie
Shunyi
安华街10号
顺义区
Map 3 C1 41

010 8149 2345 | www.isb.bj.edu.cn

With more than 1,850 students from 50 countries, ISB is Beijing's largest international school. Catering to children from pre-kindergarten (age 3) to grade 12, this school offers the International Baccalaureate programme, some Advance Placement classes and tuition in Chinese. Classes have 14 to 22 students. Facilities include libraries, science labs, a theatre, running track, gyms and weights room, tennis courts, baseball diamond and pool with diving boards.

Int'l School Of Collaborative Learning 北京协力国际学校

White Building Naidong Gongyequ Shunbai Lu
Chaoyang
顺白路奶东工业区
白楼
朝阳区
Map 3 C3 42

010 8470 9458

This small, modern kindergarten to grade 12 school follows a curriculum developed by Sidwell Friends School in Washington DC. Classes are taught in both Chinese and English. Kindergarten to grade two, grades three to four and grades five to six are grouped together. Older students are grouped together based on language abilities. The school, situated inside the White Building, has a computer lab, a media centre and a library, and sport fields.

Kinstar International Bilingual School 海嘉双语国际学校

Monet Garden Building 11, 5 Yumin Lu
Shunyi
后沙峪裕民大街5号
11号楼莫奈花园主
校区
顺义区
Map 3 D2 43

010 8041 0391 | www.kinstarschool.org
This bilingual school opened in August 2006 for children from pre-kindergarten to grade six. The bilingual pre-kindergarten and kindergarten programme is at Merlin Champagne Town Clubhouse (6 Liyuan Jie, Tianzhu Zhen, Shunyi, 010 6450 8259) with one English classroom and one Chinese classroom. At Monet Garden Main Campus, grades one to six follow a US-style curriculum. Pre-school and kindergarten students can attend three or five days a week for half or full days. Facilities include a library, computer lab, dance and calligraphy rooms, gym and playing fields.

Lycée Français International de Pékin 北京法国国际学校

Sanlitun Dong Si Jie 13
Chaoyang
三里屯东四街13号
朝阳区
Map 9 F2 44

010 6532 3498 | www.ifp.com.cn
Part of the Agency for French Education Abroad network, this kindergarten to grade 12 school follows the French curriculum including Brevet des Collèges and French Baccalaureat. Students have a history of high French Baccalaureat scores. The school has approximately 1,000 students averaging 20 pupils per class. Facilities include a theatre, gym and library. A new high school campus will open soon. The kindergarten is at 4 Sanlitun Lu, Chaoyang (010 6532 6579).

Pakistan Embassy College 巴基斯坦大使馆学校

1 Dongzhimenwai Dajie
Chaoyang
东直门外大街1号
朝阳区
Map 9 F2 45

010 6532 1905 | www.embassyofpakistan-beijing.org.cn/en/college.htm
Located inside the Pakistan Embassy, this kindergarten to year 13 embassy school has 350 students from 45 countries. It follows the British system of education until grade eight. After this, students can choose either the intermediate and secondary system of the Federal Board of Education Islamabad, Pakistan or London University's GCSE and A level systems (Edexcel). Classes are taught in English. Facilities include computer and science labs, basketball and badminton courts and a gym.

Potter's Wheel Int'l Elementary School 匠心之轮国际学校

1 Chajia Donglu Langxinzhuang
Chaoyang
郎辛庄茶家东路1号
朝阳区
Map 7 D3 46

010 8538 2803 | www.potters-wheel.cn
Beijing's first sport-based international school accepts athletic-minded children in pre-kindergarten (age 3) to grade five and online courses for grades six to 12. It follows Oak Meadow (an American curriculum) in the morning, with afternoons devoted to fine arts and sports such as tennis. Facilities include a computer lab, library, music and art rooms, kitchen, 21 tennis courts including one stadium court, pool, running track and a playground. After-school and weekend tennis lessons are available to amateurs and there's intensive tennis training for junior professional players through its International Junior Tennis Centre.

Swedish School Beijing 北京瑞典学校

Legend Garden Villas 89 Capital Airport Road
Chaoyang
首都机场路89号丽
京花园
朝阳区
Map 3 E3 47

010 6456 0826 | www.swedishschool.org.cn
Following the Swedish national curriculum, the pupil or at least one parent must speak a Scandinavian language to be accepted. Classes are taught in Swedish and have between five and 20 students. English and Chinese tuition is also on offer. The school has approximately 120 students in pre-school up to Swedish grade six. After-school activities include cooking, music and sport.

Western Academy Of Beijing 京西学校

10 Laiguangying
Chaoyang
来广营东路10号
朝阳区
Map 3 C4 48

010 8456 4155 | www.wab.edu
This school, located on Dong Lu, has over 1,400 students and 14 to 21 students per class. Following the International Baccalaureate from nursery (age 3) to grade 12, WAB is a model IT school with a wireless campus and a laptop ratio of 1:1 for grades five

to 12. Spread across a park-like campus, the provision for students is excellent, and includes libraries, art studios, sport fields, gyms, pool, climbing wall, and experimental outdoor education centre. After-school activities include sport or cultural and academic activities including Global Issues Network, Model UN and Roots & Shoots.

Honglingjin Park
5 Houbalizhuang
Chaoyang
后八里庄5号红领巾
公园
朝阳区
Map 7 E1 **49**

Yew Chung Int'l School Of Beijing 北京耀中国际学校

010 8583 3731 | www.ycis-bj.com
Affiliated with Yew Chung International Schools based in Hong Kong, this bilingual Beijing school offers education for pre-kindergarten to year 13. This school follows the National Curriculum for England leading to IGCSE or International Baccalaureate qualifications. There are 740 pupils with no more than 24 students in a class. The school has several computer and science labs, libraries, music suites, playground, gym, and new multipurpose auditorium. After-school activities include cooking, drama, dance, kung fu, drumming, Girl Scouts, swimming and sport.

University & Higher Education

Most foreign students tend to study at universities in the US or Europe, but increasing numbers are attending China's top institutions. Beijing has more than 70 universities. Peking (p.141) and Tsinghua (p.141) are arguably the best in China. Most of the schools are clustered around Wudaokou (p.96), the student area in Haidian district. While the locals must endure a rigorous admissions process, including sitting the *gaokao* (National University Entrance Examinations), expats are exempt from this and admission to these prestigious universities is pretty straightforward. An application, copies of visa and passport, school records, physical exam, photo, and proof of language proficiency is all most students need for undergraduate and graduate programmes. Language proficiency can be demonstrated by taking the Hanyu Shuiping Kaoshi (HSK) exam. Most schools require a score of level six (on a scale of one to 11).

Foreign students can expect to pay more in tuition, but fees remain markedly lower than in the United States or Europe. Tuition averages ¥23,000 ($3,200) to ¥48,000 ($6,600) annually and scholarships are available for expats. The most common are given by the Ministry of Education's China Scholarship Council (www.csc.edu.cn). This offers 100 scholarships per year to EU students, most of which bring a monthly stipend of ¥800 plus round trip airfare. Scholarships for other foreign nationals are also available, in an effort to encourage educational exchange. The Chinese government also awards the HSK Winner Scholarships (www.hsk.org.cn) for the top HSK test-scorers overseas. One scholarship is awarded per country where the test is administered.

Executive Education

Foreigners can study at Beijing's top schools without speaking a word of Mandarin. Programmes range from a few weeks to two years or more, with subjects varying from traditional Chinese medicine (TCM) to MBAs. To apply, complete the application form of your chosen institution, and provide a copy of your visa and passport, school records or diploma and photo. You'll also need to pass a physical exam. Tuition is moderate, between ¥19,000 and ¥28,00 a year for Chinese study at area universities.

2 Xisanhuan Beilu
Haidian
西三环北路2号
海淀区
Map 4 C4 **50**

Beijing Foreign Studies University (Beiwai) 北京外国语大学

010 8881 6438 | www.bfsu.edu.cn
This university teaches over 30 languages, including various strains of Chinese. Short term, bachelor's and master's programmes are available for expats. BFSU is in lively Weigongcun, which is a less crowded student area than Wudaokou. Tuition is ¥21,150 a year.

Beijing International MBA Program 北大国际MBA

Peking University
Haidian
颐和园路1号北京大
学中国经济研究中心
101室
海淀区
Map 4 B2 **51**

010 6275 4800 | www.bimba.edu.cn
BiMBA offers 18 month, full-time, 26 month part-time and two year executive MBA programmes taught in English. Graduates receive a degree from Fordham University in New York. It was ranked China's most valued part-time MBA by *Forbes* magazine from 2005 to 2007. Tuition is ¥120,000 (part-time), ¥150,000 (full time) and ¥290,000 (executive MBA).

Beijing Language & Culture University (BLCU) 北京语言大学

15 Xueyuan Lu
Haidian
学院路15号
海淀区
Map 4 D2 **52**

010 8230 3951 | www.blcu.edu.cn
BLCU accepts more foreigners each year than any other university. Short term, bachelors, masters and doctoral programmes are available. Expats mainly study Chinese and culture. Those who speak Mandarin can study IT, finance and accounting alongside Chinese students. BLCU offers online courses in Chinese and HSK training in English through www.eblcu.net. The vast campus includes basketball and tennis courts, library, gym, dining halls and shops. Tuition starts at ¥23,200 a year.

Beijing University Of Chinese Medicine 北京中医药大学

11 Beisanhuan
Dong Lu
Chaoyang
北三环东路11号
朝阳区
Map 5 B5 **53**

010 6428 6322 | www.bjucmp.edu.cn
This is one of the oldest higher learning institutions for traditional Chinese medicine (TCM). Expats can enroll for short term and undergraduate programmes in TCM, massage and acupuncture. No Mandarin is required for short term classes, but those on the undergraduate programme must take an entrance exam, and Chinese culture and language classes alongside the medical courses. Tuition is ¥30,000 a year, ¥3,400 for a one week course or ¥34,000 for a five month short term course.

The Central Academy Of Fine Arts 中央美术学院

8 Huajiadi Nan Jie
Chaoyang
花家地南街8号
朝阳区
Map 5 B5 **54**

010 6477 1019 | www.cafa.edu.cn
Foreigners need to score level four on the HSK entry exam to enroll as undergraduates, and level nine to enroll as doctoral students. Courses are available in art, art history and theory, architecture and design. Chinese study is available to non-speakers. The no-frills campus has numerous art and design studios, a library, lecture hall, language labs, multi-media classrooms and three dining halls.

Inter-University Program For Chinese Language Studies (IUP) 国际联合汉语培训项目

502 Wen Beilu
Tsinghua University
Chengfu Lu
Haidian
成府路清华大学文北
楼502室
海淀区
Map 4 C2 **55**

010 6277 1505
This university, formerly known as the Stanford Centre, was once headquartered at the University of California, Berkeley. Students must have taken two years of college Mandarin classes to attend this intensive language programme. Students can attend a 32 week, 16 week or eight week summer course and can apply, for an additional fee, to have credits transferred from Indiana University in the US. There is a student to teacher ratio of 3:1. Tuition costs ¥103,200 ($14,000) per year, ¥55,290 ($7,500) per semester and ¥31,700 ($4,300) for the summer.

Peking University (p.141)

1 Yiheyuan Lu
Haidian
颐和园路1号
海淀区
Map 4 B2 **56**

Peking University (Beida) 北京大学

010 6275 1230 | www.pku.edu.cn

This is the 'Harvard of China' according to its spiel. Peking accepts the second-largest number of expats each year, after BLCU, mainly through affiliations with foreign universities. Most study Chinese, but those who score level seven or higher on the HSK can study any subject they want. The extensive, green campus has basketball and tennis courts, a running track, cafeterias, restaurants, coffee shops, a gym, shops and a theatre. Tuition starts at ¥26,000 ($3,500) per year.

59 Zhongguancun Dajie
Haidian
中关村大街59号
海淀区
Map 4 C2 **57**

Renmin University Of China 人民大学

010 6251 1588 | www.ruc.edu.cn

Several short and long term programmes are available at this prestigious university, which is also known as Renda or the People's University of China. Its specialities are all in humanities and social sciences. Facilities include a library, dining halls and sports areas. The school organises many activities for students, including talent shows and trips.

Suite 2505A
CITIC Building, 19
Jianguomenwai Dajie
Chaoyang
建国门外大街19号国
际大厦2505A
朝阳区
Map 7 B2 **58**

Rutgers International Executive MBA 罗格斯国际EMBA 项目

010 8526 2528 | www.rutgers.cn

With so many of the expats in Beijing being high flying execs on the same pay scale they might get in London or New York, a few decide to invest their spare cash in career advancement. Rutgers offers a 14 month executive MBA programme, taught in English by Rutgers faculty. However, doing it in China isn't cheap or easy. Tuition is ¥302,250 ($41,000) and admission is competitive. Rutgers has 18 courses and each class has less than 45 students.

Chengfu Lu
Haidian
成府路
海淀区
Map 4 C4 **59**

Tsinghua University 清华大学

010 6278 4857 | www.tsinghua.edu.cn

China's answer to MIT offers short and long term Chinese language programmes, Chinese language study and international masters programmes in journalism, public policy, law, architecture and engineering that are taught in English. There are no undergraduate programmes in English, so level six on HSK must be achieved to enroll as an undergrad. Facilities include basketball and tennis courts, a running track, dining halls and shops. Student trips and special events are coordinated annually.

317a, Tower 2
Bright China Building
7 Jianguomennei
Dongcheng
建国门内大街7号光
华长安大厦2座317A
东城区
Map 7 B2 **60**

University Of Maryland 马里兰大学（中国中心）

010 6510 2600 | www.rhsmith-umd.cn

The University of Maryland offers the Smith Executive MBA programme in Beijing. The course takes 18 months and meets once a month for four consecutive days. Instruction is in English by Smith faculty, and students receive a degree from the University of Maryland's Smith School of Business. Tuition is ¥293,000 ($39,750) per year.

Special Needs Education

Many schools in Beijing can accommodate students with mild special needs. Most schools offer language support for students in several languages including English and Chinese. Australian International School of Beijing (p.130), Children's Learning Center of Beijing (p.128) and Daystar Academy (p.134) are among the schools offering English as a Second Language (ESL). Daystar Academy offers Chinese as a Second Language (CSL) while Lycée Français International de Pékin (p.138) has French as a second language.

Many international schools, like Beijing BISS International School (p.132) with its Optimal Learning Centre, and Beijing City International School (p.132) which has a learning support teacher, can assist students with mild to moderate learning difficulties, like Attention Deficit Disorder and dyslexia. Several nurseries and kindergartens like Children's Learning Center of Beijing (p.128) will accept students with mild speech problems. Many schools are open to accepting students with disabilities, provided the school is equipped to meet their requirements.

For students with more severe disabilities like autism, admission is determined after consultation of medical records and in-person interviews to access the student's needs. While most schools are willing to consider students with special needs, children with severe needs are often turned away. Only one school, Sunshine Learning Centre (below), is solely devoted to educating children with special needs.

The Parent Support Group (139 1029 7173) allows parents of children with special needs to share experiences and knowledge. The Selective Mutism Support Group (www.selectivemutismchina.gmxhome.de, or email selectivemutism.sgb@gmx.net) is a support group for families with children who have an anxiety disorder in which children have difficulty interacting in social situations including smiling, making eye contact and speaking.

Sunshine Learning Centre 阳光康复培训中心

89 Capital Airport Road, Legend Garden
Shunyi
首都机场路89号丽
京花园
顺义区
Map 3 E3 **61**

010 6454 9014 | www.dcbeijing.cn

Started in 2004 to provide an education for children with moderate and severe learning difficulties, this is the only special needs school in Beijing. In June 2007, it became part of Dulwich College (p.136). The school has seven students and three teachers, aided by a learning support team. It accepts children aged 5 to 18 and classes have one or two pupils. Classes are held from 09:00 to 15:00, Monday to Friday. Tuition is ¥147,440 ($20,000) and includes therapy time within school hours. Students have access to Dulwich College's art, music, drama and sport facilities, including the gym and pool. On Mondays, students from the International School of Beijing (p.137) run an activity programme and on Tuesdays, Sunshine's students have lunch with Dulwich College kids. Parents must provide copies of school reports in English from the past three years, previous medical reports and specialists' assessments, and liability and consent forms as part of the application process. Additionally, students will be assessed by the academic principal. The school is planning to relocate to its own campus to allow for larger enrolment in the near future.

Learning Mandarin

Your standard of life in Beijing will improve immeasurably if you can learn Mandarin. Patience and a smile will only get you so far. While locals are willing to be more accepting of foreigners than many expect, English is still spoken too rarely for residents to get by without at least a few phrases. The language centres listed are all reasonably priced, but foreigners can also learn Mandarin at one of Beijing's universities (p.139). Tuition at these tends to be between ¥19,000 and ¥28,000 a year.

Learning Mandarin		
Beijing Hutong School	010 6403 8670	www.hutong-school.com
Berlitz	010 6593 0476	www.berlitz.com
The Bridge School	010 8451 7605	www.bridgeschoolchina.com
Easy Peking	010 6538 9957	www.easypeking.com
Frontiers	010 6413 1547/8	www.frontiers.com.cn
Global Village	010 6253 7737	na
Imandarin	010 6568 8228	www.imandarin.net
Mandarin House	010 5203 6550	www.mandarinhouse.cn
New Concept Mandarin	010 8446 6455	www.newconceptmandarin.com
Taipei Language Institute	010 6461 2973	www.tli.com.tw

Transport

Other options **Getting Around** p.42, **Car** p.45

Beijing's traffic is a nightmare, and it's getting worse. At the time of the Athens Games in 2004, there were just over 2 million registered cars on the streets of the capital. By the time Beijing itself holds the games that number is expected to jump to more than 3.5 million. In 1994, traffic in the city moved at a brisk 45kph pace. Now the average speed has dropped to just 12kph, and it continues to fall.

Experts say that the city's traffic problems are not simply the result of having more cars on the road. The layout of the capital, which uses a system of six ring roads (with a seventh on the way) surrounding the cultural and political centres of the Forbidden City and Tiananmen Square, is much more symbolically than functionally effective. The city lacks great north-south thoroughfares and Changan Jie, which connects the capital from east to west is far from sufficient to handle the daily onslaught of commuters. As the former capital of the Bicycle Kingdom turns into a motor city, finding ways to ease traffic woes will be essential to Beijing's continued development.

Transportation Options

While there are many options for getting around the sprawling metropolis that is Beijing, none are ideal. Buses, while cheap, are overcrowded, slow and difficult to use if your Chinese is not at an advanced level. Bicycles and motorbikes are good choices in certain areas (especially in and around *hutong* neighbourhoods), but don't work well for long distances and can be dangerous in busy parts of the city where taxi drivers make liberal use of bike lanes. Most visitors get around the city using taxis or the subway. The subway system is currently undergoing major improvements, with four new lines to be added in 2008. By way of encouraging people to keep their cars at home, the city government has also lowered subway fares from ¥3 to ¥2. The experience is often claustrophobic, but more reliable than above ground transportation. Foreigners that don't live or work close to a subway stop generally make use of one of Beijing's 67,000 cabs. These cost ¥10 for the first three kilometres and an additional ¥2 per kilometre after that (at night, the cost goes up to ¥11 for the first three kilometres with an additional ¥3 per kilometre beyond that). Fears about dishonest drivers taking innocent foreigners for long rides around the city are seriously overstated, but even honest drivers often get lost. Knowing where you are going can save a lot of time and money.

New Drivers

As is true with any part of living in a new country, be aware of the official rules but don't be surprised or upset when the reality on the street is very different. While most drivers on the road follow traffic laws, there are always some who will cause chaos on the streets. Keep your cool and stay aware.

Do You Really Want A Car?

Other expats in Beijing choose to drive. While this proves convenient for some, many car owners in the capital find the proposition significantly more hassle than it's worth. Anyone considering driving in Beijing should take some time to think about whether or not it really makes sense for them. For families or individuals that need a break from the city on a regular basis, car ownership may be a logical choice. However, for travel within the city, driving a car is potentially much more expensive than relying on taxis. The parking situation alone should be enough to scare away a number of potential motorists. Normally, a city needs 130 parking places for every 100 cars; Beijing has only 73 slots for every 100 cars. It is not rare at all for drivers to find themselves arriving early at their destination only to spend the next hour searching in vain for a place to park.

Driving In Beijing

If you are absolutely determined to suffer the slings and arrows of car ownership, there are a number of things to be aware of. While traffic is often bearable outside the Fourth Ring Road, Changan Jie and the Second and Third Ring Roads are almost

always busy and can become carparks during morning and evening rush hours. Although there are rumours of a group called the *er huan shi yi* (Second Ring Eleven) who have purportedly circumnavigated the Second Ring Road in only 11 minutes, one would be very fortunate to make it around the loop once in two hours during peak traffic hours. Also, be aware that building complexes are not required to examine how their presence will affect traffic flow. Roads around developments (especially in the southern CBD) are often jammed. The worst slowdowns are often caused by accidents and breakdowns. Drivers more proficient in Chinese should make use of the traffic reports on the radio to avoid the worst of these.

Alcohol

Drink driving is a very serious offence in China. If you are pulled over with a blood alcohol level between 20mg per 100ml and 80mg per 100ml, you will be fined ¥500, lose six points from your licence, and forfeit your licence for one to three months. If you are caught with a blood alcohol level above 80mg per 100ml, you will be fined ¥1,800, lose your licence for six months, and may be forced to spend 10 days at your local police station. Drivers caught twice will lose their licence permanently.

Although the city's layout doesn't make for smooth traffic flow, it is relatively easy for drivers to orientate themselves. Most roads are laid out straight on either a north-south or east-west axis. The exceptions to this rule are in the Yizhuang and

Beijing traffic

Wangjing neighbourhoods where roads tend to fall in less geometric patterns. Signage in the city is usually clear, even if you are not a good Chinese speaker.

Drivers should be aware of a number of potential dangers on the road, most notably the suicidal road-crossing of pedestrians and cyclists. Traffic lights and crossings appear to have only the slightest influence on when and where people cross the street. While drivers in other countries will speed up when approaching a yellow light, doing so in Beijing is very dangerous due to the number of pedestrians who file into the road at the first possible moment. It is also typical for Beijing motorists to make left turns in the face of oncoming traffic with the expectation that cars will slow down or drive around them. Due to the unpredictability of traffic, the time it takes to go from one part of the city to another varies a great deal. At certain times, a car can make it from the CBD to Tsinghua University in Wudaokou in less than 40 minutes. At other times, it would take longer than that to drive the distance between two subway stops on Changan Jie. Getting to meetings and engagements on time requires some degree of foresight and, on occasion, psychic ability. Fortunately, traffic jams in the city are endemic to the point that Beijingers tend to be more flexible with issues of punctuality than people in other parts of the world.

Driving Habits

Drivers should be conscious of the fact that traffic laws are interpreted loosely. Never underestimate the ability of the driver next to you to do something stupid or dangerous and be especially careful when approaching pedestrian crossings or places where oncoming traffic may take a left turn. Do not expect other drivers to signal or acknowledge your right of way, and be aware that in the case of most accidents, bystanders will have a large say in determining culpability and will frequently side with Chinese drivers when there is ambiguity. Many drivers who get into accidents prefer to settle the matter with cash on the spot, rather than involve the authorities and risk losing points on their licence. However, you should recognise that doing so will cause you to forfeit any insurance claim you might wish to make. Although nearly every cab driver in the city uses their mobile phone on the road, it is technically against the law to do so.

Non-Drivers

As a motorist, be aware that pedestrians and cyclists will often cross the street without regard for their own personal safety. Crossing guards are grossly ineffective. If anything, show more caution at intersections where they are directing traffic. Raised pavements are safe for pedestrians, but cars so often make use of bike lanes that they should not be considered safe, especially in busy areas.

Traffic Rules & Regulations

You should only overtake, rather than undertake while driving. However, do not be surprised when other motorists break this rule. Speed limits vary throughout the city. Speed limits on the Second, Third and Fourth Ring Roads are 50 to 80kph. The limit on the Fifth Ring Road is 50 to 90kph. The limit on the Airport Expressway is 120kph. The limit on the Jingjingtang Expressway is 110kph. Limits are 70kph on main streets like Changan, Pingan and Qianmen. Special limits are posted in hazard zones and around schools.

Parking

Parking is a large problem throughout the city, especially in busy shopping areas. Depending on location, parking tends to cost between ¥1 and ¥10 per hour. Parking lots usually charge between 07:00 and 21:00 within the Fourth Ring Road, and car owners can normally arrange to pay monthly or annual fees for parking at their apartment complexes and work places. In most cases, annual costs for parking range from ¥500 to ¥2,000.

Petrol Stations

The top four petrol stations in China are Sinopec (China Petroleum & Chemical Corporation), CNPC (China National Petroleum Corporation), Shell and Mobil. Attendants pump your petrol for you. Some stations have non-petrol services, but there is a good deal of variation in what is provided. Prices at all four companies tend to be about the same. Petrol with octane level (marked with a 'hash') 90# is ¥4.99 per litre; 93# is ¥5.34 per litre (the national standard); 97# is ¥5.68 per litre; 98# is ¥6.27 per litre. Diesel with 0# is ¥5.29 per litre, 10# is ¥5.62 per litre.

Vehicle Leasing

If you want to lease a car, the best option is probably to hire a car with an English-speaking driver. This usually costs between $800 and $1,100 per month. Typically the best places to find information on cars for hire are in the listings of *City Weekend* (www.cityweekend.com.cn) or *That's Beijing* (www.thatsbj.com). Most car rental companies will not rent vehicles to foreigners directly. To rent a car, foreigners either must find a local Beijinger to rent the car for them, or get their company to rent the car. To be listed as a driver for a rental car, foreigners must have a Chinese driver's licence, a valid passport, a Beijing residence permit, and place a cash deposit.

Rental Costs & Tips

Deposits for month-long rentals range from ¥10,000 to ¥20,000 depending on the model. For daily rentals deposits range from ¥5,000 to ¥10,000. For Passats, Audis and Buicks the average rental price is between ¥7,000 and ¥8,000 per month or ¥400 to ¥500 per day. For Toyota Corollas the average rental price is between ¥4,000 and ¥5,000 per month or ¥180 to ¥200 per day. If a rental car breaks down, the driver should call the service centre offered by the rental company. The service centre should be able to provide on-site assistance within two hours. If the problem is serious, the rental company should provide the driver with another car. Be aware, however, that workers at the service centre will not be able to speak English. After returning a rental car, the

---

Born To Ride

Instead of driving, you can also hire a car with a driver. Depending on the model, this can cost between ¥500 and ¥3,000 per day but prices generally don't include tolls, fuel or parking fees. Hotels and furnished apartments can usually offer suggestions, and many English-speaking drivers advertise online. For hiring a full time driver (you provide the car, salaries are around ¥1,500 per month), see Driving, p.143.

---

rental company will take 20 days to check with the police about any accidents and to check the car for damages. If no fines have been incurred and no damage has been done to the car, the deposit will then be refunded. In the case of a fine or damage to the car, the renter must go to a police station to pay any fines or repair costs.

Renting A Limo

If you want to cruise Beijing in style, you can hire a limo for around $350 for eight hours. You can make your reservation at Beijing Limo (010 6546 1588). Check the website for prices on airport services and trips to the Great Wall (www.beijinglimo.com).

Company Cars

Whether or not you receive a company car or transportation stipend will depend a great deal on the company you work for and whether or not you were recruited locally. Even at top companies, less than half of local appointees receive any sort of transportation stipend, while more than 90% of executives arriving on global expat packages will be given access to a company car. Most companies are willing to offer employees a taxi stipend (usually around $200 to $500 per month) in lieu of providing a company car. However, these policies vary from company to company.

Vehicle Leasing Agents

Beijing Beiqi Taxi	010 8661 1062	www.beiqitaxi.com.cn
Beijing Beiqi Taxi	010 8766 5998	www.beiqitaxi.com.cn
Beijing YinJian Rental Company	010 8761 1468	www.yjzl.com
N.Star Rental Company - International Exhibition Center	010 6496 7388	www.bczl.com.cn
N.Star Rental Company - No 1 Automobile Service Center	010 6863 8838	www.bczl.com.cn
N.Star Rental Company - No 2 Automobile Service Center	010 6496 0916	www.bczl.com.cn
N.Star Rental Company - Wangjing	010 6475 2516	www.bczl.com.cn
N.Star Rental Company - Yayuncun	010 8499 2878	www.bczl.com.cn
N.Star Rental Company - Yuquanlu	010 8825 5826	www.bczl.com.cn
N.Star Rental Company - Zhongguancun	010 6263 8006	www.bczl.com.cn
North Peace Rental Co Ltd, Jianguomen	010 6528 0335	www.npcr.cn
Shouqi (China) Auto Lease Alliance	400 810 9090	www.sqzl.com.cn

Buying A Vehicle

Drivers have the options of importing a car, buying new or used through a dealer, or going through a private sale. Importing is probably the least attractive option (unless you desperately want a particular model), as the process is costly and the car may not pass Beijing's emissions inspection. The best deals can often be found through private sales, but these are riskier than buying at a dealership.

Buying a car in Beijing is surprisingly easy. You don't even need to be a Beijing resident; simply take your passport to the dealership. For the sake of convenience, the best places to go are 4S (sales, service, spares and survey) dealerships, which will help you through the registration process (p.147).

When buying a used car, try the same bargaining techniques (disinterest, disgust, and, occasionally, walking away) that you would at any Beijing market. Most used car dealers will offer to pay the transfer-of-ownership fee for you, but you should still be able to cut at least 10% of their initial asking price.

Private Sales

Many foreigners choose to buy used vehicles from other expats. But, if these deals go sour there is not much recourse available, so make sure you trust the seller. You will need your passport and the seller must provide a bill of sale, title, and registration.

There is no need to pay the purchase tax when buying a used car, but transfer of title can cost up to ¥900 depending on the make and model. For help buying or selling a car, check out Beijing Car Solution (www.car-solution.com).

Vehicle Finance

Car buyers who don't want to pay all at once can either go to the bank or turn to a financing company for help. Typically, financing companies charge interest rates that are about 1% higher than that of the banks (usually 6.9% over three years as opposed to 5.75% at the bank). However, they require lower downpayments (between 0% and 20% compared to 40% at most banks). Additionally, the process for getting the loan is easier than at a bank (applicants only need an ID card, proof of income and residential certificate), and processing time can be weeks faster than at a bank. Financing companies can also offer loan periods of up to five years, while banks typically expect car loans to be repaid in one to three years. Consult your dealer to find out what financing options are available to you.

Vehicle Insurance

To drive in China at the very least you need third person insurance. This will cost somewhere in the region of ¥1,000 each year. Most motorists choose to purchase insurance policies that cover damage and theft at a cost of ¥2,000 to ¥5,000 per year. Policies tend to be largely the same regardless of the insurance company. Each 4S (sales, service, spares and survey) dealership will have a particular insurance company that they work with, and can help set up your policy with that company when you buy your car. As is true elsewhere, insurance will cost more if you have a history of accidents and traffic offences.

Vehicle Insurance Companies

China Continent Property & Casualty Insurance	010 8251 5533	www.ccic-bj.com
CPIC	010 8402 4867	www.cpicbj.com
Ping An Of China Insurance	010 6621 0437	www.pa18.com
Sinosafe Insurance	010 6523 6288	www.sinosafe.com.cn

Registering A Vehicle

When buying through a dealer, much of the paperwork is done for you.
The car dealer should be willing to take you to get the car inspected at an Official Inspection Point and apply for the car's licence and plates at an Automobile Administrative Office (车辆管理所, 010 8762 5155, Public Security and Traffic Bureau, 18 Nansihuan Donglu, Chaoyang). Take your passport, residence permit, registration form, bill of sale and safety certificate. The emissions test at the inspection point costs around ¥200, while number plates and the car licence cost ¥145 and ¥20 respectively. Finally, you must pay a car tax of 8% of the total purchase price for cars made in China and 10% for imported vehicles.
Your car needs to take the emissions test every year and the sticker you receive when it passes should be displayed on the windscreen. Should the car fail the test you need to make the necessary repairs until deemed roadworthy.

Registration Services

Automobile Administrative Office	010 6839 9114
Beijing Car Purchase Surcharges Collection & Inspection Administration Office	010 6765 0033
Beijing Tax Bureau Foreign Section (to pay car user tax)	010 6779 9245
Beijing Vehicle Administration Office	010 6490 4379

Insurance

Most dealers will help you apply for insurance when you buy your car. However, you should remember that it will not be valid for 24 hours, so it may be better to leave it on the lot for a day, instead of taking to Beijing's hectic roads in an unfamiliar car.

Fines For Parking Infringements
Parking tickets range from ¥50 to ¥200. Drivers must find a nearby police station or ICBC to pay fines. Drivers will not lose points on their licence for parking infringements. You cannot pay fines over the internet.

Traffic Fines & Offences

Driving on Beijing's streets can sometimes feel like you are in a land without laws. However, there are traffic rules that prove costly when broken. Traffic violations in Beijing can result in anything from a small fine to a jail sentence. Fines should be paid promptly at your local ICBC (Industrial and Commercial Bank of China), police station, or at the location stipulated on the ticket.

Driving under the influence can result in jail time of between eight to 10 days. Driving with a suspended or cancelled licence can result in jail time of 15 days.

Driving Offences		
Parking fine	¥50 - ¥200	0 points
Driving without your licence	¥5	1 point
Not wearing seatbelt	¥50	1 point
Running a red light	¥200	3 points
Speeding		
Less than 50% over limit	¥200	3 points
More than 50% over limit	¥1,000	6 points
More than 50% over limit on expressway	¥1,800	6 points
Driving Under Influence		
Over 20mg/100ml BAL	¥500	6 points
Over 80 mg/100ml BAL	¥1,800	12 points
Driving with a suspended licence	¥200 - ¥2,000	na

Breakdowns

Breaking down in a place like Beijing can be scary, so you should always be prepared. In addition to all proper documentation, always keep a torch (and Chinese dictionary if you are not fluent) in your car and never drive without your mobile phone. If you are planning on travelling away from populated areas, make sure to take water.

If your car breaks down, move it to the side of the road quickly – if this can be done safely – and put on your hazard lights. It would add insult to injury if your car was to breakdown and you were fined (¥200) for blocking traffic. As soon as the car has been moved to a safe location, you should call a towing service. If you bought your car at a 4S dealership, they will have a road service provider that can help you. Likewise, if the car is leased or rented, the rental agency will have towing services that are available to

Recovery Services & Towing (24 hour)	
198 SOS Center	800 810 0198
Beijing Dalu Club SOS Center	010 6846 2626
Beijing Shenlong Fukang Club	800 810 0988
Gangan 'Drivers' Friends'	010 6491 2233
Wanhe SOS	010 6468 3838
Weisheng SOS Center	010 6261 5496

you. If your vehicle is not covered by either of these, there are a number of SOS services in Beijing that you can use. Write down the contact information for at least one of these and keep it in your car.

Finally, don't forget to contact your insurance company to claim reimbursement for any towing service fees. Tows are charged by distance, and a tow from Shunyi to downtown Beijing will usually cost between ¥300 and ¥400.

Traffic Accidents

Other options **Car** p.45

Road Rage ◀
Considering how many bad drivers there are in Beijing, it is surprising that levels of road rage are not higher. The most likely scenario for encountering a problem is in the event of an accident. Always do your best to be diplomatic and remain calm.

Sadly, traffic accidents are incredibly common in the Chinese capital. Reliable statistics are nearly impossible to find, but even the government mouthpiece *China Daily* admits that traffic accidents are the leading cause of death among children and teenagers in Beijing. Whether you are driving or walking along the street, be aware that the situation on the road is not some complex ballet. Traffic flow looks chaotic and dangerous because it is, not because people are just driving 'differently' from the way they do back home.

If you are in an accident, keep calm and don't panic. Stop your car in the spot that the accident occurred. If you can, take down the other driver's name, licence details, licence plate and car type. Take pictures of the car from different angles, but do not interfere with the scene. Try to enlist the help of bystanders as witnesses, but be aware that Chinese bystanders will often side with a Chinese driver if blame is ambiguous. Once you have properly documented the accident, move both cars to the side of the road or you will face a fine of ¥200 and a potential two-point deduction from your licence. If you and the other driver can decide who was at fault, it is not uncommon to try to reach an agreement about a cash settlement then and there to avoid involving the authorities. If not, police officers will assess responsibility and fines when they arrive on the scene.

Make sure to call the police (122) if the other driver doesn't have a licence, appears to be drunk, or becomes abusive. If someone at the scene is injured, call an ambulance (999) immediately.

In the event that you are pulled over or involved in an accident, you should always carry your Chinese driver's licence, your car's registration, and an insurance card when you are driving. You must report tickets or accidents to the insurance company (or to the car rental company in the case of a leased vehicle) within 48 hours. If the other driver is found to be at fault, you will pay nothing. If you are found to be at fault, you will have to pay 20% of the repair costs, as insurance only covers 80%.

Vehicle Repairs

If you purchased your vehicle from a 4S dealership (sale, service, spares and survey), it will be able to provide repair and maintenance services that are compatible with your car insurance. If you purchased the car by other means, you should check with your insurance provider for recommended garages. However, even if you choose a garage that has not been recommended, your insurance provider should still cover their share of the repair costs. You don't need to file a police report for repairs, unless the repairs are the result of a traffic accident. Car owners should take their car licence when they go for repairs.

Given the amount of available labour in China, it is surprising that there are so few motor mechanics around. This means that car owners hoping for amazing deals on repairs are likely to be disappointed. Standard procedures like changing a battery usually cost around ¥395 plus a ¥30 labour fee. Fixing broken air conditioning will cost somewhere in the region of ¥3,000 while installing airbags can set you back ¥16,000. The best insurance companies will pay 100% of the repairs without a deductible, but most car owners opt for cheaper policies that offer 80% coverage.

Vehicle Repair Services	
Beijing Bei Chen Wan Tong Trade Center	010 6443 8327
Beijing Car Trade Center	010 6443 7756
Beijing Jinlong Junjia Car Trade Company	010 6443 6878
Beijing Tengyuanxingshun Vehicle Service	010 8578 2682
Beijing Tian Yu Xiang Xing Vehicle Trade Company	010 6597 3883
Beijing Volkswagen Exhibition Center	010 6424 2955

Exploring

Exploring

Exploring

This is a city in flux. Affluent shoppers in designer labels walk among beggars, while ancient *hutongs* are tucked in the shadows of towering skyscrapers. And despite its history and traditions, change has been Beijing's one constant. It has had half a dozen names, seen dynasties demise and armies vanquished. The History section, p.3, has all the details.

The grid pattern started by the Yuan Dynasty and enhanced by the Ming Dynasty is still visible, though only two of the original nine gates to the city wall remain – Deshengmen and Zhengyangmen (today's Qianmen). Line 2 of the subway runs in a square along the Second Ring Road, marking where the city wall once stood. The nine stations with *men* at the end of their name mark where city gates used to be. Additional ring roads expand outwards, with most residents living within the Fifth Ring Road.

In the 80s, the city's tallest building was the 17 storey high Beijing Hotel. A quarter of a century on from the beginning of economic reforms, cranes dominate the skyline as Beijing remodels itself for the Olympics and beyond. Luxury hotels like the St Regis (p.36) and Ritz-Carlton (p.36) have opened, and English signs and language skills are (very) gradually becoming more common. Getting about should become more simple as the subway expands. Buses go everywhere (see www.bjbus.com or p.45) and taxis are cheap.

By 2020, Beijing will have the largest subway system in the world, with nine lines totalling 200km of track. Beijing Capital International Airport is building a new terminal, also the biggest on earth, which will whisk incoming passengers to Dongzhimen via a new airport subway line. The expansion will allow Beijing to handle more than 60 million international passengers a year. Some estimates suggest that China will become the most visited country on earth in the next decade.

It is easy to see the appeal. Beyond obvious tourist attractions like the Great Wall (p.197), Peking Opera (p.347), Tiananmen (p.162) and the Forbidden City (p.180), there are simpler pleasures to be found, like strolling through the *hutongs* in the south, having a drink in Sanlitun, rowing a boat in Houhai, or feasting in Chaoyang.

And the welcome can surprise many. Beijing doesn't have an easily identifiable image in the way that Shanghai and Hong Kong do, so many arrive not knowing what to expect. The friendliness of Beijingers (some taxi drivers aside) and their willingness to accommodate gormless, smiling westerners is one of the city's most pleasant surprises. There will be more to come.

Text & The City

Text your destination to Guanxi at 010 9588 2929 and instantly receive its address and phone number in English for ¥1 or in Chinese for an additional ¥1 (to show cab drivers).

The Great Wall (p.198)

Climb The Wall p. 197

Mao Zedong said '*Bu dao changcheng fei hao han*', or, 'You're not a real man until you climb the Great Wall'. Whether you visit the heavily restored Badaling (p.197), less crowded Simatai (p.198) and Mutianyu (Mutianyu Town, Huairou county, 010 6162 6505) or the desolate Jingshanling (Gubeikou, Luanping county, Hebei province, 031 4883 0222), seeing the Great Wall in all its glory is a must. You can even camp overnight on some sections.

Go Ride A Bike p. 44

There's no better (or scarier) way to get around than on two wheels – whether it's an old school Chinese Flying Pigeon or a new Giant. Bikes cost from ¥150 for an old beater to more than ¥21,000 for the latest imports. Just be sure to buy a huge lock as bike theft is rife (expect to buy two or three bikes a year.) Serious riders should check out Beijing Windspeed Bike Shop or Giant (p.253).

See Peking Opera p. 347

While not particularly easy on the ears, Peking Opera has been popular for more than two centuries. Those afraid of sitting through a marathon three-hour session with no intermission can opt to hear highlights. Li Yuan Theatre (Qianmen Hotel, 175 Yongan Lu, Xuanwu 010 8315 7297) is the best place for vignettes. See Theatre (p.347) for other options.

Stroll Tiananmen p. 162

Tiananmen Square has been the site of protests and celebrations throughout history. Located in the heart of Beijing, it's the world's largest patch of concrete, and a great place to watch people, fly a kite or amble about. Early birds can catch the daily flag raising ceremony at dawn.

Eat Duck p. 301

Roasted in a special oven, the skin on Peking duck is crispy, while the meat is tender. It is delicious wrapped in a thin pancake with scallions, sliced cucumbers and sweet plum sauce. Quanjude, established in 1864, is the best known (and most touristy) place to try Beijing *kaoya* (Peking duck). There are a dozen locations in Beijing but the one at 14 Qianmen Xi Dajie, Doncheng (010 6304 8987), where Mao and Nixon dined together, is the most famous.

Shop The Silk Market p. 297

Prepare to bargain hard at the Silk Market. This bustling, seven floor indoor market sells everything from pearls to silk to fake designer gear. It's a favourite with tourists and locals, and there's a Quanjude where you can tuck in to Peking duck after a day of shopping.

Play Games p. 207

On street corners and *hutongs* around town, the locals are crouched over small tables engrossed in majong or chess. Learn to play at the Chinese Culture Club (p.207) before trying your luck with the locals.

Have A Foot Massage p. 237

First your feet are soaked in hot water infused with tea and herbs. Then, while sitting in a comfy lounge chair, your feet are kneaded, patted and massaged. Head to Aibosen Blindman Massage (p.238) for a traditional and inexpensive treat.

Chow Hot Pot p. 301

Sitting around this bubbly pot of herbal broth (*huo guo*), diners place paper-thin sliced meats, noodles and vegetables in to cook, then dip them in sesame or peanut sauce. Beijingers like lamb the most, and while you can choose a non-spicy broth, locals opt for *ma la* (spicy). Try Hot Loft (8 Gongti Xi Lu, Chaoyang, 010 6501 7501) for individual servings with a good choice of broths and sauces.

Murder Some Music p. 300

Indulge in some god awful caterwauling in the privacy of your own karaoke room. Party Life (Zhengren Plaza, 9 Chaoyangmenwai Dajie, Chaoyang, 010 6708 6666) is open 24 hours and has buffet and drinks included in the room price. It's a popular place to sing western and Chinese tunes late into the night.

Gasp At Acrobats p. 347

Acrobatics has been a popular art form in China for more than 2,500 years. Head to Chaoyang Grand Theatre (p.347) to see breathtaking stunts performed every night. Alternatively, watch former flyers keep limber in a park (p.190)

Slurp Cha p. 324

For thousands of years, the Chinese have been tea-totallers. Head to Maliandao Tea Street (11 Maliandao Lu, Xuanwu, 010 6328 3014) to sample hundreds of teas or go to Confucian Teahouse (28 Guozijian Jie, Andingmenwai Dajie, Dongcheng, 010 8404 8539, to see *cha li*, the Chinese tea ceremony.

Hike The Fragrant Hills p. 190

Spend an afternoon hiking on Fragrant Hills. There's a chair lift to whisk you to the top if you don't want to climb. The view is spectacular, as is the clean, fresh air. It is especially beautiful in October and November when the leaves turn a vibrant red.

Mess About On The Water p. 191

Summer or winter, Beijing's lakes provide relaxation and entertainment. Take out a paddleboat in Chaoyang Park or head to Beihai Lake when it freezes over for skating or ice bike racing.

Buy Fakes p. 292

Whether it's software, Rolex watches, the latest Gucci bag or Burberry accessories, the Chinese are masters at creating fakes. From major markets like Silk Street (p.294) to impromptu kerbside stalls, cheap copies are everywhere – just be sure to bargain.

Explore The Tombs p. 198

The Ming Dynasty Tombs on the outskirts of town house the remains of 13 former emperors. Escape the heat with a descent into these cool catacombs. Visitors can combine their exploration with a visit to nearby sections of the Great Wall (p.197).

Learn Chinese p. 142

You don't need to be the next Dashan (a.k.a. Canadian Mark Rowswell) the *laowai* (foreigner) who mastered Mandarin and won the hearts of Chinese TV viewers, but it wouldn't hurt to learn how to say hello (*ni hao*) and thank you (*xie xie*). From pricey immersion classes at Tsinghua University (p.141) to bargain group classes at Global Village (p.142), there's a school and schedule for anyone who wants to learn a little Putonghua (Mandarin).

Fly A Kite p. 218

Buy a kite at San Shi Zhai Kite Store (Three Stones Kite Store, p.288) where the Liu family has been making bamboo frame kites for three generations. Then head to nearby Beihai Lake (p.191) and see how high you can fly.

Wander The Hutongs p. 170

There is no better way to see how the locals live than to walk the quickly disappearing *hutongs* (alleyways) of Beijing. Expect to see beer drinking, intense games of mahjong, pigeon walking, toddlers running around with *kaidangku* (pants with a slit in the crotch so youngsters can relieve themselves anywhere) and women steaming dumplings.

Enter The Forbidden City p. 180

Until 1925, no ordinary folk were allowed inside the imperial residence. This one square kilometre city warrants repeat visits, because there is simply so much to see. Try weekday mornings to avoid the crowds.

Marvel At The Temple Of Heaven p. 188

Popular with residents and tourists, this is where emperors of the Ming and Qing dynasties would come to worship and to pray for a good harvest. While the temple itself is impressive, seeing pensioners doing their morning exercise in the surrounding Tiantan Park is delightful.

Picnic At The Summer Palace p. 182

Do as Empress Dowager Cixi (p.4) did, and escape Beijing to enjoy the fresh air and peace along the tranquil Kunming Lake at the Summer Palace (p.182). Pack a picnic lunch and eat on the shore.

Meet The Giant Pandas p. 189

Head to the Beijing Zoo (p.189) and see the iconic, cuddly giant pandas. While there's plenty more to see here, including the Beijing Aquarium (p.174), the pandas are the main attraction.

Do Kung Fu p. 219

Get in shape by trying kung fu with Milun School of Traditional Kung Fu (Wangfujing, Dongcheng, 139 1072 4987, www.kungfuinchina.com). It offers bagua, taiji, sanda, xingyi and shaolin styles in its courtyard school and through private lessons in Ritan Park (p.192).

Dip In The Hot Springs p. 198

Head to the city limits and take a rejuvenating dip in soothing hot springs. Jiuhua Hot Spring Resort (p.198) is a favourite among locals. You'll be one of the few foreigners there, but signs in English will show you the way as you immerse yourself in more than 40 bubbly indoor and outdoor pools.

Learn To Bao Jiaozi p. 210

Everyone loves dumplings, so impress your guests by learning to wrap your own. The Peninsula Hotel's academy (p.35) offers 90 minute dumpling making classes, with advance reservations and a minimum of four people.

Experience The Cultural Revolution p. 293

Step back in time at The East is Red restaurant (266 Baijialou, Dong Wuhuanwai, Chaoyang, 010 6574 8289). Staff are clad in Mao suits and jubilant locals sing Mao's praises, do loyalty dances and wave little red flags. Otherwise, buy some authentic memorabilia at Panjiayuan market.

View The Wooden Buddha p. 189

The recently renovated Lama Temple (p.189) is one of Beijing's main heritage sites. It contains a brighly decorated Buddha, which is the largest in the world to be carved from a single piece of wood.

When you're lost what will you find in your pocket?

Item 71. The half-eaten chewing gum

When you reach into your pocket make sure you have one of these minature marvels to hand… far more use than a half-eaten stick of chewing gum when you're lost.

Explorer Mini Maps
Putting the city in your pocket

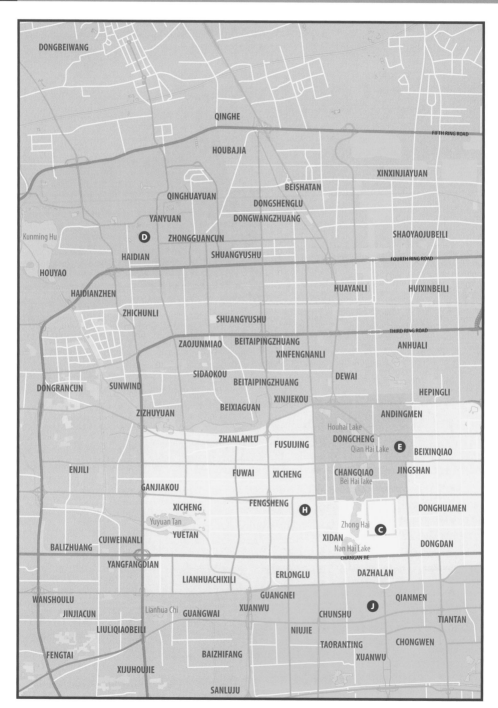

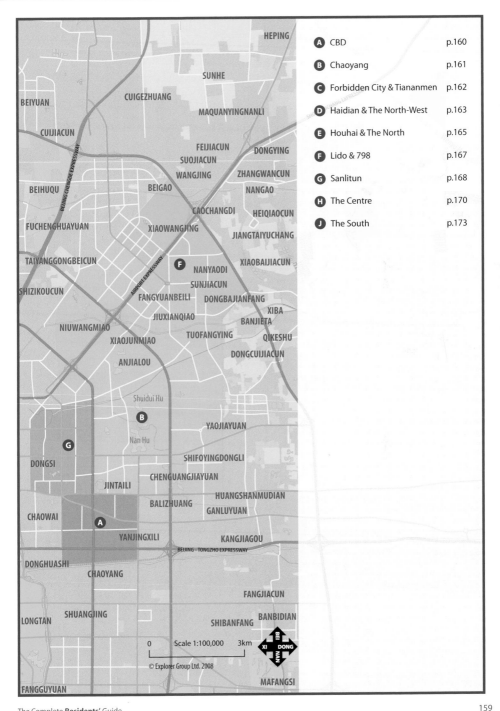

A	CBD	p.160
B	Chaoyang	p.161
C	Forbidden City & Tiananmen	p.162
D	Haidian & The North-West	p.163
E	Houhai & The North	p.165
F	Lido & 798	p.167
G	Sanlitun	p.168
H	The Centre	p.170
J	The South	p.173

Area **A** *p.158*
See also Map 7

CBD

The Lowdown
This area for earning and spending.

The Central Business District (CBD) is bordered by Chaoyang Beilu in the north, Tonghui River in the south, Dongdaqiao Lu to the west and Xidawang Lu to the east. It is part of Chaoyang district and is the centre of business activity in Beijing. It is also a good area for shopping, with the Silk Market (p.294), China World Shopping Mall (p.295), Kerry Shopping Mall (p.296), The Place (p.296) and Shin Kong Place (p.296) all in the area. The massive Jianwai SOHO (map 4 F2) complex, south of Jianguo Lu, is part of the CBD too.

The Good
A shopper's paradise, with markets for bargain hunters and designer goods for the fashion conscious, all accessible by subway.

Aside from shopping, the staggering new CCTV Tower, designed by Rem Koolhaas, is being built here and worth a visit.

This large area is sliced in half by the Third Ring Road, but Line 1 of the subway has stops near all the major points of interest, while Lines 1 and 2 intersect at Jianguomen.

This rapidly developing part of town aims to be the place for business people to meet, mingle and work. While most expats live north of here, cheaper rents and rapid expansion are luring more foreigners.

The Bad
If you live outside of Chaoyang, it's a long haul to get here.

Yong'anli Subway

Just outside the Yong'anli subway station lies the Silk Market (p.294), the largest and most popular in Beijing. Tourists and residents converge to haggle over fake goods, souvenirs, jewellery and silk. This older, quieter area is where most of the foreign embassies are found. They line the small, shady streets around Jianguomen.

The Must Dos
Check out the 'skyscreen' at The Place (p.296), one of only two in the world (the other is in Las Vegas). Haggle for souvenirs and fakes at the Silk Market (p.294).

The St Regis hotel (p.X36), a favourite among foreign diplomats, is steps from Jianguomen station. Behind the Friendship Store (p.264) on Jianguomen are family restaurants like Paul's Steak & Eggs (Xiushui Nan Jie, Jianguomenwai Dajie, Chaoyang, 010 6592 8088, www.steakeggs.com.cn) and Grandma's Kitchen (p.304), which both serve burgers, fries and homemade pies and are a short walk from the Silk Market.

Guanghua Lu

A 10 minute walk north of the Silk Market is Guanghua Lu, which has The Place (p.296). It is a massive shopping mall with a $32 million, 250m long and 30m wide TV screen suspended above the plaza. Further east on Guanghua Lu is the Kerry Centre (p.296) which includes the The Kerry Centre Hotel (p.35) Kerry Shopping Mall (p.296) and Kerry Sports (p.206), a massive gym with swimming pool, exercise classes and tennis courts.

West of The Place is the south gate of Ritan Park (p.192) which has the altar of the Temple of the Sun, one of the four royal shrines where emperors would make sacrifices to the gods. The park is often full of people fishing and practising tai chi.

Guomao Subway

One of the Guomao exits (follow the signs) empties in to the China World Trade Center (1 Jianguomenwai Dajie, 010 6505 2288, www.cwtc.com.cn), a complex of offices, residences, the China World Hotel and three floors of designer stores and restaurants. There is also an indoor ice rink.

A 15 minute walk south of Guomao is Jianwai SOHO, a complex of 16 white high-rises with all white interiors. These have apartments and offices, with 200 restaurants and shops on the lower floors. Chains of expat favourites including Annie's (p.315) are here as well as Beijing's only dark restaurant, Whale Inside Restaurant (Room 1037, Building 10, 010 5869 4235, www.whaleinside.com) where diners eat a set menu in total darkness. There's also a Jenny Lou's (p.297) and an outpost of Tongrentang (p.274), the most famous traditional Chinese medicine clinic and apothecary in Beijing.

Area **B** p.158
See also Map 5

The Lowdown
A bustling, modern, heavily developed area with a huge expat population.

The Good
There is a dizzying array of restaurants, shops and recreation. Many expats are based in the area, so it's convenient for working and socialising.

The Bad
The closest subway station is Dongzhimen, a long slog to the action at Chaoyang Park, Super Bar Street, Lucky Street and Lufthansa Centre.

The Must Dos
Wander Chaoyang Park. In the early morning, Chinese pensioners practise tai chi or sing revolutionary songs, and the afternoons are a great time to get in a pick-up game of football. Have a drink at Super Bar Street and drop by the Kempi Deli (p.264) for delicious desserts. Buy flowers at Liangma Flower Market (p.263).

Chaoyang

Similar to Lido (p.167) but more spread out, Chaoyang is a popular neighbourhood for expats to live, work and play. Set in the east, it extends roughly from Nongzhanguan Nanlu north to the Airport Expressway and Lido, and is set between the Third and Fourth Ring Road. Many expats live here for the proximity to the airport, international schools, corporate offices and nightlife.

The mammoth Chaoyang Park (p.191), with its acres of space and many activities, is a favourite meeting spot for families. Just a 10 minute walk north of the bustling Chaoyang Park West Gate is Lucky Street (Haoyun Jie) and another 10 minute walk north is Super Bar Street (Xingba Lu). All are crammed with popular clubs, bars and restaurants. A 10 minute walk south-west of Super Bar Street is the Kempinski Hotel and Lufthansa Centre on Liangmaqiao Lu. In the opposite direction on Liangmaqiao Lu is the city's only drive-in movie theatre, called, rather unimaginatively, Drive-In Movie Theatre (Liangmaqiao Lu, west of the East Fourth Ring Road, Chaoyang, 010 5165 2832, www.drive-in.net.cn). This shows Chinese and western movies nightly.

Chaoyang Park

Until the Olympic Green was built, this was the largest park in Beijing. Along the West Gate there are several good bars and clubs, including The World of Suzie Wong (p.344) and Goose & Duck Pub (p.332) and restaurants like Haiku by Hatsume (p.316) and the Italian chain, Annie's (p.315). There is also a Jenny Lou's grocery store (p.297). Inside, there's an amusement park with bouncy castle, carnival games and rides, including a ferris wheel. Patrons pay per ride or game. There are also football fields, where the French L'Equipe (www.frenchlequipe.com.cn) amateur football team plays and ClubFootball (p.213) hosts its five-a-side league on Monday to Thursday evenings and Sunday afternoons. The park also has ping pong tables, basketball, tennis and beach volleyball courts, which are all open to the public. Near the South Gate, there's also Sony ExploraScience, an interactive science museum that is popular with families.

Super Bar Street

The main rival to Bar Street in Sanlitun, Super Bar Street was built to provide more bars and restaurants for night-owl expats. The small L-shaped street off Tiantan Lu has popular eateries like Dini's Kosher Restaurant (p.320) and Biteapitta (p.320). There is also Tim's Texas Roadhouse (p.305), where runners from the Boxer Hash (www.boxerhash.com) and Hash House Harriers (www.hash.cn) meet on Sundays to go for long distance runs before tucking in to the restaurant's Tex-Mex food.

Lucky Street

Lucky Street is more of a strip mall than a street, with all the action confined to the south side of the road. It is also a little more family friendly, and has many international restaurants, including Ottoman Turkish Cuisine and South German Bakery, which bakes authentic German pastries and breads. There's also Lohao City (p.267), an organic supermarket. While it does attract a crowd after nightfall, most grab a bite to eat and then move on.

Lufthansa Centre

The Lufthansa Centre, adjacent to the Kempinski Hotel (p.35), has a multi-storey department store selling cosmetics, clothes and accessories. The 24 hour International Medical Center (p.118), two great German restaurants – Kranzler's and Paulaner Brauhaus and several shops, including a luxury car dealership are also here. Inside the Kempinski Hotel is Kempi Deli (p.264), a favourite hangout among expats who feast on some of the best pastries and desserts in town.

Area **C** *p.158*
See also Map 10

Forbidden City & Tiananmen Square

This is the centre of Beijing's universe. Once off limits to anyone outside the court and its staff, the Forbidden City (p.180) opened it's doors on October 10, 1925. For the first time, ordinary folk could look inside the former home of Ming and Qing emperors. Directly to the south, Tiananmen Square has witnessed some of the most momentous events in China's history.

The Lowdown
The most historically important area in Beijing.

The Good
Everything is within walking distance and many attractions, like Tiananmen Square and Mao's Mausoleum, are free.

The Bad
The Forbidden City and National Museum of China are so crammed with things to see that it's impossible to cover in just one day. Sites become irksomely crowded.

The Must Dos
Witness the dawn flag raising ceremony, particularly on October 1 (National Day) when people from across the country stand in silence all night, awaiting day break, to celebrate the founding of the republic.

Forbidden City

The imperial home of 24 emperors for 491 years, this is officially called The Palace Museum. About a third of the complex is open to the public, with extensive renovations due to be finished by 2020. At least one palace will be under renovation at any given time for the next 12 years.

There are three parts; the outer court, inner court and imperial garden. The emperor received visitors in the outer court, while he, the empress and eunuchs lived in the inner court. The imperial family would relax in the garden. Prepare to spend an entire day here, though even that won't be enough to see everything. Those looking for a break can turn to several restaurants inside the city's walls, but Starbucks was told to decamp in 2007. See p.180 for more.

Tiananmen Square

After Mao expanded it in 1949, Tiananmen became the world's largest public square, at 440,000sqm. It has been a gathering place during the most pivotal points in modern Chinese history – from the May Fourth Movement in 1919 to a huge party to celebrate the successful bid for the 2008 Olympics in July 2001.

Points of interest include the Monument to the People's Heroes, a marble and granite obelisk depicting people in revolt, and Chairman Mao's Memorial Hall where the big man's preserved body is on display. West of Tiananmen is the Great Hall of the People, home of the National People's Congress (China's parliament). At the north end is the Tiananmen Rostrum, where Mao declared the founding of the People's Republic of China on October 1, 1949. Each day at dawn, members of the National Liberation Army perform a flag raising ceremony that takes two minutes and seven seconds – the exact time it takes for the sun to rise. Onlookers watch in silence while vehicles driving down Changan Jie screech to a halt. A flag lowering ceremony is repeated at sunset, when the square closes. East of Tiananmen is the National Museum of China (p.186) which showcases 5,000 years of Chinese history but is currently closed for renovation until 2010. Steer clear of the friendly 'art students' who want to take you to their 'galleries' for a tour. This is a scam to get foreigners to buy fake art.

The geographical and political centre of Beijing, the square was originally little more than an ornate corridor leading through to the Forbidden City. But, starting in 1911, it was expanded at the expense of the surrounding structures (many of which were important temples and courtyards). Since 1949, the communists have made the square their own, flanking its two sides with the soviet style Great Hall of the People and the National Museum, and placing Mao's preserved body in a mausoleum at its centre.

While political meetings are no longer welcome, millions flock to the square on October 1 to celebrate the birth of the PRC. The rest of the year it is filled with tourists, kite fliers and people trying to hawk tacky Mao-related souvenirs.

Forbidden City entrance

Area **D** *p.158*
See also Map 4

Haidian & The North-West

Starting south of the Third Ring Road and extending almost to the Fifth, this vast area in the north-west is the academic and technological part of town. With dozens of universities, including China's top two; Peking (p.141) and Tsinghua (p.141), this area is home to thousands of Chinese and foreign students. Aside from cheap rent, schools and hip cafes and hangouts, there's a lot of historical ground to cover, and it's all accessible on the Line 13 light rail.

The Lowdown
An area defined by its student and Korean populations.

The area has seen rapid development in recent years, with most of the *hutongs* knocked down to make way for apartment blocks. More and more foreigners are moving to the area to be close to what's dubbed the Silicon Valley of Beijing. Tsinghua Science Park, just west of the light rail station, is home to Google's offices. Several international chains are building hotels nearby, and the foreigners who are not on expat packages know the area's assets.

The Good
A haven for the college crowd and those with limited budgets, there's enough cultural and recreational entertainment to be self contained.

Third Ring Road

East of Zaojunmiao Lu and along the Third Ring Road is the Great Bell Temple (p.187), home of the largest bell in China. This is rung every New Year's Eve and during Spring Festival. The temple also has a set of Ming-style chimes and Yuan and Song dynasty bells.

The Bad
It can feel like living on a college campus. The traffic on weekend nights is horrible and, whether by taxi or subway, it's a long haul to places like the city centre and Chaoyang.

Wudaokou

Affectionately nicknamed The Wu, this is the centre of university life in Beijing, where international students come to party and mingle. At the foot of Wudaokou light rail station lies Huaqing Jiayuan, a complex of pink high rise apartments popular with Koreans. On a clear day, you can see the mountains just north-west of town. Chengfu Lu is the main road in Wudaokou, connecting Peking University in the west, Tsinghua University in the middle and Beijing Language and Culture University in the east. The first and second floors of Huaqing Jiayuan, which face Chengfu Lu, house the most popular establishments in the neighbourhood. They offer affordable, trendy clothing stores, cheap eats, late night munchies and watering holes. The atmosphere at Lush (p.334), a 24 hour American restaurant and bar and its sister Pyro Pizza (Basement, Building 12, Huaqing Jiayuan, Caijing Dong Lu, 010 8286 6240, www.luahbeijing. com/pyro), is more American than Chinese. These offer beer pong tournaments, open mic nights and fraternity-style 'rush' weeks each semester, to help orientate new international students.

The Must Dos
Stroll through Peking University and, if it's winter, go iceskating on Weiming Lake. Visit Yuanmingyuan and the Summer Palace.

The Bridge (Second Floor, Building 12, Huaqing Jiayuan, Caijing Dong Lu, 010 8286 3094), a 24 hour coffee shop serving pastries, paninis, fresh soups, coffees and teas is a popular student hangout. The new U-Centre, a 16 storey office and apartment complex with shops on the lower floors, has more retail and dining options. There is an outpost of Grandma's Kitchen serving western food for homesick students. A 10 minute walk to the east, on the BLCU campus, is Bla Bla Bar (p.328), a steady favourite among students. There are several clubs, including Propaganda (p.337), a sweaty spot that attracts the student crowd, Club 13 (next to D-22 on Chengfu Lu, 010 8262 8077) and D-22 (p.343), a surprisingly hip music joint worth a trip across town to see live music, particularly punk bands.

Wudaokou is also home to many small Chinese language schools. With the cheapest classes in Beijing, Global Village (p.142) is a popular choice among money-strapped students, while 1on1 Mandarin (Room 503, Building 7, Huaqing Jiayuan, Chengfu Lu, 010 8286 3272, www.1on1mandarin.com) and That's Mandarin (west of Wudaokou light rail station, 136 0123 4071, www.thatsmandarin.com) also have a loyal following. Just east of the light rail station down Wangzhuang Lu is Beijing's Koreatown.

Zhongguancun

While this huge thoroughfare seems to always have bumper-to-bumper traffic, it's worth trekking across town to visit the Zhongguancun Electronics City (p.276), for any conceivable gadget or computer part. The nearby Gate City Mall (Zhongguancun Dajie, Haidian, 010 8248 6666 www.thegate.cn), Zhongguancun Mall (p.296) and shopping street have all the same stores as the malls out east, but are worth a look if you're in the area. The new subway Line 4, due to open at the end of 2008, will make this area more accessible.

Peking University & Beyond

Peking University, the 'Harvard of China' is a popular destination for Chinese tourists, who come to have their pictures taken on the sprawling campus. It is worth visiting the recently renovated Arthur M Sackler Museum of Art and Archaeology (p.185) at the campus' west gate. It houses 10,000 pieces, including a 280,000 year old pre-human skeleton, and Shang and Tang dynasty artifacts. Also try to catch a cheap play or concert at Peking University Hall (010 6275 1278, www.pku-hall.com), which hosts national and international acts all year.

Just north of Peking University is the Old Summer Palace, and Yuanmingyuan Remains Park. The park is less touristy than the Summer Palace (p.182), which can be reached from Wudaokou light rail station by bus or a ¥15 to ¥20 taxi ride. Climbing Longevity Hill will give you a good view of the park and Western mountains. Nearby is Fragrant Hill (p.190), a peaceful mountain that takes about two hours to hike up but provides breathtaking views and fresh air. At the base of the mountain are many small shops and family restaurants. Two kilometres east, are the Botanical Gardens (p.190), with 6,000 species of plants. Fragrant Hills and the Botanical Gardens are accessible by taxi or bus 333 from Yuanmingyuan Remains Park or bus 904 from Xizhimen subway station.

Beijing Zoo (p.190)

The Summer Palace (p.182)

Kunming Lake

The Aquarium (p.174)

Area **E** *p.158*
See also Map 8

Houhai & The North

Houhai is directly north of Tiananmen Square and just south of subway Line 2. Because of its proximity to the Forbidden City, this area was historically home to court officials and the city's elite. Some of their residences still stand. Today the area has noisy

The Lowdown
Dozens of bars, restaurants and clubs around three lakes.

bars and restaurants, and China's middle class and expats eager to live in *siheyuans*, traditional courtyard homes.

Historic sites include the Drum and Bell Towers (p.179) and former residences of literati and court officials, including revolutionary author Guo Morou (18 Qianhai Xijie, Xicheng, 010 6612 5392), Song Qingling, Sun Yat-sen's widow (46 Houhai

The Good
Houhai is a great place to get outdoors, by sailing on the peaceful lakes, cycling through old alleyways and strolling along the lakes.

Beiyan, 010 6404 4205), and Chinese author, Mao Dun (13 Yuanensi Hutong, Doncheng, 010 5304 4089). Prince Gong's Mansion (p.184), a courtyard home that housed Heshen, a corrupt member of Emperor Qianlong's imperial guard, can also be found in the area.

The Lama Temple and Confucius Temple are nearby, along with lesser known temples like Guanghua (31 Ya'er Hutong, Xicheng, 010 6403 5032).

Aside from the alleyways and historic sites, what attracts most people is the variety of bars and restaurants. Lotus Lane and Yandai Xiejie are two popular strips along Qianhai

The Bad
Loud music, tacky neon lights and overly eager bar-staff who try to lure you inside have transformed this once peaceful retreat into an all-night drinking spot.

Lake. The strip along the western bank of Qianhai and Houhai lakes is also popular, as well as the renovated Nanluoguxiang Hutong, east of the lakes. North of the lakes are the National Stadium (p.228) and National Aquatics Centre (p.228), known as the Water Cube, built for the 2008 Olympics.

The Lakes

The Must Dos
Have a drink and soak up the atmosphere at the rooftop Drum and Bell (p.331).

Three artificial lakes called Qianhai, Houhai and Xihai, are surrounded by more than 100 bars and restaurants and some well-preserved *hutongs*. The lakes were part of the canal system that used to run through Beijing. By day, they are an idyllic place for renting a boat or taking a leisurely stroll. While the locals complain that the noisy bars with neon lights have sent the neighbourhood downhill, Houhai and its lakes remain a favourite retreat.

The local dragon boat racing club rows here on Wednesday nights and Sunday mornings during the warmer months (p.212). On weekends, families can be seen maneuvering boats on the lakes or riding in rickshaws. Paddleboats and electric boats can be rented along the lakes at Houhai Nanyuan (010 6616 2868). River Romance (Qianhai Xiyuan, Lotus Lane, 010 6618 5806) will rent you old-style wooden boats with an oarsman, and include a musician for an extra ¥100.

Cycling along the lake is also popular. Bicycles can be rented at Sihai Dedo (8 Houhai Beiyan, 010 8401 6501) and Shuangren Yizhan (Qianhai Nanyan). For those who don't want to break a sweat, cycle rickshaws can also be rented. Be sure to haggle, and don't pay much more than ¥60 an hour. Popular restaurants include Hutong Pizza (9 Yindingqiao Hutong, Dongcheng, 010 6617 5916, www.hutongpizza.com), located in a 900 year old nunnery west of Houhai Lake, and Jiumen Xiaochi (1 Xiaoyou Hutong, Xicheng, 010 6402 5858) which sells traditional Beijing snacks on the north side of Houhai Lake.

Lotus Lane

A hub for many big, glitzy bars, with plenty of outdoor seating, night owls congregate along this strip at spots like Lotus Blue (Lotus Lane, 51-56 Dianmen Dong Dajie, 010 6617 2599) and Buffalo Bar (6 Lotus Lane, 51-14 Dianmen Xi Dajie, Xicheng, 010 6617 2242). There is also a Starbucks at the top.

The touts offering trips to nearby 'lady bars' can be annoying, as can the wandering vendors flashing laser pens at passers by. A firm 'no thanks' to the former and shake of the head to the latter is normally enough if you're not interested. Both groups can be persistent, but are rarely aggressive. Ballroom dancers can be seen nightly at the end of the strip, spinning serenely to pop waltzes in the open air. It is one of Beijing's most surreal and pleasant sights.

Yandai Xiejie
A walk down this winding, cobblestone street, with its bars, restaurants and small shops, gives an idea of what old Beijing looked like.

Nanluoguxiang
This heavily renovated *hutong* is a haven for backpackers, who flock to the cosy bars, coffee shops and restaurants that line the small, newly paved alleyways. Popular spots include the Passby Bar (p.336), eateries like Paper (p.309), cheeky Beijing-themed T-shirt vendor Plastered 8 (p.260), gig venue MAO Livehouse (p.335) and the late night snack outlet Fish Nation (p.305).

Andingmen Dong Dajie
Ditan Park (p.191) is to the north and the Confucius and Lama temples are just to the south of Andingmen Dong Dajie. Next to Yonghegong (Lama Temple) subway station, the heavily incensed Lama Temple (p.189) is a lamasery for the yellow hat lama sect of Buddhism and home of the world's largest wooden carving of Buddha. Just to the west of the Lama Temple is Confucius Temple (p.187) which houses the former academy where civil servants trained for exams to gain entrance to the court. Walk north to Andingmen Dong Dajie and Ditan Park, a favourite among kite fliers.

North Of The Third Ring Road
Cycle or take a taxi north of the Third Ring Road to visit the China Science & Technology Museum (p.185), which includes China's first space capsule and exhibits on ancient Chinese science. Continue north to see Olympic Green, the city's largest green space, which is home to the National Aquatics Centre (p.228), National Stadium and Olympic Sports Centre. West of the Olympic Sports Centre is the Chinese Ethnic Culture Park (1 Minzuyuan Lu, Chaoyang, 010 6206 3646), a theme park consisting of buildings and costumed people paying homage to China's ethnic minorities.

Jiugulou Dajie
The Drum and Bell Towers (p.179) are just east of Jiugulou Dajie. In the same square is the Drum and Bell (p.331), a bar with a rooftop terrace full of comfy couches where locals and expats enjoy a pint while soaking up the atmosphere.

Beihai Park (p.191)

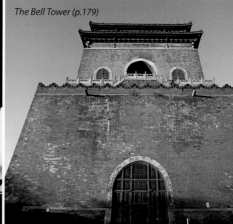
The Bell Tower (p.179)

Area **F** *p.158*
See also Map 5

Lido & 798

This area is bordered to the west by the Airport Expressway, to the east by Jiuxianqiao Lu and extends south to around the Fourth Ring Road. It was expat central when foreign families first arrived in Beijing, and before the development of villas in Shunyi (p.95). Commercial buildings, rather than historical landmarks, are the reference points in this neighbourhood. The area's nucleus is the Holiday Inn Lido (below) and its complex of shops. Lido Garden to the east and Side Park to the south offer green space to relax and play football, practise tai chi or fly a kite.

Today, this small, walkable area is still home to expat families and has foreign schools, restaurants, grocery stores, shops and hospitals. There is the largest international hospital, Beijing United Family Hospital (p.118), as well as AmCare Women's & Children's Hospital (p.116). Those who don't live in the area come to buy comfort food at Jenny Lou's (p.297), to eat at the restaurants, or drop their kids off at school. Eton International Bilingual Academy (p.129), Eton International School (p.129), International Academy of Beijing (p.137) and 3e International Kindergarten (p.128) are all here.

To the east of Jiuxianqiao Lu lies Dashanzi, better known as the 798 art district, an area that once housed top-secret weapons factories. After the state-owned land was sold in the 80s, artists, evicted from their commune at the Old Summer Palace, started to move in to the well-lit, empty factories. By the 90s the area had transformed into gallery and work spaces. In recent years, 798 has come under threat as developers realise the area's value.

The Lowdown
The place to see the latest in China's art scene and stock up on foreign comfort food.

The Good
Walking or biking around is quick and convenient. Plenty of good restaurants and leisure activities, plus a thriving cultural scene at 798.

The Bad
There's no subway stop, so cabbing it, driving, or taking a long, cramped bus ride are the only transport options.

The Must Dos
Go gallery-hopping in 798, have a coffee while browsing the books at Timezone 8 (p.254) or snack on a crepe at Vincent Café (2 Jiuxianqiao Lu, 010 8456 4823).

Holiday Inn Lido

The hotel has an arcade that includes a branch of Eric Paris Salon (p.235), the Cosmic bowling alley and Lido Pool (6 Jiangtai Lu, Chaoyang). There are many popular restaurants, including Pure Lotus (p.332) and Indian restaurant, The Taj (p.315). Down the street along the north-east side of Lido Garden is Fangyuan Xi Lu. This small street has trendy homewares shops, including Spin (number 6, 010 6437 8649, www.spinceramics.com), which sells ceramics, Kartell (number 4, 010 6436 3281, www.kartell.it), a furniture store specialising in chairs, and Kang Deco (p.271), which sells contemporary Asian furniture and offers decorating services.

Hairun International Condominiums

One block east of the Holiday Inn, these condos are home to hundreds of expats. A row of first floor shops and restaurants include a Starbucks, Coups Bakery, Jenny Lou's grocery store, family-favourite Peter's Tex-Mex Grill (2B Jiangtai Lu, 010 5135 8187) serving the thickest milkshakes in Beijing, and Tom's DVDs (p.277). This reliable DVD and CD store is in the basement of Tom's Embroidery.

Side Park

Along the north-east side of the park on Jiangtai Xi Lu are popular restaurants and bars, including Frank's Place (p.331), Il Casale (010 6436 8778) and The Cellar (010 6437 8399). Inside the park, there's a small lake and plenty of space. It is a popular meeting point for sports groups, including Beijing International Badminton Club (p.207), which plays at the indoor badminton centre across from the Rosedale Hotel on Wednesday evenings and Sunday mornings. ClubFootball's (p.213) five-a-side league play here every evening from Monday to Thursday and on Sunday afternoons.

798

This collection of galleries is so large that you could easily amble about for days. Highlights include the latest exhibits at New Long March Space (4 Jiuxianqiao Lu, 010 6438 7107, www.longmarchspace.com) and Red Gate Gallery (p.177). At Café (p.324) is a popular spot for lunch.

Area **G** *p.158*
See also Map 9

Sanlitun

Between the Second and Third Ring Roads, Sanlitun is bordered by Gongti Nanlu in the south and Liangma River to the north.

The Lowdown
This is a place for mingling. You can eat, drink and be merry daily.

Technically within Chaoyang, this area is such an expat hub that it merits it's own entry. It is close to the homes of many foreigners, who flock here for dinner and drinks. It is packed with bars, restaurants and clubs and is a favourite socialising spot, especially among singles and the college crowd. Among the neon clubs and tacky discos are many fine restaurants, cafes, shops and bars.

The Good
The dozens of watering holes make this a great area for pub crawling and club hopping.

The area can be reached from the Dongsishitiao and Dongzhimen

Sanlitun nightlife

The Bad
The traffic at weekends is horrendous and the area is overrun with rowdy and, sometimes obnoxious, foreigners at night.

subway stations on Line 2 and most of it is walkable, though strolling from north to south would take a couple of hours. There are many restaurants and clubs along Gongti Xilu and several good restaurants by Workers' Stadium. Nan Sanlitun Lu has a great cluster of restaurants south of Gongti Beilu.

The Must Dos
Watch the ballroom dancers in front of Workers' Stadium, and join in if you're brave enough. Go to happy hour at The Den (p.330) for half price pizzas and drinks specials from 17:00 to 22:00 daily. Eat a gelato at Gustomenta (p.325). Go clubbing at Cargo (p.342) and refuel next door at Bellagio (p.306) with a huge tower of their shaved-ice desserts.

Other areas to explore include the Sanlitun bar strip, Nali Mall and 3.3 Mall, and Tongli Studios, a block of bars north of Gongti Beilu. Another cluster of shops, restaurants and bars lies north of Dongzhimenwai Dajie, between Sanlitun Beixiao Jie and Sanlitun Beilu.

Workers' Stadium Area

Just off Gongti Beilu, and a five minute walk from Dongsishitiao station, is the newly renovated Workers' Stadium. Every night old Beijingers converge out front to show off their ballroom dancing skills. On the sidewalks along Gongti Beilu are glass cabinets with the day's newspapers inside.

The Kro's Nest (p.304), which serves up the largest pizzas in town, is a good spot for dinner or late night munchies. At the north gate of Workers' Stadium is the Emma/Ticketmaster window, where the city's most popular concert, sports and entertainment tickets can be bought (010 6551 6590).

Just west is Workers' Gymnasium, where concerts are often held. Gongti Xi Lu runs between Workers' Gymnasium and Workers' Stadium and has a few good night spots. Babyface (p.341), Cargo Club (p.342) and other big clubs are here, along with Gongti 100 bowling alley (p.208), a KTV club, and Bellagio (p.306), a Taiwanese restaurant that is open until 04:00 and popular among clubbers for its terrific desserts. A few metres south and across the street is Destination (p.345), a well-liked gay and lesbian club.

Continue south on Gongti Xi Lu until you reach the intersection with Gongti Nanlu, where you'll find the French Cultural Centre (Guangcai International Mansion, 18 Gongti Xi Lu, 010 6553 2627) on the north side of the street and Instituto Cervantes (1 Gongti Nanlu, 010 5879 9666) several metres east and on the south side. One block over is Blue Zoo (p.176) an aquarium with a huge coral reef that's popular with families. Walk another block east and south and you'll come to Fundazzle (p.218), a favourite play space among children, with an indoor jungle gym, ball pit and climbing wall.

Nan Sanlitun Lu

Running north to south, Nan Sanlitun Lu intersects with Gongti Beilu. South of Gongti Beilu are maze-like narrow streets, with popular restaurants like Hot Loft (4 Gongti Beilu, Chaoyang, 010 6501 7501) and Pink Loft (6 Sanlitun Lu, 010 6506 8811) and English-language bookshop and cafe, The Beijing Bookworm (p.254). An institution among expats, this shop can order hard-to-find or banned books, and has an extensive foreign magazine selection. It has monthly events like wine tastings, book signings, lectures and play readings with Beijing Playhouse (p.347), an English-language community theatre, (www.beijingplayhouse.com). There's also a weekly children's story time.

One block east is Pacific Century Place (p.296), which has a huge six-storey department store with an extensive international grocery in the basement.

On the north side of Nan Sanlitun Lu is the Sanlitun bar strip with a dozen neon lit bars. Past this strip is Nali Mall on Sanlitun Lu, a mix of small shops that includes Jiali Manicure (010 6417 8565), a favourite among expat women for a hygienic and inexpensive manicure and pedicure.

Tongli Studios Area

Just north of Sanlitun bar strip, on the west side of Nan Sanlitun Lu, is another labyrinth of streets crammed with bars and cafes, including Poachers (p.336) and The Tree (43 Sanlitun Houjie, 010 6415 1954, www.treebeijing.com) along with small eateries like Fish Nation 1 (p.305), which serves up late night fish and chips. Tongli Studios has chic bars and cafes like Bar Blu (p.342). Just north of Tongli Studios is 3.3 Shopping Mall (p.295), a five-storey mall with hundreds of cubicle-sized shops. These are all owned by local designers, and attract a young crowd looking for the latest fashions and accessories at cheap prices.

Dongzhimenwai Dajie & North

Dongzhimenwai Dajie is a large boulevard connecting Lines 2 and 13 of the subway and an important reference point. Its close proximity to two subway lines, Sanlitun and Chaoyang, international schools and corporate offices mean many expats choose to live here.

Just north of Dongzhimenwai Dajie is a cluster of cafes, restaurants and shops, nestled between Sanlitun Beixiao Jie and Sanlitun Beilu. The quiet, tree lined streets are more relaxed and attract less drinkers than Sanlitun Bar Street.

The area has several grocery stores which stock expat favourites, including a Jenny Lou's (p.297) and its competitor April Gourmet (1 Sanlitun Bei Xiaojie, 010 8455 1245). Chic French linen store Rouge Baiser-Elise (Sanlitun Xi Wu Jie, 010 6464 3530), Beijing International SOS Clinic (p.118) and great restaurants like Serve the People (p.322), Peterpan (Sanlitun Xi Wu Jie, 010 6465 1661) and Gold Barn (1 Sanlitun Bei Xiao Jie, 010 6463 7240) are also here, making it a good choice for a stroll in the evening before deciding where to dine.

Sanlitun shopping

Area **H** *p.158*
See also Map 6

The Centre

Encompassing the area inside the Second Ring Road, along where the ancient city walls once stood, this is the historic heart of Beijing. Most of the tourist attractions are in this area and it's easiest to get about by bicycle or by hopping on the subway. Changan Jie runs 40km through the heart of Beijing. This large boulevard replaced the main road into the imperial city, which was the north-south road through Tiananmen Gate (under where Mao's portrait is today). The government knocked down ancient gates to expand Changan Jie, which was completed in 1959. Today many important buildings are situated along this 80m wide road.

The Lowdown
The heart of Beijing, where many important historical and cultural sites are found.

The western part of the centre, along Fuxingmenwai Dajie, was once a maze of *hutongs* and home to princes, government officials and imperial canal waterways. It is now the city's financial centre, with mammoth new buildings and rapid development. The hundreds of courtyard homes around Financial Street have dwindled down to one, which has been renovated and turned into Whampoa Club Beijing (p.311). This Chinese restaurant is headed by Jereme Leung.

The Good
Many sights, and getting around on the subway is quick and easy.

The ancient Xizhimen gate is now an interchange station for the Lines 2 and 13 and a shopping mall distinguishable by its three curved buildings. Financial Street, Beijing's answer to Wall Street, is undergoing a ¥45billion overhaul that includes the building of the ritzy, high-end Season's Place Shopping Mall, Ritz-Carlton (p.36) and a new bar street to rival Super Bar Street and Sanlitun Bar strip.

The Bad
Sights are a long walk apart and some sections consist of block after block of offices. Sights can be crowded.

Aside from having banks and government buildings, there's lots to see including several museums such as the Capital Museum (p.185), Military Museum of the Chinese Revolution (p.186) and Beijing World Art Museum (A9 Fuxingmenwai Dajie, 010 6852 7108, www. worldartmuseum.cn) and temples, including Temple of Great Charity (Xisi Nan Dajie, east end of Fuchengmennei Dajie, 010 6616 0907), White Dagoba Temple (p.22) and Temple of Longevity, (Xisanhuan Beilu, 010 6845 6997). They are all spread out, so you'll need to be prepared to jump on and off the subway and walk several long blocks to see everything. For children, there's also the Beijing Zoo (p.189) and Beijing Planetarium (p.185).

The Must Dos
Shop in Wangfujing and eat in Guijie. Stroll along the ancient canal from Yuyuantan Park to the Summer Palace.

Wangfujing & Around

While most people come to Wangfujing to shop at the Oriental Place, the new Sung An Dong Plaza and the shops along Wangfujing Dajie, there's also some history in the area. Palaeoanthropologic relics that were found during the construction of Wangfujing are on display at the Wangfujing Paleolithic Museum Oriental Plaza (W1P3, 1 Dong Changan Jie, 010 8518 6303). If you visit the area in the evening a visit to Donghuamen Night Market, at the top of Wanfujing Dajie is worthwhile. Take your pick from scorpions and starfish on a stick to traditional treats like *tanghulu* (fruits like strawberries, pineapple and tomatoes on a stick dipped in sugar).

East of Wangfujing at Jianguomen subway station is the Ancient Observatory (p.179). It has eight bronze instruments on its roof, exhibits on the lunar calendar and the Shadow Observation House where Ming and Qing dynasty astronomers would tell the time by looking at sun shadows.

National Theatre (p.347)

Quianmen Gate

West Of Tiananmen

Full of cypress trees, Zhongshan Park (1 Zhonghua Lu, 010 6605 5431) was where Ming Emperor Yongle built the sacrificial Altar of Land and Grain. Today there's a flower garden, a Chinese restaurant, the Sun Yatsen Memorial Hall and a children's playground.

North Of The Forbidden City

Created from dirt dug up to make the city's canals, Jingshan Park sits above the Forbidden City, allowing a great view. It's also called Coal Hill because coal used to be piled up there.

East of Jingshan Park is the National Art Museum (p.177), which has traditional and contemporary art shows. West of Jingshan Park is Beihai Park (p.191). It is more than 1,000 years old and was an imperial garden for five centuries. In the mornings, older Chinese can be seen practising their tai chi. In the winter, there is ice skating on the lake and in the summer there are boats to rent.

Guijie 'Ghost Street'

Within walking distance of Dongzhimen subway station, this food street on Dongzhimennei Dajie is decorated with hundreds of red lanterns and has more than 100 restaurants. The ghost nickname was attached to this area because, years ago, vendors would stand out all night selling food under the glow of lanterns. A popular restaurant for late night eats is Hua Jia Yi Yuan (235 Dongzhimennei Dajie, Dongcheng, 010 6405 1908), which serves up home-style food like *kaomantou* (roasted buns) and *ma la xie* (spicy crayfish) in a courtyard setting.

Xidan Subway Station

Popular among young locals and teens is Xidan Shopping Center (p.296), a multi-storey mall. It has an entrance connected to the subway station and stalls crammed with retro clothes, cool shoes and jewellery. It gets crowded on the weekend, so browsing during the week is best.

Fuxingmen

Fuxingmen is a continuation of Changan Dajie. From the Fuxingmen subway station, walk west along Fuxingmen to the Capital Museum (p.185). It has 5,622 artefacts on display and exhibits on traditional Chinese art and Beijing's history as a capital. West of this is the Military Museum of the Chinese People's Revolution (9A Fuxingmenwai Dajie, 010 6686 6244), where you'll find exhibits about China's military history including weapons, Zhou Enlai's plane and Mao's limo. A five minute walk further west is the Beijing World Art Museum (A9 Fuxingmenwai Dajie, 010 6852 7108, www.worldartmuseum.cn), which has hosted several high profile international exhibits.

Just west again is the current CCTV centre. North of the CCTV building at Millennium Monument subway station is Yuyuantan Park (Xisanhuan Lu, 010 8865 3806) boasting two big play areas, cherry blossoms and Diaoyutai State Guesthouse, which foreign diplomats frequent. Still further west at Bajiao subway station is Beijing Shijingshan Amusement Park (p.174) featuring 73 rides, a faux London Bridge and miniature EPCOT ball.

Man Scam

When on Wangfujing, it may be wise to steer clear of young, flirting Chinese women offering to take you for a cup of tea, or hoping to practise their English. They are usually in front of McDonald's and aim their scam at men. If you accept the invite, you'll be taken to a teahouse or bar and after several rounds of mediocre tea and alcohol, you'll be forced to forfeit hundreds of dollars.

Fuchengmen Subway Station

From Fuchengmen subway station, walk east down Fuchengmen until you reach the White Dagoba Temple (p.22), which has many Buddhist statues and texts. Walk further down the street and you'll reach the Temple of Emperors of Successive Dynasties in China (131 Fuchengmennei Dajie, 010 6616 1141) which is one of three imperial temples in Beijing where emperors went to worship people gods, ancestors and past rulers. A 10 minute walk to the east lies the Temple of Great Charity (Xisi Nan Dajie, east end of Fuchengmennei Dajie, 010 6616 0907), the headquarters of the Chinese Buddhist Association, and across the street, the Geological Museum of China (15 Yangrou Hutong, 010 6655 7858) with a huge 5.5m high dinosaur at the front.

Xizhimen Subway Station

A short walk west from Xizhimen station along Xizhimenwai Dajie is the Beijing Zoo (p.189), home to giant pandas and the world's largest indoor aquarium. Though the animals' living conditions aren't up to scratch, it's still worth a visit. Next door is the Beijing Planetarium (p.185), with ancient and modern astronomical exhibits, solar observatory and theatre. Continue walking west and turn right on to Zhongguancun Nan Dajie where you'll see the National Library of China (010 8854 5593, www.nlc. gov.cn). Here you can browse but not borrow from a list that includes the largest collection of foreign language books in China. A short walk across from the library is the Five Pagoda Temple (24 Wutasi Cun, 010 6217 3543), which includes a stone carving museum. At the intersection of Xizhimen Nan Dajie and Zhongguancun Nan Dajie is the east gate of Zizhuyuan (Purple Bamboo Park). Walk through the small park with its stone bridges, lakes and 50 types of bamboo and exit through the north gate to get to the Temple of Longevity (Xisanhuan Beilu, 010 6845 6997), where the Empress Dowager Cixi (p.4) would stop on her way to the Summer Palace. Inside the temple is the Beijing Art Museum.

Dongbianmen Watchtower

Changan Jie

Dragon at the Ancient Observatory (p.179)

Area ❶ p.158
See also Map 12

The South

Comprised of Xuanwu, Chongwen and Fengtai districts, this area south of the Forbidden City and the Second Ring Road, is less developed than the north. Historically, the area has been the poor part of town. After the Manchurian army founded the Qing Dynasty in the 17th century, the Han Chinese were kicked out of the north of the city and sent to live in the south.

The Lowdown
The place to explore the untouched hutongs *of old Beijing.*

The south is a glimpse at what life used to be like, and is a short walk from Tiananmen or Qianmen stations. While the Temple of Heaven (p.188) and Hongqiao (Pearl) Market (p.293) are the main draws, there are also temples and *hutongs* to explore.

The Good
It's less developed, allowing foreigners to see the way the city once was.

Beijing South Railway Station (scheduled to be completed in August 2008) and Beijing West Railway Station (Lianhuachi Dong Lu, 010 5182 6253) are both in the area.

Xuanwu

Historically, shop and factory workers lived in Xuanwu, a busy commercial area. Today it has Soviet-style apartment blocks and *hutongs* on the verge of demolition. Meandering through by foot or bike is a good way to explore for a few hours. The easiest starting point is Qianmen gate. From there, head south and you'll reach Liulichang, a 750m long cultural street built in the Yuan dynasty. Here, tiles were made for the city's palaces and temples. It was the main shopping centre during the Qing dynasty and is still a popular place for shoppers. The restored street has many shops, including Rongbaozhai Bookshop, which is famous for its art supplies. Qianmen and Dazhalan *hutongs* including Bada, the former red light district, are a short walk away.

The Bad
The highlights are quite spread out, though manageable as a day long walk or bike ride.

The Must Dos
See dancing grannies in Tiantan Park, haggle at the Pearl Market, visit the Temple of Heaven.

Continue south to visit the Museum of Ancient Architecture. West of the museum is Taorangting Park, one of Beijing's oldest.

Cross the park and walk north along Caishikou Dajie and then head west down Nansheng Xi Jie to see the Fayuan Temple (p.22) on the north side of the street. Built during the Tang dynasty to commemorate soldiers lost in battle, it is the oldest temple in Beijing.

Continue west on Nanshen Xijie then north on Niu Jie to the Beijing Mosque (88 Niu Jie, 010 6353 2564). Cycle or take a taxi back to Qianmen station for tea and the nightly cultural show at Laoshe Teahouse (Buil ding 3, Qianmen Xi Dajie, 010 6303 6830, www.laosheteahouse.com), which includes Peking opera and demonstrations of traditional tea ceremonies.

Chongwen

One of Beijing's most famous landmarks, the Temple of Heaven (p.188), is in Tiantan Park, a pleasant spot full of active old folk dancing, stretching, and practising tai chi. First thing in the morning, this may be the most beautiful sight in the city. In the western part of the park is the Museum of Natural History (126 Tianqiao Nan Dajie, 010 6702 4431). Next to the park's east gate is Hongqiao Market, also called the Pearl Market (p.293), where locals and tourists haggle for gems of varying quality. North of the park and west of Chongwenmenwai Dajie is the Underground City (p.187), a maze of tunnels built underground out of fear of a Russian attack.

Fengtai

There aren't many reasons to visit this part of town, except for the Marco Polo Bridge (p.180), built in 1189, which Marco Polo praised as being one of the finest in the world, and World Park (158 Fengbao Lu, Huaxiang, 010 8361 3344, www.beijingworldpark.cn). This 46 hectare park has more than 100 models of famous landmarks, including the Eiffel Tower and Statue of Liberty.

Amusement Centres

Beijing is not blessed with an abundance of amusement centres. Instead, locals tend to spend their free time either in parks or internet cafes. The amusement parks that the city does possess, while safe, are not exactly of Disneyland standard, but should still be a fun day out for the kids.

19 Zuoanmennei
Dajie
Chongwen
左安门内大街19号
崇文区
Map 7 B4 **1**

Beijing Amusement Park 北京游乐园

010 6711 1155 | *www.bap.com.cn*

This is possibly the best amusement park in Beijing. It contains more than 100 different activities that should ensure children stay occupied for the best part of a day. Ferris wheels, rollercoasters and water rides will keep thrill seekers happy, while the more laidback will enjoy the regular dance shows and screenings on the 3D and e-motion cinemas. Admission costs ¥120 (¥80 for children). Open 09:00 to 21:00.

Wuji Beilu
Dongsihuan Lu
Chaoyang
东四环路
朝阳区
Map 7 E4 **2**

Happy Valley Amusement Park 欢乐谷游乐园

010 6738 9898 | *www.happyvalley.com.cn*

Beijing's newest amusement park offers a different approach to its rivals, with the rides and attractions divided into six themed areas based on ancient civilisations. With more than 100 different attractions, the park is more modern and well planned than others. It also boasts the Flying Rollercoaster, the country's most expensive ride, as well as an IMAX cinema and exhibition halls.

Happy Valley can get very crowded during the summer and national holidays, so it is best to visit off-season. Admission costs ¥160 for adults, ¥80 for children and is free for children under 1.2m tall. Open 09:00 to 22:00 but rides finish at 17:30.

25 Shijingshan Lu
Shijingshan District
石景山区石景山路
25号

Shijingshan Amusement Park 石景山游乐园

010 6886 2547 | *www.bs-amusement-park.com*

Located near the Bajiao subway station, this park has more than 60 rides, including a big wheel, rollercoaster and paintball area. It is surrounded by elegant scenery and eclectic buildings including an unusual, gothic-style Cinderella castle. The park also contains water-based rides including slides, wave pools, boats and children's play pools. Admission costs ¥100 for unlimited rides or ¥10 per ride. Open 08.30 to 17:00 in summer and 09:00 to 16:30 in winter.

Aquariums

While Beijing's zoo (p.189) may be prehistoric when it comes to animal treatment and conditions, the city's two aquariums are thankfully more modern. Built in the last decade, they each offer a host of marine life that should thrill and entertain anyone missing the sea.

137 Xizhimenwai
Dajie
Haidian
西直门外大街137号
海淀区
Map 4 D4 **4**

Beijing Aquarium 北京海洋馆

010 6217 6655 | *www.bj-sea.com*

For a city so far from the coast, Beijing boasts a surprisingly impressive aquarium. Unlike its neighbour, Beijing Zoo (p.189), the facility is modern and seemingly humane. Designed to resemble a giant conch shell, it houses many species, including piranhas, sharks and dolphins. It also has a large coral reef (in a tank) teeming with marine life.

The half-hourly shows performed by seals and dolphins are sure to thrill the kids, as is the petting zoo; a small tank where children can touch some of the more friendly animals. Admission is ¥100 for adults, ¥50 for students and two children can enter free with every adult. Open 09:00 to 17:00.

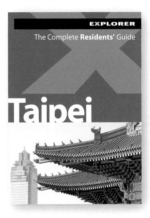

Gongti Nanmen
(Workers' Stadium
south gate)
Chaoyang
工人体育馆南门
朝阳区
Map 9 E4 **5**

Beijing Blue Zoo 北京富国海底世界

010 6591 3397 | *www.blue-zoo.com*

Opened in 1997, Beijing Blue Zoo has the longest underwater tunnel in Asia. For those interested in scuba diving, there is the chance to swim with the fish (reservations needed). The 3.5million litre main tank maintains a complete ecosystem with sharks, rays, eels, reef fish, lobsters, sea horses and starfish. In total, 18 themed tanks make it an educational experience, as do display areas devoted to endangered species including the fresh water dolphin of the Yangtze. Admission is ¥75 for adults, ¥50 for children and free for kids under 1m. Open 08:00 to 20:00.

Art Galleries

Other options **Art & Craft Supplies** p.250, **Art** p.249

The art scene in Beijing is booming. Communist-inspired art of the 60s and 70s (soldiers, guns, flags and propaganda), has largely been replaced by a blossoming contemporary movement. It takes inspiration from international and local styles and issues. Artist communities are continuing to spring up in the outskirts of the city, epitomised by the mass sprawl that is 798 (p.167), also known as Dashanzi. The workers who once laboured in this rundown area have been replaced by young and eager artists that fill the factory spaces with all manner of creations. The close proximity of the galleries and the intriguing factory buildings themselves mean hours can be spent in the area. You might even find a few hidden gems. Chinese art is becoming increasingly popular, with pieces sold around the world for millions of dollars. Some artists are clearly jumping on the bandwagon but others really are striving for originality.

The Chinese art scene may be in its infancy, but it is catching up quickly. With constantly changing owners and exhibitions, the galleries in 798 are hard to categorise, so a tour (p.193) can be helpful. While it is enjoyable to simply set off and explore the area yourself, a few of the more enduring and memorable galleries are listed below. Others of note include Amelie Gallery (www.longyibang.com), Fifth Element Gallery (www.798gallery.net) and Beijing Central Art Gallery (p. 244, www. bjcagallery.com).

Those looking for traditional Chinese art and sculpture, can find a vast array of more classical museums and galleries within the city. Internationally renowned exhibitions and artists are also appearing more regularly in Beijing, so keep an eye on the city's various listings magazines (p.51) for information.

798 Art District
4 Jiuxianqiao Lu
798
酒仙桥路4号798艺
术区
朝阳区
Map 5 E2 **6**

798 Photo Gallery 百年印象摄影画廊

010 6438 1784 | *www.798photogallery.cn*

Featuring iconic black and white photographs that capture China's development in the last few decades, this gallery is simple yet powerful. While other galleries attempt grand statements, 798 Photo Gallery lets the images do the talking. The displays are generally focused on minorities and labourers; the individuals who have been left behind by modernisation. Limited edition prints of the art are beyond most customers' price range, but the gallery sells a great selection of art books to compensate. Open 10:00 to 18:00.

2/F Gongmei Building
2 Jiuxianqiao Lu
798
酒仙桥路二号798艺
术区工美楼2层
朝阳区
Map 5 E2 **7**

A3 Gallery 阿立方画廊

010 13911 70 3704 | *www.a3gallery.com*

A new addition to 798, this small gallery displays exquisite Chinese photographs and jewellery. The first of the gallery's two rooms is dedicated to atmospheric landscape photographs, while the second features themed abstracts. Rolling exhibitions focus on themes that have caught the artists' eyes, such as the Beijing skyline, construction in the city and the minorities of China. The husband and wife team produce mesmerising images that are available to buy in a variety of sizes. Exhibitions change on a regular basis. Open Friday to Sunday, 12:00 to 18:00.

East Street
2 Jiuxianqiao Lu
798
酒仙桥路2号798东路
798艺术区
朝阳区
Map 5 E2 **8**

Asia Art Center 亚洲艺术中心

010 8459 9707 | www.asiaartcenter.org
With a sister gallery in Taipei, Asia Art Center aims to establish cultural links between mainland China, Taiwan and Hong Kong. Its three large halls generally contain a range of works, both sculpture and paintings, which lack a unified theme but are all of impressive quality. The gallery also houses a coffee shop area, making it a welcome stopping point on a walk around 798. Open Monday to Saturday, 09:00 to 17:00.

104 Caochangdi
Village
Chaoyang
崔各庄乡草场地村
104号
朝阳区
Map 5 E2 **9**

Galerie Urs Meile 麦勒画廊

010 6433 3393 | www.galerieursmeile.com
Designed by artist Ai Weiwei, this impressive complex is not only a gallery but also home to some of the artists. They are offered residency and space to work for up to six months. In partnership with its namesake in Lucerne, Switzerland, the gallery has one of the best records in Beijing for attracting top international names to share their talent and skill. Open Tuesday to Sunday, 11:00 to 18:30.

4 Juixianqiao Lu
798
酒仙桥路4号798艺
术区
朝阳区
Map 5 E2 **10**

Marella Gallery 玛蕊乐画廊

010 6433 4055 | www.marellabeijing.com
Since it opened in 2005, Marella Gallery has brought a slice of European standards to China. This small Italian gallery focuses on promoting Chinese talent by offering up-and-coming artists solo exhibitions. These artists are subsequently promoted in magazines and Marella Galleries throughout the world. Perhaps due to the cutting edge artists chosen, the exhibitions are likely to either really impress, or utterly disappoint. Enjoyable launch parties precede each new exhibition, so check the website regularly. Open Tuesday to Sunday, 10:00 to 18:00 and 11:00 to 19:00 in the summer.

1 Wusi Dajie
Dongcheng
五四大街1号
东城区
Map 8 E4 **11**

National Art Museum 中国美术馆

010 8403 3500 | www.namoc.org
A grand museum with over 50,000 pieces in its collection, the National has been revamped in recent years with the aim of exhibiting more contemporary art. Where a visit could once be described as uninspiring, now the museum displays a combination of traditional Chinese art and more modern artists. It is certainly an interesting place to spend an afternoon. Even with the influx of new material, it is probably still the large socialist artwork that will stick in your memory. Admission is ¥20 and ¥10 for students. Open 09:00 to 17:00.

National Art Museum

Chongwenmen
Dongdajie
Chongwen
崇文门东大街东便
门角楼
崇文区
Map 11 B4 **12**

Red Gate Gallery 红门画廊

010 6525 1005 | www.redgategallery.com
Located in the old Donbianmen watchtower, this gallery's ancient setting is perfectly juxtaposed with its contemporary exhibits. Established in 1991 by an Australian art historian, it has been firmly at the forefront of the Chinese art scene for the last 16 years. With 15 resident artists, the gallery produces around eight exhibitions a year, incorporating

paintings, sculptures, paper cuttings, photography, performance art and mixed media. Modern and innovative, Red Gate should be on the agenda of any art lover. Open 09:00 to 17:00.

4 Jiuxianqiao Lu
798
酒仙桥路4号798艺
术区
朝阳区
Map 5 E2 **13**

Ullens Centre For Contemporary Art (UCCA)
尤伦斯当代艺术中心
010 8459 9269 | www.ucca.org.cn
Currently the only fee-charging gallery in 798 (¥30 for adults, ¥10 for students and free for children) UCCA offers a more interactive experience for visitors. It is a large Bauhaus-inspired building with three grand halls that exhibit continually changing displays. The gallery also contains an auditorium and research room. By bringing quality equipment to Beijing, the gallery aims to attract high profile, international exhibitions to set it apart from its neighbours. UCCA also offers educational packages for adults and children. For more information check the website. Open Tuesday to Sunday, 10:00 to 18:00.

136 Nanchizi Lu
Dongcheng
南池子大街136号
东城区
Map 10 E2 **14**

Wan Fung Art Gallery 云峰画苑
010 6523 3320 | www.wanfung.com.cn
Located near Tiananmen Square in the old Ming and Qing dynasty Imperial Archives, Wan Fung focuses primarily on China's fine art scene. It regularly displays works by current Chinese masters, as well as organising exhibitions all over Asia. Regarded among the top 10 galleries in China, Wan Fung also has branches in Hong Kong, Shanghai and Guangzhou. Budding artists are able to hire the gallery space for around ¥3,000 per day, which may seem steep, but the setting is absolutely stunning. Open 10:00 to 17:00.

2 Jiuxianqiao Lu
798
酒仙桥路2号798艺
术区
朝阳区
Map 5 E2 **15**

White Space 空白空间
010 8456 2054 | www.alexanderochs-galleries.de
Only ever sparsely filled, White Space is one of the more important galleries in 798. Set up by Alexander Ochs, a German gallery owner, it has strong contacts with international artists. Popular exhibitions will often be shown in both the Beijing and Berlin branches. The gallery chooses a blend of established and rising stars, and seems to have a particular liking for monumental canvas which can fill its large wallspace. Open Tuesday to Sunday, 11:00 to 19:00.

Heritage Sites
Other options **Museums** p.184, **Art** p.249

Beijing is one of the most culturally rich cities in the world. While it's recent history is fascinating and traumatic, it's older sites are beautiful and charming. The city has six UNESCO World Heritage Sites; the Forbidden City (p.180), Summer Palace (p.182), Temple of Heaven (p.188), Great Wall (p.197), the Ming and Qing Tombs (p.198) and Peking Man Site in Zhoukoudian (010 6930 1278).
The Cultural Revolution (1966-76) was less than kind to the city and many of its temples, ancient buildings and artefacts that were deemed representative of China's imperial past did not survive. Those that did endure were preserved as the pinnacles of imperial Chinese achievement.
Since realising the financial benefits of mass tourism, the Chinese government has tried to repair and improve many of Beijing's sites and temples. Some have been tastefully renovated, keeping the traditional mood, while others have been too heavily restored – it is up to you to decide which fall into each category.

2 Dongbiaobei Hutong
Haidian
东裱褙2号
海淀区
Map 11 C3 **16**

Ancient Observatory 古观象台

010 6524 2202 | www.bjp.org.cn
Located in one of the watchtowers of the old city wall, this is one of the oldest observatories in the world. It was set up in 1442 and was fully functional up until 1929. With the arrival of foreigners, in the form of Jesuit priests, Chinese stargazing technology altered drastically. Elaborate equipment, beautifully wrought with dragons and mythical creatures, was designed during the 17th century and can still be found scattered around the site.
While these machines are largely beyond comprehension, they reveal an amazing blend of modern (at that time) technology and traditional design. Exhibits inside are not so impressive. You are unlikely to get the clear sky needed to test the equipment, but standing on this small part of the wall surrounded by the modern city can be suitably surreal. Admission costs ¥10 for adults and ¥5 for students. Open 09:00 to 16:30 and 09:00 to 18:00 in the summer.

Tiananmen Square
Dongcheng
天安门广场
东城区
Map 10 D4 **17**

Chairman Mao Memorial Hall 毛主席纪念堂

010 6513 2277
It's an odd tradition, but embalming important leaders does give visitors a real pilgrimage experience. Against his wishes, Mao joined the likes of Lenin, Stalin and Ho Chi Minh to be forever preserved and displayed, though Stalin has subsequently been placed in storage.
Visitors can join the long line of schoolchildren and patriots to get a brief glimpse of the revered leader. The speed with which you are hustled in and out means that the queues are deceptively long. Strange but memorable, it is a Beijing must. You will need to check your bag in at a building to the east of the square before you can enter. Admission is free. Open Sunday 08:30 to 11:30, and from 14:00 to 16:00 on Tuesdays and Thursdays, but times do change.

Deshengmen Jianlou
Bei'erhuan Lu
北二环路德胜门箭楼
西城区
Map 8 A1 **18**

Deshengmen 德胜门

010 6201 8073
Surrounded by the hustle and bustle of the Second Ring Road and a nearby bus depot, the 'Gate of Virtuous Triumph' is one of the few surviving gates of the old city wall. Some of Beijing's gates performed unique functions and it was Deshengmen's honour to welcome back victorious returning troops. While the Ancient Coins Museum inside is unimpressive, sitting on the rooftop bar can be a rewarding experience even with the less than peaceful environment. Admission is ¥10. Open Tuesday to Sunday, 09:00 to 16:00.

Gulou Dongdajie
Dongcheng
鼓楼东大街
东城区
Map 8 D2 **19**

Drum & Bell Towers 钟鼓楼

010 6401 2674
Timekeeping at its most grandiose, the two towers lie on the central access of the city. For centuries imperial officials and merchants rose and slept on their loud instructions.
Climbing the steep steps up to the Drum Tower you are rewarded with a great view and a half-hourly drumming demonstration. Also on display are the remains of drums past their prime, some bearing the

Chairman Mao Memorial Hall

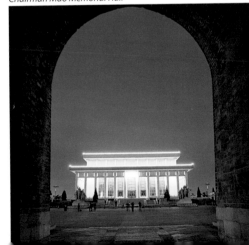

knife cuts of 19th century foreign soldiers. The Bell Tower is the thinner of the two and, unusually, made entirely of stone. It houses a 600 year old 42 tonne bell which, during Spring Festival, visitors can ring for a small fee. Adult admission costs ¥20 for the Drum Tower (students ¥10) and ¥15 for the Bell Tower (students ¥8). Open 09:00 to 17:00.

North of Tiananmen
Square
Dongcheng
天安门广场
东城区
Map 10 D2 **20**

Forbidden City 故宫

A palace (or for some a 'golden prison'), the Forbidden City was the residence of the last 24 emperors of China over a period of almost 500 years. When the capital was moved to Beijing, the emperor Yongle decided to create the ultimate home for the 'Son of Heaven'. Carefully constructed on the north to south meridian, each hall and courtyard was designed only after extensive consultation of the stars. A truly expansive complex, it runs 960m north to south, 750m east to west and took 200,000 labourers 15 years to complete.

Considered the centre of the universe, mere mortals were forbidden from entering, hence the name. Court officials were permitted during the day but at night, apart from the royal family, the only people allowed within the imperial compound were the tens of thousands of female servants, concubines and eunuchs.

Most of the buildings date from the 18th century; the palace's wooden structures were susceptible to fire and many earlier versions burnt down. Of the 8,706 rooms and halls the most important was the Hall of Supreme Harmony. For a long time it was the tallest building in Beijing; it was illegal for any building in the city to be higher than the imperial palace. It was purely ceremonial, and from the Dragon Throne within, the emperor nominally ruled his empire. Weddings, New Year processions and enthronements would all take place there, with thousands of loyal subjects paraded before the emperor.

The northern end of the compound is taken up by the imperial residence. When not involved with ceremonies, the royal families could spend their time in the beautiful gardens and rockeries, relaxing away from the formality that accompanied much of their official responsibilities.

While much of its treasures are no longer in the Forbidden City – pilfered by eunuchs, or taken to Taiwan when Chiang Kai-Shek fled in 1949 – the palace collections are still grand and impressive. Rolling exhibitions of some of the finer pieces are displayed in halls around the grounds. Every visitor to Beijing should witness this glorious vestige of the golden age of imperial China. Admission costs ¥60 for adults and ¥40 for children. Open April to October, 08:30 to 17:00 and November to March, 08:30 to 16:30.

Tiananmen Square
(west side)
Dongcheng
天安门广场西侧
东城区
Map 10 C4 **21**

Great Hall Of The People 人民大会堂

010 6309 6156

With a 10,000 seat auditorium and a 5,000 seat banquet hall, the Great Hall of the People is a somewhat intimidating building. The meeting place for the Chinese People's Assembly, it was constructed in just 10 months during 1959. The grandiose Soviet architecture is a legacy of the previously close relationship between Communist China and the USSR, but the red stars that adorn the auditorium's ceiling are a distinctly Chinese touch. In 1972 President Nixon dined there, as relations between the two countries were being restored. The auditorium has been known to host classical music recitals. Admission costs ¥30. Open 08:00 to 16:00 (closed during government sessions).

Wanpingcheng
Fengtai
宛平城
丰台区

Marco Polo Bridge 卢沟桥

010 8389 3919

This stone bridge dates back to 1189 and once spanned a busy river, which is now little more than a dry riverbed. Along its sides sit 400 stone lions which, according to folk tales, come alive after dark. The bridge is picturesque, but its importance lies not in the

Attractions

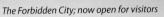

The Forbidden City; now open for visitors

fact that Marco Polo described it as the greatest bridge in the world. It was there, in 1937, that a skirmish took place marking the beginning of the War of Resistance against the Japanese invasion. The town of Wanping, located on the north side, is a beautiful dusty hamlet complete with town walls. The Anti-Japanese Memorial Hall is especially recommended. Admission costs ¥20 for adults and ¥10 for students. Open 07:00 to 19:00.

Chongwenmen
Dongdajie
Chongwen
崇文门东大街
崇文区
Map 11 B4 **23**

Ming City Walls Ruins Park 明城墙遗址公园

010 6527 0574

When Mao decided Beijing's modernisation required the sacrifice of the city walls, little was left standing. This small section, measuring a mile east to west, survived in part and was then restored in 2002 using the old brickwork. Originally constructed during the Yuan dynasty, the walls that remained until most recently were 16th century Ming dynasty creations. Located within a pleasant (free) park, the ruins have not been overly restored and look suitably dilapidated, with collapsing buttresses. The Red Gate Gallery (p.177) is especially worth visiting. Admission costs ¥10. Open 08:00 to 17:00.

Tiananmen Square
Dongcheng
天安门广场
东城区
Map 10 D4 **24**

Monument To The People's Heroes 人民英雄纪念碑

Standing between Mao's Memorial Hall (p.179) and the Forbidden City (p.180), the Monument to the People's Heroes was erected to honour China's dead. Built in 1958, the facade on this 37m stone pillar shows the struggle of the Chinese people in the face of extreme adversity. Beginning with the 19th century Opium War, the story slowly unfolds until you reach October 1949.

28 Qinghua Xilu
Haidian
清华西路28号
海淀区
Map 4 B4 **25**

Old Summer Palace (Yuanmingyuan) 圆明园

010 6262 8501

Its glorious past might have come to an abrupt end 150 years ago but Yuanmingyuan still has a lot to offer. The massive imperial compound is now a beautiful park filled with lakes and, during the warmer months, a wide variety of plant life. Interspersed with these are the ruins of buildings destroyed by the British and French armies during the Second Opium War in 1860, and kept as a symbol of the suffering caused to China by foreign aggressors. Much more damage was caused after this by locals using the site as a source of building materials. A full day can be spent walking around the park (or trying to get back out of the maze). Entry to the park costs ¥10 with ¥15 extra for the palace ruins. Open 07:00 to 19:00.

Tiananmen Square
Dongcheng
天安门广场
东城区
Map 10 D4 **26**

Qianmen Gate 前门

While it seems out of place amid the 20th century Soviet architecture of Tiananmen Square, Qianmen was a fundamental part of imperial tradition. Located at the south end of the corridor that once was Tiananmen, it was for the exclusive use of the emperor on his way to sacrifice at the Temple of Heaven. The tower, originally built in 1419 and the tallest in the city, can be climbed, walked through or just marvelled at. The photograph collection inside is well captioned in English and worth the entrance ticket alone. Just to the south is another structure called the Arrow Tower. Admission costs ¥20. Open 08:30 to 16:00.

Yiheyuan Lu
Haidian
颐和园路
海淀
Map 4 A2 **27**

Summer Palace 颐和园

010 6288 1144

The Summer Palace was a Qing dynasty retreat during the city's hotter months, but is really a colossal park, rather than a palace. At more than 300 hectares, the grounds are huge and can take anywhere from a half day to a more leisurely full day to explore. The emperor Qianlong originally enlarged and remodelled the park in the 18th century, but it was the Empress Dowager Cixi who ordered the expensive renovations after the site had been destroyed twice by foreign forces, once in 1860 and once in 1902. Constructed around the largely manmade Kunming Lake and Longevity Hill, the various buildings and structures are individually important. The beautiful Long Corridor, 728m in length, is decorated with over 10,000 paintings taken from Chinese history and legends. The Seventeen-Arched Bridge which links the central isle and its temple to the shore is just one of several fantastic bridges. The Marble Boat, completed in 1893, was built with funds allocated for the modernisation of the navy. Its construction is blamed for China's empathic defeat in the Sino-Japanese War (1894-5), but it does look pretty.

While summer sees the park filled with tourists, perhaps the best time to visit is in the depths of winter when the lake is frozen and you are able to walk across it. Admission costs ¥30 for adults and ¥20 for students. Open 06:30 to 20:00.

Tiananmen Square
Dongcheng
天安门广场
东城区
Map 10 D3 28

Tiananmen Gate 天安门城楼

The 'Gate of Heavenly Peace' has been an icon since Mao stood on it to announce the formation of the PRC on October 1, 1949. It has continued to function as a platform from where generations of Communist leaders stand to address the Chinese population and the outside world. To enter, you must first go over the bridges and under Mao's portrait. After checking your bags, you are able to ascend the gate and stand on the spot where the Chairman once waved to his adoring followers (unlike him, you will have to share the space with many others). Inside the gatehouse are exhibitions showing the progressive stages of the square's history, and images taken from political rallies held over the last 50 years. Admission costs ¥15. Open 08:30 to 16:30.

Historic Houses

Ever since the capital was moved to Beijing in the 15th century, many of China's most important and influential individuals have made the city their home. While the poor struggled to survive, living in cramped and rundown accommodation, the rich were building increasingly lavish and magnificent residences. The years, not to mention the Cultural Revolution, have not been kind to these buildings, but scattered around the city there remain fine examples of the lifestyles of the rich and the famous.

More moderate housing was expected from leaders and celebrities during the 20th century, and preserved in among Beijing's *hutongs* are the former homes of some of the gifted writers and politicians of the Republican and Communist eras.

19 Fengfu Hutong
Dongcheng
丰富胡同19号
东城区
Map 10 E1 29

Lao She's Former Residence 老舍故居

010 6559 9218
One of China's most beloved writers and author of *Rickshaw Boy*, *Tea House* and *Four Generations Under One Roof*, Lao She met with a tragic end during the Cultural Revolution. After moving back from the USA in 1949, he was first praised then persecuted for his work. Believing there was no escape he committed suicide in 1966 by leaping into one of Beijing's lakes. His study has been preserved as a fitting tribute and remains the way it was when he left that last morning, with a game of solitaire laid out and the calendar turned to August 24, 1966. The house is an excellent example of a traditional *hutong*, and one that might endure long after the rest have made way for modernisation. Admission costs ¥10. Open 08:00 to 18:00.

9 Huguosi Jie
Xicheng
护国寺街9号
西城区
Map 8 A3 30

Mei Lanfang's Former Residence 梅兰芳故居

010 6618 0351 | www.meilanfang.com.cn
Peking Opera might be unfathomable to most foreigners, but the former residence of one of its best known stars is still a great place to spend a few hours. More than 30,000 items have been preserved, including photographs, costumes, make up and art. Mei

Lanfang (1894-1961) was famed for his portrayal of passionate female roles at a time when women were not allowed on the stage. In his later life, he became a Chinese cultural ambassador, travelling around the world to promote artistic co-operation and his life was the inspiration behind the 90s film *Farewell My Concubine*. This attraction is rarely crowded. Admission costs ¥10.

14a Liuyin Jie
Xicheng
柳阴街甲14号
西城区
Map 8 B3 **31**

Prince Gong's Mansion 恭王府
010 6616 6924

A stunning example of Qing dynasty splendour and Suzhou-style gardens, this mansion gives a glimpse into the extravagant lifestyles of court officials. It was originally built for one of China's most notorious villains, He Shen. His corruption was so great that much of the blame for the fall of the Qing dynasty has been placed on his shoulders. After he was 'invited' to commit suicide, the mansion was given over to Prince Gong, a western-influenced reformer who helped broker the dubious Treaty of Peking that ended the second Opium War. A popular place for Chinese tour groups, the mansion can get crowded in the afternoon. Admission costs ¥20. Open 08:00 to 17:00.

46 Houhai Beiyan
Xicheng
后海北沿46号
西城区
Map 8 B1 **32**

Soong Ching Ling's Former Residence 宋庆龄故居
010 6404 4205

Otherwise known as Madame Sun Yatsen, Soong was one of the first Chinese women educated in the west. She became the 'first lady' of China after her husband helped found the republic. While having strong links with the KMT, her passionate advocation of women's rights after 1949 led her to be highly respected by the Communist leadership. The house, a former prince's palace, was a gift from Mao Zedong and has elegant gardens, complete with a running stream diverted from the nearby lakes. Puyi, 'the last emperor', was apparently born in the mansion which, with its stunning grounds, can form a nice detour on a walk around Houhai. Admission costs ¥20 for adults and ¥10 for students. Open 09:00 to 17:00.

Museums
Other options **Art** p.249, **Heritage Sites** p.178

With so much history and culture, it is no wonder that Beijing possesses some truly remarkable museums. Large amounts of money are being spent on improving the displays, notably the English captioning, so places that were once confusing to foreigners are now becoming more accessible.
In addition to these progressions, new museums are appearing and engaging in cultural exchanges with institutes from other countries. These exchanges have lead to an increase in the number and quality of visiting foreign exhibits.

101 Wanpingcheng
Neijie, Lugouqiao
Fengtai
卢沟桥宛平城内街
101号
丰台区

Anti-Japanese War Memorial Hall 抗日战争纪念雕塑园
010 8389 2355

Located in the ancient walled town of Wanping, the Anti-Japanese Memorial Hall is precisely what the name implies. Built next to the Marco Polo Bridge (p.180), it focuses on some of the more unsavoury aspects, real or otherwise, of the Japanese conquest of northern China in the 30 and 40s. While the captions have not been translated, it's not hard to work out the meanings of the displays. Dioramas and photographs show brutal scenes that are definitely not child-friendly.
The museum is worth visiting (in tandem with the Marco Polo Bridge), but should be treated more as a lesson on the animosity between the two countries than a historically accurate account of the conflict. Admission costs ¥15 for adults and ¥8 for students. Open 09:00 to 16:00.

Peking University
Haidian
北京大学
海淀区
Map 4 B2 **34**

Arthur M Sackler Art & Archaeology Museum
赛克勒考古与艺术博物馆

010 6275 1667 | www.sackler.org

Located on the campus of Peking University, the Arthur M Sackler Museum is more a research facility than a typical museum. Items on display, all excellently captioned, begin with the 280,000 year old fossilised remains of early man, a brown bear's skull and a rhinoceros' jaw bone. There is also Bronze Age pottery and ceramics from various dynasties of the last thousand years. With over 10,000 artefacts, and the option of hiring guides able to speak English and Japanese (¥100 per tour), it is a worthwhile place to visit. Admission costs ¥5. Open 09:00 to 17:00.

138 Xizhimenwai Dajie
Xicheng
西直门外大街138号
西城区
Map 6 D1 **35**

Beijing Planetarium 北京天文馆

010 6831 2570 | www.bjp.org.cn

In a city lacking skyward views at night, the planetarium offers a welcome reminder of what stars actually look like. The modern facilities, reopened after renovation in 2004, include 3D and 4D digital 'space theatres' to give an interactive aspect to your visit. The fourth 'D' refers to the use of smoke and seat effects. These exciting shows take you on journeys through the creation of the Solar System and on a space shuttle trip into the cosmos. The planetarium also includes the more traditional features, captioned exhibitions on the universe, and industrial sized telescopes. Admission costs: Space Theatre ¥45 (¥35 student), 3D theatre ¥30 (¥20 student), 4D Theatre ¥30 (¥20 student). Open Wednesday to Friday, 09:00 to 15:30, Saturday to Sunday, 10:00 to 16:00.

36 Dongjiaomin Xiang
Dongcheng
东郊民巷36号
东城区
Map 7 A3 **36**

Beijing Police Museum 北京警察博物馆

010 8522 5018

While you won't find out about the intimate workings of the city's cops, this museum is still an interesting place to spend some time. Exhibits stretch back to Qing dynasty armour, leading up to modern fingerprinting technology and displays of advanced weaponry. The museum is, without doubt, one-sided, but still possesses some interesting features. A memorial to police casualties, seemingly up to date, gives detailed accounts of each officer and the manner in which they died. And for an extra ¥15 you get a keyring and a chance to practise shooting moving targets with a laser gun. Admission costs ¥5. Open Tuesday to Thursday 09:00 to 16:00.

16 Fuxingmenwai
Dajie
Xicheng
复兴门外大街16号
西城区
Map 6 D3 **37**

Capital Museum 首都博物馆

010 6337 0491 | www.capitalmuseum.org.cn

With its striking modern architecture and impressive variety of exhibits, the Capital Museum has staked its claim as the best museum in Beijing. Well captioned displays are offset with informative introductions that, thankfully, don't assume everyone is an expert on Chinese history and culture. Permanent exhibits chronicle China and Beijing's past, explain folk customs and show fine examples of early ceramics, jade and calligraphy. With the National Museum (p.186) currently closed, this has become the principle museum in Beijing for cultural exchanges. Recent events have included visiting exhibitions on Ancient Greece, Gaudi, and Medieval

Capital Museum

European armour and weaponry. Admission costs ¥50 for adults and ¥25 for students. Open Tuesday to Sunday, 09:00 to 16:00.

1 Beisanhuan Zhonglu ◀
Xicheng
北三环中路1号
西城区
Map 5 F3 **38**

China Science & Technology Museum 中国科学技术馆

010 6237 1177 | www.cstm.org.cn

More for kids than adults, the China Science & Technology Museum offers a host of interactive experiences; building three is even named the Children's Science Paradise. The museum runs the gamut from ancient technology (especially focusing on the four great Chinese inventions – gunpowder, the compass, paper, and printing) to modern science, including a robot performing tai chi. It is a wonderful place to let the kids run riot for an afternoon. The museum also contains an IMAX cinema (¥30), which is unfortunately only in Chinese. Admission costs ¥30 for adults, ¥15 for students and under 12s are free. Open Tuesday to Sunday 09:00 to 16:30.

9 Fuxingmenwai ◀
Dajie
Haidian
复兴门外大街9号
海淀区
Map 6 C2 **22**

Military Museum Of The Chinese People's Revolution 中国人民革命军事博物馆

010 6686 6244

The Chinese people have been doing war for thousands of years. This museum takes visitors through the ages, from the invention of gunpwder and cunning ways of blowing things up, to Mao's old limo and more modern bits of death-dealing kit. The slant on history is slightly skewed, and certainly emphasizes the animosity towards Japan, but overall this is a museum worth visiting.

Tiananmen Square ◀
(east side)
Dongcheng
天安门广场东侧
东城区
Map 10 D4 **39**

National Museum Of China 中国国家博物馆

010 8447 4914 | www.nationalmuseum.cn/en

The National Museum is closed until 2010. Construction is apparently on schedule for renovations that will make it one of the largest museums in the world, measuring more than 70,000sqm. The facilities are being upgraded, new wings added and the museum collection significantly enlarged. Hopefully, work will also be undertaken to improve foreign language signs and captioning. Until its grand reopening, the collection is being lent out around the city so look out for special exhibitions taking place at other museums.

20 Qianmen ◀
Dongdajie
Chongwen
前门东大街20街
崇文区
Map 7 A3 **40**

Planning Exhibition Hall 北京城市规划展览馆

010 6702 4559

This simple museum offers little English captioning, but the displays are rather self explanatory. Charting the growth of Beijing and its rapid modernisation over the last 50 years, the museum exhibits huge models of the city. There is also an excellent collection of black and white photographs. Visitors can see the reshaping of the city from 1949, with the destruction of the traditional *hutongs* as well as the implication of Olympic construction. The impressive central model covers one entire level of the building. It must be viewed from the floor above, so binoculars can be useful.Admission costs ¥30. Open 09:00 to 16:00.

2/F Poly Plaza, 14 ◀
Donzhimen Nandajie
Chaoyang
东直门南大街14号保
利大厦2层
朝阳区
Map 9 C3 **41**

Poly Art Museum 保利艺术博物馆

010 8610 6500

High end, well-captioned museums are a rare commodity in Beijing so, while Poly Art Museum is smaller and more expensive than most, it is certainly worth a visit. Funded by private investors, it houses a remarkable collection, mainly retrieved from abroad. On display are bronze statues and stone carvings going back 4,000 years to the Zhou and Shang dynasties. Alongside elaborately carved figures of Buddha you will find perhaps the prize of the collection; four bronze animal heads originally located in Yuanmingyuan. They were looted during the Boxer Rebellion and only returned, to national acclaim, in 2000. Admission costs ¥50 for adults and ¥25 for students. Open 09:30 to 16:30.

62 Xidamochang
Hutong
Chongwen
西打磨厂胡同62号
崇文区
Map 7 A3 **42**

Underground City 北京地下城
010 6702 2657
Alarmed at the souring of relations with the USSR, Mao ordered the construction of an underground city where the population could flee in the event of nuclear war. Thousands of workers were dispatched to dig this escape, using only hand tools. When finally cancelled, the project covered over 85km of tunnels and included hospitals, schools and cinemas. Guides dressed in military fatigues lead you through a small section, past dark tunnels with signs that point towards distant landmarks of Beijing. While it is infuriating not to be able to explore on your own, it would be very easy to get lost in the warren of tunnels. Admission costs ¥20 for adults and ¥10 for students. Open 08:30 to 18:00.

Religious Sites
While 50 years of communism may have dented the enthusiasm of religious types in China, many temples, mosques and churches still remain. For more than 500 years, religion played a crucial role in the lives of Beijing's rich and poor. Taoism, Confucianism, Islam, Christianity and Buddhism have all played a part through the ages, and each is still represented by places of worship around the city.
Under communism, many temples and religious buildings were closed or knocked down. This policy began to change in the 80s as temples have been reopened, renovated and turned into tourist sites.

6 Baiyunguanjie
Xibianmenwai
Xuanwu
西便门外白云观街
6号
宣武区
Map 6 D3 **43**

Baiyun Guan (White Cloud Temple) 白云观
010 6346 3531
Built in 739, this Taoist temple is still active, and one of the best places to spend Spring Festival. The largest Taoist complex in Beijing, most days it is still filled with traditionally robed monks, each with long hair twisted into a topknot. Incense rises continually from its courtyards as worshippers pray for the same things that generations before them have; wealth, descendants and job prospects. Outside of festival times it draws few tourists and is a good place to come to escape the hordes. Admission costs ¥10. Open 08:30 to 16:30.

13 Guozijian Jie
Dongcheng
国子监街13号
东城区
Map 8 F1 **44**

Confucius Temple 孔子庙
010 8402 7224
Nearing the final stages of massive renovations, it will be interesting to see how the Confucius Temple changes over the next few years. The temple is almost 1,000 years old and was, until recently, largely overlooked in favour of its imposing neighbour Yonghegong (p.189). For centuries, every scholar in the Beijing area who wished to gain office had to come to the temple and the adjoining Imperial College to study and take examinations. The names of 52,000 such individuals can still be seen carved into the 198 large stelae that form one of the temple's highlights. Scholars would also come to pray for guidance at the various halls and to listen to the emperor read out the Confucian classics. Admission costs ¥10 for adults and ¥3 for students. Open 08:30 to 17:00.

31A Beisanhuan Xilu
Haidian
北三环西路A座31号
海淀区
Map 4 D4 **45**

Dazhongsi (Great Bell Temple) 大钟寺
010 6255 0819
Housing one of the biggest bells in existence, Dazhongsi is an unusually thematic Buddhist temple. Hundreds of bells, created over the last 1,000 years, fill its halls and were once rung for prosperity on New Years Eve. The bell after which the

temple is named was cast between 1403 and 1424, measures almost 7m tall, and weighs 46.5 tonnes. Covered in Buddhist sutras carved in both Chinese and Sanskrit, it can apparently be heard more than 40kms away when tolled. Since the temple is off the main tourist route, you are unlikely to have much company when you visit, making it a relaxing spot to soak up some stress-free culture. Admission costs ¥10. Open 08:30 to 16:30.

141 Chaowai Dajie
Chaoyang
朝外大街141号
朝阳区
Map 7 B2 **46**

Dongyue Miao 东岳庙
010 6551 0151

One of the more surreal and enjoyable temples in Beijing, Dongyue is filled with the personnel of the Taoist underworld. Built from 1314 to 1320, the temple contains halls representing each of the 76 departments of the afterlife. Hanging outside each hall are red prayer tablets left by Taoist worshippers hoping for divine assistance from the various immortals. Counting the tablets outside each hall may demonstrate the desires of today's Chinese; the departments of 'Bestowing Happiness', 'Accumulating Justifiable Wealth' and 'Raising Descendants' are clearly the most popular. The departments of 'Interrogating Criminals', 'Hepatitis Jaundice' and 'Suppressing Schemes' are evidently the least. Admission costs ¥10 for adults and ¥5 for students. Open 08:30 to 16:30.

88 Nui Jie
Xuanwu
牛街88号
宣武区
Map 6 E4 **47**

Niujie Mosque (Ox Street Mosque) 牛街清真寺
010 6353 2564

Beijing has more than 80 mosques and this is the oldest and most elaborate. Niujie is considered the heart of the city's Muslim population; you only need to visit on a Friday to see the size of its congregation. Built in 996, it manages to blend traditional Arabic features with Chinese architecture, which makes for a very unusual and distinct mosque. The hexagonal Watching Moon Tower is considered unique among Islamic places of worship, while the Kiln prayer hall remains intimate even when filled with more than 1,000 worshippers. Since China's Muslim population mainly heralds from the minorities of the north-west, it is interesting to be catch a glimpse of these lesser known ethnic groups. Admission costs ¥10. Open 06:00 to 19:00.

74 Wangfujing Dajie
Dongcheng
王府井大街74号
东城区
Map 10 F2 **48**

St Joseph's 圣约瑟夫天主教堂
010 6524 0634

After being granted permission to build the church by the emperor Shunzhi in 1655, St Joseph's was first destroyed by an earthquake in 1720, then by fire in 1812, and then twice by angry mobs. The current church, dating from 1904, has a distinctly gothic exterior but the interior lacks the ornate features of its European counterparts. The church courtyard is a great spot to people watch, though you will have to share the space with the many young skateboarders who use the area. Daily services are held every morning, with the church usually locked outside of these times. Admission is free. Only open during service hours, daily at 06:30, 07:00 and on Sundays at 06:30, 07:00 and 08:00.

Tiantan Park
Chaoyang
天坛东路
朝阳区
Map 12 F4 **49**

Temple Of Heaven 天坛
010 6702 8866

A contemporary of the Forbidden City (p.180), the Temple of Heaven is one of the largest temple complexes in China. Built as a place of imperial sacrifice, the emperor would make annual visits to ask the gods for favourable harvests and a disaster-free year. It is located within a massive park and at the centre of it stands the Hall of Prayer for Good Harvest, an iconic circular 38m building. It was built in 1420, though the current one is a replica made after a fire in 1889. To the south is the Circular Altar, used in sacrifices, which is an acoustic marvel. You can join the crowds testing its special

qualities by speaking into one side while a friend listens on the other. A visit will generally take several hours, so be prepared to do a lot of walking. One of the most rewarding experiences in Beijing is watching elderly residents doing their daily exercise at the park's north gate. Dancers and tai chi performers are joined by people practising kung fu and many other health related activities. You should arrive between 06:00 and 08:00 to catch them in full swing. Admission costs ¥15 for the park or ¥35 for all sites. The park is open 06:00 to 21:00 and the sites are open from 08:00 to 18:00.

Temple of Heaven

Yonghegong Lama Temple 雍和宫

12 Yonghegong Dajie
Dongcheng
雍和宫大街12号
东城区
Map 9 A1 **50**

010 6404 4499
The former residence of Emperor Prince Yongzheng, Yonghegong is Beijing's grandest temple and is filled with tourists all year round. It is, however, still possible to see monks and worshippers placing incense at the feet of the statues. Built in 1694, half of the complex was turned over to Tibetan Buddhism on Yongzheng's succession to the throne, and the other half after his death. The grand buildings blend Tibetan, Han and Mongolian architecture, and feature an impressive collection of statues, prayer wheels and Buddhist art. While the complex has many different areas worth visiting, the hall containing the 18m Maitreya Buddha, carved out from a single piece of sandalwood, is the most memorable. This temple is good to visit in combination with the more neglected Confucius Temple (p.187) nearby. Admission costs ¥25. Open 09:00 to 16:30.

Water Parks

Tuanjiehu Park 团结湖公园

16 Tuanjiehu Nanli
Chaoyang
团结湖南里16号
朝阳区
Map 7 C2 **51**

010 8597 3603
Tuanjiehu Park offers a compromise for those who want the delights of a beach without leaving the city. Its man-made beach, complete with wave machine, brings the seaside experience to Beijing. The sandy beaches (sadly lacking deckchairs) surround a massive swimming pool that is ideal for summer days. The park is also pleasant to stroll or boat around. There are several lakes and waterfalls, most of which are also man-made. Just remember, if you think a visit on a really hot day is a good idea, chances are thousands of others will too. Entry is ¥20 (¥15 for children). Open 06:30 to 21:00.

Zoos

Beijing Zoo 北京动物园

**Baishiqiao Lu,
Xizhimenwai Dajie**
Haidian
西直门外大街白石
桥路
海淀区
Map 6 D1 **52**

010 6831 4411 | *www.beijingzoo.com*
The main attractions are the pandas and, befitting their status as a national symbol, they are well treated. The other animals, however, are not. Cages are barren, small and depressing. This is a pity, as the selection of animals is actually very good, with giraffes, elephants, lions and tigers pacing their tight enclosures. Plans are underway to improve conditions, so hopefully over the next few years things will pick up. Entry is ¥15 (¥8 for students, free for kids). Open 07:30 to 18:00.

Botanical Gardens

Just to the north west of the city lie the Western Hills, a favourite relaxation spot for the rich and powerful of the last 500 years. It is here, just outside the city limits, that visitors can get a glimpse of the sheer beauty of China's wildlife. The air tastes fresher and the views are a little clearer. Whatever time of year you visit, you are likely to see stunning trees and flowers, though spring and autumn are the most inspiring. From the Wudaokou subway station on Line 13 it is a short bus ride (331) to both the sites mentioned below.

Xiangshan Nanlu
Haidian
香山南路
海淀区

Botanical Gardens 北京植物园

010 6259 1283 | www.beijingbg.com

Just north of the Fifth Ring Road, Beijing's 1,000 acre Botanical Garden has more than 6,000 varieties of plant, including a collection of exotic species kept in large greenhouses. The park is almost empty during the winter months, but as soon as the flowers begin to appear, the city folk arrive for daytrips. One of China's greatest writers, Cao Xueqin (1715-63), is said to have written his famed love story *Dream of a Red Chamber* while living there. His house can still be visited along with other cultural sites within the gardens. Positioned on one of the hilltops, commanding a spectacular view, is a Tang dynasty temple that is home to a giant sleeping (some think dying) Buddha. The gardens can be revisited many times, and are a great place to see the variety of plant life in China. The greenhouses are also good, especially if you choose to spend a few surreal winter hours in among the cacti and tropical trees. Entry is ¥5 or ¥50 for entry to the greenhouse. Both tickets are half price for children. Open 07:00 to 17:00.

Xiangshan
Haidian
香山
海淀区

Xiangshan (Fragrant Hills) 香山

010 6259 1155

Elderly Chinese people have some unusual ways of staying healthy, but a daily run up and down Xiangshan is one of the most commendable. A little further on from the Botanical Garden, Fragrant Hills is equally impressive. Its trees, bushes and flowers, peonies and plum blossom, give the whole park a pink hue in early spring, while the autumn leaves create a vibrant red that should not be missed. Unfortunately everybody else in the city knows about this too. Clambering up the steep paths can be very rewarding, both as exercise and as a way to see the many pavilions and buildings along the way. For the less hardy, a chairlift can do the climb, which would otherwise take around 40 minutes. Views from the hilltop, looking south over the distant city, remind you of the enormity of Beijing, while the walk back down may remind you of the grandness of nature. Entry is ¥10 (¥5 for students). Open 06:00 to 18:30.

Parks

Despite the smoggy summers and freezing winters, Beijingers live their lives in the open. This can be seen in the old *hutongs* and in the many parks. A fetish for exercise (particularly among the over 30s) and a culture of communal living mean that open spaces are invariably crowded with people playing cards, making music, doing stretches or just having a chat.

With strict security guarding the grass, the parks may not feel overly liberating, but they are always fully utilised. Lakes are often a key feature, as are picturesque pavilions, but the simplest, sweetest pleasure of Beijing is sitting back to view the park life. Watching a team of grannies play hackey-sack, hundreds of middle-aged couple dance to country and western, or pensioners practising their rhythmic gymnastics are sights that will win over most new residents.

Parks are generally open from early morning until near dusk, charging small fees and offering limited facilities to buy food and drink. While pets are usually allowed, bikes must be left at the gates, and activities are limited to the paved areas. Spring and summer months are particularly beautiful, as they see a blossoming of plant life with lotuses filling the ponds and trees offering welcome shade from the heat.

1 Wenjin Jie ◀
Xicheng
文津街1号
西城区
Map 8 C3 55

Beihai Park 北海

010 6403 1102
Snaking down the west side of the Forbidden City, Beijing's lakes provide a peaceful escape from the hustle and bustle of the city. An exclusive imperial garden until 1925, Beihai Park was originally designed (with a natural lake extended) under the rule of Kublai Khan.
Towering over the central islet is the 36m high White Dagoba, which was built to honour the visit of the fifth Dalai Lama in 1651 and is one of the more impressive sights on the skyline. Local residents can be seen using the space for tai chi, singing, dancing and water calligraphy, using large brushes and water on the stone cobbles. Hiring a boat and floating across the lake is definitely the most romantic way to see the park. Entry to sites is ¥20. Open 06:00 to 20:30.

Nongzhan Nanlu ◀
Chaoyang
农展南路
朝阳区
Map 7 D1 56

Chaoyang Park 朝阳公园

010 6506 5409
If the restrictions of city life leave you yearning to run around on some grass, Chaoyang Park is a good bet. One of the few parks where you are free to step off the paths, it is liberating to throw a Frisbee, kick a football or just lie down without being pestered by security guards. A massive expanse of land, the park contains lakes (with paddleboats for hire), an amusement park, basketball courts and football pitches. Even during busy summer months, its size guarantees some quiet corners. Live music events are often held there, and it will also be the site of the beach volleyball competition of the 2008 Olympics. Entry is ¥5 (students ¥2.50). Open 06:30 to 21:30.

Andingmenwai Dajie ◀
Dongcheng
安定门外大街
东城区
Map 5 A4 57

Ditan Park 地坛公园

010 6421 4657
Ditan was one of five venues formerly used for imperial sacrifices. The other four were Ritan, Tiantan, Yuetan and Shejitan. It still has its altar, but is now more accustomed to kite fliers and noisy kids. The Ming dynasty altar in the centre of the park attests to its previous function as the 'temple of earth' and, while this is worth seeing, the park is better as a place of relaxation. Go-karting, bouncy castles and merry-go-rounds supply entertainment for the children, while regular exhibitions will keep the adults amused (but don't expect much English). Entry is ¥2. Open 06:30 to 21:30.

2 Xinjiangongmen Lu ◀
Haidian
新建宫门路2号
海淀区
Map 4 A2 58

Haidian Park 海淀公园

010 6285 0282 | www.haidianpark.com
This massive expanse of land, just south-east of the Summer Palace, has recently been utilised for large music events. Summer months now see several three-day festivals including the annual Midi and jazz festivals (p.53). When not being used to host concerts, the park is good for those wanting a bit of space to run around. Fishing is available in the park's canal and there is an unimpressive amusement area for kids. Should any natural disaster befall Beijing, this is one of the places geared up to handle the crisis, and is designated as one of the city's relief centres. Entry is ¥2. Open 08:00 to 21:00.

1 Wenjin Jie ◀
Xicheng
文津街1号
西城区
Map 6 A1 59

Jingshan (Prospect Hill) 景山

010 6404 4071
Created using soil dislodged when digging the Forbidden City moat in 1420, Jingshan is one of the few raised areas in an otherwise flat city. This, on a clear day, gives it unparalleled views over the Forbidden City and nearby Beihai Park. In theory designed

to protect the imperial residence's feng shui from the ill omens of northern winds, the hill was actually the location for the last Ming emperor, Chongzhen's, death. Fleeing rebel troops he ran to the hillside but, realising it was the end, he hung himself on a nearby locust tree. A plaque marks the spot. Wait for a clear day to get the most out of a visit. Entry is ¥2. Open 06:00 to 21:00.

Ritan Lu
Chaoyang
日坛路
朝阳区
Map 11 D2 **60**

Ritan Park 日坛公园

Thanks to its location in the middle of the CBD, this small park is a favourite lunchtime retreat for embassy workers. Sitting on the remains of the ancient Altar of the Sun, Ritan is one of the city's free parks. It has an impressive climbing wall, table tennis tables, mini golf and fishing ponds. These ponds allow you to take your catch home for a small fee, and at weekends are used by big kids with remote control boats. While the park officially closes at 20:00, the west gate remains open to allow access to Stone Boat bar (p.338); a great venue next to the water for food, drinks and live music.

19 Taipingjie
Xuanwu
太平街19号
宣武区
Map 12 B4 **61**

Taoranting Gardens 陶然亭公园

010 6353 5704

Taoranting has been a public park for hundreds of years. Named after the Taoran (Joyous) Pavilion that sits within, it drew people from all walks of life who wanted to relax and discuss important issues. Poets and writers congregated during the imperial ages to compose material and write lavish praises of the pavilion. During the 20th century, revolutionaries, including Sun Yatsen and Zhou Enlai (at different times), held informal meetings to plan their uprisings. It is just as beautiful today and now includes an enormous water park and playground for children. Entry is ¥2. Open 06:00 to 20:00.

Beihai Park

Yuyuan Park

Tiantan Park

Tours & Sightseeing

Around a decade ago, the few tour operators in Beijing offered limited choice, and catered more to national tourists than foreigners. Typically, this meant large groups were led around at speed by Chinese-speaking guides. But, as the number of western visitors has increased, a host of agencies have opened, offering tours that cover all the traditional must-dos and some more specialised trips.

Activity Tours

Various Locations

Beijing Day Trips 北京周边日游

www.beijingdaytrips.com

Beijing Day Trips organises some unique outings for those who want to see the city from a sidecar. You can take a ride to the sights, cruise the capital at night or visit the Palace Museum for a glass of champagne. Each sidecar has space for two adults and one child, and comes with an English-speaking driver. The company also offers trips to *hutongs*, the Great Wall, the Summer Palace and other famous spots. During the winter months it runs trips to ski resorts.

36 Nanlishi Lu
Xicheng
南礼士路36路
西城区

Panda Tour 熊猫旅游有限公司

010 6522 2991

This firm touts its offerings at hotel counters across the city, including the Shangri-La (p.33) and the Kempinski (p.35). It organises rickshaw rides through the *hutongs*, trips to popular sights including the Great Wall and performances of Peking opera and acrobatics. Free pick-up from the major hotels and lunch are often included in the prices, which start at $25.

Art Tours

Various Locations

artWALK 北京艺术漫步

http://artwalkbeijing.com

Beijing's art scene is formidable, but artWALK helps to make it a little more accessible. The events allow people to visit galleries in a fun, social setting, and typically feature a series of lectures and performances and end with a party. Check the website for updated information on when and where the next event will be held.

Various Locations

City Discovery 城市探索

www.citydiscovery.com

The district of 798 is a warren of galleries, studios and cafes. To help you navigate this world of contemporary art, City Discovery offers a guided tour. It includes an English-speaking guide, air-conditioned mini-bus, tea break and map. Tours depart at 08:30 and 12:30 every day except Monday and cost $89 for adults or $71 for children under 10 years old.

Bicycle Tours

Various Locations

Bike China Adventures 自行车中国之旅

www.bikechina.com

Get on your bike and start pedalling; these tours start in Beijing and cover anything from 300 to 500 miles. The longest visits Shanghai and involves a sneaky flight, but if you have a spare 21 days and calves of steel, it can be one of the best ways to see China. The number of riders varies, but there are usually no more than eight people per group. Bikes can be rented if needed.

Dongcheng
景山东路12号
东城区

Cycle China 非常之旅

010 6402 5653 | www.cyclechina.com
You can ride around Beijing alone easily enough, but for those who want to have a carefully planned tour, Cycle China offers themed trips around the city. Choose from a ride around the *hutongs*, Olympic venues or night cycling. The company is branching into 'running tours' and it can also organise rickshaw rides with reputable, English speaking drivers. Tours cost between ¥150 and ¥400 per day, depending on the group size.

Culinary Tours

Various Locations

Beijing Discovery Tours 北京发现之旅

www.beijingdiscoverytours.com
For those whose interest in Chinese food goes further than ordering a number 72, Beijing offers plenty of chances to learn. Beijing Discovery organises culinary tours, starting with the selection of ingredients and ending with the eating of your handiwork. Aimed at small groups, the company can be hired to take you on sightseeing trips around Beijing and beyond. One day and multiple tours are available, and prices start at around ¥250 per person per day.

Various Locations

Imperial Tours 紫禁城之旅

www.imperialtours.net
If you're serious about Chinese food but also want to explore other cities, Imperial Tours may have the answer. Starting in Beijing, over 12 days you will visit Chengdu, Shanghai and Hong Kong, learning about regional cuisines and local sights. From dinner in a Michelin-starred restaurant and a banquet on the Great Wall, to teahouses and food markets, this isn't cheap, but should be a trip to remember. Included in the $9,000 price are domestic flights, five-star accommodation, bilingual guides, all meals, lectures and demonstrations, taxes and tips. Groups are limited to 20 people.

Other Tours

Scorpion, served rare

Room 314
2 Renminnan Lu
Chengdu, Sichuan
四川成都人民南路2号
314室

Chengdu Panda Travel 成都大熊猫观光游

028 8665 2084 | www.chinagiantpanda.com
This unusual travel company offers panda fanatics the chance to track these iconic animals. Tours from Beijing last 10 days and take in the city sights before heading to the breeding and research centres at Chengdu and Wolong. Prices depend on the standard of accommodation and time of year, but start from $1,080. Travel within China, accommodation, meals, entrance fees, English-speaking guide and insurance are included.

Various Locations

Tour Beijing 易途旅游

010 6716 0201 | www.tour-beijing.com
Traditional Chinese medicines like herbal cures, meditation and acupuncture, are growing in popularity internationally. To discover more about alternative healing, a few operators organise lessons and visits to practitioners. Tour Beijing can also arrange bird-watching trips and cruises on some of the city's lakes. Tours cost round $60 a day depending on group size.

Private Tours

Various Locations

Lune Tours 新月旅行

010 1381003 5140 | www.lunetours.com

If you are keen to focus on a particular aspect of Chinese history and culture, you may wish to hire an agency to organise a specific itinerary. These usually charge more than pre-arranged trips, but can be tailored to any theme. Lune Tours offers diverse topics such as exploring Jewish history in China. Prices vary depending on the length of the tour and your specific criteria.

Wine Tours

Other options **Alcohol** p.249

Beijing is not high on the must-see list of most oenephiles. The Chinese have been cultivating grapes for more than 4,000 years, but have a strong preference for beer and hard spirits. The local firewater, *baijiu*, is sometimes translated as 'white wine', but is a clear spirit that is about 40% alcohol. Do not expect subtle tastes and textures. It is often presented in plastic bottles that resemble paraffin containers, with a taste to match. The cheapest stuff is sold by the gallon, but even the 'top end' brands are deemed pretty foul.

China is beginning to develop its own wines, but its status is more developing world than 'new world'. Whites can be very sweet, reds can be vinegary, but some bottles are quite drinkable. Dynasty and Great Wall are the most common brands. Local labels are often much cheaper than imports, which are subject to heavy taxes. To learn a little more, get in touch with one of the firms below.

1 Nanxiaojie
Chongwen
南小街领行国际1号
楼20层1室
崇文区

Beijing E-Tours 北京新华国旅

010 6716 0201 | http://beijing.etours.cn

This is a jack of all trades outfit offering specialised theme tours and dealing with areas of Beijing that would otherwise be hard to explore. Its one day tours include antique hunting, visits to farms and agricultural parks in neighbouring villages, and wine tasting at local vineyards. For a more complete list check their website. Prices generally work out around $60 a day per person.

Various Locations

China Wine Tours 中国葡萄酒旅游

www.chinawinetours.com

This firm is based in the US, but offers tours around Beijing and the rest of China. These include the Dynasty winery in Tianjin (www.dynasty-wines.com), south-east of Beijing, and the Dragon Seal winery in Haidian (2 Yuquan Lu, 010 6821 9243).

Tour Operators

Backpacking China	Great Wall tours	010 8400 2429	www.backpackingchina.com
Beijing E-Tours	Themed tours	010 6716 0201	http://beijing.etours.cn
BeijingService.com	Cultural tours	010 5166 7026	www.beijingservice.com
Chinese Culture Club	Walking tours	010 6432 9341	www.chinesecultureclub.org
Great Wall Adventure	Great Wall tours (inc overnights)	138 1154 5162	http://greatwalladventure.com
Imperial Tours	Luxury vacations	010 8440 7162	www.imperialtours.net
Nordic Ways	Great Wall cycling	010 6592 0545	www.nordicways.com
Tour 2008	Culture tours and vacations	010 8610 6551	www.2008tour.com
Tour Beijing	Varied tours	010 6716 0201	www.tour-beijing.com
Travelchinaguide.com	Cultural tours throughout China	010 8523 6688	www.travelchinaguide.com
Wild China	Tours off the beaten track	010 6465 6602	www.wildchina.com

Various Locations

West China Adventure Tours 中国西部探险之旅
010 1358168 2703 | www.westchina.net.cn

This firm offers a little more than straight wine tours, with trips to hot spas often included. Local wine may not match up to its imported rivals, but the vineyards are still worth exploring and after the first few glasses, you may not be able to judge anyway. West China can also arrange hiking, horse riding and cultural tours. Costs range from ¥200 to ¥400 for day trips, but the larger the group, the lower the price.

Tour Operators

Beijing is awash with tour agencies, each trying to cash in on China's growing popularity. Figures for 2002 (the last year with available records) show almost 100 million international tourists. Many firms that previously focused on Chinese customers have tried to make the transition to an international market. Most have failed, or only offer large tours (complete with the ubiquitous shopping trip) and guides with dubious foreign language skills. More useful are hotels and youth hostels, which will often organise excursions, or at least offer advice and guidance for their customers.

There is, however, a growing list of reputable agencies (their level of English is generally a good test), like the ones listed. Prices vary considerably depending on the skill and qualifications of your guide, and the level of luxury of your tour. You may also be able to negotiate a lower price, depending on the time of year and the number of people in your group. With more than 14,000 tour agencies registered in China, you can shop around and chose carefully.

With most of the tours, especially the one day trips, it is possible to make arrangements yourself for a fraction of the cost. If you have the time and inclination, this might prove to be the best course, especially if you are just visiting the major sites.

The Great Wall

29

Daytrips

Daytrips

Outside Beijing, there is enough to keep even the most adventurous explorer busy for a long time. World Heritage sites like the Great Wall and the Ming Tombs are joined by hot springs, temples, ancient villages and activity filled ranches.

Camping On The Great Wall
Camping on the Great Wall is allowed at Jinshanling, so bring a tent, or just a sleeping bag in the summer, and watch the sun rise over one of man's most impressive creations.

Cuandixia

About 60km west of Beijing, the tiny village of Cuandixia is a vestige of a lost time. Built by a single extended family in the Ming dynasty, it has survived more or less intact through the last 500 years.
Resembling a crumbling hamlet, the town is only a two hour drive outside the city but with its winding alleys and picturesque buildings, it can feel like another world. The nearby hills are lined with thin paths that offer amazing views back over the village while the food and tea at the few restaurants around the town comes fresh from the nearby fields. With accommodation readily available for only ¥20 a night, those wanting to stay longer will find families ready to oblige. The accommodation is basic, but during winter the *kang* beds are blissfully warmed from below by steam, which is far better than an electric blanket. Admission to the village is ¥20. Cuandixia Village is in Zhaitang Town, Mentougou district. Call 010 6981 9333.

Goose & Duck Ranch

Before long, most city dwellers feel the need to flee. For those who can't spare the time for a holiday, the Goose & Duck Ranch is a good tonic. Just outsides the city limits, it is good for families and filled with activities including bowling, go-carting, mini golf, shooting, horse riding, swimming, archery and paddleboats. With the children occupied, parents can relax with generous helpings of free food and drink. The admission price (¥200 for adults, ¥100 for children and free for kids under 4 years old) includes transport, food, drink and most activities.
For anyone wanting a longer stay, the ranch has cabins, lodges and bungalows on offer (¥500 per adult, ¥250 per child for a weekend). To get there, simply take the free bus that leaves at 09.30 from the Goose & Duck Pub (p.332), and returns at around 18:00. Bookings need to be made three days in advance. Call 010 6067 1097 or visit www.gdclub.net.cn.

Great Wall At Badaling

Many Beijing residents will scoff at the idea of visiting Badaling rather than one of the other Great Wall sections. As the first part open for tourists in 1957, it received all of the then current wisdom on restoring a site. The difference between restoring and completely rebuilding was slim. The site is a good representation of how the wall probably looked when it was first built (largely because it is all new), but with tourists, Starbucks and a KFC added.
On the plus side, it is close to the city, has good transport links and has few difficult sections for those with either challenged mobility or motivational issues. There is also a cable car up to the wall itself. If driving, take the Badaling Expressway, exit 17, Yanqing County. Call 010 6912 1737, or visit http://badaling.gov.cn. Open daily from 07:00 to 19:00.
Much more worthy of a visit is Badaling Safari World, across the highway from the wall. While 'safari world' may be a hopeful description, it is still an interesting trip. You can see wolves, lions, tigers, bears and zebras up close and enjoying more freedom than in Beijing Zoo (p.189). Admission to the Great Wall is ¥45 (¥25 for students) and ¥70 (¥45 for students) for Safari World. Tourist bus 1 from Qianmen takes about one hour. It is open daily from 08:00 to 17:00. Call 010 6912 1842 or visit www.bdlsw.com.cn.

Great Wall From Simaitai To Jinshanling

If you are not scared by a bit of exercise and the possibility of a twisted ankle, the best way of experiencing the Great Wall is to hike the section between Simaitai (¥40) and Jinshanling (¥50).

The 10km hike takes about four hours at a comfortable pace, including the necessary photo stops, and revels in some of the grandest views in China. Visited by far fewer people than Badaling, once you leave the main entrance you will probably have much of the wall to yourself.

Its isolation is partly because it is much harder to reach than Badaling. To get to the Simaitai end, take bus 980 from Donzhimen to Miyun, then switch to a Simaitai-bound bus. To reach Jinshanling, take the Chengdu bus, which drops you at the lower gate. The Simaitai entrance is in Gubeikou Town, Miyun County. Call 010 6903 1051 or visit www.ndcnc.gov.cn.

Well Cooked Eggs
Hungry for a snack? Try one of Jiuhua's special hardboiled eggs; watch it being hoisted down a well and then cooked in the simmering waters below.

Jiuhua Hot Springs

Although it is easy to find spas and massage parlours in Beijing, those who really want to pamper themselves could consider Jiuhua Hot Springs. A short bus ride north of Lishuiqiao subway station (bus 984), they are a good spot to unwind after a stressful week.

The naturally heated waters vary in temperature, between hot and too hot, while massages, saunas and ubiquitous staged entertainment will loosen all of those tight muscles. For those with really specific issues, piping hot pools are available that have mixtures of herbs specially designed to combat troubles with your lungs, spleen and kidneys.

The adventurous might also try the fish exfoliation bath, where you lie very still as small fish eat the dead skin off your body. They may be small, but in such quantities they create a disturbingly ticklish sensation.

The basic ticket price is ¥188 for a three hour visit (including a foot or back massage), but a discount card is available, as are additional treatments. For more information check the website. It is quite expensive, but during the cold winter months, worth every *fen*. The springs are in Xiaotangshan and are open daily from 08:00 to 13:00. Call 010 6178 2288 or visit www.jiuhua.com.cn.

The Ming Tombs

The Ming tombs are about 50km north of Beijing, and often visited by tour groups in combination with the Great Wall at Badaling. They are the final resting places of 13 of China's 16 Ming emperors. The first two were buried in Nanjing, while the seventh, Jingtai, was refused a place after usurping the throne from his brother who had been captured by Mongols. He was later executed for this. The site was chosen by the third Ming emperor, Yongle (who also planned the layout of Beijing and the Forbidden City), as a place with exceptional feng shui and natural beauty, and therefore worthy of his remains. Off-limits to commoners, it was pillaged and set on fire by rebel armies marching on Beijing in 1644.

Of the tombs, only three have been opened, and the most impressive is Changling, Yongle's grave (¥45). Most of the treasures found in the tombs have been removed, so a visit is more about the ambiance and subterranean grandeur of the final resting places of the Sons of Heaven. Another highlight is the 7km Spirit Way (¥30) leading to the tombs. This is lined with statues of animals, soldiers, officials and mythical beasts, forming an honour guard for the dead. Those wanting to make the journey on their own can take the Badaling-bound tourist buses that leave from Qianmen (Bus 1-5) before 09:00.

Weekend Breaks

China's vast size means people are willing to travel further for weekends away than in other countries. If you are organised, flights can take you to all corners of the continent, but for those looking more locally, there are several options just a sleeper train away.

Beidaihe

Beijing is stifling in the summer and unless (like the emperors) you have a palace to retreat to, Beidaihe may be your best bet. This stretch of coast first became popular with foreign residents in the 19th century, and their villas can still be found. It was requisitioned by the communist party leadership after 1949 and until the turn of this century, used for their summer meetings. It's far from a tropical paradise, but it does have relatively clean water, boats and beach paraphernalia. The highlight of any trip is likely to be the seafood; every building in the town seems to be a hotel and fish restaurant. Large tanks line the streets, and customers can choose their supper from the swimming mass. Hot days see the beaches teeming with people, and with China's love of regulations, the swimming area is carefully marked and can feel annoyingly restrictive. Buses and trains leave from Beijing Railway Station on most hours during the summer months. Accommodation is plentiful and costs ¥150 to ¥200 for a double room.

Chengde

The Summer Palace at Chengde, set in impressive mountains, was one of the first in China to join the UNESCO World Heritage list. It is a fitting imperial retreat. Mountains, lakes and forests surround the palatial grounds, and either side of its 10km long walls lie some of the most beautiful temples and pavilions in China. It was built between 1703 and 1794, with different temples and halls designed for when the emperor wished to impress, appear humble, or highlight his position as Son of Heaven. The palace was in use during the summer up until 1820, when the death of emperor Jiaqing (struck by lightning here) was taken as a sign of negative feng shui, and the site was abandoned. As well as the palace grounds (¥90), eight stunning, Tibetan-influenced temples are dotted outside the walls. Five are open to the public and the Putuo Zongcheng Temple (¥40 – it's modelled on the Potala Palace in Lhasa) is the most impressive. Trains arrive regularly from Beijing Railway Station (250km away), taking around four hours. The city is cooler than the capital so best seen in the summer.

Datong

Datong is an unimpressive city, surrounded by coal mines and factories. But, there are two gems that make it worth visiting; the Yungang Grottoes and Hengshan Monastery. The grottoes were started in 453, as penitence for the previous emperor's persecution of Buddhism. They are carved into the sandstone cliffs and are some of the most stunning examples of Buddhist art in the world. Twenty grottoes, with more than 50,000 carved statues of Buddha, have been meticulously cut out of the rock. It's an amazing show of religious devotion. Even more eye-catching is the Hengshan Monastery (or Hanging Temple). It is quite literally clinging to the canyon walls. Supported by wooden pillars, the monastery's 40 halls jut out over the valley at precarious angles. Thin walkways join them, and within each beautiful structure stand Buddhist, Confucian and Taoist gods (sometimes together in harmony).

Hohhot

If you have the urge to follow in Genghis Khan's footsteps and ride horses through the grasslands of China, Hohhot is certainly the place to visit. As the capital of Inner Mongolia, it is an unimpressive, bland city, but once you get out into the surrounding countryside, it can offer you some of the most memorable experiences in China.

Three grassland areas; Xilamuren, Huitengxile and Gegentela, are close to the city and in each, visitors can hire guides and horses to explore the vast wilderness. Traditional accommodation, in the form of *yurts* (permanent nomadic tents) is also available. The city has many tour operators, so it is best to wait until you arrive before choosing one, so that you can haggle in person.

Inside the city, the 16th century Dazhao temple complex (¥20) is worth a visit. Mongolian prince Altan Khan ordered the construction of this large Tibetan Buddhist temple in 1557, and it is still active to this day (though now home to only a few dozen monks). The 400 year old Silver Buddha is one of the many highlights on display inside.

Pingyao

Ancient Pingyao has somehow survived all that the 20th century has thrown at it. The Cultural Revolution, modernisation and the internet age appear to have had little impact. One of the few remaining walled cities, Pingyao had an illustrious past. Home to Rishengchang, China's first bank, it was the financial centre of the Qing dynasty. Many of the old banks are still preserved (¥120 for a two-day ticket, students ¥60). The temples that once served Taoists, Buddhists and Confucians still stand, and the dusty streets and one storey houses are a record of imperial China. Renting a bicycle and riding into the nearby countryside is rewarded with a glimpse of life in rural China. Pingyao is on the train route between Beijing and Xi'an and has some great courtyard hostels and hotels.

Xi'an

Ever since a farmer discovered a clay head while digging a well, Xi'an has been firmly on the tourist trail. That most visitors just come to see the Terracotta Warriors is perhaps an injustice for a city that was once the capital of China and housed generations of emperors. The 8,000 statues that form the deathly honour guard for Qin Shihuang, the unifier and first emperor of China, should be visited (¥90 for adults, ¥65 for students), but there are other diversions too. Walking or cycling along the old city walls (¥40 plus ¥20 for the bike hire) is a great way of getting a view of the city. The beautiful Muslim quarter and the Great Mosque (¥15) with their thin alleyways and bazaars, reveal the city's grand Muslim past. The Small and Big Wild Goose Pagodas (¥15 and ¥25 respectively) demonstrate Xi'an's key role in the development of Chinese Buddhism. The city is less welcoming than others in China, but has a good variety of hotels and food.

Weekend Breaks

Anda Guesthouse	78 Northern Hulun, Hohhot	na
Bobs Guesthouse	85 Huan Cheng Beilu, Xi'an	029 8210 8180
Chengde Plaza Hotel	5 Chezhan Lu, Chengde	na
Datong Hotel	37 Yingbin Xilu, Datong	035 2586 8555
Garden Hotel	4 Yanyin lu, Xi'an	029 8526 1111
HaoHai International Hotel	46 Xinjian Nanlu, Datong	035 2568 6666
Harmony Guesthouse	165 NanDajie, Pingyao	135 9308 5633
Hongan International Hotel	28 Binxi lu, Datong	035 2586 6555
Hyatt Regency	156 Dong Dajie, Xi'an	029 8769 1234
Inner Mongolia Hotel	West Wulanchabu Lu, Hohhot	047 1693 8888
Pingyao Tianyuankui Hotel	73 South Street, Pingyao	na
Pingyao Yide Hotel	16 Shaxiang Jie, Pingyao	na
Qian Yang Grand Hotel	18 Pule Lu, Chengde	031 4590 7000
Shangri-La Hotel	5 Xi Lin Guole Nanlu, Hohhot	047 1336 6888
Sheng Hua Hotel	22 Wulie Lu, Chengde	031 4227 1000
Xi'an Shuyuan Youth Hostel	2 Shuncheng Xiang, Nandajiexi, Xi'an	029 8728 7720
Yamen Hostel	69 Yamen Lu, Pingyao	035 4568 3539

Exploring China

Chengdu, Leshan, Emeishan & Jiuzhaigou

Flight time: 3 hours
Best time to visit:
April to October, but
winter snow and ice is
beautiful in Jiuzhaigou.

Fiery Sichuan cuisine, some of China's best street snacks and teahouses, and a distinctive Chinese opera style are just some of Chengdu's attractions. It is also the home of the giant panda. They live in the wild in Sichuan's mountains and can be seen close-up at a breeding research centre. The Giant Buddha of Leshan and the holy Buddhist mountain, Mount Emeishan, can be visited on a day trip, but the spectacular forested valleys, waterfalls and pools of Unesco-listed Jiuzhaigou to the north deserve a few days.

Chongqing & Yangtze Cruise

Flight time: 2.5 hours
Best time to visit:
Spring and autumn.
Avoid high summer.
Winters can be drab
and cold.

Yangtze cruises have been some of the most popular tourist trips since China opened up to visitors. The completion of the towering Three Gorges Dam will raise the water level 156m when the project is finished in 2009, and a number of historic sites are being submerged. But the majesty of the cliffs remains and a visit to the dam has become a highlight on cruises. Boats sail between Chongqing, a vast city perched on cliffs, and Wuhan, downstream.

Guangzhou

Flight time: 2 hours
Best time to visit:
Any time, but it gets hot
and humid in summer.

Formerly known as Canton and famed for its cuisine, the capital of Guangdong province lies on the Pearl River Delta close to Hong Kong. It is often overlooked as a tourist destination but has many interesting sights. Shamian Island, where British and French traders were once confined, has wonderful European architecture. Nearby is fascinating Qingping Market, with its dried insects and animal parts. Yuexiu Park has the Statue of the Five Goats, the city's symbol, plus 600-year-old Zhenhai Tower and the Sun Yatsen Memorial Hall. The decorative Chen Family Temple, Six Banyan Tree Temple and a night Pearl River cruise are other highlights.

Guilin & Yangshuo

Flight time: 2 hours
Best time to visit:
Autumn and spring is
the rainy season, winter
is cool and summer
is hot.

The sharp limestone peaks of this area of south-west China rise up dramatically out of the flat paddy fields to create one of the country's most iconic landscapes. They punctuate Guilin in a series of evocatively named hills, stretching either side of the Li River to laid-back Yangshuo and beyond. Other than taking a river cruise, you can explore the area by bike, venture into caves, go rock climbing, watch cormorant fishermen or chill out in bars and cafes.

Harbin

Flight time: 2.5 hours
Best time to visit:
January, for the ice and
snow festival.

China's most north-easterly city has a strong Russian influence. It was founded by Russian railway builders constructing the trans-Manchuria rail line and settled by refugees of the Bolshevik Revolution. The onion-domed Church of St Sophia is among the period buildings which survived the Cultural Revolution. But the city's real highlight is the spectacular Ice and Snow Festival, featuring snow sculptures and colossal buildings carved from the frozen Songhua River and lit by multi-coloured fluorescent tubes.

Hong Kong (p.202)

Hong Kong

Flight time: 2.5 hours
Best time to visit:
Any time, although
summers are hot
and sticky.

A decade on from its hand-over to China, the former British colony has retained its vitality and character and is thriving under the 'one country, two systems' policy. The opening of Hong Kong Disneyland has bolstered its appeal, which centres on shopping, nightlife, culture and cuisine. Victoria Peak gives spectacular views and is a perennial favourite, along with open-air markets, Ocean Park, Repulse Bay's beaches and bistros, the Big Buddha on Lantau Island and the Symphony of Lights show. Explorer publishes a *Hong Kong Mini* guide with lots more information.

Huangshan

Flight time: 1 hour
Best time to visit:
Autumn is pretty
because of the foliage
colours but any time
of year is good, even
winter.

The pine-tree-clad craggy pinnacles of Huangshan, or Yellow Mountain, are an iconic Chinese scene gracing countless paintings and porcelain designs. Clouds often cloak the mountain, enhancing its beauty. Climbing it takes a full day, but a cable car whisks more sedentary visitors to the summit. The mountain can be combined with a visit to the nearby preserved historic villages of Xidi and Hongcun, which starred in the movie *Crouching Tiger, Hidden Dragon*.

Kashgar

Flight time: 7 hours
Best time to visit:
Spring and autumn.
Summer brings fierce
heat.

China's western outpost feels very much like a frontier city. It grew into an important staging point on the Silk Road, having been established at an oasis at the junction of the trading route's northern and southern arms. Under Islamic rule for eight centuries, it has several important Muslim edifices including the Id Kah Mosque and Abakh Hoja Tomb. The Sunday bazaar is a lively and colourful affair. A Silk Road trip may take in historic Urumqi and Turpan, where grapes grow in a fertile valley and where the ground plunges to the second-lowest point on earth.

Lhasa

Flight time: 3.5 hours
Best time to visit:
May to October

The opening of the Qinghai-Tibet Railway has brought an unprecedented rush of tourists and settlers to the Tibetan capital – so much so that authorities have had to restrict tickets to the fortress-like Potala Palace, the former winter home of the Dalai Lama, which stands on a hill overlooking the city. Among Lhasa's other historic treasures are the ancient Jokhang Temple and neighbouring Barkhor district, with its lively market and prayer-wheel-spinning pilgrims. The impressive Sera and Drepung monasteries and the Dalai Lama's summer palace, Norbulingka, from which he fled in 1959, are also worth a visit.

Lijiang, Dali & Kunming

Flight time: 2.5 hours
(Kunming), 4.5 hours
(Lijiang).
Best time to visit:
Spring and autumn.

An ancient town of cobbled streets and alleys lined by ornate wooden buildings and laced by streams, Lijiang, in north-west Yunnan, is a delight despite becoming increasingly overrun by tourists. The town is home to the Naxi minority group, whose traditions, culture and music remain strong. More minority culture can be experienced among the cafes and environs of Dali (the Bai people) and in provincial capital Kunming, where the main attraction is the Shilin Stone Forest, two hours outside the city.

Macau

Flight time: 2 hours
Best time to visit:
Any time, but summers
are hot and humid.

Macau was the oldest European colony in China, having been under Portuguese rule for more than four centuries, before it was handed back to China in 1999. Its Historic Centre has been declared a World Heritage Site by Unesco and encompasses 28 buildings and monuments, and eight squares. Gambling has been licensed for over 150 years and gaming revenue now exceeds that of Las Vegas thanks to the opening up of its casino industry and the building of new mega casino resorts. More are in the pipeline.

Shanghai

Flight time: *2.5 hours to Jinan, then two hours by bus to Qufu.*
Best time to visit: *April to October.*

Qufu

The Shandong town of Qufu has left its mark on the world as the birthplace of philosopher Confucius, whose teachings have been followed for 2,500 years. At the heart of the old town, which is Unesco listed, is a walled complex encompassing the Kong Family Mansion and Kong Miao, or Temple of Confucius. Just beyond the town is Kong Lin, or Kong Family Cemetery, a huge forested area where the great man, his sons and more than 100,000 descendants are buried.

Flight time: *3 hours*
Best time to visit: *Any time, but October to March is the peak season.*

Sanya

Sanya, on the southern tip of tropical Hainan Island, has become China's top beach resort. Big hotels line sandy bays lapped by the warm, clear waters of the South China Sea. Activities include diving in the coral-rich sea and golf on palm-fringed courses. Yalong Bay sits between two peninsulas and is where most of the top hotels are found.

Flight time: *1.5 hours*
Best time to visit: *Spring and autumn.*

Shanghai

Shanghai is China's largest city and a brash commercial hub. With teetering high-rises in the modern business district and classical European architecture in the Bund, the city has developed a reputation as one of the most exciting places in the world. Hectic nightlife, boutique hotels, fashionable stores and diverse culture are attracting visitors from China and beyond. For more information see the *Shanghai Mini* from Explorer.

Flight time: *2.5 hours*
Best time to visit: *Spring and autumn.*

Xi'an

The Terracotta Warriors, buried for 2,000 years and discovered by two farmers in 1974, are one of the world's greatest treasures and have made Xi'an a must-visit destination. The burial chambers do not disappoint, and the city has other attractions too; Xi'an was the starting point for the Silk Road and was the capital for 13 dynasties. The old city wall runs for more than 15km, enclosing the Drum Tower and Great Mosque. Beyond the wall are delights including the Big Wild Goose Pagoda.

Travel Agencies

Beijing Highlights	773 281 0927	www.beijinghighlights.com
BJS Holiday	010 5166 7711	www.bjs.com.cn
BTG International	010 9609 6798	www.btgtravel.cn
China Swan	010 6731 6393	www.china-swan.com
China Youth Travel Service	021 6433 0000	www.scyts.com.cn
CNAdventure	010 5126 8494	www.cnadventure.com
Country Holidays	010 5869 1781	www.countryholidays.com.cn
Easy Tours International Travel Service	021 6203 7070	www.easytours.cn
Easy Travel	010 5126 7266	www.easytravel.cn
eLong	400 810 1119	www.elong.net
Golden Holiday	010 6858 9990	www.goldenholiday.com
TUI	010 6517 1370	www.tui.cn
Wild China	010 6465 6602	www.wildchina.com

Activities

Sports & Activities

While the legacy of the Olympics remains to be seen, the swell of excitement it has caused has certainly thrust sports to the forefront of local minds. Meanwhile, the older generation continues to play majong and practice tai-chi in parks and underpasses all over Beijing, all through the year. Locals live their lives in public, and one of the city's great treats is to spend an afternoon strolling around and watching local life.

As the country's cultural centre, Beijing also offers plenty for the more creative and spiritual, from art to yoga. The Chinese Culture Club, mentioned throughout this book, is a good place to start (www.chinesecultureclub.org).

The growing number of foreigners means that language is becoming less of an issue, and it is easy to find classes that are conducted in English or a sports team that uses English as its common language. Activities are generally much cheaper than in the west, so it is a great opportunity to learn a new craft or try a different activity.

Beijing's hot, smoggy summers and cold, crisp winters do restrict outdoor activities somewhat, but the many new indoor facilities ensure that residents can remain active all year round. The sub-zero temperatures in winter actually add a whole new dimension to the city, and while footballers may be cursing themselves for not bringing an extra pair of long–johns, others will be relishing the chance to go ice skating on Houhai's lakes or skiing in the hills to the north. Likewise, the oppressive heat of summer presents opportunities to escape the city for fresh air, and the Great Wall offers some unbeatable hiking.

The rapid pace of change in China, and in particular Beijing, is presenting its residents with a wealth of opportunities. Like the buildings, new activities pop up on a weekly basis, so it is worth checking one of the city's many expat publications (p.51) to stay up to date.

Aerobics & Fitness Classes		
Bally Total Fitness	010 5869 0666	www.csibally.com
California Fitness	400 8100 988	www.californiafitness.com
Evolution Fitness	010 8599 7650	www.evolution-fitness.com
Kerry Sports	010 6561 8833	www.beijingkerrycentre.com
Nirvana Fitness Centre	010 6597 2008	www.nirvana.com.cn
Ozone Fitness	010 8586 9533	www.ozonefitness.com.cn
Powerhouse Gym	010 8528 2008	www.powerhousegym.com.cn

Aerobics & Fitness Classes

The city's older generation can be seen exercising outdoors all year round. Some gather to dance, others will limber up on mind-boggling roadside exercise contraptions, while more will briskly walk backwards, seemingly oblivious to the city life around them. If you don't fancy the gym, then take a leaf out of their book and head to the streets. Once you've seen a 60 year old grandmother with her ankles behind her head, your own grumbling about little aches will be put into perspective.

Otherwise, there are plenty of modern gyms (p.232) that offer well-run classes. The city has several fitness chains (see table above), many of which offer membership discounts, particularly after Chinese New Year.

Calligraphy brushes

Art Classes

Other options **Art Supplies** p.250, **Art Galleries** p.176

Beijing has a thriving art scene and a close-knit community of artists. They are generally based around a series of decommissioned military buildings in Dashanzi, Chaoyang. It was feared that this area, known as 798 (p.167), would go the way of Beijing's many *hutongs* and meet the wrecking ball, but it was recently declared a protected site. Professional artists often choose this area as their base, but for mere enthusiasts it is a great place to get a taste of contemporary Chinese art. The Chinese Culture Club offers many classes for those who want to go a step further, and put paint to canvas.

Kent Center, 29 Anjialou Liangmaqiao Lu Chaoyang 亮马桥路安家楼29号肯 特中心 朝阳区 **⊕ *Dongzhimen L2*** *Map 7 D1* **1**

Chinese Culture Club 中国文化协会

010 6432 9341 | www.chinesecultureclub.org

This group is good for people who want to deepen their understanding of Chinese culture. Check the website for details of upcoming classes, which are designed specifically for expats and are conducted in English. They include calligraphy, ink and wash painting, and Chinese landscape painting. A two hour class costs ¥120 and includes all materials. You must register for classes in advance. Outside of office hours, call 010 6432 1041.

Room 128, Estoril House, 2 Jiangtai Lu Chaoyang 将台路2号爱都大厦 128室 朝阳区 *Map 5 E3* **2**

Chinese Language & Culture School 汉语语言文化学校

010 6437 9280 | www.clcs.com.cn

This offers weekly classes in calligraphy, Chinese painting, knot making, tea ceremonies, paper cutting and playing traditional instruments. The school also coordinates a Chinese language centre, lectures and tours. Classes cost ¥100 each and can be customised for groups and individuals.

Aussie Rules Football

Aussie Rules is gradually expanding from its antipodean roots and gaining popularity around the world. Beijing is no exception. This physically demanding sport requires a range of skills, with speed, agility, coordination and strength – all integral parts of the game. And while mullets are encouraged, they are no longer compulsory. Teams consist of 18 players and games are played on an oval pitch, with four posts at each end through which points are scored.

77 Baiziwannaner Lu Chaoyang 百子湾南2路77号 朝阳区 *Map 7 D3* **3**

The Beijing Bombers

www.beijingbombers.cn

The Beijing Bombers train every Saturday afternoon from March to November at the Beijing City International School (BCIS), about 2km south of Dawanglu subway station. Sessions run from 16:00 to 18:00 in the summer and 15:30 to 17:30 at either end of the season. The club currently has a playing group of 30 to 40 blokes from Australia, China and the US, but it is open to anyone who wants to give the game a try. It is also one of the cheaper sports in town – players pay just ¥20 for each session. The Bombers play Shanghai home and away each year in their big grudge match, and some of the better players from both sides team up to form the 'China Reds', who play in the Asian Championships in exotic locales such as Thailand and Singapore. Contact Andrew Sawitsch (sang500@ yahoo.com) or Ed Smith (edsmith@bjconsultinggroup.com) for more information.

Badminton

Badminton is a hugely popular pastime in China and you will often have to dodge shuttlecocks as you take a stroll down one of Beijing's *hutongs* or wander through a park. One of the biggest appeals is that you can play almost anywhere. It is also a great opportunity to get out into the streets and soak up some atmosphere. You can buy a badminton racket at sports shops (p.284) or superstores for as little as ¥50.

True enthusiasts can reserve courts by the hour at schools and universities (p.126) for about ¥20 or join a club. Beijing International Badminton Club (Side Park Badminton Centre, 010 6433 5226) is a slightly more serious club for players with some experience.

Baseball

Various Locations

Bad News Bears
010 8557 4961 | baseballchina@yahoo.com

Baseball has been played in China since the 1800s, but was banned during the Maoist era and has been slow to make a comeback. Still, there are some opportunities to play the great American pastime in the Chinese capital. The Bad News Bears club has regular weekend games against colleges and semi-pro teams, and tends to draw the best players in the expat community. Players must buy their own uniforms and pay their share of field costs.

Basketball

Basketball is arguably the most popular sport in China, particularly among school children, who worship their home-grown hero Yao Ming and other NBA superstars like Allen Iverson. Replica shirts are a common sight, and sports stores and markets stock plenty of merchandise. When it's not too cold to play outdoors, the best games can be found on the courts of the city's parks (p.190) or universities (p.139) where getting a game is never difficult, and court time is usually free. During the winter, indoor gyms can be found at the city's international schools (p.130) and the fitness centres of large hotels and complexes like East Gate Plaza (010 6415 8797), which rents half courts by the hour for ¥50. Otherwise, you can book half a court at some gyms (p.232) and play there.

108 Chongwenmennei
Dajie
Dongcheng
崇文门内大街108号
东城区
Map 11 A4 **5**

Dongdan PE Centre 东单体育中心
010 6512 9377

These courts draw some of the better players in Beijing. If you have teams in place, you can rent indoor full courts (¥500 per hour) or half courts (¥300 per hour). Prices for outdoor courts vary. And if you want to find new players to go up against, individuals can play on the indoor (¥10 per hour) or outdoor courts (¥5 per hour) too.

Bowling

Ten-pin bowling is pretty popular and, for locals, often features with karaoke on a night out. It is a great opportunity to hang out with friends, have a few drinks and show off. Bowling is not renowned for its fitness benefits, and having easy access to booze reinforces this, but it is a great way to unwind. Beijing used to have a few 24 hour bowling alleys, but now even the biggest ones close in the early hours. The city's most famous bowling alley is Gongti 100, which is sandwiched between a row of nightclubs by the west gate of the Workers' Stadium (Map 9 E4). This has 100 lanes and some claim it is the largest in the world. Another favourite is at the Holiday Inn in Lido (p.92).

8 Gongti Xilu
Chaoyang
工体西路8号
朝阳区
Map 9 D4 **6**

Gongti 100 工体100
010 6552 2688

This enormous bowling alley, named for its number of lanes, is one of the world's largest. It can easily serve as a stop in a night of bar hopping or as an event in itself. Besides the bowling, it has a large arcade, ping pong rooms, and even some small rides for children. Bowling costs ¥30 per game per person, with an additional ¥5 for shoe rental.

Bungee Jumping

Although any claims of total safety should be taken with a pinch of salt, this activity is less dangerous than people might assume. Check listings in *City Weekend* and *That's Beijing* (p.51) for updated information on what venues are open around the city.

Wangfuijing Dajie
(by Lisheng Sports)
Dongcheng
王府井大街(利生体育
商厦旁)
东城区
Map 10 F2 **7**

Wangfujing Slingshot 王府井东方火箭文化艺术有限公司

010 6559 5259

None of Beijing's bungee jumping venues is more central than this one on Wangfujing. The thrilling 'rocket bungee' in front of Lisheng Sports is kind of a reverse bungee (you fly up) and is similar to being hurled from a jet aircraft in an ejector seat. If the ride itself is not enough to tempt you, you can view yourself on video after your launch. Tickets are ¥120 for one person and ¥300 for three people.

Camping

Other options **Outdoor Goods** p.278

The countryside around Beijing has some great camping spots, and you can get all the gear you need at Decathlon (p.285). Tents, sleeping bags and other kit can also be bought at the markets, but check them thoroughly, as you don't want to face the elements with dodgy equipment. Beijing's icy winters mean that this is mostly a summer pastime, and although the heat can become almost unbearable during the day, you may need a light jumper in the evening. Strictly speaking, you are not allowed to camp independently on the Great Wall, but many people do. Just be careful with campfires. Taking an organised tour (p.193) might be better, as you won't have to worry about legal or language issues, and you will get access to some great spots.

Various Locations

West China Tours 北京秘境旅游

135 8168 2703 | *www.westchina.net.cn*

This company will arrange everything from start to finish. West China organises trips around the country, and excursions closer to Beijing include camping on the Great Wall. English-speaking guides are on hand to help you on your way and they will even set up your tent and cook dinner. It is worth packing your own drinks to help the spirits soar, as you gaze at that rare Beijing sight – a starry sky.

Climbing

For those not afflicted by vertigo, climbing can be a thrilling way to build up muscles and enjoy a truly rewarding experience. China offers some great climbs, but getting from Beijing to Moon Hill in Yangshuo or base camp in the Himalayas can be a bit of a headache on the weekends. The mountains around Beijing have only a limited appeal for experienced climbers, but there are places in town that will help cliff hangers get their fix.

Various Locations

Angela's Ice Climbing 优度户外

136 1124 1407 | *udoadventure@hotmail.com*

Most of the outdoor walls close during the winter months, but hardcore climbers can ascend a different kind of slope. Although it remains less well-known, ice climbing has become increasingly popular in China recently. If you are interested in giving this winter mountaineering a shot, call Angela or send an e-mail to reserve a spot.

Various Locations

Dianshi Club 点石俱乐部

138 0105 2361

Rock climbing buffs should check out this group of outdoorsmen. On weekdays, they climb at the Fengyuxue Ritan Park Climbing Wall, and weekends they travel to places in the suburbs. The Ritan Park wall costs ¥10 per climb and ¥30 per day. Although the wall need not be considered dangerous, climbers should take care, as safety standards in China are not nearly as strict as they are at climbing walls in the west. See Fengyuxue entry below for more details.

Baiziwan Lu
Chaoyang
百子湾路32号苹果社区
12号楼
朝阳区
Map 7 C3 11

Exbear Indoor Climbing Wall 极度体验

010 5876 0008 | www.exbear.com

This climbing wall is challenging enough to keep keen climbers happy. Beginners are also welcome, but may initially find it daunting. Costs vary depending on the time of day. From 12:30 to 18:00 it is ¥20, from 18:00 to 23:00 it is ¥30. Shoe rental costs ¥10. Weekly climbing cards cost ¥75. It's inside 12, 32 Pingguo Community.

B1-12 Pingod
Community, 32
Baiziwan Lu
百子湾路32号苹果社区
12号楼B1
Map 7 C3 12

Extreme Experience 极度体验

010 5876 0008

Serious climbers just have to keep climbing, even in winter. The indoor wall at Extreme Experience on Baiziwan Lu is Beijing's best spot. The wall charges ¥20 before 18:00, and ¥30 after. Climbers can find all the gear they need at the attached climbing store. For serious climbers, there is an unlimited entry card: one year for ¥998, or two months for ¥300. Open 10:00 to 23:00.

Ritan Park
Chaoyang
朝阳区
Map 11 D2 14

Fengyuxue Ritan Park Climbing Wall 日坛公园风雨雪攀岩场

010 8563 5038

This relatively small wall is in the picturesque grounds of Ritan Park (p.192). Climbs cost ¥10, or ¥30 for access all day. It's generally open 10:00 to 21:00 Monday to Friday, but it is worth calling in advance as these times can change without notice.

Longtanhu Park
Dongerhuan Nanlu
Chongwen
东二环南路龙潭湖公园
崇文区
Map 7 B4 15

Longtanhu Climbing Center 龙潭湖攀岩中心

010 6718 6358

This climbing wall, which is inside the east gate of Longtanhu Park (18 Longtanhu Lu, Chongwen, 010 6714 4336), is open from 09:00 to 17:00 and costs ¥20 per climb.

Cookery Classes

West House, 3 Shajing
Hutong, Nanluoguxiang
Dongcheng
南锣鼓巷沙井胡同3号
西房
东城区
Map 8 D2 15

Hutong Cuisine 胡同烹饪

010 8401 4788 | www.hutongcuisine.com

Chinese cooking classes are offered daily (by appointment) in a traditional courtyard home. You will be taught, by chef Chun Yi, how to cook three dishes in the traditional Guangzhou or Sichuan style. Classes cost ¥180 each or ¥450 for three sessions. They take place from either 10:30 to 14:30 or 16:00 to 20:00.

Cricket

Dulwich College, Exit 7
Airport Expressway
(first left after toll)
Shunyi
机场高速公路7号出口
左转，德威学校
Map 3 C4 16

Beijing Cricket Club 北京板球俱乐部

135 5274 7032 | www.beijingcricketclub.com

Yes, it's true, you can play cricket in China. Beijing Cricket Club has existed in some form since the 80s, when a group of people from various embassies played on someone's lawn. The sport died out until 2006, when a committed bunch of fans got together to form the club, which now has 80 members who regularly prop up the bar at Frank's Place (p.331). The team plays from March to November at Dulwich College, which has the only purpose-built cricket pitch in the north of China. Games and practice take place every Sunday afternoon, with a bus available from Dongzhimen to the ground. There is a bi-annual grudge match against the Shanghai Dragons and players have the opportunity to tour in regional sixes tournaments in Hong Kong and Shanghai. Membership is ¥600 per year or ¥50 to play each week.

Cycling

Other options **Sports Goods** p.284, **Mountain Biking** p.220, **Bicycle Tours** p.193

Beijing's streets may have been taken over by cars, but bicycles remain an essential mode of transport for many. Jumping on a bike and setting out onto the crowded streets can initially be quite daunting, evoking memories of the *Wacky Races*. It is, however, a fantastic way to travel, either for commuting or for more leisurely exploring. Most of the main roads have wide cycle lanes that offer some sanctuary from the rush of motor vehicles, but it is important to beware of oncoming traffic, fellow cyclists and other potential threats such as open manholes. Cyclists tend not to wear helmets but these are available from bike shops (p.253), superstores and markets.

Giant (p.253) has stores around town and offers some of the best bikes. Supermarkets such as Carrefour (p.264) and Wal-Mart (p.297) also offer a decent range at competitive prices. Be sure to buy a good lock, as you seldom meet someone here who has not had at least one bicycle stolen. If you want to try cycling before committing to a flash new bike, try Bicycle Rental (www.bicyclekingdom.com, 133 8140 0738 for English speakers), which allows you to order bikes online, or Shuangren (130 7013 5600 / 010 6089 1616), which has three stores in Xicheng, including one opposite the Dianmen department store.

Various Locations

Beijing Mobsters 北京山地自行车俱乐部
http://themob.404.com.au

This group likes nothing more than hooning around dirt tracks, mountain paths, and muddy lanes. The only reliable contact is through Google Groups, but the page listed has lots of info about rides, pictures of previous events and other info to get you started. It's all quite fun but serious, with rides of more than 100km fairly typical.

Dance Classes

Other options **Music Lessons** p.221

Sino-Chu Wine Bar
18 Liangmahe Nanlu
Dongcheng
亮马河南路18号亮马
红酒屋
东城区
Map 9 F3 **18**

Beijing Ballroom 北京交谊舞会俱乐部
131 2102 5208 | http://groups.yahoo.com/group/beijingballroom/

On arriving in Beijing, Kevin Wiland was horrified to discover there was no good place to learn ballroom dancing. He has changed that with his club, Beijing Ballroom. It offers 'some salsa and some swing in a friendly atmosphere'. Wiland sponsors a free ballroom dance party every Saturday at 20:00 at the Sino-Chu Wine Bar (18 Liangmahe Nanlu). He also offers group and private lessons starting at ¥300 per hour.

Nine million and one

Dongcheng Cultural
Center, 111 East Jiao
Daokou Lu
Dongcheng
交道口东大街111号，
东城区文化馆
东城区
Map 8 E3 **19**

Beijing LDTX Modern Dance Co 北京雷动天下现代舞团
010 6405 4292 | www.beijingldtx.com

This is the first independent professional dance company in China, and is famous for putting on some of the most exciting and innovative dance performances in the capital. Even if you are not a professional, you can get into the action. The company sponsors training classes on weeknights and all day on Saturdays and Sundays. Individual classes are ¥40, and a 10 class pass costs ¥300.

Various Locations

The Beijing Modern Dance Company 北京现代舞团
010 6601 6107 | www.bmdc.com.cn

This may be the most prestigious modern dance company in China. Known primarily for its performances at the Chaoyang Culture Center and TNT Theatre, the BMDC holds classes for dancers of every make, model and level of experience. They are taught by members of the BMDC or invited guests.

Dragon Boat Racing

Dragon boat racing is synonymous with Chinese culture and has a history dating back centuries. The sport was invented in China and every year lavish events are held in honour of various historical figures, including the poet Qu Yuan. These festivals draw thousands of people, with local dignitaries taking on pre-race ceremonial duties, such as painting pupils on the dragon's eyes. The head sits on the boat's prow to ward off evil spirits. Boats usually sit up to 20 paddlers, a drummer and main oarsman. Although the sport is more popular in the south of China, Taiwan and Hong Kong, there is still a thriving community in Beijing.

Various Locations

Beijing Dragon Boat Club   北京龙舟俱乐部
135 0103 6116 | polo_heming@hotmail.com

This club, which is about 70% Chinese, trains on Houhai lake on Wednesday evenings in summer from 19:00 to 21:00 and on Sunday mornings from 09:30 to 11:30. These sessions are hard work but great fun and a chance to show off your paddling and singing skills to tourists and locals strolling around the lakes. The team regularly gets invited to compete in tournaments around China, where local governments provide hotels and food. These events offer a marvellous opportunity to experience a side of China that few people see. Houhai training sessions cost ¥30 and paddlers often go for a meal in a nearby restaurant afterwards.

Drama Groups

Jiangjingjiu Bar
Houhai
钟鼓楼广场疆进酒
酒吧
Map 6 F1 22

Beijing Improv 北京即兴创作俱乐部
010 8405 0124 | www.beijingimprov.com

The wild child of the Beijing theatre scene, Beijing's improv kings call themselves 'a group of folks who are committed to exercising our laughing muscles on a regular basis'. Check their website for details on upcoming performances, or get into the action yourself. Every Wednesday from 20:00 to 22:00, Beijing Improv holds workshops on improvisational theatre at the Jiangjingjiu Bar.

Various Locations

Beijing Playhouse 北京剧场
www.beijingplayhouse.com

If you think you were meant for the stage, head to the Beijing Playhouse. Run by executive director Chris Verill, the ambitious community theatre is coming off successful runs of *A Christmas Carol* and *Guys and Dolls*, and will be putting on new shows throughout 2008. There are opportunities for actors and stagehands with varying levels of skill and experience. Check out their website for updated information on how you can get into the action.

Various Locations

Cheeky Monkey Productions 顽皮猴子戏剧社

www.cheekymonkeytheater.com

Producer, writer, director and actress Elyse Ribbons is the driving force behind Cheeky Monkey, a more experimental counterpart to the Beijing Playhouse. Ribbons' company put on the original play *I Heart Beijing*, and, in early 2008, produced a theatre festival comprised of 10 minute shorts. For future original productions, Cheeky Monkey will be looking for actors, writers, and stagehands. Check the website for updated information or email Ribbons directly (elyse@iheartbeijing.com).

Football

Football is one of the most popular sports in China. While many Chinese regard the national side and local clubs with something close to disdain, they have huge respect for European club football and replica shirts are common. One team of lifeguards in Sanya in south China's Hainan province even wears the England football kit as its uniform.

Beijing has two established and well-run leagues. These run for most of the year, taking a break in the coldest winter months, but even then teams often get together for an indoor kickabout.

New arrivals can contact either the International Friendship Football Club (IFFC) or ClubFootball, and they will help assign you to a team. Alternatively, if you have a big enough gang of friends, you can form your own team and apply to join, although you will start in the lower divisions.

The IFFC has around 40 teams playing in four different 11 a side leagues every weekend. Playing standards vary, with the likes of the mighty Afrikans and Athletico Beijing fielding some highly skilled players in the first division. The lower leagues cater for slightly less blessed individuals. Some of the teams are based on nationality, while others pride themselves on their multinational make-up. Membership fees vary, but are generally ¥300 to ¥400, which includes a club strip. Expect to pay around ¥70 per match. Games are held throughout the weekend on good quality Astroturf pitches near the Rosedale Hotel in Lido or at Chaoyang Sports Stadium.

IFFC provides referees and linesmen who put up with the backchat with varying degrees of composure. Teams can be fined or even expelled from the league for excessive bad behaviour, which is not an entirely uncommon sight. You have been warned.

Unit A10, Jingdu
Business Hotel, 26
Jiuxianqiao Lu
Chaoyang
酒仙桥路26号晶都国际
酒店A10室
朝阳区
Map 5 E4 25

ClubFootball 万国群星足球俱乐部

010 5130 6893 | www.clubfootball.com.cn

ClubFootball is a well-run outfit with staff qualified with the English FA, who run coaching camps for kids throughout the year. Since 2005 it has focused on five a side football. Many of the teams in the IFFC were affiliated with ClubFootball and there continues to be a close relationship between all parties. If you are not having much luck getting into the IFFC league, contact ClubFootball for help. The five a side league involves 32 teams that play on week nights on pitches near the east gate at Chaoyang Park (p.191). Women's football is also available. Registration costs ¥100, which gets you a card that offers discounts at bars, restaurants and spas around town.

Various Locations

International Friendship Football Club 国际友好足球俱乐部

010 6234 7106 | www.iffc1994.com

Beijingers that love their football can flaunt their stuff at the IFFC's weekly matches. This enormous league boasts more than 800 members from more than 70 countries. There are 24 teams, divided into two divisions of 12, for 11 a side games. Players can join existing teams or form their own. Matches cost ¥100 or ¥50 for students. Membership costs ¥300 and team fees are ¥1,000. Check the website for updated league standings.

Frisbee

Ultimate Frisbee caters to a mixed crowd wanting good exercise and to work on a variety of throwing and catching skills. Players are not allowed to run when they have the Frisbee in their hands, and points are scored by catching the disc in your opponent's end-zone. Regulation fields are 70 yards long and 40 yards wide, with end-zones 25 yards deep. The friendly spirit of the game is reflected by the fact that players are responsible for their own foul and line calls and there are no referees. So, test your honesty and have a fling.

Various Locations

Beijing Ultimate Frisbee 北京飞盘

136 0103 6430 | www.beijingultimate.com

Although members take the games and practices very seriously, those who are new to the sport are encouraged to join in. The club practises regularly in Beijing, and occasionally organises trips to tournaments in Tianjin, Shanghai and outside China. Practices are usually held at the Beijing City International School (p.132). First-timers should call or check the website to confirm times and locations. There are no membership fees but players pay for court or pitch rental, which is split among the group and usually comes to about ¥30.

Gaelic Football

Gaelic Football looks like an amalgamation of rugby, football and Aussie Rules, played on a rectangular pitch with uprights similar to rugby posts at each end. The ball, which is round and slightly smaller than a football, can be carried for four steps and then kicked or passed with the hand or fist. Players can carry it while running, but they must bounce or drop it onto their foot after every four paces. Points are scored by putting the ball over or under the crossbar between the posts.

Western Academy
10 Laiguangying
Donglu
Chaoyang
莱广营东路10号北京
西学校
朝阳区
Map 5 E1 28

Beijing Gaelic Football Club 北京盖尔人运动家协会

139 1175 6121 | www.beijinggaa.net

Despite its obvious lack of Chinese characteristics, Gaelic Football has really taken off and the Beijing Gaelic Football Club can rightly claim to be one of the biggest sporting groups in the city. This predominantly expatriate club has both men's and women's teams that regularly tour Shanghai and elsewhere in the region. Anyone is welcome to join, and annual membership is ¥300. The club also has a page on Facebook – search for Beijing GAA.

Golf

The many top golf courses around Beijing reflect the country's rising prosperity, with more and more locals donning their plus-fours and heading out for a hack. While you can still get a full set of good quality fake clubs for around ¥1,200, golf remains an expensive pastime, with a round at one of the top courses costing as much as ¥1,000. However, you will be treated royally, and keen young caddies will scavenge in the rough to find balls from the most wayward of shots.

It is worth registering with a group such as the Beijing Golfer's Club, which gives you great discounts on green fees and access to the city's best courses. Handicaps at these clubs are available after posting five scorecards.

West of Chaobai River
Shunyi
马坡村潮白河西侧
顺义区
Map 3 C2 29

Beijing Country Golf Club 北京乡村高尔夫俱乐部

010 6940 1111 | www.bccgolf.com

Created in 1998, this club has three courses and is 30km north of Beijing on the west bank of Chaobai River. Green fees are ¥568 on weekdays and ¥888 at weekends. Annual membership costs ¥22,000.

Various Locations

Beijing Golfer's Club
www.beijing-golfers-club.org

Started in 1999, the Beijing Golfer's Club organises weekly Sunday games at courses around town, with a 10:00 tee-off. Membership (¥900 per year) has grown each year and is open to golfers of various levels. This includes invitations to over 40 events, heavily discounted green fees at some of the city's best courses and access to tournaments. Costs per game are ¥200 to ¥500 for members and ¥900 for non-members.

North of Shisanling
Ming Tombs Reservoir
昌平区十三陵水库北侧

Beijing International Golf Club 北京国际高尔夫俱乐部
010 6076 2288

Beijing's oldest course is set in a scenic spot next to the Ming Tombs Reservoir, among the hills 45km north-west of the city. The course has held major international events, including the Volvo Masters. Green fees are ¥1,400 on weekends, ¥800 Monday to Friday for men and ¥480 for ladies. Annual membership costs ¥23,000.

Beijing Country Golf
Club

Beijing Ladies Golf Club 北京女子高尔夫俱乐部
www.beijingladiesgolf.org

This ladies club welcomes all players who have at least a basic knowledge of the game to play on Thursday mornings. Annual membership fees are ¥300.

10 Xinglong Xijie
Gaobeidian
Chaoyang
高碑店兴隆西街10号
朝阳区
Map 7 F2 **33**

Beijing Meisong Golf Club 北京美松高尔夫俱乐部
010 8575 3959

Whether you want to work on your drive or just blow off some steam, the Beijing Meisong Golf Club is the place to put your clubs to good use. The large driving range has 124 tees on two different levels. Non-members pay ¥30 to ¥75 for 50 balls and ¥20 to ¥40 for club rental. If you plan to go regularly, an annual membership costing ¥8,000 gets you unlimited balls.

Pine Valley Resort
Nankou Town
Changping District
昌平区南口镇华彬庄园

Beijing Pine Valley Int'l Golf Club 华彬国际高尔夫俱乐部
010 8528 8038 | *www.pinevalley.com.cn*

This course, 60km to the north-west of Beijing, was designed by the great Jack Nicklaus and has a price tag to match. It hosted the 2007 Beijing Open and Johnnie Walker Classic, and is only open to members who pay a steep membership fee and annual duties of $1,500.

9A Nongzhan Nanlu
Chaoyang
农展南路甲9号
朝阳区
Map 7 C1 **35**

Chaoyang Kosaido Golf Club 广济堂高尔夫俱乐部
010 6501 8584

If playing an international standard course is too daunting (or a bit above your budget), this is a more accessible and cheaper option. A round costs ¥290 and club hire is available for ¥100. This nine-hole course is fairly challenging and there is also a driving range.

East Yanjiao Economic
Development Zone
燕郊经济开发区东侧

Jinghua Golf Club 京华高尔夫俱乐部
010 6159 1234

This smart course to the east of Beijing held the 2005 Volkswagen Masters and has some challenging holes with plenty of water hazards. Green fees cost ¥800.

Pine Valley Resort
Nankou Town
昌平区南口镇华彬庄园

Pine Valley Golf Resort & Country Club
华彬国际高尔夫俱乐部
010 8979 6868 | *www.pinevalley.com.cn*

This 7,000 yard course was designed by Jack Nicklaus. It is in Changping and has stunning views of the Great Wall at Badaling. It's only open to members, who must pay a $180,000 membership fee and annual dues of $1,500. Open 07:00 to 16:00.

Ritan Park
Chaoyang
日坛公园北门高尔夫
花园
朝阳区
Map 11 D2 **38**

Ritan Minature Golf Course 日坛小型高尔夫球场

010 8561 5506

For a city of Beijing's size, there is a notable lack of mini-golf courses. The happy exception is the course at Ritan Park (p.192). It is no grand affair, but makes for a great family outing or as a stop on a date. It is open from 08:00 to 19:30 and accepts international credit cards.

Hiking

Other options **Daytrips** p.197, **Outdoor Goods** p.278

A rather famous wall about an hour's drive north of Beijing offers some truly wonderful hikes with striking scenery. There are many trails on and around it, and you can easily hire a taxi to take you there. If your Mandarin language skills allow, you can negotiate with a driver to wait and pick you up at the end of your walk. Otherwise it is a good idea to sign up to a group like Beijing Hikers, which organises trips for most weekends. See the Exploring chapter, p.152 for more ideas about day trips and excursions out of the smog of the city. Try Tours & Sightseeing, p.193, for tour operators and other guides.

A 201, Kent Centre
Chaoyang
亮马桥路29号安家楼肯
特中心A201
朝阳区
Map 5 C4 **39**

Beijing Amblers

010 6432 9341 | *www.chinesecultureclub.org*

This group is part of the Chinese Culture Club (p.207), and organises weekend walks that range in cost from ¥150 to ¥400 for day trips, or more for overnight excursions. There are normally 20 to 30 people on each hike. These are organised for most weekends and usually head to scenic locations with some cultural or historical significance. The Kent Centre is at 29 Liangmaqiao Lu.

Various Locations

Beijing Hikers 北京爱山户外文化国际俱乐部

139 1002 5516 | *www.beijinghikers.com*

The Beijing Hikers take on treks in towns and villages around the capital. The group meets every Sunday, but occasionally organises overnight hikes from Saturday to Sunday. Hikers meet at 08:00 at the Starbucks outside the Holiday Inn, Lido (p.167). You should check the website or ask about fitness levels in advance, but most are suitable for all. Regular hikes cost ¥200 per person (¥150 for children under 12). Cost includes two-way transport, food and drink and professional guidance.

Hockey

National Stadium
Olympic Green
🚇 *Jishuitan L2*
Map 4 F2 **41**

Beijing Hockey Club 北京曲棍球俱乐部

Tiantan Park (p.173)

This newly formed club welcomes players of both sexes and all ages. Training and games are held on the new astroturf pitches just south of the Bird's Nest Stadium (p.228) every Saturday from 13:00. Chinese hockey players also join in the fun and you can arrange to buy equipment at the ground. Match subs cost ¥30. The club now has about 80 members and is growing rapidly, with plans to participate in tournaments around southeast Asia, including Bangkok. You can either make your own way to the pitch or meet other players at Jishuitan subway station.

Horse Riding

Sunhe Zhen
91 Shunbai Lu
Chaoyang
顺白路91号孙河镇
朝阳区
Map 3 B4 **42**

Beijing Equuleus International Riding Club
北京天星调良国际马术俱乐部
010 6432 4947 | www.equriding.com

Equuleus trains riders of all levels from those just getting started to competition show jumpers. Qualified instructors teach students the skills of dressage and show jumping. Membership costs vary from ¥2,400 for 10 lessons over three months to ¥19,200 for 110 lessons over 15 months. Check the website for updated schedules.

Ice Skating

Beijing has a few ice rinks, but it truly comes into its own over the winter months, as hordes of people head to frozen lakes such as Houhai, Beihai and Kunming. Here you can hire skates and glide around for a great Beijing experience. If skates are too mundane, try one of the more bizarre forms of ice transport, including bicycles on skates or ice chairs, which you propel over the frozen lake with a set of ski poles. These normally cost ¥15 to ¥20 per day. The lakes are shallow, so don't be concerned about the countless skaters on the ice; it somehow manages to take the strain. Around the sides of lakes such as Houhai you will also be treated to the sight of brave swimmers doing frenzied strokes around ice holes. You can always warm up afterwards with a hot drink at one of the many surrounding bars.

14A Hepingli Zhongjie
Dongcheng
和平里中街甲14号
东城区
Map 5 F3 **43**

Ditan Ice Arena 地坛紫龙祥滑冰馆
010 6429 1619

Aspiring figure skaters can practise year round here. The Champion Rink also has the distinction of being the only place in the capital where you can play the Olympic sport of curling. Shoe rental is ¥26 per hour. Call ahead to reserve a curling sheet (¥400 per hour). Open Tuesday to Friday, 13:30 to 21:00 and Saturday to Sunday, 09:00-21:00.

B2, China World Mall
Dongcheng
国贸商城B2
东城区
Map 11 F3 **44**

Le Cool Ice Skating China World 国贸溜冰场
010 6505 5776 | www.chinaworldmall.com

Le Cool is in the middle of China World Shopping Mall (p.295) one of Beijing's swankiest complexes. You can put down your shopping bags and pick up a pair of ice skates for ¥30 to ¥50 for 90 minutes. The rink also offers lessons costing ¥100 for a 40 minute session. It is in the underground shopping centre that connects Traders Hotel to China World Hotel. Open 10:00 to 22:00.

Karting

If you've had enough of sitting in Beijing taxis and want to burn some rubber, there are few better options than speeding round a track in a go-kart. While driving rules exist, they are less strictly adhered to than in most places, which is a pretty fair reflection of the city's proper streets.

Xinglong Park
Gaobeidian
Sihui
四惠高碑店兴隆公园
Map 7 F2 **45**

Sihui Go-Karting Track 四惠花园卡丁车赛车俱乐部
010 8575 1433

Sihui Go-Karting has a 550m track with enough hairpins, chicanes and straights to get your g-force fix. Races are limited to six karts at a time, and a five-minute stint costs ¥48. Helmets are provided. There is also a bar, some pool tables and plenty of places to sit, so you won't be left impatiently twiddling your thumbs waiting to get out on the tarmac again. The track is open all-year round and it is worth calling to book in advance if you have a large party. Annual membership costs ¥800 and brings a 50% discount. Members can also join a special race on the last Friday of every month.

Kids' Activities

With its busy roads, towering buildings and herds of people, new arrivals might be forgiven for fretting about their kids. Beijing, however, has much to offer to keep children safe and busy, including clubs that provide great opportunities for youngsters to make new friends. Many expat families live in Shunyi (p.95), and this large district with its wide streets is a safe place for children to play. Within the city, most parks have a playground and enough to keep even the most energetic kids occupied. International schools (p.130) also offer some excellent after-school programmes and summer courses. AJ Arts (www.aj-arts.com) offers dance and music lessons.

A10, Jingdu Hotel
Chaoyang
酒仙桥路26号晶都国际
酒店A10室
朝阳区
Map 5 E3 25

ClubFootball 万国群星足球俱乐部

010 5130 6893 | www.clubfootball.com.cn

This company has English FA qualified coaches who run football clinics for kids of all skill levels, on weekends and during the holidays. The website has full details on courses and prices, and there are new astroturf practice pitches available at Xiaowuji, near the south-east section of the Fourth Ring Road. The Jingdu hotel is at 26 Jiuxianqiao Lu. See also, entry under Football, p.213.

Various Locations

Danz Centre 北京丹安丝舞蹈中心

www.danzcentre.com

This club offers kids and teenagers dance classes, including ballet, tap, Latin and hip hop. It has campuses in Shunyi and Dongcheng, and lessons are available in English. Children's Clubhouse is at Yosemite Villas, Shunyi (010 8046 2286) and there is another site at Building B, East Gate Plaza, 9 Dongzhong Jie, Dongcheng (010 6418 5525).

Gongti Nanlu
Chaoyang
工体南路
朝阳区
Map 9 D4 48

Fundazzle 翻斗乐

010 6500 4193

This indoor playground is good for young kids, who can enjoy playing in a two-storey jungle gym, ball pits, trampolines, slides and swings. Two hours in Fundazzle costs ¥30 and includes play shoes. Counsellors are on hand to help out, and they also teach arts and crafts. Open 09:00 to 17:30.

4/F, Lifestyle Mall
Lido
酒仙桥路10号星城国际
大厦妙典时尚广
Map 5 D3 49

Sports Beijing 京体

010 6430 1412 | www.sportsbj.com

This non-profit organisation has dedicated volunteers who organise a wealth of games for kids, including rugby training, football, tennis, cheerleading, golf, gymnastics and softball. The mall is at 10 Jiuxianqiao Lu, and the location in Lido means it's very popular with expat families.

Kite Flying

The Chinese started making kites more than 2,000 years ago, and the popularity of these flying artworks has rarely waned. Initially used as a signalling device above battlefields, kiting eventually evolved into a leisure pursuit.

More so than in any country, kites in China come in all shapes and sizes, with some painstakingly contructed pieces. In fact, the country's strict airspace regulations mean the only type of helicopter you're ever likely to see flying over Beijing will probably be made of fabric and on the end of a piece of string.

Kites are a common sight, from flyovers and rooftops to Tiananmen Square and Fragrant Hills. They can be bought at many of Beijing's markets and other stores. A word of warning though, some of these kites go very high, so start winding in the string at least half an hour before that important meeting.

Laser Game
Other options **Paintballing** p.221

Block 3, Xincheng
Xiyuan, Wangjing
Chaoyang
望京新城西园3区
316楼B1
朝阳区
Map 5 E1 **50**

Beijing Startrooper Laser Tag 北京激光搏击
010 6475 8329 | www.startrooper.net
This is a popular spot for Beijingers to live out their nerdiest sci-fi fantasies. It hosts high-tech live action games in an arena filled with fog, special effects and pumping music. Unlike paintball, laser tag is completely painless and shots are unlimited. Games cost ¥40 per person. There are special prices for groups and on weekends, so call ahead or send an email. Open Monday to Friday 14:00 to 20:00; Saturday to Sunday 09:00 to 20:00.

Martial Arts
There are scores of well-trained martial arts experts in Beijing – and many more of limited ability. If you are more interested in dabbling in self-defence than becoming a killing machine, many expats find their Chinese friends willing to teach them some basics. The variety of disciplines that fit under the martial arts umbrella ensures that there is something for most tastes. In parks and streets around Beijing, clusters of people practice the mellower forms, such as tai-chi, while the more ferocious types take place in special academies. Martial arts aim to develop physical strength, coordination and flexibility, but most importantly, focus the mind and cleanse the inner body.

BCIS, Baiziwan Nanlu
Chaoyang
百子湾南路北京乐成国
际学校
朝阳区
Map 7 D3 **51**

Aikido 合气道
137 1890 1839 | www.bcis.cn
Aikido is more a state of mind than a sport based on competition. This Japanese art of self-defence uses holds, locks and principles of non-resistance to debilitate an opponent's strength. You can practise this defensive art form at the Beijing City International School on Baiziwan Nanlu every Monday and Wednesday from 08:00 to 21:30. Prices may vary, so contact the instructor's mobile.

Rm 906, Bld 9
Jianwai SOHO
Chaoyang
建外SOHO9号楼906室
朝阳区
Map 11 F3 **52**

Beijing Black Tiger Academy 北京黑老虎学院
136 8140 2122 | www.blacktigerclub.com
This martial arts training centre has some of the most experienced instructors in Beijing, including the only gracie jiu-jitsu black belt and the only muay thai boxing champion in China. The centre not only offers martial arts training, but has an additional combat conditioning programme to get students in fighting shape in less than 90 days. This is among the best regarded clubs in the city, but is certainly not for the faint of heart or students who just want to dabble. Classes are ¥750 per month (Monday to Friday evenings and Saturday to Sunday afternoons). All classes are conducted in English.

Tiantan Park (p.173)

Room 309, 3/F
1 Anding Lu
Yayuncun
亚运村安定路1号3层
309室
Map 4 F2 **53**

Beijing Jiu-Jitsu Academy 北京安帝柔术馆
130 3119 5542 | www.baxiroushu.com
Looking to get in shape, learn self-defence or become a professional fighter? Take to the mats at the Beijing Jiu-Jitsu Academy. It specialises in Brazilian jiu-jitsu, but also offers instruction in Chinese kick-boxing and mixed martial arts. At present, prospective students get a free one-week

trial for any of the academy's programmes. It is in the National Olympic Sports Centre Gymnasium near the Asian Games Village, with a training facility containing more than 80sqm of tatami-style mats. Check the website for updated prices.

Chinese Culture Club 中国文化协会

29 Anjialou
Liangmaqiao Lu
Chaoyang
亮马桥路安家楼29号
朝阳区
🚇 *Dongzhimen L2*
Map 7 D1 **1**

010 6432 9341 | *www.chinesecultureclub.org*
Regular tai chi classes are among the many events this popular club organises. Classes run all year round and are conducted in English. A full course runs for eight weeks, with eight 90 minute classes conducted by the lake in Chaoyang Park (p.191). Meet in front of the Jintai Gallery, which is on the right-hand side as you enter the west gate of the park. Call the number during the week, between 09:00 and 18:00, and 010 6432 1041 at other times.

Dadehe Kungfu Club　武之魂文化有限公司

Various Locations

010 8618 9094 | *www.dadehe.com*
This club has two locations and special classes for kids. The one in Ritan Park (p.192) is dedicated to kids' classes on Saturday mornings and charges ¥50 for 90 minutes. The other is at 2 Yangguan Guangchang Nanlu.

Tianyi Kungfu Club 天一功夫俱乐部

BCIS (2km south of
Dawanglu subway)
Baiziwan Nanlu
百子湾南路北京乐成
国际学校(大望路地
铁站南2公里)
Map 7 D3 **56**

130 5113 8804 | *www.tianyikungfu.com*
This club teaches many forms of kung fu, including shaolin, as well as self-defence techniques. The two trainers have more than 60 years of teaching experience between them. The fee of ¥500 per month includes 12 lessons. Open Tuesday and Thursday, 19:30 to 21:00 and Sunday 15:30 to 17:00.

Motorsports

Goldenport Motor Park 奥迪金港汽车公园

1 Jingang Dadao
Jinzhanxiang
Chaoyang
金盏乡金港大道1号
朝阳区

010 8433 3490 | *www.goldenport.com.cn*
It's unlikely that racing cars is covered in your auto insurance, so if the motorhead in you feels the need for speed just head out to the Goldenport Motor Park. Located a few kilometres from the airport, the park has a track where daring drivers can race their own car for ¥200 per hour. Schedules vary, so call ahead to make sure the track is available.

Mountain Biking
Other options **Cycling** p.211

The Beijing MOB 北京山地自行车俱乐部

Various Locations

http://themob.404.com.au
This group of fanatics meets every weekend for challenging rides around the outskirts of Beijing. Most riders are experienced, but the group sometimes splits into two to let the faster folks speed ahead while the slower ones (or 'mushies') catch up. The rides can be over 100km, so a day with the MOB is not for the faint-hearted. It is a hugely rewarding experience, even if you can't sit down for a while afterwards. The group meets every Saturday morning at 08:00 by the Agricultural Exhibition Centre at the end of Dongzhimenwai on the east Third Ring Road. From there a bus (adapted to take bikes on the back) drives to the starting point of the day's ride, usually an hour or so outside the city. A daytrip costs ¥100 and it is recommended that participants bring a good quality bike, although these can be rented (sometimes) for an additional ¥50. Riders must bring their own helmet, sun lotion and plenty of water, particularly

in the blistering summer heat. You can sign up to the Google group or Facebook page (search for The Beijing MOB) for weekly updates on rides and a brief description of the intended route.

Music Lessons

Other options **Music, DVDs & Videos** p.276, **Dance Classes** p.211

Most music lessons are available one-on-one. Check the classifieds in local expat magazines (p.51) for up to date listings by tutors. Beijing stands out from other cities in China for the opportunities available to aspiring rock and punk musicians. If you are interested in playing before crowds in the capital, talented acts will find excellent support through venues like MAO Livehouse (p.335), Yugong Yishan (p.344) and especially D-22 (p.343) in Wudaokou.

12 A Ruiwangfen
Haidian
瑞王坟甲12号香山附近
海淀区

Beijing Midi School Of Music 北京迷笛音乐学校
010 6259 0101 | *www.midischool.com.cn*
Take advantage of Beijing's wealth of modern musical talent at this school. Founded in 1993, it is the first in China to teach modern genres like rock, jazz, funk and fusion. The school sponsors the annual Midi Music Festival (p.53), the capital's largest rock festival, in May of each year. Annual tuition is ¥16,450.

Stone Boat Bar (south-west corner Ritan Park)
Chaoyang
日坛公园西南角石舫
酒吧
朝阳区
Map 11 D2 **60**

Gloaming 火烧云
010 6501 9986 | *www.redtmusic.com*
For a night any music lover can appreciate, check out Gloaming at the Stone Boat bar in Ritan Park (p.192). Sponsored by Red T Music, it features the best acoustic music in the city. Musicians interested in getting involved should email Ed Peto (blog@edpeto. com). This event is free to all. Check website for updated schedule.

Paintballing

Other options **Laser Game** p.219

Wanfangting Park
Fengtai
南三环中路洋桥西里甲
2号万芳亭公园
丰台区
🚇 *Huilongguan L13*

BJ Paintball 北京匹特搏
010 6979 4184 | *www.bjpaintball.com.cn*
For those without any interest in running or hiking, BJ Paintball can provide a fun way to get out of the city. The course has a good collection of hills, bunkers and grassy knolls from which to shoot at your friends and enemies. The entry fee is ¥100 per person (which includes 30 pellets) or ¥180 per person for 100 pellets. Additional pellets are ¥2 each.

1 Anding Lu
Chaoyang
安定路1号
朝阳区
Map 5 A3 **62**

Olympic Sports Centre Paintball Strike Range 奥林匹克运动中心彩弹搏击场
010 6492 1603
The 10,000m course lacks some of the better additions at BJ Paintball, but is both bigger and more central. Participants get guns and headgear with the entry fee (¥80) for a two-hour game. Extra paintball pellets cost ¥1.70 each. Paintball veterans can also rent the entire course for ¥128 per person per hour.

Pool

Many of the city's bars, including Bar Blu (p.343) at Tongli Studios and the Black Sun at Chaoyang Park West Gate, have decent pool tables. Frank's (p.331) in Lido offers weekly tournaments that draw the cockiest (if not most skilled) players in the city. If you want to play seriously, you are better off at a genuine billiards club.

40 Zhonglouwan
Gulou Dajie
Houhai
鼓楼大街钟楼湾胡同
40号（钟楼东侧）
Map 8 D2 63

Ball House 波楼酒吧

010 6407 4051
One of Beijing's most underrated bars, Ball House, in the shadow of the Drum and Bell Tower, is one of the best places in the city to play pool. It has three tables, all in better shape than you would expect for a place with cheap drinks (¥15 a beer). You can play to your heart's delight for ¥30 per hour. Open 14:00 to 03:00. Gulou Dajie is just east of the Bell Tower (p.179).

9 Minwang Hutong
Hepingli Dongjie
Dongcheng
和平里东街民旺胡同
9号 东城区
Map 9 A1 64

Xuan Long Billiards Club 轩隆台球俱乐部

010 6421 8868
Enough talk, Fast Eddie, shoot pool. Whether you're a pool shark or a billiards beginner, Xuan Long Billiards Club offers a reasonably priced venue for you to work on your game. Snooker tables go for ¥32 per hour and billiards tables for ¥20 per hour. There is no need to rush, either; the club is open 24 hours a day.

Public Speaking

3, 20/F Tower B
Tsinghua Science Park
Wudaokou
清华科技园B座20层第
三教室
五道口
🚇 *Wudaokou L13*
Map 4 C2 65

Zhongguancun Toastmasters 中关村英语演讲俱乐部

138 1048 2271 | *http://zgctm.weebly.com*
The Toastmasters are a non-profit organisation offering training in English public speaking. With 211,000 members from 90 countries, the international club tries to help its members develop leadership skills and gain confidence through impromptu speeches and constructive advice. The Beijing branch of the club welcomes any individuals looking to get ahead in their personal or professional life. Sessions run from 19:00 to 21:00 every Tuesday.

Rugby

Rugby in Beijing doesn't quite have the same following as it does in Hong Kong. However, standards have improved in recent years and the capital can now claim to have the makings of a rugby hotbed. Four or five teams play on a regular basis, including China's Agricultural University, or 'Nongda', a side which contains many Chinese national players. The Beijing Cup was launched in 2006 and involves the four expat teams.

Beijing Language &
Culture University
Haidian
Map 4 D2 66

Aardvarks Rugby Club 北京地豚橄榄球俱乐部

135 2224 8133 | *www.geocities.com/aardvarksrfc*
Keen to bust heads and take names? The Wudaokou-based Aardvarks might be the team for you. Sponsored by the Rickshaw Bar (p.337), the Aardvarks specialise in full contact rugby. The team welcomes new players, regardless of ability, age, sex, nationality or anything else. If you want to play, or perhaps just find some new drinking buddies, email aardvarksrfc@yahoo.com, or call Dave on 135 2224 8133. They are a student side, based at the Beijing Language & Culture University (p.140) in Haidian. Like the Devils (p.223), the Aardvarks welcome all players and occasionally tour in China.

Purple Jade Villas
1 Ziyu Donglu
紫玉东路1号紫玉山庄
Map 5 A1 67

Beijing Angel's Women's Rugby 北京天使女子橄榄球俱乐部

kathryn_latimer@hotmail.com
Rugby is not just for the boys in Beijing. Women who are interested in playing should email Kathryn Latimer. New players are always welcome, and practices are held each Saturday at 14:30.

Sports & Activities

Various Locations

Beijing Japanese
ishada-k@asahi.com
Only recently formed, this thriving club has grown exponentially and now boasts several talented players and speedy drinkers. Training takes place at Chaoyang Sports Stadium on Saturday afternoons at 14:00. Email Ishida Koichiro for details.

The Den
Chaoyang
朝阳区
Map 9 E4 69

Touch Rugby 触式橄榄球
010 6592 6290 | *www.beijingdevils.com*
This mixed league plays at the Western Academy of Beijing or Chaoyang Stadium on Sunday afternoons throughout the year. It is run by the Devils and a bus to the pitch is available from their base at The Den Bar. Membership costs ¥600 for adults or ¥300 for students. There are several tours, when players from the different teams group together to form a rather formidable unit. The club has won several titles and often travels to tournaments in Malaysia, Singapore, Hong Kong and Shanghai.

The International
School of Beijing
Shunyi
北京国际学校
顺义区
Map 3 C1 70

Vermilion Beijing Devils 北京鬼子英式橄榄球俱乐部
010 6592 6290 | *www.beijingdevils.com*
The Devils have led the charge in raising the profile of rugby in Beijing and the club now has around 150 members from all over the world. The team is involved in several tournaments outside the capital, including the Yellow Sea Cup – a three-team tournament with home and away games against the Shanghai Hairy Crabs and the Seoul Survivors. The competition is expected to expand to include teams from Guangzhou and Chengdu. The Devils train on Tuesdays and Thursdays, with matches on Saturdays. The Den, a bar in Sanlitun, is the club's base and many social events are held there. Annual membership is ¥600 (¥300 for students and locals), which includes a full kit, half-price beer and pizza at The Den and transport to and from training and matches. Social members are welcome and pay ¥150 for a discount card for The Den.

Running
Beijing's polluted air is not kind to runners' lungs, but some intrepid sorts do manage to get out onto the streets and parks. One outfit worth mentioning is TRIBEIJING (p.227), a triathlon club formerly known as BUTT (Beijing United Triathlon Team).

The 5:19 Bar & Grill
26 Xingba Lu, Nuren Jie
Chaoyang
女人街星吧路26号梧桐
湾酒吧
朝阳区
Map 5 D4 71

Beijing Hash House Harriers
010 8448 0896 | *www.hash.cn*
This fun loving group has been dubbed 'the drinking club with a running problem'. Race trails change from week to week, and are laid out by 'hares' who use chalk to mark out the route on the ground so the 'hounds' can follow. The fun and games culminates in the 'circle' where the hashers gather to mete out punishments and drink. The Beijing Hash House Harriers is a lively, mixed bunch that meet every Sunday come rain or shine. Starting times and location depend on the season, but all the information you need for upcoming races is posted on the group's website. Runs are usually about one or two hours long and weave through Beijing's modern skyscrapers as well as ancient *hutongs*. It usually costs ¥20 to join a race or ¥60 for a race and dinner.

Skiing & Snowboarding
Just one or two hours from Beijing (depending, of course, on traffic), there are several small ski resorts. Describing these hills as resorts may be a touch generous, but they do serve up a taste of life on the piste, albeit with a very Chinese twist. As well as skiers and snowboarders, be prepared for dog owners, lots of kebab sticks and loud pop music blaring across the slopes. You may be longing for the awe-inspiring vistas of the Alps or

the Rockies after looking down on the rather brown industrialised landscape, but plenty of fun can still be had. While there is some natural snow, most of the slopes are coated in the artificial stuff. Look out for organised trips by the likes of *That's Beijing* (p.51) and the Rickshaw Bar (p.337). These popular events cost ¥300 to ¥400 and include transport, ski hire, food and a goodie bag. Alternatively you can hire a car or minivan to take you to one of the resorts. The website www.bjski.com.cn has useful info on prices.

Badaling Ski Resort 八达岭滑雪场

Badaling Town
Yanqing County
延庆县八达岭镇

010 6501 0330

Ski fans can do much more than just hit the slopes at Badaling. Activities include water-skiing, sledging and gliding, and ice skating on the large artificial pond. Covering an area of 150 hectares, the resort has slopes and trails for skiers of all skill levels. It is 70km north of downtown Beijing. Drive along the Badaling Highway to Badaling Huaxuechang or take bus 919 from Deshengmen direct to the ski site. Ski fees are ¥50 per hour or ¥220 per day on weekdays and ¥70 per hour or ¥340 per day on weekends. Open 08:30 to 18:30.

Huaibei International Ski Resort 怀北国际滑雪场

Hefangkou Village
Huaibei Town
Huairou District
怀柔区怀北镇河防口村

010 8969 6677 | www.hbski.com

The biggest appeal of this resort is its proximity to the Great Wall, which you can easily see from the slopes on a clear day. It takes about an hour to cover the 70km from Beijing. There are more than 3km of trails, ranging from beginner to advanced, with a drop of 238m. A day on the slopes will cost ¥150 in the week, ¥200 at weekends and ¥240 on public holidays.

Jundushan Ski Resort 军都山滑雪场

Zhenshun Village
Changping District
昌平区真顺村

010 6808 7910 | www.bjski.com.cn

This resort is just 34km from the city. It has seven runs that predominantly cater for beginners, although night skiing is also possible and the 1.2km advanced lane has a gradient of 40%. Passes cost from ¥180 during the week to ¥320 on a public holiday.

Nanshan Ski Village 南山滑雪场

Shengshuitou Village
Miyun County
密云县圣水头村

010 8909 1909 | www.nanshanski.com

Around 100km from Beijing is Nanshan Ski Village, possibly the area's top resort. It has several trails, including a narrow black mogul run that may challenge even experienced skiers. There is also a snowboard park with half pipes and rails, as well as a slope for inner tubing. It offers skiing and snowboarding instruction from teachers trained by the Austrian Snowboard Association. To get there, take the bus to Mi Yun from the Dongzhimen bus stop. The ride is two hours, but it takes less than an hour by car. Prices vary, so check the website for details.

Qiaobo Ice & Snow World 乔波冰雪世界

Chaobai River Park
Shunyi
马坡村潮白河国家森
林公园
顺义区

010 8497 2568 | www.qbski.com

This is an indoor ski centre with two short slopes. It is open all year round, which gives the opportunity to practice your turns and ploughs when it's too cold to head outdoors, or too warm for any decent snow on the slopes. It's popular with local and expat families.

Wanlong Ski Resort 万龙滑雪场

Honghualiang
Hebei
河北省崇礼县红花梁

010 6553 6830 | www.wlski.com

Getting out to Wanlong is a bit of a trek. The resort is in Hebei province, 249km from Beijing (about three hours' drive). Although the distance from Beijing makes it a hassle, there is real snow. The resort has 12 runs about 2,200m long, and about 550m in height. Prices range from ¥120 for two hours to ¥260 for a full day. If you don't have a car, you can take a bus from Workers' Stadium, Ma Bian Bridge, or San Yuan Bridge. Call 010 6553 6830/31 to reserve a spot on the bus.

Social Groups
Other options **Support Groups** p.125

Since the well-liked YPHH (Young Professionals Happy Hour) stopped operating, networking events have been rare. The listings magazines (p.52) do have some up to date information though. People interested in meeting like-minded individuals might be better placed looking beyond standard networking. Contacts made running with the Hash House Harriers (p.223) or enjoying cocoa at ChocoJing (p.227) will usually be more meaningful than those made at traditional networking events.

Chaoyang Community College
Chaoyang
朝阳区社区学院
朝阳区

Beijing Sport & Social Club 北京体育社交俱乐部
134 6638 8333 | beijingssc@gmail.com
If you think competition is everything, then the Beijing Sport & Social Club is probably not for you. The club meets on the first Wednesday of every month for a night of sports and carousing. A fee of ¥50 covers all costs. Contact Baker Zhang by email if you want to be included.

3/F Low Rise Capital Mansion, 6 Xinyuan Lu (Behind Capital Club)
Chaoyang
新源南路6号京城大厦
三层 (京城俱乐部后)

INN (International Newcomers' Network) 京城俱乐部
010 8486 2225 | www.innbeijing.org
Open from 10:00 to midday on the last Monday of each month (except December), this monthly networking event provides new arrivals a chance to obtain information about living in the Chinese capital and to meet new friends. Meetings are open to all foreign passport holders.

Various Locations

The Speed Dating Specialists
www.speeddatingbeijing.spaces.live.com
One networking event that has Beijing buzzing is the speed dating nights organised by this outfit. With activities ranging from 'traditional' speed dating to often outrageous activities (including stripteases), the event is a wonderful way to break the routine and perhaps meet someone special. Check the website for updated schedules.

Squash
Other options **Sports & Leisure Facilities** p.232

Kempinski Hotel
Chaoyang
亮马桥路50号
朝阳区
Map 5 D4 81

Pulse 都市脉搏
010 6465 4474 | www.kempinski-beijing.com
Open from 06:00 to 22:30, Pulse at the Kempinksi is a good venue for squash lovers to get on the court. It attracts some of the city's better (and more serious) players. You can join the ladder or just go for a good workout.

Various Locations

Squash Ladder Club 壁球梯俱乐部
bsll.coo@uss-squash.cn
Test your physical ability and mental concentration with Beijing's largest squash club. From the greenest novice to the most seasoned veterans, squash lovers of all levels can join the club, which boasts more than 100 participants. Send inquiries by email to get updated information on where and when you can play.

225

Swimming

Swimming is very popular and there are plenty of pools. Many gyms, apartment complexes and hotels have decent swimming pools, but the most eye-catching has to belong to the Grand Hyatt (p.34) in the Oriental Plaza. Sadly, pools in the major hotels are off-limits to non-guests. The Chinese have a fondness for outdoor pools, which you can find in parks such as Chaoyang (p.92) and Tuanjiehu, complete with artificial beaches. However, these can get packed in the summer and may not be very relaxing. Pools generally require bathers to wear swimming caps, but these can usually be bought on site. There are pools at many gyms (p.232). Typically, use of these adds ¥200 to ¥1,000 to membership fees.

1 Xiedao Lu, City Seaview (Haijing) (near Lido Hotel)
Chaoyang
Map 5 F1 83
蟹岛路1号城市海景水上乐园丽都酒店附近

Crab Island Resort (City Seaview)
蟹岛度假村（城市海景水上乐园）
010 8433 9689 | www.cityseaview.net

Occupying about 60,000sqm, this is the biggest man-made beach in China. The water park offers a fair (if somewhat tacky) copy of a day at the beach with sand, waves, waterslides, and even cocktails and barbecue. It costs ¥60 for adults and ¥40 for kids under 1.4 metres tall. The resort is closed in winter, but in warmer months it is open daily from 09:00 to 20:00, and until 22:00 in July and August.

Yujinxiang Huayuan Jinzhan
Dongweilu
东苇路金盏乡郁金香花园

Merry Water World 摩锐水世界
010 8433 0606 | www.yujinxiang.com.cn

If you get bored swimming laps, get wet at Merry Water World. Rush down one of the six giant water slides, relax on the 'lazy river', or get a taste of the ocean at the wave pool. Merry Water World also features a children's pool, a lap swimming pool and several hot tubs. It costs ¥98 for adults and ¥60 for children under 1.4 metres tall.

Swimming

Ditan Swimming Pool	010 6426 4483	Indoor. Open Mon-Fri 08:30 to 15:30 and 18:30 to 21:30. Fee ¥30 (unlimited time)
Dongdan Indoor Swimming Pool	010 6523 1241	Indoor. Open 09:00 to 22:00. Fee Adults ¥30, Students and Children ¥20
Jing Guang Swimming Centre	010 6597 8888	Indoor. Open 06:00 to 23:00
Olympic Sports Centre	010 6491 2233	Indoor. Open 09:30 to 21:30. Fee ¥40 per visit or ¥100 for 10
Sino-Japanese Youth Centre	010 6468 3311	Open 08:00 to 22:00. Fee ¥68 per visit

Tennis

Many apartment complexes have courts that are free (or charge a minimal fee) but are for residents only. For the less fortunate, prices range from as little as ¥50 to as much as ¥400 per hour. Membership at the bigger clubs tends to be expensive but will include discounts or 'free' access, so can be a wise investment if you play regularly. Kerry Sports (010 6561 8833) at the Kerry Centre in Chaoyang has three indoor courts, while the Beijing Tennis Centre (010 6721 1558, www.bjtennis.com) has both indoor and outdoor courts. Hiring a court at Chaoyang Tennis Club costs ¥200 per hour. The Potter's Wheel centre (www.potters-wheel.cn, 010 8538 2803) also offer lessons.

50 Tiantan Donglu
Chongwen
天坛东路50号
崇文区
Map 7 A4 85

Beijing International Tennis Centre 北京国际网球中心
010 6715 2532

Probably the swankiest digs in town, the Beijing International Tennis Centre has five courts in excellent condition. The level of play tends to be more varied than the wealth of the players. Time on the luxury courts comes to ¥300 per hour for non-members and ¥100 per hour for members. Annual membership is ¥8,000.

**54-56 Zhongguancun
Nandajie**
Haidian
中关村南大街54–56号
海淀区
Map 6 C1 86

Capital Gymnasium 首都体育馆

010 6833 5552

Compared to the luxury of the Beijing International Tennis Centre, the courts at the Capital Gymnasium feel like a nostalgic trip back to China's more socialist past. Still, the Haidian gym offers a more budget-conscious tennis experience than its Chongwen counterpart. Time on one of the three indoor tennis courts costs ¥150 to ¥200 per hour, and visitors can also make use of the badminton courts and ping pong tables (both ¥35 per hour).

**Asian Games Village
1 Anding Lu**
Chaoyang
安定路1号亚运村奥林
匹克中心
朝阳区
Map 4 F3 87

Olympic Tennis Centre 奥林匹克网球中心

Here you can sweat on the same spot as Federer and the like, though this Olympic venue has nifty machine ventilation and fresh air circulation to keep players cool. There are 12 outdoor courts, it's open from 08:00 to 17:00 and costs ¥80 an hour to play on weekdays and ¥100 an hour on weekends.

Triathlon

This sport is for super keen athletes and covers the disciplines of running, cycling and swimming. It's no stroll in the park, but certainly something to boast about if you survive an event. Distances vary, from the 'sprint' (swim 750m, bike 20km and run 5km) to the full deal (swim 3.8km, bike 180km and then run a full marathon).

Various Locations

TRIBEIJING 北京铁人三项俱乐部

135 0113 3504 | www.tribeijing.org

TRIBEIJING (the excitable capitals are theirs, the crazy kids), is a predominantly male, expat group that meets on weekends (normally at the Pinnacle Plaza in Shunyi). Training schedules vary, but you can start limbering up early by checking the midweek emails sent out by the club, which detail weekend routes. There are also regular competitions around China that you can join for a shot at some substantial prize money. You will need your own equipment. The mobile number listed is for Patrik Li.

Wine & Chocolate Tasting

6/F East Gate Plaza B
Dongcheng
东中街29号东环广场
B座6层0–P号
东城区
Map 9 C3 88

ASC Fine Wines ASC精品葡萄酒公司

010 6418 1598 | www.asc-wines.com

This is the leading importer of wines to China. In addition to providing some of the better wines available in the country, it organises hundreds of tasting and educational events. Wine lovers interested in attending these should check the website for dates, or email Adam Steinberg. The plaza is at 29 Dongzhong Lu.

Various Locations

Bacchus Wines 北京神露洋酒公司

010 6415 7873 | http://bacchus-wines.net

Bacchus specialises in fine French wines. Its founder, Xavier Tondusson, aims to educate people about the ways in which wine can improve well-being. To this end, Bacchus sponsors wine tastings and dinners. You can sign up online to keep abreast of events.

Various Locations

ChocoJing 巧可京

www.iheartbeijing.com/chocojing.html

This is somewhere to come for cocoa beans rather than carefully selected grapes. Beijing's only chocolate appreciation society meets on a regular basis to sample the best dark chocolates, fondues, milk chocolates, pralines, crèmes and mole sauces the city has to offer. For ¥50 you get a chocolate tasting that includes coffee or tea. Check the website for upcoming events, and RSVP early to reserve your spot.

Tickets

The best ticket services
for sports events are
www.piaowutong.com
and www.piao.com.cn.

Spectator Sports

Domestic spectator sports do not have the significance that they might in western countries. While the Superbowl or Premiership get fans excited in the US and UK, a Beijinger is unlikely to be annoyed by someone from Shanghai simply because the Shanghai Sharks beat Beijing's CBA basketball team. International competitions tend to draw more interest than domestic ones, and seeing Chinese players succeed against international stars can be a big draw. The NBA has been more popular than the Chinese Basketball Association (CBA) since Yao Ming first suited up with the Houston Rockets. Liu Xiang's record-breaking sprint in the 110m hurdles at the Athens Olympics was more exciting to locals than anything in Chinese sports that year. This can be attributed to the relative youth of China's professional sports leagues. In time, football club Beijing Guoan may be discussed around water coolers, but not yet.

Sports like badminton and ping pong, where China boasts some of the world's best talent, are enormously popular, but less so when the competition features Chinese players battling against one another.

There are, however, a bevy of spectator sports available to Beijing residents who want a taste of live action. Though they may pale in comparison to the excitement surrounding Olympic events, there should be plenty going on before and after the games. More information on the Olympic venues and the full schedule for events can be found at http://en.beijing2008.cn

Minor Sports

For baseball, try Lucheng Sports School (south of Lucheng, Huangcun Town, Daxing, 010 6123 9856). For motorsports, it's Goldenport Motor Park (p.220) and horse racing fans should head to Beijing Jockey Club (Neijunzhuang Village, Xuxinzhuang Town, Tongzhou, 010 6518 2312).

Olympic Green
Haidian
奥林匹克森林公园
Map 4 F2 92

National Aquatics Centre 国家游泳中心

The National Aquatics Centre, most commonly referred to as the Water Cube, is the centrepiece for BOCOG's concept of a 'green' Olympics. The design of the eco-friendly structure was based on the natural formation of soap bubbles which trap light and heat so less energy is consumed. It covers more than 65,000sqm, and will have the capacity to seat 17,000 visitors for swimming and diving events. After the Olympics, it will be used for swimming competitions and as a recreational facility. Function during the Olympics: swimming, diving, and synchronised swimming.

Olympic Green
Haidian
奥林匹克森林公园
Map 4 F2 92

National Indoor Stadium 国家体育馆

Shaped like an unfolding Chinese fan, the National Indoor Stadium captures some of China's traditional culture in a modern building. The biggest indoor stadium in the country, the NIS will have a seating capacity of 20,000, and covers more than 80,000sqm. After the Olympics, it will be used for cultural and entertainment events and will serve as an exercise centre for local residents. Function during the Olympics: artistic gymnastics, trampolining and handball.

Olympic Green
Haidian
奥林匹克森林公园
Map 4 F2 92

National Stadium 国家体育场

The National Stadium, also known as the Bird's Nest will host the football finals, track and field events and the opening and closing ceremonies for the 2008 Olympics. The stadium, completed in March 2008, covers more than 250,000sqm and can seat more than 90,000 people. Its remarkable, nest-like exterior encloses the stadium with a series of curved, steel-net walls and was designed by Swiss architects Herzog & De Meuron and China Architecture Design Institute. After the Olympics it will be used to stage sporting events and host cultural exhibitions. Function during the Olympics: athletics and the football final.

1 Anding Lu
Chaoyang
安定路1号
朝阳区
Map 4 F2 95

Olympic Sports Centre Stadium 奥林匹克体育中心体育场

This is a multi-use stadium that will host the cross country and show jumping events of the modern pentathlon. Used to host football matches prior to the Olympics, the stadium has been completely renovated for the games, including the addition of 17,000sqm of floor space. The venue has a seating capacity of 40,000. Function during the Olympics: modern pentathlon (running and equestrian).

1 Anding Lu
Chaoyang
安定路1号
朝阳区
Map 4 F2 95

Olympic Sports Centre Gymnasium 奥林匹克体育中心体育馆

This centre was originally built for the 1990 Asian Games, but the post-renovation gym looks very little like the old, rundown stadium that once stood in its place. In keeping with the eco-friendly Olympics theme, designers equipped the venue with a new roof that will greatly reduce energy consumption.
The gymnasium will hold the preliminary and quarterfinal handball events and serve as the training venue for goal ball, wheelchair basketball, wheelchair fencing and wheelchair rugby for paralympics. It can seat 6,300 spectators. Function during the Olympics: handball.

Other Olympic Venues

Venue	Location	Event
Beach Volleyball Ground	Chaoyang Park	Beach volleyball
Beijing Institute of Technology Gymnasium	33 Zhongguancun Nanlu	Volleyball
Beijing Shooting Range Clay Target Field	Xiangshan Nan	Shooting (trap and skeet)
Beijing Shooting Range Hall	3 Futiansi Lu, Shijingshan	Shooting
Beijing University of Aeronautics & Astronautics Gymnasium	37 Xueyuan Lu	Weightlifting
Beijing University of Technology Gymnasium	100 Pingleyuan, Xidawanglu	Badminton and rhythmic gymnastics
Capital Indoor Stadium	Baishi Bridge	Volleyball
China Agricultural University Gymnasium	17 Qinghua East	Wrestling
Fengtai Softball Field	67 Fengtai Lu	Softball
Hockey Field	Olympic Green	Hockey
Laoshan Bicycle Motocross Venue	Laoshan, Shijiangshan	BMX biking
Laoshan Mountain Bike Course	Laoshan, Shijiangshan	Mountain biking
Laoshan Velodrome	Laoshan, Shijiangshan	Track cycling
National Conference Centre	Olympic Green	Fencing and modern pentathlon
Olympic Green Archery Field	Olympic Green	Archery
Peking University Gymnasium	5 Yiheyuan Lu	Table tennis
Shunyi Olympic Rowing-Canoeing Park	Mapo Village	Rowing and kayaking
Tennis Centre	Olympic Green	Tennis
Triathlon Venue	Ming Tomb Reservoir	Triathlon
University of Science & Technology Gym	30 Xueyuan Lu	Judo and taekwondo
Urban Road Cycling Course	Yongdingmen to Juyongguan	Road cycling
Workers' Indoor Arena	Gongti Lu	Boxing
Wukesong Baseball Field	Wukesong Dajie	Baseball
Wukesong Indoor Stadium	Wukesong Dajie	Baseball
Ying Tung Natatorium	Olympic Sports Centre, Anding Lu	Water polo and modern pentathlon (swimming)

Spectator Sports

Gongti Lu
Chaoyang
工体路
朝阳区
Map 7 B1 97

Workers' Stadium 工人体育场

Like the Olympics Sports Centre Gymnasium, the Workers' Stadium was originally constructed for use during the 1990 Asian Games. It has since become more famous to Beijingers for the bars and clubs surrounding it, but has a new look after its own renovations. The Beijing Institute of Architectural Design oversaw structural consolidation on the 80,000sqm, 60,000 spectator stadium. It will host the football quarter-finals and semi-finals for the 2008 games. Function during the Olympics: football.

Badminton

Just a few years ago, it would have been absurd to suggest that any badminton team had a chance against China in 2008. However, China's less than dazzling performance at the Hong Kong Open in 2007 led to some hand-wringing on the mainland. Even star player, Lin Dan, admitted that the world was catching up. Beijingers are expected to follow China's games at the Olympics (especially against the ascendant Indonesian team) with great interest. However, there are few opportunities to see the Chinese stars play, other than on the sports network, CCTV5.

Basketball

Interest in local basketball is eclipsed by the NBA. This is particularly true for Yao versus Yi showdowns, when Yao Ming's Houston Rockets take on Yi Jianlian's Milwaukee Bucks. However, since its inception in 1994, the Chinese National Basketball League (CNBL) has been steadily building a fan base. Beijing used to be home to two CBA teams, the Beijing Ducks and the Beijing Aoshen Olympians. The Olympians have since moved into the American Basketball Association and play their 'home' games in California. The Beijing Ducks used to play in the Workers' Stadium from October to March or April, but have temporarily moved to Beijing Shougang Basketball Centre as their old arena undergoes renovations for the Olympics. Fans are generally supportive, although when riled they have been known to hurl both bottles and insults at opposing players. One such display in a game between the Chinese national team and Puerto Rico prompted the IOC to ask the Beijing Organising Committee to address issues of spectator etiquette.

Shougang Basketball
Centre, 159 Fushi Lu
Shijingshan District
石景山区阜石路159号
首钢篮球中心
Map 6 B2 98

Beijing Ducks 北京金隅

010 8829 6158

The Ducks play in the North Division of the Chinese Basketball Association and in 2005 finished second in that league. Their best known player is Mengke Bateer, a Mongolian, who in 2001 was the first Chinese national to start an NBA game. He had stints with the Denver Nuggets, San Antonio Spurs and Toronto Raptors.

Football

During the 2006 football world cup, everywhere in Beijing with a TV and alcohol turned into a sports bar. Even without a horse in the race (except perhaps, whoever was playing against Japan), the entire city was transfixed.

Most Beijingers long for a day when they can be proud of the Chinese national team, but in the meantime they support the local club. Briefly called the Beijing Xiandai (after the Hyundai car company), Beijing's professional football club is once again known as Beijing Guoan. They play in the Chinese Super League, which has 15 teams. Each team plays a home and away tie against their 14 rivals, and at the end of the season, the two bottom teams drop down to the Jia League (the country's second tier), with the top two Jia teams going the other way.

Fengtai Sports Center
55 Xisihuan Nanlu
Yuegezhuang Qiao
Fengtai
Map 6 A4 99

Beijing Guoan
010 6381 1576

Although they lean towards mediocrity, the team has an army of loyal fans who attend each game in Guoan green and white. In 2007 they managed second place in the league. In the past, the team played at the Workers' Stadium but has since moved to the 33,000 seat Beijing Fengtai Stadium, as their old arena undergoes renovations for the Olympics. After August 2008, Guoan will move into fancy new digs at the National Stadium.

Table Tennis

The 90s were the golden age of Chinese table tennis when charismatic stars like Deng Yaping and Wang Nan took the ping pong world by storm. China remains dominant in the sport but today's stars do not have the same flare, and interest has declined accordingly. Domestically, the China Table Tennis Super League (CTTSL) is the top division. It is run by the Chinese Table Tennis Association, and has the greatest ping pong talent in the world. To date, however, the league has been financially unsuccessful and failed to attract much interest abroad. Tickets are not available for league events, but tickets for competitions in Beijing are often on sale at www.piao.com.cn.

Tennis

The popularity of tennis has grown with the wealth of Chinese citizens. Increasingly, young professionals are taking up the game as an alternative to table tennis, badminton and basketball. The sport will get even bigger when China produces a tennis player that can compete internationally. Beijing's biggest tennis event is the annual China Open (www.chinaopen.com.cn). For VIP packages call 010 8518 1601 or order tickets online at www.piaowutong.com.

Playing Chinese chess

Strolling in the park

Inspirational sculptures

Sports & Leisure Facilities

A decade ago, sports and leisure options were limited. Today, there are offerings to rival most international cities. At the high end are equestrian and country clubs that require annual dues greater than most Beijingers' salaries. At the other extreme are exercise amenities in parks (p.190) and universities (p.139) that can be used for free. Most of the city's gyms have annual membership fees but other venues, particularly those for basketball, tennis and ice skating, can be used on a pay-for-play basis. Most native Beijingers choose not to pay for (or cannot afford) gym memberships and entry to private clubs. Locals who do sign up tend to be young professionals.

Health Clubs

Anantara Spa	010 8118 1888	www.anantara.com
Bodhi	010 6413 0226	www.bodhi.com.cn
CHI, The Spa	010 6841 2211	www.shangri-la.com
Green Lake 1513 Spa (men only)	010 6538 1098	www.greenlake1513spa.com
I Spa	010 6178 7795	www.ispa.cn
Jiuhua Spa & Resorts	010 6178 2288	www.jiuhua.com.cn
Oriental Taipan Massage & Spa	010 6503 5701	www.taipan.com.cn
Palm Springs Spa	010 6539 8888	www.spa-international.com

Country Clubs

After Deng Xiaoping said 'to get rich is glorious', it was only a matter of time before marks of status began to appear. Golf (p.124) is becoming as important as *baijiu* for greasing the wheels of capitalism and most country clubs have a course. Clubs range a great deal in price, but are all prohibitively expensive for the average Beijinger. While ¥230 will get you some time on the green at the nine-hole course of the Chaoyang Kosaido, only members are allowed to play on the lavish greens of Pine Valley, and membership costs $180,000.

Country Clubs

Beijing Country Golf Club	West of Chaobaihe, Mapuocun	010 6940 1111
Beijing International Golf Club	North of Shisanling Reservoir	010 6076 2288
Grand Canal Golf Club	Hugezhuangxiang	010 8958 2988
Legend Holiday Golf Club	89 Shoudu Jichang Lu	010 6456 1141
Lido Country Club	6 Jiangtai Lu	010 6437 6688
Pine Valley Golf Resort & Country Club	Pine Valley Resort, Nankou Town	010 8979 6868

Gyms

Despite the image that Chinese people live long lives, Beijing is not a very healthy place. Air quality is bad, stress levels are high and beer consumption is maniacal. Gyms tend to be the best solution for most expats. Annual fees range from ¥21,000 at the St Regis to less than ¥1,000 at more humble gyms. Many apartment complexes and offices also have gym facilities. Price promotions are frequently available.

Gyms

25 Hours Fitness Club	2 Maliandao Nanjie, Nr Carrefour	010 5837 2587
Alexander City Club	1 Xiangheyuan Lu, Dongzhimen Wai	010 8440 8888
Bally Total Fitness	Bld 2, Jianwai SOHO, 39 Dongsanhuan Zhonglu	010 5869 0666
Evolution Fitness Center	1/F, Dabeiyao Property Center, 2 Dongsanhuan Nanlu	010 6567 0266
Kerry Sports Centre	2/F, Kerry Centre Hotel, 1 Guanghua Lu	010 6561 8833
Nirvana Fitness	West Wing, Great Dragon Hotel, 2 Gongti Beilu	010 6597 2008
St Regis Spa	1/F, St Regis Hotel, 21 Jianguomen Waidajie	010 6460 6688

Well-Being

The history of traditional Chinese medicine (TCM) dates back thousands of years, and many expats arrive curious about the local take on wellness and relaxation. Today, there are all manner of salons and spas popping up to primp, preen and pamper. In Beijing, with its dubious air quality, dry winters, piping hot summers and 20 million people fighting for space, the ability to switch off, unwind and forget about the world for a couple of hours is crucial.

Today there are options to suit just about every budget, from cheap and cheerful (and often questionable) venues, to luxury establishments offering indulgent treatments. As with most aspects of life in Beijing, getting pampered generally comes with 'Chinese characteristics'. Sometimes that means a sensational five-element massage to align your inner qi. Sometimes it means looking the other way when the sheets in your massage parlour are not quite clean, or the scissors in your salon not sharp or… as the saying goes, you get what you pay for.

Beauty Salons

Other options **Perfumes & Cosmetics** p.280, **Health Spas** p.236

Beijing's beauty salons offer all the usual treatments, such as waxing, massage, facials and nail treatments. The service tends to be flexible though – in many cases, even if they don't really offer something, but you want it, they'll manage a compromise. The city is dotted with hundreds of small establishments where English is rarely spoken but nothing is too much trouble. There are also a growing number of excellent facilities in four and five-star hotels. Hygiene can be an issue, especially in smaller establishments, so if you want to look good for a special occasion it's best to visit a more reputable outlet. Also beware of whitening treatments – not only do they sting, but putting peroxide on your skin is bad for it, no matter how much you look like Cleopatra afterwards.

China World Hotel
Chaoyang
建国门外大街1号
朝阳区
🚇 *Guomao L1*
Map 11 F3 **100**

Beauty Farm 美丽田园

010 6505 1238 | *www.shangri-la.com*

With locations around town, including at Seasons Place Shopping Mall, Beauty Farm is one of the nicest spots to get plucked and polished. The facials are excellent, with staff providing a consultation before every treatment to determine the exact type required. The centre also offers waxing and eyebrow shaping, as well as massage and slimming treatments. A basic facial costs around ¥400, although members receive decent discounts and regular freebies.

301 Bld B, Sunshine
100, Guanghua Lu
Chaoyang
光华路阳光100B座
301室
朝阳区
Map 7 D2 **101**

Daisy's Beauty Salon 黛丝美容院

010 5100 0557

Daisy's proudly displays 'before' and 'after' shots throughout, so it is clearly the place for a makeover. Apparently you can enter as a hairy, overweight recluse and emerge the other side silky smooth and glowing. The salon offers just about every waxing service under the sun (from ¥60 for a lip wax), as well as many facials, slimming treatments, manis, pedis and makeup for special occasions.

Hairdressers

There are hairdressing services in Beijing to suit most budgets. If you're not fussy, don't mind a crowd of curious onlookers, and have the courage of a gladiator, you can get a roadside cut for a couple of *kuai*.

If you're more inclined to trust your locks to a qualified stylist, then you're looking at a considerable increase in cost – although it does come with peace of mind. Most salons offer varying levels of service, from non-English speaking trainees through to professional stylists with years of international experience. Needless to say, price varies accordingly, with trainees charging from around ¥100 for a cut, and senior stylists starting from about

Hairdressers		
Asakura	Chaoyang	010 6506 7455
Gary Lewis Salon	Shunyi	010 8046 4410
Hair & Beauty	Various Locations	010 8470 3110
Hair Plus Concept	Dongcheng	010 8515 0700
Image Momentum	Chaoyang	010 5820 4500
Toni & Guy	Various Locations	010 6528 1568

¥300. Aside from the snip, most hairdressers offer a wide variety of beauty treatments, including waxing, manicures, pedicures and eyelash extensions.

Nali Mall, Sanlitun Beilu
Chaoyang
三里屯北路那里商场内
朝阳区
Map 9 F3 102

C de France 北京风色云边美容美发
010 6417 3029 | www.cdefrance.com
C de France was opened by Catherine Colin, who has more than 13 years of experience in the hairdressing world, including stints at Eric Paris (see below). It offers a good range of services, from hair consultations, colours and cuts through to waxing, manicures and facials. Cuts start from ¥360 (¥150 with a junior stylist), although recommendations and first visits score a 20% discount. The salon itself is very chic, with minimal white decor, upbeat music and cool stylists. There are regular events and promotions, including ladies' evenings with complimentary champagne, and TGI Friday cuts that come with a glass of red wine.

43 Nanlu, Sanlitun Beijie
Chaoyang
三里屯北街南路43号
朝阳区
Map 9 F3 103

Eric Paris Salon 爱丽克美容美发沙龙
135 0137 2971
With six branches around town, Eric Paris is a favourite among expats for its English-speaking, professional staff and reliable service. Basic cuts begin from ¥230, although a cut from a trainee means a significant discount. Hair products used include Kerastase, L'Oreal and Wella, with a dedicated Kerastase Institute recently opened at the Hilton Hotel branch (Dongfang Lu, Dongsanhuan Beilu, 137 0118 3307). Hair is serious business here and your mane is even computer analysed before being treated. Other services include nail treatments, waxing, eyelash tinting and extensions and tanning. More details are on the website, which is in Chinese but can be found by putting the salon name into a search engine.

V-0117, Villa 9
Jianwai SOHO
Chaoyang
东三环中路39号建外
SOHO9号楼V-0117
朝阳区
🚇 *Guomao L1*
Map 11 F3 104

Tony Studio 东田造型
010 5869 0050
Tony Studio at Jianwai SOHO merits a day long visit to make the most of its extensive facilities. Spread over four floors, it includes a cafe, a homewares boutique, a photo studio, and, of course, a hairdressing salon. A number of the stylists speak English, and their cuts start from ¥180. Follow up with a facial, manicure and makeup session before heading into the studio for a quick portrait photo. There's another studio at 919 Building 2, Sundongan Plaza, Wangfujing, Dongcheng. Jianwai SOHO is at 39 Dongsanhuan Zhonglu.

S106, 18 Gongti Xilu
Chaoyang
工体西路18号S106
朝阳区
🚇 *Chaoyangmen L2*
Map 9 D4 105

Vajra 画间沙龙
010 6551 6461 | www.vajra.com.hk
Headed up by a team of highly experienced stylists from the UK, Vajra is where Chinese celebs go to get their hair done. Prices reflect its exclusive nature, with cuts beginning from ¥400. However, you do get what you pay for – niceties include private rooms, a dedicated hair dye specialist, style education seminars, a nail salon, and a chic cafe serving up all manner of beverages and snacks.

Health Spas

Other options **Sports & Leisure Facilities** p.232, **Massage** p.237

Inevitably, many of the plush new spas here are in five-star hotels, but there are also many excellent independent options that are usually cheaper than their hotel counterparts. The variety in treatments is exceptional, ranging from standard Thai and Chinese aroma massages, to targeted treatments and indulgent all day rituals. These spas are increasingly catering to male patrons, with a number of men only centres opening in recent years (including Spa de Feng, C306 Sunshine 100, 2 Guanghua Lu, Chaoyang, 010 5100 1330). Pattaya is also popular with gents (www.pattaya-spa.com). Some spas will charge around ¥100 for admission, which includes use of the showers, hot tubs and saunas, and even food. Charges are then added for massages (usually between ¥200 and ¥500 for one hour) or other services. Whatever you go for, membership offers can see you pumiced, polished and pruned for a lot less than you might expect. Cheaper massage and beauty services are available at bathhouses and salons around the city, but be aware that many of these are fronts for prostitution.

Commune by the Great Wall Kempinski
Badaling Highway
长城公社凯宾斯基饭店，八达岭高速长城水关出口

Anantara Spa 水疗中心

010 8118 1888 | www.spa.anantara.com

Run by MSpa International, Anantara is about one hour's drive from Beijing, in the clubhouse at the Commune by the Great Wall Kempinski hotel. The 15 private rooms are simple but stunning in design, and many feature views of the Great Wall. Day spa packages include morning yoga, meditation, body scrubs, floral baths, aroma oil massages and a healthy lunch. Alternatively, individual treatments include massage, facials and body therapies using delicious natural products.

Shangri-La
29 Zizhuyuan Lu
Haidian
紫竹院路29号北京香格里拉饭店
海淀区
Map 4 B4 107

CHI, The Spa 水疗中心

010 6841 2211 | www.shangri-la.com

The signature spa for the Shangri La group, CHI is in the new Valley Wing of the Shangri La Hotel (p.33). You'll find Tibetan and Burmese antiques in private, self-contained spa suites with infinity bathtubs. Based on the Chinese philosophy of five elements, treatments are designed to align your qi, and begin with a consultation to determine your element type. The Empress Jade Journey is one of the more unique treatments, and includes a facial and massage using smooth crystals of jade.

5/F Block B, Taiyue Suites
16 Sanlitun Nanlu
Chaoyang
南三里屯路16号泰悦豪庭2座5层
朝阳区
Map 9 F4 108

I Spa 泰美好水疗

010 6507 1517 | www.ispa.cn

This spa has two locations in Beijing, one in Sanlitun and the other in the Napa Valley residential estate outside the north Fifth Ring Road. It is a great place to indulge in weekday lunchtime massage breaks (when discounts are offered), or lengthy weekend rituals. Both centres feature Thai-inspired design, Thai-trained therapists, and a number of Thai treatments. They also offer seasonal packages, such as the winter detox, and hangover rituals that combine massage, body scrubs, facials and aroma steams.

Area C1, Upper East Side
Central Plaza
Dongsihuan Beilu
Chaoyang
东四环北路阳光上东中环商业广场C1区
朝阳区
Map 5 D3 109

Renewal Spa Club 善泉水疗俱乐部

010 5139 5555

Renewal is one of the newest spas in town, and one of the biggest too. Guests are treated to complimentary juices and teas while receiving a consultation, before being whisked off to one of the three stunning ritual rooms – Moroccan, Asean and Oriental. Each is impeccably decorated and features treatments themed around the design. The Renewal Rejuvenating Therapy uses Romanian gold. After your treatment, you can take it easy with magazines and tea in relaxation rooms or the small cafe.

Chaoyang
小武基路甲8号1号楼
朝阳区

Zen
010 8731 2530 | *www.zenspa.com.cn*

Obscurely located in a beautiful *siheyuan* property on the east Fourth Ring Road, Zen has some indulgent treatments. Stunning rooms feature south-east Asian decor, and surround a serene, pebbled courtyard. All suites have a private bathroom and shower, and a number of the larger rooms also have spa tubs, where you can recline in waters infused with ginger, lime and lemongrass. Zen offers a range of wraps, body scrubs, facials and massage treatments, including heavenly hot and cold stone therapies.

Health Spas			
Heavenly Spa	The Westin Financial Street	Xicheng	010 6629 7878
In One Spa	Raffles	Dongcheng	010 6532 0333
LeSpa	Sofitel Wanda	Chaoyang	010 8599 6666
Palm Springs Spa	Palm Springs International Club	Chaoyang	010 6539 8888
QUAN	JW Marriott	Chaoyang	010 5908 6688
Ritz-Carlton Spa	Ritz-Carlton	Xicheng	010 6601 6666
Serenity	The Regent	Dongcheng	010 8522 1888
Thann	The Place	Chaoyang	010 6587 1384
Touch	Lido Hotel	Chaoyang	010 6430 1072

Massage
Other options **Health Spas** p.236, **Reflexology & Massage Therapy** p.124, **Sports & Leisure Facilities** p.232

While wellness spas are about an indulgent experience, many of Beijing's smaller massage centres put a greater emphasis on the treatment than the decor. That's not to say that the cheap and cheerful are unhygienic – most are very clean and neat. Dragonfly, Bodhi and Oriental Taipan are among the nicest, all offering a good range of massage and beauty services. Needless to say, Chinese massage tops the menu, but Thai and Swedish are not far behind, all for around ¥70 to ¥200 per hour. Most massage centres offer memberships, which can get you excellent discounts and some freebies. Avoid places with red lights, unless, of course, you're not actually looking for a massage at all.

12 Gongti Beilu◀
Chaoyang
工体北路12号
朝阳区
 Dongsishitiao L2
Map 9 E3 110

Bodhi Therapeutic Retreat 菩提休闲会所
010 6417 9595 | *www.bodhi.com.cn*

Bodhi is in the heart of Sanlitun, above The Olive (which serves delicious health food) and below Yoga Yard (p.242). It is very popular at all times and reservations are essential. The male and female staff are friendly and well trained in a variety of massage styles including Chinese, Thai and Ayurvedic. Treatments begin from ¥138, although large discounts are offered before 17:00, Monday to Thursday. Complimentary fresh juices, teas, other beverages and snacks are available throughout your treatment. Perhaps the only drawback of Bodhi is the super-thin walls, which mean it can be difficult to relax if you're next to a rowdy group.

60 Donghuamen Dajie◀
Dongcheng
东华门大街60号
东城区
 Tiananmen East L1
Map 10 E2 111

Dragonfly Therapeutic Retreat 悠庭保健会所
010 6593 6066

Already well established in China, Dragonfly has started branching into Europe, with a spa in Oslo. In Beijing there are three outlets across the city. The flagship Forbidden City branch is in a beautiful old two-storey building, dimly lit and simply decorated with signature Dragonfly home wares. These are for sale along with spa products in a boutique adjoining the reception. The Crystal House suite is stunning, with a private bathroom and a tree laden with teardrop crystals. The Ultimate Indulgence treatment

237

lasts for three hours and includes body, foot and head massages. Waxing services are also available, and there's a nice nail bar with manis and pedis starting from ¥120. Other locations: 1F Eastern Hotel, Sanlitun Nanlu, Chaoyang, and 888 Pinnacle Plaza, Shunyi.

B1/F Xindong Lu
Chaoyang
新东路1号B1
朝阳区
Map 9 E1 **112**

Oriental Taipan 东方大班健身中心
010 8532 2177 | www.taipan.com.cn

Popular because of its late opening hours, Oriental Taipan is a Beijing institution, with four different outlets across the city. Although nothing fancy, private rooms are clean and comfortable, and feature flat screen TVs with cable, so you can chill out with a DVD or music while enjoying your massage. A standard 90 minute foot massage costs ¥138, but there's a good range of other treatments including Thai body massage and hot stone massage, cupping, facial treatments (starting from ¥480) and nail treatments. VIP cards can get you discounts of over 20%. See the website for other locations.

Massage

99 Massage & Spa Center	703 e-Tower, Guanghua Lu	Chaoyang	010 6501 0799
Aibosen Blindman Massage	11 Liufang Beilu	Chaoyang	010 6466 1247
Dragon Foot Club	15 Jianguomennei	Dongcheng	010 6559 6957
Heping Massage	Building 1, Hairun International Building,	Chaoyang	010 6436 7370
Liangzi Sport & Fitness	2F Just Make Mansion	Chaoyang	010 6417 2272
Long Island Massage & Spa	BF Jiahui Center, 6 Jiqingli	Chaoyang	010 6551 6112
Lotus Spa	W02 Tianzhu Huayuan, Fuqian Yijie	Shunyi	010 6457 4822
Tianhe Liangzi	10 Nongzhan Nanli	Chaoyang	010 6506 2697

Meditation

If practised properly, meditation can be a great way to unwind and de-stress. Although it's widely recognised across China, particularly among members of the Buddhist community, there are limited opportunities to learn the techniques. A number of related activities including yoga, pilates and reiki incorporate some meditative principles. Mountain Yoga (p.242) includes meditation sessions in its weekend yoga retreats, and can also arrange personal meditation classes. Yoga Yard (p.242) also runs weekly meditation and chanting classes for ¥100 per session.

Nail Bars

A number of Beijing's better spas, massage centres and beauty salons have excellent nail bars, including Dragonfly (p.237), and CHI, The Spa at Shangri La (p.236). These places are generally more expensive than dedicated nail bars, with standard manicures beginning at around ¥120, and advanced bookings required. There are, however, dozens of smaller establishments that operate on a walk-in basis. If you're looking for something quick, cheap and high quality, visit one of the many nail bars on the fourth floor of Yashow Market (p.294) in Sanlitun. Set prices see manicures going for ¥20 and pedicures ¥40, with all manner of add-ons including hot oil treatments. Due to their popularity, you may find yourself waiting, especially on weekends.

101/5 Jianwai SOHO
Chaoyang
东三环中路39号建外
SOHO5号楼101室
朝阳区
🚇 *Guomao L1*
Map 11 F3 **113**

Kuka 艺术沙龙
010 5869 0868

Spread over two floors, Kuka offers a wide range of hand and nail treatments, from French tips and acrylics to hand and nail waxing. A standard mani will set you back ¥80, and you can get your hair trimmed or styled at the same time. A cut will cost a minimum of ¥280. Jianwai SOHO is at 39 Dongsanhuan Zhonglu.

Great things can come in small packages…

Perfectly proportioned to fit in your pocket, these marvellous mini guidebooks make sure you don't just get the holiday you paid for, but rather the one that you dreamed of.

Explorer Mini Visitors' Guides
Maximising your holiday, minimising your hand luggage

Abu Dhabi · Amsterdam · Bahrain · Barcelona · Beijing · Berlin · Dubai · Dublin · Geneva

EXPLORER

1/F, Tongli Studio
Bei Sanlitun Lu
Chaoyang
北三里屯路同里大
厦1层
朝阳区
🚇Dongsishitiao L2
Map 9 F3 114

Lovely Nails 爱手·爱脚美甲

010 6417 5812

The Sanlitun branch of Lovely Nails is chic, modern and super clean. The skilled staff are attentive, and you can recline in soft sofas with magazines while you wait for your polish to dry. Nails start from ¥90, and additional services include waxing, eyelash extensions, eyebrow shaping and facial tattooing. Other locations are at W06 Skyplace Market, Tianzhu Garden in Shunyi District and Taiyue Heights.

Nail Bars

Frost Nails	2F Jiezuo Dasha	Chaoyang	010 6417 9148
Nail Plus	B23 Kerry Centre, 1 Guanghua Lu	Chaoyang	010 8529 9407
Nan Nan Nails	2F Shutterbox Accessory Shop	Chaoyang	010 5135 7477
Sunshine Nails	4F Yashow Market	Chaoyang	010 6413 2426

Pilates

Other options **Yoga** p.241

Like yoga, Pilates is a new age fitness trend that has taken off in China like a bullet. And for good reason – it is one of the best ways to strengthen core muscles and build up the abs, all the while practising controlled breathing to reduce stress and relax. Although there are very few dedicated Pilates centres in Beijing, it's widely offered at hotel fitness centres. In establishments like Kerry Sports at the Kerry Centre Hotel (p.35), instructors are bilingual. At many fitness centres instruction may be exclusively in Chinese, but it's not that hard to imitate your instructor. Evolution Fitness (2 Dongsanhuan Nanlu, Chaoyang, 010 6567 0266) offers multiple Pilates classes every week. If you're planning to attend on a regular basis, you might want to invest in a gym membership (p.232). Otherwise, you can buy a 10 pass membership for ¥350. CSI Bally Fitness (Building 2, Jianwai SOHO, Chaoyang, 010 5869 0666) also holds classes every week, as does Nirvana Fitness (Zhaolong Hotel, 2 Gongti Beilu, Chaoyang, 010 6597 2008) and the Beijing YMCA Fitness Centre (13 Guangqumennei Dajie, Chongwen, 010 6719 5151).

Reiki

Although the concept of Reiki can be a little bit hard to get your head around, regulars swear by it as an intuitive form of healing and wellness. In essence, it is focused meditation used to change the flow of 'energy' and positive healing in people, rooms and situations. Some use reiki masters, for example, to establish a positive vibe in a room before a big event. Generally, however, the practice of reiki involves a reiki master changing energy in people through hand placements above the body (in reiki theory, you don't need to touch someone to change their energy). There are two different stages you must pass through before you can become a reiki master, and to get through both of them requires intensive training on a daily basis. The Expat Learning Center (3205 Building A, Soho Xian Dai Cheng, Chaoyang, 010 8580 3111, www.beijing-classes.com) holds workshops for all three different levels, costing ¥2,000 per course. Mountain Yoga (p.242) also incorporates Tera Mai Reiki courses into a number of its weekend retreats, starting from ¥1,600 per weekend. Instructor Michael Ulrich is also available for private workshops.

Stress Management

Other options **Support Groups** p.125

Moving abroad can be stressful, especially if children, pets and extended family are involved. Once in Beijing, there are all manner of issues to deal with, like communicating in Chinese, finding employment and managing household affairs. And then there is the added inconvenience of navigating a city of 20 million people. If you feel like screaming from time to time, you're not alone, and there are support services to help you through.

If you're not releasing your anger at the gym or by contorting yourself into all manner of yoga positions, try the stress management classes at the Expat Learning Center (3205 Building A, Soho Xian Dai Cheng, Chaoyang, 010 8580 3111, www.beijing-classes.com). Their intensive introduction teaches essential skills for dealing with tension in a relaxed and healthy way. The ¥3,200 course is intimate and interactive, with lots of role-playing and myth-busting. If you're after something more personal, many of the foreign hospitals have psychologists and social workers. Try Beijing United (p.118) for regular anger and stress management classes.

Tai Chi

Wander through any park in Beijing at sunrise or sunset and you'll find locals braving the elements to practice various forms of *wushu* (martial arts), the most popular being tai chi. It's a great way to reduce stress, improve balance and coordination, and ease sore muscles and joints. Other health benefits include stimulation of the central nervous system, enhanced digestion, and even the easing of constipation. At its core, tai chi is also a subtle method of self defence – if you pressed the fast forward button, those grandparents in the park might start to resemble a Jet Li film. In its slowed down mode it's a peaceful, social, way to gently exercise. If you're not ready to join in with the park practitioners, Mountain Yoga (p.242) includes tai chi in its weekend retreats. Tai Chi Workshop (1F CTS Hotel, Sanyuan Qiao, Chaoyang) conducts weekly classes for around ¥50, with translators available on request.

Chinese Culture Club 中国文化协会

29 Anjia Lou
Liangmaqiao Lu
Chaoyang
亮马桥路安家楼29号
朝阳区
Map 7 D1 **1**

010 6432 9341 | www.chinesecultureclub.org

The martial arts arm of the Chinese Culture Club holds tai chi classes every Thursday evening, costing ¥800 for ten lessons or ¥120 for an individual session. The group classes are a good way to learn the basics, with a focus on deep breathing. The same club offers classes in *qigong*, an ancient form of healing designed to balance qi through a series of postures and movements, every Monday night.

Yoga

For young Chinese, tai chi is somewhat out of date. The activity of the moment is definitely yoga, with fitness centres and private studios offering many different courses. Although yoga postures are fantastic for strengthening and toning the body, the 'sport' is also widely praised for its mental health benefits. There are six different types of yoga – hatha being the most commonly practiced in China. To complicate things, there are different branches of hatha, including iyengar (a modern interpretation) and ashtanga (a more vigorous version). Both are popular. And then there's evo yoga (less about traditional hatha poses and more about stretching) and hot yoga, done in 42 degrees, with the aim of sweating out what ails you. Most fitness centres in town offer daily classes, Evolution Fitness (p.240) offers early morning and lunch classes in addition to evening and weekend sessions.

Beijing Yoga 北京瑜伽

Room 501, 5/F Tower A
Chaoyang
SOHO新城A座5层501室
朝阳区
🚇 *Dawanglu L1*
Map 7 D2 **116**

010 5900 3192 | www.beijingyoga.com

Beijing Yoga offers classes in traditional ashtanga yoga to students of all levels. The centre also has classes in kids', prenatal, hot and hatha yoga. There are a wide range of rates depending on the type and length of your yoga training. Check the website for more details.

Bikram Hot Yoga 比克拉姆热瑜伽

5/F Building E, Pacific Century Club
Chaoyang
工体北路甲2号盈科中
心E座5层
朝阳区
Gongtibeilu
Map 9 F3 **118**

010 6539 3434 | http://bikramyogabeijing.googlepages.com
Named after yoga master Bikram Choudhury, Bikram hot yoga is based on the 26 hatha poses, but is practised in a room heated to 42 degrees, to help facilitate stretching. Classes run for 90 minutes, and are suitable for all levels of experience. Daily classes are taught by graduates from Bikram's yoga academy in the US, and cost ¥140, with a range of different membership deals available. A number of the classes are conducted in silence, so there is no talking and absolutely no mobile phones. The Pacific Century Club is at 2A Gongti Beilu.

Easy Yoga, Easy Life

503, Building 2C, Jianwai SOHO
Map 11 F3 **119**

010 5900 0850 | amieryang@163.com
This charming centre offers small classes and one-on-one teaching with professional instructors. It's a thoroughly civilised way to learn how to take better care of your body and mind. The emphasis on 'easy' that has been put into the name is certainly appropriate. The courtyard style studio, music and home-brewed flower tea help to create a peaceful atmosphere on even the most stressful Beijing day. The centre is convenient for people who work in and around the Guomao area.

Mountain Yoga 山地瑜伽

6 Gongzhufen Cun Fragrant Hills
Haidian
香山公主坟村6号
海淀区

010 6259 6702 | www.mountainyoga.cn
If you have the time, the yoga retreats run by Mountain Yoga are a fantastic way to detox and get back to nature. The holistic seasonal breaks are held in a camp by the Great Wall, to the west of Beijing. When the weather gets too cold, proceedings move to one of two centres near Fragrant Hills or an ancient Buddhist temple just outside of town. The retreats teach you about a wide range of practices, including hatha, karma, ashtanga and raja yoga, alongside tai chi workshops, and natural healing. The guesthouse at the retreat dishes up delicious vegetarian cuisine. The retreats cost from ¥500 per night.

Om Yoga 42° 静心堂

9102, 03 Lido Apartment Building
Lido
丽都公寓3号楼9102室
朝阳区
Map 5 D3 **120**

010 6437 8810 | www.omyoga42.com
At Om, bilingual classes are held in a serene room heated up to between 42 and 46 degrees. It's recommended that beginners take it easy at first, as the heat and extra blood to the brain can cause you to go a bit woozy. It is worth it in the end, with benefits (on top of those associated with normal yoga) including relief from arthritis, diabetes and thyroid disorders. A single class costs ¥150, with monthly and yearly packages available.

Yoga Yard 瑜伽苑

6F, 17 Gongti Beilu
Sanlitun
工体北路甲17号6层
朝阳区
Gongtibeilu
Map 9 E3 **121**

010 6413 0774 | www.yogayard.com
Located above Bodhi (p.237) in Sanlitun, Yoga Yard's classes include yoga for kids and prenatal yoga. Teacher training and workshops with 'celebrity' instructors and trainers are also available. If you're looking for something intimate, Yoga Yard can also provide English and Chinese instruction in the privacy of your home. Single classes cost ¥90, with memberships available.

Yoga			
Alona Studio	Room 802, Building 6 Wanda Plaza	Chaoyang	010 5820 6920
Beijing Yoga	2610 Tower D, SOHO New Town	Chaoyang	010 8589 3102
OmShanti	B11 Jianwai SOHO	Chaoyang	010 5869 2849
Yoga Club	53 Maizidian Zhengjie	Chaoyang	010 6200 0127
Yogi Yoga	Ritan Park	Chaoyang	010 8561 5506

Tiantan Park (p.173)

Beihai Park (p.191)

Huanhuan

Art (p.207)

Singing in the Long Corridor (p.188)

碩 華 畫 廊
Beijing Central Art Gallery

赵艺 Zhao Yi

纪晓峰 Ji Xiao Feng

尹俊 Yin Jun

李云 Li Yun

章华 Zhang Hua

庞永杰 Pang Yong Jie

02, Riverville Square, No.1 District One,
Tianzhu, Shunyi, Beijing, 101312.
(Airport Expressway, Yanglin 7th Exit)
北京市, 顺义天竺丽宫别墅一区1号,
温榆广场02 号. (机场高速杨林第七出口)
Telephone 电话: (86) 10 64508483
Fax/Tel 传真:(86) 10 64508646

Hotel Shop No. 2, Ground Floor,
Kempinski Hotel Beijing,
50, Liangmaqiao Road, Beijing.
北京市朝阳区,亮马桥路50号.
凯宾斯基饭店一层02店.
Telephone 电话: (86) 10 64651396

E-mail 电子邮件: artenquiry@bjcagallery.com
Website 网站: www.bjcagallery.com

Shopping

Shopping

Shopping expeditions in Beijing can veer from the best to the worst retail experience in minutes. Bargains and hidden gems lurk around every corner, but to get to them you must hurdle crowds of thousands, clingy shopkeepers, and bargaining rituals that can take up the best part of a day.

There's not much that money can't buy in the Chinese capital, from the most obscure herb that grows on the back of wild yak, to dime-a-dozen 'Gucci' handbags, to glittering sports cars – complete with a chauffeur.

Only a few short years ago, shoppers made do with a smattering of markets and Chinese-style shopping malls. But today, there's something to suit just about every taste and style, from the budget, to the boutique.

China is now home to 106 billionaires, and retailers are increasingly inclined to cater to their fat wallets. Mega malls bursting with big name brands are now commonplace in Beijing; glimmering, multi-storey beacons all making history in some way, shape or form. The Place (p.296) has the largest upside-down LCD screen in the world; Seasons Place (Map 6 D2) houses the flagship Lane Crawford (p.258) in mainland China; Shin Kong Place (Map 7 D2, www.shinkong-place.com) has only the second Fauchon gourmet supermarket in Asia. And yet, many of these glitzy malls remain ghostly empty which begs the question, is the recent boutique boom more a show of status than a shrewd business decision? Regardless, for shoppers this expansion and constant need for retailers to outdo each other promises a bright buying future.

Faking It

Beijing has a lot of fake goods. From CDs and DVDs through to North Face jackets, Gucci sandals and Tod's handbags, if it can be copied, it is. As a general rule, if it's Gucci and not sold in an authorised Gucci boutique, it's fake. It may look like the real deal on the surface, with its pretty logo and soft leather, but chances are that Gucci did not authorise a 13 year old from Hebei to sell its purses on street corners. Just don't be too surprised when the $4,000 bag you're buying for ¥40 falls apart within a few weeks of purchase.

Sale Away

Shopping malls such as Xidan (p.276), Oriental Plaza (p.296), The Place (p.296), Shin Kong Place (Map 7 D2), Twin Towers, and the China World Shopping Mall (p.295) come alive with end of season sales, often seeing prices slashed by 50% to 70%. This sometimes leads to scenes reminiscent of Pamplona's Running of the Bulls, particularly on weekends and during lunch hours. However, if you're up for a bit of jostling and queuing, then you'll no doubt walk away with some bargains.

What & Where To Buy – Quick Reference

Alcohol	p.249	Computers	p.260	Jewellery & Watches	p.270	Pets	p.280
Art	p.249	Electronics & Home App	p.261	Lingerie	p.273	Second-Hand Items	p.281
Art Supplies	p.250	Eyewear	p.262	Luggage & Leather	p.273	Shoes	p.282
Baby Items	p.251	Flowers	p.263	Medicine	p.274	Souvenirs	p.284
Beachwear	p.252	Food	p.263	Mobile Phones	p.274	Sports Goods	p.284
Bicycles	p.253	Gardens	p.265	Music, DVDs & Videos	p.276	Stationery	p.285
Books	p.254	Gifts	p.265	Musical Instruments	p.277	Tailoring	p.286
Camera Equipment	p.256	Hardware & DIY	p.265	Outdoor Goods	p.278	Textiles	p.286
Car Parts & Acc	p.256	Health Food	p.266	Party Accessories	p.279	Toys & Games	p.287
Clothes	p.257	Home Furnishings	p.267	Perfume & Cosmetics	p.280	Wedding Items	p.289

The Little People

Big foreign retailers are not completely crushing local talent. Young designers and small boutiques are springing up all over the city, to cater to an increasingly bohemian crowd.

For those who want to stand out, the best places for individual designer items and one-offs are Nali Mall (p.272), 3.3 Shopping Mall (p.295), the Ritan Office Building, and Jianwai SOHO. The only downside to these places is that sizes are aimed at locals. There are no secret size 12 jeans hidden out the back, and 34 really is the largest shoe size available.

Plastic Not Fantastic

In a bid to reduce waste and curb pollution problems, the Chinese government plans to ban shopkeepers from handing out free plastic bags. As landfill sites overflow and pollution increases, from June 2008 shoppers will be encouraged to use baskets or reusable cloth bags.

Beijing's Top Markets

Beijing has some of the country's best markets. The notorious Silk Market (p.294) draws crowds of more than 60,000 bargain-hungry shoppers every Saturday. Hongqiao (p.293), also known as The Pearl Market, sells a lot more than jewellery and pearls. It is popular with restaurateurs and chefs, thanks to the sprawling fish market in the basement and its fresh catches. Panjiayuan (p.293) is a treasure trove of antiques, art and furniture. Alien Street (p.288), in the heart of 'little Moscow', is the place to visit for silver vinyl stilettos and Halloween costumes, and Dongjiao is heaven for the thrifty, selling anything and everything at prices that you'd be ashamed to bargain down any lower.

Clothing Sizes

Big nose, big feet, big bum… foreigners can have a hard time finding clothes that cover their generous assets. Although changing diets are making the locals bigger and taller, they're still no match for the size 40 feet of your average western female. Shopping can be a frustrating experience if you try to squeeze into the same sizes as locals. It's better to just accept your proportions and head to shops that cater to your curves. For bigger sizes, the best bets are touristy markets like Yashow (p.294) and the Silk Market (p.294), as well as newer European and American designer stores, like Zara (p.260), MNG (p.259) and Levi's (p.259).

Online Shopping

Online shopping is becoming extremely popular, with a boom in sites. For books, the most popular websites are Dangdang (the biggest online book retailer in China), and Amazon. Both are in Chinese, and offer home delivery within 48 hours for a nominal fee. Site members can also opt to receive promotional updates by text message.

The local eBay, Taobao, is all the rage. Anyone can set up a shop to sell goods on the Chinese-language site, which makes for an eclectic storefront indeed. Consumers can pick up clothes and home wares, health food, IT products, books, movies and other items that are too risque to mention.

English language shopping sites are rare, although Carrefour (p.297) supermarket does have a good e-shopping site (http://e-shop.carrefour.com.cn), offering groceries, health and beauty products, home wares, clothes and electrical appliances. Minimum spend is ¥500 and home delivery is free. To order takeaway food online, try www.beijinggoodies.com.

Online Shopping

http://e-shop.carrefour.com.cn	Groceries, appliances, health and beauty products, clothes
http://home.dangdang.com	Books
www.amazon.cn	Books, CDs, DVDs
www.taobao.com	Anything and everything
www.yesasia.com	Books, music, games, toys

Refunds & Exchanges

Use common sense when shopping in China. If you're making a big purchase, like home appliances, quality clothes or a car, always ensure you get a warranty and official receipt or *fapiao*. In most cases, this will allow an exchange if your goods give up the ghost for no apparent reason. Purchases from markets can be a bit trickier – most places will exchange clothes for you if you've purchased the incorrect size, but getting your money back is unlikely (you can expect to be laughed at). If it's a concern, ask about refunds and exchanges before you buy, and get the shopkeeper to write you a guarantee about these before you hand over any cash.

Shipping

While shipping goods home is not difficult, there are a few restrictions. You are not permitted to take antiques from before 1795 out of the country, and many shipping companies prohibit you from exporting large quantities of DVDs and CDs. International branches of China Post (try the one opposite the north gate of the Workers' Stadium) can send boxed goods anywhere in the world, but will inspect your packages first. Don't bother taping your boxes before they're inspected. For faster delivery, with fewer questions asked, DHL, FedEx, and UPS (see p.112) are good (but more expensive) options, and will collect goods from your home, provided they're under a certain weight limit.

How To Pay

Cold, hard cash is still the most common form of payment for anything from a meal to a car. Carry a range of bills with you; many people consider ¥100 difficult to break (especially taxi drivers in the early morning), and it's always handy to have small notes for the subway.

ATM cards are becoming more common, but don't be surprised when you're asked to sign receipts, even though you've already entered your PIN. Most Chinese banks are part of the Union Group, which means you can use foreign ATM cards to withdraw money wherever you see the Union sign.

Souvenirs (p.284)

Some larger boutiques, international stores and restaurants also accept credit cards, although you may find that your card is 'not working' a surprising amount of the time, especially if it's American Express. Generally, your card will be working, but retailers are often told to push consumers for cash.

Bargaining

As a general rule, don't even ask about a price unless you have every intention of buying the item. If you do find something you want, don't wear your excitement on your sleeve. Instead, be nonchalant, as shopkeepers are well trained to sniff out weakness and then pounce with an inflated number.

The first price a storekeeper quotes will generally be outrageous, particularly in big, touristy markets. Aim for about one third of the initial asking price, but start bargaining at a figure considerably lower than this. Walking away is a good trick, and you'll promptly be yanked back into the store for another round of negotiation.

Most shopkeepers in markets speak English, but they'll probably pull out a calculator to facilitate proceedings. If you speak a bit of Chinese, you'll instantly get quoted much lower prices.

Alcohol

Other options **Bars** p.326, **Drinks** p.326

While there are a few speciality alcohol stores, most supermarkets and delis offer a decent enough range of booze. Carrefour (p.297) supermarkets have new and old world wines, as well as local and imported beers, spirits and mixers. Aim to pay around ¥65 for a bottle of gin or vodka, and from ¥50 for a bottle of red or white wine. These are marked with flags to help you identify the country of origin. Many Carrefour outlets hire wine professionals from the major distributors to provide customer advice at the weekends. Jenny Lou's stores (p.297) all sell a good range of wines, spirits and beer, although they're usually slightly more expensive than Carrefour at around ¥70 for the same bottle of gin. But, there are regular sales, when you can pick up a nice Aussie red for as little as ¥45. If you're really serious about your grapes, it might be best to buy direct from a distributor. They offer the widest selection, can arrange home delivery, sell wine accessories, and offer discounts for bulk orders. ASC Fine Wines (010 6418 1598, www.asc-wines.com), China's leading distributor of imported wines, has a mind boggling selection that can be ordered over the phone or from its website, with free delivery for orders over ¥200. It also hosts regular wine tastings (p.227), so you can try before you buy. Similarly, Summergate Fine Wines (010 6562 5800) has a good selection, as well as a couple of top end spirits, and offers advice and home delivery. Others worth investigating are Gelipu Wines (www. ai9.com.cn) and Jointek Fine Wines (wwwjointekwines.com).

B101, Kunlun Gallery
Xinyuan Nanlu
Chaoyang
新源南路昆仑汇地下一
层B101
朝阳区
Map 9 F2 **1**

Aussino World Wines 富隆酒业

010 6508 9008 | *www.aussino.net*

As the name suggests, Aussino does an impressive stock of Australian wines, including some interesting drops from up-and-coming boutique wineries. It also sells wines from across Europe, as well as America, Chile and Argentina. The friendly, knowledgeable staff will often have a bottle or two open in store for tastings. This is also a good place to stock up on accessories, including home wine cellars, glasses, corkscrews and decanters.

China World
Shopping Mall
Chaoyang
建国门外大街1号B1
朝阳区
Guomao L1
Map 11 F3 **2**

Ole Wines 华润超市烟酒屋

010 6505 1328 | *www.cwtc.com*

Although the Ole supermarket next door does sell alcohol, if you're after a serious wine (some in excess of ¥10,000 per bottle) then this is the place to shop. Aside from top shelf Grand Cru wines, this small shop sells quality liquor and cigars. Unfortunately, staff only speak Chinese, and when you're looking to make such a large investment it would be helpful to have advice in English.

Kerry Centre Hotel
Chaoyang
光华路1号嘉里中心饭
店大堂缤味
朝阳区
Guanghualu
Map 11 F2 **3**

Top Cellar 九福

139 1148 6749 | *www.shangri-la.com*

In three locations around town, these small shops are well stocked with interesting wines from around the world. The Bento & Berries outlet hosts tastings with free canapes every evening, and always has helpful staff on hand to recommend wines for different occasions. Other locations are at Central Park, 6 Chaowai Dajie (010 6597 0024) and Winland Plaza, 7 Jinrong Jie (010 5181 9969).

Art

Other options **Art Supplies** p.250, **Art Classes** p.207, **Art Galleries** p.176

China is the current darling of the modern art world, with collectors falling over themselves to nab a Wang Yuping original, or a photo by Sheng Qi. The attention has seen prices soar. Beijing-based artist Yue Minjun's painting, *Execution*, recently went for $5.9 million, making it the most expensive work of Chinese contemporary art ever sold. Other emerging artists include Du Xinjian, Morgan, Cao Fei, Cui Xiuwen, Chen Xinmao, Zhang Dali, and Zhong Biao. They all regularly display their works at the dozens of galleries (p.176) around town.

If you're looking to invest, these galleries are definitely your best bet – just about everything on display is for sale, and often the artists will be hanging around to talk about their works. Most Chinese art is no longer cheap, and small paintings by lesser-known artists start from a couple of thousand *kuai*.

If you're after something more along the lines of an 'original replica', then try Panjiayuan Market (p.293), with two long aisles dedicated to art. Or, try a wander around Wangfujing (p.290), where you'll be accosted by an 'art student' looking to take you back to their 'art school' within a matter of minutes. These places are not art schools, but if you like what you see, who cares? You can pay as little as ¥100 for a nice scroll.

4 Jiuxianqiao Lu
798
酒仙桥路4号
朝阳区
Map 5 D2 **4**

798 Art District 798艺术区
www.798.net.cn
Once a factory district, 798 has become one of the most highly regarded art areas in the world. This is thanks, in part, to a number of attention-grabbing openings from the likes of the Ullens Centre for Contemporary Art (p.178). The biggest art zone in Beijing, 798 (also known as Dashanzi) is home to dozens of artists' studios and modern galleries. Some of the better galleries for original art include Red T Space (www.redt-art.com), Red Gate Gallery (p.177), Yan Club Art Scene (010 8457 3506), the 798 Photo Gallery (p.176), Beijing Tokyo Art Projects (010 8457 3245), and Art Scene Beijing (010 6431 6962). Ullens also has an art education area. A particularly good time to visit is in September, during the Dangdai International Art Festival (p.54), when there are many new exhibitions.

Jia 2, Wangsiying
Chaoyang
王四营甲2号
朝阳区
Map 7 E3 **5**

Guanyintang 观音堂文化大道
010 6736 6059 | *www.no1hlj.com*
A relatively new art street, Guanyintang has more than 40 galleries, many of them with sister outlets in 798. Look out for Meedoo Gallery, Century Hanmo Gallery, Asia Art Center (p.177), Wing Gallery, Tao Gallery, Art 8 Space and more, all of which sell modern Chinese art at prices significantly lower than places closer to town. Bargaining is expected.

15 Beihuqu Lu
Anwai Beiyuan Dajie
Chaoyang
安外北苑大街北湖渠
15号
朝阳区
Map 5 C2 **6**

Liquor Factory 酒厂艺术区
Within spitting distance of the China Central Academy of Fine Arts (p.140) and the Wangjing Art Center, this sprawling district is home to hundreds of artists, many of which have created mini galleries and shops in their studios. It is a peaceful place to stroll, talk to the artists and get some perspective on the piece you're buying. It's also included on the Dangdai International Art Festival (p.54) route.

Art Supplies
Other options **Art Galleries** p.176, **Art Classes** p.207, **Art** p.249

Some galleries in the major art districts (like 798, p.250) stock a small range of art supplies, including photographic films, inks and oils. Gallery owners and staff are good

798 art district (p.250)

people to chat to if you want specialist products, as they're in regular contact with the artists roaming the city. Another good bet is Panjiayuan Market (p.293) for brushes and paper. There are also some art stores in the buildings nearby. Many of the supplies lean towards traditional Chinese calligraphy (like large horsehair brushes), and pots of black ink. For quality oils you're better off shopping at speciality stores, like those listed below.

Beijing Art Supplies 北京美术用品网

Online Only

010 8539 3027 | *www.bjarts.cn*

This new website sells a huge range of art equipment, including traditional Chinese art and painting supplies, as well as everything you might need to carve the next *Venus de Milo*. Delivery costs begin at ¥12.

Liulichang 琉璃厂

26 Hutong Xiaoxingjie
Changan Jie
Xuanwu
琉璃厂，长安街小型街
26胡同
 Chongwenmen L2
Map 7 A3 **7**

The shops on Liulichang are famous across China for selling ancient books, calligraphy products, paintings, rubbings, ink and antiques. Although the street is less than a kilometre long, it is lined with dozens of small stores selling everything you need to set up a home studio. Given its reputation, it's slightly more expensive than Shazikou (below), but bargaining is still accepted. Break up your expedition with a stop at one of the numerous teahouses en route.

Pebeo 贝碧欧

4 Jiuxianqiao Rd
Chaoyang
酒仙桥路4号
朝阳区
Map 5 D2 **8**

010 8459 9289

Just across from Contrasts Gallery in 798, Pebeo is a great place for professional art supplies. It is also full of craft products such as puff paint, sequins, and 'kid friendly' kit like water paints and non-toxic glues. Small tubes of oil paint start from around ¥40, and there are mixers, oils and bases available too. Products are all from the Pebeo range and if there's something you want that's not on display, the staff are happy to order it.

Shazikou Stationery Market 沙子口文具市场

Shazikou
Yongdingmenwai
Chongwen
永定门外沙子口
崇文区
 Chongwenmen L2

This massive wholesale and retail market is not easy to find, but it's worth the effort. It is home to the cheapest art supplies and products in town. If you are feeling lazy, then head to the street opposite the National Art Museum (p.177), where art shops sell products from this market at marked-up prices. There's a good range of water and oil paints available, as well as paper, pens, clay and ceramics.

Baby Items

There are a growing number of (expensive) speciality stores selling imported baby clothes, but most large Chinese shops and markets have a wide range for less. The Zhongyou, Xidan and Juntai department stores – all in the Xidan area – each have a floor dedicated to infant clothing. The quality is reasonable, and prices are set. The Silk Market (p.294) and Yashow (p.294) also have dozens of stores selling baby clothes, shoes and accessories and, although the quality may suffer, you can pick up an outfit for as little as ¥60. These markets are a good place to buy your baby its first little Tommy Hilfiger T-shirt, miniature Guess jeans or Converse shoes in tiny sizes.

Jacadi 亚卡迪

China World Mall
Chaoyang
建国门外大街1号NB135
朝阳区
Guomao L1
Map 11 F3 **10**

010 6505 0766 | *www.jacadi.fr*

Established in France and with numerous boutiques around the world, Jacadi is renowned for its quality infants' clothing. The dresses and jackets are stylish, well made, and items you might wear yourself if they came in larger sizes. Prices reflect the quality, with dresses starting from around ¥600. There's a special range for newborns, as well as accessories including rugs, nappy bags and blankets.

251

F5, Capital Mall
Xicheng
西直门外大街1号西环
广场5层
西城区
🚇 **Xizhimen L2**
Map 6 D1 **11**

Lijia Baby 丽家宝贝

010 5830 2400 | *www.lijiababy.com.cn*
Aside from the large store, Lijia Baby has a good website for online shopping (though it's all in Chinese). There's a pretty comprehensive range of branded clothes for babies and toddlers, as well as everything you need for the nursery, including cots, high chairs, toys, books and nappies. There's also a small range of baby food available, and cutesy items like baby sunglasses.

China World Mall
Chaoyang
建国门外大街1号NB133
朝阳区
🚇 **Guomao L1**
Map 11 F3 **12**

Miki House 米奇屋

010 6505 9652 | *www.mikihouse.co.jp*
This Japanese purveyor of infant wear stocks clothes for super cool kids. The bright outfits are emblazoned with animals, and often cutesy Japanese slogans that make no sense whatsoever. The brand varies slightly to cater to different age groups: Black Bean Baby products for newborns, Miki House First for toddlers, and Double-B Miki House for small kids. Expect to pay as much as you would for adult clothes.

Wangfujing Dajie
Dongcheng
王府井
东城区
🚇 **Wangfujing L1**
Map 10 F3 **13**

Xin Zhong Guo Children's Store 新中国儿童用品商店

www.forchildren.cn
Quite possibly Beijing's oldest, and definitely largest, children's store, this institution has been dressing kids for more than 50 years. Shopping is spread over eight floors, with toys on the first floor, clothing on the second, kids' shoes, hats and sporting goods on the third, and children's stationery on the fourth. Levels five and six are activity zones, with games and craft stations to keep the youngsters entertained. The two basement levels feature another game zone and a studio for portrait photography.

Baby Items

Benetton	China World Shopping Mall	010 6505 6810
Happy Mother	112 Xinjiekou Nandajie	010 6615 9808
Naturino	315 Rong Xiang Plaza, Tian Zhu Town	010 8046 1788
Sunny Baby Kids' Clothing	Stall 562, Jiayi Vogue Square, 3a Xinyuan Nanlu	010 6466 3028
Whale Baby	7 Gongti Nanlu	010 6551 4622

Beachwear

Other options **Sports Goods** p.284, **Clothes** p.257

Like kids' clothes, you can find basic swimming gear at most department stores. Unfortunately, with the nearest beach hundreds of kilometres away, Beijing is not renowned for its quality or stylish, beachwear. Most bikinis look as though they've been on the rack since the revolution, with garish colours and fuddy duddy cuts, and men don't fare much better. If you're not into Speedos, then your best bet is to buy swimming shorts on your next holiday.
A couple of sports shops have a better range of apparel. Li Sheng Sports Store (201 Wangfujing Jie, Dongcheng, 010 6525 6298) sells Zoke, Hot Wave and Speedo on the second floor, and the Pacific Century Department Store (Jia 2, Gongti Beilu, Chaoyang, 010 6539 3888) has a reasonable selection on the fifth floor. Decathlon (p.285) is another good bet, stocking goggles, ear and nose plugs, flippers and boards.

Various Locations

Quiksilver & Roxy

www.quiksilver.cn
Roxy and Quiksilver are possibly the only places in town to pick up trendy beachwear, as well as surf, skate and snow apparel. Although the range is small, the bikinis in Roxy are cute, colourful, and start from about ¥500. Men can pick up a pair

of board shorts for around the same price. Both stores sell some beach accessories, like sunglasses, halter tops and flip-flops, but sadly no surfboards. Locations: Quiksilver, L2 03-04 Ginza Mall, Oriental Kenzo Building, 48 Dongzhimenwai Dajie, Dongcheng (010 8447 6447). Roxy; Shop 309 SOGO Department Store, 8 Xuanwumenwai Dajie, Xuanwu (010 6310 4556).

Bicycles

They say there are nine million bicycles in Beijing. It becomes apparent pretty quickly, that this is a conservative estimate. Cycling is still one of the best ways to navigate a city that can become snarled up with traffic, and there are plenty of bike lanes to help you avoid the loopy moves of local drivers. Bike shops are a common sight, and there are a number of bike markets across the city (including Beixinqiao Bike Market, Dongsi Beidajie, Dongcheng), selling new and used bikes. Be careful if you're purchasing second hand – many used bikes on the market are actually stolen. You can pick up cheap bikes at big supermarkets such as Carrefour (p.297), with a basic bum-rattler costing around ¥200.

Small wheel and folding bikes are also gaining in popularity, because you can pop them in your backpack and avoid seeing them turn up at markets like Beixinqiao. There are a couple of small shops clustered around Houhai, where you can also rent bikes by the hour or day. See Cycling, p.211, for more.

Min Yue Jia Yuan
Yuegezhuang Beiqiao
Xisihuan
Fengtai
西四环岳各庄北桥民
岳家园
丰台区
Map 6 A4 15

Dahon Folding Bikes 大行折叠自行车
010 6087 0999 | www.dahon.cc
Even though the folding bike craze baffles many, they are an increasingly common site around Beijing, especially among young residents. Dahon sells an excellent range of folding and mountain bikes by Dahon and Yeah, with wheel size ranging from 12 to 26 inches. For a small wheeler, prices start from around ¥12,000. They also stock some biking accessories, including helmets, locks and Dahon bike bags, as well as spare bike parts.

4-18 Jiaodaokou
Dongdajie
Dongcheng
交道口东大街4-18号
东城区
Zhangzizhonglu L5
Map 8 F2 16

Giant 捷安特
010 6403 4537 | www.beijing-giant.com
The indecisive should avoid Giant – it will only lead to confusion. However, if you're a serious biker, then this is the place to shop. Beijing has more than 20 Giant outlets offering a huge range of mountain and city bikes across brands including Shimano, Topeak, Bell and Rock Shox. It also sells folding bikes, electric bikes, and all manner of accessories, including helmets.

66 Dianmen Dongdajie
Dongcheng
地安门东大街66号
东城区
Tiananmen East L1
Map 8 D3 17

Trek 崔克自行车
010 8403 6967
Frequented by dedicated cyclists, Trek is renowned for selling quality road and mountain bikes, as well as custom-made cycles for kids. The staff are all enthusiasts, apparently eating, reading and sleeping lightweight metal. It organises regular cycling events around Beijing, and will love your bike as much – and maybe even more – than you do. You can also pick up spare parts, accessories and a range of snazzy Lycra that will turn a few heads.

Bicycles		
Decathlon	3 Wenhuayuan Xilu	010 6782 6100
Forever Bicycle Store	4 Dianmen Xidajie	010 6402 0396
Windspeed	66-2 Dianmen Dongdajie, west of Nanluoguxiang	010 8403 6967

Books

Other options **Second-Hand Items** p.281

Although it's getting easier to pick up a copy of the latest bestseller, quality bookshops are still few and far between. A number of stalls around Tongli Studios in Sanlitun sell paperbacks in English, but they're usually copied, so don't be surprised if pages are missing.

Perhaps the best-known shop for English texts is the Foreign Language Bookstore on Wangfujing (it's at number 235, or call 010 6512 6911, some English is spoken). It has six floors, including a good travel section as you enter, fiction, education and music texts.

A growing number of cafes and bars also stock English language books and magazines for their customers to peruse. Thai restaurant Purple Haze (p.322) has a nice selection of novels and picture books, including a handful for kids. Blue Goat Books & Café (3 Shuimo Xinqu, Haidian, 010 6265 5069) has a good range of Chinese and English books about cinema and art; and Le Petit Gourmand (p.314) lends out books to members (membership costs ¥300 per year). International magazines and newspapers can be found at most five-star hotels, as well as at the Beijing Bookworm and Chaterhouse Booktrader.

4 Nansanlitun Lu
Chaoyang
南三里屯路4号
朝阳区
🚇 *Gongtibeilu*
Map 9 F3 **18**

The Beijing Bookworm 北京书虫

010 6586 9507 | *www.beijingbookworm.com*

With its cosy atmosphere, free Wi-Fi and shelves of English language books, this is one of Beijing's most popular cafes. Not everything you see is for sale, with most titles restricted to a lending library system. Those that are up for grabs tend to have an Asian focus, with a good collection of novels by Indian and Chinese authors. There's also an extensive range of travel guidebooks, and additional titles can be ordered. The Bookworm hosts regular author visits, talks and signings.

B107 The Place
9A Guanghua Lu
Chaoyang
光华路甲9号世贸天阶
中心B107号
朝阳区
🚇 *Guanghualu*
Map 11 E3 **19**

Chaterhouse Booktrader

010 6587 1328 | *www.chaterhouse.com.cn*

Chaterhouse is home to the largest collection of English language books in Beijing, bigger even than the collection at the Foreign Language Bookstore (see above). There's an entire shelf dedicated to imported fashion, food and sporting magazines, as well as an aisle for new releases, bestsellers, fiction, non-fiction, travel, health, kids, business and much more. Chaterhouse also sells cards, wrapping paper and other stationery.

4 Jiuxianqiao Lu
798
酒仙桥路4号大山子
艺术区
朝阳区
Map 5 D2 **20**

Timezone 8 东八时区空间

010 8456 0336 | *www.timezone8.com*

Always busy, Timezone 8 is dedicated to Chinese and English language books on art, fashion and architectu re. Although most of the texts here are imported, some are published locally – look out for the collection detailing the history of the Dashanzi (798) art district that the bookstore calls home. This is also a good place to buy arty postcards.

C17 Xichangan Jie
Xicheng
西长安街C17号
西城区
🚇 *Xidan L1*
Map 10 A3 **21**

Xidan Books Building 西单图书大厦

010 6607 8477

For the Chinese, this is the best place in town to buy books. To peruse English language publications, head to the basement where you'll find a collection of classics, alongside travel guides, maps, cookery books, and some new releases. If you're learning Chinese, there's an array of textbooks and tapes, as well as coffee table books on art, architecture and monuments.

We're all over Asia

When it's time to make the next stop on your expat Asian adventure, be sure to pack an Explorer Residents' Guide. These essential books will help you make the most of your new life in a new city.

Explorer Residents' Guides – We Know Where You Live

Camera Equipment
Other options **Electronics & Home Appliances** p.261

With the bustling port of Tianjin only a few hours away, Beijing is becoming a good place to buy cameras and photographic equipment. While you can find the odd brand store around town, the best places to purchase equipment are the shops that sell a range of makes. The small Ray Camera Market has a number of stores in Beijing, including two at Soho Xiandaicheng (010 8580 6643) and one inside Beijing Camera Equipment City (010 8814 4785). They sell the latest and greatest in Sony, Canon, Nikon, Tamron, Benro, Sigma, and Tenba, and also offer online shopping. Prices are slightly more expensive than other shops because quality is guaranteed, and staff are extremely knowledgeable. Camera accessories and equipment can also be picked up from the many Kodak stores around town, where you can get same day passport photos and print digital photos.

Camera Equipment		
Beijing Photo City	40 Wukesong Lu	010 8811 9797
Golden Lens Photography	12 Xichanganjie	010 6605 6386
Maliandao Camera Market	11 Maliandao Lu	010 6339 1618
Ray Camera Market	Various Locations	www.rayi.cn
Wande Photo Equipment	35 Cuifujiadao	010 8401 1883

40 Wukesong Lu
Haidian
五棵松路40号
海淀区
Map 6 A2 **22**

Beijing Camera Equipment City 北京摄影器材城
010 8811 9728 | *www.bjphoto.com.cn*
One of the best camera markets in Beijing, this multi-level shop is home to more than 200 independent retailers selling a huge range of digital cameras and video recorders. You will find equipment including lenses, viewfinders, tripods and more. There's a large assortment of Chinese models available, but there's also major international camera brands such as Sony, Canon, Nikon, Benro and Sigma.

180 Wangfujing Jie
Dongcheng
王府井大街180号
东城区
🚇 *Wangfujing L1*
Map 10 F3 **23**

China Photography 中国照相馆
010 6512 0623
This is one of China's most famous studios, because it was once commissioned to take a portrait of Mao. It is still a good place to visit for family photography. Most of the staff have worked in the store for longer than they care to remember, and have a few tales to tell. The shop's history and reputation make it a very popular choice for shoppers and browsers, so avoid visiting on weekends if you can.

68 Dianmen Dongdajie
Dongcheng
地安门东大街68号
东城区
🚇 *Tiananmen East L1*
Map 8 D3 **24**

Kuandi Photography 宽地摄影
010 6404 6309
It's not cheap, but Kuandi is regarded as one of the best places in town for quality portrait photography. It is frequented by many an up-and-coming star, and has a variety of photographers on the books.

Car Parts & Accessories
With more than one thousand new cars Beijing's roads every day, many auto retailers have jumped on the spare part bandwagon. A number of car markets are located around the city, most are outside the Fourth Ring Road and monstrous in size. An increasing number of foreigners are purchasing cars in Beijing and, despite the horrendous traffic, owning a car does open up a world of weekend getaways (p.199). However, if you are looking to drive to greener pastures, then you might need a Chinese-speaking friend. Very little English is spoken amongst the retailers at Beijing's auto markets and, unless you have a good Chinese technical vocab, shopping at them can become rather tedious.

East of Litang Lu, 2km
from Tian Tong Yuan
Chang Ping County
昌平区天通苑2公里立
汤路东侧

Beijing Yayuncun Auto Market 北京亚运村汽车市场

010 6176 6699 | *www.beiyacheshi.com*

This place is slightly more expensive than other auto markets around town because it boasts the largest range and most reliable service and products. This huge market sells everything including cars, spare parts, accessories, and all the associated services. Ironically, it is miles away from the city centre, so if your car does need fixing, it means a long tow.

Dongsihuan Nanlu
Chaoyang
东四环南路 小武基桥
西 欢乐谷东南侧
朝阳区
Map 2 F3 26

Shilihe Auto Market 十里河汽车配件市场

010 5107 2890

Despite its new site in Xiaowuji, this large market is still known by its previous location's moniker, Shilihe. Very popular among Beijing's taxi drivers, Shilihe offers a good range of new and used car parts at prices considerably lower than other similar markets around town. Come to browse with other petrol heads. It's south-east of Happy Valley Park (p.174), west of Xiaowuji Nanlu.

Beisihuan Donglu
Chaoyang
北四环东路
朝阳区
Map 5 C2 27

Si Yuan Qiao Car Market 四元桥汽车配件市场

010 6439 3355

This is one of Beijing's oldest car accessory markets, covering a massive 90,000sqm. The 700 stalls sell both wholesale and retail car parts and accessories. They also stock a good mix of Chinese and international auto components. There are numerous ATMs across the market to remind shoppers to buy big. If you're particularly flush, there's a car display area which also offers repairs and consultation services.

Clothes

Other options **Beachwear** p.252, **Tailoring** p.286, **Sports Goods** p.284, **Shoes** p.282, **Lingerie** p.273

Although Shanghai is still regarded as the fashion capital of China, Beijing is gradually making a name for itself thanks to recent events. These include the biannual China International Fashion Week (p.53), alongside visits and fashion shows from some of the world's most prolific designers. Last year Fendi brought out Karl Lagerfeld to celebrate the launch of a new store in Seasons Place, with a fashion parade on the Great Wall. Not long before that, the city had visits from Cavalli and Donatella Versace. Amid all the catwalk parades there have been whispers that Giorgio Armani plans to set up 30 chain stores on the Chinese mainland before the end of 2008, while the Versace empire intends to add 16 stores.

A qipao dress

Some of China's most highly regarded designers also call the capital home, including young style gurus Yang Lin and Liu Wei. While their creations are increasingly inspired by international trends, most retain a unique Chinese flavour that sees them increasingly applauded around the world.

Big Brands

Given Beijing's weather extremes, most shopping is confined to mega malls, with very few shopping streets like those found in other international cities. For the best fashion labels, the boutiques that call the Peninsula Hotel (p.35) home should not be missed. More than 50 exclusive brand stores line the lower levels of the hotel, including Bally, Bvlgari, Chanel, Hermes, Gaultier, Kenzo, Lanvin, Piaget, Tiffany, and Zegna.

The China World Shopping Mall (p.295) is also home to many of fashion's elite, including Louis Vuitton, Prada, Chloe, Burberry, Lagerfeld, Givenchy and Lacroix. Generally, the higher you go in the building, the higher the prices become – the basement levels are the best place to shop if you're after designer clothing that doesn't pack such a big price punch. Here you'll find MNG, Max & Co, Cavalli, Esprit, Kookai, and also a well-stocked Sephora for cosmetics. Similar brands can be found in Oriental Plaza (p.296), which is also home to an IT mall and fashion from the likes of French Connection, and Camper. The Place (p.296) has a growing array of mid-level boutiques, such as Zara, Mexx, Jack Jones, Hotwind, and Juicy Couture. Shin Kong Place (Map 7 D2) brandishes 938 brand boutiques from Anna Sui to Zegna. It's also home to 21 Beijing flagship stores, including a Mikimoto pearl boutique, Stuart Weitzman, Guy Laroche and Patrizia Pepe. Finally, the newly opened Seasons Place (Map 6 D2) is not only home to the likes of Versace, Louis Vuitton, Dior, Givenchy and Loewe, but is also the launching pad for Hong Kong department store Lane Crawford in mainland China, stocking threads from 600 top-end brands. So much shopping, so little time.

Botao 薄涛高级时装店

18 Dongzhimenwai Dajie
Chaoyang
东直门外大街18号
朝阳区
🚇 *Nongzhanguan*
Map 9 F2 **28**

010 6417 2472
If price is not an issue, Botao should be visited for its exclusive, haute couture clothes. A number of local designers work for the label, selling their creations in China, the US and Europe. Aside from stunning jackets and formal wear, Botao has some beautiful accessories including hats, handbags and shoes. This is the place to come for well made, locally designed pieces that won't appear anywhere else.

Hotwind 热风

L319 The Place
9 Guanghua Lu
Chaoyang
光华路9号世贸天阶L319
朝阳区
🚇 *Guanghualu*
Map 11 E2 **29**

021 5383 9521 | www.hotwind.net
The Chinese version of British label Hot Station (which has an outlet in the COFCO Plaza, 010 6513 8692), Hotwind is popular for its extensive range of affordable clothes, shoes and accessories for men and women. Women's heels start from around ¥100, with shirts going for around ¥150. In winter, you can pick up beanies and scarves on the cheap.

Juicy Couture

2 Jinchengfang Jie
Xicheng
金城坊街2号金融街购
物中心L206
西城区
🚇 *Fuxingmen L1*
Map 6 E2 **30**

010 6622 0481 | www.juicycouture.com
Juicy Couture tracksuits are renowned for unabashedly drawing attention to your rump with bold logos, gold glitter and sequins. Aside from its signature, bum-hugging velour tracksuits, the Juicy boutique at L206 in the Seasons Place also sells underwear in vibrant colours. Juicy Couture is also known for it's super-girly, eye-catching accessories and brash handbags. Think more J-Lo (and Li-Lo) than classic Audrey Hepburn.

Lane Crawford 连卡佛

2 Jinchengfang Jie
Xicheng
金城坊街2号金融街购
物中心L130
西城区
🚇 *Fuxingmen L1*
Map 6 E2 **31**

010 6622 0808
Spread over three levels in the new Seasons Place, Lane Crawford is home to clothes, shoes and accessories from more than 600 big brands. There are designs from the likes of Stella McCartney, Emilio Pucci, Maison Martin Margiela, Alexander McQueen, Marni, Miu Miu, and Givenchy. There's also an in-store computer centre, a CD bar, and grooming counter for beauty tips.

Levi's 李维斯

Building 9, Jianwai SOHO
39 Dongsanhuan
Zhonglu
Chaoyang
东三环中路39号建外
SOHO09号楼
朝阳区
Guomao L1
Map 11 F3 32

010 5869 1948

The Levi's brand doesn't require an introduction – everyone has gone through a phase of needing the red tab on their rear pocket. The large store at Jianwai SOHO sells a huge range of jeans starting from around ¥800, as well as belts, buckles, shirts and jackets. If you're into wearing your brand on your sleeve, then this is the place to shop.

Traditional dress

Mexx 麦克斯

L223 The Place
9 Guanghua Lu
Chaoyang
光华路9号世贸天阶L223
朝阳区
Guanghualu
Map 11 E2 33

010 6587 1559

Although the clothes in Mexx probably won't wow you, they're a surprisingly rare combination of affordable and stylish. The store in The Place (p.296) sells a regularly updated range of clothing, most of it casual and semi-formal, alongside a small range of shoes and accessories.

MNG 芒果

China World Mall
Chaoyang
朝阳区
Guomao L1
Map 11 F3 34

010 6505 1608 | www.cwtc.com

This boutique is popular for its large range of no-fuss women's wear, including basic vests (starting from around ¥130), through to trendy business suits, jeans, jackets and formal dresses. The accessories are good value, with bags, sunglasses, belts, scarves and jewellery all available. The sales are excellent, with 50 to 70% discount on most items. There is another store in Oriental Plaza (010 8518 7870).

Mushi 模西

107 Twin Towers
Chaoyang
建国门外大街12号双子
座大厦107
朝阳区
Yonganli L1
Map 11 E3 35

010 8529 9420 | www.mushi.com.cn

French designer Caroline Deleens creates interesting fusion clothing at Mushi, combining Chinese flair with the best of French style. She keeps things simple, with classic cuts, colour schemes dominated by black and white and adds flourishes with glittery accessories. Items can be commissioned. The Twin Towers are at 12 Jianguomenwai Dajie.

Shanghai Tang 上海唐

Grand Hyatt Beijing
Dongcheng
东长安街1号B1
东城区
Wangfujing L1
Map 10 F3 36

010 8518 0898 | www.shanghaitang.com

Famous for turning Chinese designs, materials and patterns into couture items, Shanghai Tang seems to epitomise modern Chinese chic. The Tang handbags are gorgeous, and the shop also sells a small range of T-shirts, jumpers, shirts and dresses. Tailoring is available on request, so if you're after the perfect, pricey *qipao*, then this is the place to come.

Shiatzy Chen 夏姿陈

Shin Kong Place
87 Jianguolu
Chaoyang
建国路87号新光天地
朝阳区
Dawanglu L1
Map 7 D2 37

010 6530 5888

The flagship store for Taiwanese/Chinese designer Chen, this boutique is overflowing with Asian-inspired creations. Chen's clothes are often described as encapsulating 'neo-Chinese chic', which means that the fabrics and styles, essentially would not be out of place on a Chinese catwalk. With an international following, Chen's designs don't come cheap, but their timeless nature makes them a good investment.

1227 SOHO Shangdu
Chaoyang
东大桥路8号SOHO尚都
1227号
朝阳区
🚇 *Hujialou*
Map 11 E2 **38**

Swarka 天堂眼

010 5900 3082

Transform yourself into Aishwarya Rai in the swoosh of a sari with clothes, jewellery and makeup from this Indian import store. There's a particularly good collection of mirrored bracelets, as well as ornate bindis, earrings and nose studs. While Swarka is popular with Beijing's small Indian community, you're as likely to find Chinese or western shoppers after a bit of Bollywood glitz. SOHO Shangdu is at 8 Dongdaqiao Lu.

China World Mall
Chaoyang
建国门外大街国贸商城
2座WB101
朝阳区
🚇 *Guomao L1*
Map 11 F3 **39**

Vivienne Tam 薇薇安. 谭

010 6505 0767 | *www.viviennetam.com*

One of greater China's most lauded designers, Hong Kong-born, America-based Tam whips up couture numbers for some of the world's biggest celebs. In Beijing her designs aren't cheap, but to have the Tam logo on your *qipao* is a luxury worth investing in. Aside from a beautiful range of dresses, the two stores in Beijing (also in Oriental Plaza, 010 8518 0871) feature Tam's signature Asian-inspired items, including jackets, camisoles and accessories.

The Place
9a Guanghua Lu
Chaoyang
光华路甲9号世贸天阶
朝阳区
🚇 *Guanghualu*
Map 11 E2 **40**

Zara 飒拉

010 6587 1341 | *www.zara.com*

After a highly anticipated opening, half of Beijing can now be seen wandering the streets wearing Zara. The first floor of the large shop is dedicated to women's wear – from casual to formal clothing – while the second floor is for men, with children's wear on the third. The end of season sales are worth holding out for.

Clothes		
Chanel	B1 Peninsula Hotel	010 6512 8899
Diesel	Maison Mode, 88 Xi Changan Jie	010 8391 3367
E-Land	CAT Lifestyle Mall, A10 Jiuxianqiao LU	010 5838 5400
Esprit	China World Shopping Mall	010 6505 8068
Fornarina	The Place, 9 Guanghua Lu	010 6587 1330
French Connection	The Place, 9 Guanghua Lu	010 6587 1455
Guess	The Place, 9 Guanghua Lu	010 6587 1415
Hot Station	COFCO Plaza, 8 Jianguomennei Jie	010 6513 8692
I.T.	Oriental Plaza	010 8518 6571
Jessica	China World Shopping Mall	010 6505 6671
Jimmy & Tommy	14 Dongdaqiao Lu	010 6591 1286
Kookai	Oriental Plaza	010 8518 2933
Louis Vuitton	China World Shopping Mall	010 6505 6213
Plastered 8	61 Nanluoguxiang, Dongcheng	134 8884 8855
Ports	China World Shopping Mall	010 6530 7528
Prada	L1 Peninsula Hotel	010 6559 2888
Sisley	China World Shopping Mall	010 6505 7885
Surface	Building 6, Jianwai SOHO	010 6513 8692
UCLA	L305, The 8 Gate, 19 Zhongguancun Jie	010 8248 6082
www.izzue.com	Oriental Plaza, 1 Dongchangan Jie	010 8518 6571

Computers

Other options **Electronics & Home Appliances** p.261

It is rare to see an uncluttered desk in Beijing; most are covered with an array of digital widgets. The best places to pick up such devices are the electronic markets, clustered in the north of town around Zhongguancun, or just south of the Workers' Stadium in

Dongdaqiao. These are home to hundreds of brand and speciality stores that are barely big enough to swing a mouse. Given their proximity to one another, shopkeepers are very sensitive about price and tend to know what everyone else is offering. This also means they know how much they can fleece you for. That said, bargaining is fine and you can usually get a good deal if you're making a big purchase. Some English may be spoken, but it's best to take a Mandarin speaking friend to assist with negotiations.

Etop Digital City 鼎好电子城

3 Zhongguancun Jie
Haidian
中关村大街3号
海淀区
🚇 Huangzhuang
Map 4 C2 **41**

010 8269 7799 | *www.etopone.com*
Just west of Hailong Digital Market (p.261), Etop is less crowded and has slightly cheaper prices than its neighbour, especially on the upper levels. It's also much less testing on the nerves – there are fewer trumpeting salespeople, and you won't suffer from heatstroke due to overcrowding on the weekend. It offers the same variety of products as Hailong, with brand and speciality stores in the basement and first floor, and mobile phones and games in B2. Food and drink is available on the top level.

Hailong Digital Market 海龙电子城

1 Zhongguancun Jie
Haidian
中关村大街1号
海淀区
🚇 Huangzhuang
Map 4 C2 **42**

010 8266 3883 | *www.hilon.com.cn*
The busiest electronics market in town, Hailong is always overflowing with bargain-hungry shoppers. Spread over seven floors, each level offers different wares, including PCs, Macs, MP3 players, digital cameras, printers, computer screens, software, desks and chairs. There are also a number of shops where you can get repairs done. After a hard day of bargaining, head to the seventh floor for a beer and bowl of noodles.

Hongtu Sanbao Market 宏图三胞市场

F2-F3, Building 4 9 Zhongguancun
Haidian
中关村大街9号4号楼
2-3层
海淀区
🚇 Huangzhuang
Map 4 C2 **43**

010 6256 7438 | *www.hisap.com.cn*
One of the most popular computer markets in Nanjing, Hongtu is a relative newcomer to Beijing. Rather than being composed of small independent stores, it sells IT and digital goods in a supermarket fashion – you can browse the long aisles and pick up goods as they tickle your fancy. The sales staff are very knowledgeable, and the crowds are not as intrusive as other computer markets around town. There are 11 stores across Beijing, in Xizhimen, Chaowai Jie, Beisanhuan and Xidan.

Zhongguancun E-Plaza 中关村E世界广场

11 Zhongguancun
Haidian
中关村大街11号
海淀区
🚇 Huangzhuang
Map 4 C2 **44**

010 6268 1858 | *www.bjemall.cn/main.php*
The newest electronics market in Zhongguancun is a gleaming monolith packed to the rafters with computer products and digital goods. In terms of the number of stalls, the E-Plaza blows both Hailong and Etop out of the water. However, you do pay for the pleasure – it's more expensive, and there's less scope for bargaining.

Computers		
Apple Centre	Rai Se Plaza, 126 Jianguo Lu	010 6566 2068
Bainaohui	10 Chaowai Dajie	010 6599 5912
Johnson Computer Connections	312 Pinnacle Plaza	010 8046 3358

Electronics & Home Appliances

Other options **Camera Equipment** p.256, **Computers** p.260

In many homes in Beijing you'll find a TV and DVD player in every room, alongside all manner of entertainment systems and gaming consoles. Without private gardens, and with the weather extremes, people tend to spend a lot of time indoors and need their pads to be kitted out accordingly.

Many of Beijing's shopping malls and supermarkets, including Carrefour (p.297), sell a good range of electronics and home appliances. However, the three largest retailers are Gome, Suning (www.suningshop.com) and Dazhong – all of which have outlets around town. In general, the first two stores are more highly regarded in terms of quality. They're also notably cheaper than Dazhong. All three have a similar product range, covering everything from mobile phones and digital cameras to white goods and smaller household appliances. Although prices are marked, bargaining is common. So if you're making a large purchase, you should be able to negotiate the price. It's also worth asking for a couple of smaller goods to be thrown in for free. Gome offers online shopping (www.gome.com.cn).

Electronics & Home Appliances

Bang & Olufsen	Oriental Plaza, 1 Dongcha Nanjie	010 8518 6808
Bose	Oriental Plaza, 1 Dongcha Nanjie	010 8518 6885
Dazhong	130 Nanhuzhongyuan, Wangjing	010 6472 8629
Gome	Dongsanhuan Zhonglu, 200m west of Shuangjing Qiao	010 8778 2242
Suning	5 Balizhuang Dongli	010 6557 9966

Eyewear
Other options **Sports Goods** p.284

Wearing glasses is no longer regarded as an essential medical aid in Beijing, but is instead a fashion statement that, it is believed, makes you look more intelligent. Today, the biggest designers produce some truly trendy frames. Choose from a huge variety, including classic black rims from Chanel and minimal steel frames from D&G. While you still get the odd shop selling 'Mao glasses' (the ones that take up half your face and leave a permanent groove on your nose), most spectacle shops in Beijing are moving with the times, and stock the latest frames in a variety of colours and sizes.

0336, Building 3
Jianwai SOHO
Chaoyang
建外SOHO3号楼0336
朝阳区
🚇 *Guomao L1*
Map 11 F3 **45**

Baodao Optical 宝岛眼镜
010 5869 2778 | *www.baodao.com.cn*
With more than 70 stores around town, Baodao is one of Beijing's largest chain stores. The majority are clustered in Chaoyang and Haidian (try 114 Zhichun Lu, Haidian, 010 6263 2389). The largest store is located in Jianwai SOHO, where shoppers can have eye tests and buy sunglasses, spectacles, contact lenses and eye care products. Filling a lens prescription takes around four days, and frames start from ¥200.

B117, Building A
The Place
Chaoyang
光华路9号世贸天阶A座
B117，朝阳区
🚇 *Guanghualu*
Map 11 E2 **46**

Lens Crafters 亮视点眼镜
010 6587 1508
Although it is relatively new to Beijing, Lens Crafters already has over 60 shops across the city. The store at Capital Shopping Mall (33 Guangshun Beidajie, Chaoyang, 010 8472 2574) is also worth a look. The burgeoning popularity of the chain is mainly due to the quality of its designer frames, including Bulgari, Prada, D&G and LV, in addition to the fast and efficient services. The Place is at 9 Guanghua Lu.

Nr Panjiayuan Bridge
Sanhuan
三环路东南侧劲松桥
南，潘家园桥附近
朝阳区
🚇 *Jinsong*
Map 7 C4 **47**

Panjiayuan International Glasses City 潘家园的国际眼镜城
Aptly occupying the former site of the Beijing Glass Factory, this multi-storey market contains hundreds of independent retailers. Some sell big brands, but most sell locally made frames. A pair of non-branded prescription glasses will set you back between ¥400 and ¥600 – about 50% less than other eyewear shops around town. The quality can be patchy and service is not always as attentive as it should be, but you can't beat the prices.

Flowers

Other options **Gardens** p.265

Around the main hospitals, the many smaller flower shops often also sell fruit and cigarettes – essential pick-me-ups for every patient.

The larger flower markets sell everything from bouquets, pot plants and outdoor furniture to fish, birds and even pet bugs. The best time to shop for flowers is in the evening, when most stalls will slash their prices to get rid of their daily stock. Many shops also offer wrapping and there are now a number of large websites dedicated solely to delivery services. Try www.cnflowernet.com, which offers same or next day delivery, or free delivery in major cities.

9 Maizidian Lu
Chaoyang
麦子店路9号
朝阳区
🚇 *Maizizhanxilu*
Map 5 C4 48

Lai Tai Flower & Plant Market 莱太花卉市场

010 6463 6554
Located next to Lady Street clothes market, Lai Tai is the largest wholesale flower market in town. It sells everything from exotic imported flowers, to locally grown bunches and bonsais. Florists are on hand to help with arrangements. Wrapping and delivery are available for a fee. The flower market adjoins an equally huge plant market, where you can pick up small cacti for a couple of *kuai* or huge outdoor palm trees for a couple of thousand.

Dongsanhuan Beilu
Chaoyang
东三环北路亮马河南岸
朝阳区
🚇 *Liangmahe*
Map 5 C4 49

Liangma Flower Market 亮马花卉市场

010 6504 2446
This is a good, central place to pick up flowers. The shops tends to focus on popular Asian stems like lilies, but aside from the fresh flower arrangements, you'll also find dried displays and some interesting vases. Visit in the evening to pick up a bargain; you'll bump into storekeepers in the street selling their flowers at highly discounted prices.

3 Xiaoguan Beili
Chaoyang
小关北里3号
朝阳区
Map 5 C4 50

Yayuncun Flower Exhibition Market 亚运村花卉市场

010 6489 2556
On the south bank of Liangma river, this is one of the more expensive flower markets in town, because it is home to one of the largest collections of imported flowers. Depending on the season, stalls sell buds from Korea, Taiwan, Holland and Australia. If you're into bonsai, there's an excellent collection, as well as garden gnomes and other accessories.

South-west of
Yuquanying intersection
Nansanhuan
Fengtai
南三环玉泉营路口南
丰台区
Map 5 A3 51

Yuquanying Flower Market 玉泉营花卉展销厅

010 6253 8637
The flower market is one wing of the Yuquanying, which has stalls selling building materials, home furnishings and light fittings. The range of flowers available is mind-boggling. It's all here; from fresh to fake, foreign to local, alongside an extensive range of pot plants, fish, and pet bugs. Bargaining is recommended.

Food

The range and quality of produce available in Beijing has improved drastically in recent years. Aside from the numerous hotel delis selling sliced meats, cheese and other imported products, many restaurants also sell specialty goods direct to customers. La Fattoria (5 Phoenix City, Shuguang Xili, Chaoyang, 010 5866 7072), has shelves of Italian products including Limoncello, coffee, pasta and an extensive range of quality olive oil, that customers can take home. They also wholesale delicious home-smoked meats. Call for a takeaway menu. Popular Belgian restaurant Morel's

263

(p.312) also has a separate cafe and bakery where customers can pick up authentic ingredients and deli products.

Various Locations

Carrefour 家乐福

010 6760 9911 | www.carrefour.com.cn

With several locations around town, outlets of this French-owned supermarket chain usually have at least one aisle of imported products, including alcohol, coffee, cheese, cereal, tinned produce and jams. It also stocks a good range of Japanese and Korean products, including beverages and condiments like wasabi. The organic section is particularly impressive but, queues can be horrendous.

7 Sanlitun Lu
Chaoyang
三里屯路7号
朝阳区
Liangmahe
Map 7 F2 **53**

Friendship Supermarket 友谊超市

010 6532 1871

Slightly more expensive than Jenny Lou's (p.297), the Friendship Supermarkets are still popular for imported products including alcohol, spices and cereals. They're also good for fresh and cured meats and seafood, as well as dairy and organic produce. The Sanlitun store is linked to a large DVD shop and bakery.

Basement of 3.3
33 Sanlitun Lu
Chaoyang
三里屯路33号3.3时尚
购物大厦地下一层
朝阳区
Gongtibeilu
Map 9 F2 **54**

Heping Supermarket 和平超市

010 6417 3333

In the basement of 3.3 Mall (p.295) in Sanlitun, Heping has a few nice features that other shops lack. The Italian gourmet section, courtesy of Agrilangia, sells organic pastas and sauces starting from around ¥60 a tub. There is also a shelf of products past their use by date that you can pick up for around half price. The deli selection is small (there is usually only one type of meat and a couple of cheeses), but there is a good array of wines and beverages. Herbs like mint and basil are also on sale for ¥10 a pot.

Various Locations

Jenny Lou's 婕妮璐食品店

010 6501 6249

This fast expanding network of import stores seems to be setting up shop in expat enclaves across town. There's a small fresh fruit and veg counter in every store, as well as reasonably priced deli goods including cheeses and meats. The Chaoyang Park store sells DVDs and has a Chef To Go counter for delicious roasted chickens with all the condiments. These are, in theory, available for delivery after 20:00, but there's rarely one left by then. The Jianwai SOHO branch (010 5869 2326) has a small sandwich counter for takeaway salads and rolls. See also p.297.

Kempinski Hotel
Chaoyang
北京燕莎中心凯宾斯基
酒店1层
朝阳区
Liangmahe
Map 5 C4 **56**

Kempi Deli 凯宾面包房

010 6465 3388 | www.kempinski-beijing.com

This is one of the oldest delis in Beijing, and still one of the most popular, thanks to its cosy cafe. Lunch and dinner customers can eat in or take away gourmet sandwiches, vegetable and meat pies, home-made bread, delightful cakes, and excellent deli products like cured meats, cheese, pasta and pickles. Visit after 20:00 for half price goods.

Food		
April Gourmet	Various Locations	010 8406 4132
Boucherie Michel	1 Jiezuo Building, Xingfucun Zhonglu	010 6417 0489
Lion Mart	1F The Somerset, 46 Liangmaqiao Lu	010 8440 1143
Schindler's German Food Centre	15 Zaoying Beili, Maizidian	010 6591 9370

China World Mall
1 Jianguomenwai Jie
Chaoyang
建国门外大街1号国贸
商城ED101
朝阳区
🚇 **Guomao L1**
Map 11 F3 **57**

Ole 华润万家生活超市

010 6505 8295

The range of imported products at the various Ole supermarkets is hard to beat. There are shelves dedicated to organic fruit and vegetables (about double the price of normal supermarket produce), a bakery counter with cakes and fresh breads, a counter for sushi and sake, packaged cheeses, coffee, sweets, cereals and toiletries. It is, however, one of the more costly places in town, with some items around 30% more expensive than Carrefour.

Gardens

Other options **Hardware & DIY** p.265, **Flowers** p.263

In the centre of town, it's rare to find apartments or houses with a balcony or garden; the sheer force of numbers meaning that most spaces are occupied by humans, rather than plants.
However, there is a trend towards outdoor living, particularly in the residential complexes around Shunyi (p.95). While purchasing plants is relatively painless (see Flowers, p.263), finding cheap, durable outdoor furniture can be quite an ordeal. A number of the small stores opposite the Lady Street market can custom-make outdoor chairs and tables for around ¥2,000 per table. Your best bet for quality outdoor furniture, however, is Dadizheyang (Jingshun Lu, Chaoyang, 010 8459 3665). Again, pieces can be custom-made, or ready-made pieces can be purchased for around half the price of items in Lady Street. As an added bonus, the store is next to a number of shops selling glorious ceramic pots, perfect for holding large plants.
For convenience, it's hard to beat B&Q (p.266), which has a number of megastores around town. The shop is not cheap, with your average hammock costing around ¥1,500, but it sells a reasonable range of products, including barbecues, swing chairs and table umbrellas. Just make sure whatever you buy is weather-proof.

Gifts

Many an expat has endured, and barely survived, Christmas shopping in Beijing's markets and malls. In terms of the variety and price of gifts on offer, you can't go wrong at places like Panjiayuan (p.293). Not only does this massive market sell all manner of art and furniture, but a number of aisles are dedicated to Chinese trinkets and jewellery. The upper levels of the Silk Market (p.294) and Yashow (p.294) also stock a good range of souvenirs – think lanterns, Mao bags, pillowcases, jewellery and chopstick sets. If you're looking for more upmarket offerings, Shanghai Tang (p.259) has a nice range of notebooks, photo albums and other trinkets, albeit at western prices. But, you are paying for quality and it's unlikely the piece you buy can be found at the Silk Market.

Mao at Panjiayuan Market (p.293)

Hardware & DIY

Other options **Outdoor Goods** p.278

With the recent boom in Beijing real estate, every man and his dog is trying home improvement. The range, price and quality of goods varies wildly, from cheap and cheerful local markets, to modern designs in IKEA. The two main areas for DIY products are Beishihuan and Shilihe, where you can find markets bursting with building materials and home furnishings. The outlets around Shilihe are particularly good value and near a number of markets selling outdoor furniture, including garden tables, chairs, hammocks and swings.

117 Xisihuan Beilu
Haidian
西四环北路117号
海淀区
Map 6 A1 **58**

B&Q 百安居

010 8846 6611 | *www.bnq.com.cn*
There are six B&Q outlets in Beijing, spanning the districts of Haidian, Chaoyang, Xuanwu and even Yizhuang Economic Development Zone. The furniture and DIY accessories are generally less fancy than those found in IKEA, but they rate well for convenience. You can pick up window fittings, bathroom accessories, bench tops, and even timber in a range of sizes and conditions.

Dayangfang Lu
Dongsanhuan Nanlu
Chaoyang
东三环南路大洋坊路
朝阳区

Shilihe Hardware Market 十里河五金建材市场

www.zjchy.com.cn
This street, just east of Shilihe Bridge, is home to several markets and shops catering to your every DIY desire. These include Minle Hardware, Minhexing Hardware, Shilihe Light Market, Jinlaisheng Hardware Market, Easy Home, Baojia Building Material & Accessory Market, Zhaolong Hardware Market, Caixuan Hardware Market, Minlong Crockery Market and Rainbow Curtain Market.

Each outlet could occupy you for a day, so it's best to arrive with a plan of action and a calculator for bargaining. Minle sells everything from nails and hammers to lamp fittings, toilet bowls, and even the kitchen sink.

Hardware & DIY		
Aika	75 Chengshousi Lu	010 6765 7187
	36A Liangmaqiao Lu	010 6432 1125
	66 Beixiangbin Lu, Guangshun Bei Dajie	010 8490 4695
	119 Xisihuan Beilu	010 8845 7900
B&Q	Jianxiang Store, 200m south of Jianxiangqiao	010 6235 6611
	66 Xiangbin Lu, Laiguangying	010 8490 4848
	31 Guangqu Lu	010 8776 8811
	10 Maliandao Lu	010 6331 6611
	117 Xisihuan Beilu	010 8846 6611
Orient Home	Xisanqidian	010 8271 1166
	28 Chaoyang Lu	010 6547 6880
	Bajiaodian, 168 Fushi Lu, Shijingshan	010 6886 2886
	55 Laiguangying Xi Lu, Wuhuan Lu	010 8495 0800
	Lujiayingdian, 1 Nan sihuna Dong Lu	010 8769 9007
	55 Xisanhuan Nanlu	010 8366 6611

Health Food

Other options **Food** p.263, **Health Clubs** p.232

The average non-smoker in Beijing has the lungs of a geriatric nicotine addict, so it's no wonder the health market is booming. Most residents consume all manner of herbs, pills and potions to retain some sign of vitality. Traditional Chinese medicine (TCM) shops are exciting places to find a cure – as long as you know what you want. If not, the roots and herbs that fill jars and line shelves will be cause for confusion. For similar pills with convenient English packaging, try the health food section in Watson's pharmacies across Beijing where you can pick up all manner of vitamins at

266

prices similar to those in the west. You can also find fitness supplements, like protein powder, fibre and Chinese-versions of Berocca. Some supermarkets, like Carrefour (p.297) and Ole (p.265), also have small shelves for vitamins, although the range is generally limited to a single supplier.

De Run Wu Grocery Store 德润屋

813 Danshui Town
Chaoyang
顺黄路甲3号淡水小镇
813室
朝阳区

010 8459 0809 | *www.derunwuorganic.com*
Like Lohao (below), this grocery store stocks a wide range of farm fresh organic produce as well as dry goods and health food products, including health bars, vitamins and dietary supplements. It offers free home delivery inside the Fifth Ring Road. If you want to go in person, Danshui Town is on Shunhuang Lu.

Lohao City 乐活城

52 Jingshun Lu
Chaoyang
京顺路52号
朝阳区
Map 5 E1 61

010 8459 0134 | *www.lohaocity.com*
This organic food shop has three outlets across Beijing. Their product range includes organic alcohol, cooking oils, dry foods, fruit and vegetables, meat, and baby food. The stores are also a good place to pick up imported vitamins and health supplements, with a complete range listed online. Lohao City also offers free home delivery. Other locations are at Building B4, 29 Haoyunjie, Zaoyinglu, Chaoyang (010 5867 0265) and F1, Landgent International Apartments, Nanerlu, Baiziwanlu, Chaoyang (010 8772 4133).

Home Furnishings & Accessories
Other options **Hardware & DIY** p.265

Beijing is full of places to buy furniture. Whether it's authentic Ming and Qing Dynasty pieces, or the latest by Italian designers, there are stores and markets to suit every taste and budget. While kitting out a house with products from markets or stores like IKEA (p.268) and Carrefour (p.297) can be cheap, those who want to go all out will have no problem spending their money. COFCO Plaza (p.296) has many European showrooms including, Camerich and Euro-Home (see table, p.271).

There are plenty of options for children's furniture including Flexa, the Danish company that makes durable wooden pieces without sharp corners and HABA, that sells whimsical lighting and play tents.

There are dozens of antique stores in Beijing, though reproductions abound and are sometimes just as nice for half the price. If you buy any antiques, make sure you have a stamp of authenticity to show that it is legal for export – anything from before 1795 can't be taken out of the country. Liulichang in Xuanwu district is a great place to search for authentic antiques and reproductions. Gaobeidian Antique Furniture Village has more than 200 manufacturers and retailers selling Ming and Qing Dynasty reproductions and some authentic pieces. Beijing Cunyi Huayi Furniture sells opium beds, tables and chairs. For smaller furniture, head to Panjiayuan (p.293), also known as the Dirt Market, or to Baoguosi Flea Market, which has antiques, old toys and lots of cultural revolution knick-knacks. You should bring your bargaining skills. For DIY fans there are plenty of stores like Aika, B&Q (p.266) and Orient Home that sell tools, paints, plaster, wood, tiles, nails, showerheads and appliances.

If you want accessories like pillows and curtains made, head to Neighbor's Linens, which can make delicate curtains and pillows. An average size curtain costs approximately ¥560 while pillows cost ¥60 for the cover or ¥70 with stuffing. For tailor-made linens, Rouge Baiser makes duvet covers, sheets, pillowcases, tablecloths and napkins. Those looking for custom furniture, should head to Radiance, which will make just about anything, or stall 45A of Chaowai Antique Furniture Market, which makes high chairs, wardrobes and beds free of lead paint. E West Home sells old and modern Shanghai furniture and can custom-make sofas and ivory pieces. For re-upholstery services, check out the tailors at Silk Market (p.294) and Yashow (p.294). For the creatively challenged, there's help; Dara offers design services. Other stores worth considering are Chang & Biorck (www.changbiorck.com) Boloni (www.kebao.cn), and Leslie's Fidelity Interiors (lesliefidelity@yahoo.com).

Dara 家大家业

2 Jiuxianqiao Lu
798
酒仙桥路2号798艺术区
大山子
朝阳区
Map 5 D2 **62**

010 6434 5382 | www.dara.com.cn

Dara is an expat favourite, offering items with a distinctly Chinese twist on European style. From antiques to modern art, many find it difficult to leave empty handed, especially once the lamps and cushions have been spotted. Design services are also available, should you fancy creating a unique piece.

Ferranini Studio 法尼尼家居中心

Cultural Centre
Chaoyang
东土城路9号中国国际
文化交流中心1层
朝阳区
Map 5 B4 **63**

010 6448 1888

This Italian shop features kitchens and accessories from stainless steel sinks to lacquer cabinets. The store has everything you need for a great cooking space. Brands include Ariston, Franke and Indesit. The friendly staff speak English. The store is on the ground floor of the China International Cultural Exchange Centre, at 9 Dongtucheng Lu.

Ideal Idea 意德法家家居体验馆

South Dongtucheng Lu
Chaoyang
东土城路南口
朝阳区
Map 5 B4 **64**

010 6429 5588

For contemporary furniture with high prices, head to Ideal Idea. The five floor showroom carries cutting-edge European designs for the kitchen, bathroom and living room, including trendy tiles, bold wallpaper and velvet sofas.

IKEA 宜家家居

59 Futong Dong Lu
Chaoyang
阜通东路59号
朝阳区
Map 5 C3 **65**

800 810 5679 | www.ikea.com/cn/en

Although it's considered basic in many other countries, IKEA is a sign of good taste in Beijing. If you've seen modern Chinese furniture, you might agree. This huge building has become a weekend destination where middle class families come to look, buy, eat and – much to the entertainment of foreign shoppers – sleep in the beds and on the sofas. The large store follows the standard IKEA layout with one-way traffic through kitchen, office, bedroom, living room and children's displays, before leading to a basement where the bigger goods are stored. The kitchen utensils are generally reasonably priced, with cups and mugs selling for a couple of *kuai*. However sofas, beds and tables are pretty expensive – a small two-seat sofa bed costs at least ¥1,000. Aside from all the furniture, IKEA has a great range of DIY devices, including storage boxes, tools, curtains, rugs and more. Home delivery is available for ¥50.

Tea should be served in style

Illinois Home 伊利诺依家居

1 Jingang Dadao
Chaoyang
金港大道1号
朝阳区

010 8433 4969

Illinois Home is a good stop if your taste isn't too conventional. It sells home wares guaranteed to pep up your pad, such as colourful chairs and stainless steel kitchen utensils, injecting style into the most austere of homes. It may be pricier than its rival IKEA but the collection tends to have a more individual feel, with cheaper accessories if you can't stretch to that enormous sofa.

RADIANCE
ONE STOP SHOPPING
A TRUE CHINESE EXPERIENCE

Furniture, Lamps, Carpets, Gifts and More...

64 Yongdingmenwai
Chongwen
永定门外大街64号
崇文区
Map 12 D4 67

Longshuncheng Chinese Furniture Shop 龙顺成中式家具
010 6722 5608
Shop where the big man shops. Chinese President Hu Jintao's government compound is reportedly exclusively kitted out with Chinese furniture from this place. Expect high prices.

2 Jiuxianqiao Lu
798
酒仙桥路2号大山子
798艺术区
朝阳区
Map 5 D2 68

Mooi Living Style
010 8459 9566
This is somewhere to get rare, old fashioned European and local pieces. The shop carries antiques from the 30s and 40s alongside retro Chinese, German and Scandinavian furniture. It also has a small cafe where you can take a break from shopping, with a coffee and pastry.

29 Xiaoyun
Chaoyang
霄云路29号
朝阳区
Map 5 C4 69

QM Furniture 曲美家具
010 6464 6301 | www.qumei.com
This ultra trendy, Danish-owned furniture and homeware shop sells beautiful, modern items for those with deep pockets. Contemporary and minimalist are the general themes, and the quality is top of the range. Apart from furniture, a carefully selected collection of bedding, kitchen items, cushions, rugs and lamps are displayed.

5 Dongtucheng Lu
Chaoyang
东土城路5号
朝阳区

Snaidero 施奈德橱柜中心
010 6429 4180
This Italian store sells tailor-made kitchens. Its showroom includes examples of the styles and amenities that can be included in a custom kitchen. Some of the designs are a bit unusual, including cabinets made of high gloss metalised lacquer in a variety of bright hues. Snaidero also sells everything from ovens to dishwashers. Brands include Pininfarina and Candy.

Jewellery & Watches

While pearls and jade are the most popular jewellery, diamonds, gold, silver and gemstones are widely available. You can shop at international boutiques like Cartier, Hiersun and Tiffany & Co or smaller, local shops that sell unique costume, precious and semi-precious jewellery.

For fun and unusual items, the stalls at Nali Mall (p.272) have some interesting finds, as do the street vendors in Sanlitun and Wudaokou, who set up their displays on blankets. Of course, knock-offs of all the major designers are on sale for ridiculously low prices at the Silk Market (p.294) and Hongqiao (Pearl) Market (p.293). For authentic pieces, check out Fanghua Pearls at the Pearl Market (p.293).

Panjiayuan (p.293)

If you've been to the shops but don't see what you like, there are many places that allow you to design your own jewellery. JMax Handmade Jewellery and Shayne's Treasures (see table) let you pick out your own materials and create your own designs. Prices are very reasonable and turnaround time is quick. There's also a handmade jewellery beginner's course offered in Beijing that lasts six weeks (139 1017 2722, www.shoudesigns.com). Students learn basic techniques of making pieces, get educated about Beijing suppliers and receive advice on starting their own home business. Tuition is ¥2,500.

Home Furnishings & Accessories

Aika	75 Chengshousi Lu	010 6765 7187
	36A Liangmaqiao Lu	010 6432 1125
Alessi	NB142 China World Trade Center Mall	010 8229 0009
Beijing Cunyi Huayi Furniture	Xiaodian 89, Jinzhan	010 8433 3220
Blissliving	1043-1045, 3.3 Fashion Mall, 33 Sanlitun Lu	010 5136 5296
Camerich	B3, COFCO Plaza, 8 Jianguomennei Dajie	010 6527 8510
Carrefour	11 Malian Dao	010 6332 2155
	15, Zone 2, Fangchengyuan, Fangzhuang	010 6790 9911
	6 Beisanhuan Dong Lu	010 8460 1043
	54A Baishiqiao Lu (east of Beijing Zoo)	010 8836 2729
	56A Zhongguancun Plaza	010 5172 1516
	31 Guangqu Lu	010 5190 9508
Chief Chop	B058, 3.3 Fushi Mansion, 33 Sanlitun Lu	139 0119 3954
Dara	Caochangdi	010 6432 5217
	Dashanzi 798 Art District, 2 Jiuxianqiao Lu	010 6434 5382
	Upper East Side, 6 Dongsihuan Beilu	010 5130 7506
	Shop 3, Building 1, 6 Chaoyangmenwai Dajie	010 6597 0650
	17 Gongti Beilu	010 6417 9365
DC Design Beijing Ltd	30 Dong Zhong Jie, Dongzhimen	010 6417 6628
E West Home	52 Gaobeidian Dajie	010 8579 2248
emo+	Building 4, Room 103, Soho New Town, 88 Jianguo Lu	010 8589 2787
Euro-Home	B1-B6, COFCO Plaza, 8 Jianguomennei Dajie	010 6526 3965
Flexa	First Floor, Dazhongsi Lanjing Lijia	010 8211 7233
Gome	Basement level, COFCO Plaza, 8 Jianguomennei Dajie	010 6524 2726
	31 Beisanhuan Xilu	010 6207 1731
HABA	Basement level, COFCO Plaza, 8 Jianguomennei Dajie	010 6526 3279
Home Shop	1119 SOHO Shangdu, 8 Gongti Donglu	010 5869 2366
IKEA	59 Futong Donglu	010 6479 2345
Illinois Home	63-1 Xisihuan Beilu	010 8846 5238
	10 Dongsanhuan Zhonglu	010 8771 2597
	9 Dongsihuan Nanlu	010 6730 5375
	1 Zhigang Lu, Jinzhanxiang	010 8433 4969
	208C B2 Tier Plaza, Zhongguancun	010 5986 3589
	1/F Aijia Shijie Furniture Exhibition Center, Dongsanhuan	010 6431 7153
Kang Deco	Room 9104, Lido Place, 6 Jiangtai Lu	010 6437 6330
Kartell	4 Fangyuan Xilu	010 6436 3281
Lock & Lock	The Place, 9 Guanghua Lu	na
Luxman	Basement Level, COFCO Plaza, 8 Jianguomennei Dajie	010 8511 8727
Neighbor's Linens	Lido Plaza, 6 Jiangtai Lu	010 6430 1100
PIV:style	China World Shopping Mall	010 6505 0375
	B150 Gate City Mall, Zhongguancun	010 6505 0375
Potato & Co	China World Shopping Mall	010 8405 0098
Radiance ▶ p.269	9 Kaifa Jie, Xi Baixinzhuang	010 8049 6400
Red Star Macalline	193 Dajiaoting Qiao	010 8795 1515
Rouge Baiser	Sanlitun Xiwujie (near International SOS Clinic)	010 6464 3530
Spin Ceramics	6 Fangyuan West Lu	010 6437 8649
Sunstyle	East 1, Nangao Lu	010 6431 0020
Tupperware	B21, Zhongguancun Shopping Street	010 5172 1478
Villa Lifestyle	W-8 Tianyun Plaza, Tianzhu Garden	010 6457 1922
Vita Furniture ▶ p.101	2-2 Jinbao Dajie	010 8511 1616
Wal-Mart Supercentre	B1-2 Fl, 48 Zhichun Lu	010 5873 3666

Fake Rolexes and other top brands are available at the Silk Market, complete with sweeping motion and lots of fake bling. Be sure to bargain hard; a ladies' Rolex with sweeping motion goes for about ¥60 while a man's sells for ¥80.

3 Shajin Hutong (off Nanluoguxiang Hutong)
Dongcheng
沙井胡同3号（南锣鼓巷附近）
东城区
Map 7 C1 **71**

DIY (Chuang Yi Fang) 创意坊
010 8403 9648

With jewellery designed by Li Hong, this shop stocks colourful beaded necklaces, silver earrings and cute flower rings. Customers can order pieces to be made in their favourite colours. The store also stocks men's jewellery, including silver and copper rings and silver bracelets with Chinese characters. The service is friendly and the prices are reasonable.

1 Ritan Beilu
Chaoyang
日坛北路1号
朝阳区
Map 11 D2 **72**

Shard Box 慎德阁
010 8561 3712

This small shop sells jewellery boxes and pieces made from crushed Cultural Revolution-era porcelain inlaid in wood, silver and ivory. These unique creations make great gifts and meaningful souvenirs. There is a second store at 2 Jiangtai Lu, Chaoyang (010 5135 7638).

9 Kaifa Jie
Baixinzhuang
Shunyi
白新庄开发街9号
顺义区
Map 3 C1 **73**

Shayne's Treasures
010 8046 7086 | shaynestreasures@gmail.com

The shop has well-priced combinations of pearls, Swarovski crystal and old jade, as well as reproductions of famous and fashionable pieces. Many have a Beijing theme, like silver Chinese virtue bracelets, gold character pendants, and silver cufflinks inlaid with working abacuses. The owner, Shayne Hannum, has lived in Beijing since 1985 and has spent years designing jewellery. Customers can design their own pieces in silver or gold and choose from a variety of stones. Cleaning, repairs, resizing, redesigns and ear piercing are all available.

9 Kaifa Jie
Baixinzhuang
Shunyi
白新庄开发街9号
顺义区
Map 3 C1 **74**

Things Of The Jing 西东之东西
136 9151 3985 | www.thingsofthejing.com

Owner and designer Gabrielle Harris uses silver, pearls, jade, turquoise and amber to create great jewellery and gifts. Her best sellers are the 'feudal ladies' and double happiness candle holders. Her shop also does corporate gifts and customised pieces. Things of the Jing displays are also in The Orchard (Shun Beilu, Hegezhuang Village, 010 6433 6270), Kang Deco (Room 9104, Lido Place, 6 Jiangtai Lu, Chaoyang, 010 6437 6330) and The Beijing Bookworm (p.254).

Jewellery & Watches

Agatha	A107, The Malls at Oriental Plaza, 1 Dong Changan Jie	010 8518 6303
Bvlgari	126 Shin Kong Place, 87 Jianguo Lu	010 6530 8888
Cartier	Various Locations	010 6512 8404
Hiersun	AA29, The Malls at Oriental Plaza, 1 Dong Changan Jie	010 8518 5120
JMax Handmade Jewellery	17 Nanluoguxiang	134 6666 2024
Nali Mall	Sanlitun Beijie	010 6415 2663
Omega	Various Locations	010 6587 1387
On Pedder	Shin Kong Place, 89 Jianguo Lu	na
Rolex	5/F Tower E1, Oriental Plaza, 1 Dong Changan Jie	010 8518 3128
Swarovski	Various Locations	010 8518 6790
Swatch	Zhongguancun Plaza	010 5172 1637
Tiffany & Co	The Palace Hotel, Shop GF 10, 8 Goldfish Lane, Wangfujing	010 6512 9048

Lingerie

Other options **Clothes** p.257

There are plenty of places to buy lingerie. Lane Crawford (p.258), Sogo (p.273), Parkson (p.273) and other major department stores sell pricey international brands. For every day, moderately priced bras and underwear, check out Calvin Klein, Jockey (next to the Carrefour in Zhongguancun) and La Senza. Jockey also sells long underwear in the winter.

Most of the bras sold in Beijing are padded and it may be difficult to find larger sizes. Shirley of Hollywood sells bras up to 38DD and includes international brands like Yeefer, Love Kylie and New Look. Super Bra sells international brands like 6ixty 8ight, Jockey and Victoria's Secret.

For men, boxers and briefs are available at major department stores and designer boutiques. For bargain underwear, Carrefour (p.297) and Wal-Mart (p.297) also have a large selection for men and women. For fetish underwear (and toys) explore The Sex Store, G Spot, and Adam & Eve.

Lingerie		
Adam & Eve	84 Xinjiekou Lu	010 6613 8219
Calvin Klein	Peninsula Hotel, 8 Jinyu Hutong, Wangfujing	010 8667 0270
G Spot	37 Dongdaqiao Lu	010 8562 7687
La Senza	3/F, Ginza Mall, Dongzhimenwai Dajie	010 8454 9663
The Sex Store	23 Dongdaqiao Lu	010 8562 4853
Shirley of Hollywood	Zhongguancun Gate City Mall	010 8161 2403
Super Bra	60 Nanluoguxiang	010 6402 5058

Luggage & Leather

While you can find luxurious luggage at designer shops like Louis Vuitton (p.260) and cheap, fake designer suitcases at the Silk Market (p.294) and Pearl Market (p.293), there are few stores selling anything in between.

Tumi (www.tumi.com) luggage can be found inside the Golden Resources Shopping Mall (p.295) while Samsonite (www.samsonite.com) bags can be found in Lufthansa Shopping Center (p.292), Parkson (101 Fuxingmennei Dajie, Haidian, 010 6601 3377) and Sogo (8 Xuanwumenwai Dajie, Xuanwu, 010 6310 3388). Furla (010 6505 5978, www.furla.com) in shop 115 of the China World Shopping Mall (p.295) is good too. An authorised Samsonite repair shop is at Room 908, Guomao Building, 21 Jianguomenwai Dajie, Chaoyang (010 6505 1133).

For leather purses, wallets and accessories, all the luxury brands carry a wide, but pricey selection. Practically every mall in Beijing has a luxury store with leather goods. Some locally run stores (see Su Ren) are good for mid-range items. For imitation leather and copies of designer brands, Silk Market (p.294) and Yashow Market (p.294) carry a vast selection at low prices. When it comes to a really good fake, it's all about the details. Check the inner lining – it should be stitched, not glued, and any labels should be stitched as well. Some brands, like Louis Vuitton, have date codes or serial numbers. More than likely, if you're not buying leather goods from the designers' boutiques, then you're a buying a fake.

Various Locations

Su Ren 素人

www.su-ren.com

Established in 1993, this shop stocks leather shoes and wallets, but the best items are their handbags. The shop, (the name means 'simple people'), describes its leather goods as 'unadorned and reserved…classical and bold.' It's the go-to place in Beijing when you don't want to spend a fortune on high quality leather. There are stores at 18,

---

Mini Explorer

Don't let the size of this little star fool you – it's full of insider info, maps, contacts, tips and facts for visitors. From shops to spas, bars to bargains and everything in between, the Mini Explorer range helps you get the most out of your stay in the city, however long you're there for.

58 Gongti Beilu, Chaoyang (010 8700 0099) and Apartment 3, Building 49, Dongdasifu Lu, Chaoyang (010 8700 0088).

Medicine
Other options **General Medical Care** p.113

Whether it's for a cough, a fever or cuts and bruises, over-the-counter medication is easy to find. Watson's stocks a variety of western medicines and basic first aid supplies. For prescription drugs, hospital pharmacies are good. Those at Beijing United Family Hospital (p.118), Beijing Vista Clinic and International Medical Center are open 24 hours. Many drugs that require a prescription in the west are sold over the counter, including the pain reliever Tramadol. Some pharmacies, like Beijing United Family Hospital, have direct billing with insurance companies for easier payment. The doctors and pharmacists at the hospitals listed can speak English and provide advice to patients. The other pharmacies may have one or two people who speak English.

Various Locations

Tongrentang 同仁堂
www.tongrentang.com/en
The original building at Dazhalan is Beijing's oldest apothecary. Founded in 1669, it still sells the same remedies it sold to Qing and Ming Dynasty emperors. There are no western medicines here, just all manner of traditional Chinese herbs. TCM doctors are also on hand to treat sick patients. There are stores at 24 Dazhalan, Xuanwu (010 6301 4883) and Room 15, Building 7, Jianwai SOHO, 39 Dongsanhuan Zhong Lu, Chaoyang (010 5869 1171).

267 Wangfujing Dajie
Dongcheng
王府井大街267号
东城区
🚇 *Wangfujing L1*
Map 10 F1 **75**

Wangfujing Pharmaceutical Store 王府井医药商店
010 6525 2322
The first floor stocks traditional Chinese medicines and western over-the-counter drugs. The second floor sells medical supplies and equipment like crutches and wheelchairs. Because it is in the bustling Wangfujing area, the pharmacists are accustomed to dealing with tourists and expats.

Medical Centres

Beijing United Family Hospital	Pinnacle Plaza, Tian Zhu Real Estate Development Zone	010 8046 5432
	B1, The St Regis Residence, 21 Jianguomenwai Dajie	010 8532 1221
	2 Jiangtai Lu	010 6433 3960
Beijing Vista Clinic	B29, The Kerry Centre, 1 Guanghua Lu	010 8529 6618
Golden Elephant Medicine	114 Xidan Bei Dajie	010 6607 7021
International Medical Center	S106, 1/F Lufthansa Centre, 50 Liangmaqiao Lu	010 6465 1561
Watson's	CC17, Oriental Plaza, 1 Dongchangan Jie	010 8518 6426

Mobile Phones
Other options **Telephone** p.108

Mobiles are very popular here. To work in China, your handset must be a GSM phone that uses a SIM card. The exception being dual-band GSMs from north America; these won't work.
Motorola, Nokia, Samsung and Sony Ericsson are all readily available. When shopping for a phone, it's essential to bargain. Ignore any prices that might be on display. Do your homework first and have an idea of what kind of phone you want. Be wary of any unusual models the sales clerk may try to sell you, as these are often poor quality phones that they just need to get rid of.

Dry Cleaners p.74
Divorce Lawyers p.108

Written by residents, these unique guidebooks are packed with insider info, from arriving in a new destination to making it your home and everything in between.

Explorer Residents' Guides
We Know Where You Live

You can buy a phone almost anywhere. Xidan, Wudaokou and Wangfujing are good areas to start. Phones are relatively inexpensive (about ¥300 to ¥500) though the latest styles will cost more. For second-hand phones, try Grand World Second Electrical Market (Nuren Jie, Chaoyang, 010 8448 4336). It's inside Laitai Flower Market (p.294). Here, you'll pay a fraction of the cost of a new phone. Most people choose a pay-as-you-go plan. Pre-paid phone cards are available all around town at 7-Eleven and newsagents and come in ¥50 or ¥100 denominations.

Lucky Numbers
Chinese superstitions ensure that telephone numbers that include the number eight cost more than those without. Save the punch-out card the SIM card comes with. If your phone is lost or stolen, you can use this to reactivate your old number.

8 Chaoyangmenwai
Chaoyang
朝阳门外大街8号
朝阳区
Map 7 B2 **76**

Landao 蓝岛大厦
010 8563 4422
This electronics store sells the latest mobile phones and gadgets alongside other electrical appliances. It will also be able to help you set up your mobile service. An advantage to coming here is assured authenticity and quality.

Oriental Plaza
Dongcheng
东长安街东方广场
东城区
Ⓜ *Wangfujing L1*
Map 10 F3 **77**

Vertu 沃尔图
The ultimate in mobile technology is stocked here, including diamond encrusted models. These eye-wateringly expensive phones come with a 24 hour personal Vertu concierge service. The hefty price ensures you get a quality phone and bragging rights among your chums. Oriental Plaza is at the south end of Wangfujing, at 1 Dong Changan Jie.

131 Xidan Bei Dajie
Xicheng
西单北大街131号
西城区
Ⓜ *Xidan L1*
Map 10 A1 **78**

Xidan Science & Technology Shopping Mall 西单科技广场
010 6651 9639
This place is a text addicts delight; it's a whole mall for mobile phones. There are more than 20 stores packed with names like Nokia and Samsung. Authenticity, good service and repairs are guaranteed. Accessories like batteries and chargers are also sold. Don't forget to bargain.

3 Haidian Dajie
Haidian
海淀大街3号
海淀区
Map 4 C3 **79**

Zhongguancun Electronics City 中关村电子城
This bustling market sells every conceivable electronic gadget, including mobile phones, batteries and accessories. Bargain hard and inspect everything carefully to ensure you're getting an authentic item, with all its necessary parts. Ask for a receipt in case your bargain phone breaks within days of purchase.

Various Locations

Zoomflight 中复电讯
010 6585 2322 | www.zoomflight.com.cn
With 58 outlets dotted across the city, chances are there's a location near you. It's one of the most popular places to buy the latest models at competitive prices (and with warranties). Service is friendly and there is a wide variety of phones in stock.

Music, DVDs & Videos
The proliferation of music download websites means fewer people are turning to music stores. While international retailers like HMV and Virgin don't exist here, there's a thriving local and underground scene. Prices for CDs are much, much less than in the west, but sometimes the CDs are copies. A quick scan at the cover often reveals typos. DVDs are readily available on street corners throughout Beijing. It seems that the minute a movie is released or a television show is aired in the west, it's already on

DVD in Beijing. Since DVDs and CDs are so cheap, videotapes are virtually non-existent. For domestic and international CDs and DVDs check out FAB, which is the closest thing to a music megastore. For cheap but high quality, reliable CDs and DVDs, everyone goes to Tom's DVDs, which is cleverly hidden in the basement of Tom's Embroidery. For underground, rock, indie or punk music, Fusheng Records and Sugar Jar are the best bets.

Tom's DVDs 汤姆DVD店

Awaiting Mandopop melodies

2 Jiangtai Lu
Chaoyang
将台路2号
朝阳区
Map 5 D3 **80**

010 5135 7487

Tom's has long been a favourite among the expat crowd, and you can be assured that if you visit on a weekend, you'll be shoulder to shoulder. DVD 5s (lower quality) cost ¥10 while DVD 9s (better quality) are ¥20 and are normally as good as pirated products get. There is a wide selection of new releases, hundreds of older titles, children's movies, foreign movies and a whole floor dedicated to CDs and music videos. Tom's is in the small car park 20m from the Lido market, next door to the Sculpting in Time Café, down a set of steep metal steps, below a 'Tom's Embroidery' sign.

Music, DVDs & Videos		
FAB	G/F Malls at Oriental Plaza, 1 Dong Changan Jie	010 8518 8905
Fusheng Records	South-east corner of the Pinganli intersection	010 6613 6182
Sugar Jar	2 Jiuxianqiao Lu, 798	010 6433 1449

Musical Instruments

Other options **Music Lessons** p.221, **Music, DVDs & Videos** p.276

The Xinjiekou area has a number of music shops. Fierce (64 Xinjiekou Nandajie, 010 6304 2708, www.bjfierce.com) has kitted out most of the famous acts to hit town, including Norah Jones. It has an impressive drum and cymbal section and carries brands like Pearl, LP, Sabian and Slingerland. Heng Yun Music (105 Xinjiekou Nan Dajie, 010 6618 8745, www.hengyun.com) specialises in classical Chinese kit like the *erhu*, a three-stringed instrument. It also sells mid-range guitars like Ibanez and Jackson and rents instruments. Yangshi Yueqi (122 Xinjiekou Nan Dajie, 010 6615 8552, www.bjysyq.com) also sells quality traditional instruments. Sunny (98 Xinjiekou Nan Dajie, 010 6616 3316) has an assortment of brass and wind instruments that come in a rainbow of colours. Ask for Yang Jing, who will sort you out. For used pianos, head to Ao Yue Piano Center. The Yilun Piano Center (48-1 Zhongguancun Nan Dajie, 010 6218 3582) also sells reconditioned pianos, most of which are under 10 years old. Steinway (88 Guangqumennei Dajie, 010 6716 4658) does some very fancy pieces, and Tom Lee Music (57 Tiantan Lu, 010 6702 0099) sells most modern instruments imaginable.

Ao Yue Piano Center 奥乐钢琴中心

Jianxiang Qiao
Chaoyang
北四环路健翔桥东北角
朝阳区
Map 4 E2 **81**

010 6492 4835

This shop sells pianos wholesale, including Yamaha, Kawai and local brands like Xinghai and Zhujiang. It also rents out new and second-hand pianos by the day and month. Piano tuning is available, and there are three practice rooms. Jianxiang Qiao is on Beisihuan Lu.

Various Locations

Parson's Music 柏斯琴行

www.parsonsmusic.com

This chain music megastore sells pianos, wind, stringed, percussion, electric and traditional Chinese instruments. Brands include Casio and Schimmel. Shops can be found at 4006-4011, Golden Resources Mall (p.295, 010 8887 4340); 53-4 Xisanhuan Beilu, Haidian (010 6873 2880); 4/F Floor, Wanjiao Plaza, Nanhu Beilu, Wangjing, Chaoyang (010 8471 3688); and A404-405, Metro City, 189 Dongsihuan Zhonglu, Chaoyang (010 6722 8100).

Outdoor Goods

Other options **Sports Goods** p.284, **Camping** p.209, **Hardware & DIY** p.265

Whether you're hitting the slopes or going on a camping trip, there are plenty of places to get supplies. While the Silk Market (p.294), Yashow Market (p.294) and others sells knock-offs of Columbia, North Face and the like, if you really want gear that won't let you down at 10,000 feet, it's probably worth buying the real thing. Decathlon (p.285) sells durable camping, hiking and skiing gear at low prices. Fishermen head to Bibo.

For hiking, mountain climbing and camping, head to Italian store Dolomite or Nice Days Outdoor Gear Store. For hard-to-find items like snakebite kits and biodegradable soap, try Extreme Beyond.

The staff at all these stores are knowledgeable and have people who speak English. Demokratic, Sanfo and Snow Fever organise trips.

Outdoor Goods		
Dolomite	3078, 3/F Golden Resources Mall, 1 Yuanda Lu	010 8889 2642
Extreme Beyond	A6 Gongti Donglu	010 6506 5121
Snow Fever	Dadushi Shangyejie, Changping	010 6707 1085
Sunwind Outdoor	6A Xiangjun Beili, Dongsanhuan Beilu	010 6585 8278

Golden Resources Mall
Haidian
远大路1号金源时代购
物中心三层3100
海淀区
Map 4 A4 82

Bibo 碧波渔具

010 8886 1286

Bibo markets itself as a real fisherman's friend, and stocks high quality kit and clobber from Japan, Korea and Taiwan. Rods, lines, nets, bait and tackle boxes are all available, along with the tackle itself, and, if your Chinese is up to scratch, a little advice on where to go. It also offers delivery.

Central Plaza
Dongsihuan Beilu
Chaoyang
东四环北路中环广场
A座东区8号
朝阳区
Map 5 D4 83

Demokratic

010 5130 7173 | *www.demokratic.com*

This shop sells gear for beginner and expert snowboarders alike. It carries a range of items for men and women, including snowboards, clothes, padding, bindings, goggles and boots. Brands include Burton, Oakley (it's the exclusive retailer in Beijing for prescription eyewear), Coal, DC and RED. The store also offers snowboarding classes for all levels.

1-4 Chaoyangmennei
Bei Xiaojie
Dongcheng
朝阳门内北小街1-4
东城区
Map 11 B2 84

Nice Days Outdoor Gear Store 遇见时光户外用品

010 8406 9499

This shop stocks a wide selection of camping, mountaineering and outdoor gear like backpacks and hiking boots. It sells Chinese and international brands like Wolverine, Columbia and Montrail. The staff are friendly but expect to pay western prices for this genuine gear.

Various Locations

Sanfo 三夫户外用品

www.sanfo.com

Specialising in outdoor and camping gear, this shop sells ropes, harnesses and shoes. The Madian store has a rock climbing wall, so shoppers can test the equipment before buying. Some gear is available for rent. Sanfo also organises weekend and week-long hiking and camping trips. Branches can be found at Jinzhiqiao Dasha (north-west corner of China World Shopping Mall), Jianguomenwai Dajie, Chaoyang (010 6507 9298) and Building 5, 4 Madian Nancun, Beisanhuan Zhong Lu, Chaoyang (010 6201 5550).

Party Accessories

Other options **Party Organisers** p.348

It can be hard to find helium balloons and other party favourites. It's often easiest to hire out planners that can entertain and help plan shindigs. If you plan to have a small, simple party at home, then most supermarkets have you covered. They sell paper plates, cups and napkins, along with balloons and sometimes noise makers and hats. For decorations, head to markets like Yashow (p.294). On the third floor there's a stall crammed with everything you'll need. In October, it carries one of the largest collections of Halloween costumes, decorations and accessories.

Kids Plus also has a large assortment of costumes year round, as well as invitations, party hats and horns. For loot bags, head to Exquisite Bakery, which also sells baking and decorating products. If you're after balloons, Big Dog Balloon Party Shop (Room 102, Unit 4, Building 3, District C1, Upper East Side, 6 Dongsihuan Beilu, Chaoyang, 010 5130 7088, www.bigdogparty.cn) has inflatables galore, including balloon sculptures. For Halloween, Fancy That (C3, 118A Shunhuang Lu, Sunhexiang, 010 8459 3241, www. fancythat.com.cn) rents and sells costumes. Wal-Mart (p.297), Carrefour (p.297) and, oddly enough, B&Q (p.266) have small selections of Halloween costumes, accessories and pumpkins for carving. Live Christmas trees can be bought at the plant market on Nuren Jie and artificial trees and decorations are sold at Carrefour, Wal-Mart and some local supermarkets.

The St Regis (p.36), The Ritz-Carlton (p.36) and other hotels also offer outside catering, as do many expat restaurants like Fish Nation (p.305) and Comptoirs de France (p.313). For more caterers see p.348.

60 Guangqu Donglu
Chaoyang
广渠东路60号
朝阳区

Bounceabout 北京天仁达莱工贸有限公司

010 8770 4047 | www.bjtrdl.com

This company rents inflatable bouncy castles and rock climbing walls. Fill your little ones with fizzy pop and chocolate and watch the vomiting ensue. Alternatively, you may fancy a bounce yourself; you're never too old. Rentals are not cheap, but kids do tend to get giddy with excitement, and it ensures a memorable soiree.

Shop 7, Riverville Square
Shunyi
天竺温榆广场7号
顺义区
Map 3 D3 87

Exquisite Bakery 南炉食品屋

138 1180 1180 | www.exquisite-bakery.com

This bakery sells themed cakes, cute cupcakes and decorated cookies as well as baking trays and decorations. Party supplies like goodie bags and paper goods are also available. The staff are friendly and speak English.

701 Pinnacle Plaza
Shunyi
日祥广场701
顺义区
Map 8 D2 88

Kids Plus 格林塔儿童用品商店

010 8046 4572

This store is a kids' paradise, with cool imported toys, board games, a variety of costumes sold all year, and party supplies like hats, horns, stickers, greeting cards and invitations. Prices are a bit steep, but the staff speak excellent English.

Various Locations

Mr Magic 魔术先生
800 429 8765 | *www.mrmagic.com*

Mr Magic can help you plan the best party, from princess and pirate themes to Harry Potter and Santa. His fee includes a magic show, treasure hunt, circle games, crazy dance, and fashion show. And if you want a petting zoo or to rent carnival rides, Mr. Magic has those too. Prize bags, face painters, balloon animals and bouncy castles are also on offer. Discounts for schools and charities are available.

Perfumes & Cosmetics

Smelling good and looking pretty are becoming easier thanks to a bevy of international brands, readily available in department stores and dedicated shops. Department stores like Sogo (8 Xuanwumenwai Dajie, Xuanwu, 010 6310 3388) offer a wide selection of cosmetic counters with Clinique, Estee Lauder and Shiseido on offer. There is an import tax applied to luxury goods, including cosmetics and perfumes, meaning prices can be up to 35% higher than back home. Lane Crawford (p.258) carries Dior and Stella McCartney, and has a men's grooming bar that sells soaps and shaving gear.

Most supermarkets and pharmacies have an aisle dedicated to skin care, and always have a large section for the gentleman, as beauty products are popular among Chinese males. Be careful when purchasing foundations and moisturisers, as many include whitening agents. Pale skin is prized, so many products have built-in whiteners that bleach the skin. The Eric Paris Salon (p.235) has the city's only Keratase Institute, which offers treatments and products for sale.

There are several chains and international shops like Fruits & Passion, L'Occitane and Stenders that sell shower gels, body lotions and soaps in dozens of flavours. Most hotel hair salons and chains like Toni & Guy (p.235) and Eric Paris (p.235), carry international haircare products like Paul Mitchell. Avoid buying them at markets as they are likely to be fakes or expired. Hotel spas (p.236) are another great place, as they usually have luxury products for sale in their gift shops.

The Ritz-Carlton (p.36) and Peninsula Hotel (p.35) both sell their own shampoos, conditioners and soaps in their gift shops.

For the widest range of international perfumes, head to major department stores or to a branch of Sephora.

Perfumes & Cosmetics

Fruits & Passion	Various Locations	010 8518 6064
Korres	The Place, 9 Guanghua Lu	010 6587 1255
L'Occitane	Various Locations	010 6269 6178
M.A.C.	The Place, 9 Guanghua Lu	010 6587 1598
Red Earth	Various Locations	010 8391 3685
Sephora	Various Locations	010 8472 9388
Stenders Soap Factory	China World Shopping Mall	010 6505 1918
Thann Spa	The Place, 9 Guanghua Lu	010 6587 1384

Pets
Other options **Pets** p.280

Whether its cats, dogs, fish or snakes you're after, the choice here is vast. But no matter how cute the puppies, turtles and rabbits look outside subway stations and on street corners, it's not a good idea to buy them. Most are sick and unvaccinated, and die after purchase. It's better to stick with established shops and breeders. When visiting breeders, ask to see their registration and licence from the Agricultural Bureau.

Otherwise, try the International Centre for Veterinary Services (p.106) or Dr. Tony Beck at Beijing Ornamental Animal Hospital (p.106, 010 6202 3827), for recommendations. There are several places to adopt cats, like Carepets (http://carepets.blog.com.cn) and Cat Friends (135 0131 5988, www.beijingcat.org). Both rescue, train, vaccinate and de-worm cats before putting them up for adoption. There's also the Beijing Human and Animal Environmental Education Centre (010 5129 8676, www.animalschina.org), a private shelter that rescues animals and helps find them a new home. The International Centre for Veterinary Services offers regular workshops on how to adopt pets in Beijing. Otherwise, several markets and pet shops are listed in the table.

Many places sell pet supplies. International pet foods and treats are readily available in local supermarkets. Imported specialty food and supplies are available at pet hospitals, markets, Hip Dog Club and Qiqi Pets.

Shop 7, Central Park
6 Chaoyangmenwai
Chaoyang
朝阳门外大街6号新城
国际7号
朝阳区
Map 11 F1 **89**

Hip Dog Club 宠物用品
010 6533 6814
This shop sells a variety of imported dog supplies and a range of homemade biscuits. To make sure your pup has a birthday to remember, the store also sells pork liver, beef, lamb and chicken birthday cakes. Be sure to order in advance. It also offers obedience training.

Pets

Aisida Dog Market	8A Fatou, Wangsiying Town	010 6736 6155
Dasenlin Flower Market	5 Zaojunmiao	010 6211 9255
Guanyuan Fish & Bird Market	North of Fuchengmen	na
Laitai Flower Market	9 Maizidian Xilu	010 6463 6145
Pet Care Shop & Grooming Parlour	A118 Shunhuang Lu, Sunhe Xiang	010 8459 3083
Prime Pet Shop	Huizhong Beili, Yayuncun	010 6485 5577
Qiqi Pets	8 Laiguangying Donglu	010 8142 2927
Tian Yu Fish Market	Tuanjiehu Lu	na
Yiya Pet Store & Hospital	34 Gongti Beilu	010 6552 6178

Second-Hand Items
Other options **Books** p.254

Chinese Takeaway
The three wheeled silver carts that can be seen around town, which are typically overflowing with cardboard boxes and Styrofoam, will take anything with a resale value. Just hail one down and show them what you've got. They may charge a few kuai to take bigger items.

Buying second-hand goods is a relatively new phenomenon in Beijing, so there aren't many options. Most locals don't understand why someone would dress scruffily if they could afford not to, and the idea of wearing someone else's old clobber is associated with being poor, but the idea is slowly catching on among the city's youth.

A good selection can be found on the local Craigslist (www.craigslist.com), and eBay (www.ebay.com) sites, and many listings are bilingual. Then there's Taobao (www.taobao.com), China's answer to eBay. If you want to skip the shipping, City Weekend (www.cityweekend.com.cn) and That's Beijing (www.thebeijinger.com) have message boards where anyone can list items for sale (with pictures) for free.

If you want to get rid of your stuff, but don't want to do it online, several companies will haul away your possessions, including Beijing Ganjia Recycling Company (010 6292 7146) and Beijing Fangzhou Recycling Company (010 8885 1670). These places speak Chinese only.

There are many charities, particularly orphanages, which accept used clothing and, sometimes, furniture. The Salvation Army (Room 102, Unit D, Shemao Apartment, 2 Guanghuali, Chaoyang, 010 6586 9331, www.salvation.org.hk) accepts donations of used clothes.

Vintage cameras

6 Yandai Xiejie, Houhai
Xicheng
后海烟袋斜街6号
西城区
Map 8 C2 **90**

China Vintage 中国葡萄酒
133 6628 5573
This small, hip shop sells a range of second-hand clothes like vintage T-shirts and jeans. It mostly caters to men but there is a small selection for women. Prices are reasonable and the service is friendly.

Store 5137, 3.3 Fashion Mall, 33 Sanlitun Lu
Chaoyang
三里屯33号3. 3时尚商城5137店
朝阳区
Map 7 C1 **91**

China's First Celebrities' Second-Hand (Pre-Owned) Goods Shop 明星二手店
010 5136 5507
This store stocks clothes and accessories worn by celebrities at photo shoots and in movies. Photos and certificates prove the authenticity of each item. Prices range from a few hundred *kuai* to thousands for jackets, boots and accessories. The store donates a portion of its proceeds to local charities like Hope Project, which helps to build schools in remote villages.

108/5 Sankongjian
Chaoyang
北四环东路亚运村三空间5号楼108室
朝阳区
Map 5 C3 **92**

Discover 发现服装饰品二手奢侈品交流店
131 6428 8125
This boutique carries women's designer cast-offs like Burberry, Marc Jacobs and Prada, with handbags, shoes and clothes for sale. Expect to pay a fraction of the price you would pay in a real boutique for these gently used items. Sankongjian is on Beisihuan Donglu.

Laitai Flower Market
Nuren Jie
Chaoyang
女人街莱太花卉市场
朝阳区
Map 5 D4 **93**

Grand World Secondhand Electrical Market 大世界二手电器城
010 8448 4336
Three floors of second-hand goods make this a bargain hunter's paradise. Goods include mobile phones, TVs, CD players and turntables. Be sure to bargain hard and inspect products carefully, and always turn on what you intend to buy and have a play in store. Request a receipt in case your gadget breaks soon after taking it home.

101/18, Huayang Jiayuan
Chaoyang
六里屯北里姚家园路华阳家园18号楼101
朝阳区
Map 7 D1 **94**

NU2YU Baby Shop NU2YU国际精品妇幼用品调剂空间
010 6508 2388 | www.nu2yubabyshop.com
Run by Karen Patterson, this shop sells second-hand baby and toddler toys and furniture. Anyone can buy, sell, or rent items; some of which are hard to find in Beijing. Karen doesn't just buy any old tat, and has been known to turn items down (though these are given to local orphanages). The store is open Sunday to Thursday and by appointment for browsing and purchasing. If you are donating items, you must call or email first. The building is on Yaojiayuan Lu.

Shoes
Other options **Beachwear** p.252, **Sports Goods** p.284, **Clothes** p.257

Finding shoes is easy, but finding your size can prove tricky. Most places only carry up to size 38 for women and 44 for men. Some don't even come close, but international chains carry larger sizes. Burberry, Gucci and Louis Vuitton also carry a small selection of designer shoes, while their respective knockoffs can be found in markets (p.292). Department stores like Lane Crawford (p.258), Parkson (101 Fuxingmennei Dajie,

Haidian, 010 6601 3377) and Sogo (8 Xuanwumenwai Dajie, Xuanwu, 010 6310 3388) also have extensive collections for men and women. Carrefour (p.297), Wal-Mart (p.297) and local supermarkets carry cheap shoes and trainers. For factory rejects, try stall B1-098 at Yashow Market (p.294), which carries brands like Steve Madden and Michael Kors. For wholesale bargains try Europe & Asia Handbag Wholesaler (200m south of Andingmen Qiao, Dongcheng, 010 6401 3897), which carries leather shoes and boots for men and women, but their sizes only go up to 39. Remember to bargain.
There are several places that can custom-make shoes for reasonable prices including Pi'erman Maoyi. Bring a picture or the shoes you want duplicated to the store. It can take up to six weeks to make a pair. Shoes cost an average of ¥400 and boots ¥800. If you need repairs, there are plenty of shops throughout the city including expat favourite Lido Shoe Repair (Room 206A, Holiday Inn Lido, 6 Jiangtai Lu, Chaoyang, 010 6437 6688).

Acupuncture 艾克佩克

M3027 Shin Kong Place
Chaoyang
建国路87号新光天地
3楼M3027
朝阳区
🚇 *Dawanglu L1*
Map 7 D2 **95**

010 6533 1181
This hip line of coloured trainers from London made its way to Beijing in 2007. There are two shops in town selling trainers, caps, T-shirts and teddy bears all sporting the 'A' logo. The designs are bright and simple. Shin Kong Place (Map 7 D2) is at 87 Jianguo Lu. The other branch is at Jiamao Shopping Mall, 1F, Xizhimenwai Dajie, Xihuan Plaza, Chaoyang.

CPU 服饰专卖店

D3060 Shin Kong Place
Chaoyang
建国路87号新光天地
D座3060
朝阳区
🚇 *Dawanglu L1*
Map 7 D2 **96**

010 6533 1545
This store has a variety of well-known international brands like Dr Martens and Birkenstock. In a city where it's hard to find larger shoes sizes, it stocks men's shoes in sizes up to 45 and women's up to 39, so your big clumsy western feet should fit just fine. The service is friendly too. Shin Kong Place (Map 7 D2) is at 87 Jianguo Lu, where you'll also find Acupuncture (see above).

Crocs 卡骆驰专卖店

B105, The Place
Chaoyang
光华路甲9号世贸天阶
中心B105号
朝阳区
🚇 *Yonganli L1*
Map 11 E2 **97**

010 5869 6970
Hated by many, mocked by more, these durable rubbery shoes (made of a patented material called 'croslite') have become a recent sensation. The quirky shoes come in over a dozen colours for men, women and children, but go sock-less in them for too long and your friends may begin to back away when they see you. The Place is at 9 Guanghua Lu.

Deal 迪欧主题潮流鞋店

28 Gulou Dong Dajie
Dongcheng
鼓楼东大街28号
东城区
Map 8 D2 **98**

010 6402 8262 | *www.dealkicks.com*
With two floors of shoes in museum-style glass displays, this is the place to come for limited edition Nike and Adidas shoes. Be prepared to shell out several thousand *kuai* for these coveted versions. The shop also offers online sales and mail ordering through its website.

Shoes		
Aldo	The Place, 9 Guanghua Lu	010 6587 1578
An De Li Si	3.3 Shopping Center, 33 Sanlitun Beijie	138 0132 8747
Easy Spirit	The Malls at Oriental Plaza, 1 Dong Changan Jie	010 8518 8987
Pi'erman Maoyi	37 Gulou Dongdajie	010 6404 1406
Rong Xin Tailor & Boutique	2/F Friendship Supermarket, 7 Sanlitun Lu	010 6532 7913
Skechers	Zhongguancun Gate City Mall	www.skechers.com
Wanzhong Machine Trim Shoe Shop	Yashow Market, 58 Gongti Beilu	136 9121 9943

Jolly Buddha

Souvenirs

Souvenirs are not hard to find. And occasionally, hawkers trying to flog you jade, Olympic T-shirts, Mao watches or photocopied versions of the *Little Red Book* are very hard to avoid. Anything bought off a street corner is almost guaranteed to be a fake.

That said, avoid the high-priced souvenirs at the airport, hotels and tourist sites like the Great Wall. Even the government-run Friendship Store (p.264), which used to be the only place foreigners could shop for goods, tends to have stiff prices, though at least authenticity is guaranteed.

Unsurprisingly, for pearls, the best place is the Pearl Market (p.293), particularly Fanghua (Shop 4318, 010 6718 7888, www.fanghua. com). You're more likely to find cultured pearls than natural ones in Chinese markets. Real pearls should feel gritty, not smooth and their lustre will not appear chalky or dusty. If you really want a thorough check, examine the pearls with a jeweller's loupe, the mini eye piece that will magnify the surface so you can check for imperfections. For jade, either the Silk Market (p.294) or Pearl Market (p.293) will do.

If you want to skip the markets, check out the small shops in Yangrou Hutong in Xicheng. It has a cluster of jewellery shops specialising in jade. Brighter, more vivid colours tend to be higher quality and more expensive. Air bubbles cannot be seen in real jade.

And for tea, head to Tea Street Market (Maliandao, Chayecheng, Xuanwu) or Wuyutai Tea Shop (186 Wangfujing Dajie, Dongcheng, 010 6525 4961), which opened in the Qing Dynasty.

For Cultural Revolution items like Mao suits and little red books, Panjiayuan Market (p.293) is most likely to have the real deal. For silk, head to the Silk Market or Panjiayuan (see Textiles p.286 for more). For everything else, including chopsticks, seals with your name carved in Chinese, scrolls, postcards and kites, the Silk Market and Pearl Market are worth a visit.

Sports Goods
Other options **Outdoor Goods** p.278

There are a plethora of Adidas, Nike, Puma and Reebok stores throughout the city, as well as Chinese chains like Anta (www.anta.com.cn) and Sports 100 (www.sports100. com.cn). They all sell basketball, football and running kit and clothes, and can be found in most malls.

For bargain prices, head to Sports Equipment Street on Tiyuguan Xi Lu in Chongwen. It is packed with small shops selling everything from yoga mats to swords. You will also find some fake replica kits.

If you're after golf clubs, then head to Beijing Honma Golf Service Store. For men's ice hockey gear, there's really only one place – The Ice Zone (Second Floor, River Garden Clubhouse, 7 Yujang Lu, Shunyi, 010 8046 6092, www.icezonechina.com). Here, a set of gloves, trousers, shinguards, elbow and shoulder pads will set you back somewhere in the region of ¥1,800.

For fake or replica sports clothing, head to Silk Market (p.294) or Beijing Longteng Athletics Thing at Alien Street Market (p.288, then stall 1290, or try calling the owner on 139 1042 4388).

Various Locations ◄ ## Decathlon 迪卡侬
www.decathlon.com.cn
Part of a huge French chain, Decathlon is the place to buy genuine, good quality kit for the entire family. While it doesn't stock many men's sports shoes in big sizes, their selection of equipment covers ball and racquet sports and athletics. It also has a good selection of camping equipment, including tents, sleeping bags and portable barbecues. Shops can be found at 195 Dongsihuan Zhonglu (010 8777 8788) and Wenhuayuan Xilu, Beijing Economic Technological Development Area, south-east Fifth Ring Road (010 6782 6100).

302 Dongsi Bei Dajie ◄ ## Fly 法拉艾
Dongcheng
东四北大街302号
东城区
Map 9 A3 **99**
010 6402 2151 | www.skatehere.com
This is the place for skateboarding gear, including Nike SB, Nike's signature skateboarding line. The shop stocks men's clothes only and includes brands like Adio, Stussy, Trimvir, LRG and Circa. There's also a collection of decks, wheels and trucks to complete your street style.

Various Locations ◄ ## Sports 100 运动100
www.sports100.com.cn
The Chinese megastore carries well-known brands at reasonable prices. It sells men's and women's (teens and up) basketball, football and running attire and shoes, including larger sizes. The staff are friendly and there are frequent sales. Branches can be found at 100 Ginza Mall, 48 Dongzhimenwai Dajie, Chaoyang, (010 8447 7117) and Oriental Plaza, 1 Dong Changan Jie, Dongcheng, (010 8518 6740).

Sports Goods

Adidas	Malls at Oriental Plaza, 1 Dong Changan Jie	010 8518 6753
Beijing Honma Golf Service Store	Stall 5, Kerry Centre Mall, 1 Guanghua Lu	010 8529 9448
Lacoste	Shops at Oriental Plaza, NBB68, 1 Dong Changan Jie	010 8515 0275
	15 Fuxingmenwai Dajie	010 6802 8851
	3 Chongwenmenwai Dajie	010 6708 9825
	40 Zhongguancun Dajie	010 6257 6688
Nike Golf	Malls at Oriental Plaza, 1 Dong Changan Jie	010 8578 6713
Puma	L133-134, The Place, 9 Guanghua Lu	na

Stationery

If you want smart stationery, you may be disappointed. Most paper, pens and organisers tend to be Hello Kitty or other cheap varieties. For everyday school and office supplies, there is Staples, the US chain. It offers boxes of ballpoint pens, paper, calculators, office furniture and, of course, staples. Most supermarkets (p.297) have school and office supplies too. For photocopying, there are plenty of independent shops, and Kinko's, which is open 24 hours. For high end writing implements, there's Mont Blanc and for fashionable stationery, there's a small selection at Kate Spade, while Shanghai Tang (p.259) has leather notebooks costing from $45 to $200.

Stationery

Kate Spade	China World Shopping Mall	010 6505 5665
Kinko's	11A Xiangjun Beili, Dongsanhuan Lu	010 6595 8050
Mont Blanc	Various Locations	010 8214 8486
Shanghai Tang	Shop 3 & 5, Grand Hyatt Hotel, 1 Dong Changan Jie	010 8518 7228
Staples	93 Caochangdi	800 610 0999

Tailoring

Other options **Tailors** p.102, **Clothes** p.257, **Textiles** p.286

You don't need to have a million bucks to look it here. With so many tailors, getting simple alterations and elaborate bespoke suits is easy, quick and inexpensive. Tailors across town will make just about anything – from wedding dresses to seat cushions. The process of being fitted, and tweaking a garment to your tastes, is a princely experience, and something that should be tried if you ever need a special outfit. Many will also knock up extravagant items of fancy dress, should you be in the mood. Markets like Yashow (p.294), which has dozens of tailors on the third floor, and Silk Market (p.294) can assist. Some places, like Dave's Custom Tailoring, can make Saville Row style suits.

You can buy material separately (see Textiles, below). Once you have this, head to your chosen tailor, who will take your measurements. You can bring along sketches, patterns or photos from magazines, or your own suits or dresses if you'd like them copied. Many tailors speak enough English to communicate, but bringing pictures and samples is best. Expect one or two alteration sessions to get everything right.

Be sure to bargain hard to get the best prices. You may still spend several thousands, but custom tailoring in Beijing is much cheaper than other countries. The turnaround time on garments can be as little as 24 hours and as much as several weeks, though most good tailors take one or two weeks to complete your order.

Friends are a great source for recommendations, and many expats turn to Sunny (Huo Youquan). She has helped humble expats and Condoleezza Rice look good. Shanghai Tang (p.259) takes seven to 10 days to make a garment. Blanc de Chine, which sells Chinese designer clothing like *qipaos* and Mao suits, offers tailoring.

There are also international outlets specialising in bespoke suits, including Dunhill (which has several branches) and Paul Rousseau. At Thomas Pink's shops, men and women can have their own custom shirts made and men can design their own English silk ties.

Tailoring

Blanc de Chine	115-117, Kerry Centre, 1 Guanghua Lu	010 8529 9450
Dave's Custom Tailoring	104 Kerry Centre, 1 Guanghua Lu	010 8529 9433
Dunhill	Various Locations	010 6515 8053
Lisa Tailor	Stall 5011, 3.3 Fashion Mall, 33 Sanlitun Beijie	139 1079 8183
Paul Rousseau	206 Fortune Plaza, 7 Dongsanhuan Zhonglu	010 6530 9182
Senli & Mae	Yaxing Building, 46A Liangmaqiao Lu	139 1009 2419
Shanghai Tang	Shop 3 & 5, Grand Hyatt Hotel, 1 Dong Changan Jie	010 8518 7228
Shanghai Xu	AA10, Malls at Oriental Plaza, 1 Dong Changan Jie	010 8518 6376
Sunny (Huo Youquan)	Stall 3066, Yashow Market, 58 Gongti Beilu	010 6415 1726
Thomas Pink	Various Locations	010 6622 0451
Xiao Fei Tailor & Fabric Shop	Room 103, Building 1, 35 Xinyuan Jie	010 8455 1939
Yin's Fashion Tailor	Resident Committee's Community Center, 15 Xueyuan Lu	010 8237 2950

Textiles

Other options **Souvenirs** p.284, **Tailoring** p.286

Buying fabric in Beijing is easy and cheap. The speciality is silk, but cashmere, cottons and blends can all be found. Prices start about ¥13 per metre though bargaining is a must.

The best place to go for fabrics is Muxiyuan Market. It has a good range from the finest silk for dresses to fabrics for upholstering chairs. For knitters, Lidea sells more than 100 kinds of woollen thread. For curtains, bed sheets and other household fabric, Jingjusishi Fabric Market is the place to go.

To make sure you're buying real silk, take a loose thread and ignite it with a lighter. If it's real, it will turn to ash and smell like burning hair. If it's fake, it will melt or smell like paper. You should look for a fabric identification tag on the bolt of silk. There will be five digits starting with the number one. It's not necessary to buy the entire bolt; a few metres will be enough for trousers or a dress.

Muxiyuan Fabric Market

Nestled in rows in outdoor shacks and tents, this place sells every type of fabric imaginable. Bartering is essential to get the best prices. The stalls are grouped by the items they sell, with buttons on one aisle, ribbons on another and silk on another. Whether you need zippers, elastic, sewing patterns or fabric, it's all here and all cheap. Though the service is not the friendliest, be persistent and you'll get some good deals. It's on Nansanhuan Lu in Fengtai.

Textiles

Bayunxiang Silk Clothing Shop	90 Zhonglouwan	010 6402 9512
Beixin Jingfeng Fabric	4-23 Jiaodaokou Dongdajie	010 6404 2658
Daxin Textiles Co	North-east corner of Dongsi crossing	010 8602 3919
Jingjusishi Fabric Market	Section 1, Jiancai Jingmao Mansion, 14 Dongtucheng Lu	010 6427 4730
Lidea	China World Shopping Mall	010 6505 6350
Linfuxiang Fabric	324 Andingmennei Dajie	010 6404 5747
Qianxiangyi (Beijing Silk Street)	50 Dazhalan Xi Jie, Qianmen	010 6301 6658
Ruifuxiang	180 Wangfujing Dajie	010 6523 2807
Ruifuxiang	5 Qianmen Dazhalan	010 6303 5313
Shantung Silk	357 Chaoyangmennei Xiaojie	010 6523 2440
Wansha Cashmere Store	14-2 Dongshidongkou Dajie	010 6512 7090

Toys & Games

Beijing has plenty to keep little emperors and empresses entertained, whether you're looking for traditional toys made by hand or the latest PlayStation games. The one-child policy has created a tendency to indulge children, and the growing wealth of parents encourages them to provide luxuries they missed out on. Jack Toys, stuck in the back of Jenny Lou's (p.264), has a balloon delivery service, along with some arty, creative distractions and the usual kiddie kit. Kids Plus does a decent line in costumes for ¥200, though it tends to be pricier than Jack Toys.

Lego has three stores in the city, for those in need of a fix of bricks. Besides the store in the table, there is one in the Lufthansa Centre (p.292; Lufthansa has got lots of other toy shops too) and one at Pacific Century Place.

T.O.T.S (The Original Toy Store) sells gear to help junior grow up clever, rather than a social incompetent staring at the flashing lights of a games console. It sells Plan Toys (www.plantoys.com) and others that claim to help development. China World, where T.O.T.S is based, is a good spot for toy stores.

Silks at Silk Market (p.294)

Laofanjie Shichang
Chaoyang
雅宝路老番街市场
朝阳区
Map 6 B2 **100**

Alien Street Market 老番街市场

This is regrettably neither manned by, nor a vendor of, aliens of any sort. It does, however, have stall holders that are keen for a bit of haggling. Inspect the toys carefully though, as among the bargains are some items of truly shoddy quality, and others that may be dangerous. Laofanjie Shichang is on Yabao Lu.

38 Guozijian
Dongcheng
国子监38号
东城区

Bannerman Tang's Toys & Crafts 盛唐轩传统玩具店
010 8404 7179

The talented Tang family of toymakers have been making playthings for five generations. The tiny shop specialises in handmade toys. Most of the figures are human or animal, and made of clay, paper and cloth. Each toy takes days to make, and many are delightful.

4/F Sung An Dong
Plaza, Wangfujing
Dongcheng
王府井新东安商场4层
东城区
🚇 *Wangfujing L1*
Map 7 A2 **102**

Crayola Activity Centre 卡幼乐儿童活动中心
www.crayola.cc

This 2,000sqm mini children's mall and activity centre has a place for kids to play, with drop-in craft projects and fun amenities like glass windows to paint on. There is a 32 seat theatre for kids to play dress up, and an art room with easels, and lots of kid-friendly favourites on sale. The retail portion of the store sells Crayola art products, Barbie, books and musical instruments. There's even a Harry Potter Magic Store.

L408, The Place
Chaoyang
光华路9号 世贸天
阶L408
朝阳区
Map 7 D2 **103**

Playism 玩主义
010 6587 1385

This store sells many items for toddlers, but the coolest toys are the driveable cars, including a mini red Ferrari, complete with racing tyres. They are so cool adults may want a go too. It also stocks toys for older children, including telescopes and Crayola products. The Place is at 9 Guanghua Lu.

25 Dianmen Xi Dajie
Xicheng
地安门西大街25号
西城区
Map 8 A3 **104**

San Shi Zhai Kite Store (Three Stones Kite Store) 三石斋风筝店
010 8404 4505

At this shop you'll find hand-made and hand-painted kites crafted from bamboo, silk or paper (prices change accordingly) and most are shaped into birds, dragons and butterflies, with the odd flying fish thrown in for good measure. Some kites can fly as high as 1,000m, and several metres long. The store also does repairs.

Zhongguancun Mall
Haidian
中关村新中关购物中
心421
海淀区
Map 4 C3 **105**

Warner Brothers Studio Store 华纳兄弟专门店

The only Warner Brothers store in Beijing, the small shop is crammed with Bugs Bunnys and Daffy Ducks. There is an extensive DVD collection including *Batman*, *The Dirty Harry* series, *Superman*, *Gremlins*, and *The Goonies*. There's a small collection of children's clothes and baby accessories. The shop also carries book bags, stationery and chopsticks.

Toys & Games

Buyi Wanou	Building 43, Dongdaqiao Lu	010 8563 6735
Jack Toys	Pinnacle Plaza, Tianzhu Real Estate Development Zone	136 8330 0568
Kids Plus	Pinnacle Plaza, Tianzhu Real Estate Development Zone	010 8046 4572
Lego	Various Locations	www.lego.com
New China Children's Store	168 Wangfujing Dajie	010 6528 1774
Park Classic Toys	1/F, Huixin Building, 6 Xiangjun Beilu	010 6506 8952
T.O.T.S.	China World Shopping Mall	010 6505 4548
Tianle Toy Market	136 Fahuasi Jie	na
Toy & Game	China World Shopping Mall	010 6505 1911

Wedding Items

Weddings are big business in China but expats find the paperwork and formalities can be daunting. Xiyan Wedding Planner Company (010 8403 7030 ext 8300) helps plan religious, civil and traditional Chinese weddings. From finding a priest to booking a hall to designing invitations, they do it all. FIORE Design Studio (Unit 601, Level 6, Tower W2, Oriental Plaza, 1 Dong Changan Jie, Dongcheng, 400 618 5527) specialises in wedding decorations and will do custom flower arrangements.

Off the peg wedding dresses can be bought from La Vincci and NE Tiger, while custom-made bridal, bridesmaid and page boy outfits are on sale at Galatea Bridal. It has more than 100 samples for shoppers to try before a tailor-made dress is commissioned.

The China International Wedding Attire Exhibition (www.chinawedding.com.cn) might offer inspiration, but it mostly caters to distributors and stores.

Traditionally, a *hong bao* (red envelope stuffed with money) is given in lieu of wedding gifts.

Wedding Items

Galatea Bridal	3/F Building 12, Jianwai SOHO, 39 Dongsanhuan Zhonglu	010 5869 7887
La Vincci	Soho New Town, 88 Jianguo Lu	010 8776 0680
NE Tiger	AA31-AA33, Malls at Oriental Plaza, 1 Dong Changan Jie	010 8518 6397
New Wedding Shopping Center	109 Xidan Bei Dajie	010 6605 2123
S-JOY	Room 337, Friendship Store Office, Jianguomenwai Dajie	135 2199 9137

Dazhong (p.262)

Mao kitsch

Books (p.254)

Areas To Shop

Shopping streets in the city tend to have a selection of everything, with women's fashion – both designer and thrifty bohemian – accounting for a great percentage of shops. Wangfujing is Beijing's answer to London's Oxford Street, but should by no means be the final stop on a shopping spree. Ancient or brand new, plastic tack or designer finery, it can all be found in Beijing.

Dongcheng
东城区
Map 9 A4 **106**

Dongsi Beidajie 东四北大街

Dongsi Beidajie shopping street, along with Wangfujing (p.290) and Xidan (p.291), completes the trio of main shopping areas in the city centre. It adds a touch of boutique originality missing from the other two. For those looking for something a bit different, this is the place to visit. Independent shops and boutiques have a bohemian feel and it is a great place for ferreting out hidden gems. Open daily 08:00 to 19:00.

Xuanwu
宣武区
🚇 *Qianmen*
Map 10 D4 **107**

Qianmen Dajie & Dazhalan 前门大街&大栅栏

This has been a shopping strip for more than 500 years, and remains one of the most memorable experiences in the city. Flashy lights, neon signs and cheap clothes stores vie for space amongst the Chinese restaurants and *hutongs* that snake off to the side. The street is under renovation and due for completion by the Olympics when it should hopefully be a little cleaner. Qianmen Dajie runs north to south from the bottom of Tiananmen Square and is intersected by the famous Dazhalan Hutong, where ancient Chinese medicine shops, fine silk clothing and age-old handicrafts are crowded together. The red lanterns and bustle along both streets make for a quintessential Chinese experience, especially after dark. Shops are open daily from 08:30 to 18:00.

Chaoyang
朝阳区

Tian Ze Lu 天泽路

Inconspicuous Tian Ze Lu hides some of the most useful, and interesting, shops you might need. The most famous is the Women's Market (Nu Ren Jie). It is a little grubby, but offers cheap clothes and shoes in unusual styles. It is geared towards Chinese buyers, so larger sizes are difficult to find. It is tucked away behind the conspicuous Flower Market (p.263), down a set of steps. On the top floor is a huge golfing equipment store. The basement is a treasure trove of Chinese furniture, home wares and decorations. Outside and opposite the entrance to the Women's Market are food stalls and a hotpot restaurant. To the right of the Flower Market when facing it is a small parking area and an O-Mart stationery store. On the opposite side of Tian Ze Lu is Super Bar Street, which has many international and Chinese restaurants. There is also a second-hand electronics market, which is a great place to buy reconditioned mobile phones. Shops are open from 09:00 to 18:00.

Dongcheng
东城区
🚇 *Wangfujing L1*
Map 10 F2 **109**

Wangfujing 王府井

This is the city's best known shopping area. The mostly pedestrianised street is always busy, but that's part of its charm. Street cafes are full to bursting and water fountains put on elaborate shows along the wide boulevard. Most places are authentic (but pricey), although cheaper goods can be found at the northern end. The city's biggest bookstore, the Wangfujing Bookstore (see p.254) has lots

Wanfujing

Places To Shop

Fingering the goods

of English language publications, particularly travel tomes, while the Oriental Plaza (p.296) is Wangfujing's most popular mall. At the northern end of the street is the Wangfujing Food Market. Opposite the market is a large mobile phone mall. Shops are open daily from 08:00 to 22:00.

Dongcheng
东城区
🚇 *Xidan L1*
Map 10 A2 `110`

Xidan 西单

This is one of Beijing's most popular shopping streets, and a rather unusual mishmash of ultra-modern and downright dingy. The Grand Pacific department store undoubtedly falls into the former, with its glittering Dior and Calvin Klein perfume stands. It stocks good quality everything, including clothes, homewares, sporting goods and designer jewellery. On the opposite side of the street is a rather bizarre selection of cheap clothing outlets, with Adidas, Nike and Reebok at the southern end. The Xidan Department Store, while not as well stocked as the Grand Pacific, does have some nice jewellery and handbags. In between the two is the Xidan Shopping Centre, which is worth the visit for the experience. Like a flea market or jumble sale, it is packed with a mixture of tack and rather nice, affordable clothes. For those in search of electronics, don't miss the Xidan Sci-Tech Square.

The Xidan Cultural Square forms the centre of the area, and is a massive complex of rather un-cultural (but fun) activities including a cinema, bowling alley, swimming pool and climbing wall. The area has loads of places to eat, including street food and Chinese, American and Japanese fastfood chains. Shops are open daily from 08:00 to 22:00.

Xicheng
西城区
Map 8 A1 `111`

Xinjiekou Clothing Street 新街口服装街

Stretching all the way from the Second to the Third Ring Roads, Xinjiekou Clothing Street is often over-looked, but it contains some fantastic shops at decent prices. You can find great, cheap clothing (predominantly women's) that has an individuality often missing from other markets and outlets. It is renowned among Beijing's fashionable but financially limited women as one of the best places to pick up a bargain. Xinjiekou is also well-known for its music and DVD stores and eateries. Shops are open daily from 10:00 to 20:00.

Haidian
海淀区
Map 4 C2 `112`

Zhongguancun Zone 中关村商圈

The Zhongguancun Zone, which stretches from Baishiqiao Lu to Haidian Lu, is in fact a beehive of vast malls, hi-tech businesses and higher learning establishments packed into one area. Often dubbed China's Silicon Valley, the area is a hub of all things electronic, from televisions to computers. Bargaining is a big part of buying, and because the choice is enormous it's best to know roughly what you want before arriving. Shops are open daily from 09:00 to 21:00.

Department Stores

Western-style department stores have not been received with the same enthusiasm as shopping malls. Those that do exist generally attract the expat crowd and are reserved for those with deep pockets or shoppers looking for something special. Cosmetics and perfume are the biggest draws, generally found on the ground floor and stocking top international brands. Most department stores are in busy shopping districts such as Xidan and Wangfujing (see Areas To Shop above and left). Another, different type of department store is the electronics centres. Names such as Gome and Dazhong are scattered across the city, usually denoted by large flags and red balloons. They sell everything that needs batteries or has a plug and are the best place to go for televisions, household electrical items or cameras, with no need to bargain.

Landao Department Store 蓝岛商场

8 Chaoyangmenwai
Dajie
Chaoyang
朝阳门外大街8号
朝阳区
🚇 *Chaoyangmen L2*
Map 11 E1 113

010 8563 4422

In contrast to many other department stores in Beijing, Landao sells mainly Chinese brands and is a fabulous place to get a bargain. For those after something affordable and of better quality than at the markets (p.292), this is a good option. Cosmetics, home wares, perfumes, jewellery, and clothes for the whole family are spread across its busy but pleasant floors. In winter this is arguably the best place to buy a warm, reasonably priced coat (head to the back of the third floor). Open daily 09:00 to 21:00.

Lufthansa Shopping Centre 燕莎购物中心

50 Liangmaqiao Lu
Chaoyang
亮马桥路50号
朝阳区
Map 5 C4 114

010 6465 1188

This is possibly Beijing's best-known department store, and it stands proudly alongside the east Third Ring Road, next to the Kempinski Hotel (p.35). It is home to a wide selection of top quality products, including clothes, a delightful baby section, shoes and bags, homeware items – including fine quality bedding – jewellery, Chinese ornaments, jade items, and a huge toy section. A few eateries run around the outside of the store, including the ever-popular Paulaner Brauhaus German restaurant. Inside, the Lufthansa boasts Beijing's most mouth-watering Italian icecream flavours (on the fourth floor). There is a substantial car park outside. Open 09:00 to 21:00 Monday to Friday and 09:00 to 21:30 Saturday to Sunday.

One World Department Store 世都百货

99 Wangfujing Dajie
Dongcheng
王府井大街99号
东城区
🚇 *Wangfujing L1*
Map 10 F3 115

010 6526 7890

This glamorous department store has marble floors and shimmering lights, providing a plush setting. There is a mixture of international and Chinese brands - good quality at steep prices is the general theme. Christian Dior and Versace are available, while unique clothing lines come from more obscure - but by no means less interesting - Chinese designers. Amid the women's wear on the second floor is a tasteful, but over-priced, cafe. A great selection of imported children's toys can be found on the fourth floor. Open daily 10:00 to 22:00.

Markets

Beijing's markets are a must-try for expats, on a par with hiking the Great Wall (p.198), flying a kite in Tiananmen Square (p.162) or soaking up the history of the Forbidden City (p.180). However, you'll soon realise that there is more to Beijing's scene than the tourist traps of the Silk and Yashow markets, with their fake brands and pushy vendors, although these certainly have their place. Antiques, paintings, electronics, flowers, clothes and the latest footwear fashions can all be found by those in the know.

Bainahui Electronics Market 百脑汇电子市场

8 Chaoyangmenwai
Dajie
Chaoyang
朝阳门外大街8号
朝阳区
🚇 *Chaoyangmen L2*
Map 11 E1 116

While not quite in the same league as Zhongguancun (p.296), Bainahui has a wide selection and, most importantly, a good reputation. The six floors contain computers with associated gadgets, mobile phones, MP3 players, gaming systems and other techy bits. You will need to bargain, but most vendors start at reasonable prices. Be sure to get a receipt, but if you want to risk it, you may get a cheaper price without one. You'll also need to take a store card, so you can exchange items without problems. It is advisable to wear light clothes, as the building seems to suffer from a heat problem in both summer and winter. Open daily 09:00 to 18:00.

Beijing Curio City 北京古玩城

21 Donsanhuan Nanlu
Chaoyang
东三环南路21号
朝阳区
Map 7 D4 **117**

010 6774 7711
For those who don't want their home filled with IKEA, this market is a fantastic place to find antiques and curios with lots of character. Curio City has a good reputation for selling many original pieces, although the increase in tour groups has lowered the standard somewhat. It is still a great place to peruse the old furniture, clocks, paintings, jade, pottery, ornaments and other collectables that fill its four floors. Vendors start their prices high, so be prepared for a long bargaining session. Open daily 09:30 to 18:00.

Beijing Zoo Clothing Market 北京动物园服装市场

Xizhimenwai Dajie
Xicheng
西直门外大街
西城区
🚇 *Fuchengmen L2*
Map 6 D1 **118**

010 8835 2668
Claustrophobics are best advised to steer clear of the Zoo Clothing Market, especially on weekends when stampedes are part of the experience. Opposite the zoo, above the bus station, is this colossal, shabby-looking market. The second floor is dedicated to women's fashions which are the best reasons to go. For those weary of half hour bargaining sessions in the tourist markets, price tags come as a welcome treat, especially with such small numbers on them. Most tops and jackets however, are one size only, so may not fit westerners. The same can be said for the third floor jeans stalls. The fourth floor men's section is limited compared to the fabulous women's selection, but does have some good, well-priced suits. Food options are pretty limited too, so go on a full stomach. The area around the Zoo Market has other shopping opportunities, including the Wantong New World Commodities Fair, housed in the unmistakable cucumber-shaped buildings linked to the Fuchengmen subway station on Line 2 (exit D). From there it's a short taxi ride to the Zoo Clothing Market.

Panjiayuan 潘家园

18 Huawei Lu
Panjiayuan Lu
Chaoyang
潘家园路华威里18号
朝阳区
Map 7 C4 **119**

This open-air market is crammed full of thousands of stalls selling a fascinating array of jade, agate, old books, furniture, coins, ceramics, ornaments, Cultural Revolution memorabilia and decorative items from many of China's ethnic minorities. It is a bustling, intriguing marketplace, though many of the wares are not genuine. On weekends, one end of the market opens to artists, who sell their works for decent prices. There is a mixture of modern and traditional Chinese styles on offer. The antique area is open daily 08:00 to 18:00, with the art area open on Saturdays and Sundays from 05:00 to 18:00.

Pearl Market (Hongqiao Market) 虹桥市场

Tian Tan Dong Lu
Chongwen
天坛东路
崇文区
Map 7 A4 **120**

010 6711 9130
Just a precious stone's throw from the Temple of Heaven (p.188), Beijing's Pearl Market is, as you might expect, the best place to buy pearls and jewellery. While the rest of the market sells similar items to Silk (p.294) and Yashow (p.294), it is the stones and pearls that make this place stand out. The third floor is an Aladdin's cave of fresh water pearls, jade, antiques, handicrafts and ornaments, with the fourth floor devoted to pricier, more upmarket stones. The second floor is home to a grand selection of bags, suitcases, wallets, silk items and shoes, and is a fantastic place to buy gifts. The standard market fare on the first floor

Panjiayuan Market

includes cosmetics, fake watches and mobile phone accessories. The basement is home to a potent, but interesting, collection of foods. As with all of the city's markets, don't be afraid to bargain hard or you will pay grossly over the odds. Open daily 08:30 to 19:30.

8 Xiushui Dongjie
Chaoyang
秀水东街8号
朝阳区
Yonganli L1
Map 11 C3 121

Silk Market (Xiushui) 秀水街

010 5169 8800 | *www.xiushui.com.cn/english.*
This is the most popular market in Beijing for tourists. The indoor market has six floors of cheap, fake goods of varying degrees of quality. The basement offers the best selection of copied shoes, boots, bags and suitcases in the city, but you have to bargain hard (and not mind being grabbed at by the elbow by over-zealous vendors).

Silk Market

Men's and women's clothes deck out the ground and first floors while silk, tailoring services and children's clothes can be found on the second floor. The third floor has sunglasses, watches and pearls, although the Pearl Market (p.293) is a better option for the latter.

As with most indoor markets, the top floor has a foodcourt, each stall selling pretty much the same as its neighbour. There are several over-priced and not particularly pleasant cafes outside. There is a small car park, but public transport is more convenient. Open daily 09:00 to 21:00.

58 Gongti Beilu
Sanlitun
工体北路58号
朝阳区
Chaoyangmen L2
Map 9 E3 122

Yashow & New Yashow 雅秀服装城

010 6416 8945
These two markets are almost identical, but New Yashow is considerably less crowded and has fewer stalls. The large square buildings have several themed floors, ranging from clothing and shoes to bags and tea sets. Silk, copied designer clothes and jackets, a nail salon, pearls and home wares are the main attractions for the bus loads of people that pour through the doors. Late afternoons are the best time to visit, as the coaches have departed for the day.

Both markets have large Chinese-style foodcourts on the top floor, but for something a bit different try the Paris Baguette outside New Yashow. You can get ready-made sandwiches as well as baked goods to take home. New Yashow is on Chaoyangmen Waidajie. Open daily 09:00 to 21:00.

Other Markets

Baoguosi Flea Market	North end of Guanganmennei Dajie	Xuanwu
Beisihuan Lighting Market	Nanhu Liugongzhucun, Laiguangying Xiang	Chaoyang
Chaowai Antique Furniture Market	43 Huwai Beili	Chaoyang
Chengwaicheng Furniture Market	303 Chengshousi Lu (north-east of Xiaocun Qian on Nansihuan)	Fengtai
Gaobeidian Antique Furniture Village	435 Gaobeidian Gu Jiajucun	Chaoyang
Huasheng Laotian Qiao	Shiliheqiao (south-east corner of Panjiayuan)	Chaoyang
International Textile Market	9 Houcun, Dahongmen Lu	Fengtai
Laitai Flower Market	9 Maizidian Xi Lu	Chaoyang
Shilihe Lighting Market	East side of Shilihe Qiao, Dongsanhuan Nanlu	Chaoyang
Xinji Yuan Stone Market	Nansanhuan Dong Lu	Chaoyang

Shopping Malls

New shopping malls appear to sprout up from the smoggy streets every day. They are seen as an advancement of the Chinese middle classes and a sign of prosperity and modernisation. While Beijing's ultra-pricey centres of consumerism are a sparkly sign of the country's development, many malls have perhaps come too soon. The Chinese love to peruse, but it is only a select few who can afford the high-end goods. Mall culture in Beijing is most definitely a western import, with architecture adopting the generic blend of marble, glass and soft lighting seen everywhere. As a rule, shopping malls house the most elite shops, with international brands occupying prime space. The opening hours are a perk for shopaholics; malls are open seven days a week until 21:00 or 22:00. Weekends are the busiest time to visit.

3.3 (San San) Shopping Mall 3. 3服饰　大厦

33 Sanlitun Beijie
Sanlitun
三里屯北街33号
朝阳区
Map 9 F2 **123**

010 6417 8886 | *www.3d3.cn*

The 3.3 Shopping Mall is easily found on Sanlitun's Bar Street. Fronted by bright neon lighting, this mall has 300 stores on five floors. It is aimed at women, although there are a few men's shops too, and houses a wonderful selection of funky, home-grown boutiques, as well as the latest fashions from Korea and Japan. The basement floor is not yet full, but there are some unique home decoration stores selling Chinese art and sculpture, clocks, candles and handicrafts. Despite its relatively good prices and unique products, 3.3 is rarely crowded. There is a Xinjiang-style restaurant on the top floor and a cafe on the ground floor. Parking can be a problem and is limited to vacant street spaces, which incur the standard public parking fees. Open daily, 09:30 to 23:00.

China World Shopping Mall 国贸商城

1 Jianguomenwai Dajie
Chaoyang
建国门外大街1号
朝阳区
🚇 *Guomao L1*
Map 11 E1 **124**

010 6505 2288 | *www.cwtc.com*

Housed in the China World Trade Centre complex, this is one of the city's best-known and most prestigious malls. It covers 60,000sqm over four floors and has its own indoor ice skating rink (p.217). The mall boasts more than 200 shops which lean towards designer clothes, furniture and children's toys. The decor and architecture is plush, with brands such as Gucci, Prada, and Dior, though more affordable stores can also be found. There are lots of eateries, ranging from fastfood outlets (featuring the whole cast of American imports) to cafes and international restaurants. A directory of all the mall's shops can be found on the website. There are thousands of parking spaces. Open daily, 10:00 to 22:00.

Golden Resources Shopping Mall 金源时代购物中心

Yuanda Lu
Haidian
远大路
海淀区
Map 4 A4 **125**

010 8887 5888

To grasp the sheer enormity of the world's second largest (smaller only than its counterpart in Dongguan), you need to consider a few figures. There are 230 escalators, more than 1,000 shops, a skating rink, car park with 10,000 spaces and food courts covering an area the size of two football pitches. Despite its size, the mall is still relatively unheard of among expats, perhaps due to the fact that

The Place (p.296)

few stores accept foreign credit cards. Listing what you can find inside the mall is futile, as the array of goods is so vast. Price tags however, tend to have a lot of digits. The mall hasn't attracted truly big international names, but there are plenty of lesser-known imported goods. It is an experience and as yet, not too crowded. Open daily, 09:30 to 21:00.

1 Dongchangan Jie
Dongcheng
东长安街1号
东城区
🚇 *Wangfujing L1*
Map 7 A2 126

Oriental Plaza 东方广场
010 8518 6363 | www.orientalplaza.com
This is Beijing's best-known and most visited mall. It sits on prime real estate in the heart of the Wangfujing area and is a hub of food, entertainment and shopping. The mall is divided into six themed zones; Market Square, Metro City, Garden Court, International Boulevard, Wonderful World and Sky Avenue. Top fashion names such as Vera Moda, Max Mara, Valentino, Paul Smith and Bally glitter alongside Swarovski, Apple computers, a huge Nikon store and the city's largest CD and DVD shop. The Wonderful World zone (dedicated to all things sporting and entertaining) even has Volkswagen and Audi stores.
There are hundreds of eating options, ranging from food courts to cafes to exclusive restaurants. Those with grumbling stomachs should head to the Metro City zone where Gourmet Street offers an eye-popping selection of international food. The zone is also home to the Sony ExploraScience Museum. The 1,800 space car park charges ¥2.5 per half hour. Open daily, 09:30 to 22:00.

9A Guanghua Lu
Chaoyang
光华路甲9号
朝阳区
Map 7 C2 127

The Place 世贸天阶
010 8595 1755
This is probably the city's most architecturally impressive mall. The huge overhead movie screen is its most distinguishing feature, playing a spool of sea creatures swimming above you. Shops such as MNG (p.259), Miss Sixty, French Connection and Zara (p.260) are among the brands available, along with Adidas, the Swiss Perfumery Shop and M.A.C makeup. Affordable boutique jewellery stands line the floors, where you can pick up some nice trinkets.
Food outlets are rare, although there is a Japanese restaurant on the top floor of the left-hand building. The mall also puts on arguably the best Christmas show in the city, with lights and a 10m tree to get shoppers into the festive feeling. Open daily, 10:00 to 22:00.

12 Zhongguancun
Nandajie
Haidian
中关村南大街12号
海淀区
Map 4 C3 128

Zhongguancun Mall 中关村购物中心
Amid the electronics fervour of the Zhongguancun hi-tech area, this new mall is characterised by good quality products at discounted prices. It is next to Carrefour (p.297) and is a great place to hunt for home ware items, furnishings, sporting equipment, branded clothing outlets and unique boutiques. There is a decent selection of eateries inside, including a Haagen Dazs icecream parlour. Open daily, 09:00 to 21:00.

Shopping Malls

Capital Shopping Mall	Wangjing, 33 Guangshun Beidajie	010 8472 2574
CAT Lifestyle Mall	Star City, 10 Jiuxianqiao Lu	010 5838 5555
COFCO Plaza	Jianguo Men Nei Dajie 8	010 6526 6666
Kerry Mall	1 Guanghua Lu	010 8391 3311
Pacific Century Place	2a Gongti Beilu	010 6539 3888
Peninsula Hotel	8 Goldfish Lane	010 8516 2888
Shin Yong Place	87 Jiango Lu	010 6530 5888
Xidan Shopping Center	132 Xidan Baidajie	010 6602 5016

Supermarkets & Hypermarkets

With the exception of the small chain of Jenny Lou stores that stock some imported items, supermarkets are different to what most expats are used to. The big chains tend to be crowded and stressful, particularly Carrefour, although most endure a visit at least once. Local produce markets, while basic, are best for fresh fruit and vegetables, as the fresh goods sold in the big hypermarkets are often below par. They are dotted all over the city. Meat and fish aren't refrigerated, so it's best to stick to the supermarkets for these, particularly in the summer.

Various Locations

7-Eleven 便利店

www.7-11bj.com.cn

There are 55 branches dotted throughout Beijing. They sell the very barest of essentials, but more branches are offering fresh milk and bread. If you're looking for chocolate, nuts or boiled meats, then this is the place to go, although they do have a selection of toiletries. The website is in Chinese, but has a store locator map on the homepage.

31 Guangqu Lu
Chaoyang
广渠路31号
朝阳区
Map 11 D2 **129**

Carrefour 家乐福

010 5190 9580 | *www.carrefour.com.cn*

Carrefour is the big name in Beijing's supermarkets. As stressful, congested and hectic as it is, you'll find extremely varied goods on offer. Customers are normally shepherded upstairs first, to the homewares, clothing, electrical and hardware items. These tend to be reasonably priced and of good quality. Downstairs, the food selection is aimed towards Chinese customers, although there is a small aisle of imported fare. The fruit and vegetables are not particularly fresh, but the organic vegetable section is considerably better. Meat and fish are generally still wriggling, so the squeamish might want to steer clear. There is a fairly good array of toiletries, although some feminine products and spray deodorants are not sold. Delivery is available. Other stores can be found at 11 Maliandao Lu, Xuanwu (010 6332 2155); Fangyuan Building, 56 Zhongguancun Nandajie, Haidian (010 8836 2729); Zhongguancun Plaza, Haidian (010 5172 1517) and 6 Beisanhuan Donglu, Chaoyang (010 8460 1013).

6 Sanlitun Beixiaojie
Chaoyang
三里屯北小街6号
朝阳区
Map 7 D1 **130**

Jenny Lou's 婕妮璐食品店

010 6461 6928

Most expats crave home comforts at some point. This is where Jenny Lou steps in. These small supermarkets are a godsend to foreigners, and sell a fantastic assortment of imported goods. They are considerably pricier than the local supermarkets, but you get what you pay for. The Lido branch has a particularly good wine selection, while the Sanlitun, Ritan and Chaoyang branches have better cheese and deli counters. The Chaoyang branch also has a wonderful bakery. Fresh fruit and vegetables are overpriced but considerably better than Carrefour. While the Sanlitun store closes at 22:00, the others are all open from 08:00 to midnight. Other stores can be found at the west gate of Chaoyang Park (010 6501 6249); Building 4, Jianwai SOHO, Chaoyang (010 5869 2253); 4 Ritan Beilu, Chaoyang (010 8563 2316) and 1 Nongzhanquan Nanlu (010 6507 5207).

B1 Wanda Plaza
Jianguo Lu Plaza, 93
Jianguo Lu
Chaoyang
建国路93号万达广场B1
朝阳区
Map 7 D2 **131**

Wal-Mart 沃尔玛

010 5960 3566 | *www.wal-martchina.com*

The American brand has found its way to China and there are now branches scattered across the city. It stocks the hardware and homeware items that have made it so popular across the pond. As with all Beijing imports, Wal-Mart now has a definite 'Chinese' flavour. Stores are open from 07:30 to 22:00. There are two others, one at B1, Ground Floor, Top Real Garden Plaza, Xuanwai Jie, Xuanwu (010 6316 8905), and another at B1, Ground and First Floors, 4th Mansion, 48 A Zhichun Lu, Haidian (010 5873 3666).

since 1947

CRI ENGLISH

91.5FM, 846AM and 1008AM in Beijing
www.crienglish.com

Going Out

Going Out

Beijing's nightlife peaks on Friday and Saturday nights, when whole areas come alive with inviting music, neon lights and throngs of people. Alcohol flows freely, although prices do tend to be over-inflated in expat drinking areas like Sanlitun. There are bars and clubs that are very Chinese, and others frequented mainly by expats, students and tourists. This is more a question of taste than discrimination, and everyone is welcome in every venue.

Nightlife begins late, and until 23:00 you're likely to have the place to yourself. Bars don't tend to close until the last customer has stumbled out the door. There is currently a bar and nightclub boom with new places popping up every week, so check local magazines (p.51) for new venues. Most bars don't charge entrance fees, although clubs sometimes charge up to ¥100 per person.

KTV (karaoke bars) are much-loved across China. Groups hire private booths to sing (and drink) their hearts out, content in the knowledge that only friends can hear. Most are kitsch and flashy, but usually fun. Try The Bank (p.341), Tango (p.343) or Goose & Duck (p.332).

The exceptionally low cost of DVDs means cinema (p.346) is not popular, but can make a good option for families with children. English-language cinemas can be found, but are priced as they might be in the west, and are often noisy.

Beijing's many theatres (p.347) often host western plays, concerts and ballet as well as showing plenty of Chinese entertainment. Tourists tend to enjoy the Beijing opera, while the acrobatics shows are a big hit with all ages and nationalities.

Closing Time
Restaurants generally close early, while bars and clubs stay open late. Restaurants tend to take a break after lunch and stop serving dinner at around 21:00 (with the exception of more touristy or upmarket places). Finding a Chinese restaurant open in the mid afternoon is rare but foreign restaurants stay open later. Bars and clubs open mid evening, get going late, and close when the last punter goes home. Most places stay open over weekends and national holidays

Eating Out

Beijing's dining scene can satisfy most cravings. There are restaurants offering fare from most corners of the globe. Every type of Chinese cuisine is represented too. Sichuan restaurants abound, as do Xinjiang and Yunnan cuisine. Meanwhile, the flood of expats and their accompanying palates has created a market for international food. Hotels offer familiar western fare, but you can also find charming restaurants serving mouthwatering Brazilian delicacies or diet busting Tex-Mex dishes.

Finding an early western breakfast is impossible outside of hotels (unlike brunches, which are plentiful). You may find that many of the Chinese restaurants you frequent in the evening rent their space out to morning cooks who drum up wonton soup, steamed dumplings, or long, deep-fried doughnuts served with a bowl of savoury rice porridge. These breakfasts are typically washed down with a hot cup of sweet soymilk. A popular street breakfast is *jianbing* (see Street Food, p.303).

Choices for lunch and dinner are more varied. Popular restaurants always draw a crowd, regardless of the day of the week. Opening hours vary, but expect service between 10:00 and 21:00. Some local restaurants close between 14:00 and 16:00. International restaurants typically run seasonal promotions – turkey dinners at Christmas, or set

Cuisine List – Quick Reference

African	p.304	Fusion	p.314	Mediterranean	p.319
American	p.304	Indian	p.314	Middle Eastern	p.320
British	p.305	Italian	p.315	Russian	p.321
Caribbean	p.305	Japanese	p.316	Spanish	p.321
Chinese	p.305	Korean	p.317	Thai	p.322
European	p.311	Latin American	p.317	Vegetarian	p.322
French	p.313	Malaysian	p.318	Vietnamese	p.323

menus on Valentine's Day, for example. The five-star hotels have regular promotions, usually featuring guest chefs. For those with children, there are several child-friendly eateries. Most places in Shunyi are equipped with booster chairs and menus for kids. International places tend to be clustered in the CBD, Sanlitun, and Lido.

Chinese Cuisine

Discounts
Some foreign restaurants offer loyalty cards, which award 10% discounts. New restaurants, bars, and clubs often provide discount vouchers in expat magazines (p.51). Most bars have happy hours (normally starting between 19:00 and 21:00) where local beers such as Qingdao are cheaper.

Chinese cuisine takes many different forms, but the most influential genres are referred to as the 'eight cuisines'. These are Shandong, Sichuan, Guangdong, Fujian, Jiangsu, Zhejiang, Hunan, and Anhui. Distinctions are a complex result of geography, cooking traditions and ingredients, and each has its own sub categories.
Beijing does not make the big eight, but that does not mean the capital lacks gastronomic merit. The most famous dish is Peking duck, also known as Beijing roast duck. The meal consists of a wood-fire roasted ex-quacker, sliced at the table and served with bamboo baskets of rice pancakes. Diners place slices of duck, cucumber, spring onions, crushed garlic, and plum sauce inside, and wrap everything up into a roll. Beijing is also known for imperial cuisine. Local chefs developed a complex cooking style devoted to fresh ingredients to please generations of emperors. Elaborate vegetable carvings are an aesthetic reminder of this culinary discipline. Hot pot is another popular dish locally, and is something like an Oriental fondue. You get a skewer and raw ingredients like sliced meat, cabbage and potatoes then add them to a boiling pot of soup.

Chinese Cuisine

Beijing	Huajia Yiyuan	p.308
Cantonese & Dim Sum	Din Tai Fung	p.306
	Horizon	p.308
	Xian Lao Man	p.311
Contemporary	Paper	p.309
	People 8	p.309
	Whampoa Club	p.311
Hakka	Han Cang	p.308
Hotpot	Ding Ding Xiang	p.306
	Sange Guizhou Ren	p.310
Imperial	Red Capital Club	p.310
Mixed	Da Li Courtyard	p.306
	Kuan Dian	p.308
	Sansheng Wanwu	p.310
	Xiao Wang Fu	p.311
Peking Duck	Da Dong Kaoya Dian	p.306
	Liqun	p.308
	Made In China	p.309
Shanxi	Noodle Loft	p.309
	Paomo Guan	p.309
Sichuan	Baguo Buyi	p.305
	Sichuan Representative Restaurant	p.310
	Source	p.310
	South Beauty	p.311
	Xiongdi	p.311
Taiwanese	Bellagio	p.306
Xinjiang	Crescent Moon Muslim Restaurant	p.306
Yunnan	No Name	p.309

Perhaps the most popular Chinese cuisine (one of the eight) is Sichuan. Regional interpretations sometimes tone down the spice for Beijing's northern palates. Dumplings and dim sum are popular staples of Cantonese (Guangzhou) food. This is the stuff that is most typically exported to the west, and is likely to have the most recognisable dishes. Shanxi restaurants should placate those with a fondness for noodles. For an interesting experience in local cuisine, sign up for a Chinese cooking class (p.210). Several places offer instruction in English, and hotels sometimes host special classes.

Delivery & Takeaways

Most restaurants will deliver to within a few kilometres, though ordering usually requires some level of Mandarin. Western restaurants in the embassy districts and the CBD can often take orders in English. American sandwich chain Subway (010 8283 8918) boasts that it will deliver any order, even a cookie. Similarly, McDonald's will deliver all meals except breakfast. Upscale restaurants typically do not offer individual delivery or takeaway.

Beijing Goodies (www.beijinggoodies.com), has struck up partnerships with several excellent restaurants, and you can order dishes from their menus online at the company's website. Service charges range from ¥20 to ¥150 and vary by location.

Hygiene

Hygiene standards run the gamut. Some upscale restaurants have open kitchens and strict cleanliness standards, but local dives and street vendors are part of the Beijing experience. Raw meat lying uncovered in the sun or a less than sparkling set of bowls and plates are to be expected at such establishments. Trust your intuition. If you see something has been left uncovered for a long period of time or you suspect your meat has not been cooked at a high enough temperature, send it back or leave it. Your stomach will thank you for your caution. If you are worried about offending, apologise for your weak foreign constitution rather than scolding your hosts for their hygiene standards.

Special Deals & Theme Nights

Most international restaurants have special offers for holidays like Christmas, Thanksgiving and Easter. Expat favourite Steak & Eggs (Xiushui Nanjie, Jianguomenwai, 010 6592 8088, www.steakeggs.com.cn) does popular Thanksgiving specials. Hotel restaurants also have regular promotions celebrating specific regional and international cuisines. Several bars and pubs throw green dye in a pint to celebrate St Patrick's Day. And like every other city on earth, Beijing has Irish bars. Try Durty Nellies (p.331) or Paddy O'Shea's (p.336). Regular quiz nights are offered at Bar Blu (p.342) and Sequoia Café (44 Guanghua Lu, 010 6501 5503). Student district bars, Lush (p.334) and D-22 (p.343), host open mic nights and movie screenings. The best place for special events is The Bookworm (p.324), on the south side of Sanlitun. It hosts book talks by local and international authors, screens documentaries, and even holds live classical music events. The partitioned layout, with three generously sized rooms, means there is always an escape route if the event isn't what you expected.

The Yellow Star
The natty yellow star seen to the right highlighs places that merit extra praise. It might be the atmosphere, the food, the cocktails, the music or the crowd, but any review that you see with the star attached marks somewhere that's a bit special.

Tax & Service Charges

Upmarket hotel bars and restaurants sometimes add service charges. The typical rate is 15%. Service charges should be stated, often in small print, at the bottom of menus.

Tipping

Tipping doesn't happen. Culturally, the practice is anathema, partly because it hints at superiority and a lack of respect, and partly because self sufficiency is so prized. Those who try to leave a few extra *kuai* often find shocked waiters return their money, and may even chase them down the street.

Vegetarian Food

Chinese restaurants offer many dishes that appear to be meat free, but may dissatisfy veggies. Several vegetable dishes contain pieces of chopped pork or beef that are not stated in the menu. Other dishes may be alternately fried or sauteed in animal fat as opposed to vegetable or peanut oil. Chinese cuisine isn't necessarily over laden with meat products, but the absence of any meat whatsoever is rare. Any upscale restaurant will cater to specific orders or try Pure Lotus (p.322), a popular vegetarian restaurant, with English speaking staff who can explain dishes.

Street Food

For an adventurous street food experience, visit the night market at Deng Shi Kou, at the northern end of Wangfujing (p.290). This outdoor market showcases an unrivalled selection of street food, everything from deep friend crickets to sauteed tripe. Avoid food poisoning by sticking to items that are freshly cooked at bacteria-killing temperatures prior to serving. Around Beijing, the most common types of street food are *chuan'r*, kebabs of meat or seafood, and *jianbing*, a flour-based crepe spread with egg, plum sauce, hot sauce, chopped spring onions, and coriander, all folded over a crispy fried wafer. *Jianbing* is often eaten at breakfast, but can be found at all hours of the day. *Baozi*, steamed buns stuffed with fillings like pork and cabbage, spicy tofu, or sweet red bean paste, are very popular, as are steamed dumplings. In Sanlitin, Fish Nation (p.305) is the best place for takeaway fish and chips at 02:00. Nearby, Kebab Republic (1/F Tongli Studio, Sanlitun, 010 6417 4119) offers late night shawarmas.

Candied yams

Street food (p.303)

Capital Theatre (p.347)

African

22 Xingba Lu
Laitaihua Jie
Chaoyang
星吧路22号莱太花街
朝阳区
Map 5 D3 🔳

Pili Pili 比利必利
010 8448 4332

Pili Pili offers spicy African food, with a focus on barbecue and West African cuisine, plus a few Egyptian dishes. A good selection of cocktails and plenty of diplomats make for an interesting night out. Granted, the dancing acts aren't always great, but where else in Beijing can you buy gifts straight from sub Sahara? Prices are reasonable, and quality ranges from dismal spaghetti to excellent spicy skewers of assorted meats. Open until 02:00 and decorated with African art, Pili Pili is a good start to a night drinking in one of the many nearby bars. Most of the art is for sale.

American

Chaoyang Gongyuan
Xilu
Chaoyang
朝阳公园西路
朝阳区
Map 5 D4 🔳

Chef Too 美西西餐厅
010 6591 8676

Beijing is a town where you'll be hard pressed to find a diner, much less one with good coffee. One of the nicer American restaurants in town, Chef Too bills itself as 'fine neighborhood dining'. Excellent service and wonderful food are let down slightly by the prices. It offers great steaks and one of the best brunches in town. The set business lunch is a bargain, and be sure to ask about the specials.

1-2/F Building B
Jianwai SOHO, 39
Dongsanhuan Zhonglu
Chaoyang
东三环中路39号建外
SOHOB座1-2层
朝阳区
Map 7 D3 🔳

Grandma's Kitchen 祖母的厨房
010 5869 3055

If you were to pick a restaurant that encompassed 'comfort food' for north American expats, this might be it. Straddling the line between homestyle American cuisine and high-end diner, Grandma's Kitchen provides shakes, griddles, and mac n cheese. The popular breakfasts are served all day, but their dinner entrees are worth a try too. Open 07:30 to 23:00. There is another restaurant at 47-2 Nanchizi Dajie, Tiananmen (010 6528 2790) which is open from 08:00 to 22:30.

201, Building 1, China
View Building, Gongti
Beilu
Chaoyang
工体北路中国红街
1号201
朝阳区
Map 9 E3 🔳

Hooters 猫头鹰餐厅
010 6585 8787 | www.hooters.com

The staple of the American experience has made it to Beijing, bringing its greasy jalapeno chili cheese fries and 119 sauce. Peppy, scantily-clad servers with a desire to please are at the beck and call of foreigners and locals at this 'American Owl Restaurant' – the translation for 'Hooters' in Chinese. This is a slightly different experience than in the US, and is more likely to attract people for the dependable American-style food. It is, however, one of the few places where even your vegetables are deep-fried.

Gongti Beimen
Workers' Stadium
north gate
Chaoyang
工人体育场北门
朝阳区
Map 9 E3 🔳

Kro's Nest 乌巢
010 6553 5253

Kro's Nest pizzas are highly-coveted. The bubbly crusts and cheesy goodness remind many north Americans of the wonderfully greasy pizzas back home. On the downside, the salads are a little expensive and the difference between their thin crust and thick crust is mostly in the name. The restaurant itself is

Dumplings

a charming party place (open until 02:00 at weekends) filled with booths, and the two laid-back young owners are often around. Delivery isn't yet available.

One East On Third 东方路一号西餐厅

Hilton Beijing
Chaoyang
东方路1号
朝阳区
Map 5 C4 **6**

010 5865 5000 | www.beijing.hilton.com

This isn't your average hotel restaurant. One East on Third boasts the largest selection of American wines in town, and a classic interior to accompany the outstanding steaks. Prices are steep, but the blackened prawns and dessert selection make up for the toll on your wallet. It suffers from uneven service, but is still the closest thing you can find to an upmarket American steakhouse. This is a popular place for impressing clients.

Tim's Texas Roadhouse 西部牛仔餐吧

**27 Xingba Lu
(near Nurenjie)**
Chaoyang
星吧路27号 (女人街
附近)
朝阳区
Map 5 D3 **7**

010 6461 1141

Pool table, dartboards, regular events, and slightly kitschy country and western decor – all you would expect from somewhere with Texas in the name. This is a great place to catch the game, grab a burger, dine on barbecue dishes or try the Cajun chicken. Portions are large, in keeping with the American theme, but prices are decent. The staff even make a mean cocktail.

British

Fish Nation 1 鱼邦

43 Sanlitun Nanlu
Sanlitun
三里屯南路43号
三里屯
Map 9 F2 **8**

010 6415 0119

There are two locations offering massive pieces of hot battered fish served with vinegary chips. The newer restaurant in the up and coming Nanluoguxiang neighbourhood is nicer than the small-but-beloved spot in Sanlitun. It even serves decent pizza and breakfasts. Open late for those looking for a bite after a night out, both have a wide selection of beers. Tartar sauce, ketchup and garlic sauce are available, and local tastes have been accommodated with the inclusion of tempura-battered offerings. Don't expect a date to be impressed by the decor, but for a fast taste of the UK, Fish Nation can't be beaten. They even print their own newspapers to wrap their greasy goods in. The other branch is at 31 Jiaodaokou, Nanluoguxiang (010 6401 3249).

Caribbean

Trader Vic's 垂德维客餐厅

**3/F Building C, China
International Trade
Center, 6 Jianguomen
Waidajie**
Chaoyang
建国门外大街6号中国国
际贸易中心C座
朝阳区
Map 11 F3 **9**

010 5869 5336 | www.tradervicschina.com

This is a bright addition to the area near Jianwai SOHO. Beijing now has a bit of over-the-top Caribbean and Polynesian – tiki torches, canoes, and all. However, it is tucked away on the second floor of an intimidating office complex and can be a bit hard to find. Though prices are on the high side for many dishes, the food is great, the drinks are stiff, and the staff are friendly. Standards like Hawaiian pork chops, barbecued chicken, crab wontons, and a wide range of desserts are available, and though the dishes aren't likely to wow anyone, the swanky surroundings and overwhelming kitsch might.

Chinese

Baguo Buyi 巴国布衣

89-3 Dianmendong Dajie
Dongcheng
地安门东大街89-3号
东城区
Map 8 D3 **10**

010 6400 8888

Arrive before 20:00 to catch the nightly mask-changing show. Diners gather on the stairwell around a small stage to watch the lively Sichuanese performance, which involves split-second mask changes choreographed to traditional music. The performer of the day walks among audience members and performs the magic trick up close, much to the crowd's delight. All the regular Sichuan favourites are here, and the *dandan mian* – yellow noodles served in a spicy broth, are especially tasty.

Bellagio 鹿港小镇

6 Gongti Xilu
Chaoyang
工体西路6号
朝阳区
Map 9 D4 **11**

010 6551 3553
Shaved ice desserts and salty Taiwanese dishes are the main attraction at Bellagio. The stylish restaurant draws a mixed crowd of hip young Chinese and expats from the nearby clubs. Bellagio has a strict aesthetic that extends to its staff – everyone sports an ultra short, spiky haircut. Do not miss out on the Taiwanese stewed minced pork or dragon beans stir-fried with garlic. Those with a sweet tooth can order the mango shaved ice or the peanut ice smoothie (it tastes like a frozen Reese's Peanut Butter Cup).

Crescent Moon Muslim Restaurant 弯弯的月亮

16 Dongsi Liu Tiao
Dongcheng
东四六条16号
东城区
Map 9 A4 **12**

010 6400 5281
Xinjiang is in China's far north west and borders the Tibet autonomous region. Many of its minority groups are Muslim, and the food has a distinctly Middle Eastern flavour. The Uigher staff dish up homemade yogurt and generous mutton kebabs. The *dapanji*, a stew of chicken, potatoes, onions, and peppers served with traditional Xinjiang naan bread, is popular for groups. The restaurant is scruffy, but clean and authentic.

Da Dong Kaoya Dian 大董烤鸭店

International Plaza
22a Dongsi Shi Tiao
Chaoyang
东四十条甲22号南新仓
国际大厦1-2层
朝阳区
🚇 *Dongsishitiao L2*
Map 9 B3 **13**

010 5169 0329
Da Dong makes superb Peking duck. The expansive Nanxincang restaurant has the bright fluorescent lighting that plagues most Chinese restaurants, but the decor, screens with bamboo calligraphy and wooden furniture, is unobtrusive. On display behind glass windows near the entrance is a wood burning oven roasting succulent ducks. As with most duck restaurants, you should place your order when you make reservations. This is an excellent place for large groups.

Da Li Courtyard 大里院子

67 Xiaojingchang
Hutong
Dongcheng
鼓楼东大街小经厂胡
同67号
东城区
🚇 *Beixinqiao L5*
Map 8 E2 **14**

010 8404 1430
A courtyard gem in the heart of Beijing's old *hutongs*, Da Li serves set menus that favour larger groups. You'll find that small groups get less choice, but pay similar prices. The alfresco dining in the central courtyard is wonderful during the summer, while rooms lining the perimeter stave off the cold in winter. The decor is traditional Chinese, with the odd retro poster thrown in for good measure. The *hutong* runs off Gulou Dong Dajie.

Din Tai Fung 鼎泰丰餐厅

24 Xinyuan Xili
Zhongjie
Chaoyang
新源西里中街24号
朝阳区
Map 9 E1 **15**

010 6462 4592
This dumpling chain had humble beginnings in Taiwan, but vaulted to international prominence when *The New York Times* named it one of the best restaurants in the world back in the mid 90s. The must-order dish is *xiaolongbao*; savoury, soup-filled pork dumplings in delicate, thin wrappers. The large restaurant has a lively atmosphere and is a popular place for diplomatic families.

Ding Ding Xiang 鼎鼎香

1/F, 14 Dong Zhong Jie
Dongcheng
东中街14号1层
东城区
Map 9 C2 **16**

010 6417 2546
Hotpot meals are DIY affairs – diners chose from an assortment of raw dishes, including sliced meat, cabbage, and potatoes, then add them to a boiling pot of soup. At Ding Ding Xiang, you get individual hotpots. This is a departure from the group atmosphere

of regular joints, where a giant pot of boiling soup is placed in the middle of the table for all to enjoy. However, this method comes with its advantages; you can order your preferred soup base, and you're assured everything is yours for the taking. The sesame dipping sauce is some of the best in town.

Han Cang 汉仓客家菜

12 Qianhai Nan Yan
Houhai
前海南沿12号
后海
Map 8 C2 **17**

010 6404 2259
The short wooden stools can be uncomfortable during a long dinner, but hopefully your attention will be on the succulent Hakka dishes, rather than your aching backside. Popular dishes are grilled shrimp served in a bucket of rock salt and the foil-wrapped fish. The restaurant is on the banks of Qianhai, near the Starbucks on Lotus Lane, and offers alfresco dining during warmer months. Han Cang is a great place to take a date or a large group of friends.

Horizon 海天阁

Kerry Centre Hotel
Chaoyang
光华路1号嘉里中心
饭店
朝阳区
 Guomao L1
Map 11 F2 **18**

010 6561 8833 | *www.shangri-la.com*
Horizon is the answer to all those Cantonese diehards who moan that Beijing is devoid of good dim sum. The all-you-can-eat weekday buffet draws crowds with its perfectly steamed shrimp dumplings. The menu also carries Sichuan specialties. The main part of the restaurant is spacious and lively, while private rooms tucked around the corner are good for intimate conversations. Banquet facilities are also available. The traditional Chinese decor brings to mind colonial tastes. A small bridge connects the entrance to the restaurant, and patterned carpets, satin textiles, and dark wood furniture abound.

Huajia Yiyuan 花家怡园

235 Dongzhimennei Dajie
Dongcheng
东直门内大街235号
东城区
Beixinqiao L5
Map 9 A2 **19**

010 6403 0677
Huajia Yiyuan draws a crowd of mandopop stars with its succulent cuisine and raucous ambiance. The restaurant is housed in a large, converted courtyard. Smaller rooms lining the perimeter make for intimate dining spots, while the central, alfresco space is great for lively conversations. The chrysanthemum fish, a meticulously carved, breaded and deep-fried fish served with sweet and sour sauce, is great for larger groups. The house draught beer, in black, amber, and green (yes, really), is the beverage of choice.

Kuan Dian 宽店

153 Jiugulou Dajie
Dongcheng
旧鼓楼大街153号
东城区
Gulou
Map 8 C2 **20**

010 8404 0523
Beijingers are militant about the quality of their grilled chicken wings, and Kuan Dian appears to have passed the test. The tiny restaurant is so popular, you often have to book tables in advance. Wings are served non-spicy, spicy, and extra spicy. Everyone washes down the finger food with bottles of Tsingdao beer. For a splash of variety, it also serves a tasty dish of mashed potatoes and *laohu cai*, a spicy salad of sliced coriander, cucumber and peppers.

Liqun 丽群烤鸭店

11 Zhengyi Lubei Xiang Feng
Dongcheng
正义路北11号翔凤胡同
东城区
Map 12 E1 **21**

010 6705 5578
Liqun is a duck roasting institution. You once had to navigate a maze of *hutong* homes to get to the humble courtyard restaurant. These were recently torn down, leaving Liqun amid a sad pile of rubble. But modernisation worked fast, and a new paved road allows cabs to pull up to the door. Liqun employs traditional roasting techniques, using smoky wood to infuse ducks with a fruity flavour. Despite the barebones decor, it has attracted diplomats and Chinese celebrities (as evidenced by photos lining the entrance hall). It has even garnered praise from visiting foodies like Anthony Bourdain.

Made In China 长安一号

Grand Hyatt Beijing
Chongwen
东长安街1号君悦大
酒店
崇文区
🚇 *Wangfujing L1*
Map 10 E3 **22**

010 8518 1234 | www.beijing.grand.hyatt.com

Made In China serves some of the best Peking duck in town. It may not be terribly romantic or claim that an American hotel chain outperforms local outlets in the city's signature dish, but in this case it's true. The restaurant has stunning decor, featuring a central wood-fired stove and L-shaped open kitchen. The staff are top notch, and come to your table at the hint of a frown. Always book ahead, as it is permanently packed; even on weekdays. When making reservations, order your duck in advance - prep time and roasting clocks in at more than an hour. This gastronomic experience comes at a price, so expect to pay upwards of ¥300 per person.

No Name 无名酒吧

1 Dajinsi Hutong
Houhai
大金丝胡同1号
后海
🚇 *Gulou*
Map 8 C2 **23**

010 6618 6061

This is the best Yunnan restaurant in Houhai. You should head straight for a table on the glassed-in balcony overlooking the traditional rooftops of neighbouring courtyards. Service is friendly, but slow. Any dish wrapped in a banana leaf is a good bet, and a bowl of 'crossing the bridge' noodles is a local favourite. Dishes are reasonably priced, but come with expensive drinks.

Noodle Loft 面酷

3 Heping Xijie
Chaoyang
和平西街3号
朝阳区
🚇 *Yonghegong L5*
Map 9 F3 **24**

010 5130 9655

Watching the flurry of cooking activity in the large open kitchen is half the fun of dining at Noodle Loft. The fresh Shanxi noodles and fusion dishes complete the experience. There is upbeat background music and a stylish orange and grey interior. Popular dishes include *qiao mian mao erduo* (pasta shaped like cat's ears stir-fried with chopped meat).

Paomo Guan 泡馍馆

53 Chaonei Nanxiaojie
Dongcheng
朝内南小街53号
东城区
Map 11 B2 **25**

010 6559 8135

Judging by the height of seats in Paomo Guan, Shanxi people must be tiny. This quaint restaurant serves tasty Shanxi favourites, including fluffy noodles and hearty baked bread stuffed with chopped meat – something akin to a hamburger crossed with a shawarma. *Mijiu*, a warm rice wine, is a popular beverage with deceptively high alcohol content.

Paper 纯白餐厅

138 Guloudong Dajie
Dongcheng
鼓楼东大街138号
东城区
🚇 *Beixinqiao L5*
Map 8 E2 **26**

010 8401 5080

This stylish restaurant is minimalist deluxe. White dominates – walls, floors, tables, chairs, even the tiger lilies in the entrance. The ambiance is accordingly hushed, with soft lounge music playing in the background. There is also an iPod deck on hand for customers who want to play their own tunes. Paper serves contemporary cuisine in set menus. Owner Cho, whose stylish additions to Beijing include Bed Bar (p.328) and Café Sambal (p.318), claims that all ingredients at this upscale eatery are organic.

People 8 人间玄八

2/F 18 Jianguomenwai
Chaoyang
建国门外大街18号2层
朝阳区
🚇 *Jianguomen L1*
Map 11 D4 **27**

010 6515 8585

The first task is to find the entrance to this restaurant, which is unmarked but for a couple of stones leading seemingly into a wall, hidden behind a mini bamboo forest. But, as you approach you'll

Door Policy

There is a very relaxed attitude to dress codes. Door policies are rare and IDs are almost never checked. Foreigners are unlikely to be confronted by bouncers, and are generally treated with a tolerance that few other cities can claim. Winters are cold and you will need to dress up warm, but most places offer free, trustworthy coat checks.

see a well hidden door. Once inside, the pitch-black interior deprives you of sight, but your eyes will adjust. Take your time climbing the stairs to the restaurant and don't walk into the mirror at the top (it happens). Menu items like miso soup and stir-fried beef are served in small portions, so order several dishes. The interior looks black and trendily 'post industrial' in the dining room, with a few bare twigs offering artistically mimimalist decoration. The bar area has some very comfortable low seating, which it may be hard to leave. If labyrinthine journeys and dining in the dark are less than appealing, visit during lunchtime - the set meal is an excellent deal and the entire place is swathed in light that filters through the glass panelled ceiling.

Red Capital Club 新红资俱乐部

66 Dongsi Jiu Tian
Dongcheng
东四九条66号
东城区
📷 *Dongsishitiao L2*
Map 9 A3 28

010 6591 8888 | *www.redcapitalclub.com.cn*

Red Capital Club is decked out in kitsch, authentic Cultural Revolution memorabilia. There is even a vintage Red Flag limo parked outside. Housed in a restored Chinese courtyard, this is a great place to take visitors. The retro cigar and cocktail lounge is decked out in furnishings originally used by the central government in the 50s. Meals are served banquet style and feature the favourite dishes of Mao and Deng. You should call ahead to work out a menu if your group has less than 10 people.

Sange Guizhou Ren 三个贵州人

8 Gongti Xi Lu
Chaoyang
工体西路8号
朝阳区
Map 9 D4 29

010 6551 8517

This restaurant attracts a hip Chinese crowd with its cool interior and Guizhou cuisine. Hotpot is a house speciality and the spicy ribs, grilled to tender perfection, are not to be missed. Staff members clad in traditional ethnic clothing add a splash of colour to the surroundings.

Sansheng Wanwu 广福馆

27 Yandai Xie Jie
Houhai
烟袋斜街27号
后海
Map 8 C2 30

010 6404 2778

This tiny restaurant tucked away in an alley near Houhai is a great place for an intimate dinner party. A group of about 10 will ensure you get the entire place to yourself. Make reservations, as the dinner is a set menu. The wine selection is nothing fancy, so oenophiles may want to bring their own bottles. Dishes are light and fresh, following the traditional order of Chinese meals, with starches like rice or noodles served at the end to ensure everyone is full.

Sichuan Representative Restaurant 川办餐厅

5 Gongyuan Tou Tiao
Jianguomennei Daijie
Dongcheng
建国门内大街贡院头条
5号，东城区
📷 *Jianguomen L1*
Map 11 C3 31

010 6512 2277

This is the best place to get an authentic Sichuanese meal. The restaurant is attached to the provincial government office, and chefs and staff are all from the area. Prices are incredibly affordable. The expansive main room and lively atmosphere make it a great place for large dinner parties. Menus have Chinese and English, with accompanying photos to help decode the dishes.

Source 都江源

14 Banchang Hutong
Jiaodaokou Dajie
Dongcheng
交道口大街板厂胡同
14号
东城区
Map 8 E3 32

010 6400 3736 | *www.yanclub.com*

This beautiful courtyard restaurant, with intimate rooms and traditional Chinese decor, is good for group dinners. During the day, head to the back of the restaurant and dine next to lattice windows overlooking nearby courtyards. The ambiance follows the furnishings, with traditional Peking and Kunqu opera music playing softly in the background. Lunch and dinner are set menus that change weekly. Wandering through the nearby *hutong* area to find Source is a delight in itself.

Various Locations

South Beauty 俏江南

010 8447 6171 | *www.qiaojiangnan.com*

This popular chain is a good standby for Sichuan food. Clean surroundings, a foreigner-friendly menu and the (limited) English skills of staff make it a good spot for newcomers. Dishes like *lazi ji* (crispy cubes of chicken served with large, intimidating peppers) and *kungpao* chicken are perennial favourites.

23A Jingrong Dajie
Xicheng
金融大街甲23号
西城区
🚇 *Fuxingmen L1*
Map 6 E2 34

Whampoa Club 黄浦会中餐厅

010 8808 8828

Headed by star chef Jereme Leung, this second Whampoa follows in the successful footsteps of its sister restaurant in Shanghai. In Beijing, Leung focuses on modern interpretations of Beijing and Shandong cuisines. The tasting menus include innovative dishes like beancurd and vegetable roll with foie gras terrine, oven-baked black cod, Beijing-style fermented bean paste and pork with handmade noodles. The upscale courtyard setting features a dining room done in shades of white, blue and black, beneath a glass-bottomed goldfish pond.

252 Andingmenwai
Dajie
Dongcheng
安定门外大街252号
东城区
🚇 *Andingmen L2*
Map 8 E2 35

Xian Lao Man 馅老满

010 6404 6944

This dumpling restaurant is always packed. The expansive menu offers something for everyone – from standbys like pork and cabbage, to adventurous fillings like peanuts, cabbage, and white rice. The menu is entirely in Chinese and paper copies are placed on each table. Diners are supposed to tick off their dishes and hand them to passing staff. Apart from dumplings, the restaurant also serves tasty sweet and sour pork, and tangy 'eight treasures spinach' – a cold dish of sauteed spinach served with soy sauce, vinegar, and pine nuts.

Ritan Park
Chaoyang
光华路东里2号楼
朝阳区
Map 11 D2 36

Xiao Wang Fu 小王府

010 8561 7859

A meal at this cosy restaurant is a wonderful way to end a day in the great outdoors. The menu includes familiar hearty dishes like Beijing duck, crispy fried tofu, and stir-fried chicken wings. The environs are upscale, with stylish decor and a second floor that overlooks nearby Ritan Park.

121 Gulou Dong Dajie
Dongcheng
鼓楼东大街121号
东城区
🚇 *Beixinqiao L5*
Map 8 D2 37

Xiongdi 巴渝兄弟川菜

010 6405 6681

Xiongdi is known for its basic decor, lax hygiene and stellar Sichuan food. Order the standards – *kungpao* chicken, stir-fried beans, or *mala dofu* (cubes of soft tofu served with a spicy sauce), and you won't be disappointed. Private rooms in the back can accommodate groups of eight or more. Remember that, presumably in the interest of plumbing, there is a strict 'liquids only' policy in the bathrooms.

European

Other options **French** p.313, **Italian** p.315, **Mediterranean** p.319, **Russian** p.321, **Spanish** p.321

2/F China World Hotel
Chaoyang
建国门外大街1号中国
大饭店2层，朝阳区
🚇 *Guomao L1*
Map 11 F3 38

Aria 阿丽雅酒吧

010 6505 2266 | *www.shangri-la.com*

Up a spiral staircase and past the beautiful bar is a restaurant that consistently exceeds expectations, offering regularly changing selections and 'new French, modern European' cuisine. The set menus change weekly, and feature items such as confit of rabbit, tortellini turf and surf with roasted duck, and desserts like upside down apple tart. It also features a chef trained in several French Michelin-starred restaurants. This is a great place to impress a date or client, or a good spot to lunch near the China World Trade Centre.

Blu Lobster

Blu Lobster 蓝韵西餐厅

Shangri-La Hotel
29 Zizhuyuan Lu
Haidian
紫竹院路29号香格里
拉饭店
海淀区
Map 4 B4 **39**

010 6841 2211 | *www.shangri-la.com*

This is one of the more expensive restaurants in Beijing, and it's easy to spend ¥700 per person before drinks. It is, however, one of the few must-tries if you want experimental fusion featuring foams, test tubes, and watermelon gazpacho. There is excellent seafood, but Blu Lobster offers more, including an amazing mango and pineapple ravioli (as a dessert) that will take your breath away. Service and presentation are almost flawless.

Café Europa 欧洲屋

Shop 1113, 1/F Building
11, Jianwai SOHO
Chaoyang
建外SOHO11号楼1层
1113商铺
朝阳区
Map 7 D3 **40**

010 5869 5663 | *www.cafeeuropa.cn*

This bistro can be hard to find in the maze-like Jianwai SOHO, but persevere and you'll find a decent cafe with plenty to offer. The prices and service are average, but food and decor are a cut above. Try the steaks or one of the items from the rotating Chef's Recommendations and enjoy a bottle from the surprising wine list, with plenty of choices available by the glass. The chocolate mousse is also particularly good. Set business lunches are available, making it a great meeting spot.

Café St Laurent 圣罗兰西餐厅

6 Xingfu Yicun
Chaoyang
幸福一村6号
朝阳区
Map 9 E3 **41**

010 6413 0086

During the day, the patio of popular club Alfa (p.329) turns into Café St Laurent, a relaxing spot for brunch. The chef from the Canadian embassy lends his expertise to create subtle and high-quality cuisine. The menu combines the traditional with a little something extra; the pancakes are lemon ricotta, the bloody marys are served with wasabi, the French toast is caramelised, and their excellent smoothies are served in large shot glasses.

Morel's 莫劳龙玺西餐

Gongtibeilu, opposite
Workers' Stadium north
gate
Chaoyang
工人体育场北门对面
朝阳区
Map 9 E3 **42**

010 6416 8802

This charming Belgian bistro, right across from the Workers' Stadium, serves French and Belgian cuisine in cosy surroundings. Morel's is a favourite with long-standing expats, who remember when high-quality authentic European cuisine was scarce. The standard has not changed, but the competition has increased. Still, the food is quite good; most people rave about their steaks, which come with a variety of sauces, and their wide array of Belgian beers.

P&O's One

4 Dongfang Lu
Chaoyang
东方路4号
朝阳区
Map 7 C1 **43**

010 8455 2611

Perhaps not the best place for a vegetarian, this is one of the few places in town serving authentic Austrian cuisine. The many meat options include the *zwiebelrostbrat*, (beef with onions and potatoes), and chicken cordon bleu. For dessert try the *nusspalatschinken*, a pancake with chocolate and nuts. This restaurant is fairly pricey, but worth it for the responsive service and decent surroundings.

Pacifico 帕思菲克餐厅酒吧

4/F Uptown Office
Plaza
Chaoyang
青年路朝阳路尚街时尚
广场4层
朝阳区
Map 7 F2 44

010 8559 2886

Pacifico boasts one of the largest outdoor terraces in town, and also features a 'Drums of Tahiti' dance troupe for entertainment. The food ranges from fairly standard European classics including steaks and pastas, to dishes influenced by the South Seas, like the duck with lychee. Set meals (starting at ¥60) are a bargain, with reasonable drinks and desserts. It is on the corner of Chaoyang and Qingnian.

French

Brasserie Flo 福楼

2/F Rainbow Plaza
16 Dongsanhuan Beilu
Chaoyang
东三环北路16号隆博
广场2层
朝阳区
Map 7 C1 45

010 6595 5135 | www.flo.cn

A Beijing institution, and frequent winner of local 'best French restaurant' awards, Flo is consistently good and impressively large – with prices to match. Fresh, imported oysters, escargot, excellent salads and steaks are all on the menu. This is a great place to impress with its sunny terrace, good set meals and wine list offering France's finest. Desserts from the in-house confectioners are some of the best in Beijing, and the chef's speciality of sauerkraut and goose liver is definitely worth a try.

Café de la Poste 云游驿

58 Yonghegong Dajie
Dongcheng
雍和宫大街58号
东城区
Map 8 E2 46

010 6402 7047

Another great little *hutong* restaurant near Nanluoguxiang. Step inside and you are transported to a French cafe. Casual and a little crowded with French expats, expect 'meat and potatoes' cuisine instead of anything too highbrow. Steaks are excellent, as is the selection of cheeses. Prices are affordable, even after you've spent too much in the local boutiques, and range from ¥30 for a starter to ¥80 for a main. Inviting and quaint, Café de la Poste is a great little place to kick back, but be prepared for the smoky environment.

Comptoirs de France 法派

35 Dongzhimen
Waidajie
Dongcheng
东直门外大街35号东
湖别墅
朝阳区
Map 8 C3 47

010 6461 1525 | www.comptoirsdefrance.com

Set in the East Lake Villas complex, this is the best bakery in town, serving a wide variety of pastries, coffee, amazing hot chocolate, and some decent sandwiches. Comptoirs de France is inexpensive, with plenty of smaller treats costing less than ¥10. Homemade icecream and interesting chocolates (including some flavoured with Szechuan peppercorn) help to make this cafe the best spot for a quick breakfast or some tasty gifts.

Fauchon 馥颂美食精品店

B1-F2 Shin Kong Place
87 Jianguo Lu
Chaoyang
建国路87号新光天地
B1-F2
朝阳区
Map 7 D2 48

010 6533 1266 | www.fauchon.com

Spread across three floors, you can start with the cafe, make your way down to the deli, and finally take home some goods from the market on the bottom floor. It's easy to overspend on French delicacies at this pricey establishment. Breads, cheeses, chocolates, and pastries from the other floors complement the more substantial offerings from the cafe. The buffet is a reasonably-priced alternative to the wince-inducing prices of small a la carte portions. However, you get what you pay for, so expect some of the most beautiful food and surroundings this side of Paris. Don't miss the variety of *madeleines*.

Le Petit Gourmand 小美食家

3/F Tongli Studio
Sanlitun
同里3层
三里屯
Map 9 F2 **49**

010 6417 6095 | www.lepetitgourmand.com.cn
This is bar, restaurant and lending library is a nice contrast to the gaudy Sanlitun area. It offers savoury and sweet crepes and steaks at reasonable prices. The comfortable, enclosed balcony is a great spot to catch up on your reading and sip a latte. If you get really into your book, you can become a member and borrow it. Membership costs ¥150 for six months or ¥250 for a year.

Le Pré Lenôtre

Wanda Plaza
93 Jianguo Lu
Chaoyang
建国路93号万达广场
朝阳区
Map 7 D2 **50**

010 8599 6666 | www.sofitel-asia.com
This is the newest, and possibly finest, French restaurant in town. Located in the Sofitel Hotel (p.36), Le Pré Lenôtre is a collaboration between the hotel and the Lenôtre haute cuisine brand. The sumptuous surroundings are slightly over the top, but dishes like prawn ravioli or salad with passion fruit dressing are definitely worth a try. It is expensive, but the quality seafood and excellent service justify the cost. This is an excellent place for taking a date, or wooing that difficult client while enjoying a bottle of wine from the extensive selection.

Fusion

The Courtyard 四合院

95 Donghuamen Dajie
Forbidden City
东华门大街95号
故宫
Map 10 E2 **51**

010 6526 8883 | www.courtyardbeijing.com
Upscale and trendy, The Courtyard is one of the most romantic restaurants in Beijing. It's not as eclectic as the Green T House (below), but offers a much better location, with views of the Forbidden City and an outstanding wine list. Modern fusion doesn't have to be completely wild, and there are plenty of restrained options on the menu. Pricing is on a par with other restaurants in this class, as is the excellent service and elegant decor.

Green T House 紫云轩

6 Gongti Xilu
Chaoyang
工体西路6号
朝阳区
Map 9 D4 **52**

010 6552 8310 | www.greenteahouse.com.cn
Surreal meets feng shui at Green T House, resulting in a unique dining experience. This high-end restaurant has innovative design, ambient candle lighting, lie-down seating, and intriguing bathrooms. The restaurant is a great venue to impress visitors, boasting Asian cuisine that uses green tea to memorable effect. Prices are steep, even by international standards, and staff are militant about the no photography policy.

Jasmine 茉莉

Gongti Donglu
Opposite Gate 9 of
Workers' Stadium
Chaoyang
工体东路工人体育场
9号门对面
朝阳区
Map 9 E4 **53**

010 6553 8608
The food is eclipsed by the decor, but the location and hip factor of this mainly-Chinese restaurant are hard to beat. Plush velvet, large windows, chandeliers and high ceilings create a fashionable (but affordable) spot. The food focuses on updated presentations of fairly standard dishes and drinks are good, if a bit strong. Prices are cheaper than the Green T House or The Courtyard (both above), and many appreciate the more laidback service.

Indian

Ganges Lido 恒河印度餐厅丽都店

5 Hairun Apartments
Lido
海润国际公寓5号商铺
朝阳区
Map 5 D3 **54**

010 5135 8353 | http://ganges-restaurant.com
Reasonable food at reasonable prices has made Ganges the most prominent Indian restaurant chain in Beijing. The three locations may have different decor, but offer essentially the same versions of classic dishes – the *palak paneer* is decent and the

naan is served piping hot. Ignore the Bollywood videos (if you can), and enjoy a quick lunch. Be prepared to spend some time choosing; there are more than 300 dishes on the menu. Stick to the classics for best results. Other locations at B138A, The Place, 9 Guanghua Lu, Chaoyang (010 6587 2999) and Ganges Wudaokou, 160 Chengfu Lu, San Cai Tang, Haidian (010 6262 7944).

Mirch Masala 马沙拉之香印度餐厅

60-2 Nanluoguxiang
Dongcheng
南锣鼓巷60-2
东城区
Map 8 E2 **55**

010 6406 4347 | www.mirchmasala.com.cn
Mirch Masala may not offer the most authentic food, but it's comfortable and great for dropping in after a browse around Nanluoguxiang. It is often busy, especially at weekends, so consider making a reservation. Service is prompt and friendly, and the decor is modern. You don't need to be afraid of breaking the bank; most dishes are quite inexpensive, with naan for around ¥10. Be prepared for wildly different spice levels, with insanely hot vindaloos contrasting with many mildly spiced dishes.

Taj Pavilion At Guomao 泰姬楼国贸店

L1-28 China World Trade Center, 1 Jianguomenwai Dajie
Chaoyang
建国门外大街1号中国国际贸易中心L1-2
朝阳区
Map 11 F3 **56**

010 6505 5866
This restaurant offers arguably the best Indian cuisine in Beijing. Elegant seating, excellent service, and competitive prices combine to create an impressive experience. The Taj Pavilion aims to satisfy all of your taste buds, delighting patrons with its authentic curries, tandoori chicken, and sweet kashmiri naan. Sip a mango lassi to cool your tongue. The other restaurant is at Taj Pavilion at Lido, 3/F, Holiday Inn Lido, Lido Place, Jichanglu, Jiangtailu (010 6436 7678).

Italian
Other options **Mediterranean** p.319

Alla Osteria 意尚意大利餐厅

SOHO Shangdu 1112 8 Dongdaqiao Lu
Chaoyang
东大桥路8号SOHO尚都1112
朝阳区
Map 11 E2 **57**

010 5900 3112
This is a classic Italian with a wide menu. Start off with some excellent flatbread, move onto a delicious rocket salad, sample some baked aubergine or Milanese lamb, and make sure you check out the wine cellar. Set lunches are excellent value at ¥68. An open kitchen adds a touch of class to this laid-back restaurant, and you can see the preparation that goes into each item. Service is efficient, and the pastas are reliably excellent.

Annie's 安妮意大利餐厅

Various Locations

010 6591 1931 | www.annies.com.cn
Annie's is a powerhouse of the Beijing Italian scene. It is frequently voted 'favourite Italian', but the food might not be winning any awards for authenticity. However, the family-friendly atmosphere, large portions, great locations, and unfussy menu selections ensure that crowds gather at Annie's. Take your kids to one of the rare places that offers high chairs and play areas. Annie's has restaurants in Chaoyang, Lido and Riviera, check the website for locations.

Capone's 卡邦意大利餐厅

L404A, 4/F The Place 9 Guanghua Lu
Chaoyang
光华路9号世贸天阶A座4层L404A
朝阳区
Map 11 E2 **59**

010 6587 1526 | www.capones.com.cn
Swanky and sexy, this bar and restaurant offers some interesting dishes, even if portions are on the small side. There is excellent service and great music, but fairly high prices. Unlike Annie's (above), you won't find many families dining, but you can expect to see some well-heeled Beijingers enjoying baked sea bass, squid ink ravioli, tiramisu and a good wine list. Be sure to bring friends who can dance to help you enjoy the jazz band.

Cepe 意味轩

Ritz-Carlton
Xicheng
金融街金城坊东街1号
丽思卡尔顿饭店
西城区
Fuxingmen L1
Map 6 E3 **60**

010 6629 6996 | www.ritzcarlton.com

Offering sophisticated northern Italian fare, Cepe specialises in mushrooms of all shapes, sizes, and varieties – and grows many in the house humidor. The rich, roasted portobellos are among the most popular varieties. You may need a reservation during peak hours, as the crowds can be heavy becuase of the location in the Financial District. Excellent service, inventive cuisine, and some of Beijing's more interesting desserts (lavender icecream, for example) make for a great party or special occasion venue.

L'Isola 益顺客

**201 Pacific Century
Place, A2 Gongti Beilu**
Chaoyang
工体北路甲2号盈科中
心商场2层201单元
朝阳区
Map 9 E3 **61**

010 6539 3773

Upscale yet cosy, you'll enjoy the homemade pastas and set lunches that cost ¥69 for two courses, or ¥96 for three. Well-seasoned entrees, fresh mozzarella, and flavourful sauces complement the great views of the Sanlitun area. The restaurant offers a romantic alternative to the many bland Italian options that abound in Beijing. Fantastic fresh breads, knowledgeable service, and an extensive wine selection will make even a jaded cynic happy.

La Fattoria 法朵莉亚

**Shop 5, Phoenix
Xintiandi**
Shuguang Xili
曙光西里凤凰新天地
5号商铺
Map 5 D3 **62**

010 5866 7072

You will probably see some Italians eating in La Fattoria – always a good sign, especially since the first branch of this restaurant is in Italy. Not the easiest place to find, it's worth the effort for some Neapolitan favourites like homemade sausage, rigatoni alla genovese, and rum cake. The complimentary glass of wine is a neat touch, and while the decor isn't impressive, it is warm and intimate. Prices are reasonable and you're likely to return, if only for the pleasant service.

Luce 路溪

138 Jiugulou Dajie
Xicheng
旧鼓楼大街138号
西城区
Map 8 C1 **63**

010 8402 4417 | www.luceluna.com

Houhai has plenty of bars but lacks nice places to eat, which makes Luce a refreshing find. The well-designed interior manages to be snazzy without being imposing, and the same can be said of the food. Mushroom risotto, plenty of interesting pastas, and succulent grilled meats lead up to some excellent desserts, including mocha crème brulee. Patient staff and decent prices complete the picture. There is a nightclub next door, if those post-dinner drinks inspire some dancing.

Japanese

Haiku By Hatsune 隐泉之语

**8 Chaoyang Xilu
Inside Block 8**
Chaoyang
朝阳西路8号8号楼
朝阳区
Map 7 D1 **64**

010 6508 8585 | www.block8.cn

This place is chef Alan Wong's second step towards total domination of the fancy fusion market. Thanks to the overflowing tables of the original Hatsune (see top of next page), the famed chef decided to open a second, high-end Japanese restaurant in Beijing. It is housed in the elegant surroundings on the third floor of Block 8, and adds some new fusion elements to traditional Japanese food. The menu has some overlaps with the original Hatsune, with similarly innovative sushi options, but also adds favourites like *yakitori* (Japanese grill) and Japanese tapas. However, those looking to stick with more traditional Japanese morsels, like sashimi, will not be disappointed, and everything is fresh and prepared with Wong's signature care and attention to detail. The restaurant is fully licensed, and has a decent range of wines and sake.

Hatsune 隐泉日本料理

2\F Heqiao Building
Chaoyang
光华东路甲8号C座和乔
大厦2层
朝阳区
Map 7 D2 **65**

010 6581 3939

Hatsune's fresh, creative sushi options are just one highlight of the wonderful Japanese dining experience, explaining why reservations are strongly recommended at all times. Water, stones and sleek black provide the Zen surroundings for your meal. The award-winning sushi combines western and Japanese styles, with wasabi challenge rolls, spicy 119 rolls and Beijing duck rolls. Sushi this good comes at a price though, which is why many advise enjoying lunch instead of dinner; the complete lunch bento boxes are a great deal. And when you order, don't overlook their steak teppanyaki or Hatsune-exclusive sake. The building is at A8 Guanghua Donglu.

Tokugawa 德川家日本料理

Shuangjing 16
Dongsanhuanzhong
Chaoyang
东三环中路16号双井
地点不唯一
Map 7 C3 **66**

010 8776 2765

This all-you-can-eat (and drink) chain of sushi joints is sure to satisfy even the largest appetite. The food might not be the freshest or the most authentic, but you can't argue with the prices, with buffets costing ¥68 to ¥200 depending on the time of day and food offered. Service can be lacklustre and the decor won't win any prizes, but the sashimi is decent and the drinks (sake or beer) are quite good. Tokugawa is a great spot for large parties of any sort. There are other restaurants at Guanghua Lu, Bldg D Shimao Apartments, 9 Guanghualu, (010 6506 6199) and Zhongguancun, 2/F Huantai Building, 12 Zhongguancun Nandajie, (010 6210 9096).

Korean

Saveurs de Corée 韩香馆

29 Nanluoguxiang
Dongcheng
南锣鼓巷29号
东城区
Map 8 E2 **67**

010 6401 6083 | *www.saveursdecoree.com.cn*

Try a reasonably-priced set meal at this cute bistro, especially if you haven't sampled Korean food before. Nanluoguxiang has plenty of options, but few match Saveurs de Corée for its modern and healthy take on Asian cuisine. Beef marinated in pear? Pork with pumpkin? It isn't traditional, but it is delicious. Drinks like green tea latte and cinnamon tea are on hand if you'd prefer to relax a bit in the cosy, if sometimes smoky, cafe.

Sorabol 萨拉伯尔

Liangmahe, 2/F
Liangmahe Building, 8
Dongsanhuan Beilu
Chaoyang
东三环北路8号亮马河
大厦2层
朝阳区
Map 7 C1 **68**

010 6590 0630 | *www.sorabolrestaurants.com*

This smart chain has two restaurants, both known for their interiors, pleasant staff, reasonable prices and excellent food. The *bulgogi*, sometimes called simply 'Korean barbecue' is impressive. These thin slices of marinated beef are second only to *kimchi* in the Korean diet. If you're still hungry, you might like to try the *banfa*, which is similar to fried rice, only mixed with *kimchi* and hot sauce. There are many Korean options in town, but this is among the best. The other restaurant is in the Lufthansa Centre (010 6465 3388).

Latin American

A Che 切

28 Dongzhimenwai
Dajie
Sanlitun
东直门外大街28号
三里屯
Map 9 E2 **69**

010 6417 2201 | *www.a-che.com.cn*

This place is great for food away from the bustle of Sanlitun. The 'old clothes' beef is excellent, as are the sandwiches. Well-priced set menus are available, at ¥60 for two courses or ¥78 for three, while the wine list offers more Spanish and Chilean wines than anywhere else in the city. Cuban modern art adds colour to the walls, while on Friday nights a Cuban three-piece band adds colour to the dancefloor.

Alameda 阿拉梅达

Tongli Studios
Sanlitun Houjie
Sanlitun
三里屯后街同里
三里屯
Map 9 F2 70

010 6417 8084

Regularly hailed as one of the city's best restaurants, Alameda is a favourite lunch spot in Sanlitun. The ¥60 lunch set menu (¥158 for dinner) is one reason, as is the lively atmosphere and well-made contemporary cuisine. Roasted chicken with paprika, pumpkin soup, excellent scallops, steaks, and a wide selection of desserts and wine have made its popularity a bit of a curse; reservations may be needed, service can be a little slow, and it can get a bit loud.

El Fogoncito 福客多

01-02, Wanda Plaza
93 Jianguo Lu
Chaoyang
建国路93号万达广场
19号楼01-02
朝阳区
Map 7 D2 71

010 820 6551 | *www.fogoncito.com*

It's hard to find decent Mexican food in Beijing, so El Fogoncito is doing well. Unfortunately, those looking for decent guacamole or even spicy salsa will be disappointed. While the food is pretty good, those who like their Mexican with a kick will find many dishes bland. But, the decor is modern and sleek, the service is pleasant and prices are affordable.

Garden Of Delights 饕餮源

53 Donganmen Dajie
Dongcheng
东安门大街53号
东城区
Map 10 F2 72

010 5138 5688 | *www.gardenofdelights.com.cn*

This is one of the best restaurants around Wanfujing. Garden of Delights offers sophisticated Latin American cuisine in a lovely environment, filled with Renaissance prints. From the duck filet with white chocolate to the chocolate tower dessert, the food is decent, as is the presentation. Staff are friendly and knowledgeable. Prices are high, considering the fairly small portions. The restaurant is easy to miss, so it's worth calling ahead for directions.

Rio Brazilian BBQ 里约巴西烤肉

9-13, Building 5
Dongzhimennei Dajie
Dongcheng
东直门内大街5号楼
9-13, 东城区
🚇 *Dongzhimen L13*
Map 9 B2 73

010 8406 4368 | *www.riobbq.com*

Rio Brazilian BBQ will make both your mouth and wallet happy – it's an all-you-can-eat buffet with meat carved directly from skewers, and a large salad bar. Rates start at ¥48 per person, and the meat can be a little tough or over spiced, but it is a fun dining experience. Drinks are cheap too. You may find the service a bit disappointing, but the live music can be entertaining, and it is only a short walk from Dongzhimen subway station.

Malaysian, Burmese & Singaporean

Other options **Chinese** p.305, **Thai** p.322

Awana 阿瓦娜餐厅

32 Tianze Lu, Xingba Lu
Chaoyang
星吧路天泽路32号
朝阳区
Map 5 C4 74

010 6462 0004

In a town filled with kebabs, Awana serves some of the best. The satay bar offers a choice of meats, some of them free-range and all of them tender, served with some excellent dipping sauces. Prices are reasonable, the interior is stylish, and the staff are eager, if a bit overbearing. The appetiser sampler for two can easily work for three. Awana is owned in part by the Malaysian Tourism Board, which may help explain why it stands out over most of the other options in the Nurenjie area.

Café Sambal

43 Doufuchi Hutong
Jiugulou Dajie
Houhai
旧鼓楼大街豆腐池胡
同43号
后海
Map 8 D1 75

010 6400 4875 | *www.cafesambal.com*

Café Sambal receives consistently rave reviews for its chic *hutong* location and excellent interior design, as well as dishes like beef *rendang* and the speciality *kapitan* chicken. Small portions and high prices make the wonderful mango rolls seem like less of a bargain. Café Sambal can become quite busy, but the wide drinks selection and spicy curries might make up for the wait.

Java & Yangon 印度尼西亚和缅甸菜

Sanlitun Xiwujie
Sanlitun
三里屯西五街
三里屯
Map 9 F2 **76**

010 8451 7489

Right across from the German embassy and not far from Sanlitun Bar Street is the only place in Beijing for Burmese food. Java & Yangon also serves Indonesian cuisine, and though it might not be a good place for a date, it's perfectly suitable for a quick meal. Set menus are available, and prices are cheap, so you can have your fill of curries, noodles, bamboo shoots with coconut milk, or vanilla chicken breast soup. Service is fairly prompt, if a bit distant, but the green papaya salad alone is worth the trip.

Lau Pa Sak 老巴刹

Xindong Lu, opposite
the Canadian Embassy
Chaoyang
新东路加拿大使馆对面
朝阳区
Map 9 E2 **77**

010 6417 0952

Limited menu, tricky to find, uninspiring decor… so why is this place so busy? It must be the excellent Singaporean street food at hard to beat prices. The service is friendly, but the highlight is the food. Everything is great; condensed milk coffee, satay, noodles, curry chicken, *hainan* chicken, and best of all, the *laksa* (spicy noodle soup). Arrive early and beat the large groups of homesick Singaporeans and embassy workers who have made this a popular lunch spot.

Sambal Urban 马来西亚餐厅

Shop 6, Phoenix
Xintiandi, Shuguang Xili
Chaoyang
曙光西里凤凰新天地
6号商铺
朝阳区
Map 5 64 **78**

010 5866 8538 | *www.cafesambal.com*

Owned and managed by the same folks as Café Sambal (p.318), this newer and harder to find location offers fancier digs, but much of the same food. The focus is on seafood, like the delectable chilli crab, which you may need to order in advance. The peanut sauce, mojitos, and mango rolls are excellent, but be prepared for fairly small portions and pretty high prices.

Mediterranean

Other options **Italian** p.315, **Spanish** p.321

Athena 雅典娜西餐厅

1 Sanlitun Xiwujie
Sanlitun
三里屯西五街1号
三里屯
Map 9 F2 **79**

010 6464 6036

Not far from the main Sanlitun Bar Street is this cute restaurant serving all of your favourite Greek dishes. The only real place in Beijing for Greek food, there's no doubt that the chefs could hold their own in their homeland. There are decent lamb kebabs, tzatziki and baklava, but try the corncake with feta cheese for an interesting appetiser. Large enough for a group, with some smaller tables for more intimate occasions, the prices are reasonable and the staff are helpful.

Med 地中海餐厅

8 Chaoyang Xi Lu
inside Block 8
Chaoyang
朝阳西路8号8号楼
朝阳区
Map 7 D1 **80**

010 6508 8585 | *www.block8.cn*

Beautiful, if unfulfilling, Med is a stylish addition to Block 8 (p.342). With gourmet twists on Mediterranean food, the menu includes a wide assortment of wood-fired pizzas, Moroccan-spiced chicken, roasted feta, bacon-wrapped calamari, and the usual appetisers. The real stand-outs are the desserts, like panna cotta and chocolate soup. Prices are a bit high, but service is decent and the design is certainly impressive. Med is a fun place to start a night at the clubs near Chaoyang Park.

The Olive 橄榄树西餐厅

17 Gongti Beilu
Chaoyang
工体北路17号
朝阳区
Map 9 E3 **81**

010 6417 9669

Not far from the Workers' Stadium, The Olive serves some of the best European and Mediterranean food in town. In pleasant weather you can dine outdoors on the terrace, and enjoy one of their excellent fresh juices or smoothies. Weekend brunch is also available, with dishes including the popular avocado and cream cheese bagel. Service is genuine, and the appetiser sampler (mixed breads and dips) shouldn't be missed; it can easily serve four people. Prices are fairly standard for healthy cuisine in a nice, unfrilly, atmosphere.

1/F Trio Building
Jiangtai Xilu
Chaoyang
将台西路珀丽酒店1层
朝阳区
Map 5 D3 82

Salt 盐
010 6437 8457 | www.saltrestaurantbeijing.com

The gimmick is the salt, of course, with several varieties at each table. However, the food itself hardly requires any, thanks to the interesting spices and combinations; pork loin with rosemary and guava, tuna tartare with coconut foam, cured duck salad, and one of the best souffles in town. Service is uniformly excellent, and prices are reasonable; try a set meal for ¥68 to ¥168, depending on whether you dine for lunch or dinner, and whether you want two or three courses. An open kitchen compensates for the minimal decor, making this one of the best places in the Lido area.

Middle Eastern
Other options **African** p.304, **Indian** p.314

While Middle Eastern dishes are relatively rare, the places listed are among the best in the city. Another option is food from the Xinjiang region in China's far north west. There are many Muslims among the minority ethnic Chinese groups that live in the region, and their cuisine has a distincly Arabian flavour, mixed with Chinese influences. The Crescent Moon Muslim Restaurant (p.306) is a good example.

A30 Tianze Lu
(near Nuren Jie)
Chaoyang
天泽路甲30号(女人街)
朝阳区
Map 5 D3 83

Biteapitta 吧嗒饼
010 6467 2961 | ilovepitta@biteapitta.com

Head to Biteapitta for fresh pitta so good it's supplied to the local grocery stores. You can also buy it straight from the restaurant. Falafel is a great bargain, but also try the baba ganoush pitta and the fresh mint lemonade. Located near Dini's (below), this is the superior place for a quick bite or something to go. Authentic and inexpensive, the staff are friendly and the owner is almost always around.

32 Tianze Lu
(near Nuren Jie)
Chaoyang
将台乡天泽路32号(女
人街附近)
朝阳区
Map 5 D3 84

Dini's 蒂妮犹太餐厅
010 6461 6220 | www.kosherbeijing.com

Dini's is the best kosher restaurant in town, but unfortunately that isn't saying much – it is also the only kosher restaurant in town. All of the food adheres to Jewish dietary laws, and Dini's is also smoke free. You may, however, be surprised to see how few traditional Jewish dishes are on the menu. Sushi? Pasta? Burgers? Chinese? The food can be a bit bland, and the desserts are certainly lacking, but the matzoh ball soup is exactly what you'd want. Prices are higher than you might expect, but the staff are friendly.

B7 Xiushui Nanjie
Jianguomenwai
Chaoyang
建国门外秀水南街
乙7号
朝阳区
Map 11 E3 85

Istanbul 伊斯坦布
010 6503 2700 | www.kebabs24.com

Next door to Grandma's Kitchen (p.304), this restaurant is an often overlooked option on Xiushui Nanjie. Istanbul is a Middle Eastern-style joint providing healthy and exotic food at reasonable prices. It offers the classic appetisers, such as hummus, and *cacik*, a wonderful yoghurt sauce. The exotic pastas are surprisingly good, and you should try the mint teas. The restaurant is somewhat cramped, but you can order food through a delivery service or to take away.

Rumi 入迷餐厅

1A Gongti Beilu
Chaoyang
工体北路甲1号
朝阳区
Map 9 E3 **86**

010 8454 3838

Rumi provides startling, exotic, mouthwatering Persian cuisine in a classic Middle Eastern environment. For the adventurous there is *fenjensan* (chicken in a walnut and pomegranate sauce), hummus with spicy ground beef, and an excellent *ghormeh sabzi* (beef with red kidney beans and fenugreek). For the faint hearted, try the classic lamb, beef, and chicken kebabs, hot sandwiches or the surprisingly good cheeseburgers. Some dishes allow for vegetarian substitutes and all the meat is halal. The menu is comprehensive and reasonable, though the combo platters aren't a great bargain. Finish off your meal with shisha, available in many flavours.

Sahara 撒哈拉餐厅

Courtyard 4
Gongti Beilu
Chaoyang
工体北路4号院
朝阳区
Map 9 E3 **87**

010 6507 3521

Belly dancing, shisha and comfortable booths are all on hand at Sahara. It somehow looks much smaller than it is, but the decor is fairly authentic. However, the North African food is uneven and a bit pricey – the excellent Turkish salad gives way to mediocre and badly-presented meats. Buffets are available for those with large appetites, and though no alcohol is served, you can bring your own at no charge. Service at Sahara is helpful if inconsistent, so your best bet may be to bring a group and share a selection of dishes.

Russian

Traktirr Pushkin 彼得堡俄式餐厅

5-15 Dongzhimennei
Dajie
Sanlitun
东直门内大街5-15号
三里屯
Dongzhimen L2
Map 9 B2 **88**

010 8407 8158

You can't have a Russian restaurant without a huge vodka selection, and Traktirr Pushkin definitely delivers. Along with copious amounts of booze, you'll find traditional and modern Russian cuisine including the usual suspects like chicken kiev. Luckily, you won't need to queue on icy street corners for black bread – it is delivered to your table with cheese and sour cream. The staff have name tags in Russian and their English isn't exactly fluent, so you might have to order in a variety of languages, with some pointing thrown in.

White Nights 白夜西餐

13a Beizhong Jie
Dongcheng
北中街甲13号
Map 9 C2 **89**

010 8402 9595

Much like Traktirr (above), the portions are large and the prices fair, but the food at White Nights is a just a little bit better. However, you might find the service is glummer than a Moscow winter. The ¥5 beers are hard to beat, and the outdoor patio is pleasant in warmer weather.

Spanish

Other options **Mediterranean** p.319

Mare 古老海西餐厅

14 Xindong Lu
Sanlitun
新东路14号
三里屯
Map 9 E2 **90**

010 6417 1459

Mare offers modern Spanish fusion cuisine which isn't quite as expensive as Mare Nostrum (p.322). It is, however, almost as good and certainly easier to find. The wine list might not be up to expectations, but the paella (served only on Sundays) and the wide variety of tapas, are sure to tempt. The chicken stuffed with foie gras and the chocolate lava cake are also excellent. Mare's upmarket atmosphere and outstanding staff have helped make it one of the most romantic spots in town.

Mare Nostrum 橄榄园西班牙餐厅

6a Chaoyangmenwai
Dajie, Vantone Center 2/F
Chaoyang
朝阳门外大街甲6号万通
中心2层
朝阳区
Map 7 A2 **91**

010 5907 0088

Mare Nostrum's Michelin-star chef cooks up some phenomenal Catalonian tapas, but it doesn't come cheap. Squid with citrus; ham and mushroom croquettes; truffled potatoes and restaurant speciality *cochinillo* (roast suckling pig) all satisfy with careful presentation. Every detail has been addressed, with the possible exception of the service, which might not meet those Michelin in standards just yet. It is definitely worth looking for if you have the budget, but the odd location (it's in an office building) can be a bit off-putting.

Thai

Purple Haze Bistro 紫苏庭泰式餐吧

201, Building 3, China
View, Corner Gongti
Dong & Beilu
Chaoyang
工体北路中国红街3号
201, 朝阳区
Map 9 E3 **92**

010 6501 9345 | www.purplehaze.com.cn

Purple Haze operates a chain of reasonably-priced and popular eateries throughout Beijing. Their newest location continues the theme, with lounge-like surroundings and decent Thai food. Those familiar with the real thing may be disappointed, as most of the flavours are quite muddied, but that's sadly true of all of Beijing's Thai restaurants. The green papaya salad, lime chicken curry, and coconut and galangal chicken soup are best. Free Wi-Fi and live jazz on Wednesdays will help you overlook the indifferent service.

Serve The People 为人民服务

010 8454 4580

While many visitors consider the food pretty average, this neighbourhood favourite attracts a regular crowd from nearby Sanlitun for its excellent beef salad and pad thai. The pineapple fried rice is tasty, and the desserts are good value. Portions are generous, beer is inexpensive, and the patio is a good place to people watch. Friendly staff and a somewhat kitschy interior have sealed Serve The People's reputation.

Thai Thai 泰泰餐厅

010 6437 3480

A relative newcomer, this is probably the largest and best-designed Thai restaurant in town. Spread over two floors, the beautiful lighting, silk curtains, and Thai ornaments are surprisingly lovely, as is the food. As in other local restaurants, your appreciation will depend on your love of kaffir lime leaves, Thai basil, and other similarly difficult to find ingredients. The larb gai, tom yum goong soup, and curries are a cut above other spots, though prices are a bit higher. Thai Thai even has a cute gift shop.

Vegetarian

Bodhi-Sake 菩提缘素食斋

010 6355 7348

Set in the courtyard of a Buddhist temple, this restaurant is known for its vegetarian versions of popular meat dishes, including mock Peking duck. Soothing chants from the temple help put you in a peaceful frame of mind, while the library and art studio nearby help make this one of the best alternative places for a date. It is proud to be completely smoke-free. The prices won't offend, and the service is excellent.

Pure Lotus II 静心莲

010 8703 6668

Frequently voted 'best vegetarian' by local expat magazines, Pure Lotus is run by Buddhist monks – and it shows, in everything from the carefully prepared food to the pleasant, easygoing service. Prices are a bit higher than you might expect for a restaurant behind a warehouse. The tofu and mushroom-based dishes are uniformly excellent, making real meats look bad on occasion, and the unique handmade dishes and tables add another touch of class. There is another branch in Nongzhanguan Nanlu (010 6592 3627).

Vietnamese

7 Sanlitun Beilu (Behind 3.3 Mall)
Sanlitun
三里屯北里7号 (3. 3商场后侧)
三里屯
Map 9 F2 97

La Maison de Marguerite 玛格利特
010 6417 8288
La Maison de Marguerite offers French and Vietnamese food in comfortable surroundings with colonial flair. Caramelised ginger chicken, prune pork stew, lime and coriander salmon, and mango duck go far beyond traditional bowls of *pho*. The Vietnamese influences are clearer in the spring rolls and Saigon soup. Slow service adds to the relaxed and nostalgic feel, as long as you aren't in a hurry. Prices are around ¥50 to ¥70 for most main courses.

1 Chaoyang Gongyuan Xilu
Chaoyang
朝阳公园西路1号
朝阳区
Map 7 D1 98

Muse 妙
010 6586 3188
Popular with expats, this restaurant near Chaoyang Park, offers Vietnamese cuisine with a Parisian influence. The food isn't spectacular, and prices vary widely, but service is efficient and the menu pleases most diners. The Vietnamese coffee (with condensed milk) is excellent, as are the spring rolls and cold coconut shrimp soup. Though it can feel cramped and smoky at times, Muse still offers some of the best Vietnamese food in east Beijing. The set meals are a great bargain.

22 Qianhai Dongyan
Houhai
前海东沿22号
后海
Map 8 C3 99

Nuage 庆云楼
010 6401 9581
Trendy Nuage continues to impress out-of-towners and locals alike. Slightly hidden from the bustle of Houhai but still on the lakeside, it has splendid views and a wonderful interior (rickshaws for tables). These facts make up for the woefully inconsistent service and uneven food. The papaya salad is a good bet, as are the spring rolls and the lemongrass chicken.

Sugared Fruit

Time for tea

Cafes & Coffee Shops

Coffee is still a relatively new thing in China, and often the appeal of a cafe is more to do with its location than its cappuccino. Starbucks has a strong presence, but Chinese imitators UBC and SPR can be found across the city. Dotted between the galleries of 798 (p.176) are some of the best cafes in town. Those that line Nanluogu Xiang are unexceptional, but the street has a pleasant atmosphere. Wudaokou (p.96) and Sanlitun (p.168) also boast some quiet and relaxing spots to grab a coffee. Most cafes sell alcohol, staying open until midnight or until the last customer leaves. But, they tend to maintain their relaxed atmosphere, leaving raucous behaviour for bars and nightclubs. Most cafes have a good selection of light western meals and consider themselves family friendly, but parents expecting children's menus or baby changing facilities will be disappointed.

Jiuxianqiao Lu
Dashazi, Number 4 Gate
798
酒仙桥路4号大山子
798 & 丽都
Map 5 E2 `100`

At Café 爱特咖啡

010 6438 7264 | www.atcafe.com.cn

A favourite of the art crowd, the At Café is in the heart of 798. Like the galleries around it, the cafe shows signs of its first incarnation as a factory. Old cable drums and piping remain, while huge holes have been preserved in the brickwork of the partition wall. Posters of previous exhibitions cover the remaining wall space. The menu is high quality and alongside the usual sandwiches, pasta and pizza are chef's specials like goose liver salad. The coffee is Italian Illy brand and all wines are imported. Prices are reasonable with a cappuccino costing ¥18. Wi-Fi is available.

Building 4, Nan
Sanlitun Road
Sanlitun
南三里屯路4号楼
朝阳区
Map 9 F3 `101`

The Bookworm 书虫

010 6586 9507 | www.chinabookworm.com

Conversation and the clacking of laptops form the audio backdrop at this booklovers' haunt. Members can borrow from the 14,000 used books lining the walls. There is also a small range of new books, all free of airport trash. Easy chairs and sofas fill the back room, while the main room has a bar and small dining tables. The menu has decent wines and a wide range of dishes, all named after literary giants, like the Hemingway Cheesecake. There are lectures and a weekly open mic poetry night in a third room. This is an important centre of expat life and carries a few books that have snuck past the censor. Membership costs ¥300 per year. Entry and Wi-Fi are free.

Building 1, 1/F Huaqing
Jiayuan
Wudaokou
华清嘉园1号楼1层
五道口
🚇 *Wudaokou L13*
Map 4 C2 `102`

Cava Coffee 卡瓦小镇咖啡馆

010 8286 7297 | www.cava.net.cn

The quietly chatting clientele and autumnal colours lend warmth to Cava Coffee, making it an enjoyable and popular place. Its wooden flooring gives it a cosy feel and the low-key music adds atmosphere. Coffees, teas, smoothies and milkshakes are available, alongside a large selection of beers (including Belgian Trappist beer Chimay), wines, spirits and cocktails. The food menu includes fried breakfasts, soups, salads, sandwiches and pastas, and there is a reasonable selection of cakes. Customers can also make use of a piano and Wi-Fi.

26 Chaowainan Jie
Chaoyang
朝外南街26号（朝阳门
外大街附近）
朝阳区
🚇 *Chaoyangmen L2*
Map 11 D1 `103`

Goodwood Coffee 良木缘咖啡

010 8565 3700

Goodwood has a grandeur that is nicely balanced by decorative quirks like statuettes of grinning Rastafarians. The decor is just on the right side of tasteful and opposite a secluded balcony lies a row of unusual high-backed booths. Several international coffees are available, including Jamaican, Mexican and Sumatran, along with teas and soft drinks. The cafe is fully licensed, sells several German beers and has a decent list of imported wines. There are two French set menus (both featuring Caviar) and Wi-Fi is available.

24 Sanlitun Bei Jie
Chaoyang
三里屯北街24号
朝阳区
Map 9 F2 **104**

Gustomenta 古斯曼冰淇淋

010 6592 2978 | www.gustomenta.com.cn

For a taste of Italy, this is the full package, with walls as brightly coloured as the icecreams. The gelatos, containing less than 4% fat, are made on site by the Italian owner's brother, in 30 flavours and from natural ingredients. A range of beautiful sundaes is available, costing from ¥50 to ¥80, while a single scoop cone is ¥12. The cafe also serves food and alcohol. Wi-Fi is available.

Various Locations

Sculpting In Time 雕刻时光

010 5135 8108 | www.sitcoffee.com

This chain is popular with foreigners and there are seven branches in total, with no two quite alike. But there are common trends, such as wooden floorboards, plentiful sofas and similar menus. Breakfasts, sandwiches and pasta are on offer, but the standard is unspectacular. Alcohol is available. Besides Illy coffee, there are herbal and fruit teas. Wi-Fi is available.

Shuangqing Lu
(behind shops west of
Caijing East)
Wudaokou
双清路
五道口
🚇 **Wudaokou L13**
Map 4 D2 **106**

Space For Imagination 盒子咖啡馆

010 6279 1280 | www.hzcafe.com

This is a quiet place to escape the endless stream of students tramping about Wudaokou. It's comfortably furnished and dimly lit but not gloomy, with pictures of Chinese ethnic minority farmers from Yunnan and Guizhou lining the walls. The stereo plays Brazilian jazz and other relaxing world music. On Tuesdays and Saturdays, independent and world films are shown on a projector screen. There is an extensive coffee menu, with standard teas, beers, wine and cocktails all available. The food menu features sandwiches, soups, pasta, pizza, steaks and some Asian dishes.

Gongtibeilu, east of
Workers' Gym north gate
Dongcheng
工体北路工人体育场北
门东侧
东城区
Map 9 D3 **107**

Tasty Taste 泰笛黛斯

010 6551 1822 | www.tastytaste.com.cn

There is one reason for going to Tasty Taste – its huge array of delicious cakes. Black forest gateau, tiramisu and French cheese mousse cake are a few of the 30 or so delicacies available. Chinese attempts at western desserts often produce delicious looking, but atrocious tasting, cakes – this isn't the case here. The atmosphere is quiet and the decor is plain but pleasant. The menu also includes standard teas and coffees, as well as sandwiches and filled croissants.

89 Nanluoguxiang
Dongcheng
南锣鼓巷89号
东城区
Map 8 E3 **108**

Three Trees Café 三棵树

010 8401 9868

Three Trees Café is a bright and comfortable place to stop for a coffee on Beijing's popular Nanluoguxiang. There are several questionably upholstered sofas and the natural light makes a welcome change from the dimly lit cafes elsewhere. The menu includes fresh fruit, sandwiches, pasta, soup and pizza. You'll find several international coffees on offer, along with standard teas, smoothies, milkshakes, fruit juices, foreign beers and an average selection of cocktails. Wi-Fi is available.

Wudaoying Hutong
Dongcheng
雍和宫西五道营胡同
东城区
Map 8 F1 **109**

Vineyard Café 葡萄院儿

010 6402 7961 | www.vineyardcafe.cn

The Vineyard Café serves some of the best western food in Beijing, including a mean fried breakfast. It also does burgers, pasta, Indian dishes and moussaka. There is a decent wine list and some hard-to-find tipples like Old Speckled Hen. The atmosphere is relaxed, with huge sofas in the back room, a glass-roofed inner courtyard, and tasteful wooden furniture. Expats form the majority of the clientele. It also screens classic films and delivers food. Prices are fair and Wi-Fi is available.

Cocktail Bars
The city is more inclined towards wine bars and beery pubs than cocktail joints, although most bars do have a cocktail menu. Kokomo (p.333), the rooftop Sanlitun bar, mixes up mean drinks. The World of Suzie Wong Club (p.344) near the east gate of Chaoyang Park (p.191) is a big favourite amongst foreigners and has a long, fruity list of concoctions.

Drinks

Other options **Alcohol** p.249

Beijing is a boozy town, and both expats and Chinese like a drink. Culturally, it is frowned upon to decline the sauce when offered by a host. Beer is the most common tipple, and Qingdao (Tsing Tao) is ubiquitous. It's a crisp lager that has been exported for many years, and measures up against western brews. *Baijiu* is the notorious local firewater. You will hear it called Chinese 'white wine', but it is a merciless spirit of around 40% ABV. It tastes like schnapps mixed with battery acid. Foreign wine is expensive, as it attracts a hefty import tax, and local wine is still developing, but worth trying. Bars run the gamut from shabby *hutong* holes with a couple of broken chairs to trendy spots that wouldn't be out of place in London or New York. There is no excuse for being unsociable.

Drinking & Driving

In the run up to the Olympics, many local Chinese bars and restaurants strung up posters showing a cartoon policeman warning patrons against drinking and driving. Beijing drivers are prohibited from driving with a blood alcohol content higher than100mg of alcohol per 100ml of blood. Roughly three bottles of beer would put the average person over the limit. The Chinese licence is based on a 12 point deduction system. If you are stopped for driving under the influence you will lose six points if you are mildly intoxicated, and all 12 if you are heavily inebriated. Penalties for drink driving range from ¥200 to ¥2,000, as well as arrest and jail time.

Sports Bars
Sports bars are surprisingly few and far between. One notable exception is Frank's Place (p.331), which has a gourmet restaurant upstairs, sports bar on the ground floor and a wine bar in the basement. Also regularly showing sports is the recently relocated Goose & Duck (p.332). It has a great selection of big screens.

Bars & Pubs

Other options **Nightclubs** p.341

The bar scene offers live music, famous DJs, opulent splendour and seedy dens, and new spots have been opening up regularly in recent years. Some are more popular with foreigners, especially in Sanlitun, others with the Chinese, such as around the Workers' Stadium. Most are independent, but there are also some in hotels.

Generally speaking, bars have a happy, friendly atmosphere. Even the snottier ones, like the 'superclubs' in the Workers' Stadium area, don't have strict dress codes. Most bars and nightclubs stay open until the last customer leaves. Clubs usually charge a cover. In theory, the minimum drinking age is 18, but there is no enforcement. Alcohol is inexpensive. The price of a 330ml bottle of Qingdao, China's national beer, ranges from ¥10 to ¥30. A spirit and mixer usually costs ¥20 to ¥30. Shooters go from ¥10 to ¥30, cocktails ¥20 to ¥50. All bars have cocktail menus. Not all make them well. Two of the better cocktail bars are Kokomo (p.333) and Q Bar (p.337).

Some bars offer a good selection of foreign wines. A glass of the house stuff is usually ¥30, a bottle ¥120. The better imported bottles are typically ¥150 to ¥300. Whisky is popular in China and many venues have a good selection of single malts, such as Glenmorangie and Glenlivet.

161 Lanqiying (near Da Waguan Restaurant)
Wudaokou
蓝旗营161号
五道口
Map 4 C2 **110**

13 Club 13俱乐部
010 8262 8077 | *www.myspace.cn/13clubinchina*
The crowd-surfing capital of Beijing's live music scene, every existing shade of rock keeps the heart of this club beating. Thrash metal, punk and ska boom from the speakers, while a huge array of lights paint psychedelic patterns. There is graffiti on the walls and the floor is packed with students using cheap beer as dance fuel. Bands can be seen nearly every night, so music lovers won't regret a visit.

180 Degrees 180度酒吧

010 8261 3366

Pass between the two neon pillars and you will enter the largest bar in Haidian. The decoration is the same as many of the Workers' Stadium clubs, but the atmosphere is definitely friendlier and you'll find drinkers of all ages. Not daring to pick sides in the Beijing music dispute, the DJs flit between house, RnB and hip-hop. With so much floor space you don't have to worry about other people getting under your feet, so this place is great for anyone sick of the city crowds.

Take your pick

18 Zhongguancun Beidajie
Haidian
中关村北大街18号
海淀区
Map 4 C2 **111**

Alfa 阿尔法

010 6413 0086

Alfa holds the best 80s night in town and despite the fact it's the only 80s night around, it is still good. A little bit of older and newer music creeps in too, but the fluorescent decade remains the theme. There are fountains in the outer courtyard, with booths veiling you from other patrons. The interior is simple, with chairs, a dance floor and not much else. Alfa becomes Café St Laurent (p.312) during the day, a restaurant serving French cuisine until 16:00. Fridays play host to the 80s night and entry is free. Wi-Fi is available.

6 Xinfuyicun (west of Workers' Stadium north gate)
Chaoyang
幸福一村6号(工人体育场北门西侧)
朝阳区
Map 9 E3 **112**

Angel 唐会俱乐部

010 6552 8888 | *www.tangclub-bj.com*

Come to Angel to find sultry babes, handsome guys and lashings of glitz. The intricate neon tubes and other bits of design flair make this place pretty distinctive. Angel also stands out as it has more space in crucial places, such as in the private rooms which have their own DJ booths. It is a unique touch. Some big name acts like Judge Jules and John Digweed have come through, and more look set to take to the decks in the future.

Gongti Xi Men Workers' Stadium west gate
Chaoyang
工人体育场西门
朝阳区
Map 9 D4 **113**

Aperitivo 意式餐吧

010 6417 7793

Europeans can't seem to stay out of this minimalist venue, which is good for a pre-night out bite and or warm up drink. With bare floorboards, comfortable red chairs and sleek wooden tables, the decor is simple but refined. It sells the usual Italian dishes, including various versions of bruschetta. Charmingly, the music provides a backdrop rather than a challenge to conversation. Open from 10:00, this is a great place for coffee and Wi-Fi during the day, or a few drinks before heading on to dance.

43 Beisanlitun Nan (bar strip behind Sanlitun Lu)
Sanlitun
北三里屯南43号(三里屯路后酒吧街)
三里屯
Map 9 F3 **114**

Area 空间俱乐部

010 6437 6158

This is a far worthier candidate for the name Bed Bar than the place itself (p.328). Both venues have beds, but Area has them in abundance – sprawling in tiers, each one surrounded by veils, making for a comfortable and truly unique atmosphere. Recline in splendour as you watch people take to the central dancefloor, where sets are frequently provided by international DJs. Area is a good choice for the more discerning bar goer, and drink prices reflect the unusually luxuriant surroundings.

Fangyuan Xilu (behind Pascucci restaurant)
Chaoyang
芳园西路(帕斯古奇餐厅后)
朝阳区
Map 5 D3 **115**

Azucar Bar 阿苏卡音乐食坊

Yandaixie Jie
Houhai
后海烟袋斜街
Map 8 C2 **116**

010 8402 7477 | *azucarpub@hotmail.com*
You have to hunt for substance in the numerous bars around Houhai but Azucar has it. You won't find the meaning of life, but you will avoid irritating touts and atrocious musicians. With its fleet of old sofas, jazzy music, a fussball table and the occasional classic film poster, this is a good choice for retro fans. The food isn't up to much, but the drinks are all fine and reasonably priced for the area.

Ball House 波楼酒吧

40 Zhonglou Wan
Hutong, off Gulou
East Jie
Dongcheng
鼓楼东街钟楼湾胡同
40号
东城区
Map 8 D2 **119**

010 6407 4051
Ball House is something of a well-kept secret. It calls itself a pool hall but the layout is too fabulous for such a description. There are three pool tables and three table football tables, including a novelty mini pitch with just two lines of tiny players per side. Pool is ¥30 for an hour and football is free. You'll find wooden staircases leading to three little balconies, decked out with cushions and one even has a telescope pointing through a skylight. This is no place for wild partying, but great to visit with a group of friends for some peaceful chatting, sofa-lounging and pool playing.

Bar One

Dongfang Lu
100m east of Hilton
Chaoyang
东三环北路东方路希尔
顿酒店东100米
朝阳区
Map 5 C4 **123**

010 8455 2611
Bar One attracts a slightly older crowd, mainly made up of expats. It is a comfortable place to enjoy a few moderately priced drinks, and there's a small dancefloor for those keen to bounce about to the hip-hop, house and rock hits. There are also VIP rooms upstairs, where customers can recline on comfortable leather couches. Downstairs you'll find a cafe which sells pastries and Austrian food to soak up the booze.

Bed Bar 床吧

17 Zhangwang Hutong
Xicheng
张旺胡同17号
西城区
🚇 *Guloudajie L2*
Map 8 D1 **124**

010 8400 1554
Spectacularly comfortable (there are beds dotted about the place to cuddle up on), and divided into various little rooms to boost mystery and privacy, this is a great place to chill out or dance. Bed straddles the fence between quiet and boisterous. There's a dancefloor for those that want to move to the electronic music, and little rooms dotted around the exterior that are more conducive to conversation. There are also good, moderately priced cocktails.

Beer Mania 麦霓啤酒吧

Taiyue Hotel 1/F, South
Sanlitun Road
Sanlitun
南三里屯路泰悦豪庭
酒店1层
三里屯
Map 9 F4 **125**

010 6585 0786 | *http://beermania.todayinchina.com*
Beer connoisseurs will not feel misled by the name. In this small, specialist establishment there are more than 70 imported bottled Belgian beers and 100 other types including draught and international brands. The music is relaxing, the furniture is traditional and decoration comes by way of classic film posters. In addition to the standard snacks, the bar has a secondary speciality of waffles, with a variety of toppings. There is a computer where customers can surf the internet for free and Wi-Fi is available. The usual wines, spirits and soft drinks can also be purchased.

Bla Bla Bar

Beijing Language &
Culture University
Haidian
成府路学生会
海淀区
Map 4 D2 **126**

010 6239 7033 | *www.blablabar.cn*
This is Beijing's main hot spot for international student mingling. In the middle of the Beijing Language & Culture University, Bla Bla Bar has a long standing reputation as a venue for high spirits and low prices. The decor will suit people who prefer their trainers a bit scruffy, with the occasional piece of graffiti to brighten things up. Live bands play regularly, and there's an outdoor patio.

Butterfly 蝶 吧

Beisanlitun Nan
Sanlitun
北三里屯南
三里屯
Map 9 E3 127

010 6417 6357

This bar is unbelievably similar to the Kai Club (p.333) next door, right down to the pole on the dancefloor regularly buffed by drunken wannabe-strippers. Regardless, if they copied the formula they got the atmosphere right too. It's not huge, or impressively decorated, but the drinks are cheap, with bottles of Qingdao costing ¥10. A spiral staircase joins the floor to a balcony. There are plenty of cocktails and no cover charge, the music is pretty standard, with RnB and hip-hop.

The Capital Club 京城俱乐部

South Sanlitun Lu
Chaoyang
南三里屯路
朝阳区
Map 9 F4 128

010 8595 2751

Capital Club offers fine wines in a quiet, elegant environment. The menu features names such as Pomerol Reserve, Chateau Latour and a Chateau Lafite Rothschild (at ¥7,800). The decoration is traditional, with comfortable, wine-coloured chairs. Upstairs there are a few private rooms with televisions, and more comfortable seating. With its unobtrusive jazz soundtrack, this is a good place to talk business over a spectacular bottle of wine.

Casa Blanca 卡萨布兰卡

14 Nanyan, west of
Yinding Bridge
Houhai
银锭桥西南沿14号
后海
Map 8 C2 129

010 6613 1929

Huge murals of European scenery line the walls of this bar and the menu features pizza, pasta, sandwiches and snacks. There is a growing wine list alongside the other alcoholic drinks, including international beers and cocktails that are priced from ¥30 to ¥45. A Xinjiang musician performs a mix of modern Chinese pop hits and folk music every day. The staff are friendly and though the atmosphere isn't enchanting, it is colourful.

Casa Habana 哈瓦那之家

Jinglun Hotel, 3
Jianguomen Waidajie
Chaoyang
建国门外大街3号京
伦饭店
朝阳区
Map 11 F3 130

010 6595 0888 | *casahabana@hotmail.com*

All things Cuban await the visitor to Casa Habana. In pride of place among portraits of famous cigar lovers, including Che Guevara, naturally, is the owner's certificate of specialisation in Cuban cigars. All of these, which cost up to ¥2,000, are imported from Cuba. The island's music, rum and coffee can also be enjoyed. The club offers a walk-in humidor and lockers to store cigars for future enjoyment. Recline on one of the leather couches and ride a puff of smoke into paradise.

CD Jazz Café CD爵士俱乐部

16 Nongzhanguan Lu
(next to Sheraton)
Chaoyang
东三环农展馆路16号
（喜来登长城饭店）
朝阳区
Map 7 31 131

010 6506 8288

CD Jazz Café is, unsurprisingly, a great place to watch live jazz. The standard of music is good, with local and international musicians playing, and customers that are listening, rather than talking. Drinks are moderately priced and there is a cover charge on Fridays and Saturdays. The decor is pretty standard, with plenty of jazz memorabilia. It's not a huge bar but the atmosphere is relaxed and anonymous, with no pretentious jabber or snobby side glances.

Centro 炫酷

Kerry Centre Hotel
Chaoyang
光华路1号嘉里中心
饭店
朝阳区
🚇 *Guomao L1*
Map 11 F2 132

010 6561 8833 | *www.shangri-la.com*

Centro drains your wallet but delivers a dose of chic in return. A stamping ground for Beijing's rich and famous, the main draw is the cocktails. The menu is extensive, providing classic and modern recipes and (equally important), the staff know how to mix their drinks. Luxurious furniture and seductive lighting host an older crowd in the week, but on Fridays and Saturdays the kids come by. There's daily live jazz, except on

Sundays, when the mood goes Latin. You'll find special offers on selected cocktails on Mondays, Wednesdays and Thursdays, and the waitresses may be the most attractive in the city.

2/F, Tongli Studio
Beisanlitun Nan
Sanlitun
北三里屯南同里2层
三里屯
Map 9 F3 **133**

Cheers 酒吧

135 2044 6062 | cheersbjchina@yahoo.com.cn

Has the homely, pub feel of its television namesake, despite being wedged between the bars of the Sanlitun strip. There is daily live music, with western rock and alternative on weekdays and Xinjiang fusion rhythms at the weekend. It's all very compact, with a tiny stage and dancefloor with just enough room for a pool table. A pleasantly attitude-free place for a drink.

Shangri-La Hotel, 29
Zizhuyuan Lu
Haidian
紫竹院路29号香格里拉
饭店，海淀区
Map 4 B4 **134**

Cloud Nine 九霄云外

010 6841 2211 | www.shangri-la.com

Shangri-La is a mythical mountain paradise, and the hotel's bar, Cloud Nine, delivers on the promise suggested by the name. Naturally, you will need to dress smartly to be admitted into this den of expensive comfort. Benefits include splendour, regular live music and a spectacular drinks menu. A slice of heaven at a snip of the price.

4 Xiyan
Xihai
西海西沿4号
（地铁站250米）
后海
🚇 *Jishuitan L2*
Map 8 A1 **136**

Club Obiwan 润堤啤酒屋

010 6617 3231 | www.clubobiwan.com.cn

Many lament that lakeside Houhai has been swarmed by cheap bars and the accompanying desperate touts. However, the next door lake, Xihai, is relatively unscathed, and Obiwan is a great place to enjoy it. A rooftop terrace affords a view of the lake and there are two floors below. Beijing's best Reggae night takes place every Sunday and features a sizzling Jamaican barbecue. There are film nights on Thursdays and an open deck night on Wednesdays. Drink prices are cheap to moderate. It is 250m south of the subway.

Zhixin Lu
Wudaokou
志新路
五道口
Map 4 E2 **137**

Club Taku

131 2656 7320

Students and all the alcohol you can drink. In the standard spirit of such watering holes, this is a ramshackle establishment but the chairs are comfortable, the dancefloor is adequate and the music is one size fits all. Drink as much as you can manage on Thursdays for a fixed price.

78 South Sanlitun Lu
Sanlitun
南三里屯路78号
三里屯
Map 9 F4 **139**

Cross Lounge Bar 法雨

010 6586 5277 | www.bjcrossclub.com

Splendour and refinement come at a price at the Cross Lounge Bar. The third floor VIP section is for members only (annual membership starts at ¥11,200) and features a well-stocked humidor, pool table and balcony seating overlooking the live band. The menu features several pages of wines exceeding ¥1,000 and running up to ¥8,750 for a Chateau Haut Brion. Cuisine is French style, featuring dishes like fois gras and beef tenderloin with goose liver. This is a luxurious retreat for high-rollers but, with main courses priced in the ¥100 region, the more moderately-waged are not excluded.

4A Gongti East Lu
Chaoyang
工体东路甲4号（城市
宾馆北侧）
朝阳区
Map 9 E3 **140**

The Den 敦煌西餐厅

010 6592 6290

Sport, raucousness and late night pizza consumption are the main draws of the aptly-named Den. Sport is broadcast constantly on two reasonably sized televisions and framed sports shirts form the decoration. There is a daily happy hour from 17:00 to 22:00, when pizzas and all drinks are half price. Don't let the extensive food menu fool you into thinking this is some stuffy restaurant; come evening the music blares. Apart from 06:00 to 08:00 when they clean, it's open all day.

Dos Kolegas 两个好朋友酒吧

Liang Ma Qiao Lu
(south-east of cinema)
Chaoyang
亮马桥路(电影院东南侧)
朝阳区
Map 5 D4 **141**

136 9118 0119 | www.2kolegas.com

Bursting with character and the sounds of local rising music stars, this is a high quality venue for people who hate high quality venues. Beaten up but comfortable sofas, art prints, band posters and lizard prints form the decor. It's popular with Chinese and expat music lovers all year, but in the summer it goes into overdrive. Not only is there outdoor seating, but you can enjoy green grass and clean air, as the bar is tucked into the corner of Beijing's only drive-in cinema. Live bands play on most nights (usually punk or rock) with experimental electronic on Tuesdays. It also sells several real ales.

Drum & Bell 鼓钟咖啡馆

41 Zhonglouwan
Hutong (west of Drum
& Bell towers)
Dongcheng
钟楼湾胡同41号(钟鼓楼西侧)
东城区
Map 8 D2 **142**

010 8403 3600 | bjdrumandbellbar@yahoo.com.cn

This is one of the most comfortable places to chill out and enjoy cheap drinks. There's a roof terrace joined to the bar by a treacherously steep staircase and the decorations are mostly second-hand. Separated from the main bar by a glass partition is another room full of battered sofas, wood carvings and gloriously crumbling walls. Drinks are cheap and there's a host of imaginatively named shooters going for ¥10. The music includes Latin, reggae, funk and jazz.

Durty Nellies 爱尔兰酒吧

Liangmaqiao Flower
Market
Chaoyang
北三环东路，花卉市场底层
朝阳区
Map 5 C4 **143**

010 6593 5050 | www.durtynellies.cn

This is the kind of place where, with a few visits, everyone will know your name. A loyal crowd of Guinness fans form part of the furniture at Beijing's oldest Irish pub. The black stuff is on draught, and Irish beef stew, shepherds pie and fish and chips are among the authentic dishes on the menu, which also dabbles with Mexican and burgers. Nicely decorated, comfortably large and with a pool table, this is a pub with a homely feel.

East Shore Jazz Café 东岸咖啡

2 Shishahai Nanyan
Dianmen Waidajie
Houhai
地安门外大街什刹海
南沿2号
后海
Map 8 C2 **144**

010 8403 2131 | eastshorelivejazz@yahoo.com.cn

Another contender for best bar in Houhai, live jazz plays every night from Thursday to Sunday and there's no cover charge. The walls are decked with photos of performers and a semi-acoustic guitar is sunk into the wall behind glass. The atmosphere is chatty without disrupting the music and in summer there's a roof terrace and great views of the lake.

Face 妃思

Dongcaoyuan
Gongti Nanlu
Chaoyang
工体南路东草园(塞万提斯学院后)
朝阳区
Map 9 E4 **145**

010 6551 6738 | www.facebars.com

Face has a well planned and coordinated interior, well chosen items on the menu and staff who know how to make them properly. Artefacts from all over Asia blend with tasteful use of brightly coloured furnishings to make your eyes as happy as your taste buds. Raised Chinese beds hark back to the days of inns on the Silk Route. Recline and let history envelope you in this retreat from urban mayhem. Head behind the Cervantes Institute to find it.

Frank's Place 万龙富兰克酒吧

Jiangtai Xi Lu
Lido
将台西路
丽都
Map 5 D3 **146**

010 6437 8399 | www.trio-beijing.com.cn

This is a big hit with sports fans and Lido expats. If you're missing the feel of bars back home, or desperate to keep up with the Premiership, you'll like Frank's Place. It is a veteran of the Beijing bar scene, opening in 1989. It recently reopened at Trio in a venue that most prefer. Divided into four sections, you can chat quietly on the raised deck overlooking the garden, view sports on flat screen televisions in the bar, play pool and darts in the back area and in the summer, enjoy the outdoor terrace. The drinks, food and service all come recommended.

Get Lucky Bar 豪运酒吧

1 Jiuba Jie, Nuren Jie
Chaoyang
女人街酒吧街1号
Map 5 C4 **147**

010 8448 3335 | www.haoyun1996.com

Daily live music and ¥100 for all the beer you can drink are the main attractions here. The chairs and tables don't really match the vibe, but are comfortable enough and the venue is spacious. The unlimited beer is a home brew made according to a German recipe. It's a nice tipple available in dark and blonde. This isn't the main player on the live music circuit, but plenty of bands visit and the friendly service makes it a worthwhile stop.

Golden Club

2/F Tongli Studio
Beisanlitun Nan
Sanlitun
北三里屯南同里2层
三里屯
Map 9 F3 **148**

010 6413 2698

This is another newcomer bidding for a slice of the Sanlitun action, but Golden Club isn't just a clone of better bars. There's a sculpture that looks like a huge crystal exploding, and a mural depicting women and tigers to distract you from the cramped conditions. Qingdao beer is ¥20 a bottle, which is maybe a little ambitious for what the bar offers, but the cocktails are good and the place is so near all the other Sanlitun watering holes that a quick stop won't hurt.

Goose & Duck 鹅和鸭

S1, Greenlake
International Towers
Chaoyang
朝阳公园东门碧湖居国
际公寓S1
朝阳区
Map 7 D1 **149**

010 5928 3045 | www.gdclub.net.cn

Goose & Duck can keep sports fans entertained for days. A fairly spacious place, the decor is functional but there's limitless gimmickry to keep you hooked. Flat screen TVs broadcast sports and there are KTV rooms, a golf simulator, billiards, live music, authentic pub grub, air hockey, an outdoor terrace, catered parties, DJs, ladies nights and table tennis tournaments. It has virtually everything that a pub could offer, and if you do tear yourself away, there's a food delivery service.

Hai Bar 海吧

36 Yandaixie Jie
Houhai
烟袋斜街36号
Map 8 C2 **150**

010 6403 4913

Hai means sea, where most of the restaurant's Fujian-style food originates. But it also refers to the English 'high', which aptly describes its roof terrace, the loftiest by Houhai lake. The drinks list is uninspiring and prices are moderate. The food is fine but the best reason for a visit is to enjoy the views. This is an average bar with a splendid vista.

Huxleys 德彼酒吧

16 Yandaixie Jie (alley
between Yin Ding
Bridge & Dianmen)
Houhai
烟袋斜街16号 (连接银
锭桥至地安门胡同)
Map 8 C2 **151**

010 6402 7825

A trip to Huxleys is essential for newcomers to Beijing's bar scene. This was where the phrase 'shut up, just drink' was born. Since then, the slogan has encouraged hordes of students into near-fatal intoxication in this tumbledown shack. The tiny wall space is covered with knockoff *Simpsons* posters and graffiti. And all the shooters are there, including the Taiwan Duck Fart (whisky, Kahlua and Baileys). Besides that, it's the cheapest place to drink in Houhai.

i-Ultra Lounge

Block 8
Chaoyang
朝阳公园西侧8号公寓
区，朝阳区
Map 7 D1 **152**

010 6508 8585 | www.block8.cn

There's no questioning the style of i-Ultra Lounge, with its backlit table tops, post-modern chandeliers and sculpted seating. There's no questioning the pinch of the price either, but the management realises customers won't stay just because it looks pretty.

The bartenders mix good cocktails and indulge in some flaring (bottle juggling). The drinks menu is longer than your face is likely to be in the morning, when you realise how much you spent. Unfiltered sake, or nigori, provides the kick to their speciality Japanese cocktails. There is a daily happy hour from 18:00 to 21:00. Block 8 is by the west gate of Chaoyang Park.

2 Zhongku Hutong
off Gulou East
Dongcheng
鼓楼东钟库胡同2号
Map 8 D2 **153**

Jiangjinjiu 疆进酒

010 8405 0124 | www.jiangjinjiu.com
This is the place for an authentic Chinese folk music experience. Live bands play every Wednesday, Friday, Saturday and Sunday. Most Chinese people are Han Chinese, but there are 55 minority groups, such as the Bai and Uighur people. They all have their own traditional music, and you can hear it at Jiangjinjiu. The place is small but nicely decorated with instruments, art work and children's pictures. There is an upstairs area with beanbags, sofas and cushions. Most of the clientele are Chinese, but foreigners are welcome. Food from a nearby Yunnan restaurant is also available.

Beisanlitun Nan
Sanlitun
北三里屯南
三里屯
Map 9 E3 **154**

Kai Club 开

010 6416 6254
The original and best, Kai is crammed with students (and some grown-ups reliving their youth). Cheap drinks draw huge crowds, but the DJs work the music well, playing anything from breakbeat to old school classics. All the fun you'll have will distract you from the lack of decor. White spirits and a splash – including Red Bull – go for ¥10, as do bottles of Qingdao.

4/F Tongli Studio
Beisanlitun Nan
Sanlitun
北三里屯南同里4层
三里屯
Map 9 F3 **155**

Kokomo 卡勒比风情鸡尾酒餐吧

010 6413 1019 | kokomobeijing@gmail.com
Kokomo has the biggest roof terrace in town, and some of the best cocktails too. In the summer it's a great place to enjoy the night air with a frozen daiquiri, and a canopy goes over the terrace in winter. You can see the Caribbean theme in the cocktail and food menus, or hear it through the speakers. It's mostly calypso and reggae, and while other genres get played, there's a no hip-hop policy. Brazilian bands play every Thursday, while weekend evenings are drum n bass and classic dance hits. Wi-Fi is available and ¥88 will buy you a cocktail, appetiser and main course.

5 Nanguanfang Hutong
Houhai
南官房胡同5号
后海
Map 8 C2 **156**

La Baie des Anges 天使港湾休闲酒吧

010 6657 1605 | www.la-baie-des-anges.com
Another great Houhai bar. The furniture and decor are modern and stylish, featuring landscape paintings, mostly of the French countryside. The music is finely tuned by the brothers who run the place, but generally features jazz and French music on Wednesdays. The menu is French too, including pate and croque monsieurs, all ably made. The wine list is all French, and bottles range in price up to ¥4,000. There are regular theme nights and Wi-Fi is available.

Jiangtai West
798 & Lido
将台路西
798 & 丽都
Map 5 D3 **157**

La Cave 乐．卡瓦酒窖

010 6437 1242
A Korean run (and staffed) wine bar, boasting many vintages that you'll struggle to find elsewhere. There are more than 150 different drops, which go up to ¥2,000 in price. The decoration is tasteful, although a shade forbidding. Snacks such as cheese and crackers with salami and olives adorn the menu. It's mainly frequented by Korean patrons but the staff speak sufficient English to entertain westerners. The menu features Mediterranean fare with a lunch special for ¥88.

LAN 蘭会所

4/F LG Twin Towers, B12
Jianguomen Waidajie
Chaoyang
建国门外大街乙12号
LG双子座F层
朝阳区
Map 11 E3 158

010 5109 6012 | www.lanbeijing.com

The brainchild of designer Philippe Starck, LAN is a venue that provides food and drink for sophisticated tastes and music for cultured ears. Live music can be heard on most nights. Monday is ladies night, featuring two-for-one cocktails. Refreshingly, there is also a gentlemen's night on Wednesdays, where admission is free for men but ¥100 for women. Admission fees are reversed on Saturdays, when the resident DJ spins house hits. A must visit, if only to say you've danced in a masterpiece.

Latinos 拉其诺酒吧

A12 Nanxincang
south-west corner
Chaoyang
东四十条22号南新仓特
色街A12
朝阳区
Map 9 B3 159

010 6409 6997 | www.latinosclubchina.com

A spacious place to get fruity, Latinos brings salsa dancing to beginners and experts alike. Professional shows precede free salsa lessons every Wednesday. Other lessons are available on Tuesdays and Thursdays. The decor is simple and the dancefloor is wide open for twirling fellow salsa fans. There is a resident band, a ladies night on Tuesdays, and the mojitos really have all the trimmings.

Liana 离岸三十酒吧

30 Yandaixie Jie (alley
between Yin Ding
Bridge & Dianmen)
Houhai
烟袋斜街30号(连接银
锭桥至地安门胡同)
Map 8 C2 160

010 8405 0847

This is a cute little place, that opened recently on the enchanting alley leading away from Yinding Bridge. Fairy lights frame the entrance and there's a tree inside by the bar. The cocktails are wild, especially the flaming B52. There's a gorgeous roof terrace for the summer months and for the rest of the time there's a small but comfortable indoor section with chairs that swallow you like quicksand. It also has a huge pizza menu with 60 different varieties on offer. There are other western and Chinese dishes available, but the main reason for a trip here is the cocktails and insouciance.

Loco 塞亚咖啡厅

1/F Xijiao Hotel
Wudaokou
王庄路18号西郊宾馆
4楼1层
五道口
Map 4 D2 161

010 6232 2288

Loco is a small Korean bar with a big personality that pulls in an international crowd. The decoration is simple but stylish, with wooden chairs, tables and a couple of booths. According to the management, the main attraction – apart from Korean pop music – is the Mexican food, although choice is limited. Korean dishes are also served. Shisha pipes are available, along with beer, wines and spirits, as well as Korean *soju*, an alcoholic rice drink similar to Japanese sake. Customers in need of a distraction can make use of a selection of board games.

Lush

2/F Huaqingjiayuan
above 02 Sun Books
Wudaokou
华清嘉园1号楼2层
五道口
🚇 *Wudaokou L13*
Map 4 C2 162

010 8286 3566 | www.lushbeijing.com

A quiet relaxed eatery by day, this bar goes wild when the sun goes down. The decor is cheap, cheerful and comfortable, but it's the students who provide the colour. Lush is open 24 hours and serves tastes of home, including fried breakfasts, chilli wedges and chocolate mud pie. There are films shown on Mondays, quizzes on Wednesdays, live music on Fridays and an open mic night on Sundays. Expect crowds on weekend evenings.

Maggie's 美琪

South gate Ritan Park
Guanghua Lu
Chaoyang
光华路日坛公园南门
朝阳区
Map 11 D2 163

010 8562 8142 | www.maggiesbar.com

Maggie's is a Beijing legend for its comical seediness and determination to survive (it has relocated four times). The crowd tends to be older, with middle aged expats putting the moves on local girls, spurred on by the sight of scantily clad dancers. The claims about the quality of music are dubious, but it does have fantastic hotdogs.

3 Weigongcun Lu
Haidian
魏公村路3号
海淀区
Map 4 C4 **164**

Magic Rock 魔岩酒吧
010 6845 1142

Magic Rock is a popular drinking den for Beijing's climbing enthusiasts. As well as serving suds to make you merry of an evening, it organises climbing trips to mountains on the city's periphery. It is decorated with ropes, harnesses and pictures of climbers, to give customers that taste of being half way up a mountain. It also organises events such as New Years Eve parties.

111 Gulou Dong Da
Jie, Jiaodaokou
Dongcheng
鼓楼东大街交道口
东城区
🚇 *Beixinqiao L5*
Map 8 E2 **165**

MAO Livehouse 光芒酒吧
010 6402 5080 | *www.maolive.com*

MAO has a bar area and mezzanine where you can hide from the screaming of guitars on the surprisingly large stage. A three-tiered floor ensures decent views for everyone. The acts are a mix of local and international, mostly playing rock and punk. Graffiti covers some of the walls. Elsewhere there are posters of bands and opposite the bar there's a trippy mural by a Japanese artist. Drinks are reasonably priced and there's usually a cover charge.

Building 7, Sanlitun
North Lu
Sanlitun
三里屯北街7号楼
三里屯
Map 9 F2 **166**

Mingle 名格酒吧
010 6417 0090

This new bar is billed as classy, but the waitresses are dressed as PVC-uniformed nurses, French maids and policewomen. The music policy is no RnB or hiphop, but instead delivers house, techno and other electronic tunes. There are several theme nights, including acid jazz on Mondays and Tuesdays, singles night on Wednesdays, and live Latin music on Thursdays. The 80s feel extends beyond the waitresses' attire to the decor, but the cocktails are generally good and the prices reasonable.

The arty interiors of LAN

Nanjie 南街酒吧

South Sanlitun Lu
Sanlitun
南三里屯路
朝阳区
Map 9 F4 168

010 6413 0963

Beijing's rapid development forced this heavily graffitied bar to move to Sanlitun. Now it's cleaner and looks more respectable, with black tables and couches, but the party atmosphere survives. The music schedule, provided by house DJs, is rock on Wednesday, reggae, Latin and hip-hop on Thursday, with alternative rock, indie and new wave on Friday. Bars serve drinks upstairs and downstairs, including a famous array of lewdly-named shooters that are ¥10 each or 12 for ¥100. Snacks are available. The bar is just behind The Bookworm (p.254).

No Name Bar 无名酒吧

1 Dajinsi Hutong
Houhai
大金丝胡同1号
后海
Map 8 C2 169

010 6401 8541

This was the first bar to open in Houhai and many feel it's a shame the others followed. Tacky venues may have appeared, but No Name still offers class and a mellow atmosphere. Decorated with beautiful Yunnanese curios, basket chairs and glass-topped tables, world music completes the atmosphere. Shisha pipes are available in apple or strawberry, and Yunnan dishes are served at the nearby restaurant. To find the bar, look for the one-storey building draped with leaves, just south west of the Yinding Bridge between Houhai and Qianhai lakes.

Paddy O'Shea's 爱尔兰酒吧

28 Dongzhimen
Waidajie
Chaoyang
东直门外大街28号
朝阳区
Map 9 E2 170

010 6415 6389 | www.paddyosheas.com

The crowds at Beijing's newest Irish bar continue to swell. This is partly due to the disco upstairs (Shenanigans) where 80s and 90s hits blare all weekend. There's draught Guinness, of course, and plasma TVs showing sport. The menu includes a Jameson whisky-doused steak, Irish stew and some Gaelic interpretations of international favourites like tiramisu. Other perks include a pool table and Kilkenny ale. A friendly crowd awaits.

Passby Bar 过客

108 Nanluoguxiang
Dongcheng
南锣鼓巷108号
东城区
Map 8 E3 171

010 8403 8004 | www.passbybar.com

Passby is one of the more popular bars on Nanluoguxiang. There is an outdoor seating area sheltered by a clear roof, and a cosy balcony above the bar itself. The soundtrack tends to be jazz, world music or traditional Chinese. With lots of bookshelves and rustic wooden furniture, this is a good bar for demolishing a bottle of whisky while chewing over the philosophical cud. There is also a good food menu, featuring European and Chinese dishes.

Pepper Bar 辣椒酒吧

Chaoyang Park
west gate
Chaoyang
朝阳公园西门2号
朝阳区
Map 7 D1 172

010 6592 0788 | jerry0110@126.com

The bartenders spin bottles here quicker than the DJ spins vinyl. The flashy bar show even involves a little flame throwing. You don't have to wait for someone to order a cocktail to enjoy this floorshow. It takes place at the same time every night and the results get dished out for free. There's a roof terrace that is great in the summer and the decor inside is red and decadent. The only problem is the less than imaginative music, but this bar still pulls in the crowds.

Poachers 友谊青年吧

43 Beisanlitun Nan
Sanlitun
北三里屯南43号
三里屯
Map 9 F3 173

010 6417 2632 | www.poachers.com.cn

Poachers is generally considered a good place to take a break from being single. It has the feel of an indie club, but that doesn't stop the music veering off on pop tangents. No matter the tunes, it pulls in crowds of young Chinese and expat drinkers. The drinks are cheap, with prices plastered on the bottles to save you the bother of holding a menu. A couple of murals inject some verve into the club's bare brick and concrete design, while the raised stage makes for great people watching – or dancing if you feel the urge. There is a cover charge at weekends.

St Regis Hotel
Chaoyang
建国门外大街21号北京
国际俱乐部饭店
🚇 *Jianguomen L1*
Map 11 F3 **174**

Press Club Bar 记者吧

010 6460 6688 | www.stregis.com/beijing
Connect with history in this luxurious monument to foreign correspondents. Bookshelves heave under leather-bound volumes, comfortable chairs cushion your weight, while low lighting and a marble fireplace complete the tasteful decor of this upscale bar. Of course, you'll be drinking in the presence of legendary journalists – or their photos at least. The menu features eight different bloody marys and a fine selection of single malt whiskies. This hotel bar has seating for 55 and features live music, and is a great place to recline in sophisticated comfort.

Huaqing Jiayuan
Wudaokou
华清嘉园
五道口
Map 4 C2 **175**

Propaganda 五角星酒吧

010 8286 3991
Propaganda has one purpose – to be a place where students, and some older revellers, can grind to non-stop hip-hop. Drinks are dirt cheap but some customers have complained of unusually severe hangovers, so bottled beers are a safe policy. The format works and this place is constantly packed with wild, dancing, bright young things.

Basement, Building 12
Huaqing Jiayuan
Wudaokou
华清嘉园12号楼底层
五道口
Map 4 C2 **176**

Pyro Pizza 品诺比萨

010 8286 6240 | www.lushbeijing.com/pyro
The pizzas are tasty and the booze menu is basic, making this a popular spot in the student district. The fact that it serves Stella Artois and Guinness helps too. The decor is plain, with wooden chairs and benches and photos of drunken debauchery speckling the walls. Three televisions broadcast sport and the music goes in all directions. Happy hour runs daily from 22:00 to midnight and delivery is available around the area from 11:00 to 22:00.

6/F Eastern Inn Hotel
South Sanlitun Road
Sanlitun
南三里屯路逸羽连锁
酒店6层
朝阳区
Map 9 F4 **177**

Q Bar Q吧

010 6595 9239 | www.qbarbeijing.com
This place evokes a glamour-drenched bar from 30s Shanghai. It's stylish and modern, but with a flavour of Oriental mystery. Six floors up, the ample roof terrace provides a view, while droplet-shaped lights and designer sofas are interspersed with palm trees inside. The huge cocktail menu features 20 different martinis and an extensive range of other classics. Music is relaxed, usually jazz, except on weekend evenings when the tempo speeds up. Popular with the expat crowd, this is a great place for mingling or enjoying an open air drink in the summer. There are also regular sets by foreign DJs.

South Sanlitun Lu
Sanlitun
三里屯南路
朝阳区
Map 9 F3 **178**

The Rickshaw 生活园意大利餐厅

010 6500 4330
This is a pleasant spot for a drink and some awesome Mexican food. It's open 24 hours, and has a decent range of western beers. There's a nice balcony by a huge glass window, which would be improved by a better view. Besides the extensive Mexican menu, including burritos, quesadillas and chimichangas, you can also enjoy big breakfasts and deep-fried Snickers bars. There's a pool table upstairs and Wi-Fi is available.

199 Andingmen Dajie
Dongcheng
安定门大街199号
东城区
Map 8 E1 **179**

Room 101 友情部落西餐厅

010 6402 7532
Absolutely unconnected with Orwell's 1984, there's a curiously nautical theme in the layout, but a relaxed feel pervades. The menu features all manner of Gallic delicacies and there are three happy hours, including one between 04:00 and 05:00. Customers, mostly European and American, are regularly entertained with live jazz funk.

South Sanlitun Road
Sanlitun
南三里屯路
朝阳区
Map 9 F4 180

Salsa Caribe 莎莎卡利宾拉丁俱乐部

010 6507 7821

Hugely popular with Beijing's Italian and Spanish crowds, this bar offers free salsa lessons from 19:30 to 21:00 every day. And if you can't get the hang of it, you can watch the professionals later. The Venezuelan house band performs daily until midnight, when dance and rock tracks get slipped between the salsa classics. A big venue with a big balcony, the interior is dark but the atmosphere bright. Snacks are available and the mojitos are good.

66 Nanluoguxiang
Dongcheng
南锣鼓巷66号
东城区
Map 8 E2 181

Salud 老伍

010 6402 5086

Beijing's premiere tapas bar is also one of the better venues for electronic music. In addition to regular DJ nights, the management hosts live bands every Wednesday. The decor is warm, with wooden chairs and floorboards, and a balcony with sofas. The house speciality is fruit infused Havana Club rum, available in several flavours for ¥20 a shot. The tapas is good and drinks are inexpensive. What really makes this bar popular, especially with the European crowd, are the savvy DJs.

Unit 5, 51 Dianmen West Jie
Xicheng
地安门西街51号5单元
西城区
Map 8 C3 182

Sex & Da City 欲望都市

010 6612 5046 | www.sexanddacity.com

As the name suggest, this is not a bar that's big on subtlety, but it's fairly inoffensive. Go-go girls work the poles, but their clothes stay on. The decor is pretty unremarkable, although there are some cosy booths on the second floor, for which a varying minimum charge must be paid. The drinks menu is a little pricey, the music is usually RnB and most of the customers are Chinese.

Beisanlitun Nan
Chaoyang
北三里屯南
朝阳区
Map 9 F3 183

Shooters 速特酒吧

010 6416 3726

This bar has no qualms about its aims, serving up an arsenal of different shots at ¥10 a pop – with predictable results. But the crowd is jolly rather than lairy, and happy to jig about to standard dance hits. You may hear YMCA, and it may be met with excited arm movements. The decor is plain, the drinks are cheap and the bar is usually packed. Sanlitun's other bars are nearby, should it all get a bit much.

Ritan Park, Ritan Lu
Chaoyang
日坛路日坛公园
朝阳区
Map 11 D2 184

Stone Boat 石舫

010 6501 9986 | stoneboatcafe@126.com

This really is a stone boat, set among the weeping willows on Ritan Park's scenic lake. Indoor space is limited but pretty, with wooden beams painted in a traditional style. During the summer, the outdoor seating and live music make this a winning venue. It is an equally enjoyable spot day or night, with a clean, car-free atmosphere. Snacks are available, as is party catering (with a day's notice). Live music runs from April to October and Wi-Fi is available. Email stoneboatcafe@126.com for inclusion on the gig mailing list.

43 Beisanlitun Nanlu
Sanlitun
北三里屯南43号
三里屯
Map 9 E3 185

The Tree 隐蔽的树

010 6415 1954 | www.treebeijing.com

Equally worthy as a bar or restaurant, The Tree sells delicious pizzas, 40 Belgian beers, and other tipples rarely found in Beijing, like Newcastle Brown Ale. The house beer, Tree Ale is worth a taste. The pizzas are served fresh from a stone oven, but diners seeking something else can choose from a range of dishes including croque monsieurs, soups and salmon steaks. There's a warm atmosphere and occasional live music. To find it, walk up Sanlitun Houjie, take the first left, then walk around the Youyi youth hostel.

Bars & Pubs

Waiting For Godot 等待戈多咖啡馆

Building 4, 24
Jiaodaokou Dongdajie
Xicheng
交道口东大街24号
4号楼
西城区
Map 8 F2 186

010 6407 3093

This is part bar, part cafe, part gallery. The window is dressed with an array of arty pieces and many more are for sale inside. Also for sale are art cinema DVDs, jazz CDs and some arresting notebooks. The soundtrack is all jazz, but the backbone of this venue's extraordinarily laid back vibe is its sheer originality. Quiet, refined and with posters designed by the owner, it's a great place to indulge in highbrow chat.

White Rabbit 小白兔酒吧

C2 Haoyun Jie, 29
Zaoying Lu, Maizidian
Chaoyang
麦子店枣营路29号好
运街C2
朝阳区
Map 5 D4 187

133 2112 3678

While not visually as stunning as Alice's wonderland, White Rabbit does have psychedelics flowing from the speakers. The music is exceptional and includes high quality house. It is one of a handful of clubs in Beijing to offer drum n bass. It's also one of the few to host a gay night – Queeressence on Thursdays. The drinks are pretty cheap. White Rabbit is a great place for anyone serious about electronic music.

Writers Bar 作家酒吧

Raffles
Dongcheng
东长安街33号北京饭店
莱佛士
东城区
🚇 *Wangfujing L1*
Map 10 E3 188

010 6526 3388 | www.beijing.raffles.com

The pristine interior looks exactly as it might when the luminaries it honours visited. Scribes who have stayed at Raffles include George Bernard Shaw, Edgar Snow and Chinese novelist Guo Mo Ruo. The historic building has stood in its place since 1917, and the decor looks unchanged, with Persian rugs, wooden arm chairs and elegant curtains. The menu features caviar, oysters, cocktails and cigars, and the pink gins are excellent.

Chaoyang nightlife

Hilton Hotel
Chaoyang
东三环北路东方路1号
希尔顿饭店
🚇 *Dongzhimen L2*
Map 5 C4 189

Zeta Bar 颐达吧

010 5865 5000 | *www.hilton.com*

Zeta is a bar in a hotel, rather than a hotel bar. It's an important difference, and one that means this is a spot for revelry, rather than being sensible. The design is glamorous, with bottles hanging in cages behind the curvaceous bar, and a carpet you're glad it's someone else's job to clean. It offers cheap prices during happy hour and has some good live acts. Women get free sparkling wine on Fridays, when the glamour goes out the window, and this otherwise upmarket spot has its ladies' night.

Quiz Nights

Trivia in Beijing is far from trivial. Teams stake out their turf religiously, and victors lord it over their defeated opponents with free booze when the games are done. This may not be the best place to make a friend, as it's where some bitter rivalries are born. Sometimes, just having the brains isn't enough; you have to show them off.

Match wits against Beijing's brightest and most knowledgeable at the weekly events at Sanlitun's Bar Blu (p.342). This quiz features probably the hardest questions of all the weekly trivia nights, but winners are rewarded with a bottle of their favourite liquor and bragging rights, at least until the following Wednesday rolls around. The quiz starts at 21:00, but arrive a little bit early to reserve a table and enjoy Bar Blu's famous happy hour specials.

Quiz Nights		
Bar Blu (p.342) Quiz Night	010 6417 4124	Wednesdays 21:00-23:00
Lush (p.334) Trivia Night	010 8286 3566	Wednesdays 20:00-22:30
Tim's Texas Trivia Night	010 6591 9161	Tuesdays 20:00-22:30

The Wudaokou-based quiz night at Lush is perfect for students who need to get away from their studies and show how much they have learned. Regarded by many as the rowdiest of the capital's quiz nights, Lush's trivia night provides a great opportunity to meet new people while showing off your knowledge of Russian pop stars and Pakistani resistance leaders.

On Tuesdays, Tim's Texas BBQ joins in. Although some in Beijing have remarked that the food at Tim's Texas has been on the decline, the trivia contests should still be enough to get you back in the saddle. Unlike the largely British-themed questions at Bar Blu, Tim's Texas BBQ offers a contest that's perfect for red-blooded Americans.

Nightclub lighting

Chow down

Nightclubs

The quality of nightclubs in Beijing falls short of those in Shanghai, but the scene is hip in its own way. For one thing, it is very affordable. Cover charges are rarely more than ¥50 or ¥100 and usually come with a free drink or cocktail. International DJs make regular appearances at larger venues, which sometimes drives up entrance fees, but the cost of a spirit and mixer will rarely top ¥50.

Clubs attract mixed groups, both foreign and local, and stay open till the wee hours. Design and decor tends to be flashy and OTT, but then nightclubs aren't known for subtlety. If thumping techno leaves your eardrums aching, the live punk and rock scene gets healthy support from venues across the city. MAO Livehouse (p.335), D-22 (p.343), and Yugong Yishan (p.344) have secured a reputation for showcasing quality live acts from a wide variety of genres. At the other end of the spectrum, there are plenty of posh clubs serving proper cocktails to well-heeled clientele.

Babi 芭比俱乐部

010 6551 3338 | www.babiclub.com

Many people think this club's geographical spread – with venues in Shanghai and Guangzhou – gives it a special perspective. Other people think it's just like all the other clubs. There is an overlap; VIP tables, flashing lights, fairly generic tunes, and a seated mezzanine, but there are differences in these common elements. The bar is rounder and whoever chose the coloured lights dared to break away from the red that dominates everywhere else. This place intends to feel more fun than those of its neighbours, who like to treat customers mean to keep them keen.

Babyface

010 6551 9081 | www.babyface.com.cn

Babyface is hugely popular. Space is sparse despite its size because it is permanently packed, mostly with Chinese clubbers. Babyface provided the blueprint for other superclubs, with booths, private rooms, flashing lights and high prices. Some find the service unfriendly. Scantily clad girls are often drafted in to dance on the podiums and it attracts big name DJs. There is a cover charge to enter and another venue at Triumph Plaza, Xizhimen Waidajie, Xicheng (010 8801 6848).

Banana 巴娜娜

010 6528 3636

Shaping the scene rather than moulding to it, Banana has long been attracting discerning house music enthusiasts. The layout is less bland than the hordes of imitators, with a balcony overlooking one of the city's bigger dancefloors. Not only is it a good size, but it bounces like a trampoline. Seriously. Banana sees itself as one of the first clubs to get international acts and continues to play host to DJs such as Paul Van Dyke. Upstairs is the Spicy Lounge which offers a bar and a different sound.

The Bank

010 6553 1998

Local clubbers were disappointed with The Bank's debut, which featured a popular Shanghai DJ spinning well below his usual standards. Recent months have seen a turnaround in fortunes however, and international DJs are beginning to fill the roster. Accordingly, the DJ booth, complete with huge video screens, has pride of place on the gigantic dancefloor. The second floor lounge overlooks the dancefloor, and VIP rooms occupy the third. Drink prices are high.

Bar Blu 蓝吧

010 6417 4124

4-5/F Tongli Studio
Sanlitun Beijie
Sanlitun
三里屯北街同里4-5层
三里屯
Map 9 F3 **122**

Bar Blu is a scruffy, popular club with cheap drinks. The music doesn't stray far from the latest pop and hip-hop, and in response, the tiny dancefloor is usually packed with a mix of expats and local Chinese, many of them young women. As the name implies, there's plenty of blue lighting, though the haze of cigarette smoke softens the effect. The huge rooftop bar is an excellent place for laidback drinks and late-night chats, and gets particularly busy during the summer. Standard pub food is available to help you refuel for the next round on the dancefloor. Aside from the weekend grinding, Monday's happy hour game, where patrons buzz-in for drink deals, is a longstanding favourite, as is Wednesday's quiz night (p.340).

Block 8 诗景画意

010 6508 8585 | www.block8.cn

8 Chaoyang Gong
Yuanximen
Chaoyang
朝阳公园西门8号
朝阳区
Map 7 D1 **193**

This entertainment complex is the hub of the action around Chaoyang Park's west gate. It houses popular Japanese restaurant Haiku by Hatsune (p.316), Med (p.319), and i-Ultra Lounge (p.332). The modern decor of i-Ultra Lounge is marred only by the bikini-clad go-go girls that dance on raised platforms opposite the DJ. Block 8 also houses the latest addition to China's upscale bar scene, an outdoor patio called The Beach. It is a favourite with the beautiful people, who go to see and be seen while reclining on beds or lounging in cabanas. Block 8 is one place where you may have to cough up hefty cover charges at the door, or pay steep minimum prices for a table. Even if the swankiness isn't to your taste, it's worth visiting once.

Cargo Club 酒吧

010 6551 6898

6 Gongti Xilu
Chaoyang
工体西路6号
朝阳区
Map 9 D4 **194**

Cargo's deluge of neon lights might do permanent damage to your retinas but, for many, it's worth the risk. Cargo hosts international DJs that spin mainstream house. Wealthy Chinese, foreign clubbers, and other pretty young things dominate the dance floors and occupy space at the VIP tables. For those seeking a break from thumping beats and casual posing, there's a KTV lounge. On your way out, be careful not to stumble on the Porsches or BMWs in the carpark – the high rolling clientele can turn ugly fast.

China Doll 中国娃娃

010 6415 8695 | www.chinadoll.com

2/F Tongli, Sanlitun
Beijie
Sanlitun
三里屯北街同里2层
三里屯
Map 9 F3 **195**

China Doll's decor says it all. A video loop projected on several walls shows near nude, nubile men and women contorting themselves into intriguing positions underwater. Table lamps bear paintings featuring traditional Chinese characters in positions that would give Kama Sutra fans a run for their money. In short, the two-storey club exudes sex. However, the clientele is generally similar to those you would find at less explicit places. Crowds are on the younger side, and the music is usually funk or house, with the occasional drum n bass night.

Club 88

010 6413 0913

43 South Sanlitun
North Road
Sanlitun
南三里屯北街43号
三里屯
Map 9 F3 **135**

A newcomer to the strip, Club 88 stands out for not being a hip-hop and RnB club. Chinese and western DJs spin hits covering genres like breakbeat, techno and house. Other than that, it looks pretty cheap, but the decor is at least reflected in the price. A bottle of Qingdao goes for a mere ¥10. There are a few couches, a couple of booths and a moderately sized dancefloor.

Coco Banana 巴那那

010 8599 9999

Same club different entrance. Coco Banana is an offshoot of the Banana Club (p.341). Limitations include cramped conditions, but go-go girls perform to get clubbers in the mood for house and techno. Like most of the Workers' Stadium clubs, Coco Banana gets its share of big name DJs. John Digweed visited recently. The decor is modern and flashy with plenty of glitz. Beers are club prices and there's a cover to enter.

Gongti Xi Men
Chaoyang
工体西门
朝阳区
Map 9 D4 **138**

Cutie Club 美丽会

010 6552 9988 | www.cutieclub.cn

The one thing distinguishing the Cutie Club from the rest of the superclubs is a curious array of plastic cylinders running along the bar and the tables. Otherwise it's the same; predominantly red colour scheme, designer chairs and sofas, light shows, booths on the ground floor and a balcony. The drinks menu is impressive though, with a vast selection of whiskies. The music is mainly hip-hop and RnB. Bottled beers cost ¥30 and there is a cover charge to enter.

Gongti West Lu
Workers' Stadium
west gate
Chaoyang
工体西路，工人体育
场西门
朝阳区
Map 9 D4 **196**

D-22

010 6265 3177 | www.d22beijing.com

Another live music mainstay, D-22 is devoted to promoting new talent. It is a not-for-profit organisation. It is also run as a workshop for musicians and filmmakers and a place for international musicians to collaborate with local rising stars. It delivers on its ethos with a great atmosphere and entertaining acts. You can see live music on most nights and up to five bands on Saturdays. It's fairly spacious with a balcony overlooking the stage. Film lovers can enjoy screenings on Wednesday and Thursday evenings. If you like live music, you need to visit this bar.

242 Chengfu Lu
Wudaokou
成府路242号
五道口
🚇 *Wudaokou L13*
Map 4 C2 **197**

Mix 密克斯

010 6530 2889

Mix is a meat market. The bar, along with its neighbour Vic's (p.344), offers a winning combination of pop and hip-hop, beautiful waiting staff and plenty of booze. The bouncers may be the beefiest Chinese men you'll ever encounter, and they are fierce. The occasional brawl or bar fight breaks out on rowdy nights. Mix is partitioned into several areas, each featuring different music. So you can flit from room to room chasing, or hiding, depending on your intentions.

Gongti Beilu
Chaoyang
工体北路工人体育场
北门
朝阳区
Map 9 D3 **167**

Sòng Music Bar & Kitchen 颂音乐餐吧

010 6587 1311 | www.songbeijing.cn

Sòng is one of the most stylish additions to Beijing's club scene. Designed by sculptor Zhong Sòng, it features gorgeous, undulating wood that mimics paddy fields and boosts acoustics. The other half of the Sòng team is Neebing, a pioneer of electronic music. Sòng is not another meat market – it is a club that delivers good music in tasteful, original surroundings. The resident DJ is Nils Krogh, a Swedish nu-jazz musician who spins, plays live keyboard, and bowls over anyone with an appreciation for avant-garde musical talent.

B108, The Place
9 Guanghua Lu
Chaoyang
光华路9号世贸天阶
B108
朝阳区
Map 11 E1 **200**

Tango 糖果

010 6428 2288 | www.tanguo.com

Tango is a fair distance from the main nightclub strip and the cavernous club is the sole entertainment venue at the entrance to Ditan Park. Despite the location, it draws a loyal following with its large dancefloor and top DJs spinning tunes far into the night. The bar is actually open 24 hours and has well trained staff. Tango made wise choices

79 Hepingli Xijie
Dongcheng
和平里西街79号
东城区
🚇 *Yonghegong L2*
Map 5 A4 **201**

with design, eschewing go-go girls and excess neon and the distracting frills coveted by other nightclubs.

Vic's 威克斯

*Gongti Beimen, Workers'
Stadium north gate
Chaoyang
工体北门工人体育场
北门
朝阳区
Map 9 E3* 202

010 5293 0333 | www.vics.com.cn

This dance club throws down the hip-hop, lures booty shakers, and rakes in a tidy profit every weekend. The clientele is a mix of young expats (including kids from international schools, capitalising on lax ID policies) and hip Chinese drinkers. Vic's stands opposite Mix (p.343), and the clubs are often referred to as a team. Recent renovations have made it one of Beijing's largest clubs, but beware the dim interior and flashing lights; many a high-heeled girl has taken a tumble on the neon pink catwalk connecting the dancefloor to the chill out lounge. As with Mix, some mean Chinese bodyguards man the entrance. It is not a good idea to argue or be aggressive, as fights have been known to break out between clientele and bouncers.

The World Of Suzie Wong 苏西黄

*Chaoyang Park
west gate
Chaoyang
朝阳公园西门
朝阳区
Map 7 D1* 203

010 6500 3377 | www.suziewong.com.cn

East meets west with twists of 1930s Shanghai and 'classic dynasty culture' in Suzie Wong's. The split level upstairs has empty bird cages and red lanterns dangling from traditionally painted beams, as well as an outdoor balcony for the summer months. Decorative philosophy aside, this is a place where singles meet and move to house music. Drinks are club prices, ¥35 for a beer, and the menu features some impressive champagnes. It has won more awards in Beijing's listings magazines than any other club in the city. Come for the splendour, stay for the opium den vibe. Entry costs ¥100.

Yugong Yishan 愚公移山

*3 Zhangzi Zhong Lu
Dongcheng
张自忠路3号
东城区*
🚇 *Zhangzizhonglu L5
Map 8 F3* 204

010 6404 2711 | www.yugongyishan.com

Even as a no-frills club on an obscure patch of pavement near the Workers' Stadium, Yugong Yishan attracted a loyal following. It was known for its impressive selection of live music, spanning international acts and local talent, but that location is now a parking lot. Some people decry the new space as too slick and upmarket. Some say the drinks are overpriced. Others are just relieved that Yugong Yishan now offers a clean bathroom. But no one is complaining about the acts, which continue to be top notch.

The World of Suzie Wong

Gay & Lesbian

Beijing is, in some ways, gay and lesbian friendly. The community is open to fellow G&L expats, and hate crimes are rare. Discussion of gay topics can elicit giggles from local Chinese, which may appear disrespectful, but are generally just a sign of nervousness and a lack of experience of talking about such issues.

However, non-discrimination laws are still limited, so many gays and lesbians keep quiet about their sexuality (especially with their employers). Gay men are also barred from adopting children. One phrase that may crop up in local papers is MSM. This quaint abbreviation stands for 'men who have sex with men'. It's a phrase that some members of the local gay community believe amounts to a denial of homosexuality's existence. Often, Chinese 'MSM' have wives and children.

Despite the fact that homosexuality was classified as a mental disorder until 2001, there is a pretty strong gay scene in China , and many popular bars are considered to be gay-friendly. There are, of course, some more 'sceney' LGBT spots such as Destination and West Wing (see below) but on the whole, a night painting the town pink will be low-key and relaxed. Mainstream club White Rabbit (p.339) offers a gay night on Thursdays and you'll find most of the larger, music-focused venues such as The World of Suzie Wong (p.344) are open minded.

Quick word of warning; 'Peking duck' is local slang for rent boys, so be careful where you order it.

Jushi Dasha
Gongti Beilu
Chaoyang
工体北路巨石大厦
朝阳区
Map 9 C3 `205`

Cosmo 科兹莫酒吧

010 5190 8918

Cosmo is friendly to gay, lesbian, straight, and bi club goers. Unlike often claustrophobic Destination (p.345), the grand daddy of Beijing gay bars, Cosmo features vaulted ceilings and plenty of space to get your groove on. Special drinks include the Rainbow shot and the (snigger) Cosmo-BJ.

3 Shajing Hutong
Nanluoguxiang
Dongcheng
南锣鼓巷沙井胡同3号
东城区
Map 8 D2 `206`

Desert Oasis Bar 沙漠绿洲

010 6403 7856

This is not strictly a gay bar, but does attract members of the Chinese lesbian community. Tucked away on popular cafe street Nanluoguxiang, it offers a charming, cosy environment, with a rooftop for warmer days, and plenty of nooks and crannies for intimate chats over fruit juice or beer. They also serve Chinese versions of pizza and pasta.

7 Gongti Xi Lu
Chaoyang
工体西路7号
朝阳区
Map 9 D4 `207`

Destination 目的地

010 6551 5138 | *www.bjdestination.com*

Destination is Beijing's hippest gay bar. On most nights you'll find a sprinkling of lesbians and straight folk, but they are far outnumbered by international and Chinese gay men, mostly in their 20s and 30s. There is a small bar, separate from the main one, mixing healthy fruit juices and smoothies for those taking a break from the music. Destination's trump card is the bouncing dancefloor – an adventure when it's packed with people gyrating to the house and techno tunes.

Deshengmen Tower
Xicheng
德胜门城楼
西城区
Map 6 C1 `208`

West Wing Bar 西厢房

010 8208 2836

This is Beijing's biggest lesbian bar. It is actually half bar, half teahouse, swathed in simple lounge decor. The clientele is unpretentious and the atmosphere is friendly. It is a good place to dance, hang out, and meet new people. Bizarrely, along with DVD stations you'll also find a punching bag in the basement room.

Cabaret & Strip Shows

There are lady bars, escort services and visible prostitution in Beijing. Some lady bars are more or less harmless, with clients paying attractive waiting staff to sit, drink and chat with them. These are aimed at Chinese and expat audiences, and the women who work in them are a mix of nationalities. There are also certain massage parlours where 'happy endings' are offered in the form of a helping hand (swathed in a latex glove, of course). But amid all of this, strip clubs and cabarets are somehow lacking. Previous Chinese laws, which cracked down on the production of pornographic material by threatening the death penalty, may have something to do with the noted absence.

Cinemas

Despite the rampant sale of pirate DVDs, there are still many places around town offering traditional movie experiences. China has a limit on the number of foreign films screened in domestic theatres. These are typically shown in their original language, with Chinese subtitles. Those that make it to big screens are often missing footage, thanks to strict censorship policies. James Bond finally made it through the censors with the last instalment, *Casino Royale*. Previous Bond movies had been vetoed by censors, including 2002's *Die Another Day*, which was rejected for portraying North Korea, an ally of China, as a haven for gangsters. News outlets reported *Casino Royale* would be uncensored and uncut, but Beijing viewers were quick to notice missing footage during a violent stairwell scene.

Release dates tend to lag behind, with the exception of big-ticket items such as *Harry Potter*. Getting information on screenings is a hassle; most theatres have answering machines reeling off show times, but all information is in Chinese. Websites are also in Chinese, but may be easier to navigate. Cherry Lane Movies screens plenty of classic and contemporary Chinese films with English subtitles, while cultural centres and select bars offer avant-garde and foreign language films.

Cinemas

Cherry Lane Movies	29 Liangma Qiao Lu, Anjia Lou, the Kent Center	010 6430 5318
China Film Archives Art Cinema	Room 1213, 3 Wenhuiyuan Lu, Xiaoxitian	010 6225 4422
Drive-In Cinema	100 Daliangmaqiao	010 6431 9595
French Culture Centre	16 Gongti Xilu	010 6553 2627
Hart Centre of Arts	4 Jiuxianqiao Lu	010 6435 3570
Instituto Cervantes	1A Gongti Nanlu	010 5879 9666
Italian Embassy Cultural Office	2 Sanlitun Dongerjie	010 6532 5015
Mexican Embassy Cultural Office	5 Sanlitun Dongwujie	010 6532 2574
Star City	B1/F Oriental Plaza, Wangfujing Dajie	010 8518 6778
Stellar International Complex	5/F Golden Resources Shopping Center	010 8887 2743
UME International Cineplex	44 Kexueyuan Nanlu	010 8211 5566
Wanda Cinema	93 Jianguo Lu	010 5960 3399

Comedy

Comedy acts come to Beijing several times a year and usually draw a healthy crowd. The most common one is Chopsticks, a travelling show that brings English-speaking comedians (mostly American) to Asia. Listings magazines (p.51) have details of upcoming shows. There are no comedy clubs in town, but for those who would like to work on their routines, Beijing Improv (www.beijingimprov.com) holds workshops and the occasional show at Xinjiang Music Bar (West of Drum & Bell Tower Square, 2 Zhongku Alley, Gulou, 010 8405 0124), and sometimes at Yugong Yishan (p.344).

Entertainment

Concerts & Live Music

Beijing has tended to attract one-hit wonders or pop stars of decades past. Thankfully, this is slowly changing. Recently, the city has hosted urban hip-hop and underground musicians like Ziggy Marley, Sonic Youth, NOFX, Pretty Girls Make Graves and The Roots. All of these acts played at The Star Live, a hip little bar with decent acoustics and a knack for drawing good musicians.

The Beijing Concert Hall offers classical and traditional Chinese concerts, as does the Conservatory of Music and Forbidden City Concert Hall.

Beijing also hosts several annual music festivals, notably the Beijing Pop Music Festival (www.beijingpopfestival.com), an outdoor event held at the end of summer in Chaoyang Park, and the popular Midi Modern Music Festival held in Haidian Park. Midi may be cancelled in 2008 due to the Olympics. Those parched for classical music will be happy to know the city is home to the International Festival Chorus (www.beijingifc.org), which gives stunning performances three times a year. The chorus often perform with various international guests. For good bars with live acts, try D-22 (p.343), MAO Livehouse (p.335) and Yugong Yishan (p.344).

The ticket website www.piao.com.cn is good for tickets, as venues themselves can be sloppy with their customer service.

Concerts & Live Music

Beijing Concert Hall	1 Beixinhua Jie	Xicheng	010 6605 7006
Central Conservatory of Music	43 Baojiajie	Xicheng	010 6642 5702
Forbidden City Concert Hall	Zhongshan Park	Dongcheng	010 6559 8285
The Star Live	3/F Tango, 79 Hepingli Xijie	Dongcheng	010 6428 2288

Theatre
Other options **Drama Groups** p.212

Beijing's performing arts range from the sublime, to the staggering, via the ridiculous. You can see experimental theatre, acrobatics that defy the laws of physics, traditional operas that verge on camp and, occasionally some English-language am-dram.

For Peking opera head to theatres in either Changan or Chaoyang. The former does full-length shows, but three hours may prove too much for first time visitors; Peking opera is not generally easy on the ears. Chaoyang does highlight shows, which give a taste of the action, and is probably the best spot to see acrobatics. Tiandi Theatre does acrobatics shows too.

Theatre

Beijing Exhibition Theatre	135 Xizhimenwai Dajie	010 6835 4455
Beijing Peking Opera Theatre	30 Haihu Xili	010 6724 8222
Beijing People's Art Theatre	22 Wangfujing Jie	010 6512 1598
Beijing Playhouse	www.beijingplayhouse.com	137 1890 8922
Capital Theatre	22 Wangfujing Dajie	010 6524 9847
The Central Academy of Drama	39 Dong Mianhua Hutong	010 8404 6174
Changan Grand Theatre	7 Jianguomennai Dajie	010 6510 1308
Chaoyang Theatre	36 Dongsanhuan Beilu	010 6507 2421
Li Yuan Theatre	Qianmen Hotel, 175 Yongan Lu	010 8315 7297
Lin Zhaohua Drama Studio	Peking University Theatre Research Institute	010 6275 3253
National Grand Theatre	Behind Great Hall of the People Changan Avenue	na
National Theatre Company of China	45 Mao'er Hutong, Di'an Men	010 6403 1099
Tiandi Theatre	10 Dongzhimen Nandajie	010 6416 9893
TNT (The Nine Theatres)	17 Jintaili, Chaoyangmenwai	010 8599 6011

The Capital Theatre is your best bet for contemporary Chinese theatre, and the National Grand Theatre is worth a trip, just to see inside the space age shell. English and other foreign language works play rarely, so local listings magazines (p.51) are worth checking for the latest thespian activities. Beijing Playhouse is the sole English community group in town.

Party Organisers

Big events thrown by embassies and chambers of commerce are common. Limited space (and the lack of ovens) often means lavish private parties are rare; many opt for private rooms at restaurants. However, determined society doyennes will find plenty of support. ASC Fines Wines (p.227) will deliver boxes of wine to your doorstep within hours of an order. For dinner, the best cuts of meat are at Schindler's German Food Centre (p.264) and Boucherie Michel (1 Jiezuo Bldg, Xingfucun Zhonglu, 010 6417 0489). You can head to the north end of Dianmenwai Dajie, next to the Bell Tower, to find stores selling chefs uniforms, meat thermometers and other bits and pieces. The best bets for dinner napkins and extra wine glasses are Jenny Lou's (p.297) and April Gourmet (1 Sanlitun Beixiaojie, 010 8455 1245). Finally, to ensure a smooth evening, negotiate some overtime with your *ayi*, or ask a friend to recommend somebody.

Super Dos

For the party of a lifetime, parts of the Great Wall and Tiananmen Rostrum can be hired, though you'll need to go through a hotel like the St Regis (p.36) or the Ritz-Carlton (p.36). Destination companies like Destination Asia (www.destination-asia.com), Destination China (010 6588 5296, www.destinationchina.biz) or Pacific World (010 6568 8522, www.pacificworld.com) can also help. You will, however, need a big budget of at least $500,000, so make sure you enjoy yourself.

Caterers

Many five-star hotels offer excellent catering services, but at premium prices. Popular alternatives include Indian Kitchen, which has an extensive catering arm and Schindler's German Food Centre, which can supply sandwiches or a full barbecue. Expats in the know trust Li, a former chef for the Italian Embassy. He can shop for ingredients, bring staff to your house and create an Italian meal. A recent quote for a party of 10 was ¥1,400 per head. Most major hotels sell Thanksgiving, Christmas and Spring Festival hampers stuffed with goodies. Thanksgiving turkeys and Christmas hams and all the trimmings can be bought from Jenny Lou's, Kempi Deli and Lido Deli. Peter's Tex-Mex Grill sells cooked turkeys and baked pies, while Mrs Shanen's sells pies year round and gingerbread-making kits at Christmas. Halloween, Christmas, Valentine's and Easter chocolates can be purchased at the The Patisserie at the Grand Hyatt.

Caterers	
Chef Li	135 2047 2156
Indian Kitchen	010 6460 9366
Jenny Lou's	010 5135 8338
Kempi Deli	010 6465 3388
Lido Deli	010 6437 6688
Mrs Shanen's	010 8046 4301
The Patisserie	010 8518 1234
Peter's Tex-Mex Grill	010 5135 8187
Schindler's German Food Centre	010 6591 9370

Various Locations ◄ **Richard's Banquet Catering** 金日葵宴会外卖服务公司

010 8430 1623 | *www.richardscatering.com.cn*

This caterer can be hired for kids' and adults' parties. For kids, it does birthday cakes shaped like cars, planes or footballs, kid-friendly food and kiddie dishware. They also do magic shows. For adults, they can prepare Chinese and western dishes.

Capital Theatre (p.347)

Red Theatre

Waiting for showtime

National Grand Theatre (p.347)

Opera Masks

DIGITALGLOBE™

C L E A R L Y   T H E   B E S T

61 cm QuickBird Imagery is the highest resolution satellite imagery available. We offer products and resorces to both existing GIS users and the entire next generation of mapping and multimedia applications.

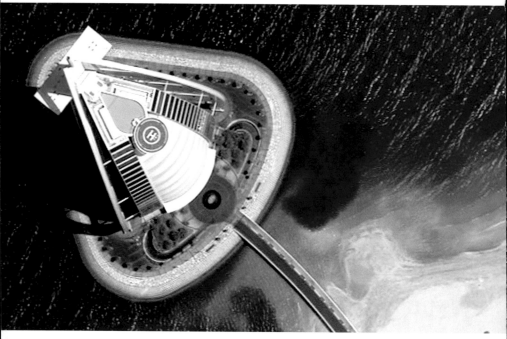

Burj Al Arab, Scale 1:2500, dated May 2003 © DigitalGlobe

MAPSgeosystems

DigitalGlobe's Master Reseller serving the Middle East and East, Central and West Africa

MAPS (UAE), Corniche Plaza 1, P.O. Box 5232, Sharjah, UAE.
Tel : +971 6 5725411, Fax : +971 6 5724057
www.maps-geosystems.com

For further details, please contact quickbird@maps-geosystems.com

Maps

Maps

User's Guide

For new arrivals, Beijing can appear a daunting city. Its size, congestion and sheer foreignness are significant obstacles, but they should not stop you from exploring. The ring roads that spread out from the centre make understanding the city simpler, and much of the area within the Fourth Ring Road is based on a grid pattern. Just don't underestimate the distances between points.

The maps that begin on p.360 cover the city on two scales. The outer areas are covered on a scale of 45,000 to one (45,000:1). This means that 1mm on the map is equivalent to 45,000mm (or 45 metres) on Beijing's streets. The more central areas are covered in more detail, on a scale of 15,000:1 (so 1mm is equal to 15m). The sheet cut index, on p.358 shows exactly where is covered.

There are also coloured annotations on these maps. They mark places that are mentioned in the book, and the different colours correspond to different chapters. So, **21** on Map 12 C1 is the Liqun restaurant (see p.308 for review) in Going Out. **21** on Map 10, C4 is the Great Hall of the People (see p.180) in Exploring. If you're near a cluster of annotations and want to now what they are, simply turn to the relevant chapter and count through the icons in the margin.

Until your Mandarin gets up to scratch, whenever you get in a taxi, you should have your destination written in Chinese. Hotel concierges are used to jotting down addresses for befuddled foriegners, but once you're out of hotels and into your own home, you can use the street and area index (p.356).

To help orientation, a few major landmarks have been given extra prominence, and a 3D drawing. These are the Temple of Heaven, the Gate of Heavenly Peace (the main entrance to the Forbidden City) and the old CCTV tower. And, to help offer a bigger picture, page 355 gives an overview of the city's outer lying areas, and the facing page shows the whole of China.

Compass Points

The compass points below will become familiar navigation tools during your time in Beijing. Street names tend to change over their course, adding bei or nan to denote north or south.

Online Maps

Beijing is not well served for online maps. This is epitomized by the official website for Beijing Subways (www.bjsubway.com), which has a list of stations and travelling times, but no map. The people on the Olympic organizing committee are a little more webly wise, and have a basic, but navigable effort at http://en.beijing2008.cn/emap. Google maps (http://maps.google.com) only manages the area around the Chinese capital. Google Earth (http://earth.google.com) is a better bet, and allows you to zoom in.

Map Legend

🏨	Hotel/Resort
⬜	Education
⬜	Park/Garden
✚	Hospital
⬜	Shopping
🏛	Heritage/Museum
⬜	Industrial Area
⬜	Agriculture
▬	Pedestrian Area
⬜	Built up Area/Building
⬜	Land

DONGSI	Area name
▬▬▬	Highway
▬▬▬	Major Road
▬▬▬	Secondary Road
▬▬▬	Other Road
▬ ▬ ▬	Under Construction
—○—	Metro Line 1
—○—	Metro Line 2
—○—	Metro Line 5
—○—	Metro Line 13
—☐—	Railway
✈	International Airport
★	Place of Interest

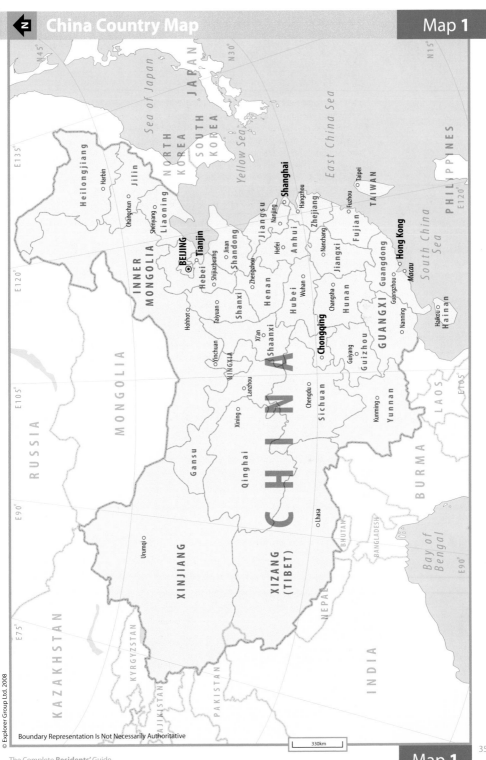

Boundary Representation Is Not Necessarily Authoritative

330km

Temple of Heaven (p.188)

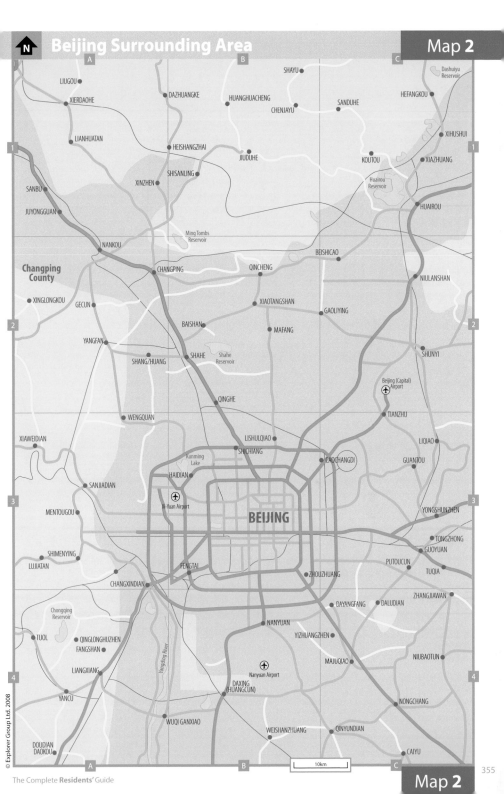

LIUGOU

XIERDAOHE

DAZHUANGKE

SHAYU

HUANGHUACHENG

CHENJAYU

SANDUHE

HEFANGKOU

Dashuiyu Reservoir

XIHUSHUI

LIANHUATAN

HEISHANGZHAI

JIUDUHE

KOUTOU

XIAZHUANG

SANBU

XINZHEN

SHISANLING

SHISHANLING

Huairou Reservoir

HUAIROU

JUYONGGUAN

NANKOU

Ming Tombs Reservoir

BEISHICAO

Changping County

CHANGPING

QINCHENG

NIULANSHAN

XINGLONGKOU

GECUN

XIAOTANGSHAN

GAOLIYING

BAISHAN

MAFANG

SHUNYI

YANGFAN

SHANGZHUANG

SHAHE

Shahe Reservoir

QINGHE

Beijing (Capital) Airport

XIAWEIDIAN

WENGQUAN

TIANZHU

LISHULQIAO

LIQIAO

SHICHIANG

CAOCHANGDI

GUANTOU

SANJIADIAN

Kunming Lake

HAIDIAN

Xi-Yuan Airport

YONGSHUNZHEN

MENTOUGOU

BEIJING

TONGZHONG

GUOYUAN

SHIMENYING

PUTOUCUN

TUQIA

LUJIATAN

FENGTAI

ZHOUZHUANG

ZHANGJIAWAN

CHANGXINDIAN

DAYANGFANG

DALUDIAN

Chongqing Reservoir

NANYUAN

YIZHUANGZHEN

TUOL

QINGLONGHUZHEN

FANGSHAN

MAJUQIAO

NIUBAOTUN

LIANGXIANG

YANCU

Nanyuan Airport

DAXING (HUANGCUN)

NONGCHANG

Yongding River

WUQI GANXIAO

WEISHANZHUANG

QINYUNDIAN

DOUDIAN DAOKOU

CAIYU

10km

Street Index

Street Name	Chinese	Map Ref
Qiansili Jinsong Nanlu	劲松南路	13-E3
Shijiazhuang Expressway	京石高速公路	6-A4
Shijingshan Lu	石景山路	6-A2
Shoudujichang Highway	首都机场高速公路	5-E1
Shoudujichang Lu	首都机场路	5-E1
Shoudutiyuguan Nanlu	首都体育馆南路	6-C1
Songyu Nanlu	松榆南路华威南路	7-D4
Suzhou Jie	苏州街	4-B3
Tianshuiyuan Jie	甜水园街	7-D1
Tiantan Donglu	天坛东路	13-A4
Tiantan Lu	天坛路	13-A2
Tonghui Beilu	通惠北路	7-D3
Wangfujing Dajie	王府井大街	10-F1
Wuhuan Lu	五环路	4-E2
Xiangheyuan Lu	香河园路	5-B4
Xichangan Jie	西长安街	10-E3
Xidan Beidajie	西单北大街	10-A2
Xidawang Lu	西大望路	7-D4
Xin Donglu	新东路	9-E1
Xinjiekou Beidajie	新街口北大街	8-A1
Xinjiekou Nandajie	新街口南大街	8-A2
Xisanhuan Beilu	西三环北路	6-B1
Xisanhuan Zhonglu	西三环中路	6-B2
Xisi Beidajie	西四北大街	6-E2
Xisihuan Beiu	西四环北路	4-A4
Xisihuan Zhonglu	西四环中路	6-A3
Xiwuhuan Lu	西五环路	4-E2
Xizhimennei Dajie	西直门内大街	6-E1
Xuanwumen Dongdajie	宣武门东大街	6-F3
Xuanwumen Neidajie	宣武门内大街	6-E3
Xuanwumen Waidajie	宣武门外大街	12-A3
Xuanwumen Xidajie	宣武门西大街	6-E3
Xuanwumennei Dajie	宣武门内大街	10-A4
Xueqing Lu	学清路	4-D1
Xueyuan Lu	学院路	4-D3
Xuwumen Waidajie	宣武门外大街	6-E4
Yangfangdian Lu	羊坊店路	6-C3
Yaojiayuan Lu	姚家园路	7-F1
Yiheyuan Lu	颐和园路	4-B2
Yongdingmen Dongbinhe Lu	永定门东滨河路	7-A4
Youanmen Dongbinhe Lu	右安门东滨河路	6-F4
Youanmennei Dajie	右安门内大街	6-E4
Yuanda Lu	远大路	4-A4
Yuanmingyuan Xilu	圆明园西路	4-A1

Street Name	Chinese	Map Ref
Zhangzizhong Lu	张自忠路	8-F3
Zhengyi Lu	正义路	7-A3
Zhongguancun Beidajie	中关村北大街	4-C2
Zhongguancun Dajie	中关村大街	4-C3
Zhongguancun Donglu	中关村东路	4-C3
Zhongguancun Nandajie	中关村南大街	4-C4
Zhushikou Dongdajie	珠市口东大街	12-F2
Zhushikou Xidajie	珠市口西大街	12-D2
Zizhuyuan Lu	紫竹院路	6-C1
Zuoanmen Xibinhe Lu	左安门西滨河路	7-B4

Area Name	Chinese	Map Ref
Andingmen	安定门	8-F1
Anhuali	安华里	5-A3
Banqiao	板桥	7-F1
Beihai	北海	8-C3
CBD	中央商业区	11-F7
Chaowai	朝阳门外大街	7-B2
Chaoyang	朝阳区	13-E1
Chongwai	崇文门外	12-F1
Chongwen	崇文区	12-F3
Dongcheng	东城区	11-B3
Dongdan	东单	7-B1
Dongsi	东四	7-B1
Fengsheng	丰盛	6-E2
Fengtai	丰台区	6-A4
Financial District	金融街	6-D2
Forbidden City	故宫	10-D1
Haidian	海淀区	4-A3
Heping	和平	5-A4
Houhai	后海	8-C2
Houshayu	后沙峪	3-D1
Lido	丽都	5-E2
Niujie	牛街	6-E4
Qianmen	前门	12-E1
Sanlitiun	三里屯	9-E1
Shunyi	顺义区	3-D2
Sunhe	孙河	3-C3
Tiananmen Square	天安门广场	10-D3
Wudaoku	五道口	4-D2
Xicheng	西城	6-E2
Xidan	西单	6-E2
Zhongguancun	中关村	4-C2

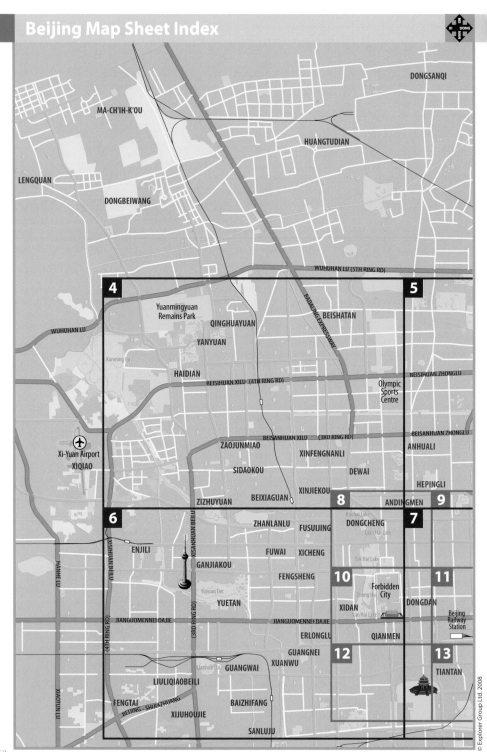

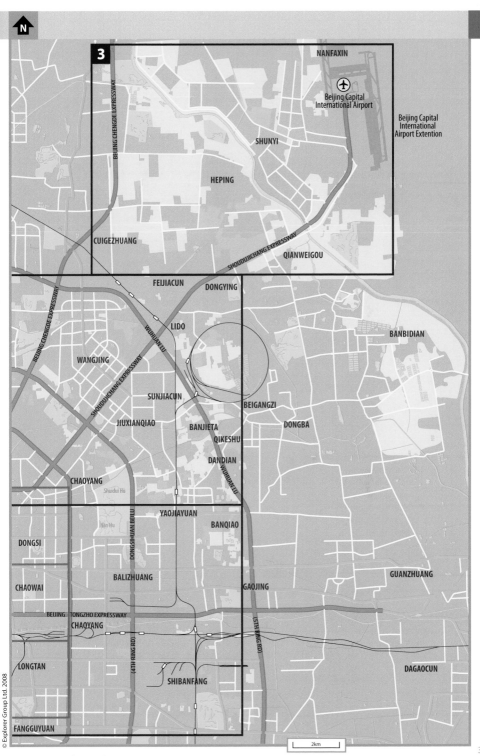

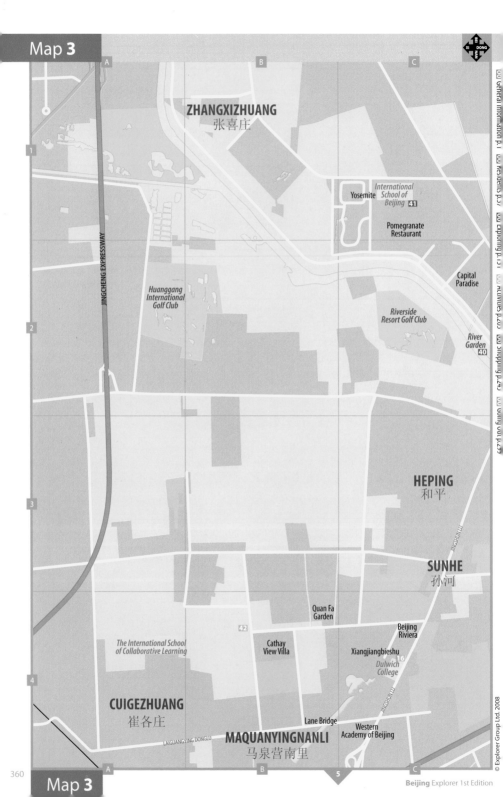

Map **3**

ZHANGXIZHUANG
张喜庄

International
School of
Beijing **41**

Yosemite

Pomegranate
Restaurant

Capital
Paradise

Huanggang
International
Golf Club

Riverside
Resort Golf Club

River
Garden
40

HEPING
和平

SUNHE
孙河

Quan Fa
Garden

Beijing
Riviera

42

The International School
of Collaborative Learning

Cathay
View Villa

Xiangjiangbieshu

Dulwich
College

16

CUIGEZHUANG
崔各庄

Lane Bridge

Western
Academy of Beijing

LAIGUANGYING DONGLU

MAQUANYINGNANLI
马泉营南里

JINGCHENG EXPRESSWAY

© Explorer Group Ltd. 2008

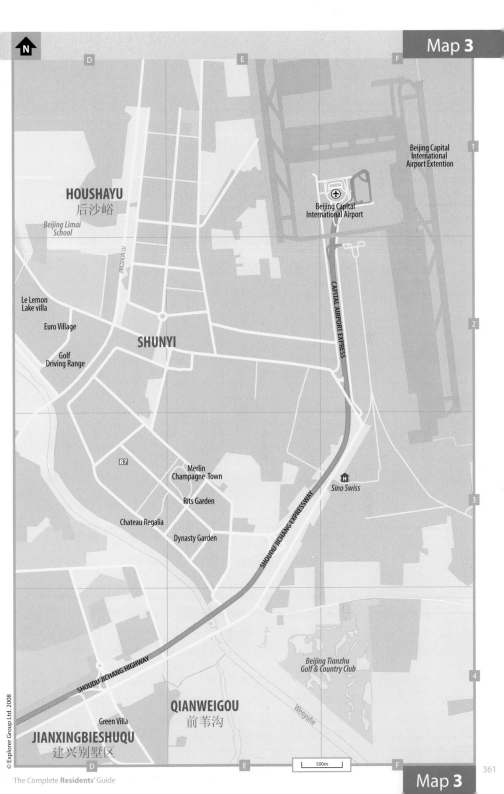

Map **3**

N

D E F

HOUSHAYU
后沙峪

Beijing Limai
School

Beijing Capital
International
Airport Extention

1

Beijing Capital
International Airport

Le Lemon
Lake villa

Euro Village

SHUNYI

Golf
Driving Range

2

CAPITAL AIRPORT EXPRESS

87

Merlin
Champagne Town

Rits Garden

Chateau Regalia

Dynasty Garden

Sino Swiss

3

SHOUDU JICHANG EXPRESSWAY

SHOUDU JICHANG HIGHWAY

Beijing Tianzhu
Golf & Country Club

Wenyuhe

4

QIANWEIGOU
前苇沟

Green Villa

JIANXINGBIESHUQU
建兴别墅区

500m

D E F

© Explorer Group Ltd. 2008

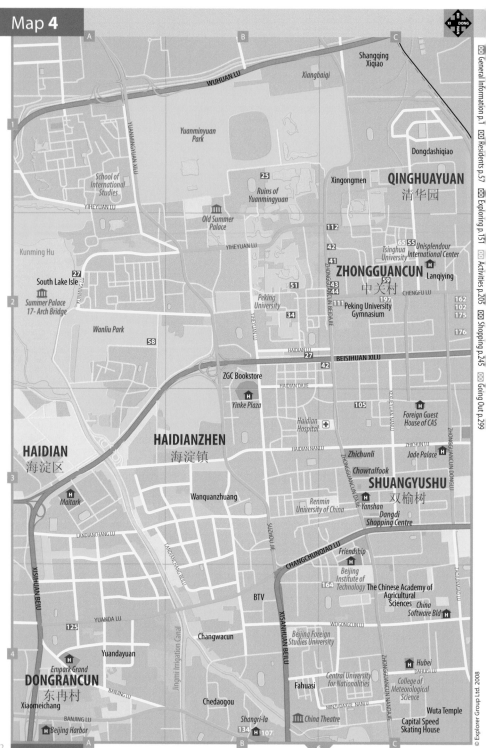

Map **4**

WUHUAN LU

Shangqing
Xiqiao

Xiangbaiqi

Dongdashiqiao

Yuanminyuan
Park

Xingongmen **QINGHUAYUAN**
清华园

25

School of
International
Studies

Ruins of
Yuanmingyuan

112

YIHEYUAN LU

🏛 Old Summer
Palace

42

Tsinghua
University **65** **55** Unisplendour
International Center

YIHEYUAN LU

41

ZHONGGUANCUN
中关村

Kunming Hu **59**

Lanqiying

27

South Lake Isle

51

43 CHENGFU LU

44

🏛 Summer Palace
17- Arch Bridge

Peking
University

111 **197** Peking University
Gymnasium

162
102
175

Wanliu Park

34

176

58

HAIDIAN LU

27

BEISIHUAN XILU

42

ZGC Bookstore

HAIDIAN DAJIE

HAIDIANZHEN
海淀镇

105 Foreign Guest
House of CAS

🏨 Yinke Plaza

Haidian ✚
Hospital

HAIDIAN
海淀区

HAIDIAN NANLU

Zhichunli ZHICHUN LU 🏨 Jade Palace

Chowtaifook

🏨 Maitark

Wanquanzhuang

SHUANGYUSHU
双榆树

LANDIANCHANG LU

Renmin
University of China 🏨 Yanshan Dangdi
Shopping Centre

CHANGCHUNQIAO LU

Friendship

BTV

🏨 Beijing
Institute of
Technology The Chinese Academy of
Agricultural
Sciences China
Software Bld 🏨

164

WEIGONGCUN LU

YUANDA LU

125

Changwacun

Beijing Foreign
Studies University

Yuandayuan

🏨 Empark Grand

DONGRANCUN
东冉村

Fahuasi

Central University
for Nationalities

🏨 Hubei

DAHUISI LU

College of
Meteorological
Science

Xiaomeichang

BANJING LU

Chedaogou

MINZUDAXUE NANLU

Wuta Temple

BANJING LU

Shangri-la 🏛 China Theatre

Capital Speed
Skating House

🏨 Beijing Harbor

134

🏨 **107**

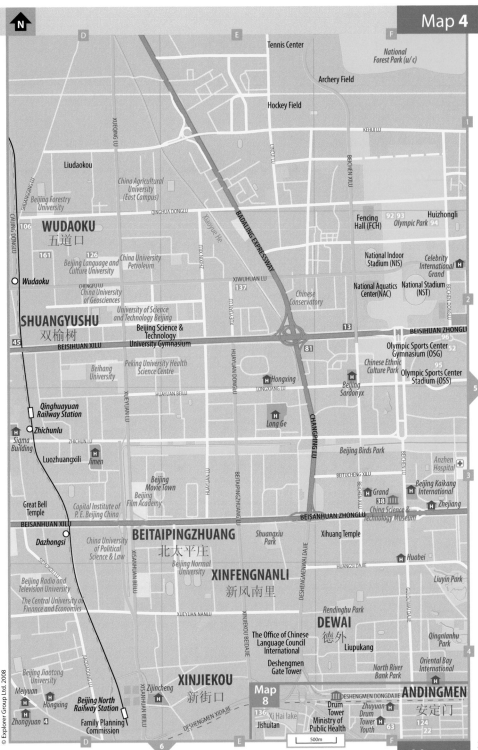

Map **4**

© Explorer Group Ltd. 2008

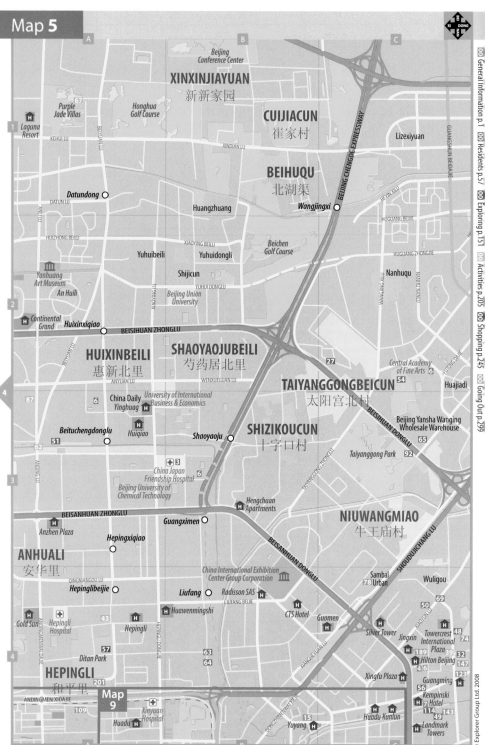

Map **5**

XI DONG

General Information p.1 | Residents p.57 | Exploring p.151 | Activities p.205 | Shopping p.245 | Going Out p.299

© Explorer Group Ltd. 2008

XINXINJIAYUAN
新新家园

Beijing
Conference Center

CUIJIACUN
崔家村

Lizexiyuan

Laguna
Resort

KEHUI LU

Purple
Jade Villas

Honghua
Golf Course

BEIDAN LU

XINDIAN LU

BEIHUQU
北湖渠

BEIJING CHENGDE EXPRESSWAY

GUANGSHUN BEIDAJIE

Datundong

DATUN LU

ANLI LU

Huangzhuang

Wangjingxi

HEJIN XILU

HUGUANG BEIJIE

HUIZHONG BEILU

XIAOYING BEILU

Beichen
Golf Course

HUGUANG ZHONGJIE

Yuhuibeili

Yuhuidongli

Nanhuqu

NANHU NANLU

Yanhuang
Art Museum

Shijicun

An Huili

YUHUI DONGLU

WANGJING XILU

Beijing Union
University

Continental
Grand

Huixinxiqiao

BEISIHUAN ZHONGLU

BEITUAN LU

HUIXINBEILI
惠新北里

ANYUAN LU

SHAOYAOJUBEILI
芍药居北里

WENXUEGUAN LU

27

Central Academy
of Fine Arts

HUTONG DAJIE

54

TAIYANGGONGBEICUN
太阳宫北村

Huajiadi

BEISIHUAN DONGLU

China Daily
Yinghuag

University of International
Business & Economics

87

6

Beituchengdonglu

SHIZIKOUCUN
十字口村

Beijing Yansha Wanging
Wholesale Warehouse

ANDING LU

51

Huiqiao

Shaoyaoju

TAIYANGGONG ZHONGLU

65

62

Taiyanggong Park

92

China Japan
Friendship Hospital

3

G

Hengchuan
Apartments

NIUWANGMIAO
牛王庙村

SHOUDUJICHANG LU

Beijing University
of Chemical Technology

BEISANHUAN ZHONGLU

Guangximen

Anzhen Plaza

Hepingxiqiao

BEISANHUAN DONGLU

Sambal
Urban

78

Wuligou

ANHUALI
安华里

QINGNIANGOU LU

China International Exhibition
Center Group Corporation

50

69

Hepinglibeijie

Liufang

Radisson SAS

XIANGHE YUAN LU

Silver Tower

Jingxin

189

Towercrest
International
Plaza

48

74

Huawenmingshi

LIUFANG BEIJIE

CTS Hotel

39

32

Gold Sun

ANDINGMEN WAIDAJIE

Hepingli
Hospital

43

Hepingli

HEPINGLI DONGJIE

63

Guomen

147

Hilton Beijing

46

123

57

Ditan Park

64

Xingfu Plaza

Guangming

56

Kempinski
Hotel

HEPINGLI
和平里

201

**Map
9**

ANDINGMEN XIDAJIE

Xinyuan
Hospital

DONGZHIMEN WAI DAJIE

15

Yuyang

Haadu Kunlun

114

143

49

Landmark
Towers

109

Huadu

7

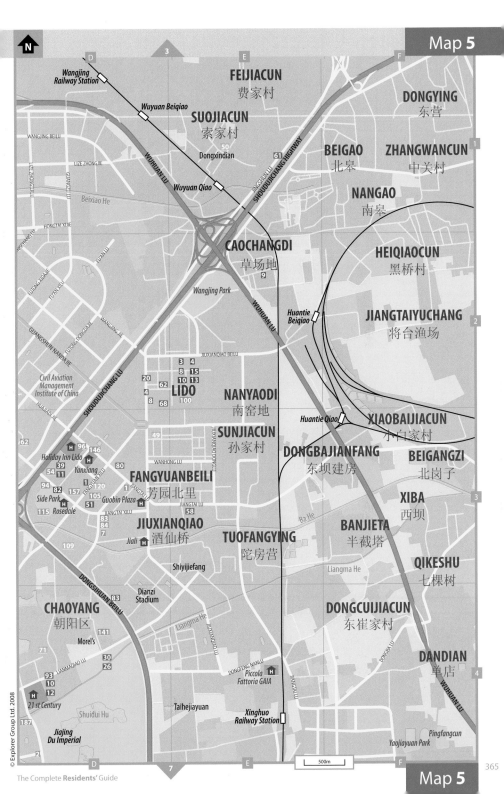

Map 5

FEIJIACUN
费家村

DONGYING
东营

SUOJIACUN
索家村

BEIGAO
北皋

ZHANGWANCUN
中关村

Dongxindian

NANGAO
南皋

CAOCHANGDI
草场地

HEIQIAOCUN
黑桥村

Wangjing Park

JIANGTAIYUCHANG
将台渔场

Huantie
Beiqiao

NANYAODI
南窑地

LIDO

Huantie Qiao

XIAOBAIJIACUN
小白家村

BEIGANGZI
北岗子

SUNJIACUN
孙家村

DONGBAJIANFANG
东坝建房

FANGYUANBEILI
芳园北里

XIBA
西坝

Holiday Inn Lido
Yanxiang

Side Park
Rosedale

Guobin Plaza

BANJIETA
半截塔

JIUXIANQIAO
酒仙桥

TUOFANGYING
陀房营

QIKESHU
七棵树

Jiali

Shiyijiefang

Dianzi
Stadium

DONGCUIJIACUN
东崔家村

CHAOYANG
朝阳区

DANDIAN
单店

Morel's

Piccola
Fattoria GAIA

Jiajing
Du Imperial

Xinghuo
Railway Station

Pingfangcun

Yaojiayuan Park

WUHUAN LU

SHOUDUJICHANG HIGHWAY

Wangjing
Railway Station

Wuyuan Beiqiao

Wuyuan Qiao

Beixiao He

21 st Century

Taihejiayuan

Shuidui Hu

500m

© Explorer Group Ltd. 2008

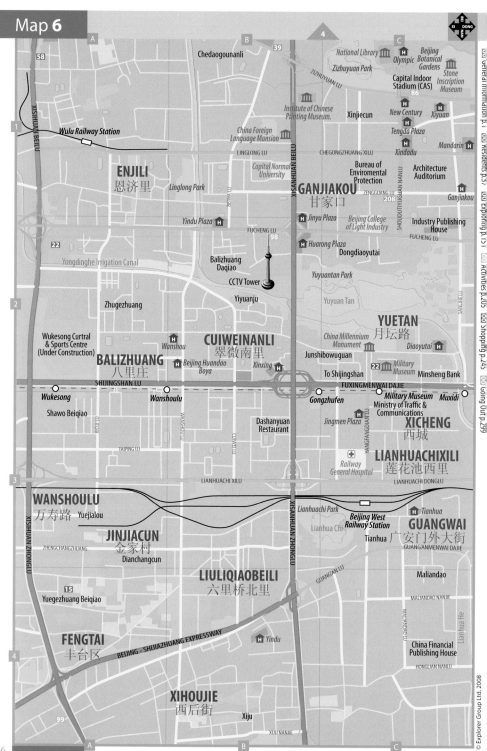

Map **6**

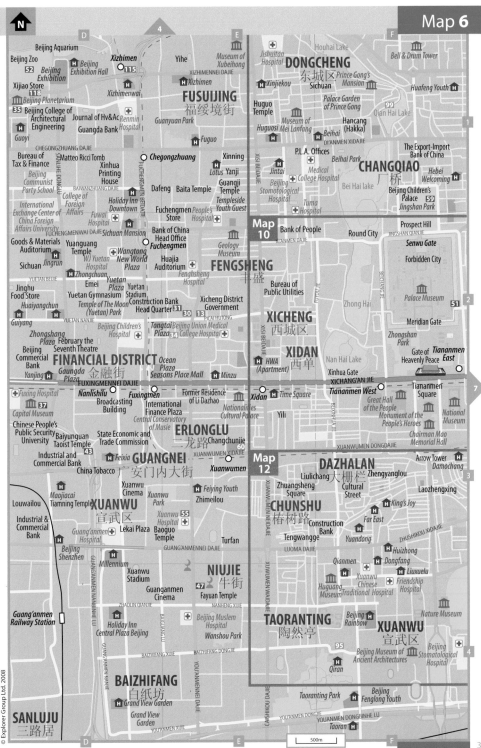

Map **6**

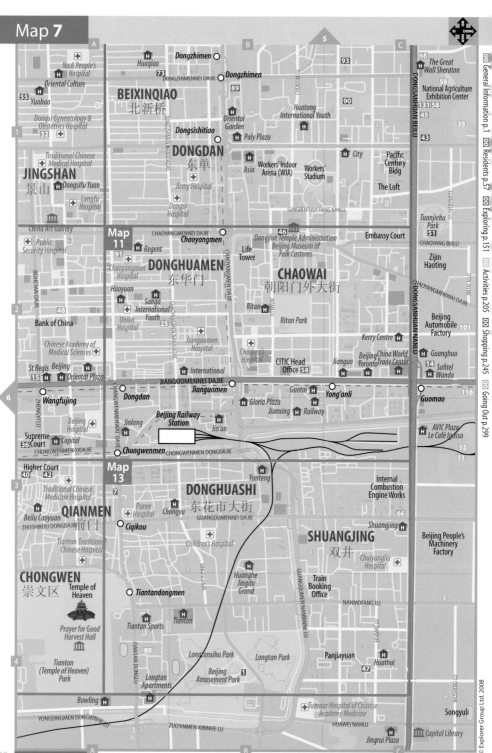

Map **7**

No.6 People's Hospital

Oriental Culture

55 Yuohao

Dongsi Gyneacology & Obstetrics Hospital

32

Huaqiao

73

DONGZHIMENNEI DAJIE

BEIXINQIAO
北新桥

Dongsishitiao

DONGDAN
东单

Traditional Chinese Medical Hospital

JINGSHAN
景山

Dongsifu Yuan

Longfu Hospital

China Art Gallery

Public Security Hospital

Map 11

BEIHUAN DAJIE

Bank of China

48

Chinese Academy of Medical Sciences

St Regis Beijing

15

Oriental Plaza

Dongzhimen

Dongzhimen

89

Oriental Garden

Paly Plaza

Asia

Army Hospital

Dongsi Hospital

CHAOYANGMENNEI DAJIE

Chaoyangmen

Regent

91

Chaoyangmen Hospital

DONGHUAMEN
东华门

Haoyuan

Sanga International Youth

25

Union Hospital

Jianguomen Hospital

International

JIANGUOMENNEI DAJIE

93

Huatong International Youth

90

City

Workers' Indoor Arena (WIA)

Workers' Stadium

GONGRENTIYUCHANG NANLU

Dongyue Temple Administration
Beijing Museum of Folk Customs

Life Tower

CHAOWAI
朝阳门外大街

Ritan

Ritan Park

Children's Hospital

CITIC Head Office 58

46

Pacific Century Bldg

The Loft

Embassy Court

Zijin Haoting

Beijing Automobile Factory

Kerry Centre

Jianguo

Beijing Toronto

China World Trade Center

Guomao

Tuanjiehu Park
51

CHAOYANG BEILU

101

Guanghua

14 Sofitel Wanda

68 The Great Wall Sheraton

58 National Agriculture Exhibition Center

131 58

45

43

35

DONGSANHUAN BEILU

DONGSANHUAN NANLU

Wangfujing

ZHENGYILU

Beijing Hospital

Supreme Court 36

Capital

CHONGWENMEN XIDAJIE

Higher Court
40   42

Traditional Chinese Medicine Hospital

Beilu Caoyuan

QIANMEN
前门

ZHUSHIKOU DONGDAJIE

Tiantan Traditional Chinese Hospital

CHONGWEN
崇文区

Temple of Heaven

Prayer for Good Harvest Hall

Tiantan (Temple of Heaven) Park

Bowling

Dongdan

Jinlang

Jianguomen

Beijing Railway Station

Jin'an

Chongwenmen

CHONGWENMEN DONGDAJIE

Map 13

7

Puren Hospital

Chongyu

Ciqikou

Children's Hospital

DONGHUASHI
东花市大街

GUANGQUMENNEI DAJIE

Tiantandongmen

Tiantan Sports

85

Longtanxihu Park

Longtan Apartments

YONGDINGMEN DONGBINHE LU

Gloria Plaza

Jianxing

Railway

Yunteng

Chongyu

Huanghe Jingdu Grand

XINGGUO JIE

Tiantan

Beijing Amusement Park

1

ZUO'ANMEN XIBINHE LU

Guotai

Yong'anli

Jin'an

SHUANGJING

Shuangjing

66

SHUANGJING
双井

Chuiyangliu Hospital

Train Booking Office

NANMOFANG LU

Panjiayuan

47

Longtan Park

Huathai

Guomao

116

AVIC Plaza
Le Café Joosso

12

11

Internal Combustion Engine Works

Beijing People's Machinery Factory

Tumour Hospital of Chinese Academy Medicine

HUAWEI NANLU

Jingrui Plaza

Songyuli

Capital Library

© Explorer Group Ltd. 2008

TIANTAN DONGLU

GUANGQUMEN NANXIAN LU

General Information p.1   Residents p.57   Exploring p.151   Activities p.205   Shopping p.245   Going Out p.299

Map **7**

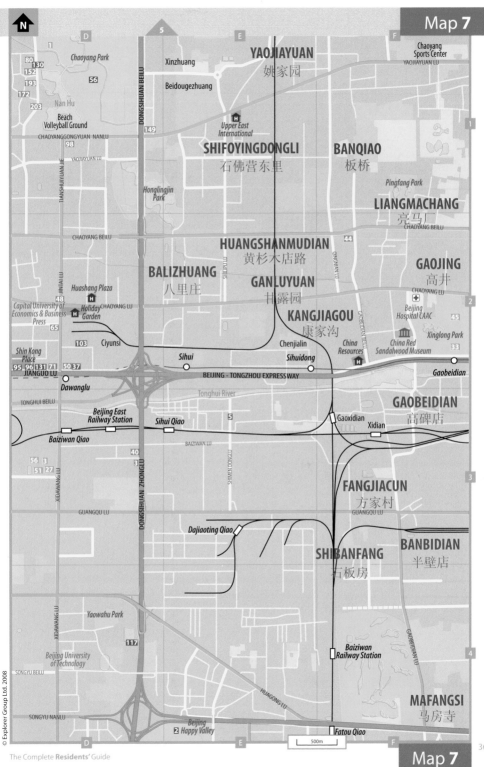

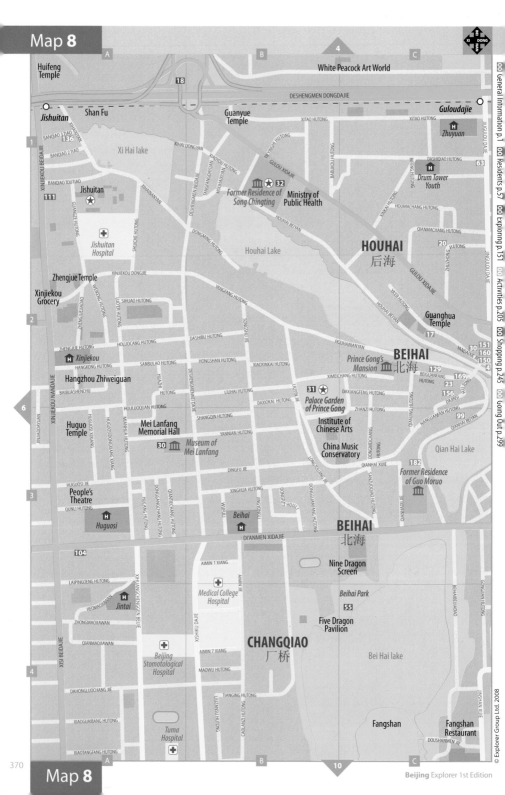

Map **8**

Huifeng
Temple

White Peacock Art World

18

DESHENGMEN DONGDAJIE

Jishuitan

Shan Fu

Guanyue
Temple

XITAO HUTONG

XITAO HUTONG

Guloudajie

Zhuyuan

BANQIAO 1 TIAO

BANQIAO 2 TIAO

Xi Hai lake

XIHAI DONGYAN

TIE TINGOI HUTONG

GULOU XIDAJIE

BABUXIOU HUTONG

DASHIQIAO HUTONG

63

BANQIAO TOUTIAO

Jishuitan

111

KIAOGU HUTONG

TANGFANGANYAN

Former Residence of
Song Chingting

32

Ministry of
Public Health

Drum Tower
Youth

HOUMACHANG HUTONG

Jishuitan
Hospital

DONGMING HUTONG

HOUHAI BEIYAN

QIANMACHANG HUTONG

Houhai Lake

HOUHAI

后海

20

HUTONG

XINJIEKOU DONGJIE

Zhengjue Temple

Xinjiekou
Grocery

YANGFANG HUTONG

SIHUAO HUTONG

GULOU XIDAJIE

Guanghua
Temple

17

ZHENGJUE HUTONG

HOLUOCANG HUTONG

DA SHIBUT HUTONG

HOUHAINAN YAN

30

151
160
150

Xinjiekou

SANBULAO HUTONG

HONGSHAN HUTONG

XIAODXINKAI HUTONG

Prince Gong's
Mansion

BEIHAI

北海

129

169

4

Hangzhou Zhiweiguan

XIMEICHANG HUTONG

BEGUANFANG
HUTONG

23

BAIBUASHENCHU

LIUHAI HUTONG

DAXIANGFENG HUTONG

156

Huguo
Temple

HOULUOQUAN HUTONG

SHANGQIN HUTONG

DAXIOKAI HUTONG

31

Palace Garden
of Prince Gong

ZHANZI HUTONG

99

Mei Lanfang
Memorial Hall

YANNIAN HUTONG

Institute of
Chinese Arts

Qian Hai Lake

30

Museum of
Mei Lanfang

DINGFU JIE

China Music
Conservatory

QIANHAI XUJIE

182

Former Residence
of Guo Moruo

People's
Theatre

XINGHUA HUTONG

QUNLI HUTONG

Beihai

BEIHAI

北海

Huguosi

DI'ANMEN XIDAJIE

104

AIMIN 1 XIANG

Nine Dragon
Screen

LAIPINGOENG HUTONG

Jintai

Medical College
Hospital

Beihai Park

55

ZHONGMAOJIAWAN

Five Dragon
Pavilion

QIANMAOJIAWAN

CHANGQIAO

厂桥

Bei Hai lake

Beijing
Stomotological
Hospital

AIMIN 7 XIANG

MAOWU HUTONG

DAHONGLUOCHANG JIE

TIANGING HUTONG

XIAOGUAIBANG HUTONG

Tuma
Hospital

Fangshan

Fangshan
Restaurant

DOUSHANMEN JIE

XIAOTANGFANG HUTONG

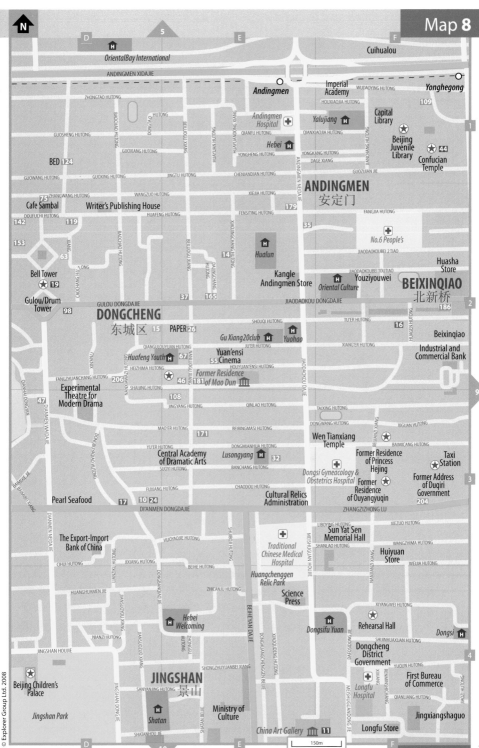

Map **8**

N

D
E
F

OrientalBay International
Cuihualou

ANDINGMEN XIDAJIE

ZHONGTAO HUTONG
Andingmen
Imperial
Academy
WUDAOYING HUTONG
Yonghegong

HOUXIAOJIA HUTONG

1

BAOCHAO HUTONG
DONGCAO HUTONG
BELUOGU XIANG
JINGTU HUTONG XIANG
HAJYA XIANG SOUTH XIANG
Andingmen
Hospital
Yalujiang
Capital
Library
109

GUOSHENG HUTONG
QIANFU HUTONG
QIANXIAOJIA HUTONG

GUOXIANG HUTONG
Hebei
Beijing
Juvenile
Library
44

BED 124
YONGHENG HUTONG
YONGKANG HUTONG
DAGE XIANG
Confucian
Temple

GUOWANG HUTONG
GUOXING HUTONG
JINGTU HUTONG
CHENJIANDIAN HUTONG
GUOZIJIAN JIE

WANGZUO HUTONG

75 ZHANGWANG HUTONG
XIEJIA HUTONG
ANDINGMEN
安定门

Cafe Sambal
Writer's Publishing House

DOUFUCHI HUTONG
HUAFENG HUTONG
FENSITING HUTONG
FANGJIA HUTONG

142
119
179

153
XIAOJINGCHANG HUTONG
No.6 People's

BAOCHAO HUTONG
35
JIAODAOKOUBEI 2 TIAO

63
14
Huasha
Store

Bell Tower
19
BELUOGU XIANG
DAJINGCHANG HUTONG
Kangle
Andingmen Store
Youziyouwei
JIAODAOKOUBEI TOUTIAO
186
BEIXINQIAO
北新桥

Gulou/Drum
Tower
98
37
165
JIAODAOKOU DONGDAJIE
Oriental Culture

GULOU DONGDAJIE

DONGCHENG
东城区
15
PAPER 26
SHOUQI HUTONG
TU'ER HUTONG
16
Beixinqiao

QIANGULOULOUYUAN HUTONG
Gu Xiang20club
Yuohao
JU'ER HUTONG
XIANG'ER HUTONG
Industrial and
Commercial Bank

Huafeng Youth
67
Yuan'ensi
Cinema
55
HOUYUAN'ENSI HUTONG

HEIZHIMA HUTONG
9

FANGZHUANCHANG HUTONG
206
46
181
Former Residence
of Mao Dun
JIAODAOKOU DAJIE

Experimental
Theatre for
Modern Drama
SHAIJING HUTONG
108
JINGYANG HUTONG
QINLAO HUTONG

47
TAIXING HUTONG

MAO'ER HUTONG
BEIBINGMASI HUTONG
DONGWANG HUTONG

171
YU'ER HUTONG
XIGUAN HUTONG

Central Academy
of Dramatic Arts
Lusongyang
32
Wen Tianxiang
Temple
BAIMICANG HUTONG

SUOYI HUTONG
BANCHANG HUTONG
Former Residence
of Princess
Hejing
Taxi
Station

Pearl Seafood
17
10 24
FUXIANG HUTONG
CHAODOU HUTONG
Dongsi Gynaecology &
Obstetrics Hospital
Former
Residence
of Ouyangyuqin
Former Address
of Duqiri
Government
204

DI'ANMEN DONGDAJIE
ZHANGZIZHONG LU

The Export-Import
Bank of China
HUOYAOJIE HUTONG
LIBOYING HUTONG
Sun Yat Sen
Memorial Hall
XIEZUO HUTONG

CHUI HUTONG
JIXIANG HUTONG
Traditional
Chinese Medical
Hospital
SHANLAO HUTONG
WANGZHIMA HUTONG
Huiyuan
Store
WEIJIA HUTONG

HUANGHUAMEN JIE
BEIHE HUTONG
Huangchenggen
Relic Park

ZHICANJU HUTONG
Science
Press
XIYANGWEI HUTONG

HUANGHUAMEN JIE
Hebei
Welcoming
Dongsifu Yuan
Rehearsal Hall
SHIJINHUAXUAN HUTONG
Dongsi

NIANZI HUTONG
Dongcheng
District
Government
YUQUN HUTONG

JINGSHAN HOUJIE
JINGSHAN
景山

Beijing Children's
Palace
Longfu
Hospital
First Bureau
of Commerce

Jingshan Park
Shatan
Ministry of
Culture
Longfu Store
Jingxiangshaguo

SHATANHOUJIE
China Art Gallery
11
150m
4

D
10
E
F

Map **8**

Map **9**

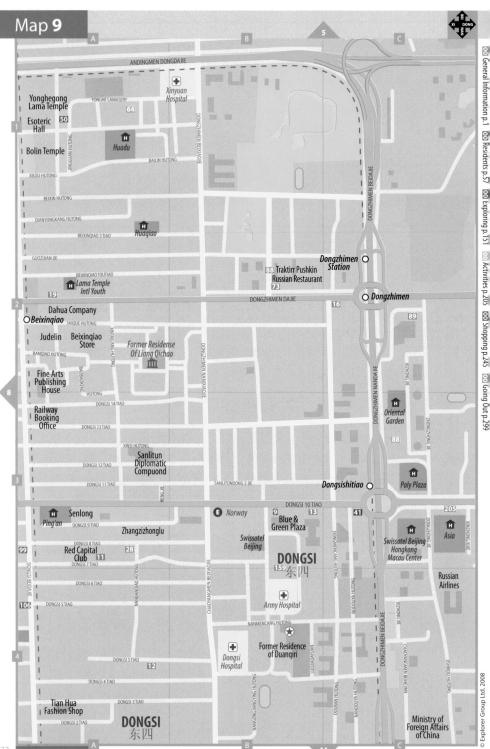

ANDINGMEN DONGDAJIE

Yonghegong
Lama Temple
YONGHE LAMASERY
64

Xinyuan
Hospital

Esoteric
Hall **50**

Bolin Temple

Huadu

BAILIN HUTONG

XILOU HUTONG

BEIXIN HUTONG

QIANYONGKANG HUTONG

BEIXINQIAO 3 TIAO

Huaqiao

GUOZIJIAN JIE

BEIXINQIAO TOUTIAO

Lama Temple
Intl Youth
19

Traktirr Pushkin
Russian Restaurant **88**
73

Dongzhimen
Station

Dongzhimen

DONGZHIMEN DAJIE **16**

89

Dahua Company

Beixinqiao   SHIQUE HUTONG

Judelin   Beixinqiao
Store

BANQIAO HUTONG

Former Residense
Of Liang Qichao

Fine Arts
Publishing
House

DONGSI 14 TIAO

Railway
Booking
Office   DONGSI 13 TIAO

XINSI HUTONG

Sanlitun
Diplomatic
Compuond

DONGSI 12 TIAO

DONGSI 11 TIAO   SANLITUNDONG 2 JIE

Oriental
Garden

88

Dongsishitiao

Paly Plaza

DONGSI 10 TIAO   **205**

Ping'an   Senlong   **E** Norway   **9**   Blue & **13**   **41**
DONGSI 9 TIAO   Green Plaza

Zhangzizhonglu

DONGSI 8 TIAO

Red Capital   **28**
Club   **11**
DONGSI 7 TIAO

Swissotel
Beijing

Swissotel Beijing
Hongkong
Macau Center

Asia

99

DONGSI 6 TIAO

DONGSI
东四
159

Russian
Airlines

106   DONGSI 5 TIAO

Army Hospital

NANMENCANG HUTONG

DONGSI 5 TIAO   **12**

Dongsi
Hospital

Former Residence
of Duanqiri

DONGSI 4 TIAO

DONGSI 3 TIAO

Tian Hua
Fashion Shop

DONGSI 2 TIAO

DONGSI
东四

Ministry of
Foreign Affairs
of China

00 General Information p.1   00 Residents p.57   00 Exploring p.151   00 Activities p.205   00 Shopping p.245   00 Going Out p.299

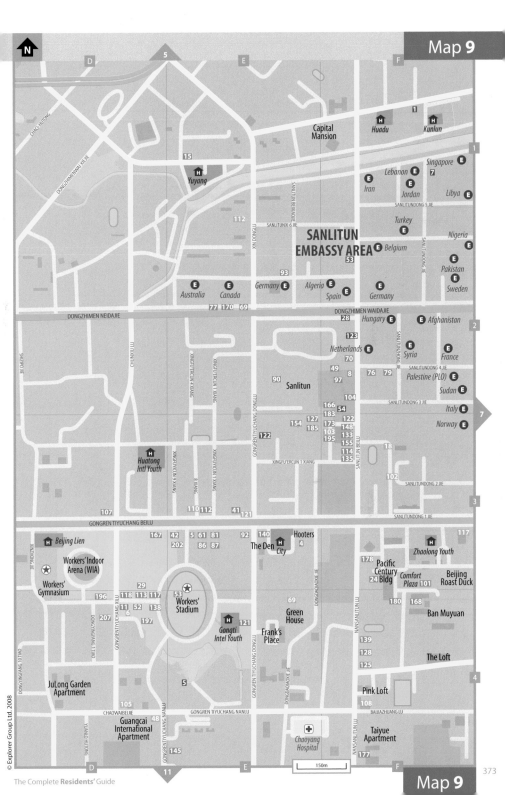

Map **9**

N

Map **9**

Capital Mansion

Huadu 🏨

Kunlun 🏨

1

Yuyang 🏨

15

Singapore E

7

Lebanon E

Iran E

Jordan E

Libya E

SANLITUNDONG 5 JIE

112

Turkey E

SANLITUN BEIXIAOJIE

SANLITUNXI 6 JIE

XIN DONGLU

**SANLITUN
EMBASSY AREA** E Belgium

53

Nigeria

E

Australia E

Canada E

Germany E

93

Algeria E

Spain E

Germany E

SANLITUNDONG JIE

Pakistan

E

Sweden

E

DONGZHIMEN NEIDAJIE

77 170 69

DONGZHIMEN WAIDAJIE

28

Hungary E

E Afghanistan

2

123

Netherlands E

70

CHUNXIU LU

XINGFUERCUN 4 XIANG

XINGFUERCUN 1 XIANG

90

Sanlitun

49

8

97

104

SANLITUNDONG 4 JIE

Syria E

76 79

Palestine (PLO) E E

Sudan E

E France

SANLITUNDONG 3 JIE

Italy E

Norway E

7

GONGRENTIYUCHANG DONGLU

166 54

183

127 173 122

185 148

103 133

195 155

114

135

18

XINGFU'ERCUN 1 XIANG

SANLITUN BEILU

154

122

SANLITUNDONG 2 JIE

102

XINGFUYICUN 9 XIANG

8 XIANG

XINGFUYICUN 1 XIANG

Huatong
Intl Youth 🏨

SANLITUNDONG 1 JIE

107

110 112

41 121

GONGREN TIYUCHANG BEILU

167

42

5 61 81

92

140

Hooters

117

202

86 87

The Den

53

4

Zhaolong Youth 🏨

🏨 Beijing Lien

City 🏨

178

Pacific
Century
Bldg

24

Comfort
Plaza

101

Beijing
Roast Duck

Workers' Indoor
Arena (WIA)

⭐

Workers'
Gymnasium

29

GONGRENTIYUCHANG XILU

DONGSIZHIQIAO LU

196

118 113 117

11 52

6

138

⭐

Workers'
Stadium

69

Green
House

180 168

Ban Muyuan

207

197

139

DONGZHIMEN WAIDAJIE

NANSANLITUN LU

128

125

The Loft

JuLong Garden
Apartment

5

Gongti
Intel Youth 🏨

121

Frank's
Place

DONGZHONGJIE

DONGYINGFANG 10 TIAO

DONGYINGFANG 1 TIAO

TAIYUAN BEILI DINGBEI

105

CHAOWAIBEIJIE

48

Guangcai
International
Apartment

145

GONGRENTIYUCHANG NANLU

GONGREN TIYUCHANG NANLU

DONGZHIMEN WAIDAJIE

DONGSANHUANBEILU

Pink Loft

108

BAIJIAZHUANG LU

4

Chaoyang
Hospital ✚

NANSANLITUN LU

Taiyue
Apartment

177

D

11

E

F

150m

© Explorer Group Ltd. 2008

The Complete **Residents'** Guide

373

Map **10**

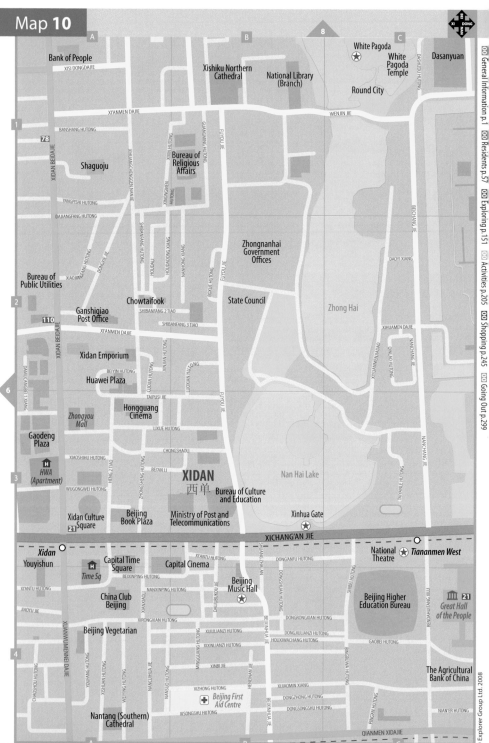

A **B** 8 **C**

White Pagoda

Bank of People
XISI DONGDAJIE

Xishiku Northern
Cathedral

National Library
(Branch)

White
Pagoda
Temple

Dasanyuan

DASHIZHU HUTONG

Round City

XI'ANMEN DAJIE

WENJIN JIE

1

BANSHANG HUTONG

78

Shaguoju

XIDAN BEIDAJIE

XIHUANGCHENGGEN NANJIE

GUANGMING HUTONG

FUYOU JIE

Bureau of
Religious
Affairs

XINGMEN HUTONG

YANGPISHI HUTONG

DAJIANGFANG HUTONG

BEICHANG JIE

DAOYI XIANG

SHIBANFANG HUTONG

HOUDAXIANG

NANHONG XIANG

BOXUE HUTONG

FUYOU JIE

Zhongnanhai
Government
Offices

Bureau of
Public Utilities

XIAO'AN

DONGKE JIE

2

Chowtaifook

SHIBANFANG 2 TIAO

State Council

Zhong Hai

XIHUAMEN DAJIE

110

Ganshiqiao
Post Office

XIDAN BEIDAJIE

SHIBANFANG 3 TIAO

XI'ANMEN DAJIE

XITIANMENDAJIE

QINLAO HUTONG

NANCHANG JIE

Xidan Emporium

XINLIAN HUTONG

BEIYIN HUTONG

6

DAMUCANGBEI XIANG

Huawei Plaza

CAIDIA HUTONG

LIUDIAN HUTONG

TAIPUSI JIE

FUYOU JIE

Zhongyou
Mall

Hongguang
Cinema

LIXUE HUTONG

Gaodeng
Plaza

XIAOSHIHU HUTONG

CHONGSHAOLI

NANCHANG JIE

H
HWA
(Apartment)

HENG 2 TIAO

ZHONGSHENG HUTONG

BEI'AN LI

XIDAN
西单

Nan Hai Lake

TAIYANLE HUTONG

3

WUGONGWEI HUTONG

Bureau of Culture
and Education

Xidan Culture
21 Square

Beijing
Book Plaza

Ministry of Post and
Telecommunications

Xinhua Gate

XICHANG'AN JIE

Xidan
Youyishun

Capital Time
Square

Capital Cinema

XI'ANTU HUTONG

SHUANG ZHA LAN

DONG'ANFU HUTONG

National
Theatre

Tiananmen West

XI'ANTU HUTONG

H
Time Sq

BEIXINPING HUTONG

NANXINPING HUTONG

DONGSHIAN HUTONG

SHIBEI HUTONG

MIX PANJIA HUTONG

China Club
Beijing

XIANMENWEI NEI DAJIE

MINXIANG

XIRONGXIAN HUTONG

DALIUBUKOU JIE

Beijing
Music Hall

Beijing Higher
Education Bureau

Great Hall
of the People

21

JIAOYU JIE

XIANGMEN DAJIE

DONGRONGXIAN HUTONG

Beijing Vegetarian

XIJIULIANZI HUTONG

DONGJIULIANZI HUTONG

4

CHAOSHOU HUTONG

YOUFANG HUTONG

XISHAN HUTONG

WEIYING JIE

NANKUJHUA JIE

XINXINLIANZI HUTONG

XINBI JIE

HOUXIWACHANG HUTONG

BINGBUWA HUTONG

GAOBEI HUTONG

The Agricultural
Bank of China

XIZHONG HUTONG

XUJIAOMIN XIANG

NIAN'ER HUTONG

Beijing First
Aid Centre

XISONGSHU HUTONG

DONGZHONG HUTONG

PINGAN HUTONG

Nantang (Southern)
Cathedral

BEIXINHUA JIE

DONGSONGSHU HUTONG

QIANMEN XIDAJIE

Map **10**

A **B** 12 **C**

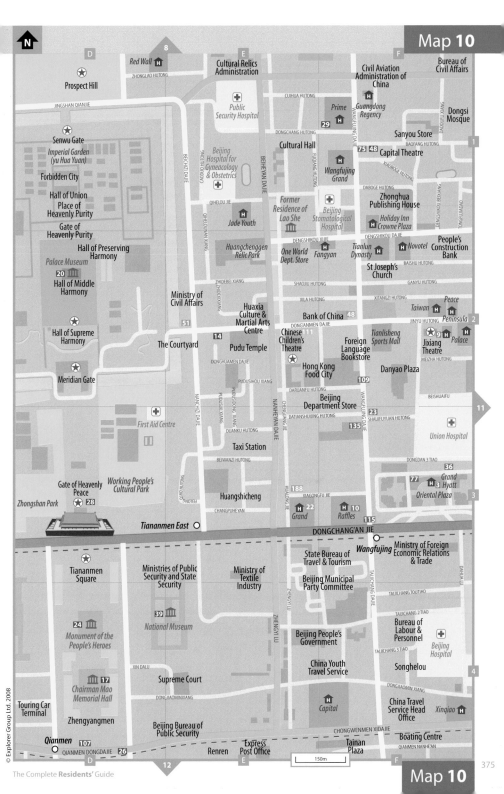

Map **10**

N

Red Wall
ZHONGLAO HUTONG

Prospect Hill

Cultural Relics
Administration

Public
Security Hospital

CUIHUA HUTONG

Civil Aviation
Administration of
China

Bureau of
Civil Affairs

BAOFANG HUTONG

DADUOTI XIANG

Prime

29

Guangdong
Regency

Dongsi
Mosque

JINGSHAN QIANJIE

DONGCHANG HUTONG

WANGFUJING DAJIE

Senwu Gate

Imperial Garden
(yu Hua Yuan)

Cultural Hall

Wangfujing
Grand

Sanyou Store

75 48 Capital Theatre

XIAOBOGE HUTONG

1

BAOFANG HUTONG

Forbidden City

Hall of Union

Place of
Heavenly Purity

Gate of
Heavenly Purity

BEIHEIAN DAJIE

FUQIANG HUTONG

DABOGE HUTONG

Zhonghua
Publishing House

DENGSHIKOU BEIXIANG

DENGSHIKOU XIDAJIE

Holiday Inn
Crowne Plaza

Beijing
Hospital for
Gyneacology
& Obstetrics

QIHELOU JIE

Former
Residence of
Lao She

Beijing
Stomatological
Hospital

Jade Youth

Hall of Preserving
Harmony

Palace Museum

20

Hall of Middle
Harmony

Huangchenggen
Relic Park

QIHELONAN XIANG

ZHIDEBEI XIANG

One World
Dept. Store

DENGSHIKOU XIJIE

Fangyan

Tianlun
Dynasty

Novotel

People's
Construction
Bank

St Joseph's
Church

BAISHU HUTONG

Ministry of
Civil Affairs

51

SHAOJIU HUTONG

GANYU HUTONG

Hall of Supreme
Harmony

The Courtyard

14

Huaxia
Culture &
Martial Arts
Centre

Pudu Temple

XILA HUTONG

Bank of China

DONG'ANMEN DAJIE

48

XITANGZI HUTONG

Taiwan

JINYU HUTONG

Peace

Peninsula

Meridian Gate

NANCHIZI DAJIE

PUDUSIXIANG

PUDUSIHOU XIANG

Chinese
Children's
Theatre

Hong Kong
Food City

DONGHUAMEN DAJIE

NANHEYAN DAJIE

CHENGXIA JIE

Foreign
Language
Bookstore

Tianlisheng
Sports Mall

Jixiang
Theatre

9

Palace

MEIZHA HUTONG

Danyao Plaza

First Aid Centre

DUANKU HUTONG

Taxi Station

BEIWANZI HUTONG

DARUANFU HUTONG

DATIANSHUIJING HUTONG

Beijing
Department Store

109

23

SHAUIFUYUAN HUTONG

135

BEISHUAIFU

11

Union Hospital

Gate of Heavenly
Peace

Working People's
Cultural Park

Zhongshan Park

28

SHUIHI HUTONG

Huangshicheng

CHANGPUHEYAN

XIAGONGFU JIE

188

HUALONG JIE

DONGDAN 3 TIAO

36

77

3

Grand
Hyatt

Oriental Plaza

Grand

22

Raffles

10

115

Tiananmen East

DONGCHANG'AN JIE

State Bureau of
Travel & Tourism

Wangfujing

Ministry of Foreign
Economic Relations
& Trade

Tiananmen
Square

Ministries of Public
Security and State
Security

Ministry of
Textile
Industry

Beijing Municipal
Party Committee

TAIJICHANG DAJIE

DAHUA LU

24

Monument of the
People's Heroes

39

National Museum

ZHENGYI LU

Z-ZHENGYI LU

Beijing People's
Government

TAIJICHANG TOUTIAO

TAIJICHANG 2 TIAO

Bureau of
Labour &
Personnel

Beijing
Hospital

China Youth
Travel Service

TAIJICHANG 3 TIAO

17

Chairman Mao
Memorial Hall

Supreme Court

DONGJIAOMINXIANG

Songhelou

DONGJIAOMIN XIANG

4

Zhengyangmen

XIN DALU

Capital

China Travel
Service Head
Office

Xinqiao

Touring Car
Terminal

Beijing Bureau of
Public Security

CHONGWENMEN XIDAJIE

Qianmen

107

QIANMEN DONGDAJIE

26

Renren

Express
Post Office

Tainan
Plaza

Boating Centre

QIANMEN NANHE'AN

150m

12

© Explorer Group Ltd. 2008

375

Map **10**

Map **11**

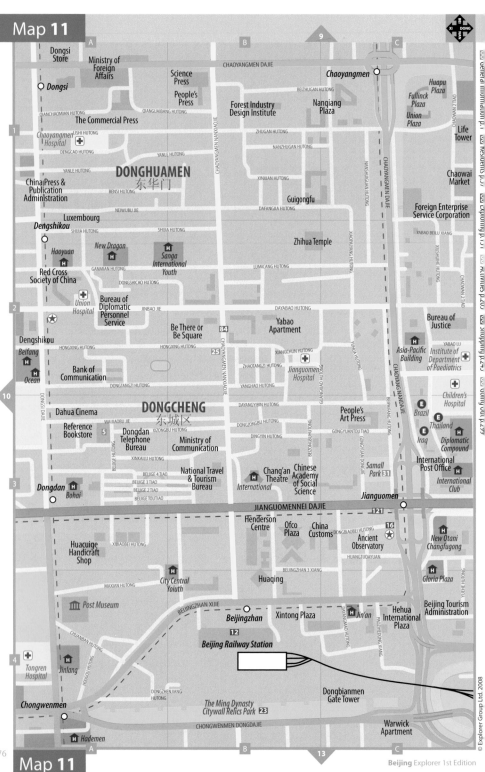

A

B

C

CHAOYANGMEN DAJIE

Dongsi
Store

Ministry of
Foreign
Affairs

Science
Press

People's
Press

Chaoyangmen

Huapu
Plaza

Fullinck
Plaza

Union
Plaza

○ *Dongsi*

BEIZHUGAN HUTONG

Forest Industry
Design Institute

Nanqiang
Plaza

Life
Tower

QIANCHAOMIAN HUTONG

QIANGUAIBANG HUTONG

ZHUGAN HUTONG

The Commercial Press

LISHI HUTONG

Chaoyangmen
Hospital

NANZHUGAN HUTONG

Chaowai
Market

DENGCAO HUTONG

YANLE HUTONG

XINXIAN HUTONG

Foreign Enterprise
Service Corporation

YANLE HUTONG

DONGHUAMEN
东华门

China Press &
Publication
Administration

BENSI HUTONG

Guigongfu

YABAO BEILU XIANG

NEIWUBU JIE

DAFANGJIA HUTONG

Luxembourg

Dengshikou

SHIJIA HUTONG

SHIJIA HUTONG

Zhihua Temple

Haoyuan

New Dragan

Sanga
International
Youth

Red Cross
Society of China

GANMIAN HUTONG

LUMICANG HUTONG

DONGSHICAO HUTONG

Union
Hospital

Bureau of
Diplomatic
Personnel
Service

JINBAO JIE

DAYABAO HUTONG

Bureau of
Justice

Dengshikou

Be There or
Be Square

84

Yabao
Apartment

YABAO LU

Beifang

HONGXING HUTONG

HONGXING HUTONG

XIANGCHUN HUTONG

Asia-Pacific
Building

Institute of
Department
of Paediatrics

Ocean

25

ZHAOTANGZI HUTONG

Jianguomen
Hospital

Bank of
Communication

DONGTANGZI HUTONG

YANGHAO HUTONG

Children's
Hospital

DONGCHENG
东城区

DAYANGYIBIN HUTONG

People's
Art Press

Brazil

Dahua Cinema

WAIJIAOBU JIE

DONGZONGBU HUTONG

Thailand

Reference
Bookstore

5

Dongdan
Telephone
Bureau

XIZONGBU JIE

Ministry of
Communication

DINGYIN HUTONG

GONGYUANTOU TIAO

Iraq

Diplomatic
Compound

XINKAILU HUTONG

Small
Park 31

International
Post Office

National Travel
& Tourism
Bureau

BEIJIGE 4 TIAO

Chang'an
Theatre

Chinese
Academy
of Social
Science

International
Club

Dongdan

BEIJIGE 3 TIAO
BEIJIGE 2 TIAO
BEIJIGE TOUTIAO

Bohai

International

Jianguomen

○

JIANGUOMENNEI DAJIE

121

Henderson
Centre

Ofco
Plaza

China
Customs

DONGBIAOBEI HUTONG

16

New Otani
Changfugong

Huacuige
Handicraft
Shop

XIBIAOBEI HUTONG

Ancient
Observatory

HUANGTUDAYUAN

Gloria Plaza

City Central
Yoiuth

Huaqing

BEIJINGZHAN 3 XIANG

Beijing Tourism
Administration

MAXIAN HUTONG

📖 *Post Museum*

BEIJINGZHAN XIJIE

Xintong Plaza

Jin'an

Hehua
International
Plaza

CHUANBAN HUTONG

Beijingzhan

12

Beijing Railway Station

Tongren
Hospital

Jinlang

Chongwenmen

DONGZHENJIANG
HUTONG

The Ming Dynasty
Citywall Relics Park 23

Dongbianmen
Gate Tower

Warwick
Apartment

CHONGWENMEN DONGDAJIE

Hademen

Map **11**   **Beijing** Explorer 1st Edition

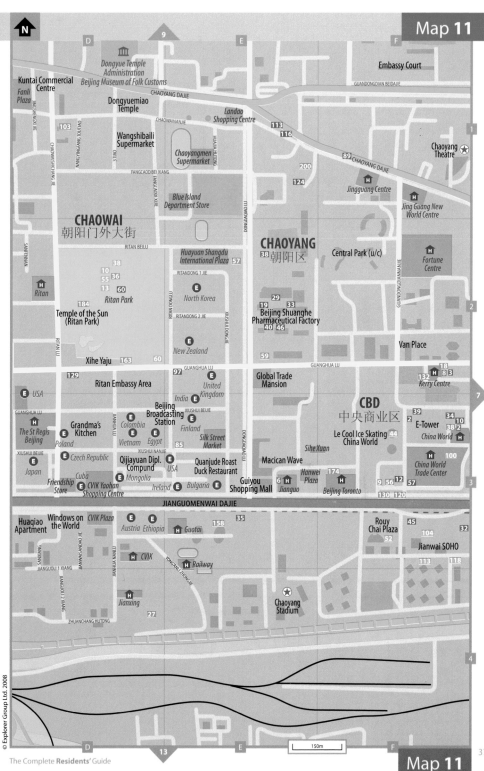

Map 11

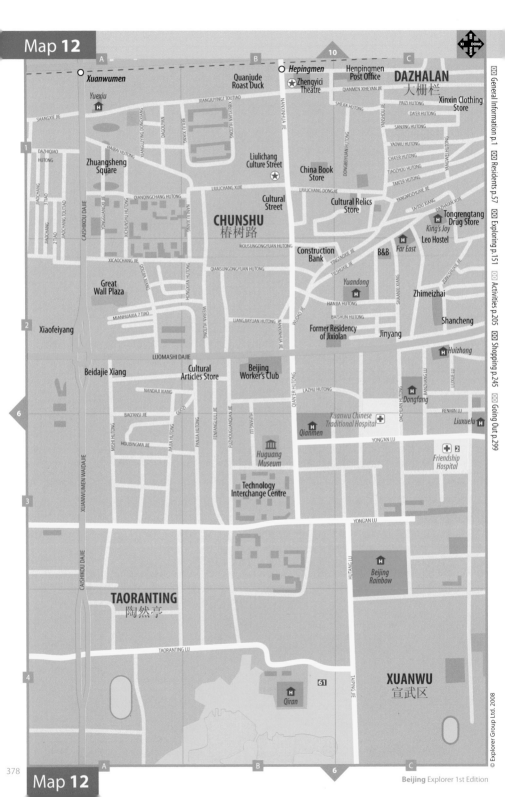

Map **12**

General Information p.1 | Residents p.57 | Exploring p.151 | Activities p.205 | Shopping p.245 | Going Out p.299

Explorer Group Ltd. 2008

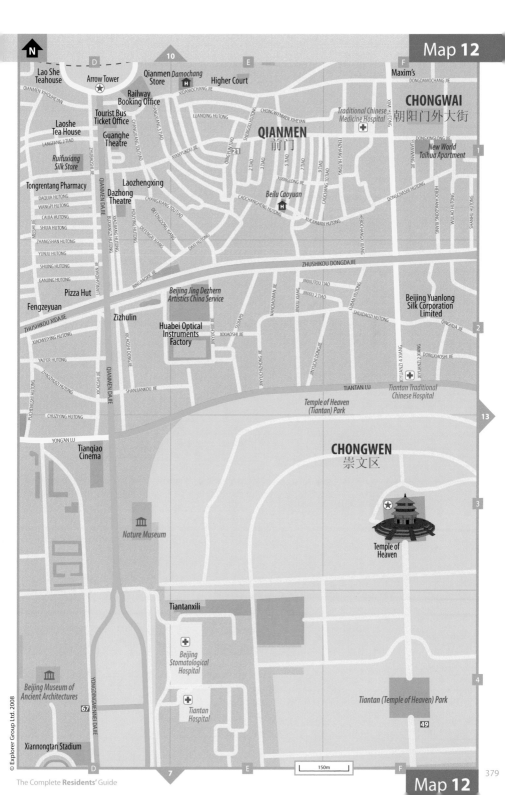

Lao She
Teahouse

Arrow Tower
★

Qianmen *Damochang*
Store

Higher Court

Maxim's

DONGDAMOCHANG JIE

QIANMEN XIHOUHEYAN

Railway
Booking Office

XIDAMOCHANG JIE

CHONGWAI
朝阳门外大街

Tourist Bus
Ticket Office

LUANQING HUTONG

CHONGWENMEN XIHEYAN

Traditional Chinese
Medicine Hospital
✚

Laoshe
Tea House

Guanghe
Theatre

QIANMEN
前门

DONGXINGLONG JIE

LANGFANG 2 TIAO

XIANYUKOU JIE

New World
Taihua Apartment

*Ruifuxiang
Silk Store*

1

Tongrentang Pharmacy

Laozhengxing

Dazhong
Theatre

XIXINGLONG JIE

DAQIUA HUTONG

CHANGXIANG TOUTIAO

Beilu Caoyuan
✚

CAOCHANGHENG HUTONG

WANGPI HUTONG

CAIBA HUTONG

KUEJIAWAN HUTONG

MEISHI JIE

ZHANGSHAN HUTONG

YUNJU HUTONG

SHIJING HUTONG

ZHUSHIKOU DONGDAJIE

GANJING HUTONG

JINXIUTOU TIAO

Pizza Hut

Beijing Jing Dezhern
Artistics China Service

JINXIU 2 TIAO

Beijing Yuanlong
Silk Corporation
Limited

Fengzeyuan

Zizhulin

SHIJIADAOZI HUTONG

QINGHUA JIE

ZHUSHIKOU XIDAJIE

Huabei Optical
Instruments
Factory

XIXIAOSHI JIE

2

XIAOWELYING HUTONG

YAO'ER HUTONG

SHANJIANKOU JIE

TIANTAN LU

*Tiantan Traditional
Chinese Hospital*

CHUZIYING HUTONG

TIANTAN LU

Temple of Heaven
(Tiantan) Park

13

YONG'AN LU

Tianqiao
Cinema

CHONGWEN
崇文区

3

Temple of
Heaven

✚

Nature Museum

Tiantanxili

4

✚

Beijing
Stomatological
Hospital

Beijing Museum of
Ancient Architectures

67

✚

Tiantan (Temple of Heaven) Park

Tiantan
Hospital

49

Xiannongtan Stadium

D   7   E   150m   F

Map **13**

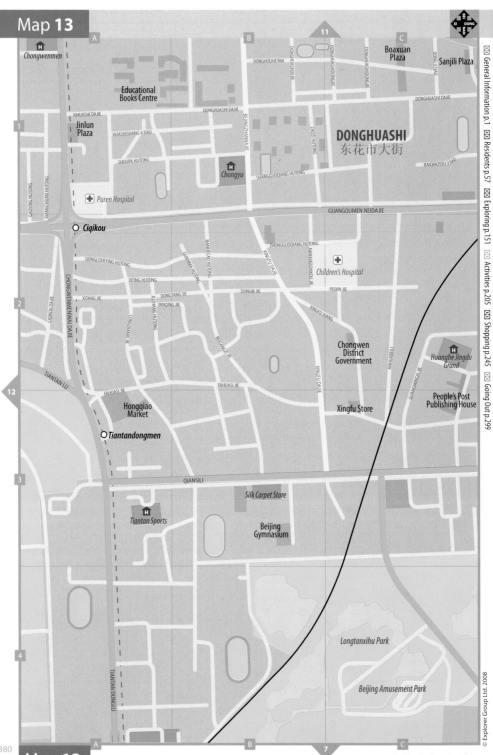

H Chongwenmen

Educational
Books Centre

DONGHOUHEYAN

DONGHUASHIDONGJIE

DONGHUASHIDONGJIE

DONG 3 TIAO

Boaxuan
Plaza

Sanjili Plaza

DONGHUASHI DAJIE

XIHUASHI DAJIE

DONGHUASHI DAJIE

BEIJINGZHANNA JIE

ZAOZI HUTONG

DONGHUASHI
东花市大街

Jinlun
Plaza

HUASHISHANG 4 TIAO

BAIQIAOTOU HUTONG

CHILE HUTONG

SHOUPA HUTONG

H Chongyu

SHANGGUOQIANG HUTONG

✚ Puren Hospital

GUANGQUMEN NEIDAJIE

○ **Ciqikou**

ZHONGGUOQIANG HUTONG

DONGLISHIYING HUTONG

NANHECAO HUTONG

GUNIMA HUTONG

XINGFU DAJIE

MANJIAKOSHIDOU JIE

✚ Children's Hospital

XITING HUTONG

JIUTING HUTONG

DONGTANG JIE

DONGBI JIE

PEIXIN JIE

XITANG JIE

YANQING JIE

XINGFU XIANG

Chongwen
District
Government

ANHUABELI

H Huanghe Jingdu
Grand

CONGGANG JIE

BEIJIANCA JIE

FAHUASI JIE

XINGFU DAJIE

GUANGMINGLU JIE

People's Post
Publishing House

TIANTAN LU

FAHUASI JIE

FAHUASI JIE

CHONGWENMENWAI DAJIE

CHIKOU DAJIE

Hongqiao
Market

Xingfu Store

○ **Tiantandongmen**

QIANSILI

Silk Carpet Store

H Tiantan Sports

Beijing
Gymnasium

TIANTAN DONGLU

Longtanxihu Park

Beijing Amusement Park

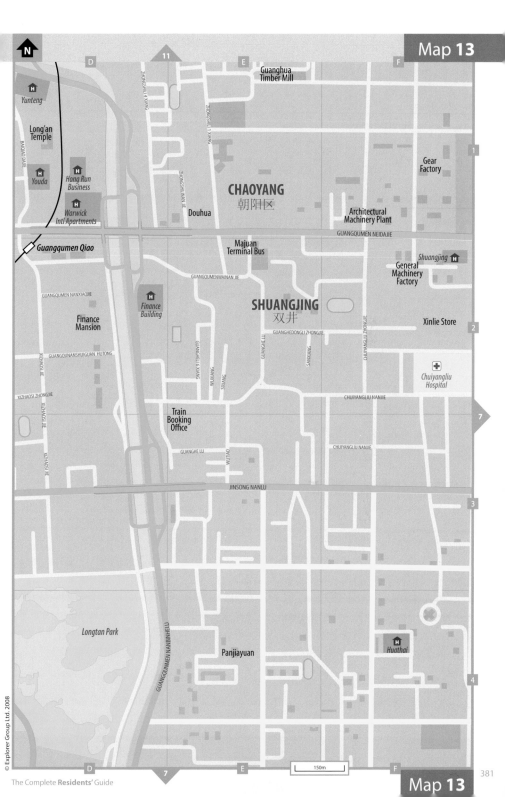

Map **13**

© Explorer Group Ltd. 2008

Not big, but very clever…

Perfectly proportioned to fit in your pocket,
this marvellous mini guidebook makes sure
you don't just get the holiday you paid for
but rather the one that you dreamed of.

Beijing Mini Visitors' Guide
Maximising your holiday, minimising your hand luggage

Index

Index

Index

Index

Index

Index

Residents' Guides

All you need to know about living, working and enjoying life in these
exciting destinations

Mini Guides
The perfect pocket-sized
Visitors' Guides

Mini Maps
Wherever you are,
never get lost again

Photography Books
Beautiful cities caught through the lens

Calendars
The time, the place, and the date

Maps
Wherever you are, never get lost again

Activity and Lifestyle Guides
Drive, trek, dive and swim... life will never be boring again

Retail sales
Our books are available in most good bookshops around the world, and are also available online at Amazon.co.uk and Amazon.com. If you would like to enquire about any of our international distributors, please contact retail@explorerpublishing.com

Bulk sales and customisation
All our products are available for bulk sales with customisation options. For discount rates and further information, please contact corporatesales@explorerpublishing.com

Licensing and digital sales
All our content, maps and photography are available for print or digital use. For licensing enquiries please contact licensing@explorerpublishing.com

Ahmed Mainodin
AKA: Mystery Man
We can never recognise Ahmed because of his constantly changing facial hair. He waltzes in with big lambchop sideburns one day, a handlebar moustache the next, and a neatly trimmed goatee after that. So far we've had no objections to his hirsute chameleonisms, but we'll definitely draw the line at a monobrow.

Ajay Krishnan R
AKA: Web Wonder
Ajay's mum and dad knew he was going to be an IT genius when they found him reconfiguring his Commodore 64 at the tender age of 2. He went on to become the technology consultant on all three Matrix films, and counts Keanu as a close personal friend.

Alex Jeffries
AKA: Easy Rider
Alex is happiest when dressed in leather from head to toe with a humming machine between his thighs – just like any other motorbike enthusiast. Whenever he's not speeding along the Hatta Road at full throttle, he can be found at his beloved Mac, still dressed in leather.

Alistair MacKenzie
AKA: Media Mogul
If only Alistair could take the paperless office one step further and achieve the officeless office he would be the happiest publisher alive. Wireless access from a remote spot somewhere in the Hajar Mountains would suit this intrepid explorer – less traffic, lots of fresh air, and wearing sandals all day – the perfect work environment!

Andrew Burgess
AKA: The Charmer
Andrew gave up his career test-driving Lamborghinis around rural Gloucestershire to move to Dubai where he now schmoozes Explorer's corporate clients and moonlights as a DJ. A lifelong Toffeeman, rumour has it he was recently involved in an attempted coup aimed at reinstating Howard Kendall.

Annabel Clough
AKA: Bollywood Babe
Taking a short break from her successful career in Bollywood, Annabel livens up the Explorer office with her spontaneous dance routines and random passionate outpouring of song. If there is a whiff of drama or a hint of romance, Annabel's famed vocal chords and nifty footwork will bring a touch of glamour to Al Quoz.

Andrea Fust
AKA: Mother Superior
By day Andrea is the most efficient manager in the world and by night she replaces the boardroom for her board and wows the pants off the dudes in Ski Dubai. Literally. Back in the office she definitely wears the trousers!

Bahrudeen Abdul
AKA: The Stallion
Having tired of creating abstract sculptures out of papier maché and candy canes, Bahrudeen turned to the art of computer programming. After honing his skills in the southern Andes for three years he grew bored of Patagonian winters, and landed a job here, 'The Home of 01010101 Creative Freedom'.

Ben Merrett
AKA: Big Ben
After a short (or tall as the case may have been) career as a human statue, Ben tired of the pigeons choosing him, rather than his namesake, as a public convenience and decided to fly the nest to seek his fortune in foreign lands. Not only is he big on personality but he brings in the big bucks with his bulk!

Cherry Enriquez
AKA: Bean Counter
With the team's penchant for sweets and pastries, it's good to know we have Cherry on top of our accounting cake. The local confectioner is always paid on time, so we're guaranteed great gateaux for every special occasion.

Claire England
AKA: Whip Cracker
No longer able to freeload off the fact that she once appeared in a Robbie Williams video, Claire now puts her creative skills to better use – looking up rude words in the dictionary! A child of English nobility, Claire is quite the lady – unless she's down at Rock Bottom.

Darwin Lovitos
AKA: The Philosopher

We are firm believers in our own Darwinism theory at Explorer – enthusiasm, organisation and a great sense of humour can evolve into a wonderful thing. He may not have the big beard (except on weekends) , but Darwin is just as wise as his namesake.

David Quinn
AKA: Sharp Shooter

After a short stint as a children's TV presenter was robbed from David because he developed an allergy to sticky back plastic, he made his way to sandier pastures. Now that he's thinking outside the box, nothing gets past the man with the sharpest pencil in town.

Derrick Pereira
AKA: The Returnimator

After leaving Explorer in 2003, Derrick's life took a dramatic downturn – his dog ran away, his prized bonsai tree died and he got kicked out of his thrash metal band. Since rejoining us, things are looking up and he just found out he's won $10 million in a Nigerian sweepstakes competition. And he's got the desk by the window!

Enrico Maullon
AKA: The Crooner

Frequently mistaken for his near-namesake Enrique Iglesias, Enrico decided to capitalise and is now a regular stand-in for the Latin heartthrob. If he's ever missing from the office, it usually means he's off performing for millions of adoring fans on another stadium tour of America.

Firos Khan
AKA: Big Smiler
Previously a body double in kung fu movies, including several appearances in close up scenes for Steven Seagal's moustache. He also once tore down a restaurant with his bare hands after they served him a mild curry by mistake.

Grace Carnay
AKA: Manila Ice

It's just as well the office is so close to a movie theatre, because Grace is always keen to catch the latest Hollywood offering from Brad Pitt, who she admires purely for his acting ability, of course. Her ice cool exterior conceals a tempestuous passion for jazz, which fuels her frenzied typing speed.

Hashim MM
AKA: Speedy Gonzales

They don't come much faster than Hashim – he's so speedy with his mouse that scientists are struggling to create a computer that can keep up with him. His nimble fingers leave his keyboard smouldering (he gets through three a week), and his go-faster stripes make him almost invisible to the naked eye when he moves.

Helen Spearman
AKA: Little Miss Sunshine

With her bubbly laugh and permanent smile, Helen is a much-needed ray of sunshine in the office when we're all grumpy and facing harrowing deadlines. It's almost impossible to think that she ever loses her temper or shows a dark side... although put her behind the wheel of a car, and you've got instant road rage.

Henry Hilos
AKA: The Quiet Man

Henry can rarely be seen from behind his large obstructive screen but when you do catch a glimpse you'll be sure to get a smile. Lighthearted Henry keeps all those glossy pages filled with pretty pictures for something to look at when you can't be bothered to read.

Iain Young
AKA: 'The Cat'

Iain follows in the fine tradition of Scots with safe hands – Alan Rough, Andy Goram, Jim Leighton on a good day – but breaking into the Explorer XI has proved frustrating. There's no match on a Mac, but that Al Huzaifa ringer doesn't half make himself big.

Ieyad Charaf
AKA: Fashion Designer

When we hired Ieyad as a top designer, we didn't realise we'd be getting his designer tops too! By far the snappiest dresser in the office, you'd be hard-pressed to beat his impeccably ironed shirts.

401

Ingrid Cupido
AKA: The Karaoke Queen
Ingrid has a voice to match her starlet name. She'll put any Pop Idols to shame once behind the mike, and she's pretty nifty on a keyboard too. She certainly gets our vote if she decides to go pro; just remember you saw her here first.

Ivan Rodrigues
AKA: The Aviator
After making a mint in the airline market, Ivan came to Explorer where he works for pleasure, not money. That's his story, anyway. We know that he is actually a corporate spy from a rival company and that his multi-level spreadsheets are really elaborate codes designed to confuse us.

Jake Marsico
AKA: Don Calzone
Jake spent the last 10 years on the tiny triangular Mediterranean island of Samoza, honing his traditional cooking techniques and perfecting his Italian. Now, whenever he returns to his native America, he impresses his buddies by effortlessly zapping a hot dog to perfection in any microwave, anywhere, anytime.

Jane Roberts
AKA: The Oracle
After working in an undisclosed role in the government, Jane brought her super sleuth skills to Explorer. Whatever the question, she knows what, where, who, how and when, but her encyclopaedic knowledge is only impressive until you realise she just makes things up randomly.

Jayde Fernandes
AKA: Pop Idol
Jayde's idol is Britney Spears, and he recently shaved his head to show solidarity with the troubled star. When he's not checking his dome for stubble, or practising the dance moves to 'Baby One More Time' in front of the bathroom mirror, he actually manages to get some designing done.

Johny Mathew
AKA: The Hawker
Caring Johny used to nurse wounded eagles back to health and teach them how to fly again before trying his luck in merchandising. Fortunately his skills in the field have come in handy at Explorer, where his efforts to improve our book sales have been a soaring success.

Joy Tubog
AKA: Joyburgh
Don't let her saintly office behaviour deceive you. Joy has the habit of jumping up and down while screaming 'Jumanji' the instant anyone mentions Robin Williams and his hair sweater. Thankfully, her volleyball team has learned to utilize her 'uniqueness' when it's her turn to spike the ball.

Juby Jose
AKA: The Nutcracker
After years as a ballet teacher, Juby decided on mapping out a completely different career path, charting the UAE's ever-changing road network. Plotting products to illuminate the whole of the Middle East, she now works alongside the all-singing, all-dancing Madathil brothers, and cracks any nut that steps out of line.

Kate Fox
AKA: Contacts Collector
Kate swooped into the office like the UK equivalent of Wonderwoman, minus the tights of course (it's much too hot for that), but armed with a superhuman marketing brain. Even though she's just arrived, she is already a regular on the Dubai social scene – she is helping to blast Explorer into the stratosphere, one champagne-soaked networking party at a time.

Kathryn Calderon
AKA: Miss Moneypenny
With her high-flying banking background, Kathryn is an invaluable member of the team. During her lunchtimes she conducts 'get rich quick' seminars that, she says, will make us so much money that we'll be able to retire early and spend our days reading books instead of making them. We're still waiting...

Katie Drynan
AKA: The Irish Deputy
This Irish lass is full of sass, fresh from her previous role as the four leaf clover mascot for the Irish ladies' rugby team. Katie provides the Explorer office with lots of Celtic banter and unlimited Irish charm.

Kelly Tesoro
AKA: Leading Lady
Kelly's former career as a Korean soapstar babe set her in good stead for the daily dramas at the bold and beautiful Explorer office. As our lovely receptionist she's on stage all day and her winning smile never slips.

Matt Farquharson
AKA: Hack Hunter
A career of tuppence-a-word hackery ended when Matt arrived in Dubai to cover a maggot wranglers' convention. He misguidedly thinks he's clever because he once wrote for some grown-up English papers.

Kiran Melwani
AKA: Bow Selector
Like a modern-day Robin Hood (right down to the green tights and band of merry men), Kiran's mission in life is to distribute Explorer's wealth of knowledge to the fact-hungry readers of the world. Just make sure you never do anything to upset her – rumour has it she's a pretty mean shot with that bow and arrow.

Mathew Samuel
AKA: Mr Modest
Matt's penchant for the entrepreneurial life began with a pair of red braces and a filofax when still a child. That yearning for the cut and thrust of commerce has brought him to Dubai, where he made a fortune in the sand-selling business before semi-retiring at Explorer.

Laura Zuffa
AKA: Travelling Salesgirl
Laura's passport is covered in more stamps than Kofi Annan's, and there isn't a city, country or continent that she won't travel to. With a smile that makes grown men weep, our girl on the frontlines always brings home the beef bacon.

Michael Dominic
AKA: The Godfather
Master of his domain, dapper Michael rules over the bookstores of the GCC with a firm hand and a warm smile. He's got spies everywhere so woe betide a hapless shop assistant who displays an Explorer title upside down...

Lennie Mangalino
AKA: Shaker Maker
With a giant spring in her step and music in her heart it's hard to not to swing to the beat when Lennie passes by in the office. She loves her Lambada... and Samba... and Salsa and anything else she can get the sales team shaking their hips to.

Michael Samuel
AKA: Gordon Gekko
We have a feeling this mild mannered master of mathematics has a wild side. He hasn't witnessed an Explorer party yet but the office agrees that once the karaoke machine is out, Michael will be the maestro. Watch out Dubai!

Mannie Lugtu
AKA: Distribution Demon
When the travelling circus rode into town, their master juggler Mannie decided to leave the Big Top and explore Dubai instead. He may have swapped his balls for our books but his juggling skills still come in handy.

Mimi Stankova
AKA: Mind Controller
A master of mind control, Mimi's siren-like voice lulls people into doing whatever she asks. Her steely reserve and endless patience mean recalcitrant reporters and persistent PR people are putty in her hands, delivering whatever she wants, whenever she wants it.

Maricar Ong
AKA: Pocket Docket
A pint-sized dynamo of ruthless efficiency, Maricar gets the job done before anyone else notices it needed doing. If this most able assistant is absent for a moment, it sends a surge of blind panic through the Explorer ranks.

Mohammed Sameer
AKA: Man in the Van
Known as MS, short for Microsoft, Sameer can pick apart a PC like a thief with a lock, which is why we keep him out of finance and pounding Dubai's roads in the unmissable Explorer van – so we can always spot him coming.

Najumudeen Kuttathundil
AKA: The Groove
If it weren't for Najumudeen, our stock of books would be lying in a massive pile of rubble in our warehouse. Thankfully, through hours of crunk dancing and forklift racing with Mohammed T, Najumudeen has perfected the art of organisation and currently holds the title for fastest forklift slalom in the UAE.

Rafi Jamal
AKA: Soap Star
After a walk on part in The Bold and the Beautiful, Rafi swapped the Hollywood Hills for the Hajar Mountains. Although he left the glitz behind, he still mingles with high society, moonlighting as a male gigolo and impressing Dubai's ladies with his fancy footwork.

Rafi VP
AKA: Party Trickster
After developing a rare allergy to sunlight in his teens, Rafi started to lose a few centimeters of height every year. He now stands just 30cm tall, and does his best work in our dingy basement wearing a pair of infrared goggles. His favourite party trick is to fold himself into a briefcase.

Noushad Madathil
AKA: Map Daddy
Where would Explorer be without the mercurial Madathil brothers? Lost in the Empty Quarter, that's where. Quieter than a mute dormouse, Noushad prefers to let his Photoshop layers, and brother Zain, do all the talking. A true Map Daddy.

Richard Greig
AKA: Sir Lancelot
Chivalrous to the last, Richard's dream of being a medieval knight suffered a setback after being born several centuries too late. His stellar parliamentary career remains intact, and he is in the process of creating a new party with the aim of abolishing all onions and onion-related produce.

Pamela Afram
AKA: Lady of Arabia
After an ill-fated accident playing Lawrence of Arabia's love interest in a play in Jumeira, Pamela found solace in the Explorer office. Her first paycheque went on a set of shiny new gleamers and she is now back to her bright and smiley self and is solely responsible for lighting up one half of the office!

Roshni Ahuja
AKA: Bright Spark
Never failing to brighten up the office with her colourful get-up, Roshni definitely puts the 'it' in the IT department. She's a perennially pleasant, profound programmer with peerless panache, and she does her job with plenty of pep and piles of pizzazz.

Pamela Grist
AKA: Happy Snapper
If a picture can speak a thousand words then Pam's photos say a lot about her - through her lens she manages to find the beauty in everything – even this motley crew. And when the camera never lies, thankfully Photoshop can.

Sean Kearns
AKA: The Tall Guy
Big Sean, as he's affectionately known, is so laid back he actually spends most of his time lying down (unless he's on a camping trip, when his ridiculously small tent forces him to sleep on his hands and knees). Despite the rest of us constantly tripping over his lanky frame, when the job requires someone who will work flat out, he always rises to the editorial occasion.

Pete Maloney
AKA: Graphic Guru
Image conscious he may be, but when Pete has his designs on something you can bet he's gonna get it! He's the king of chat up lines, ladies – if he ever opens a conversation with 'D'you come here often?' then brace yourself for the Maloney magic.

Shabsir M
AKA: Sticky Wicket
Shabsir is a valuable player on the Indian national cricket team, so instead of working you'll usually find him autographing cricket balls for crazed fans around the world. We don't mind though – if ever a retailer is stumped because they run out of stock, he knocks them for six with his speedy delivery.

Mohammed Shaji
AKA: Design Demon

After years designing sweet wrappers and cereal boxes, Shaji realised it was time for a break. So where does a health conscious, T-shirt-loving young designer go next? Explorer of course! Sadly, now he's so busy he has little time to play caroms or travel the world.

Steve Jones
AKA: Golden Boy

Our resident Kiwi lives in a nine-bedroom mansion and is already planning an extension. His winning smile has caused many a knee to weaken in Bur Dubai but sadly for the ladies, he's hopelessly devoted to his clients.

Shan Kumar
AKA: Caped Crusader

Not dissimilar to the Batman's beacon, Explorer shines a giant X into the skies over Al Quoz in times of need. Luckily for us, Shan battled for days through the sand and warehouse units to save the day at our shiny new office. What a hero!

Tim Binks
AKA: Class Clown

El Binksmeisterooney is such a sharp wit, he often has fellow Explorers gushing tea from their noses in convulsions of mirth. Years spent hiking across the Middle East have given him an encyclopaedic knowledge of rock formations and elaborate hair.

Shawn Jackson Zuzarte
AKA: Paper Plumber

If you thought rocket science was hard, try rearranging the chaotic babble that flows from the editorial team! If it weren't for Shawn, most of our books would require a kaleidoscope to read correctly so we're keeping him and his jazz hands under wraps.

Tom Jordan
AKA: The True Professional

Explorer's resident thesp, Tom delivers lines almost as well as he cuts them. His early promise on the pantomime circuit was rewarded with an all-action role in hit UK drama Heartbeat. He's still living off the royalties – and the fact he shared a sandwich with Kenneth Branagh.

Shyrell Tamayo
AKA: Fashion Princess

We've never seen Shyrell wearing the same thing twice – her clothes collection is so large that her husband has to keep all his things in a shoebox. She runs Designlab like clockwork, because being late for deadlines is SO last season.

Tracy Fitzgerald
AKA: 'La Dona'

Tracy is a queenpin Catalan mafiosa and ringleader for the 'pescadora' clan, a nefarious group that runs a sushi smuggling operation between the Costa Brava and Ras Al Khaimah. She is not to be crossed. Rival clans will find themselves fed fish, and then fed to the fishes.

Sobia Gulzad
AKA: High Flyer

If Sobia's exam results in economics and management are anything to go by, she's destined to become a member of the global jet set. Her pursuit of glamour is almost more relentless than her pursuit of success, and in her time away from reading The Wealth of Nations she shops for designer handbags and that elusive perfect shade of lipgloss.

Sunita Lakhiani
AKA: Designlass

Initially suspicious of having a female in their midst, the boys in Designlab now treat Sunita like one of their own. A big shame for her, because they treat each other pretty damn bad!

Zainudheen Madathil
AKA: Map Master

Often confused with retired footballer Zinedine Zidane because of his dexterous displays and a bad head-butting habit, Zain tackles design with the mouse skills of a star striker. Maps are his goal and despite getting red-penned a few times, when he shoots, he scores.

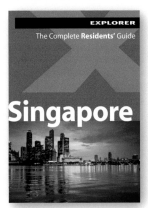

The *Beijing Explorer* Team
Lead Editor Matt Farquharson
Deputy Editor Helen Spearman
Editorial Assistant Ingrid Cupido
Designer Jayde Fernandes
Cartographers Ramlath Kambravan, Sudeer Mekkatu,
Sunita Lakhiani, Zainudheen Madathil
Photographers Victor Romero, Matt Farquharson,
Peter Ellegard, Marko Ferenc, Julien Wagner
Proofers Jo Holden-MacDonald, Kaye Holland, Audrey Lee

Publisher
Alistair MacKenzie
Associate Publisher Claire England

Editorial
Group Editor Jane Roberts
Lead Editors David Quinn, Matt Farquharson,
Sean Kearns, Tim Binks, Tom Jordan
Deputy Editors Helen Spearman, Jakob Marsico,
Katie Drynan, Pamela Afram, Richard Greig, Tracy Fitzgerald
Senior Editorial Assistant Mimi Stankova
Editorial Assistants Grace Carnay, Ingrid Cupido, Kathryn Calderon

Design
Creative Director Pete Maloney
Art Director Ieyad Charaf
Design Manager Alex Jeffries
Senior Designer Iain Young
Layout Manager Jayde Fernandes
Designers Hashim Moideen, Mohammed Shaji
Rafi VP, Shawn Jackson Zuzarte
Cartography Manager Zainudheen Madathil
Cartographers Juby Jose, Noushad Madathil, Sunita Lakhiani
Traffic Manager Maricar Ong
Production Coordinator Joy Tubog

Photography
Photography Manager Pamela Grist
Photographer Victor Romero
Image Editor Henry Hilos

Sales & Marketing
Media Sales Area Managers Laura Zuffa, Stephen Jones
GCC Retail Sales Manager Michael Dominic
Global Partners Sales Manager Andrew Burgess
Corporate Sales Executive Ben Merrett
Marketing Manager Kate Fox
Marketing Executive Annabel Clough
Digital Content Manager Derrick Pereira
International Retail Sales Manager Ivan Rodrigues
Retail Sales Coordinator Kiran Melwani, Sobia Gulzad
Retail Sales Supervisor Mathew Samuel
Retail Sales Merchandiser Johny Mathew, Shan Kumar
Sales & Marketing Coordinator Lennie Mangalino
Senior Distribution Executives Ahmed Mainodin, Firos Khan
Warehouse Assistant Najumudeen K.I.
Drivers Mohammed Sameer, Shabsir Madathil

Finance & Administration
Finance Manager Michael Samuel
HR & Administration Manager Andrea Fust
Admin Manager Shyrell Tamayo
Junior Accountant Cherry Enriquez
Accountants Assistant Darwin Lovitas
Administrators Enrico Maullon, Kelly Tesoro
Driver Rafi Jamal, Mannie Lugtu

IT
IT Administrator Ajay Krishnan
Senior Software Engineer Bahrudeen Abdul
Software Engineer Roshni Ahuja

Contact Us

Reader Response
If you have any comments and suggestions, fill out
our online reader response form and you could win prizes.
Log on to **www.explorerpublishing.com**

General Enquiries
We'd love to hear your thoughts and answer any questions
you have about this book or any other Explorer product.
Contact us at **info@explorerpublishing.com**

Careers
If you fancy yourself as an Explorer, send your CV
(stating the position you're interested in) to
jobs@explorerpublishing.com

Designlab & Contract Publishing
For enquiries about Explorer's Contract Publishing arm
and design services contact
designlab@explorerpublishing.com

PR & Marketing
For PR and marketing enquries contact
marketing@explorerpublishing.com
pr@explorerpublishing.com

Corporate Sales
For bulk sales and customisation options, for this book or
any Explorer product, contact
sales@explorerpublishing.com

Advertising & Sponsorship
For advertising and sponsorship, contact
media@explorerpublishing.com

Explorer Publishing & Distribution
PO Box 34275, Dubai, United Arab Emirates
www.explorerpublishing.com

Phone: +971 (0)4 340 8805
Fax: +971 (0)4 340 8806

Emergency Numbers

Ambulance	120
Fire	119
Police	110
Police Traffic	122
Public Security Bureau Division For Foreigners	010 8402 0101
City Emergency Power Supply Bureau	95598
Amex	800 744 0106
MasterCard	800 110 7309
Visa	800 110 2911

Landmark Hotels

Bamboo Garden Hotel	010 5852 0088
China World	010 6505 2266
Grand Hyatt	010 8518 1234
Hilton	010 5865 5000
Hotel Côté Cour	010 6512 8020
Jianguo	010 6500 2233
Kempinski	010 6465 3388
Kerry Centre	010 6561 8833
Peninsula	010 8516 2888
Raffles	010 6526 3388
Red Capital Residence	010 8403 5308
Regent	010 8522 1888
Ritz-Carlton	010 6601 6666
Sofitel Wanda	010 8599 6666
St Regis	010 6460 6688

Embassies & Consulates

Australia	010 6532 2331
Belgium	010 6532 1736
Brazil	010 6532 2881
Canada	010 6532 3536
France	010 8532 8080
Gabon	010 6532 2810
Germany	010 8532 9000
India	010 6532 1908
Ireland	010 6532 2691
Italy	010 6532 2131
Japan	010 6532 2361
Liberia	010 6532 5617
Myanmar	010 6532 0359
The Netherlands	010 6532 0200
New Zealand	010 6532 2731
Nigeria	010 6532 3631
North Korea	010 6532 1186
Pakistan	010 6532 2504
Russia	010 6532 1381
Singapore	010 6532 3926
South Korea	010 6505 2608
Spain	010 6532 3629
Sweden	010 6532 9790
Thailand	010 6532 1749
UK	010 5192 4000
USA	010 6532 3831

Capital Airport Information

Lost & Found	010 6454 0110
Enquiries	010 6454 1100
Complaints	010 6456 1200

Public Holidays

New Year's Day	Jan 1
Spring Festival	Feb 7-9
International Women's Day	Mar 8
Qingming Festival	Apr 5
Labour Day	May 1
National Youth Day	May 4
CPC Founding Day	Jul 1
International Children's Day	Jun 1
Dragon Boat Festival	Jun 8
Army Day	Aug 1
Mid-Autumn Festival	Sep 14
National Day	Oct 01

Medical Services

Beijing Union Hospital	010 6529 5284
Beijing United Family Hospital (24 hr hotline)	010 6433 2345
Beijing Vista Clinic	010 8529 6618
Hong Kong International Medical Clinic	010 6553 2288
International SOS (24 hr alarm centre)	010 6462 9100

City Information

Directory Inquiries	114
http://english.visitbeijing.com.cn	Tourist Authority
Tourist Hotline	010 6513 0828
www.chinaview.cn	State news service
www.cityweekend.com.cn/beijing	Listings magazine
www.danwei.org	Urban life in China
www.ebeijing.gov.cn	Municipality website
www.sexybeijing.tv	Internet TV station
www.thebeijinger.com	Listings magazine
www.thebeijingguide.com	Virtual travel guide

Airlines

Air China	010 6656 9226
Air France	400 880 8808
British Airways	400 650 0073
China Eastern Airlines	95808
China Southern Airlines	95539
Continental Airlines	010 8527 6696
Dragon Air	400 881 0288
Japan Airlines	400 888 0808
Korean Air	400 658 8888
Malaysia Airlines	010 6505 2081
Qantas	800 819 0089
Shanghai Airlines	010 6459 0901
Singapore Airlines	010 6505 2233
Thai Airways	010 8515 0088
United Airlines	800 810 8282